Public
Education
in the
United States
From
Revolution
to Reform

Public Education in the United States

From Revolution to Reform

R. Freeman Butts

Holt,
Rinehart
and
Winston

New York Chicago San Francisco Dallas
Montreal Toronto London Sydney

Acknowledgments

Small portions of this book have been based upon or adapted from published articles I wrote in the course of finishing *Public Education in the United States*. Permission to borrow from such materials is thankfully acknowledged:

To the Regional Commissioner, U.S. Office of Education, Kansas City, Missouri, for "Compulsory Education: History, Current Status, and Trends," published in the proceedings of a regional conference on compulsory education, December 3, 1975.

To the College Entrance Examination Board for "The Search for Purpose in American Education," *College Board Review*, No. 98, Winter 1975–1976, pp. 2–19.

To Phi Delta Kappa for "Once Again the Question for Liberal Public Educators: Whose Twilight?" *Phi Delta Kappan* (Special Bicentennial Issue), Vol. 58, No. 1, September 1976, pp. 4–14.

To *Educational Theory* for "Public Education in a Pluralistic Society," Vol. 27, No. 1, Winter 1977, pp. 3–11.

To McGraw-Hill Book Company for "Historical Perspective on Civic Education in the United States," in National Task Force on Citizenship Education, *Education for Responsible Citizenship*, 1977, pp. 47–68.

Library of Congress Cataloging in Publication Data

Butts, Robert Freeman, 1910–
  Public education in the United States.

  Bibliography: p. 399
  1. Public schools—United States—History. I. Title.
LA212.B84   379.73   77-18180
ISBN 0-03-013656-3

    9   0   1   038   9   8   7   6   5   4   3   2

Preface

For more than two decades the writing and the teaching of the history of education in the United States have been undergoing fundamental revision. Two general approaches or moods have been popular. One is a "culturalist" approach, which argues that the history of education has been focused too narrowly upon schooling as an institution and has neglected all the other agencies in U.S. society that educate young and adult alike. Schools, relatively, have played a much smaller role in the broader stream of education in American culture than is usually assumed. Thus, much attention, and rightly so, has been devoted by historians of the culturalist mode to the educative efforts of family, church, community, library, press, museum, camp, radio, television, and the like. The battle to highlight the nonschool agencies of education is well on its way to being won. So much so, I believe, that balance needs to be restored by reemphasis upon the historic role of public schools.

The other revisionist mood, which arose from the unrest and disaffection of the late 1960s and early 1970s, takes a socially radical view of the history of education. Interestingly enough, it does refocus attention upon the public schools, but primarily it purports to show how badly they have *mis*educated the people of the United States. Far from playing a minor role in the past, public schools have played a major role in promoting the wrong values and in forcing the oppressive attitudes of the dominant economic and political classes upon the defenseless and reluctant lower classes. In the typical radical mode, the schools are seen as willing agents of the established order, and thus are useless as instruments for the needed uprooting of traditional social institutions. Therefore, their role should be reduced or, indeed *in extremis*, they should be abolished, for the schools, like the society, are racist, materialistic, exploitative, capitalistic, class-biased, and irredeemably bureaucratic.

Now, I find it very useful for some historians of education to be concentrating on the nonschool agencies of U.S. education. This helps us see the schools in relation to other important aspects of cultural and intellectual history. I find it useful also for some historians to be concentrating on the seamier side of our educational past. This forestalls a superpatriotic or self-congratulatory paean of praise for our worthy ancestors. But I do not believe that either approach gives us the kind of history we need for the future. Public education was *not* a minor force in the past, and it need not be in the future. It is *not* an unrelieved blot upon the historical record, and it need not be in the future.

I believe that, on balance, the history of public education has been of such major significance in the formation of modern American civilization that it deserves special study in its own right. Recent historical scholarship makes it clear that not all the achievements of public education in the past are to be lauded, nor are all the motives of the founders of public education to be suspect. Public education was not built solely by idealistic reformers, nor solely by calculating schemers who used their rhetoric to hide their real intentions to exploit or control the lower classes. The history of education in the United States should not glorify crusaders of the past as persons who bequeathed us an untouchable heritage, nor should it impeach them as perpetrators of dirty educational tricks upon the American people.

Recent research undertaken by scores of scholars in U.S. history in general and in the history of education in particular now enable us to formulate a new interpretative synthesis to replace the one embedded in the 1919 introductory textbook by Ellwood P. Cubberley, *Public Education in the United States*, which dominated the field from the 1920s to the 1940s. We need to modify Cubberley's essentially optimistic and naive image of the "public school triumphant," and we need a more balanced conception of the dynamics of social change than that portrayed in the pessimistic and narrowly class-oriented framework promoted by radical historians during the past decade. I do not believe that either the culturalist approach or the radical approach will appropriately revise Cubberley or produce the conceptual framework that is necessary.

I believe that the best hope for a critical reassessment of the history of public education is within a framework that views public education as an essential ingredient of the persistent tensions created by three basic themes in American civilization: the cohesive value claims of a democratic political community summed up in the constitutional ideals of liberty, equality, justice, and obligation for the public good; the pluralistic loyalties that give particular identity and coherence to the different segments of society that arise from diversities of religion, language, culture, ethnicity, race, and locality; and the long-term worldwide modernization process that has been pushing all Western societies for more than 200 years toward national centralization, popular participation, industrialization, urbanization, and secularization.

The role of public education as a contributor to and as a result of these tensions forms the conceptual framework for this book. The interaction of these often divergent trends, especially the twin drives to cultural pluralism and to political cohesion, has resulted in chronic conflicts and cleavages over the control and practices of education. To single out any one of these factors, such as industrial urbanization or social stratification, to explain what happened to education at any particular time or place is to miss the complicated and subtle interplay of these several ingredients, which can be separated only for purposes of discussion.

This book, then, is an interpretative history of public education viewed in the context of the social, political, economic, religious, and intellectual development of American civilization during the 200 years from 1776 to 1976. It is divided into four parts of roughly equal chronological periods of 50 years each. The dates are, of course, arbitrary, but there is a certain rationale for such periodization beyond mere convenience for the reader.

We begin in Part I with the origins and meaning of public education during the first half century of the founding of the Republic. The Revolutionary generation set the tone that permeated much of the subsequent normative calls for public education to promote the values of the newly framed political community. We then turn in Parts II, III, and IV to what happened to the idea of the public school as the training ground for political community in the course of 150 years of ethnic and racial turmoil, religious confrontations, massive immigration, democratic and egalitarian aspiration, industrial urbanization and class conflict, national consolidation, and proliferation of knowledge and technology. The characteristic mix of these elements in each of the subsequent 50-year periods is briefly described in the introductions to Parts II, III, and IV.

I have tried to produce this history of public education as a record based on sound historical scholarship as well as a defensible conceptual framework of social change. It is my hope that it will be of value to students, the teaching profession, policy leaders, and the general public as they seek to develop coherent policies to guide public education in the future.

This book was begun while I was William F. Russell Professor in the Foundations of Education at Teachers College, Columbia University, from which I was "graduated" in 1975. I was enabled to continue research related to the book with the aid of a Rockefeller Foundation Humanities Fellowship (1975–1976). It was completed in the 1976–1978 period under the hospitable auspices of San Jose State University, where I was Visiting Distinguished Professor of Education, and of Stanford University, where I was a Visiting Scholar.

I gratefully acknowledge the many ways in which the men and women of these several institutions facilitated my work, but with no implication, of course, that they are in any way responsible for its outcome. Above all others, however, my thanks go to my administrative associate at Teachers College, Myrtle Augustin, whose unexcelled assistance made the book possible despite the changes in our "work places." Hers has been the commitment of the true professional.

Palo Alto, California   R.F.B.
January 1978

Contents

part I
The Promise of
the American
Revolution

1776-1826

Public Education in the Formation of Political Community

The idea of public education in its modern sense can be traced to many different sources in Western civilization. Some form of public schooling has been part of the nation-building process of all modern states, and usually some ingredients have been borrowed from others. Universal primary education designed to reach virtually all of a country's population is a distinctive creation of modern political systems. The purpose of this book is to examine the distinctive ingredients that have shaped the character and goals of public schooling in the United States since the beginning of the Republic.

Colonial Authority for Education

U.S. historians of education of the 1920s and 1930s, symbolized by Ellwood P. Cubberley of Stanford University, looked to the New England colonies for the origins of U.S. public education, citing laws passed in Massachusetts in 1642 and 1647. There was, to be sure, some truth in this view. The colonial governments *did* have authority over the education of the people, if they wished to apply it. Of course, the source of this authority ultimately was the English king and parliament, which had been increasingly concerned with schools and universities in England since the middle of the sixteenth century. Thus the colonial legislatures of Massachusetts, Connecticut, and New Hampshire enacted laws requiring parents to see to it that their children learned to read, learned the capital laws, knew the orthodox catechism, and became skilled in a trade. They soon also began to require towns to appoint

3

teachers and even to pay them out of local taxes if the townspeople so voted; naturally, such public teachers would be under the "vigilant eye" of the town authorities.

This control over education seemed only natural to the Puritans and Congregationalists of New England, whose view of community life centered about their Calvinistic religious and moral values. They were convinced that education—at least literacy—was necessary in order to learn to read the Bible, which contained the grounds of their faith; it was necessary, they believed, for salvation and for membership in the true Christian common-wealth. They had no difficulty accepting the Reformation doctrines of Cal-vinist and Anglican alike which stated that civil government had a legitimate authority to preserve, protect, and extend the true religion. "An establish-ment of religion" characterized most of the colonies in the seventeenth cen-tury—Congregationalism in the major New England colonies, Anglicanism in the major southern colonies. The state could thus legitimately enforce the doctrines and worship of the established church upon all the people, punish those who refused to abide by these, and levy taxes to support the preachers and teachers of the church, whether the taxpayer believed in its tenets or not.

There was *some* truth, then, in the notion that the *idea* of public edu-cation had sprouted in seventeenth-century New England. It was true that governmental authority was legitimately concerned with a public education that would serve the interests of church and commonwealth; that public wel-fare overshadowed the rights of parents and children, so that colonial authori-ties could legally compel parents to have their children educated; and that civil authorities could control and financially support teachers as well as ministers (who indeed were often the same person). Similar governmental authority could have been exerted in the South and was in fact exerted with regard to orphans and poor children. However, it did not generally extend to compulsory education for all children nor to levying taxes for the support of schools.

The Growth of Pluralism

Important as these precedents for public education were, however, the trends of the eighteenth century served to overshadow the idea that schooling should be public in purpose, public in access, public in control, and public in support. All four of these ingredients of public education were weakened in the colonies during the first three quarters of the eighteenth century. The growing wave of immigration from many countries of northern Europe brought increasingly heterogeneous groups of people to this country—people different in their religious beliefs, language, and culture from the predomi-nantly Puritan and Anglican population of the seventeenth century. Quakers, Methodists, Baptists, Moravians, and Mennonites began to talk about reli-gious freedom and object to laws aimed at enhancing the established church by means of compulsory schooling and taxation. Presbyterians, Lutherans, Catholics, and Dutch Reformed who did not oppose establishments as such nevertheless wanted their taxes to go to support their own clergy. Finally, Germans, Dutch, French, Swedes, and Danes wanted schools in their own languages rather than in English.

In addition to the growing heterogeneity of religion and language, the population was branching out from the eastern seaboard into the western sections of the colonies. This development meant the beginnings of regional or sectional interests and a growth of localism that served to weaken the community solidarity that had marked the New England towns of the seventeenth century. Thus, while religious diversity led to greater demands for the free exercise of religion, it also diluted the civic sense of community that had originally impelled the major New England colonies to promote public education. In response to the pressures of the newer groups, the colonial governments in the eighteenth century began to allow religious and charitable societies to build, maintain, and conduct their own schools with little governmental vigilance.

Similarly, the colonial governments gave more freedom to entrepreneurial teachers to establish a variety of alternative private schools that would appeal to the commercial interests of young people seeking jobs in the cities. Legislatures granted charters to merchants and landowners to incorporate themselves as boards of trustees to buy land, erect buildings, appoint teachers, and generally operate their own schools. These corporations, often known as academies, sprang up to attract the children of a growing middle class who could afford to pay the fees. Cultural and religious diversity, though not yet based upon an equality of mutual respect later to be idealized by a doctrine of cultural pluralism, certainly had the effect of diluting the idea of a common public education where it had begun to prosper under the impetus of a homogeneous population and an established religion.

The idea of a common public education promoted under the auspices of a colony-wide government was further weakened in the course of the eighteenth century by the movement of people to unsettled regions too far from the central towns for children to be able to attend school there. If schooling were to be available at all, it would have to be offered in local "district" schools. The colonial governments eventually responded by permitting the local districts to manage their own schools. This represented a kind of victory for decentralization, but no guarantee that schools of quality would be maintained nor that schools would be maintained at all.

Thus, by the middle of the eighteenth century, the "public" purpose of education that had based the welfare of the commonwealth upon the doctrines of an established church was giving way to the "private" purposes of a variety of religious beliefs seeking freedom from government control. The idea of public support of "free" town schools available to all and financed at least in part by tax funds was giving way to the practice of "free" charity

schools intended for poor children and supported by religious or philanthropic societies (such as the Society for the Propagation of the Gospel in
Foreign Parts); those who could afford the tuition had the option of sending
their children to incorporated academies or proprietary teachers. At the same
time, government management and operation of schools were increasingly giving way to control by private boards of managers. Public access to town
schools, open at least in theory to all the children of the community, was
being superseded by schools intended primarily for children of similar religious, linguistic, cultural, or social backgrounds.

A New Kind of Public Education Required

What would have happened to the mid-eighteenth century idea of
religiously motivated private education if the American Revolution had not
transpired is a matter of speculation. Possibly it would have maintained itself
for a longer period of time than it did; and the experience of the United
States would then have paralleled more closely the slower and more tortuous
developments in England itself. But with the Revolution came a reversal of
attitudes. The major historical significance of the Revolution for education
was that it redefined the meaning of political community in such a way that
within two decades (1) a new republican political system was designed and
established; (2) a new conception of republican citizenship was formulated
to fit the new political system; and (3) a new conception of a politically
motivated public education was proposed to strengthen the new Republic
and bind together the increasingly heterogeneous population into a viable
political community.

U.S. historians of the 1920s and 1930s attributed the causes of the
American Revolution to social and economic forces; today the tendency of
historians is to view the changes that the Revolutionaries sought as above all
political reforms, not a fundamental overturning of social classes nor a radical redistribution of the economic sources of wealth or production. In the
last quarter of the eighteenth century there were indeed changes in social
organization that tended to blur class lines, but there was no overwhelming
tide of egalitarianism that swept away traditional forms of status or wealth.

The Revolution did not divide the people cleanly along class lines.
There were upper-class people on both sides and lower-class people on both
sides. The Patriot cause attracted those who resented the power and privilege
exercised by British officialdom and who hoped for better opportunities in
life through freedom from British control. The Loyalist cause attracted people
who had already profited from the English rule and who feared oppression
or retaliation from triumphant Patriots. "Class" was a relatively loose term
during the Revolutionary era. Greater class conflict did appear, however,

during the nineteenth century when industrialization, urbanization, and immigration combined to sharpen and widen economic and social disparities between newcomers and "natives."

Religion in the Revolutionary Era

Another shift in historical thinking concerning the later eighteenth-century conception of public education has to do with the role of religion in the Revolutionary era. The usual interpretation has been that the Revolution involved great gains for religious freedom, thus paving the way for secular public education. Recent research has indeed confirmed the growth of freedom of religious worship for minority *Protestant* sects and an increasing separation of particular churches from the protection or support of the state. But the majority of people during and shortly after the Revolution were inclined to believe that there was a common Protestant-Christian cohesion that should underlie the new nation.

The religious revival known as the Great Awakening that swept the colonies in the mid-eighteenth century forged a common outlook that promoted a kind of liberty of religious conscience within Protestantism; but it also assumed that Protestant beliefs of whatever variety were superior to the Roman Catholic, Jewish, Islamic, or any of the naturalistic beliefs of American Indians, Africans, or Asians. All such groups were looked upon as legitimate objects of missionary efforts to bring them to see the light or of legal restrictions upon their freedom of operation, even in a republican form of government.

The "separatist" Protestant sects like the Quakers, Baptists, and Methodists often joined with radical deists to break the hold of Congregationalists upon the New England governments or the hold of Anglicans upon southern governments, but the struggle to disestablish the entrenched churches was long and bitter. Efforts were made in several of the new states to prevent complete disestablishment by offering the benefits of state authority to several or to *all* Protestant churches so that they could compel support for their clergy by taxing their own memberships. This was the principle of general assessment, with the option not of exemption from the religious tax but simply of indicating to which church the taxes should go. I have called this a "multiple" establishment of religion.[1] It was this principle that James Madison was eventually able to defeat in Virginia by his support of Thomas Jefferson's Bill for Religious Freedom, but it took seven years of bitter political fighting to achieve the bill's passage in 1786.

In general, in the decade following 1776, the legal bonds between the established churches and the new states were broken or severely weakened. By the time of the adoption of the Bill of Rights in 1791, nine of the original 13 states had formally declared for religious freedom and separation of church and state. Four continued legally to affirm freedom of religious conscience, but maintained the right to enforce taxation for religious purposes by authorizing each church to support its own clergy. Laws or constitutional amendments were eventually approved in Maryland, Connecticut, New Hampshire, and Massachusetts, enabling these states to catch up with the others and to uphold the spirit of the First Amendment.

Despite the legal and constitutional battles that divided the jealous Protestant sects over questions of taxation and religious freedom, the dominant tone of spiritual righteousness led the churches to believe that *Protestant* morality, frugality, self-denial, and benevolence should infuse the teaching of all schools, public and private. Theological fine points and complex distinctions between interpretations of predestination or baptism began to be less important than winning sinners over to the Christian faith. People began to believe that the *common* elements of Christianity could be distilled from the many denominations within Protestantism. The onset of the Revolution encouraged the growth of this feeling. After all, evangelical "new lights" like Congregationalist Jonathan Edwards and Anglican George Whitefield could both preach a Christian faith calling for a moral regeneration to counteract drunkenness, licentiousness, dishonesty, violence, and degradation and be joined by Methodist and Baptist preachers. And the more rational intellectualist "old lights" could readily join in the attacks on social or moral degeneracy.

Indeed, it is increasingly agreed among historians that the widespread assault by clergymen of many different faiths on vice, corruption, and worldly affluence in the 1760s and 1770s helped to mold a common and unifying ideological fervor that supported the Revolution itself. People of different faiths were being mobilized to unite in supporting the Revolution as a means of rooting out the profiteering, pride, arrogance, and infidelity which they associated with haughty British officialdom and colonial collaborators. As Gordon S. Wood puts it, "Independence thus became not only political but moral—Revolution, republicanism, and regeneration all blended in American thinking."[2]

Political Goals of the Revolution

Above all, however, the Revolution was political. It had moral, religious, economic, and military ingredients, to be sure, but as Bernard Bailyn, Gordon S. Wood, Edmund Morgan, Robert R. Palmer, and many other historians of the Revolution have agreed, the original flash point in the 1770s and the sustained reformation of institutions in the 1780s and 1790s coalesced about the political. As so often happens, the igniting sparks were conditions or events which mobilized people to act suddenly and decisively. What the colonists acted *against* were abuses of power and of privilege. What they formulated to take their place were the goals of liberty, equality, and public virtue. These became not only ideological and passionate rallying cries for insurrection and war, but political principles which were debated, discussed, defined, and redefined. Eventually these goals were incorporated into the political community, the constitutional order, and the governments of the independent states and eventually the new nation. The political remedies for the real and fancied political abuses go to the heart of the new conceptions of citizenship and of public education that came out of the Revolution. Together they helped to define the process of political and educational modernization that distinguished the United States from the other modernizing nations of the West.

Liberty / Though the meaning of liberty is enormously complex and even abstract, especially in a revolutionary era, there was a consistent thread in eighteenth-century English and American republicanism. Liberty was not so much conceived of as the private right of individuals to act in freedom from any governmental control; rather, it was seen as the right of the people collectively to exert political power free from the restrictions of royal power or officialdom or from a governmental authority in which the people did not participate. The "people" were viewed as principally a homogeneous body, represented in England in the House of Commons and in the colonies in the elected assemblies, both arrayed against the power of crown or nobility.

Participation by the people in the elective and the governing processes was the essence of republican liberty. The prime purpose of government was to "secure the blessings of liberty" for the people and to protect their natural rights. The more radical republicans believed that self-government could be achieved only in small states where direct participation was possible; others believed that the representative assembly or legislature, in contrast to the magistrate or executive, was the essence of liberty. Thus when colonial spokesmen in the 1770s argued for a public education devoted to liberty, they most often meant education for elective self-government based upon consent of the "people" in contrast to rule by a privileged monarchy, nobility, or external authorities. Seldom were the arguments for public education stated in terms that education ought to promote the civil liberties of private individuals or of minority groups as against governmental agencies or majorities, even in a *republican* state. The notion grew but slowly that "education for liberty" might mean preparation to exercise and protect the basic freedoms of religion, press, assembly, trial by jury, security of person, due process, and the other guarantees of the Bill of Rights of 1791.

This is important to remember when judging the liberalism of the founding fathers and the early advocates of public education. Since the "people" were assumed by radical republicans in 1776 to be united in their opposition to the privileges of hereditary or military rulers, there was assumed to be no real conflict between private liberty and public liberty.[3] Their belief that private liberty and public liberty were one and the same explained why the radicals could condone the coercion of individuals and minority groups by public bodies in the name of liberty—that is, in the name of the people; why the radicals of the Georgia legislature could declare youth studying in monarchical Europe to be aliens; why the radicals of Pennsylvania could set up a council of censors to guard against the exploitation by powerful landed and commercial interests inimical to those of the people; and even why Jefferson 40 years after the Declaration of Independence could proscribe all but Republican books and teaching at the University of Virginia on the ground that Federalist views would threaten the "liberty" of the people.

Equality / Equality was to be the remedy for the special privileges of the ruling elites, whose snobbishness, arrogance, pretensions, and contempt for the "people" infuriated the middle classes, the yeomen, the professionals, and the artisans of the towns and countryside. Again, "equality" was an elusive term. Then, as now, it sometimes meant that all persons should have an equal chance or opportunity to develop their talents and not be handicapped by inherited status of family, property, or class. Sometimes it seemed to imply that a rough equality of condition would be a desirable thing, but seldom was there great stress on *economic* leveling. More often *political* equality was the goal, for it was widely believed that there were bound to be natural intellectual or social differences or distinctions based upon ability. The important thing was to keep the avenues of mobility open so that "artificial" differences of property, wealth, or status would not harden into *political* hierarchies and privileges as they had in the ancient regimes of Europe. Rewards were to be made upon the basis of achievement and merit in a society in which equality of opportunity was kept open through the political process and especially through public educational systems where all children would have the opportunity to make the most of their natural talents.

No one would argue that the founding fathers defined with exactitude what they meant when they declared that "all men are created equal," nor that the amorphous dictum has been faithfully carried out in practice. But Edmund Morgan argues that the creed of equality achieved a kind of consensus during the Revolutionary period that has had a powerful and pervasive influence ever since:

> The creed of equality did not give men equality, but invited them to claim it, invited them not to know their place and keep it, but to seek and demand a better place. Yet the conflicts resulting from such demands have generally, though not always, stopped short of large-scale violence and have generally eventuated in a greater degree of actual equality.[4]

For 200 years the creed of equality and the creed of public education have gone together, each bound to the other with extraordinary fidelity. Like the creed of equality, the creed of public education has often been charged with being merely rhetoric, and the search for alternatives has been prolonged and pervasive. But over and over again, the idea of public education, born in the Revolution, has been called upon to help promote social, economic, and political equality while alternatives to public education, whether charitable, philanthropic, entrepreneurial, or religious, have persistently had to face the charge that they promote inequality.

Just as the Revolution did not confer equality but invited the people to claim it, so did the Revolution generate the political *values* of public education without putting them into practice. These were generalized values which successive generations sought to bring into actuality, but always with shortcomings in practice and usually neglecting to encompass some old or new group which eventually claimed to be included in the benefits of equality. In some cases, these were groups that the originators of the idea of equality did not or could not mean to include.

The Public Good / The third republican ingredient in the process of overcoming the abuses of power and privilege personified by British officialdom was the need for developing public virtue among the people as a means of furthering the public good. Pleas for devotion to the public good echoed throughout the Revolutionary period. There was little doubt that a republican form of government required the individual to sacrifice personal interests for the greater good of the community. Indeed, the ideal of a *commonwealth,* a democratic corporate society in which the common good was the chief end of government, could be solidly built only upon the public commitments of and the sense of community achieved by the citizens of the commonwealth, the people. The development of self-sacrifice, loyalty, patriotism, and moral regeneration on the part of the people was therefore one of the most important requirements for achieving the Revolution and building a secure republic. Nothing less than creating new persons would do, for while monarchical authority can be based upon fear of punishment, a republic must be founded upon the willingness of individuals to put the public good above private desires. And how better to promote the common weal than through a common education? the public good than through public schools?

The republicans of the 1770s expressed the idealistic hope that a republican government could somehow bring out the best in the people, indeed induce them to achieve a kind of political regeneration in the same way that the evangelical clergy preached that a change of heart could achieve spiritual salvation. Just as the church and the gospel could be the instruments of salvation, so the republican state could be an instrument of political reform and an agency for promoting public virtue.

With liberty, equality, and the public good in the forefront of their ideological zeal, the Revolutionaries mobilized to win independence from the British. For two decades, while fighting the war and then creating the new nation, they set about to transform their political institutions. They sought to transform education as part of the larger political transformation—to make it public where it had been private; to make it uniformly republican where it had been ideologically or culturally pluralistic; to make it serve liberty and equality where it had fostered elitism or special privilege; to make it serve the public good where it had been a badge of personal preferment.

Public Education in the Independent States

The most exciting and engrossing political activity following the Declaration of Independence centered upon the making of the new state constitutions. By the middle of 1777, 10 states had produced new constitutions proclaiming their independent republican status. Massachusetts could not agree until 1780; Connecticut and Rhode Island felt satisfied that a revision of their charters took the British crown and parliament out of their futures; and Vermont's uncertain status was only finally settled with its admission to the Union in 1791. Of the first 14 states, 7 had specific provisions for education in their early constitutions: Pennsylvania (1776), North Carolina (1776), Georgia (1777), Vermont (1777), Massachusetts (1780), New Hampshire (revision of 1784), and Delaware (revision of 1792).

The First State Constitutions

Interestingly enough, the most radically republican states and the most forthright on the separation of church and state were also the first to include provisions for education. Pennsylvania's constitution of 1776 is generally recognized to be the most radical and populist of the early state constitutions. It provided for a popularly elected and unicameral legislature, put heavy restraints upon the executive and judicial powers of the magistracy, provided for annual elections and a referendum on all laws, spelled out the civil liberties in a declaration of rights, and stressed the accountability of all officials to the people. Thus were liberty and equality to be enshrined in the organic law. But the nurture of such values was to lie with legislators who devoutly believed in God, with a separately elected council of censors who would act as ombudsmen for the people every seven years, and with laws to promote the public virtue. To this end Sections 44 and 45 stated:

> A school or schools shall be established in every county by the legislature, for the convenient instruction of youth, with such salaries to the masters, paid by the public, as may enable them to instruct youth at low prices; and all useful learning shall be duly encouraged and promoted in one or more universities.

> Laws for the encouragement of virtue, and prevention of vice and immorality, shall be made and constantly kept in force, . . .

Similar provisions for public schooling were incorporated into the politically radical and religiously liberal constitutions of North Carolina (1776) and Georgia (1777) and in the constitution first proposed for Vermont (1777). Unfortunately, few verbatim records exist of the debates that surrounded the forming of the original state constitutions, so the intentions of the framers with regard to educational provisions must be inferred from the general meaning of republicanism derived from other sources. The reasons other states did not include education are similarly conjectural. Much was probably made of the argument that the states already *had* the power to support and control education, as indicated by the long history of educational legislation passed by virtually all colonial legislatures. Whatever the specific reasons, the fact remains that several of the new state legislatures had little hesitation in passing laws having to do with schools, colleges, and universities (notably Massachusetts, Connecticut, New York, Pennsylvania, Georgia, Maryland, and North Carolina).

Just why Virginia did not include education in its first constitution is not clear, but it soon became a matter of public debate in perhaps the most spectacular failure of a newly independent state to enact a public school law. Possibly such a law was not included because radical and conservative forces were evenly matched, or because Thomas Jefferson's legislative proposal so fully spelled out republican and secular principles that political and religious conservatives feared that liberty and equality were being carried too far. Jefferson was convinced that the Virginia constitution of 1776 had not gone far enough in reforming the aristocratic institutions and class distinctions inherited from British rule. Thus, in 1779, he proposed bills for the elimination of primogeniture and entail, for religious freedom, and for public education, all viewed as agencies for regaining and regenerating the liberty, equality, and public virtue he believed the Revolution was designed to achieve.

Jefferson saw more keenly than anyone up to his time that public schools aiming to serve the whole citizenry must be under government direction and free from religious, sectarian, or private control. He believed too that education under public control must extend from the lowest to the highest levels and include a comprehensive system of elementary and secondary schools capped by a state university. Others had been concerned to achieve direct government control of one or more levels of schools, but Jefferson saw the need for a complete system of public education. These proposals were a part of his general concern to revise the whole code of laws in Virginia to bring them into line with the needs of an independent and republican state and a democratic form of society; they would thus do away with the political, economic, and social injustices of a colonial society based upon aristocratic privilege and class distinctions.

Later State Constitutions

The second wave of state constitution-making, heralded by the Massachusetts constitution of 1780, may be regarded as more conservative than the radical activity that took place in 1776–1777. This is exemplified by John Adams' arguments that the powers of the elected popular assembly should be balanced by an upper house of the legislature where men of "wisdom and learning" or of wealth and property would counteract the more egalitarian leanings of the ordinary people. This began the process of looking upon the "people" as possessing differing and conflicting economic or political interests rather than as a homogeneous body united in opposition to the hereditary ruling classes. The point is that many conservatives and radicals agreed that the states should promote public education on behalf of liberty, equality, and the public good, despite their differences with regard to the precise meaning of those terms when it came to questions of representation, separation of powers, checks and balances, bicameralism, and other matters of republican constitution-making.

The Massachusetts constitution of 1780, largely formulated by Adams, put it this way, and New Hampshire followed suit in its revision of 1784:

> Wisdom and knowledge, as well as virtue, diffused generally among the body of the people, being necessary for the preservation of their rights and liberties; and as these depend on spreading the opportunities and advantages of education in the various parts of the country, and among the different orders of the people, it shall be the duty of legislatures and magistrates, in all future periods of this commonwealth, to cherish the interests of literature and the sciences, and all seminaries of them; especially the university at Cambridge, public schools and grammar schools in the towns . . . to countenance and inculcate the principles of humanity and general benevolence, public and private charity, industry and frugality, honesty and punctuality in their dealings; sincerity, good humor, and all social affections, and generous sentiments, among the people.[5]

Differences between conservatives and radicals did arise and became extremely important. For example, when the conservatives ousted the radicals from power in Pennsylvania in the 1780s, they retreated from the idea of public support for a common school system for all and changed the educational provision in the constitution of 1790 so that it limited free education to the poor. Crucially important was the fact that the framers of the state constitutions defined a meaning of sovereignty that was to launch the states rapidly into the modern world and provide a pattern that would be widely influential. The British had moved sovereign power from the crown to the legislature. The United States went further, transferring sovereignty to the "people" as the ultimate authority and designating the fundamental law or constitution to be superior to the operating government.

Throughout the first decade of this complex, fluid, and sometimes baffling process of working out a new republican political system, public education was often, in a remarkably potent way, hit upon as a critical factor. It was seen as a nurturer of the public good in the making of a new political community, as a constituent part of the new constitutional orders of the independent states, and as indispensable for a citizenry that would elect the governing authorities and would participate in the actual functioning of government. To specify education as an integral element in so many state constitutions in the 1770s, while the war was being fought, was a considerable achievement. It implied a recognition of the political importance of education long before public education was widely put into practice in the middle of the nineteenth century. The Revolutionary era set the stage for the prominent role public education came to play in virtually every state constitution as the number of states grew from 13 to 50.[6]

Public Education and the Emerging Political Community

In contrast to the process of state constitution-making that absorbed the creative political energies of so many people in the 1770s, the matter of creating a national political community and a national constitutional order attracted relatively little attention until the mid-1780s. From 1774 onward, the Continental Congress engendered a cohesiveness necessary to fight and win the war. While the Congress drew up and adopted the Articles of Confederation in 1777, ratification by all the states did not come until 1781. In the course of this process, however, there was little of the intellectual and political ferment that marked the state constitutional debates.

Articles of Confederation

One cannot read the Articles of Confederation today without realizing the power of state prerogatives and the limiting, even grudging, delegation of powers to the "central government," which consisted only of the Congress. These powers had to do primarily with foreign relations, war and peace, disputes among states, trade with Indians, coinage of money, and intercommunication, whereas the states maintained powers over taxation, trade, and all other internal affairs. Article I adopted the name "The United States of America," but Article II made united action difficult: "Each state retains its sovereignty, freedom, and independence, and every power, jurisdiction, and right which is not by this confederation expressly delegated to the United States in Congress assembled."

In the early 1780s, distrust of any central or remote government was still widely felt, and in a time of depression, economic insecurity, paper money, and rampant land speculation, this distrust was likely to extend to *any* government. Radicals worried that the Continental Congress might try to become another British parliament; and conservatives were all too ready to blame impetuous state legislatures for undermining property rights. On top of this, the gradual crystallizing of regional voting blocs in the Continental Congress began to carve out fairly cohesive sectional interests representing quasi-legislative parties of New England, the middle states, and the South that successively dominated the Congress in the dozen years of its existence. In view of these complex loyalties—state versus federal, North versus South, East versus West—it is remarkable that the Articles of Confederation and Perpetual Union served as well as they did during the critical period of the 1780s.

Most historians agree that one of the most significant actions of the Continental Congress under the Articles of Confederation was the formulation of policies governing the disposition of public lands eventually ceded to the federal government by the states that had claims to western land. Led by New York, and followed by Connecticut, Massachusetts, and Virginia, the United States came into possession of millions of acres of land north of the Ohio and east of the Mississippi rivers. The policies for the disposal of the land and the governing of the territories were formulated by two committees of Congress, both of which were originally headed by Thomas Jefferson. Both ordinances as eventually adopted contained significant provisions for public education.

The first ordinance to be put into effect, the Land Ordinance of 1785, provided for the survey of the public lands into rectangular townships six miles square, each consisting of 36 sections of 640 acres each; the sixteenth section (in the middle of each district) was to be reserved "for the maintenance of public schools within the said township" when the lands were sold. This was a notable step in the direction of public support for public schools, in general line with policies long adopted in New England and conforming to Jefferson's own bill of 1779 for public education in Virginia. It set a policy which was to have considerable long-range influence, even though the financial returns were eventually much less than the originators expected. One reason for this was persistent land speculation by private companies, which often resulted in financial returns for speculators at the expense of the public coffers for support of schools.

Northwest Ordinance / Indeed, it was the aggressive tactics of the Ohio Land Company that prompted Congress to adopt policies for the governing of the western lands. Jefferson's original committee report of 1784 on governing the territory had proposed the eventual self-government of trans-Appalachian states on a basis of equality with the original states. The first draft even included a prohibition of slavery in all proposed states, but Jefferson's fellow-southerners forced the deletion of this part, and the proposal was never put into operation. Instead, under pressure from the Ohio Company to sell a million and a half acres of land north of the Ohio in the summer of 1787, the

Congress adopted on July 13 the Northwest Ordinance, creating the governmental machinery for not less than three states and not more than five states in the territory north of the Ohio and east of the Mississippi. Whenever any such proposed state had 60,000 free inhabitants, it was to be admitted to the Union "on an equal footing with the original states."

In what amounted to a kind of bill of rights, the Ordinance set forth several articles of compact to guarantee permanently a republican constitutional order of the new states as they were added to the Union: the free exercise of religion, the rights of habeas corpus, trial by jury, proportional representation of the people in the legislature, judicial proceedings, no cruel or unusual punishment, no deprivation of liberty or property except by due process, and no slavery or involuntary servitude (except that fugitive slaves from any of the original states could be lawfully reclaimed).

Article III contained two sentences: one is the deservedly famous and well-remembered provision about schools, and the other is the equally deserved but often forgotten provision about good faith with the Indians:

> Religion, morality, and knowledge being necessary to good government and the happiness of mankind, schools and the means of education shall forever be encouraged. The utmost good faith shall always be observed towards the Indians; their lands and property shall never be taken from them without their consent; and in their property, rights, and liberty they never shall be invaded or disturbed, unless in just and lawful wars authorized by Congress; but laws founded in justice and humanity shall, from time to time, be made, for preventing wrongs being done to them and for preserving peace and friendship with them.

In one bold and hasty stroke, the federal government laid down the rules for applying to the new states of the old Northwest Territory the principles of liberty, equality, and the public good that infused the republican state constitutions of the 1770s and early 1780s. The old conception that new territories acquired by established governments should be treated as colonies for the good of the latter was abrogated. New states were to be equals of the old. Indeed, the new states of this particular region were *not* to be slave states, and they were to promote public education as well as the civil rights and civil liberties that republican governments ought to protect among Indians as well as white citizens. One could argue that the whole business was immoral and illegal as far as the Indians were concerned. But given the subsequent history of 200 years, the principles stated by the Northwest Ordinance were still far in advance of the actual history of unfair dealings with Indians.

Some people would say that the high ideals of the Northwest Ordinance were sullied by the financial wheeling and dealing among corruptible Continental Congress members undertaken by the promoters of the Ohio Company, principally by General Rufus Putnam and the Reverend Manassah Cutler. Within a few days of the passage of the Northwest Ordinance in July 1787, a contract was agreed upon by Congress to sell some 1,500,000 acres to the

Ohio Company for about nine cents an acre rather than the one dollar per acre envisioned in the Land Ordinance of 1785. The Ohio Company "advisers" also played a part in proposing the articles of the Northwest Ordinance that would make the Ohio territory attractive as the land of opportunity for sober, law-abiding, and liberty-loving New England settlers. The contract which was eventually signed in October 1787 not only set aside the sixteenth section of land for support of public schools but two whole townships for the purposes of a university. In addition, land section 29 was reserved "for purposes of religion," a provision Jefferson would surely not have agreed to if he had still been in Congress at the time. But the religious provision would be attractive to New Englanders, who had not yet abolished their religious establishments; also popular with New Englanders would be the antislavery provision promoted especially by the Harvard-educated notables Nathan Dane and Rufus King.

Thus at the outset of formulating federal policy with respect to public education, the high goals of liberty, equality, and the public good were marred in practice by financial, private, and selfish interests. One can be cynical about the goals themselves; one can ignore the sullying motivations of the greedy; or one can recognize that both motivations were probably inherent in a democratic political process which involved the art of compromise where factional or group interests were strongly in contention. In any case, the high ideals were eventually fixed in the constitutional order of 1789 and the Bill of Rights of 1791 as claimants upon future generations. Here again the achievement brought about by the political process was enormously significant, but it fell far short of embodying all of the Revolutionary ideals for public education, for blacks, or for Indians.

Constitutional Convention

Despite the prominent place given to public education in the land ordinances during the final days of the Continental Congress, the subject of education received surprisingly little attention in the deliberations of the Constitutional Convention in Philadelphia, and subsequently no explicit mention in the Constitution. The reasons for this are still unclear, and much painstaking research may be necessary to arrive at fully supportable conclusions. So far, at least, the lack of evidence still requires that the generalizations be based upon inference rather than substantive proof.

My own conclusions go something like this. By the summer of 1787, it had been pretty well decided that if *any* government was to take major responsibility for the control and support of education, it was to be the state governments. After all, the several states by now had had a full decade of independent existence and experience in running their internal affairs, having delegated to Congress limited and often ill-defined powers to deal solely with external and foreign affairs. As we have seen, roughly half of the original states provided for education in their state constitutions, and virtually all had legislated in some manner on educational matters.

The passage of the Northwest Ordinance in July 1787 by the Continental Congress in New York at the very time that the Constitutional Convention was deliberating in Philadelphia may well have meant to delegates that there was nothing further to debate: education was a matter for the states to promote with the encouragement of the federal government and with the aid of proceeds from the sale of public lands. We know that these views represented Jefferson, whose ideas on state support and control of public education had been well known since 1779. What Jefferson might have proposed had he been at the Constitutional Convention cannot be stated for sure, but the Virginia plan for a new constitution, presented by Governor Edmund Randolph and drafted by James Madison, carried no explicit provision for the control of education by the proposed federal government. Madison, who had just gone through the exhausting campaign to get Jefferson's bill for religious freedom passed in Virginia, largely reflected Jefferson's views.

Apparently the only recorded mention of education as a subject of debate in the Convention was in a proposal by Charles Pinckney of South Carolina that the new Congress be empowered to "establish and provide for a national university at the seat of government of the United States." In the later debates on the powers of Congress, Madison supported Pinckney in advocating that the federal government "establish seminaries for the promotion of literature, and the arts and sciences." The Convention's Committee of Detail never reported out these proposals.

It is frustrating to find so little said about education in the Constitutional Convention, for this leaves to speculation or inference the reasons why. Some framers, especially those with strong nationalistic leanings, undoubtedly thought that the new federal government would inherently have implied powers to deal with education, even as the Continental Congress had done. Those who took an antifederalist[7] view believed that states or local governments should be the proper repositories of power over education. Still others undoubtedly believed that education should be left to the private efforts of interested groups or to the religious enterprise of the several churches or denominations or to the charitable and philanthropic instincts of individuals or groups of many kinds. There were no doubt still others who believed that there were more urgent and more important problems than education for the Convention to deal with, such as the interests of small states versus the interests of large states; the respective powers of the legislature and the executive; the House of Representatives *vis-à-vis* the Senate; sectional rivalries centering on slavery, land, or banking; or state versus federal powers.

But running through all shades of opinion by the mid-1780s was an uneasy feeling that *something* had to be done about the political process at both the state and the national levels. Warnings of an impending crisis were being sounded throughout the land in press, pulpit, and coffee house. High prices, corruption in high places, bribery and pay-offs to public officials, vast economic disparities between the rich and the poor, hucksterism among land speculators, arbitrary confiscation of property, reckless issuance of paper money by capricious legislatures, the decline of religion and public virtue— all of these ills fed people's long-held suspicions of political power and tempted many to believe that unrestrained state legislatures or majority rule at home were little better than an unrestrained crown or parliament abroad.

The earlier republican faith that the "people" were basically virtuous or could be made so if only they were given liberty to rule themselves began to weaken in the face of the monumental problems that were piling up after the 13 states had experienced independence for a decade. Increasingly, thoughtful people of a federalist persuasion began to argue that liberty alone or religion alone or education alone could not assure a sound political community; constitutional reform and the strengthening of political institutions themselves were required in order to remedy the excesses of unrestrained liberty and equality. Paramount among such reforms of state governments were a strengthening of the executive and judicial branches to balance the legislative and the strengthening of the senate to balance the popularly elected assembly. The Massachusetts constitution of 1780 presaged this feeling, but by the mid-1780s it was widely believed that reforms in the state governments alone were not enough, that change must also extend upward to the central government. As historian Gordon S. Wood has noted, state governments no longer seemed capable of creating virtuous laws and citizens. The calling of the Constitutional Convention was thus the culmination of a decade of trial and error in the process of constitution-making.

Ambiguity Under the Constitution

Historians are divided as to the essential meaning of the Constitution of 1787–1789 with regard to the Revolution. In general, Wood argues that the Constitution was an aristocratic repudiation of the democratic ideology of the Revolution. Bernard Bailyn, however, believes that the Constitution was not so much a repudiation as it was "a second generation expression of the original ideological impulses of the Revolution applied to the everyday, practical problems of the 1789s."[8] Jack P. Greene argues that the Constitution was less a repudiation than a fulfillment of the principles of 1776.[9]

Whatever views are taken of this question, the fact is that the Constitution was debated, drawn up, and ratified with virtually no mention of the role of the federal government in the area of elementary or secondary education. Political modernization took place in the United States within a period of less than two decades, with education viewed as a function of the states or of private or religious groups. Such an approach was in striking contrast to those of the major countries of Western Europe. With the French Revolution, France, for example, moved rapidly to destroy a rigidly stratified and aristocratic social order by instituting an egalitarian society within a powerful central state which was intended to maintain and control a centralized system of universal education. Before the educational proposals could fairly be instituted, however, the First Republic gave way to empire and then monarchy; thus for 100 years public education prospered when democratic or liberal forces were in power and languished when the monarchy, empire, church, or reactionary political forces were in power. In the German states, centralized and aristocratic public education was a tool of the ruling classes, receiving a short-lived democratic shot in the arm during the brief but unsuccessful liberal revolutions of the nineteenth century. In England, public education lagged far behind as the British moved more slowly into modern political forms, marked by universal suffrage, effective executive government, an independent civil bureaucracy, and competitive political parties.[10]

Because the United States moved rapidly into the modern political world, with relatively little violent upheaval on the French pattern and with relatively little centralized repression on the German model, the place of education in the new political order was discussed and debated more fully outside than inside the Constitutional Convention in Philadelphia and the ratifying conventions of the states. Debates within the Philadelphia Convention and the subsequent state conventions centered upon reconciling the widely different interests represented by federalists and antifederalists. Until these were worked out, the role of education would remain uncertain even in theory.

Uncertain Role of Education / The course of events between 1787 and 1789 in effect brought about an agreement to try Madison's middle ground between a strongly centralized and consolidated nation and a loose collection of independent sovereign states. As a result, it was extremely difficult to define with precision what the role of education ought to be in view of a compromise "federal" political system whose allocation of powers and function was still largely to be worked out. If Alexander Hamilton's or John Jay's strongly central government had clearly won out, it might have been fairly easy to design a centralized system of national education. Or if the New Jersey plan to alter somewhat the Articles of Confederation but leave the states fundamentally alone (as Patrick Henry, Samuel Adams, Richard Henry Lee, George Mason, and Elbridge Gerry advocated) had prevailed, authority over education would clearly have remained exclusively in state or in private hands.

But these extreme alternatives did not win. Out of the clash of federalist and antifederalist views came a new constitutional order that created a new federal government but did not automatically or immediately create a new or unified sense of political community. The problem for education, therefore, was how to help develop the social cohesion and sense of community required of a republican *nation* while the schools remained in state, private, or religious hands. Convention delegates were so engrossed in the federalist-antifederalist question and in the political process of winning an argument or reconciling differences that education was either ignored or postponed until the more basic question of union or disunion was settled.

In the end Madison's compromise won the day, especially when he came to agree with Jefferson that a specific bill of rights was desirable and promised that one of the first acts of the new Congress would be to draw up a bill of rights; this promise he promptly and personally carried out in the summer of 1789. What was happening was that a new conception of liberty was being formulated, the consequences of which could not be foreseen at the time. Liberty was no longer to be confined simply to the older Whig meaning, that is, the right of the people to participate in the legislative process through elected representatives. Liberty was now being extended to mean the protection of the private freedoms of individuals and minority groups against encroachments by the government itself, especially the legislature. This view of liberty also projected the idea that a liberal government would be an active protector of individuals from any threat of tyranny, if need be even from the majority itself.

Meanwhile, public men and educators began the process of redefining the role of education in the new republic. There were differences of opinion, of course, but also much ambiguity and much uncertainty. Many federalists who might have been expected to argue for a centralized educational system did not do so; stemming from aristocratic backgrounds, they were not enthusiastic about making education available to the lowly along with the well placed. On the other hand, most antifederalists who were likely to be in favor of universal common education as a means of inculcating republican virtues did not want the schools controlled by a new and feared national government.

Proposals for a federally controlled system of education were relatively few, therefore, although they did come in the decade following the adoption of the Constitution. Whatever views they espoused regarding the control or organization of education, most proposals agreed that a new public education should be developed that would instill the republican values of liberty, equality, and the public good. On these matters there was an increasing consensus among federalists and antifederalists alike before the Constitution was adopted, and among Federalists and Republicans after it was adopted. But just how to implement the new civic role that was envisioned for education continued to be a matter for intense public debate.

The whole problem was immensely complicated. The abstract goals of the projected political community described in the Declaration of Independence, the Preamble to the Constitution, and the Bill of Rights could easily be regarded as the political values that public education ought to promote. But the varying practices of the constitutional orders being worked out for over 50 years at the federal and state levels made it extremely difficult for common or uniform systems of education to be organized and promoted. Thus the public and educators alike were left with the problem of designing systems of education that would be able to promote the common values of an as yet inchoate national political community and yet be organized, controlled, and supported by the very real and often conflicting state constitutional orders manned by local public officials little schooled in the art or science of politics. No wonder the Revolutionary era could be long on rhetoric concerning the need for a common public education, but short on practical programs of schooling that would change the political rhetoric into reality.

Notes

1. R. Freeman Butts, *The American Tradition in Religion and Education* (Boston: Beacon, 1950).
2. Gordon S. Wood, *The Creation of the American Republic, 1776–1787* (Chapel Hill: University of North Carolina Perss, 1969), p. 117.
3. Wood, p. 61.
4. Edmund Morgan, "Conflict and Consensus in the American Revolution," in Stephen G. Kurtz and James H. Hutson, eds., *Essays on the American Revolution* (Chapel Hill: University of North Carolina Press, 1973), p. 308.
5. *The Federal and State Constitutions, Colonial Charters, and Other Organic Laws of the States, Territories, and Colonies Now or Heretofore Forming the United States of America*, Francis Newton Thorpe, comp. (Washington, D.C.: Government Printing Office, 1909, Vol. 3), pp. 1907–1908.
6. See U.S. Department of Health, Education and Welfare, Office of Education, *State Constitutional Provisions and Selected Legal Materials Relating to Public School Finance* (Washington, D.C.: Government Printing Office, 1973).
7. I use the lower case "federalist" and "antifederalist" to refer to the debates surrounding the adoption of the Constitution in 1787–1789; "Federalist" is capitalized when it refers to the emerging political party of the late 1790s that coagulated in opposition to the Jeffersonian Republican party of 1800. Recent historical scholarship sees no easy connection between federalist and Federalist, nor between antifederalist and Republican. All professed to be republicans.
8. Bernard Bailyn, "The Central Themes of the American Revolution," in Kurtz and Hutson, p. 22.
9. Jack P. Greene, review of *The Creation of the American Republic* by Gordon S. Wood, *New York Times Book Review*, October 26, 1969.
10. See R. Freeman Butts, *The Education of the West* (New York: McGraw-Hill, 1973).

2 The Educational Dream: Unum

A New Education for the New Republic

During much of the first Revolutionary decade following 1776, the spirit of national unity forged by common opposition to the British tended to prevail over the forces of disunity. Enthusiasm for the destiny of the new nation was reflected, as we have seen, in the state constitutions, and faith in the rule of the people was strong. Republican governments could indeed create the republican man, and under the rule of liberty, equality, and public virtue, the obscure, downtrodden peasant of a hierarchical European society could become the self-respecting, independent yeoman of a free United States. The French essayist Michel de Crèvecoeur's *Letters from an American Farmer* captured this optimism. In what may have been one of the earliest and most favorable views of the "melting pot" theory of assimilation, Crèvecoeur described this new man, the American:

> *He* is an American, who leaving behind him all his ancient prejudices and manners, receives new ones from the new mode of life he has embraced, the new government he obeys, and the new rank he holds. . . . Here individuals of all nations are melted into a new race of men, whose labours and posterity will one day cause great changes in the world.[1]

Despite this generous and idealistic dream of a new race of free men populating a new land of freedom and equality, the melting pot reality, of course, did not always match the dream. It was more likely to be replaced by a second type of assimilation, where the predominantly homogeneous English communities felt threatened by a flood of ethnically cohesive "foreigners." As early as the 1750s, Benjamin Franklin urged the large numbers of "clannish" Germans who had settled in Pennsylvania to disperse themselves more widely throughout the colony and to learn English. In the early 1780s, Jefferson worried about group immigration from the absolute monarchies of Europe, whose members would either maintain their authoritarian views or throw off all government restraint in favor of anarchy; and Washington, while President, expressed doubts about immigrants settling in a body.

These attitudes on the part of the founding fathers have been characterized as expressing a second kind of assimilationist view called Anglo-conformity, which has been defined as "the desirability of maintaining English institutions (as modified by the American Revolution), the English language, and English-oriented cultural patterns as dominant and standard in American life."[2] While it is clear that the founding fathers maintained a basic loyalty to the English language and literature, it is a bit extreme to say they favored "English-oriented cultural patterns" at a time when English rule was being overthrown, English political institutions were being reformed, the established Church of England was being rejected, English arrogance and aristocratic manners were being sloughed off, attendance at English educational institutions was frowned upon, and a new American English was developing.

We need not reject the definition just given of "Anglo-conformity" as it applied to the Revolutionary era, but we should not have the idea that those who reflected this attitude were implacable foes of anything non-English or that they displayed an inflexible determination to require rigid conformity to all things English. The dominant Revolutionary mood was rather a determination to achieve an *American republicanism*, drawing from English and non-English sources alike and rejecting monarchical and antidemocratic actions, whether from English or non-English sources. The ideas of Anglo-conformity and melting pot assimilation were thus genuinely mixed up in the attitudes of the Revolutionary generations. The fact is that the white population by 1800, though still predominantly English and Protestant, had absorbed fairly large numbers of German and Scotch-Irish along with smaller numbers of Dutch, French, Swedes, Swiss, Irish, Poles, and other immigrants. The more difficult problems of assimilation began in the 1820s, but even so the United States maintained a basically open door policy on immigration for the first 100 years of its history.

The problem facing the Revolutionary generation was not so much the cultural assimilation of massive groups of foreigners as it was the welding into a cohesive, national whole the politically diverse regional, sectional, and state factions that had joined together in fighting the Revolution. To this end, it was widely felt that the role of education should be to stress the *common values* of a republican government and a democratic society. In many different ways the stress was thus put upon uniform, homogeneous, thoroughgoing systems of education devoted to the republican purposes of public liberty, public equality, and the public good.

All this required a public education whose prime purpose would be the continuous process of strengthening the cohesive democratic republicanism that had characterized the decade that began with the Revolution, but was being eroded and threatened during the second decade. The new nation established by the Constitution needed this social cohesion even more than did the independent states proclaimed by the Declaration of Independence and the Articles of Confederation. The motto *"E Pluribus Unum"* was the prime goal still to be achieved by education in the hearts and minds of the new Americans even more than it was a factual statement describing the establishment of one nation out of many independent states. *"Unum"* embodied the sentiments behind the major proposals for education in the new republic, although *"Pluribus"* continued to describe the reality of educational practice to the end of the nation's first half century.

Early Proposals for Educational Reform

There was an interesting progression in the tone as well as content of the major proposals for educational reform during the first two decades after the Revolution of 1776. They all stressed a public system rather than private systems of education to meet the needs of the new republican society, but Jefferson's early plan was confined to a particular state, as was consistent with the 1770s. Then, as the need for greater national unity led to the Constitutional debates, the educational proposals of the 1780s began to call upon education to promote a more uniform national spirit; yet still people had not embraced the logic of a nationally controlled educational system. But by the end of the 1790s with their attendant political turmoil, the most widely publicized educational plans were candidly calling for a uniform national system of public education to promote *Unum* over *Pluribus*. As it turned out, Jefferson's earlier plan for a state system, though not achieved in his time, came closer to eventual U.S. practice than did the later proposals.

Jefferson's Plan of 1779

Jefferson's proposal for a system of public elementary and secondary schools was introduced in his *Bill for the More General Diffusion of Knowledge* in the Virginia assembly in 1779. He based his argument for public schools upon the grounds that a free society devoted to achieving the natural rights of its citizens could be maintained and tyranny prevented only if the people were well educated. Wise laws would be made and well administered only if capable persons had equal opportunity to achieve a liberal education without regard to wealth or social status. Therefore, all children of free citizens should have a chance at education at public expense.

Jefferson proposed that the citizens of each county in the state elect three aldermen to maintain schools in the county and that counties be divided into hundreds (or wards), in each of which an elementary school would be operated at county expense. The aldermen were to appoint an overseer (or superintendent) over every 10 of the district schools; his duties were to appoint teachers, visit the schools, supervise the teaching, and examine the pupils. Teachers' salaries and board and lodging were to be paid by public funds derived from taxes levied upon the ward residents, and all free children were to be entitled to attend school free of charge for at least three years and as much longer at private expense as their parents wished. The curriculum Jefferson proposed was to consist of reading, writing, arithmetic, and the history of Greece, Rome, England, and the United States. Notable in this connection was the secular character of the curriculum, with history to be substituted for religious instruction and reading of the Bible.

Jefferson also provided for a system of grammar or secondary schools. The state was to be divided into regional districts consisting of several counties each, and in each regional district a grammar school was to be established. The schools were to be under the supervision of a public board of visitors, who were to appoint teachers, visit schools, examine students, and provide for the acquisition of land and the building of the schools. The maintenance of the schools was to be paid for by private tuition, but the best students from the elementary schools were to be selected and sent to the grammar schools at public expense. These "public foundationers" should be examined each year, with only the highest achievers continuing their education at public expense; finally, the best student in each grammar school was to be chosen to attend the College of William and Mary for a full college course at public expense.

The curriculum of the grammar schools was to consist of Latin, Greek, English, geography, and higher arithmetic—a typical college preparatory program, but again omitting religious instruction. Whereas this was not a proposal for entirely free secondary education, it was a far cry from the attitude of Governor William Berkeley, who 100 years earlier exclaimed that he thanked God there were no free schools in Virginia to be the seed beds of disobedience and heresy against the state and the church.

To complete his proposals for a public system of education, Jefferson introduced a bill in the legislature in 1779 to amend the charter of the College of William and Mary so as to bring it under direct civil direction. Arguing that the college had not fulfilled the expectations of the public for nearly 100 years, and that its public service role would be important under a changed form of government, Jefferson proposed that the board of visitors be reduced in number and be appointed by vote of the legislature.

These changes would have had the effect of transforming the college

from a private corporation into a public corporation and would have made
the sectarian college into a secular state university; but thwarting Jefferson's
efforts were the orthodoxies and rigidities of established religion and class
distinctions. Until these patterns were changed to provide for separation of
church and state and more equal opportunity in political, economic, and
social participation, Jefferson found it difficult to make much headway in the
reform of education. The state of Virginia was not yet ready to venture into
genuinely public education at any level.

Probably more illuminating than the organizational details of Jefferson's
proposals was his rationale for public education as the wellspring of equality,
liberty, and the public good. Some years after the failure of his bill in the
Virginia legislature, Jefferson wrote:

> By that part of our plan which prescribes the selection of the youths of
> genius from among the classes of the poor, we hope to avail the state of
> those talents which nature has sown as liberally among the poor as the rich,
> but which perish without use, if not sought for and cultivated.—But of the
> views of this law none is more important, none more legitimate, than that of
> rendering the people the safe, as they are the ultimate, guardians of their
> own liberty. . . . In every government of earth is some trace of human weak-
> ness, some germ of corruption and degeneracy, which cunning will discover,
> and wickedness insensibly open, cultivate and improve. Every government
> degenerates when trusted to the rulers of the people alone. The people them-
> selves therefore are its only safe depositories. And to render even them safe
> their minds must be improved to a certain degree. This indeed is not all that
> is necessary, though it be essentially necessary. An amendment of our con-
> stitution must here come in aid of the public education. The influence over
> government must be shared among all the people.[3]

Jefferson's words, almost prophetic of the dangers of a Watergate syndrome,
anticipated the growing unease of the 1780s over the future of the Republic.

Benjamin Rush on Republican Education

In the hectic days of growing crisis and disenchantment with the Articles
of Confederation that led to the calling of the Constitutional Convention and
the subsequent adoption of the Constitution, two major statements on education published by prominent Americans reflected the urgency of rekindling a
common sense of public virtue among people in all stations of life. The first
was by Benjamin Rush, patriot, educator, physician, and liberal reformer.
Rush had formidable credentials: educated at Princeton and Edinburgh,
teacher of chemistry at the University of Pennsylvania, signer of the Declaration of Independence, proponent of the Constitution in the Pennsylvania convention, advocate of temperance and prison reform, and vigorous opponent
of slavery and capital punishment. In 1786 he proposed a plan for the establishment of public schools in the state of Pennsylvania, elaborating on this
plan by describing the mode of education he believed was proper in a republic.

Acknowledging that his proposals for "free schools" followed the examples of Scotland and New England, Rush's plan for a total system of public education for Pennsylvania sounded remarkably like that of Jefferson's for Virginia but on a larger scale. Free schools were to be established in every township or district for the teaching of reading and writing, in English and German, and arithmetic. Rush was a kind of *cultural pluralist* in his belief that children of the same religious sect and nation should be educated together as much as possible, but he was by all means a *political monist* in his advocacy of republicanism. Academies were to be established in every county to prepare youth for college through instruction in the classical languages. Four state colleges were to be distributed throughout the state (one for the Germans, at Mannheim) to teach the liberal arts and sciences; and a state university at the capital was to give instruction in the professions of law, medicine, divinity, and other advanced studies. Since every member of the community benefits from the diffusion of virtue and knowledge and the prevention of crime and vice, every member of the community ought to pay taxes for the support of public schools.

Rush's stress throughout was to "tie the state together by one system of education." He apparently did not have a proposal for *national* control of education through a central government, but his general essay in 1786 emphasized the need for the kind of education in the states that would produce the common sentiments necessary for achieving a truly national political community. In this respect Rush set the pattern which many of the educational reform plans were to follow: the necessity for a general and uniform system of education to render the mass of the people homogeneous in their political beliefs and loyalties to republican government.[4]

In another respect Rush's plan differed from most of the other well-publicized reform plans of the period, though it probably was congenial to most of the religious leaders of the day. In a fairly short introduction to his essay, Rush reflected the conventional wisdom of the Protestant majority, namely: religion is the foundation of virtue; virtue is the foundation of liberty; liberty is the object of all republican governments; therefore, a republican education should promote religion as well as virtue and liberty. Rush thus echoed the Revolutionary conjoining of religion and liberty that marked the 1770s. He even argued for the use of the Bible as a school textbook.

But he passed over hurriedly the knotty problem posed by denominational differences of religious interpretation. Rush's Presbyterian proclivities led him to favor the intellectual and moral order that comes from the discipline of a particular church, but his belief in religious freedom led him to avoid the issue of *which* church was to set the rules. He timidly left it to "the persons entrusted with the education of youth to inculcate upon them a strict conformity to that mode of worship which is most agreeable to their consciences or the inclinations of their parents."[5] Virtually all the other reformers of the late eighteenth century adopted the secular and less popular view that public education should not be involved in religious instruction. The Protestant majority was not required really to face this issue in public education for nearly another half century when a rapidly growing Catholic immigration forced the issue.

When Rush turned to the inculcating of republican principles, he had no timid doubts or qualms about logical inconsistencies. He warmed to his theme:

> NEXT to the duty which young men owe to their Creator, I wish to see a SUPREME REGARD TO THEIR COUNTRY inculcated. . . . Let our pupil be taught that he does not belong to himself, but that he is public property. Let him be taught to love his family, but let him be taught at the same time that he must forsake and even forget them when the welfare of his country requires it.
>
> He must watch for the state as if its liberties depended upon his vigilance alone, but he must do this in such a manner as not to defraud his creditors or neglect his family. . . . He must be taught that there can be no durable liberty but in a republic. . . .[6]

These words echoed the republican themes of public virtue of the 1770s, albeit "liberty" was not explicitly defined, and "virtue" had a noticeable Calvinist ring to its call for physical, mental, and moral discipline.

Rush had no difficulty reconciling the strict discipline of youth and the responsibilities of adult citizenship in a republic. Indeed, one was the prerequisite of the other, and if parents did not exercise the discipline, the schools must. In concluding his recital of what some today would call middle-class values, Rush cited as distasteful boarding schools for boys, taverns, and theaters—also beneficiaries of middle-class values. Summarizing his plan, Rush wrote: "From the observations that have been made it is plain that I consider it as possible to convert men into republican machines. This must be done if we expect them to perform their parts properly in the great machine of the government of the state."[7]

In one short paragraph in his general essay, Rush referred to the education of women, stressing the need for instructing them in the principles of liberty and government and the obligations of patriotism. In a special essay on female education presented at the Young Ladies' Academy in Philadelphia in July 1787 (while the Constitutional Convention was in session), Rush made a special point that the system for educating young women in America should be radically different from that inherited from Britain. The education of women here should be much more useful and more related to the new republic. Women should be educated to deal more directly with their husband's property, with the instruction of children, with the principles of liberty and government, and with running their own households, since they were not likely to have servants. Thus female education should be less ornamental and more practical, with stress placed on the English language (rather than French), writing, accounts, bookkeeping, geography, history, biography, travel, and natural philosophy rather than novel reading, instrumental music, dancing, and drawing. Of course, instruction in the principles of the different sects of Christianity was to have a firm place in the curriculum.

Rush concluded his general essay by noting the effects of religion, liberty, and education, one upon the other, and all upon the welfare of the government. In an impassioned plea to act *now*, Rush urged the citizens of Pennsylvania to establish public schools in every part of the state while the memories of the Revolution were still warm, while the spirit of liberty still pervaded the state, and *before* untoward changes occurred as the result of the sudden rise of a despotic junto or of "artful pedagogues" who might seek to prevent the establishment of public schools in favor of their own private "nurseries of party spirit." Fearful of a sprouting of rampant pluralism, Rush was apparently willing to embrace an authoritarian nationalism as a means of keeping the new republic welded together.

Noah Webster's Proposals for Reform

Much less a reformer of social causes than Rush, but even more a reformer of language and culture, Noah Webster wrote a series of essays on education at roughly the same time and with a surprisingly similar ring to the calls for public virtue and liberty as the goals of education. For some two decades after his graduation from Yale in 1778 Webster expressed many of the ideals of republican government that had marked the early Revolutionary period. He seemed well impressed by the Enlightenment ideas of Jean Jacques Rousseau, Claude Helvétius, and Thomas Paine, and he was a great advocate of cultural as well as political independence from Britain. As a teacher in Goshen, New York, he got the idea of reforming the teaching of English to adapt it to American idioms, usage, and pronunciation and at the same time of trying to overcome provincial dialects in an effort to establish a common American language. Cultural and literary nationalism went hand in hand with cultural and literary independence, as it was later to do in the newly independent nations of Asia and Africa in the twentieth century. Webster's speller (1783), grammar (1784), and reader (1785) formed a grandiose *A Grammatical Institute of the English Language*, which sold several million copies during the next 100 years. Perhaps more than any other individual, Noah Webster Americanized the elementary school curriculum in reading and writing.

In 1787–1788, during his younger and more liberal days when his pamphleteering interest in politics and cultural reform was high, Webster wrote a series of articles on education for the magazine he edited, *American Magazine*. These were published in 1790 as an essay "On the Education of Youth in America." The close connection of education, morality, and government was a dominant theme throughout:

Our constitutions of civil government are not yet firmly established; our national character is not yet formed; and it is an object of vast magnitude that systems of education should be adopted and pursued which may not only diffuse a knowledge of the sciences but may implant in the minds of the American youth the principles of virtue and of liberty and inspire them with just and liberal ideas of government and with an inviolable attachment to their own country.[8]

At this stage of his career Webster still assumed that the supreme power in a republican government should be the legislature whose elected members reflect the true interests of the people in their capacity as law-makers:

Education should therefore be the first care of a legislature, not merely the institution of schools but the furnishing of them with the best men for teachers. A good system of education should be the first article in the code of political regulations, for it is much easier to introduce and establish an effectual system for preserving morals than to correct by penal statutes the ill effects of a bad system.[9]

In line with his strong belief in cultural independence and nationalism, it is not surprising that Webster saw education as a prime molder of a distinctive and patriotic American character. A national spirit, a national consciousness, and a common set of national manners were the first order of business for education in a republic; the best means of achieving these qualities of cohesion to unite a heterogeneous people when the common danger of war had subsided was a public school system. The young Webster even had the notion that there should be an equitable distribution of property along with a system of public education as the basic foundations of a republican government.[10]

Unfortunately, Webster was to lose some of his early optimism concerning republican government. Like many Americans, he reacted with repugnance to the excesses of the French Revolution. From the late 1790s until his death in 1843 he became much more conservative and disenchanted with the popular assemblies in the states, and an ardent Federalism suffused his writing and lecturing during his last 40 years. In his essay of 1787–1788, Webster had opposed the use of the Bible as a school book, but as he became more politically conservative he stressed more and more the moral virtues of Christianity. In 1798 he added a moral catechism to his speller in which he spelled out the virtues of humility, mercy, purity, peace-making, justice, generosity, gratitude, truth, charity, almsgiving, frugality, economy, industry, and cheerfulness.

He also added "A Federal Catechism." After describing the faults of monarchy and the objections to aristocracy, Webster cited the defects of direct democracy in popular assemblies and went on to recount the blessings of a "representative republic" in which the people elected deputies to make the laws for them. He was echoing the views of the dominant conservative Federalists of his day.

Despite their differences in attitude toward the mob or the crowd and toward the use of the Bible in schools, Webster agreed with Rush in deploring too much attention to the classics, stressing the importance of English as a practical as well as a literary tool for Americans, favoring a more useful education for females, opposing the education of an American in a foreign country, and favoring a widespread education as a bulwark against crime (most convicted criminals were deemed to be foreigners). Above all, Webster stressed the need for a common education on a national scale (but without mentioning its support or control by the central government) to overcome the particularisms of the different sections of the United States.

Later Proposals for Educational Reform

Though Rush and Webster were probably the most eloquent spokesmen writing specifically about public education during the immediate formative years of the Constitution, they were not alone.

Robert Coram on Equality of Opportunity

In the very first years of the new republic, a proposal was published that went well beyond Rush and Webster in its greater stress upon equality over liberty and public virtue. It also went beyond them in arguing for free compulsory elementary education on a national scale. At the age of 30, Robert Coram had become an ardent antifederalist editor and publisher in Wilmington, Delaware. In 1791 he published "Political Inquiries: to which is Added, a Plan for the General Establishment of Schools throughout the United States." Though at the opposite political pole from Noah Webster, Coram agreed with his fellow-editor on the importance of public education. In fact, Coram quoted Webster approvingly and at length on the civic role of public education in a republic.

But Coram came at the problem of education from a long and involved analysis of the relation of property to government. In an emotional and passionate attack upon Sir William Blackstone's theory of the origin of private property, Coram rejected the notion that property had to be vested in individuals if agriculture and civilization were to prosper. He pointed out that American Indians pursued agriculture but still held land in common and enjoyed the fruits of their labor. Thus, it is labor that constitutes the right to property, not the natural right of possession. In the transition from a state of nature to a state of civil society, landed property was the result of arbitrary acts of government which in turn divested propertyless men of their rights to citizenship. Thus the vast majority of men have been cheated out of their right to the soil, and this unequal distribution of land was the parent of most of the disorders besetting governments. This truth offered a foundation upon which to build a system of equal education—that is, a state which obliged citizens to give up their natural right to property must preserve their civil liberties so that they could acquire the *means* to obtain some property. That means is *knowledge* of some art or science, which can alone enable citizens to support themselves and provide for subsistence in civil society. Therefore schools should be provided equally for all in order that all persons might acquire the knowledge necessary for their sustenance. And such schooling should be free and compulsory, not left to the accident of wealth or to the whims or indifference of parents:

> Education, then, ought to be secured by government to every class of citizens, to every child in the state. . . .
> Education should not be left to the caprice or negligence of parents, to chance, or confined to the children of wealthy citizens; it is a shame, a scandal to civilized society, that part only of the citizens should be sent to colleges and universities to learn to cheat the rest of their liberties.[11]

Throughout Coram's essay there is deep concern for the poor. He attacked the vagrancy and poor laws of England (where he was born) whose government made the mass of people poor and then persecuted them as vagabonds for being poor. Everyone should support the government, but each should be *able* to pay a tax before being compelled to do it as a duty.

Like the good antifederalist that he was, Coram lamented the inequities of rural education as compared with that of the towns. He saw that if the miserable rural schools for farmers were not improved and made equal with the town schools, the urban mercantile classes, with their greater ability to provide education for their children, would always control the government. He believed, therefore, that the schools must be incorporated into the government; they must be public, not private, and they must be available everywhere, free to all, and supported by public taxes:

> The necessity of a reformation in the country schools is too obvious to be insisted on, and the first step to such reformation will be by turning private schools into public ones. The schools should be public, for several reasons—1st. Because, as has been before said, every citizen has an equal right to subsistence and ought to have an equal opportunity of acquiring knowledge. 2d. Because public schools are easiest maintained, as the burden falls upon all the citizens. . . .
> Let public schools then be established in every county of the United States, at least as many as are necessary for the present population; and let those schools be supported by a general tax. Let the objects of those schools be to teach the rudiments of the English language, writing, bookkeeping, mathematics, natural history, mechanics, and husbandry—and let every scholar be admitted gratis and kept in a state of subordination without respect to persons. . . .
> To demonstrate the practicability of establishing public schools throughout the United States, let us suppose the states to be divided into districts

according to the population, and let every district support one school by a tax on the acre on all lands within the district.[12]

And like the good antifederalist that he was, Coram gave no hint that it would be the federal government that would divide the states into districts. He presumably wanted a common national system but not a federally managed system. He agreed with Webster that no specific religious faiths be taught, and he wanted no foreign languages in his elementary schools. Indeed, he made no mention of secondary schools, and the only references to colleges were as places where the privileged youth learned to cheat the poor. Coram was thus an egalitarian antifederalist echoing the radical republicanism of the 1770s. While he quoted Webster approvingly, he cannily picked up Webster's offhand reference to a distribution of lands and virtually made it into an argument that every citizen ought to possess a freehold! And the best protector against inequality was an equal education. Without an equal education available to all, a distribution of lands, however equal at first, would soon become unequal if education reverted into the hands of the few. If equality required a certain amount of uniformity in education, so be it. Uniformity meant commonality.

George Washington on Education for the Public Good

While Coram's republican antifederalism led him to stress equality in education as diffused by a general system of elementary schools throughout the nation, the Federalist view, following the establishment of the Union under the new Constitution, was more likely to stress the public good. By this was meant the need to achieve a sense of community that transcended the rivalries of sections and regions that had reasserted themselves after the war. This had been a prime argument of the federalist advocates of a stronger and more centralized national government in the first place. In the forefront of those who envisioned this unifying role of education was George Washington himself. With regard to elementary or secondary education, he spoke only vaguely of the value of "wide diffusion of knowledge," but he returned many times to the theme that a national university under the auspices of the federal government would bring together the future leaders of the nation for a common education in science and literature at the advanced levels.

In his first annual message to Congress in 1790, Washington urged the Congress to patronize and promote science and literature.[13] While he seemed reluctant to use the word "schools," it was a remarkable statement of the need for an education that would teach the people to know and value their rights as a prime means of developing a sense of community upon which the leader could draw. Washington guardedly left it to the Congress to decide whether to promote science and literature by aiding "seminaries of learning already established, by the institution of a national university, *or by any other expedients*."[14] But Congress apparently was little impressed, replying vaguely that literature and science *are* essential for the preservation of a free Constitution and the security of a free government.

In May 1790, a motion was made in the House of Representatives to refer Washington's proposals to a select committee, but it was opposed as going beyond the Constitution. The only recorded voice in favor was that of John Page, Republican from Virginia, lifelong friend and supporter of Jefferson, and later governor of Virginia, who argued that a Constitutional amendment should be passed if Congress did not already have the right to promote science and literature, for, "on the diffusion of knowledge and literature depend the liberties of this country, and the preservation of the Constitution."[15] But the House adjourned without a decision on the motion.

Toward the end of his second administration Washington came back to his favorite theme of a national university and even flirted with the idea that Congress ought to promote public education at the lower levels as well. Washington hinted in some of his correspondence that he favored Congressional support for general public education, but, curiously, this never got into his official messages. In a letter to the governor of Virginia in 1795, Washington again referred to his desire to contribute to a national university, but also slipped into the use of the term "universal public education" which he believed should be adopted in the United States.[16]

In a similar vein, Washington sent a draft of his proposed Farewell Address in a private letter to Alexander Hamilton a few days before sending it to the newspapers in September 1796. He again referred to "Education *generally*" as a subject he wished had been included in the early draft of the document; he went on to repeat his reasons for wanting a federal university to promote national unity and asked Hamilton to insert such a section in the draft. Hamilton replied that he thought the university proposal should be put into the President's regular message to Congress at the opening of its next session and that the general suggestion about education be retained in the Farewell Address. Washington apparently complied. In his final message to Congress he said:

> The more homogeneous our Citizens can be made in these particulars, the greater will be our prospect of permanent union; and a primary object of such a National Institution should be, the education of our Youth in the science of *Government*. In a Republic, what species of knowledge can be equally important? and what duty, more pressing on its Legislature, than to patronize a plan for communicating it to those, who are to be the future guardians of the liberties of the Country?[17]

But when it came to the Farewell Address as finally drafted, Washington spoke neither of a "plan for universal education" nor "education *generally*," but only of "institutions for the general diffusion of knowledge." The Farewell Address has often been taken as a great state document on foreign affairs cautioning the people of the United States against entangling alliances, but the first and major part had to do with the urgency of national unity, the dangers of sectional strife and "the spirit of party generally," and the "necessity of reciprocal checks in the exercise of political power."

It was in this setting that Washington paid his respects to the importance of religion and morality in holding the society together, and it was in this connection that his "general suggestion respecting education" did indeed come into the Farewell Address:

> Of all the dispositions and habits which lead to political prosperity, Religion and morality are indispensable supports. . . . reason and experience both forbid us to expect that National morality can prevail in exclusion of religious principle.
> 'Tis substantially true, that virtue or morality is a necessary spring of popular government. . . .
> Promote then, as an object of primary importance, Institutions for the general diffusion of knowledge. In proportion as the structure of a government gives force to public opinion, it is essential that public opinion should be enlightened.[18]

Granted the political usages of appeals to religion that have marked most Presidential addresses since Washington's time, this conjunction of religion, morality, and education as bulwarks to a republican government undoubtedly reflected the dominant views of the vast majority of Americans in 1796. But this linkage worked both for and against the spread of the idea of public education. It was no particular obstacle to a Rush or a Webster or a Washington, but it *was* an obstacle to a Jefferson and to many of his followers in the ranks of the emerging Republican party in its contests with the Federalists.

Advocates of a National System of Public Education

While Washington was stating his public beliefs about education in the most general (some would say platitudinous) terms, a band of intellectuals was about to probe much more deeply into "the best system of liberal education adapted to the genius of the government of the United States." This was the topic for an essay contest conducted by the American Philosophical Society, whose president was Thomas Jefferson in the year Washington retired as President of the United States. Not surprisingly, the two essay winners were Jeffersonian in their advocacy of thoroughgoing systems of public education, but scarcely Jeffersonian in their proposals that there should be a *national* system of education under federal auspices.

The two winners of the American Philosophical Society's contest wrote the longest and the most detailed plans that appeared during the two Revolutionary decades. They were also the most radical in their proposals for a national system of education, and therefore they were probably the least influential, for the idea of federal control of education never did overcome the state and local loyalties and the private and religious values of the majority of the American people. But the logic of their views at the end of the 1790s was impeccable. If state systems of public education were the proper accompaniments of the coming to independence of the several states, and if those states after a decade of separate independence saw the necessity of a stronger federal union, then there should be a federal system of education to support the new national political community of which the new federal government was the Constitutional embodiment. So argued the two Samuels who shared the prize, though neither turned out to be a very good prophet.

Samuel Harrison Smith / The youngest of the writers on educational reform in the Revolutionary period was Samuel Harrison Smith, a graduate of the University of Pennsylvania at age 15 in 1787, and age 25 when he won the prize. For many years he was editor of the *National Intelligencer*, a pro-Jefferson newspaper in Philadelphia. After a long and prolix discussion of the close connection among virtue, wisdom, and happiness as the goals of education, Smith summarized his principles of compulsory education as follows:

> It is the duty of a nation to superintend and even to coerce the education of children and that high considerations of expediency not only justify but dictate the establishment of a system which shall place under a control, independent of and superior to parental authority, the education of children. . . .
>
> Guided by these principles it is proposed:
>
> I.   That the period of education be from 5 to 18.
>
> II.   That every male child, without exception, be educated.
>
> III. That the instructor in every district be directed to attend to the faithful execution of this injunction. That it be made punishable by law in a parent to neglect offering his child to the preceptor for instruction.
>
> IV.   That every parent who wishes to deviate in the education of his children from the established system be made responsible for devoting to the education of his children as much time as the established system prescribes.
>
> V.   That a fund be raised from the citizens in the ratio of their property.
>
> VI.   That the system be composed of primary schools, of colleges, and of a *University*.[19]

Smith went on to elaborate the usual content of curriculum in the primary schools. He included at the upper levels (ages 10–18) the duty "to commit to memory and frequently to repeat the Constitution and the fundamental laws of the United States." He echoed Jefferson's plan in urging that the top boys in the primary schools be selected for the colleges and supported at public expense and that one out of ten be promoted to the national university and similarly supported at public expense. Finally, he proposed that a 14-member national board of literature and science be established by law to superintend the national system of education from top to bottom, including the selection of textbooks for all schools and colleges.

A close link was obviously to exist between the professors in the national university and the national board. The board in the first instance was to be established by law (presumably by Congress) and thereafter chosen by the professors in the university and approved by the colleges. The professional interlocking of the whole system was to be further enhanced by an appointment process in which the professors of the university chose the professors of the colleges, and the professors of the colleges chose the preceptors of the primary schools.

The young and unrealistic Smith could imagine only one serious objection to his plan—its expense. He simply argued that the amount of taxes required for a liberal compensation to professors and preceptors would be a tiny fraction of the total wealth of the country. He apparently could not anticipate that parents could object to compulsory education or that states-righters would take offense at having their school teachers and college professors appointed by outsiders in a national university and their textbooks selected by a national board. With respect to female education, the young Smith took the cowardly way out by simply saying it was too controversial to discuss. But his instincts concerning the political role of education were humane and enlightened even if a bit grandiloquent. In the perspective of history he should have been listened to in at least one respect. The United States would have had an enhanced moral influence in the world if it had relied more upon a "liberal and just education" to produce harmony at home and less upon its physical strength abroad:

> Scarcely a century can elapse before the population of America will be equal and her power superior to that of Europe. Should the principles be then established, which have been contemplated, . . . we may expect to see America too enlightened and virtuous to spread the horrors of war over the face of any country and too magnanimous and powerful to suffer its existence where she can prevent it. Let us, then, with rapture anticipate the era when the triumph of peace and the prevalence of virtue shall be rendered secure by the diffusion of useful knowledge.[20]

Such was the rapturous dream of the good that public education could bring to the world if only it were universally practiced at home.

Samuel Knox / The other winner of the American Philosophical Society's award, Samuel Knox, was much more modest in his rhetoric and more respectful of address to his readers, as befitted one who had just recently come to the United States when he wrote his long essay. A graduate of the University of Glasgow and a Presbyterian minister, Knox undoubtedly was influenced by the Scottish experience with a national system of schools; but, remarkably, he seemed to stress all three of the major Revolutionary goals— the public good, civil liberty, and equality. And as latecomers are often superpatriotic, Knox was the most nationalistic in proposing a centralized system of public schools throughout the country, what he called "an entire, general, uniform, national plan" of public education.

In his essay published in 1799, Knox made a great point of divorcing religion from public education in order to allow the pursuit of science and literature free from religious history and prejudice. No public funds should go to the support of religious teachers, but he urged the state to encourage the local districts to provide a more equal education by offering them state funds to pay the teachers if they constructed their own school buildings. As might be expected of a Presbyterian minister, he favored "preserving submission to the well directed discipline and progressive improvement of academical instruction."

Indeed, in his general essay Knox made much of the need for discipline. Indulgent parents pampered their children too much, so he found "public education" in a school under the authority of a teacher preferable to private tutoring at home. He was not talking about *free* public education offered at public expense except for a few boys, but he *was* talking about school education established and superintended by state and national authorities as the best means for discovering those of ability and merit who would be prime candidates for political leadership.

Not only would a uniform plan of education aid in the socializing and selection of leaders for public office, but it would help to iron out the inequalities caused by local differences and diversity of population. To achieve this national harmony and unity Knox went beyond all other contemporary plans in advocating a complete national system of educational institutions with a national board of education at the top—in effect projecting upon the whole nation what eventually became the basic ladder system of public education in the several states:

> In order to found, lay out, and carry into effect the several seminaries, let *a board of education* be incorporated under the sanction of the united authority of the states. These gentlemen should be nominated and appointed in every state, either by the united government or by the respective state assemblies: one or two in each state might be sufficient. Their office should not only be to preside over the general interests of literary instruction, to digest, direct, and arrange an uniform system in all its parts and to correspond in such a manner as to support the general and united interests of education, but more especially, in their individual capacity, to preside with regard to it in those states in which they were resident.
>
> Hence they might very properly be styled "Presidents of literary instruction and Members of the board of national education."[21]

Though Knox's plan for public education was extraordinary for its scope and inclusiveness, there was little extraordinary in his specifications for curriculum or method with regard to achieving the goals of liberty, equality, and public good. The primary school subjects were to be the usual ones, and four years seemed sufficient (ages 8–12). The county academies (ages 12–15) would be strictly college preparatory boarding schools specializing in Latin, Greek, and mathematics. The state colleges (one in each state) would offer the traditional liberal arts leading to the bachelor of arts degree. The national university would boast professors in all the major fields of knowledge of the day, except theology. One interesting and fairly novel feature was the proposal that a number of poor boys should be selected from the primary schools to go on to the academies and state colleges at public expense provided they became teachers. But otherwise the assumption seemed to be that the objectives of the Revolution could be achieved in public education if only the predominant kind of education then being offered in the private schools and colleges could be made available on a wide scale to all parts of the population (except that Knox apparently did not include girls beyond the primary schools, and he obviously did not have in mind blacks or Indians).

Knox's organizational plan went so far beyond the practice of the day that it actually stood little chance of realization. It did envision, however, that what he and others called a "uniform plan" could "be productive of not only harmony of sentiments, unity of taste and manners, but also the patriotic principles of genuine federalism amongst the scattered and variegated citizens of this extensive republic."

This constant reference to uniformity, the size of the country, and diversity of population reflected the problems facing a newly independent nation trying to achieve a sense of community and national identity in the late eighteenth century. The same problems faced the newly independent states of Asia and Africa in the late twentieth century. The search for community in the face of great diversity is an enormous burden to load upon education at any time. The United States might have had better luck if it had responded with more alacrity to the pleas and dreams of its Revolutionary reformers. But it did not do so. Perhaps it could not have done so. In any case, *Unum* was the dream envisioned by the advocates of public education in the first decades of the Revolutionary era, but *Pluribus* remained the social and political reality which educators had to face as the early nineteenth century got underway.

Notes

1. Michel de Crèvecoeur (J. Hector St. John), quoted in Milton M. Gordon, *Assimilation in American Life: The Role of Race, Religion, and National Origins* (New York: Oxford, 1964), p. 116.
2. Gordon, p. 88.
3. Thomas Jefferson, *Notes on the State of Virginia*, 2d American edition (Philadelphia: Mathew Carey, 1794), pp. 215–216.
4. Benjamin Rush, "A Plan for the Establishment of Public Schools . . . ," in Frederick Rudolph, ed., *Essays on Education in the Early Republic* (Cambridge, Mass.: The Belknap Press of Harvard University Press, 1965), p. 10.

5. Rush, in Rudolph, p. 12.
6. Rush, in Rudolph, pp. 13–15.
7. Rush, in Rudolph, p. 17.
8. Noah Webster, "On the Education of Youth in America," in Rudolph, p. 45.
9. Webster, in Rudolph, p. 64.
10. Webster, in Rudolph, pp. 65–66.
11. Robert Coram, "Political Inquiries: . . . a Plan for the Establishment of Schools Throughout the United States," in Rudolph, pp. 112–113.
12. Coram, in Rudolph, pp. 137–140.
13. George Washington, First Address to Congress, 1790, in John C. Fitzpatrick, ed., *The Writings of George Washington* (Washington, D.C.: Government Printing Office, 1940), Vol. 30, p. 493.
14. Washington, First Address to Congress, in Fitzpatrick, Vol. 30, p. 494 (italics added).
15. *Annals of the U.S. Congress*, First Congress, II, pp. 1550–1551.
16. Washington, Letter to the Governor of Virginia, 1795, in Fitzpatrick, Vol. 34, pp. 149–150.
17. Washington, Message to Congress, 1796, in Fitzpatrick, Vol. 35, pp. 316–317.
18. Washington, Farewell Address, 1796, in Fitzpatrick, Vol. 35, pp. 229–230.
19. Samuel Harrison Smith, "Remarks on Education . . . ," in Rudolph, p. 210.
20. Smith, in Rudolph, pp. 219–223.
21. Samuel Knox, "An Essay on the Best System of Liberal Education . . . ," in Rudolph, pp. 317–320.

The Educational Reality: Pluribus

Competing Claims Upon Education

In the half century between the Declaration of Independence in 1776 and Jefferson's death in 1826, the grand hopes for a common public education were only faintly realized on the state and local levels and virtually not at all on the national level. The goal of educational *Unum* was still far in the future; the practice of educational *Pluribus* remained the predominant reality, as it had in the Colonial period. But during the early nineteenth century, momentum was gathering for using the instrument of the new state governments to promote education, especially elementary and higher education. These efforts were uneven in different parts of the country and in different sections of the several states. They were sporadic in effect, often originating with the passage of laws, ordinances, or resolutions, but with indifferent results or long delays in their implementation. They often were directed at specific groups in the population, the poor at the bottom or the privileged at the top. And the actions of the state governments were often closely intertwined with private, philanthropic, or religious efforts. But by the middle of the nineteenth century, the cause of common public education was winning widespread support, especially in New England and New York, and was to sweep most of the country in the 100 years after 1826.

Education for a Sense of National Identity

In general, this restless searching for a greater role for public education in U.S. society was part of the broader movement toward nationhood and incipient modernization that began in the last quarter of the eighteenth

43

century and dominated the later nineteenth century. We have already seen how national independence spurred a reassessment of the role that education ought to play in an independent republic. These ideas continued to be promulgated in public statements for generation after generation until they filtered into attitudes and beliefs as well as legislation—formless though they might be when it came to actual practice. The principal educational problem as seen by the public men of the Revolutionary period was how to instill the idea that a pluralistic "we" could all become Americans and thus achieve a sense of national identity in the midst of great diversity. They began the search for an educational underpinning for democratic republican institutions. The idea began to emerge that free, universal, compulsory common schooling was indeed that educational underpinning.

Thus the school books were rewritten, as they have been in virtually all newly independent nations, to play up the glorious history, achievements, superior qualities, and special mission of the United States in the world. Sparked by Noah Webster's Americanization of reading, spelling, and grammar textbooks, a succession of new texts in geography, arithmetic, and history followed. They reflected the same kind of republican nationalism displayed by Benjamin Rush and Robert Coram. Ruth Elson documents with great detail her generalizations:

> All books agree that the American nation politically expressed is the apostle of liberty, a liberty personified, apostrophized, sung to, set up in God-like glory, but rarely defined. To discover what liberty means in these books is a murky problem. The child reader could be certain that it is glorious, it is American, it is to be revered, and it deserves his primary loyalty. But for the child to find out from these books what this liberty is would be astonishing.[1]

The schools were thus obviously expected to engender a national identity, usually through an exaggerated spirit of nationalism. This goal was seldom debated and usually did not distinguish public from private schools during the early period. But, the question of "patriotism" on the part of ethnic minorities was not the burning or violent problem that it became later in the nineteenth and twentieth centuries. The reason is that there was a very high degree of ethnic homogeneity at the time of the Revolution. Perhaps as many as 85 percent of Americans had roots in the British Isles. This was just beginning to change in the 1820s, and some rumblings of "nativism" appeared, but the enormous problems of effecting social cohesion in the face of a rapidly growing immigration were yet to appear. When they did come, with successive waves of immigration that mounted from the 1830s onward, the role of public education versus private education was right in the middle.

Economic Modernization

What did raise the question of public versus private education in the first quarter of the nineteenth century were matters stemming from class distinctions (centering upon what to do about the poor in the cities) and religious diversity (arising from the tremendous growth of the several Protestant sects). Compared with the range of socioeconomic differences among upper and lower classes in most European countries, the gap in the United States was not nearly so extreme. The pyramid of social classes here was flatter than those of European countries. Yet, as economic modernization took the form of expanding factories that drew new workers to the rapidly growing urban centers, the numbers of the laboring poor began almost to overwhelm the cities, as they were already doing in the factory towns of England. The spectacle of vast numbers of ragged children haunting the streets of New York, Philadelphia, and Boston prompted feelings of fear, revulsion, and contempt or of pity and charity among the more privileged elements of the community. Educational solutions ranged from charity schools of religious societies to philanthropic schools aided by public funds to public schools under government control. But almost everywhere one of the remedies for poverty was seen to be the extension of education. People in the United States turned more quickly to public schools for this purpose than did the English.

We shall have more to say about the problem of the poor as a factor in the growth of the public school in later chapters as we see how poverty and immigration together put to a severe test the very notion of a common school as a basic ingredient of a democratic society. At this point, it need be said only that the first generation of workers who came to the early factories in the first quarter of the nineteenth century came from a predominantly rural and village type of society accustomed to a traditional culture. They were largely unfamiliar with the new requirements of coordinated group discipline, orderliness, careful work habits, and punctuality demanded by factory work and industrialization wherever they appeared in modernizing societies. Such demands were often inhumanely and brutally enforced, but any society moving to industrialize requires a discipline and regularity of habits that are in sharp contrast to the more informal patterns of life in a rural or agrarian culture, which can survive irregular work habits, tardiness, frequent absences, gambling, drinking, festivity, and long holidays.

The profit motives of greedy employers and factory owners could and did exacerbate the differences in life-styles and work ethics between themselves and their employees. Yet the underlying tensions between the preindustrial cultures of traditional peoples and the requirements of a factory system were there as a basic element in the modernization process—unlovely and unwanted by many, but there. And similar tensions recurred with every wave of immigrants to the United States for the next 150 years.[2]

Political Modernization

In addition to the early surge in economic growth represented by a lively commerce and an industry that increased productivity, specialization, and diversification, the United States moved to modernize politically. The greatest leap, as we have seen, was the creation of a legitimate constitutional order, rapidly followed by an extraordinary expansion of the suffrage and popular participation, both integral parts of a modern political system. The development of a recognizable competitive party system also quickly followed under the organizing initiative of the Jeffersonian Republicans toward the end of the 1790s. Their strenuous efforts to remove property qualifications for voting led to a remarkable increase in the white male electorate by the end of the 1820s and the beginning of the Jacksonian era. The competitive efforts of the second-generation Federalists to meet the Republican challenge helped to account for the increase in the numbers of people actually voting in the early part of the nineteenth century.

While in theory the development of a competitive party system is a sign of political modernity, it is also true that the intense spirit of party rivalry in the fledgling United States helped to hold back the development of an inclusive and effective system of public education, another sure sign of modernity. Gains made by the Republicans in a state or city would often be nullified by the coming to power of the Federalists, and vice versa. The slow process of passing educational laws or the delays in putting them into effect were often the results of intense partisan feeling. By and large, the Republican dreams and hopes of the 1790s were clouded by a rising conservative reaction in the first decades of the nineteenth century. While the conservatives could not wrest the White House from the Jeffersonians, certainly they were able to hold off definitive and effective action at the state and city levels in many parts of the country.

In general, the public school idea was largely Republican and Jeffersonian from the 1770s to the 1790s. After 1800, a strong conservative consensus arose upon which the public school ideal foundered in favor of private, religious, and charity schools until the Republican ideals were refurbished by the reformers of the 1830s.

However, the case for or against public education was by no means drawn up along rigidly Republican or Federalist lines. It was the antagonistic interplay of these groups that often stood in the way of agreement. Or it was a difference in motivation in particular times and places. Republicans interested in extending public primary schools to all would oppose the charity efforts of Federalists to concentrate on the poor. Federalists interested in gaining public support for private higher education would oppose the efforts of Republican legislatures to establish public colleges under state control. Intense partisan rivalry gave zest to the *political* process, but it often made the *governing* process more difficult, especially when the political institutions were still in a formative stage.

What did seem to happen was that liberty (still largely defined as popular participation) was on the increase, and equality (defined as social mobility) was also fairly widely accepted, but the conception of the public good, so prominent in early Republican ideology, was eroding as aggressive private enterprisers began to dominate the politicians. Whereas the goal of the elite in the Revolutionary era was to work in public affairs, the elite of later generations turned more and more to commerce and industry. The political system, especially at the federal level, adopted more and more the passive stance of responding to pressures. Unlike the governments of many newly independent countries of the twentieth century, the federal government neglected to play a leadership role in modernization by planning and directing the course of national development.

Thus, in the United States economic modernization was pushed by private enterprise with only sporadic, disconnected, and unpredictable aid from the federal and state governments. Abroad, it was actively directed and promoted, for example, by the centralized governments of Napoleon and the Prussian rulers. Political modernization in the form of civil and military bureaucracies was similarly speeded up by these autocratic governments. The United States was far ahead in those aspects of political modernization having to do with popular political participation and the differentiation of political structures according to legislative, executive, and judicial functions. But governing bodies in the United States were much less efficient than their European counterparts, especially at the federal level, because of the lack of a differentiated, specialized, and professional civil service. Most obvious, however, was the fact that U.S. governments (whether state or federal) had little capability or even desire to coordinate the localisms and the pluralisms that were veering off in many different directions in the early nineteenth century.

Religious Revival

What *was* certain, and what was both a strength and a weakness, was the fact that the uncertainty about the role of government in modernization and national development was counterbalanced by an enormous vitality in what political scientists call social "infrastructure." People began to organize themselves voluntarily into all kinds of groups for all kinds of purposes— political, religious, cultural, literary, philanthropic, cooperative, professional, scientific, fraternal. Sometimes this was done because there were no government agencies available to meet a need, and sometimes because the people felt they could do the job better than government could. Among these groups, the early labor organizations might have had a strong influence upon the growth of public education, but they proved to be politically as well as economically weak until much later in the century. The voluntary organizations that proved to be the most active and the most influential in U.S. education during this as well as later periods were the religious organizations.

One of the most intriguing developments of the early post-Revolutionary period was a vast expansion of religious influence throughout the country, sometimes known as the Second Great Awakening or even the Protestant

Counterreformation. This revival has been regarded as a conservative movement by Protestant ministers designed to recapture some of the authority that had been diverted from them to the Patriot cause during the Revolution. Its manifestations were often found in revival meetings that swept up thousands in an emotional expression of faith and piety. It engendered a spirit of mission that sent preachers to the remote parts of the country as well as to the cities, prompted churches to establish charity schools and colleges, and sparked the first major U.S. missionary efforts in Asia and Africa.

The enormous success of the Protestant churches in gathering great numbers of persons into their fold is attributed to the organizational talents of the Methodists, followed by the Baptists. The genius of the movement, as analyzed by Donald G. Mathews, was the ability to organize thousands of people into hundreds of small groups that managed to hold together even after the preachers who had recruited them moved on.[3] While the Baptists and Methodists organized thousands of new religious societies, the Presbyterians and Congregationalists followed with hundreds of missionary societies, all serving as a unifying factor in creating a common sense of moral community.

The upshot was that the moral tone of the country became even more Christian and Protestant than it had been during the early Revolutionary era when a secular and civic republicanism seemed to envelop the Christian along with the deistic and secular leanings of the Jeffersonians. But in the post-Revolutionary period the permeation of U.S. culture by the Second Great Awakening made religion a more important influence than civic republicanism. In any case, it was patent to most people that the United States *was* a Christian (and they meant Protestant) nation that could tolerate different creeds as long as they were Christian.

The official disestablishment of the privileged churches and the separation of church and state in the federal Constitution and in most of the state constitutions had taken place on the wave of republican liberalism. The Great Awakening did not reverse these achievements, but it did reaffirm the belief that morality and religion were virtually synonymous as goals of education, whether public or private. During the period under consideration, the predominant view was that all children should be grounded in the fundamentals of religion that virtually all Protestant denominations could agree upon—the Bible; or at least that textbooks should mirror the biblical lessons as basic to good conduct and good citizenship. In some places sectarian instruction began to be challenged before 1830, but interdenominational Protestantism was the rule in public schools until the middle of the century.

If the Jeffersonian ideal of secular civic education had dominated the U.S. scene more thoroughly in the early national period, it is possible that the ideals of the public good would have speeded the political modernization of the United States. But it was not to be, in large part because the religious revival surely slowed the growth of public education at the secondary and higher levels. The judgment about the role of religion in speeding or slowing the growth of elementary public schools is harder to make because of the variety of circumstances in the various states and regions. In Pennsylvania, Virginia, and New York, religious interests were slow to accept the idea of public schools under state auspices. In the western regions, even where sectarian rivalries tended to block the establishment of state universities as threats to their denominational colleges, the various Protestant groups were able to work together to agitate for the establishment of public common schools, feeling reasonably sure that they would reflect a nondenominational Protestant consensus.[4]

Slavery and Antislavery Movements

While the role of religion in the development and modernization of the United States may be ambiguous, the role of slavery and racism is not. Slavery was an immoral affront to the Revolutionary ideals of civil liberty and civic equality; it also contradicted the religious equality of all persons in the sight of God as preached by the early evangelicals following the lead of such Quakers as John Wise, John Woolman, and Anthony Benezet. Moreover, slavery was in most respects a traditional and antimodern phenomenon. It was based upon classifications of race, color, and kinship rather than upon achievement and performance; it excluded blacks from participation in government and the political process; it represented the widest possible gap between classes and castes; and it divided a nation that had recently and bravely set out upon the road to a free, equal, and just society.[5]

During the 1770s and 1780s, antislavery movements gathered momentum as many whites and blacks in both the North and South sought to bring into practice the Revolutionary preachings of both secular and religious leaders. The federal government had compromised on the issue. The Declaration of Independence did not condemn the slave trade as originally proposed by Jefferson, and the prohibition of slavery in the Northwest Territories by the Ordinance of 1787 was accompanied by the stipulation that slave owners could legally recover any of their slaves who escaped to the new states. The Constitution adopted this formula, along with that of counting a slave as three-fourths of a free white, and outlawed the slave trade only after 20 years. Since the federal Constitution was at best ambiguous and at worst contradictory of the Revolutionary ideals, the problem devolved upon the states, which soon began to divide up legally and constitutionally into North and South on the issue. And since public education was by definition a matter of state governmental policy and legislation, the future of public education for blacks as well as for whites in the United States was indelibly affected by these early decisions.

Connecticut outlawed the slave trade in 1771 and Rhode Island in 1774, but the first state to abolish slavery within its borders was Pennsylvania, in a law of 1780 which proclaimed the principle of equality and the presumption of freedom for everyone in the future except for those slaves who were registered by their owners. In providing for gradual emancipation, Pennsylvania still upheld the rights of slave holders to recapture fugitive slaves. A New Jersey law of 1788 required slave owners to teach their slaves to read. New York enacted a gradual abolition act in 1799. Massachusetts abolished slavery by judicial decision under the bill of rights of its constitution of 1780. By 1805, all of the states north of the Mason-Dixon line had made some provision for emancipation, and by 1830 legal Negro slavery was all but wiped out in the North.

These legal provisions did not, of course, abolish social discrimination or prejudice or remove all legal liabilities from free Negroes, but they did go a long way to reflect the Revolutionary ideals of liberty and equality as applied to blacks as well as whites. Many of the northern states went on to pass personal liberty laws to protect blacks as well as whites, specifically with respect to trial by jury and habeas corpus. These laws eventually formed an important backdrop for the Fourteenth Amendment's broad guarantee in 1868 of due process and equal protection of the laws which was eventually applied to public education by the Supreme Court in 1954.

Significant Legislative Steps
Toward Public Education

In response to these competing claims, the attention given to public education in the first 50 years of the Republic was characterized by a great deal of written and oral rhetoric, many proposals and generalized plans, a good deal of petitioning of public bodies at state and town levels, much committee reporting, and even some passage of legislation pointing to new government policies. The actual results were not momentous, but they were significant in several states and cities, and they set the stage for the onrushing developments of the next 50 years. The rest of this chapter will illustrate some of the more significant events and trends.

By and large Massachusetts and to a lesser extent Connecticut continued to take the lead in point of timing and influence upon other parts of the country, especially the Middle West. New York illustrated an interesting interplay between state and city that forecast some of the complexities of the whole process of modernizing education in an increasingly urbanized society. Pennsylvania was still slower to live up to its earlier liberalism, and while the southern states were replete with brave plans, they somehow seemed to confine their interest in public education to charity education for the poor at one extreme and to higher education for the well-to-do at the other.

Underlying almost all the planning and agitating was the growing feeling that private and voluntary efforts were not going to do the job of educating the growing numbers of poor in the cities. While some people welcomed the idea that government efforts must be strengthened and broadened and others resisted it, the period ended with solid movements toward public control and public support. Vast numbers of charity schools, subscription schools, religious schools, Sunday schools, infant schools, academies, and proprietary schools began either to receive some public funds, or feel the competition from free public schools, or lose their private character and transform themselves into public institutions. Indeed, even where government agencies like towns and villages were supposed to set up common schools under state prodding or the carrot of state financial aid, the differences in quality, performance, and length of schooling remained enormous. Educational *Pluribus* still reigned, but somewhat less certainly.

New England

Massachusetts / As the 1780s began and the Revolutionary War was coming to a close, the Colonial tradition of public schooling in Massachusetts faced one of its most severe tests. Money was short, and many towns did not reopen their public schools. Yet the constitution of 1780 enjoined the legislature to promote education. One way the legislature did this was to charter private academies like Andover and to support Harvard College. Another way was to reassert through state authority the commandments of the Colonial general court—many of which dated back to 1642—to the towns to conduct schools. Echoing the Colonial laws, Massachusetts passed in 1789 a fairly comprehensive law requiring all towns of 50 householders to provide an elementary schoolmaster to teach the 3 R's and "decent behavior" for at least six months a year; in towns of 100 householders, elementary school was to be operated for 12 months; and towns of 200 householders were required to provide a grammar school teacher for instruction in English, Latin, and Greek for children who had already learned to read English. Such masters had to have a college education and produce a certificate of qualifications and good morals from a "settled" (religiously established) minister or selectman.

The law authorized the towns to divide themselves into smaller districts which could receive tax funds from the towns for their schools. Elementary school teachers also had to have certificates of good morals, and all teachers had to be U.S. citizens. Echoing the Massachusetts constitution of 1780, this act enjoined upon all teachers of private as well as public schools the predominant social, political and moral values to which their certificates would testify. The assumption was that they would be Protestant Christian and would stress

> the principles of piety, justice, and a sacred regard to truth, love to their country, humanity, and universal benevolence, sobriety, industry and frugality, chastity, moderation and temperance, and those other virtues which are

the ornament of human society, and the basis upon which the Republican Constitution is structured.[6]

Boston / The town of Boston quickly responded by approving a special committee's report and passing its own law to bring order and system into the city schools. In addition to the Latin grammar schools, reading schools and writing schools were to be located in convenient parts of the city, providing for both boys and girls from the age of 7 to 14. Boston followed the recommendation of Samuel Adams, who was chairman of the committee, that the school committee be elected by ballot, consist of 12 members (one from each ward) in addition to the selectmen, and be responsible for visiting the schools, examining students, and generally supervising the operation of the schools. Public control had been spelled out in no uncertain terms, and such control was based upon the current democratic elective process.

Behind this development was a growing feeling that public rather than private education should become the principal instrument of education in a republican society; therefore a special agency of government seemed to be needed (a school committee or a board of education) to give its undivided attention to school matters. The egalitarian views that gave preference to public rather than private schools had been expressed in an earlier report adopted by a Boston town meeting in 1784 which exerted its jurisdiction over the appointment of private schoolmasters in the interests of equality. It allowed "for the present" continuation of the practice of paying private schoolmasters to teach poor children free, but its preference for the public schools was clear.

By 1800 the state of Massachusetts gave the local districts the power to levy taxes and in 1817 full corporate powers to run schools. This further decentralized the whole support and control of public education. Unenthusiastic towns were permitted to do little. Supportive towns like Salem, Newburyport, Portland, and Boston could go the other way and extend the availability of education downward to children as young as 4 years. Or they could reach upward and establish new types of secondary schools to operate alongside the Latin grammar schools. Boston did this by establishing an English Classical School in 1821, which became known as the English High School for boys.

The extension of public school services did not come easily, of course. There were always opponents. Some people argued that the charity schools of the churches or the voluntary organizations such as the Sunday schools could take care of the poor, and the private schools could take care of the rest. The Boston Society for the Moral and Religious Instruction of the Poor was an example, but in 1816 the Society found that three fourths of its students could not read, so they asked the town meeting to establish elementary public schools for children between the ages of 4 and 7. By 1817 it was found that 2400 children attended eight public schools, 4000 attended 160 private schools, and 500 attended no school. Conservatives, led by Charles Bulfinch and Harrison Gray Otis, argued that the 500 could easily be taken into the present schools, that the responsibility was a private and not a public matter, and that, besides, the town could not afford more schools.[7] The public school forces attracted adherents as diverse as James Savage, egalitarian Republican, Elisha Ticknor, orthodox Federalist, and William Ellery Channing, liberal Unitarian reformer.

The public school group eventually won, and a reluctant school committee was forced to establish a primary school board. To their surprise, if not chagrin, they found that parents flocked to the new public schools, and new ones soon had to be opened. Motives were varied, of course. The appeal of neighborhood schools close to home was great, and some people probably wanted their neighborhoods improved by the presence of schools. Some leaders undoubtedly wanted to impose their Protestant moral and religious values upon the poor, while others undoubtedly, and just as sincerely, believed that in a democratic society children of the poor and the rich should be educated together in common schools.

For a Daniel Webster, grandiloquent Federalist lawyer who wanted public schools to promote social stability, there was a William Manning, Jeffersonian Republican farmer who wanted public schools in order to keep the few from ruling the many. For a Federalist politician like Josiah Quincy, the mayor of Boston, who wanted public schools to promote republican rights and obligations, there was an educator and legislator like James G. Carter, who wanted the state rather than the town or district to improve public schools and thus assure the common people of an education as good as that the rich received in their private schools or academies. Carter proposed that the state establish teacher colleges to be the prime movers in the reform of public education:

> An institution for the education of teachers . . . would form a part, and a very important part of the free school system. It would be, moreover, precisely that portion of the system, which would be under the direction of the State whether the others are or not. Because we should thus secure at once, an uniform, intelligent and independent tribunal for decisions on the qualifications of teachers. Because we should thus relieve the clergy of an invidious task, and ensure to the public competent teachers, if such could be found or prepared. An institution for this purpose would become by its influence on society, and particularly on the young, an engine to sway the public sentiment, the public morals, and the public religion, more powerful than any other in the possession of government. It should, therefore, be responsible immediately to them. . . . If it be not undertaken by the public and for public purposes, it will be undertaken by individuals for private purposes.[8]

So it went in Massachusetts. In 1826 and 1827, the legislature passed new laws that required the towns to elect special school committees, required the support of public schools by taxes, established religious neutrality in the curriculum and textbooks, and deprived the clergy of official supervisory or visiting powers, but asked them to join selectmen and school committees in urging attendance at the public schools. With these exceptions the law of 1827 repeated the importance of the social, political, and moral values specified in the law of 1789. Official values persisted; the mechanisms of public education proliferated.

Connecticut / Developments in Connecticut were somewhat different from those in Massachusetts. A Connecticut school law of 1796 provided a mixed means of public school support that ranged from local taxes, special fees from residents and parents whose children attended school to the special largesse that Connecticut received from the sale of its public lands in the western reserve of northern Ohio. Connecticut thus built what seemed to be an ample common school fund whose proceeds could be distributed to towns and districts, and many other states copied this practice. Connecticut's special circumstance prompted the legislature to rely less heavily on taxation, even discontinuing taxes in 1821 for some 30 years. Rhode Island passed its first common school law in 1800, repealed it in 1803, and finally got around to a permissive law in 1823. Not all towns and districts energetically and eagerly obeyed the new legislation, of course, but the mandate was becoming clearer. In the following decades, under the cudgeling of Horace Mann in Massachusetts and Henry Barnard in Rhode Island and Connecticut, compliance became the rule.

New York

New York State / In the quarter century between 1795 and 1820, New York State moved from a practically nonexistent school system to one which rivaled that of Massachusetts. Prior to 1795, the pattern of educational support was mostly private, with sporadic attempts by churches and associations here and there to educate small groups of the poor. In the early years following the Revolution, the educational ideas of New Englanders who had settled in the state as well as a French Republican ideology strongly influenced the case for a public school system. In response to these demands, the legislature in 1784 created the University of the State of New York as a comprehensive body for building a unified school system from the elementary school to the college level.

Traditional indifference, the impoverishment caused by the Revolution, and opposition to school taxation combined, however, to block these early moves toward public schools. A law offering state aid to districts that supported schools through their own efforts was finally secured in 1795, but it was neither adequate nor lasting, expiring five years after passage. The first years of the nineteenth century saw continuing agitation for public schools. Governors' messages, statements of the board of regents of the university, pamphlets, and resolutions urged the adoption and extension of principles which had been enunciated in the law of 1795. A partial victory was secured with the establishment in 1805 of a permanent school fund, but the interest from this fund lay unused pending further legislation. Finally, in 1812, a comprehensive school law was enacted providing for an apportionment of interest from the state fund to those districts that raised equal sums by local effort. Districts were also responsible for taxing themselves for the maintenance and repair of a school site and building. Thus, a pattern developed according to which the state subsidized what was principally a local effort to maintain schools.

The law of 1812 was an important victory; yet it too proved increasingly inadequate during the next few decades. A principal shortcoming lay in the fact that the legislature in 1814 had approved the practice of meeting school deficits by assessing the parents of students with the device known as a rate bill. Although the law had provided that parents unable to afford the fee could be excused, the taint of pauperism associated with being excused prevented many people from taking advantage of the provision.

New York was the first state really to concern itself with the development of a centralized school organization. Moreover, New York was also the first state to create the office of superintendent of common schools. His duties, according to the law of 1812, involved preparing plans for improving the common school system, reporting and overseeing the use of school moneys, and providing information concerning the schools to the legislature. In the succeeding two decades a few states followed the leadership of New York and created similar positions; but it was between 1830 and 1850, when every northern state and some southern states created similar offices, that the practice really took root.

Early state boards of education had much the same function. Once again, as has already been cited, New York created the first such body when the board of regents of the University of the State of New York was established in 1784. Although the original legislation, and the law reorganizing this board in 1787, had assigned the regents broad educational responsibilities at all levels, they chose to concern themselves primarily with higher education.

New York City / While in New York State the attitude of the people toward public education was much like that of Massachusetts, New York City was quite a different matter. New York City had a much more heterogeneous population in the 1790s, and its school system, if anything, was more pluralistic. As so clearly documented by Carl Kaestle the most popular form of primary education was offered in scores of "common pay schools" run by enterprising teachers for profit.[9] When an organization of these teachers, several of whom were Republicans, sought a share of the state funds from the common council, the Federalist-dominated council turned them down, decided not to establish government schools, and instead gave support to religious charity schools, which adopted the term "free schools," run by the several

Protestant denominations. This action was a repudiation of the Republican proposals of the 1780s and 1790s, and it reflected the views of New York Federalists that government should aid private colleges for the elite and charity schools for the poor. It also suggested a strong orientation toward old England rather than New England. New York City leaders were Anglican and Quaker, whereas the educational leaders of upstate New York were from Connecticut and Massachusetts.

New York City thus took its own route. Unlike Boston, which opted for public schools over private ones, the public-spirited citizens of New York City took a nondenominational, philanthropic, and essentially private approach to common schools. This was appropriate to the Quaker views of the principal organizers of the New York Free School Society in 1805, which opened its first school in 1806 to teach poor children who were not otherwise cared for by the sectarian schools of specific denominations. Two years later the school began to accept *all* poor children, and soon it was sharing state funds with other charitable agencies. But when the Baptist Bethel Church began to expand *its* schools and claimed public funds, the Free School Society argued to the city and the state that public funds should *not* go to sectarian institutions but only to *nondenominational* institutions like itself. It argued with good republican rhetoric that New York City should have *common* schools for all children, rich and poor alike, and that all state aid to New York City should therefore go to the Free School Society which would become the Public School Society for this purpose. In 1825 it promised common schools

> where kindlier feelings between the children of these respective classes may be begotten; where the indigent may be excited to emulate the cleanliness, decorum and mental improvement of those in better circumstances; and where the children of our wealthiest citizens will have an opportunity of witnessing and sympathizing, more than they now do, with the wants and privations of their fellows of the same age.[10]

The state legislature authorized the change in 1826. Thus at the same time that Massachusetts was passing its most comprehensive state laws for public schools to be run by government agencies, New York was willing to let a private society do the job with public funds. While Boston was beginning to systematize and standardize its schools for greater efficiency by means of the public school committee, a similar process was being started in an urban setting in New York under the private auspices of the Public School Society. The modernization process associated with bureaucratization was underway in both instances. Carl Kaestle summarizes it this way:

> The Public School Society had been the main agent of this systematization, which involved the expansion and consolidation of schools, the extension of curriculum and age groups, articulation between levels, and, in theory at least, the standardization of students' treatment and teachers' performance. . . . The bureaucratic ethic and the moral mission of the schoolmen arose from the same problem—the rapid expansion and diversifi-

cation of the population—and they tended toward the same result—a vigorously conformist system.[11]

In the next few decades the common schools of New York City would shift from private control to public control under further pressures to take care of massive immigration and an exceedingly complex religious factionalism between Protestants and newly arrived Catholics. Kaestle's analysis of the leaders of the Public School Society is that they were a conservative-minded elite seeking to improve the morals as well as the minds of the lower classes in the direction of a majoritarian, middle-class Protestant ethic. Diane Ravitch takes a more generous view of the first 25 years of the Society. She recognizes the self-interest involved, but also accepts the fact that some of the trustees at least moved from a patronizing stance to a genuinely liberal view that had room for a common education with full public support:

> In its early years, the trustees saw schooling as a bounty which they were graciously making available to unfortunate members of the community, just as other boards had undertaken to provide charity hospitals. Their overt condescension and their patronizing concentration on the morals and habits of their pupils gave way over the years to a different conception of schooling. In time, the trustees came to assert that lack of education kept some men ignorant and poor and that schooling was therefore a right of free men. This transformation in their rhetoric caused the trustees eventually to espouse common schooling for all children, rich and poor, and to demand full public support for their schools. The evolution of the Society's rationale for schooling reciprocally affected public attitudes; the idea, nourished by the Society, that education was a democratic right and a *public* responsibility eventually contributed to the Society's downfall.[12]

When the Free School Society asked to be incorporated in 1805, it based its case to the legislature on the argument that the poor deserved charity. A quarter of a century later their appeal for public funds was based on the argument that common schooling is every person's political and social right. Though this may have been in part a self-serving argument designed to obtain greater public support for their schools, it also reflected the political realities of a public opinion that would now respond not merely to the charitable appeal for the poor but the political appeal for equality and the public good. The Society trustees had found the right public argument, but the days of the private instrumentality proved to be numbered. The more they argued that their schools should become truly common schools, the more likely it was that the instrumentality would be the government.

Pennsylvania

Pennsylvania was even slower than New York City in moving from a pluralist and charitable approach to a public and governmental approach. Indeed, even so redoubtable an exponent of public education as Benjamin Rush turned to the education of the poor in urban Philadelphia as a more likely candidate for public funds than the statewide school system he had earlier proposed. In fact, Rush even arrived at a very modern-sounding voucher system for the use of tax funds by the various religious communities to spur them to adopt "alternatives" to the common public school system:

> the children of parents of the same religious denominations should be educated together in order that they may be instructed with the more ease in the principles and forms of their respective churches. By these means the schools will come more immediately under the inspection of the ministers of the city, and thereby religion and learning be more intimately connected.
>
> Let the money to be raised for the support of the schools be lodged in the hands of the city treasurer, to be appropriated in the following manner: Let a certain number of persons of each religious society be appointed trustees of the free schools of their respective churches, and let a draft signed by the president of a quorum of these trustees be a voucher to the treasurer to issue three or four pounds a year for every scholar who is educated by them.[13]

In the 1790s Rush and other philanthropic persons threw themselves into organizing voluntary subscription societies to provide free education for the poor: a Sunday School Society, the Philadelphia Society for the Free Instruction of Indigent Boys, which later became the Philadelphia Society for the Establishment and Support of Charity Schools, and others. Within a decade the Pennsylvania legislature passed the law of 1802 to supply public funds for the free education of poor children. In this case parents or guardians adjudged by the overseers of the poor to be unable to afford the cost could send their children to any school in their neighborhood and the tuition would be paid out of poor taxes or road taxes. Where there were no overseers of the poor, the supervisors of highways were charged with the task! This was scarcely an anticipation of the importance highway busing was to play in public schooling 150 years later.

In the course of the next two decades the campaign for truly public schools began to gain headway in Pennsylvania, supported by such liberal intellectuals as the literary Nicholas Biddle, who served in the legislature in 1810–1811, and Walter Johnson, a teacher who became a mining engineer. After lengthy and heated debate, the legislature authorized the city of Philadelphia to establish a school system in 1818. But 10 more years were to pass before the Pennsylvania Society for the Promotion of Public Schools was even formed. The pluralism and diversity of the religious forces in Pennsylvania held stubbornly to their denominational schools and to charity schools for the poor. The legislative battles to put common school ideals into law were not to take place in Pennsylvania until the succeeding decade.

Southern States

Meanwhile, in the states south of Pennsylvania, public participation in education was confined to the operation of charity and pauper schools, despite sporadic plans, appeals, and legislative efforts on behalf of public schools. In the liberal republican momentum of the Revolutionary era, Georgia established in 1785 a state university along the model of New York's, in the sense that public schools were to be part of a complete system of organized education supervised by the academic senate of the university. All statutes and acts of the academic senate were to be approved or disallowed by the legislature. While all officers of the institution were required to be Christians (Protestant), no one was to be excluded because of "their speculative sentiments in religion, or being of a different religious profession." There was no mention of race, of course. The intent was obviously state control of public education, and the stated goals were the welfare of the state with accent on the public good. As happened so often, however, the University of Georgia did not really begin to function until 1800, and the idea of a state system of schools somehow got lost. The concentration of public funds on higher education for the few and lower education for the poor won out.

In 1803 the city council of Washington, D.C., established a board of education to pay the cost of educating poor children of the city. The high purposes seem today somewhat incongruous with the proposed source of the funds:

> Impressed with the inseparable connection between the education of youth and the prevalence of pure morals, with the duties of all communities to place within the reach of the poor as well as the rich the inestimable blessing of knowledge, and with the high necessity of establishing at the seat of general government proper seminaries of learning, . . .
> . . . *be it enacted* . . . that so much of the net proceeds of taxes laid, or to be laid on slaves, on dogs, on licenses for carriages and hacks, for ordinaries and taverns, for retailing of wines and spirituous liquors, for billiard tables, for theatrical and other public amusements, for hawkers and pedlars, be appropriated as the trustees may decide to be necessary for the education of the poor of the city . . .[14]

In 1810 the Virginia legislature established a literary fund for the encouragement of learning, the sources to be escheats, confiscations, fines, penalties, and forfeitures. The next year the fund was limited to schools for the education of the poor in each county of the state. When in 1816 the fund unexpectedly grew much larger from repayment of a debt by the federal government, a genuine clamor led to a bill in 1817 to establish a state board of public education to establish primary schools and academies throughout the state, three new colleges, and a state university. The bill passed the house with especially strong support from the western counties, but was defeated in the senate. An act confined to education for the poor was passed in 1818. A decade later, one more small step was taken toward a common school when local districts were given permission to use their literary fund allocations to establish free schools for all white children.

State school funds were established in South Carolina in 1811, Maryland in 1813, New Jersey in 1816, and Delaware in 1817. An exceptional report to the legislature of North Carolina in 1817 was presented by a committee headed by Archibald De Bow Murphey, state senator, judge, and active reformer. The committee examined not only the Virginia bill of 1817, but the plans of the national convention in France and the school laws and practices of New England. They came up with a comprehensive proposal that showed strong similarities to these and to Jefferson's educational proposal of 1779. Considerably different from Jefferson's plan was the proposal for much greater centralized control by a state board of public instruction—a sign, as Wilson Smith points out, of the need for leadership and direction from a central authority if education was to lead the way to public improvement.[15] Murphey sensed the values of bureaucracy in modernization, but the legislature did not. His plan for a thorough system of primary and secondary schools leading to the University of North Carolina was not approved. The "war of party spirit" which Murphey hoped had lessened after 20 years had not ended, and the panic of 1819 dampened the spirit of Republican reform.

Education for Blacks: The Major Blind Spot

Despite these early steps toward public education in the post-Revolutionary period, there was very little consideration given to the need for education for black freemen or slaves. To be sure, some of the states of the North moved gradually to include Negroes in their early public school legislation, and there were some early efforts to admit Negroes to mixed public schools. But as the Revolutionary fervor and the antislavery movement waned in the North as well as in the South between 1790 and 1810, either the laws assigned Negro pupils to separate schools or local custom excluded them altogether. There were few takers for the proposal in 1795 by James Sullivan, Democratic Republican legislator and later governor of Massachusetts, that blacks and whites should receive the same education in order to enable blacks eventually to exercise their freedom and enter fully into the political process:

> As there is no way to eradicate the prejudice which education has fixed in the minds of the white against the black people, otherwise than by raising the blacks, by means of mental improvements, nearly to the same grade with the whites, the emancipation of the slaves in the United America must be slow in its progress, and ages must be employed in the business. The time necessary to effect this purpose must be extensive, at least, as that in which slavery has been endured here. The children of the slaves must, at the public expence, be educated in the same manner as the children of their masters; being at the same schools, &c., . . . we do not know but that giving them the same prospects, placing them under the force of the same motives, and conferring upon them the same advantages for the space of time in which 3 or 4 generations shall rise and fall, will so mend the race, and so increase their powers of perception, and so strengthen their faculty for comparing ideas,

and understanding the nature and connexion of the external things with which man is surrounded on this globe, as that they may exceed the white people.[16]

Northern States

New York permitted local districts to segregate Negro pupils; Pennsylvania and Ohio authorized local districts to provide separate schools wherever at least 20 Negro children were to be taken care of; and New England school committees regularly assigned Negro children to separate schools. This reluctance to provide a common public education for blacks in the North was the result of indifference or prejudice, and it was heightened by the still uncertain future of public education itself in the several states. The real drive for public education had not yet begun in New York, Pennsylvania, or even New England. Thus private schools were in the saddle, and philanthropy was directing charity schools in a few places at poor blacks as well as poor whites.

Some of the early antislavery societies had stressed education. The Pennsylvania Society for Promoting the Abolition of Slavery emphasized schooling as early as 1789, and in 1795 petitioned the legislature to provide mixed free schools in the rural regions and special schools for blacks in the towns; 25 years later the school fund was opened to separate black schools. The New York Manumission Society established an African Free School Society in 1787, which was later taken over by the Free School Society as part of its publicly supported system. In Boston, where blacks had attended the public schools but in very small numbers, a curious reversal took place. As early as 1787 blacks had asked the Massachusetts legislature for special funds for black schools, since they felt they were discriminated against in the Boston schools, but the legislature refused. So the blacks turned in 1798 to the city, demanding separate schools for their children. In the course of the next three decades a segregated system of black schools became an established part of the public school system of Boston.[17] The major difference was that the black community had itself worked for this eventuality.

Southern States

In general, separate schools for blacks were widespread in the North by 1830. Then with the upswing of the abolition movement in the 1830s, the question of integrated or mixed public schools, that is, a genuinely *common* school, came vigorously to the fore in the North, a development scarcely considered in the South until the Reconstruction period following the Civil War. The dominant tradition in the South had been to use the law to prevent slave owners from educating their slaves. A South Carolina law of 1740 had made it a crime to teach a slave to read; a similar law was passed in Georgia in 1770. Sympathetic or lenient owners, however, had made it possible for some slaves (perhaps as many as 5 percent or more) to obtain a proficiency in reading, often with the help of white women, or particularly of white children, and freed slaves.[18] The evidence that white children were often the "teachers" of slaves gives credence to the latter-day beliefs that white children would relish integrated schools far more than their bigoted parents if they were encouraged or even permitted to take part.[19]

Increasing historical evidence points to the widespread and extremely deep desire for education by black slaves as well as by freedmen themselves. Indeed, education for the slave became a top priority of the freedmen in the South despite the enormous obstacles put in the way. By 1810 there were some 100,000 free Negroes in the South, nearly 10 percent of the black population and nearly 5 percent of the free population. The opportunity to gain freedom by joining the British forces during the war and the liberal evangelical efforts of southern Methodist and Baptist abolitionists in the 1780s had helped the continuing process of escape to freedom by the slaves unaided by whites. Even the laws of nearly all of the states forbidding voluntary manumission by slave owners were softened. Thousands of slaves were thus freed by egalitarian-minded owners or by the court petitions of the slaves themselves.

The freedmen turned avidly to establish their own institutions; next to churches they sought schools. In a few cases (Baltimore and Alexandria, Virginia) integrated schools were possible for a few years, but the general rule was obviously black schools, sometimes run by Quakers or other evangelical whites, but very often by the black communities themselves. Freedmen saw education as *the* major road to improvement of their condition and participation in U.S. society.[20]

In 1800, however, the regression had set in, and the freedoms of the "free" Negroes were definitely restricted on all sides. The slim chance opened up in the wake of Revolutionary ardor that public education might be extended to blacks in the South was gone, not to be revived until the Reconstruction period. "Universal free public education" was meant for whites only. With the exception of a very few persons and a few cases, the story of the trend toward public control and public support of education to the mid-1820s was white only. This was the major blind spot in the advocacy of public education. Benjamin Rush and Noah Webster advocated abolition of slavery, and they urged the extension of public education, but they did not seem to put the two together explicitly.

Jefferson's Dilemma

In fact, the most resplendent of all the advocates of liberty, equality, and public education did not apply those principles to slaves, to blacks, or to Indians. Jefferson admired the nobility, courage, and intelligence of the American Indians, but assumed that their way of life was inferior and should give way to white civilization. The civilized or Americanized Indian could be incorporated into U.S. society, but not the black. Jefferson found fault with slavery and several times voiced his belief in its basic illegality, immorality, and inhumanity. He even insisted upon the desirability of the human rights of Negroes as a race.

In 1776 Jefferson's draft for Virginia's constitution contained a clause prohibiting the future importation of slaves into Virginia; in his draft of a new constitution in 1783, he would have given freedom to children of slaves born after 1800; and he voted for the 1784 preliminary draft of the Northwest Ordinance prohibiting slavery in those territories. In his later years, however, Jefferson never aggressively campaigned for abolition or joined antislavery organizations, nor did he seek equal rights to education for slaves or freedmen, and he never freed all of his own slaves. He was convinced, as were probably the vast majority of whites, of the inherent intellectual and physical inferiority of the black race. His only solution seemed to be that blacks should be recolonized to Africa; he did not embrace the idea of an integrated society, the social and political accompaniment of the common school. Unfortunately for the hopes for an integrated society, the predominant scientific and anthropological themes of the day were trumpeting the racial superiority themes of white over black.[21]

David Brion Davis has found Jefferson's stand on slavery exceedingly ambiguous. On one hand:

> One must emphasize that he gave occasional and extremely quiet encouragement to Negro education and to antislavery opinion among the planter class. . . . No one can deny that Jefferson's democratic ideals were of monumental importance for the later antislavery cause.[22]

But Davis concludes:

> Jefferson was attuned to the values. loyalties, sanctions, taboos, and expectations of Virginia's wealthiest families, most of whom owned more than one hundred slaves. To a large extent he shared their collective sense of propriety, their moral imperatives, their definitions of available options. . . .
> Despite his glimpses of a more humane and just world, he could not doubt the basic legitimacy of his social universe. He knew that any serious threat to slavery was also a threat to this universe, however he might wish to dissociate the two. He was, to be sure, equivocal and indecisive; because of his immense prestige, he thereby sanctiond equivocation and indecision. But when the chips were down, as in the Missouri crisis, he threw his weight behind slavery's expansion, and bequeathed to the South the image of antislavery as a Federalist mask for political and economic exploitation. If early antislavery became identified with political partisanship and with conservatives like Hamilton, Jay, and Rufus King, it was partly by default.[23]

In sum, the struggle for public education was caught up in the tragic dichotomies with which the Republic was still struggling. The history of public education would be so much easier to write if only all the proponents had been praiseworthy and all the opponents blameworthy. If only the Jeffersonian Republicans had not only believed in public education for the common people but also in freedom for blacks and all other races and ethnic minorities to attend common schools at public expense with federal as well as state support. Or if only the Federalists who *were* for the abolition of slavery *and* for a strong federal government *and* for public education of the poor had been more concerned for all the common people and less concerned for favoritism to the privileged elite and private enterprise at whatever cost. But this was not to be.

Republicans were often for the common person and for common education, but only for the *white* common person; and they were often for state control and support of education, but they bitterly defended states' rights (to enforce slavery and prohibit black education) against any threat from the federal government. On their part, Federalists often tried to use the organs of state government to aid private educational agencies and confine public education to the poor so that the classes would not be mixed. But they also took the lead next to the Quakers in the antislavery movement and were ever more ready to use the federal government to promote economic modernization and national development when the states lagged. There were, however, two essential points of agreement: both believed increasingly in *some kind of public education* over a private education; and up to the end of the 1820s, both agreed that if any kind of education were to be provided for blacks as well as whites in public or in private schools, it should be done separately.

Notes

1. Ruth Miller Elson, *Guardians of Tradition: American Schoolbooks of the Nineteenth Century* (Lincoln: University of Nebraska Press, 1964), p. 285.
2. Herbert C. Gutman, "Work, Culture, and Society in Industrializing America, 1815–1919," *American Historical Review*, 78(3):531–588. See also Gutman's *Work, Culture, and Society in Industrializing America* (New York: Knopf, 1976).
3. Donald G. Mathews, "The Second Great Awakening as an Organizing Process, 1780–1830: An Hypothesis," *American Quarterly*, Spring 1969, 21(1):39–40.
4. Timothy L. Smith, "Protestant Schooling and American Nationality, 1800–1850," *The Journal of American History*, March 1967, 53(4): 687. For the next period, see David B. Tyack, "The Kingdom of God and the Common School: Protestant Ministers and the Educational Awakening of the West," *Harvard Educational Review*, Fall 1966, 36: 447–469.

5. Clinton Rossiter, *The American Quest, 1790–1860: An Emerging Nation in Search of Identity* (New York: Harcourt, 1971), pp. 291–293.

6. Daniel Calhoun, ed., *The Educating of Americans: A Documentary History* (Boston: Houghton Mifflin, 1969), pp. 233–234.

7. For the details of this controversy, see Stanley K. Schultz, *The Culture Factory: Boston Public Schools, 1789–1860* (New York: Oxford, 1973), pp. 25–44.

8. James G. Carter, quoted in Calhoun, pp. 182–183.

9. See Carl F. Kaestle, *The Evolution of an Urban School System, New York City, 1750–1850* (Cambridge, Mass.: Harvard University Press, 1973), p. 44.

10. Kaestle, p. 85.

11. Kaestle, pp. 160–161.

12. Diane Ravitch, *The Great School Wars: New York City, 1805–1973: A History of the Public Schools as Battlefield of Social Change* (New York: Basic Books, 1974), p. 10.

13. Robert H. Bremner, ed., *Children and Youth in America: A Documentary History*, Volume I: 1600–1865 (Cambridge, Mass.: Harvard University Press, 1970), p. 250.

14. Quoted in Bremner, pp. 251–252.

15. Wilson Smith, ed., *Theories of Education in Early America, 1655–1819* (Indianapolis: Bobbs-Merrill, 1973), p. 362.

16. Quoted in Bremner, pp. 337–338.

17. For the details, see Schultz, Chap. 7.

18. Eugene D. Genovese, *Roll, Jordan, Roll: The World the Slaves Made* (New York: Pantheon, 1972), pp. 563–564.

19. Winthrop D. Jordan, *White Over Black: American Attitudes Toward the Negro, 1550–1812* (Baltimore: Penguin, 1968), p. 353.

20. Ira Berlin, *Slaves Without Masters: The Free Negro in the Antebellum South* (New York: Pantheon, 1974), p. 78.

21. Jordan, pp. 429–511.

22. David Brion Davis, *The Problem of Slavery in the Age of Revolution, 1770–1823* (Ithaca, N.Y.: Cornell University Press, 1975), p. 171.

23. Davis, pp. 182–184.

part II
Building Blocks
of Public
Education

1826-1876

Introduction

The consensus of historians is that the middle decades of the nineteenth century were of particular significance in the development of American public education. It was during these years that the idea of free, universal, and common education was so widely proclaimed and that the practices of the public elementary schools were adapted to accommodate this philosophy. But having acknowledged this, the consensus of historians today breaks rather sharply into different, even contradictory, explanations of the reasons why the common school movement gained such momentum and what it meant for the U.S. society of that time and for the present day. This is not the place for an analysis of the historiographical disputes among historians of U.S. education. Much attention has been given to them in recent years and some of the literature is cited in the Bibliographic Notes (pp. 00–00). The purpose here is to sketch briefly a conceptual framework that I believe will aid in the understanding of a most complicated and often baffling historical phenomenon.

The common school movement was neither the inevitable unfolding of a natural historical process embodying progress, enlightenment, and democracy, nor was it the instrument of an exploiting capitalist class, calculated and designed primarily to mold a working class for the benefit of the employers. Neither the linear evolutionary model of earlier historians of education nor the class-oriented model of recent revisionist historians offers a definitive explanation. Each has a contribution to make, but each is inconclusive and somewhat misleading.

I believe the development of U.S. public education is best described as the result of a three-way tension, often amounting to confrontation, among three basic and persistent elements in American life: commitment to the republican goals for a cohesive and unified democratic political community; the pluralistic loyalties that give identity and coherence to different groups in the society—but which also often tend to divide or separate on the bases of locality, religion, race, or ethnic origin; and the long-term modernization process that was gathering momentum in all societies of Western civilization in the course of the nineteenth century. As a result of the political process involving these several push-and-pull elements in various places and times, the common school movement took form. (See Figure 1.) Under some combinations of the political ABC's, the dispersion of the common school idea took the form of dissemination, diffusion, or proliferation throughout many parts of the country between 1826 and 1876. Under different combinations it took on the other meaning of dispersion: It broke apart, dissipated, separated, disintegrated, or never appeared at all.

By and large, when the commitment to unity or cohesion was strong, the common school movement was seen as a safeguard or protector of the search for building the legitimacy and authority of the democratic political

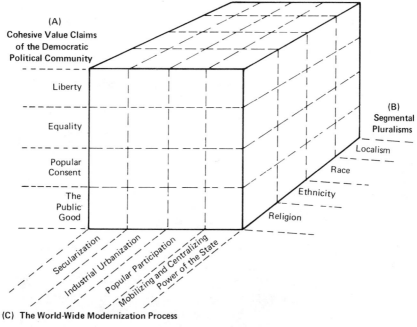

Figure 1. The Triform Building Blocks of U.S. Public Education (the Political A B C's).

community. Governor De Witt Clinton of New York called the common school the "Palladium of our Freedoms." But when an excessive stress was put on the imposition of a static belief or behavior, the common school led to a stultifying conformity and the suppression of natural differences. When the pluralisms of locality or religion or ethnicity were strong, the tendency was for different groups to establish their own homogeneous private schools or to adapt public school systems to their own differences and peculiarities. If these attempts became excessive, this pathological pluralism threatened to produce what I call "disjunctivitis," a translative term to denote a societal disease in which rampant separatism or isolationism can endanger the health and well-being of the larger political community itself.

Sometimes the pressures for modernization served to underline the forces of cohesion and legitimacy promised by the Revolution, but sometimes they tended to undermine them; at other times they demanded a cessation of pluralism, or exaggerated it. Modernization was thus an ambiguous process; it could be creative in devising new forms of social organization, or it could be destructive of traditional institutions valued by pluralism. By and large, the weight of the modernizing trends tended to promote the proclaimed values of the public school movement, and vice versa. This interchange was not always seen, then or now, as a *desirable* partnership, but I believe the linkage is clear. The danger was that the drive to make education public and modern might undercut the legitimate cohesive goals of a democratic political community on one side or suffocate the legitimate cultural aspirations of pluralistic groups on the other.

I have said a great deal about the original goals of the democratic political community in the first three chapters of this book. The Revolutionary ideals of liberty, equality, and obligation to the public good took on new colorations in the middle of the nineteenth century as they brushed up against the dynamic forces of modernization and pluralism. Public schooling and modernization are dealt with in Chapter 4; pluralism and schooling, in Chapters 5 and 6.

Characteristic Aspects of Modernization

The common school movement that gained remarkable headway in the middle decades of the nineteenth century could do so because it was, by and large, aided by the major forces that can usefully be classified under the term "modernization." The common school movement was in fact one of the major expressions of that development in the United States. Five general characteristics of a modernizing society are briefly previewed here.[1]

Centralizing Power of the Nation-State

A basic feature of all modernizing societies was the growing power of the nation-state, and its mobilizing and centralizing power in relation to other institutions of society: economic, religious, kinship, and voluntary. The process of rationalizing political authority into a single integrated polity to coordinate the centrifugal particularisms of locality, region, or pluralistic groups has been one of the most difficult yet characteristic aspects of the modernization process, wherever it has occurred, from the sixteenth century to the present. The more modern the society, the greater the capacity of.the political system to influence the whole range of its social and economic affairs. The major agencies relied upon to achieve political community and nation building were highly organized administrative and military bureaucracies, differentiated political structures designed to channelize more effectively the legislative, executive, and judicial functions of the political system, and large-scale educational systems. Organized education has thus been called upon to provide the civic education that would socialize the populace by instilling the values and attitudes required to maintain the political system, to help in the recruitment of the leaders, and to provide the professional training for those who manage the complex institutions of a modern nation-state.

Popular Participation

A second characteristic of modernizing societies was the active involvement of ever-increasing numbers of people of all classes in political, economic, and social affairs. This trend was greatly accelerated by the democratic revolutions that swept Europe and America in the eighteenth and nineteenth centuries, and swept Africa and Asia in the twentieth century. Whether the form of government is constitutional monarchy, representative democracy, socialism, communism, or military dictatorship, mass participation in public affairs has become a means of mobilizing the populace into greater group effort on behalf of the "public good," however that might be defined. The entire political spectrum from left to right now paid more attention to the power of the people than ever before. Mass participation in public affairs often led to basic changes in access to education and, in turn, the prevalence of mass education led to changes in the character of the participation.

Industrial Urbanization

A third characteristic of the transformation from a traditional to a modern society, and the one most commonly referred to as the basic impetus leading to modernization, was the shift from an agrarian society to a citified society. This was accompanied by a shift from agriculture and other primary means of production to commerce, to the market system, and to power-driven machine production in factory and city. These trends were related to the mechanization and technical improvements in agriculture itself as well as to the growth of industrial urbanism; rural transformation, if not actually preceding industrialization, at least accompanied it.

Leadership in industrial modernization was sometimes taken over by capitalist entrepreneurs of the middle classes, helped more or less by the cooperation of weak or minimal governments, and sometimes by strong governments under control of the ruling elites led by modern-minded monarchs, military factions, or socialist or communist parties. As the magnets of industrialization and urbanization continued to attract more and more people around the world, organized education became intimately involved in promoting the one while desperately trying to cope with the other.

Impact of Secular Knowledge

A fourth aspect of modernization may be summed up in the term "secularization." Modern societies are the direct beneficiaries of the scientific revolution in knowledge, initiated in the sixteenth and seventeenth centuries, accelerating in the eighteenth and nineteenth centuries, and exploding in the twentieth century. Secularization applied not only to the physical and natural sciences, but also to the humanities, the social sciences, and the arts. It implied reliance upon rational methods of inquiry freed from the exactions of inflexible religious dogma, supernatural revelation, or mystical insights peculiar to a limited few. It applied not only to the systematic organization of knowledge for practical purposes in mechanical and industrial production, transportation and communication, and economic distribution based upon inventions and technical specialization, but also to rational solutions of problems in social and political affairs.[2]

Political scientists Gabriel Almond and G. Bingham Powell apply the term directly to the problem-solving process of modern politics, as contrasted to a traditional reliance upon custom or inherited fiat:

> Secularization is the process whereby men become increasingly rational, analytical, and empirical in their political action. . . . whereby traditional orientations and attitudes give way to more dynamic decision-making processes involving the gathering of information, the evaluation of information, the laying out of alternative courses of action, the selection of a course of action from among these possible courses, and the means whereby one tests whether or not a given course of action is producing the consequences which were intended.[3]

Faith in Large-Scale School Systems

The fifth characteristic of a modern society in contrast to a traditional society was a faith in and reliance upon organized systems of schooling available to ever-increasing numbers of the population. An elaborate, organized educational system that embraced a large part of the total population was a radical departure from tradition; as fashioned by modernizing societies, it was an innovation that older societies could not visualize, let alone try to establish. Organized public education was tightly interwoven with the other characteristics of modernity previously mentioned. It was an indispensable part of the process by which Western society modernized itself in the eighteenth and nineteenth centuries and by which it effected its impact upon the rest of the world in the nineteenth and twentieth centuries.

Public education was thus composed of sometimes conflicting ingredients that flowed from the value claims of political democracy and from the modernization process still further complicated by the pushing and pulling demands of pluralism.

Segmental Pluralisms

From the beginning of the Republic, pluralism was viewed both as one of the glories of a society devoted to freedom and openness and as one of the divisive threats to the unity required for the survival of democratic institutions. Historian Michael Kammen defines a plural society as "a polity containing distinct cleavages amongst diverse population groups."[4] He refers to the "unstable pluralism" that might threaten the very authority of the polity because of the conflict between racial, religious, or regional groups, each having its own political party, "its own faction, each sect its own school, and each dogmatist his own ideology." He speaks also of "stable pluralism:"

> Stable pluralism requires a strong *underpinning* of legitimacy. A plural society is best insured by the rule of law—law made within the framework of an explicit constitution by elected representatives, executed by a partially autonomous administrative staff, and adjudicated by an independent judiciary. Insofar as all of these were created in 1787 and achieved in 1789, those dates do distinguish a genuine watershed in American history.[5]

This need to cultivate psychological as well as political legitimacy among diverse groups was one of the prime motives for promoting the common school movement to counteract the growing pluralism of mid-nineteenth century United States:

> Physical expansion and the injection of new immigrants made Jacksonian America far more heterogeneous than anything Jefferson, Rush, or Webster might wildly have envisioned. After the 1820's, when manhood suffrage became widespread, ethnic and religious differences tended to become the more important sources of political conflict. By the 1840's a nativist reaction reflexively screamed shrill notes of alarm at the prospect of unstable pluralism verging upon chaos.[6]

Another perspective on pluralism, which is especially illuminating to the understanding of the successes and failures of the public school movement in the middle nineteenth century, is the concept of segmentation so perceptively portrayed by Robert H. Wiebe:

> What segmentation denotes is a configuration of small social units—primary circles of identity, values, associations, and goals—that have sufficient authority to dominate the terms of their most important relationships with the world outside.[7]

The segments of the mid-nineteenth century increasingly centered around "island communities" based upon distinctive locality, religious belief, or ethnic affiliation of national origin or race.

National Cohesion and the Segments

Wiebe also points out that although these "small, hard pieces" of social life cultivated differences, hatreds, and barriers, they nevertheless built a remarkably resilient society based upon a few fundamental agreements that reached across the social compartments. One of the sources of agreement was the set of common public ideas that groups carried with them as they moved incessantly about the vast North American Continent in the nineteenth century:

> Because strange people constituted an omnipresent threat to the commu-
> nity in an era of mobility, members devoted particular attention to the sifting
> of newcomers. . . . they came to rely upon shorthand devices that sorted people
> by their surface characteristics: their skin color, their demeanor, their public
> habits. These very surface qualities, in fact, were the ones they emphasized
> in the rearing of their children. . . . Political parties and religious denomi-
> nations, the public school movement . . . all relied upon a small set of prin-
> ciples and procedures—a kernel of truths—that could enable people widely
> dispersed and scarcely in communication to pursue their activities with a
> firm sense of common purpose. A carefully marked Bible or Blackstone,
> Theodore Weld on slavery or Horace Mann on education held the essentials,
> and an unwavering dedication to the simple truth completed the links of an
> effective, if almost invisible institution.[8]

Wiebe cites five conditions that sustained and supported the persistent segmentation of American life: (1) The vast expanse of land enabled the social segments to solve their conflicts by moving away from each other, by separating rather than accommodating. (2) An increasing cultural diversity accentuated the values placed upon difference and particularism of the various segments. (3) Military security enabled people generally to go separately about their business without constantly regrouping to fend off an enemy. (4) The lack of "institutions of general competence"—such as a strong national government, or church, or financial institution—led to a "triumphant particularism" of local autonomy and reliance upon voluntary agencies. (5) Economic abundance, though not insuring equality, did assure a wide diffusion of economic rewards among most ranges of the population.

The strengthening of this pluralistic fragmentation threatened to nullify the promise of national cohesion inherited from the Revolutionary era, a cohesion revived in the early decades of the nineteenth century when the calls for a new national loyalty and new reforms crossing denominational, state, and regional lines were briefly sounded but hardly resurrected:

> By the 1830's rhetorical nationalism was increasingly lost among cries
> of community interest, state interest, occasional sectional interest. . . .
> Around 1850 . . . was the culmination of a process of hardening, multiply-
> ing segmentation.[9]

The public school movement between the 1830s and the 1850s was a response to this growing tension between "rhetorical nationalism" and "hardening, multiplying segmentation."

Liberty and equality redefined. The people of the United States were constantly faced with internal dissension; there were recurring tugs to break apart as well as to live apart. In many places and in many respects, pluralistic groups interpreted liberty, equality, and the public good to be confined to their own particular segments and to be denied to those outside. Liberty, defined by the founders to mean the will of the whole people, was taken in the mid-nineteenth century to apply to the autonomy of the segment *against* the will of the whole people. Rather than uniting the people, liberty was dividing and insulating them, misapplied as a keep-out sign to protect private enterprise. Equality, stated by the founders to apply to "all men," was narrowly interpreted to apply to one's own segment where people were alike. So, equality became a segmented quality identified by homogeneity: You treat others equally if they are like you: if they are not like you, they are inferior; and to be worthy of being treated equally they must become like you, that is, be assimilated.

Those who would fraternize found it difficult to cross pluralistic segment boundaries, especially when they were based upon ethnic differences. Racial lines excluded crossovers on the basis of inferiority, for those of different skin color could *never* become one of the group. Therefore, *they* must be inherently inferior and thus refused the full privileges of liberty and equality, and certainly of fraternity.

In Wiebe's view, segmentation thus prevented most U.S. citizens of the mid-nineteenth century from viewing the nation as a whole society. Their idea of national citizenship was encompassed by their loyalties to locality, state, region, religion, ethnic identity, or race. To be sure, "those others" were there, and perhaps they had more or less a legal right to be there and to claim some of the legal rights of citizenship, but their genuine *membership* and belongingness had to pass the test of their ability and willingness to adopt the "right" views and behaviors of their adopted group:

> Citizenship and membership, a relatively simple equation in France, formed the components of an exceedingly complex problem in America. Although every citizen could claim a basic set of legal rights, some of these citizens would almost certainly remain outsiders. Actual membership was determined by additional tests of religion, perhaps, or race or language or behavior, tests that varied considerably among segments and over time. Each generation passed to the next an open question of who really belonged to American society.[10]

When the founders' dream of a unified, cohesive, whole republican society was confronted by the segmental tests of religion, race, language, and behavior, the role for public education became infinitely more complex and difficult than the founders could have imagined. No longer would simple literacy, moral values, history, or study of the forms of government fill the public need. Segmentation raised all sorts of questions: Literacy in *what* language? *Whose* moral values based on *what* religion? *Whose* history? Study of *what* government? The common school movement constantly had to face such questions pertaining to its role in building civic cohesion in a society marked by diversity and particularism.

Such a segmented society also made it difficult for a clearly defined class consciousness to develop as it did in the more homogeneous societies of Europe, where the distinctions between privileged landowners, middle classes, and working classes were so definitely marked. Instead, the successive waves of immigrant workingmen to the United States found themselves divided into pluralistic segments that gave more meaning to their lives than did working-class culture in general. This meant that the middle classes, who had already assimilated or were rapidly doing so during the middle decades of the nineteenth century, had the advantage in defining the values of the cohesive elements in U.S. social, political, and economic structures.

The middle classes, by adopting "equality" as a hallmark of their segmental social level, could legitimate their efforts to correct the "faults" of both the lower and upper classes. They could argue that the poor and the more affluent workingmen should learn the "good citizenship" values of hard work, cleanliness, thrift, and sobriety, and that the rich and the aristocrats should learn the values of humility, goodwill, and respect for others. In both cases, the values of equality would be served, and the common school could be an admirable instrument for the mixing of all classes in society. In fact, the goal of public education might well be to elevate the poor to a happier level. Of course it did not work out exactly that way, but the *promise* of equality was a powerful force in the "American Dream" and in actually shaping U.S. society, even though formed through middle-class leadership. In the long run, the United States became more and more a "middle class" society.

The public good diminished. Segmental pluralism also had its effect upon the Revolutionary era's faith in the obligation to the public good as a basic value of republicanism. In the middle decades of the nineteenth century the conception of the public good was likely to be narrowed and limited to one's own segment rather than identified with the whole society or the whole Republic as the founders had visualized. The individual was a good citizen if he or she performed duties at the local level or within his or her segment. Local taxes might be justified to help pay for the local neighborhood school, but not for those other districts in the state and surely not for out-of-state schools. Segmental pluralism stood stubbornly in the way of developing state systems of education and adamantly resisted a federal system.

In other words, the revolutionary dream of obligation to the public good became in the mid-nineteenth century a contest for control of the "public thing," a domain to be fought over, contested, negotiated, bargained, lobbied, and eventually to be paid off. The "public" was something "out there." The revolutionary model in which the best men were the public men was replaced by the new image of the public official as being generally ineffective or indeed corrupt. The idea of patriotism became associated far more often with military affairs and international wars than with one's civic responsibilities for the affairs of the whole society. And what it was to be an "American" was far more easily interpreted as the characteristic description of one's own familiar segmented group rather than as an overall name that included all those others with their strange languages, customs, looks, and beliefs.

Persistent Ambivalence About Pluralism

So, there was a constant tug of war, not only between groups of like-minded people of common national or racial origin, but also within each individual. One voice said: "This is the land of freedom and equality and opportunity; all are welcome and should have equal right to live their lives as they wish." Another voice said: "But those newcomers are so different, so poor, so ignorant, so coarse that they are a threat to *our* way of life and the values *we* cherish." What should be done? Keep them out? No, that would deny the values this country was founded on. Let them behave any way they wish? No, they must not be allowed to live in ignorance or defiance of our laws, for then they will be tempted to take our property or commit crimes upon our persons. The solution, then, is to educate them to become good citizens and decent persons. And the best instrument for this purpose is the common public school.

There was a similar tug of war between and among the groups of new-comers: "We came to this new country to escape the limitations of the old country and we want a better life for ourselves and our children. So we want to learn from you who have already made it what we need to know and do as well. But your language is different, your religion is different, your habits and dress and expectation of behavior are different, and many of us do not want to give up what is familiar and valued by us. So, we are not sure about your common school. Maybe we don't need any schooling at all. Or if we do, maybe it should be in our own schools, taught in our own language, and teaching the religious doctrines of our tradition. Some of us want to hurry up and become Americans; others of us don't want to change that fast—or that much."

Nearly all were thus faced with these complex dilemmas. Newcomers had to decide how far they should go in trying to be like established citizens so that they could help maintain a stable and just political community. And old-time Americans had to decide how much difference they could tolerate in the interests of cultural freedom. The common school reformers came down fairly firmly on the side of "commonness." They were impressed and sometimes appalled by the "hardening" of segmentation that developed in the middle period of the nineteenth century. They sought to counteract the consolidation of separatist segmentation, not only by means of making the common school free and available, but also by making it compulsory and secular. Some groups among newcomers resisted the common school movement because they saw it as a threat to their language, their religion, their ethnic identity, or their national background. Other groups, like black freedmen, tried to take advantage of the common school, but were largely thwarted during this period in both the North and the South. Still others struggled over who should control the schools, public *and* private, and what should be the extent of local autonomy and separatism with regard to state or federal commonness. These several pluralisms were so complicated and so intermingled in the minds of people during the middle and late nineteenth century that their ramifications can only·be suggested in a brief discussion here. Four of these pluralisms are examined in Chapters 5 and 6—religion, ethnicity, race, and localism—and, significantly, these continue to agitate discussions of educational policy to the present day.

With this general perspective on the triformity of the U.S. experience in the middle of the nineteenth century, we are ready to look more closely at the dispersion of education during that period. On a foundation of the several building blocks of political community, modernization, and segmental pluralism, the people of the United States hammered out the fundamentals of an elementary school system that sought first to be free, universal, and common, and later became compulsory and secular.

Notes

1. R. Freeman Butts, *The Education of the West: A Formative Chapter in the History of Civilization* (New York: McGraw-Hill, 1973), Part III.
2. C. E. Black, *The Dynamics of Modernization: A Study in Comparative History* (New York: Harper & Row, 1966), p. 7.
3. Gabriel Almond and G. Bingham Powell, Jr., *Comparative Politics; A Developmental Approach* (Boston: Little, Brown, 1966), pp. 24–25.
4. Michael Kammen, *People of Paradox: An Inquiry Concerning the Origins of American Civilization* (New York: Vintage Books, 1973), pp. 60–61.
5. Kammen, p. 85.
6. Kammen, p. 75.
7. Robert H. Wiebe, *The Segmented Society: An Introduction to the Meaning of America* (New York: Oxford, 1975), p. x.
8. Wiebe, pp. 21–22.
9. Wiebe, p. 45.
10. Wiebe, pp. 94–95.

4 The Common School:
Palladium of the Republic

In 1826, the year that Thomas Jefferson died, Governor De Witt Clinton addressed the New York legislature on the subject of public education. Both in words and acts he symbolized not only the continuity of political ideas from the Revolutionary era but also the drive to modernize U.S. society. He represented in his own person the "public man" who moved in his thinking from reliance upon free education as a private charity to support of free education as a government obligation. While mayor of New York City, Clinton helped organize the philanthropic Free School Society in 1805; while governor in the 1820s, he became the foremost spokesman for state-sponsored public education. A Democratic-Republican in liberal ideology, he gained considerable Federalist support for his activist state programs and thereby lost partisan Republican support in New York City. On behalf of a democratic political community he could address the legislature thus in 1826:

> The first duty of government, and the surest evidence of good government, is the encouragement of education. A general diffusion of knowledge is the precursor and protector of republican institutions; and in it we must confide as the conservative power that will watch over our liberties, and guard them against fraud, intrigue, corruption and violence. . . .
>
> I consider the system of our common schools as the palladium of our freedom; for no reasonable apprehension can be entertained of its subversion, as long as the great body of the people are enlightened by education. To increase the funds, to extend the benefits, and to remedy the defects of this excellent system, is worthy of your most deliberate attention.[1]

Clinton did not live to witness the bitter struggle between Catholics and Protestants over "this excellent system" in New York City in the 1830s and

1840s (see Chap. 5). His brave words about the common school and republican institutions were to be put to the severe test of religious and ethnic pluralism. But his own vision of "republican institutions" was pluralistic in the sense that he was devoted to state rather than federal action in building political community and in modernizing the economy. In this respect he was at once a follower of the Jeffersonian ideal of political education and a harbinger of the pluralism of the United States that would look to state governments rather than to the federal government to promote public education. But Clinton did move out of the segmental pluralism that would seek to hold education within the control of religious, ethnic, or social class boundaries. In this respect he tried to summon the claims of both democratic political cohesion and modernization in support of a state system of common schooling. Thus, he helped in the 1820s to state the case for the common school movement, a case that was very largely put into effect in several states from the 1830s to the 1850s by a remarkable band of modernizing educational reformers.

The Mobilizing and Centralizing Power of the State

By the middle of the nineteenth century there was a discernible movement in the United States toward governmental action to modernize society and education, but its focus was primarily the pluralistic state governments rather than a cohesive national government. The national government in this country did not take the lead in political or economic modernization as early as did some European governments, notably those of France and Prussia. In fact, the federal government of the United States was relatively weak until its mobilizing power was tested and ultimately strengthened by the Civil War era. Modernization was typically a process initiated and directed "from above" in Europe, whereas it was pushed "from below" in the United States by the pluralistic segments, by capitalistic private enterprises, and by state governments.

On the economic side of modernization, mid-nineteenth-century United States proceeded rapidly and viably: enormous growth of production, transportation, capital investment, and employment opportunities. Despite the periodic business depressions, the trends of all basic economic indicators were generally upward. But in this process the national government played a lesser part in economic modernization than in other countries. With respect to *political* modernization, state governments made great strides in citizen representation (discussed primarily under the next section on popular participation), but the federal government lagged behind the states in efficiency and capability. In a striking phrase, Clinton Rossiter put it this way: *"The nation boomed; the political system of the nation languished."*[2] The principal reason for this was the rise of economic viability under the parallel auspices of pluralistic capitalism and of pluralistic segments that could not or would not put the claims of a whole democratic political community above their particular interests:

> The one genuinely troublesome defect in the American pattern of representation (a defeat, in large part, of its virtues) was the steady erosion in popular esteem of the concept of the public interest that had been a touchstone of policy in the years of Washington, Adams, and Jefferson. While pluralism and localism are two characteristics of a truly representative system, each got quite out of hand in the heady days of Jacksonian democracy.[3]

Thus, by the middle of the nineteenth century the national government was becoming less and less active, especially when compared with governments elsewhere. By 1850,

> In terms of parties, elections, suffrage, and popular participation, politics was an ever more zestful undertaking. . . . in terms of *governing*, however, of making important public choices for the nation and seeing them through to reality, politics in America was an ever more withered affair.[4]

Thus it was that educational reformers of the antebellum period turned to the *states* to promote free, universal, and common education, attempting to build common school systems that would fulfill both the claims of the revolutionary political community and the claims of a booming modernizing society. They were not wholly successful, of course, but they did make remarkable progress. Then, in the 1860s, after the federal government had survived the Civil War, which in itself was the ultimate test of pluralistic segmentation, a new generation of reformers attempted to mobilize the federal government on behalf of public education. Although they lost the immediate battle for an active federal role in elementary and secondary education, they instigated a process of federal intervention that was eventually to have widespread effect.

Revisions of State Constitutions

I think it is fair to say that the mid-century educational reformers were, by and large, responsive to the forces of modernization they saw at work, and indicated this by their claims of advancing political cohesion (at the state level) in order to ward off what they recognized as the dangers of excessive pluralism at the local and private levels. They saw that the authority and legitimate obligation of state governments to promote education had to be strengthened if large numbers of people were to become capable of coping with the rapid growth of population, of cities, of industry, and of the new knowledge that marked the modernization process. One progressive step was the effort to reorient political institutions toward the realities of modernization. This was the theme of the second round of state constitutional revisions, which took place from the mid-1840s to the mid-1850s. Legislators in this

Jacksonian era were aware of the need to expand educational opportunity so that a wider public franchise would be justified. As a result, educational provisions were included in all the new state constitutions and were added to the older constitutions.

In one way or another virtually every state put into its constitution a general statement about the importance of education to the maintenance of good government and free institutions, and obligated the legislature to provide an appropriate system of schools. The most widespread designation of purpose was that the schools should be "public," or "free," or "common"; and that the system should be "efficient," "thorough," "uniform," "general," or "open to all." In all cases the state's responsibility for providing education was explicitly expressed as the legislature's duty to "establish," or "maintain," or "support" the schools. The most common administrative instruments for enforcing such provisions were state boards of education, state superintendents of education, and state funds for the support or encouragement of public schools. These revisions in state constitutions were a phase of the more general trend toward the bureaucratization of other branches or departments of state governments as legislators sought to promote the modernization of economic and social development within their jurisdictions.

The most heated controversies in the state constitutional conventions had to do with religious and racial pluralism. Generally, the state constitutions prohibited the use of public funds for religious schools, but were either silent or ambiguous about racial equality until after the Civil War. These subjects will be discussed in Chapters 5 and 6.

Crusaders for the Common School

Revisions of old constitutions and the writing of new ones involved only a fraction of the time and effort required to mobilize support of state action on behalf of free, universal, common school systems. Much energy was expended by a seemingly tireless band of aggressive and public-minded school persons who delivered untold numbers of speeches before thousands of citizens and teachers, wrote inexhaustible supplies of articles and reports, and organized voluntary groups galore to propagandize for public schools. Many of these volunteers were subsequently appointed or elected to influential posts in state and city school systems, and continued their efforts from those vantage points. Among these in New England were James G. Carter and Horace Mann in Massachusetts (usually the pace setter) and Henry Barnard in Connecticut and in Rhode Island. The new states of the West produced Samuel Lewis, Samuel Galloway, and Calvin Stowe in Ohio, Caleb Mills in Indiana, Ninian Edwards in Illinois, John D. Pierce and Isaac Crary in Michigan, and John Swett in California. The upper South boasted Calvin Wiley in North Carolina, Robert Breckenridge in Kentucky, and Charles Fenton Mercer in Virginia.

The organized channels for discussion, agitation, and even lobbying were typified by the American Lyceum (founded 1826), the Pennsylvania Society for the Promotion of Public Schools (1827), the Western Academic Institute and Board of Education, and the American Institute of Instruction (1830). Besides articles in newspapers, popular periodicals, and literary magazines, new professional journals devoted to the continuing discussion of things educational made their appearance: William Russell's *American Journal of Education* (1826–1829), Horace Mann's *Common School Journal*, Henry Barnard's *Connecticut Common School Journal*, and eventually the most massive of all, Barnard's *American Journal of Education* (1855–1881). The "common school movement" or the "common school revival" were almost constant themes seeking to mobilize public opinion as well as the professional interest of teachers on behalf of what amounted in some minds to a "common school crusade." It often gathered the emotional momentum of the other crusading reform movements of the day such as those devoted to improving the conditions of the blind, the handicapped, the poor, the imprisoned, disadvantaged women and orphans, or to attacking the evils of slavery, liquor, crime, and war.

Merger of Modernization and Revolutionary Ideals

The argument that free, universal common schools could only be achieved by state action was supported by the historic revolutionary idealism devoted to republican governments in general. This was further reinforced by the growing realization that a rapidly modernizing society needed to emphasize the consolidating and centralizing power of political communities larger than local villages, towns, districts, or cities. With this merging of the general ideology of the Revolutionary era with the urgent pressure of rapid modernization, it was inevitable that bureaucratic types of organization would emerge, whether they were public agencies or private corporations.

It was argued that to assure that public schools serve the common good, they should be *common* schools in which all classes of children could attend together and learn together the common language (English) and common political values essential to good citizenship in a republican society. The children would thus learn how to live together without distinctions such as rich or poor, good manners or bad, religious conviction, or national origin. Thus, in a republican society where government authority rests on the will of the people, the school must be universal and open to all if it is to be genuinely common. The only way that *all* children could be served in common was to make the schooling free to all, and the only way it could be free to all was to provide it at public expense.

Public Funding / The school reformers argued that the payment of tuition or rate bills by the well-to-do and the offering of free places to the poor who declared themselves to be paupers would simply preserve the class systems of Europe. Class distinctions could be obliterated only when a "free school" no longer meant a charity school for the poor but one in which *all* children would be offered an education in common without fee or tuition cost. The only way *that* could be done was to support the schools by public taxes levied upon everyone in proportion to their ability to pay. The older sources of public school support drew on common school funds derived from the sale of public land, or licenses, or fines, or other indirect sources, but these resources were insufficient for financing the large-scale educational systems that were needed. Only direct taxation would supply the necessary funds and the most common form was, of course, the real property tax. By dint of persistent, sometimes contentious, pressure from reformers in town after town and state after state, an increasing number of school districts began to tax themselves for public school support. But many school districts were reluctant or refused to do so.

To alleviate the funding problem state legislatures were importuned not only to *permit* local districts to tax themselves, but also to encourage them to do so by dangling a promise of state aid if they did. And, finally, when legislatures could see no other way to carry out their constitutional mandates to provide "thorough and efficient systems" of education for the whole state, they passed laws *requiring* local districts to tax themselves in order to support public schools. This was a long, arduous, and complicated process, often meeting stubborn opposition from local districts or from private or religious groups who argued vehemently that their liberty was being violated. But, gradually and persistently, the claims for the public good, political cohesion, and equality of opportunity won out over the claims for personal or pluralistic liberty. The freedom of local districts to ignore the need for free schooling for their children was abrogated by the mandate of the wider political community on behalf of the larger public good so that a whole population would be enlightened by education offered equally to all.

Centralization of Control / Thus, it was determined that free, universal, and common schooling could not be genuinely achieved if its control were left entirely in the hands of local communities (democratic localism), or in the hands of charitable or philanthropic bodies (paternalistic voluntarism), or religious bodies (parochial voluntarism), or private boards of trustees (corporate voluntarism), or profit-seeking entrepreneurs (proprietary voluntarism). Instead, it was decided that a modern society devoted to republican methods of government would be better served by a kind of democratic centralism in which the *authority* for public education rested with the *state* government, but the day-to-day management or administration of the schools was delegated to the local districts, which could more conveniently exercise the subsystem autonomy in accordance with the overall direction and planning of the central authority of the state. So, local community control of an extremely decentralized sort, exemplified by the early nineteenth-century district system, was gradually circumscribed by requirements stipulated in state constitutions, in state codes of laws passed by the legislatures, in state regulations and directives issued by elected or appointed state boards of education, and in policies adopted by state departments of education headed by elected or appointed state superintendents or commissioners of schools.

Though this process of state control began in the 1820s (as mentioned in Chapter 3), a greater measure of effective practice was largely developed in the 1840s and 1850s. Under the prodding of James G. Carter, Massachusetts established its state board of education in 1837 and appointed Horace Mann as secretary; Connecticut followed suit in 1839, with Henry Barnard as secretary. Both men were convinced that state governments would better serve the values of the broader political community than could the segmented localism of the districts or the segmented pluralism of religious or class affiliations. Both believed that modernization might be easier to effect if education were made a state function rather than left to private or local segments. Barnard was more traditional than Mann in favoring specific religious instruction, and was also more conservative in adhering to the values of industrial capitalism as a modernizing force. Mann was more the passionate crusader, more zealous in supporting the separation of church and state, and unremitting in his devotion to the ideal of the common school. He viewed the latter as an elixir of reform that could at once strengthen the common bonds of cohesive citizenship, maintain the values of the Republic, and yet provide the intellectual basis for individual development and social progress. He clung adamantly to these beliefs despite the rampant pluralists who attacked him so bitterly and whom he fought so vehemently.

Pluralistic Resistance to State Control

Resistance to centralization of educational power in the hands of the state came not only from religious pluralists but from "localists," those who held firmly and devoutly to the view that local control of schools was a significant display of pure democracy in action. Such a view was consonant with the philosophy of the Jacksonian Democrats, who typically opposed monopoly whether in private or government hands and who feared the consolidation of political power "out there." A good example was the first Democratic governor of Massachusetts, Marcus Morton, who shared Mann's devotion to the common schools but argued *against* the directive power of the new state board of education over which he presided. In his message of 1840 to the legislature, he expressed a localist view of community control over common schools that sounded remarkably like the pluralist arguments of the 1970s (see Chap. 12), which claimed that

> the responsibility for their management should rest upon the inhabitants of the towns. And the more immediately they are brought under the control of those for whose benefit they are established, and at whose expense they are

supported, the more deep and active will be the feelings engendered in their favor, and the more certain and universal will be their beneficial agency. In the town and district meetings, those little pure democracies, where our citizens first learn the rudiments and the practical operation of free institutions, may safely and rightly be placed the directions and the government of these invaluable seminaries.[5]

The Committee on Education of the Massachusetts House of Representatives followed the governor's message with a bill for abolishing the board of education and the projected normal schools under its control, arguing that they were French- and Prussian-like attempts to exert political influence over the schools and the minds of the people by strengthening the hands of the government rather than simply being a means for diffusing knowledge. The legislators also argued against any central direction to instruction in morals or religion which, along with the political, must be "a right exclusively and jealously reserved by our own laws to every parent."[6] This argument anticipated by 100 years the appeal to the rights of parents to guide their children's upbringing. (See Chap. 10.)

The House Committee was echoing, less eloquently, the views expressed the year before by Orestes Brownson in his new *Boston Quarterly Review*. In reviewing Mann's second annual report, Brownson—erstwhile liberal and reformer but soon to claim that U.S. democracy would be safe only in the hands of the Catholic Church—argued that since all education must be religious and political, it must not be in the hands of *any* government body, least of all one that imitated despotic Prussia or had leanings toward Protestantism. All that the *state* government should do was to provide financial support; all else should be left to the smallest possible unit:

> The selection of teachers, the choice of studies and of books to be read or studied, all that pertains to the methods of teaching and the matters to be taught or learned are best left to the school district. In these matters, the district should be paramount to the state. . . . The more exclusively the whole matter of the school is brought under the control of the families specially interested in it, the more efficient will the school be. . . . Wherever there is a power to be exercised, there should always be a concentration of it in as few hands as possible.[7]

This is an excellent early statement of the principle of "subsidiarity," defined by John Coons and his colleagues in 1970 as a general policy preference for decentralizing decision making and locating it within the smallest community competent to discharge it. The term "subsidiarity" implies respect for divergent community behaviors based upon group preference.[8] Thus, decentralization and subsidiarity have close affinity to social segmentation and cultural pluralism. Brownson summed up this view in telling phrases:

> Government is not in this country, and cannot be, the educator of the people. In education, as in religion, we must rely mainly on the voluntary system. If this be an evil, it is an evil inseparable from our form of govern-

ment. Government here must be restricted to material interests and forbidden to concern itself with what belongs to the spiritual culture of the community. It has of right no control over our opinions, literary, moral, political, philosophical, or religious. Its province is to reflect, not to lead, nor to create the general will. It, therefore, must not be installed the educator of the people.[9]

Government the Prime Educator of the People

This view that "government is not the educator of the people" reflected admirably the growing pluralism of the mid-nineteenth century. It appealed to the growing individualism of the day because it stressed freedom from government control. But it did not reflect or take into account the claims of the larger political community on behalf of education for equality and for the public good. Thus, it departed radically from the intent of the founders of the Republic, namely, that republican government could and must be the surest educator of the people. It was to these claims that Horace Mann and other school reformers appealed. The bill to abolish the state board of education and normal schools in Massachusetts was narrowly defeated. The board under Mann's influence gained in strength and in support during the decade of the 1840s.

In his tenth annual report in 1847, Mann returned to his often repeated belief that it was necessary for government to be the prime educator of the people through the agency of the common school because on it depended the welfare of the republican society itself:

> I believe in the existence of a great, immutable principle of natural law, or natural ethics . . . which proves the *absolute right* of every human being that comes into the world to an education; and which, of course, proves the correlative duty of every government to see that the means of that education are provided for all. . . . under a republican government, it seems clear that the minimum of this education can never be less than such as is sufficient to qualify each citizen for the civil and social duties he will be called to discharge. . . .
> The society of which we necessarily constitute a part must be preserved; and, in order to preserve it, we must not look merely to what one individual or family needs, but to what the whole community needs; not merely to what one generation needs, but to the wants of a succession of generations.[10]

Here, then, in the struggle for state promotion of the common school were the beginnings of a long-lasting confrontation between the cohesive push to strengthen the political community by positive governmental action and the pluralistic pull to rely upon voluntary, family, or local community action. Each side had its contingent of "public-spirited" and humanitarian-minded persons; and each had a share of self-serving, ambitious, and power-hungry persons. But the gathering consensus prior to the Civil War was that free, universal, common schooling was essential to the welfare of the republic and that it should be advanced by the active stimulus and direction of state governments.

During the Civil War and subsequent reconstruction there were even strenuous attempts to give the federal government a more active and positive role as an educator of the people, but with few exceptions these were not very successful. In the antebellum period, the legitimacy of state action was generally strengthened vis-à-vis local community pluralism and parochial parental voluntarism. The rights of children to a public education under the protection of public authority were gradually accepted as legitimate. The growth of popular participation in public affairs and of industrial urbanization, each in its own modernizing way, increased the momentum toward "thorough and efficient" public school systems.

Popular Participation in Public Affairs

The turbulence caused by war and territorial expansion of the United States in the first half of the nineteenth century accentuated the necessity for a commonly educated electorate. Factional interests were so deeply engrained and political entities so disparate that only a sense of national political community could restore harmony. As settlers in the West and immigrants in the East were enfranchised, political participation accelerated. Swept along in the rush toward modernization and an expanded suffrage, the common school movement both profited from and speeded along popular participation in public affairs.

The public school reformers were aided in this process not only by the logic that a modern society required a more active, centralized state government (a Whig proclivity), but also by the phenomenal growth of political participation by an ever-expanding proportion of the population (a Democratic article of faith). To be sure, "popular participation" really meant *white male* participation for most of the mid-1800 period; nevertheless, compared with any other country on earth at that time, more men took part in U.S. political affairs and repeatedly voted in elections. Between the presidential elections of the 1820s and the 1850s nearly universal white suffrage was attained in 27 states. Of the other states, only six imposed small poll taxes, and only one retained a considerable property qualification. Much of this gain for popular suffrage was won by aggressive political action on the part of northern and southern independent farmers, urban workingmen, Irish and German immigrants, and Jeffersonian-oriented intellectuals who had adopted the name of Democratic Party. These groups proceeded to elect Andrew Jackson in 1828, and dominated the presidency until the election of Abraham Lincoln in 1860.

It is difficult to characterize the policy differences of whole parties over a period of two generations, but a few generalizations are in order for the three or four decades prior to the Civil War. The Democratic/Republicans-turned-Democrats were political modernizers in their adherence to democratic participation in the political process, extension of the suffrage to all free men, equality of opportunity in social and economic affairs, and their faith in popular and practical education. Democrats were typically economic traditionalists, however, believing in a social order based on agrarian self-sufficiency and the primacy of local governments as the guarantors of liberty. They were deeply suspicious of unitary central governments (whether state or federal), and they tended to view private corporations as instruments of special privilege or monopoly in restraint of individual enterprise.

The Federalists-turned-Whigs were modernists in their willingness for economic and national development to be pursued actively by business and commercial enterprisers, aided by strong central governments that would encourage banks, sound money, trade, and urbanization. But the Whigs were likely to be traditional with regard to respect for the established religions of Protestant persuasion and for the leadership role of intellectual, professional, and social elites in public affairs. The interesting thing was that Whigs also believed in the popular practical education that was purported to be the special blessing of the common school.

Political Consensus—The Common School

The Democrats may have often opposed central state government control of schools, but they were *for* the common school as a means of opportunity for the poor and working classes, and as an "equalizer" that would restrain the "uppity" upper classes. In their turn, the Whigs believed that local communities needed the prodding of a beneficent state leadership to excite an ardor for providing schools, but they also were often *for* common schools open to rich and poor alike. This was atypical of other elites worldwide. The counterparts of Whigs in Prussia, England, or France under their respective monarchies did not generally argue for public schools that would serve in common the children of both the well-to-do classes and the working classes. All European countries typically built two-track systems of schools: a common school system for the "common people" who were to be the workers; and a secondary school system for the middle and professional classes who were headed for managerial positions in society.

Whigs / Now the question arises as to why U.S. political leaders came to agree on a common school system that would serve all classes of society. Why did the Whigs, for example, not only concur with the idea of free, universal, common schooling, but also often take the lead in putting the idea into practice? One view is that the Whig school reformers were motivated by the desire to impose their capitalist middle-class values upon the working classes and the immigrants in order to make them into obedient, prompt, and passive factory workers for the greater benefit of the factory owners. For example, Michael B. Katz concludes his study of school reform in mid-century Massachusetts by saying

> the extension and reform of education in mid-nineteenth century were not a potpourri of democracy, rationalism, and humanitarianism. They were the attempt of a coalition of the social leaders, status-anxious parents, and status-hungry educators to impose educational innovation, each for his own reasons, upon a reluctant community.[11]

If this were the whole story or even the most important part of the story, why didn't the school reformers and upper classes impose an aristocratic, two-track system upon the communities, as was the case at that time in Prussia, France, and England? I believe that the answer lies in their recognition of the realities of the political process in the mid-1800 period. Even if Whigs did not believe their own rhetoric about republican institutions and the common schools (and many of them did), they could not have hoped to succeed with a rhetoric of aristocracy, or of autocracy, or of inequality. There were too many Democrats who would have thrown them out of office, and there were too many Whigs who would have found such arguments an affront to their own genuine adherence to the inherited ideals of the democratic political community.

No—the truth is that a genuine consensus reaching across the spectrum of political beliefs and political parties was being gradually hammered out in the course of the middle period. Battles were fought by elected representatives in thousands of town meetings, or city councils, or school districts, and in hundreds of state legislative sessions during this period. Sometimes the reformers won, sometimes they lost, but the trend was unmistakable. And gradually a consensus evolved—sometimes hesitantly, sometimes rapidly—that free, universal, common schools did support and were necessary for the health of a free society based upon popular participation in public affairs.

Democrats / Of course proponents of common schools worked on their behalf for different reasons, and there has been considerable debate among historians of education regarding the role of various groups in the common school movement. The balance sheet for the mid-1800 period seems to me to be something like this: In the late 1820s, some of the more persuasive arguments in favor of the common schools came from the newly formed political parties organized by workingmen's associations in the major cities of the country. Workingmen turned to political action in protest against the new industrial and factory conditions that had lowered their salaries and thrown many out of work. They stressed common schooling as a major means of achieving the equality that the Revolution had promised. But direct political action soon proved a failure, and by the early 1830s the workingmen were turning to the trade union movement to improve working conditions and wages for artisans and mechanics.

The new Democratic party picked up the arguments—and most of the voters—of the workingmen's parties and the trade unions (which collapsed in the Panic of 1837). Democrats originally promoted the cause of public schools in the several states when they came to power and when they took part in the constitutional conventions, but that policy changed. By the late 1830s, Democrats were chafing under the threats of too much *state* control over their pluralistic freedoms of economic and social action, and they rallied to the banners of *local* control in the name of liberty as well as equality.

So, it was the Whigs who adopted the cause of promoting common schools under more aggressive *state* direction. They did so not only on behalf of the same loyalties to liberty and equality, but also on behalf of the public good of the greater community as well as of themselves. On the matter of extending free, universal, common schools under state auspices, their arguments won wider appeal than those of the Democrats, and their expertise in political organization won support in state after state by the 1850s. The Whigs, in effect, adopted much of the political arsenal of the Democrats' ideology on common education, much as the Democrats had profited from adopting platforms from the workingmen's associations which in turn had been patterned on the revolutionary ideals.

In the two decades during which this "radicalization process" took place, emotion-laden statements on education stemmed from fairly extreme political poles. Two such statements illustrate the diversity of political opinions: the report of a workingmen's committee of Philadelphia in 1830, and Horace Mann's last annual report in 1848. The first was presumably influenced by a radical Democratic orientation; the second, by the more conservative Whig outlook two decades later.

Workingmen on Equal Liberties / The demand for "equal liberties" was the essence of the workingmen's argument:

> The original element of *despotism* is a MONOPOLY OF TALENT, which consigns the multitude to comparative ignorance, and secures the balance of knowledge on the side of the rich and the rulers. . . . it follows as a necessary consequence . . . that this monopoly should be broken up, and that the means of equal knowledge (the only security for equal liberty) should be rendered, by legal provision, the common property of all classes. . . .
>
> It appears, therefore, to the committee that there can be no real liberty without a wide diffusion of real intelligence; that the members of a republic should all be alike instructed in the nature and character of their equal rights and duties, as human beings and as citizens. . . .[12]

These were the sentiments that underlay the proposals for legislation to establish a system of common schools, which the workingmen's committee submitted to the Pennsylvania legislature in 1830. The bill was not passed until 1834, but it was significant that the major opposition to passing it, along with its tax provisions, came from pluralistic elements among the Democrats, principally the German-speaking religious groups. And when it came time to defend the common school act against those who would repeal it, it was the anti-Jackson, anti-Democrat Whig Thaddeus Stevens who turned the tide in favor of keeping the common school act alive.

Horace Mann on the Common School as Equalizer / So it was in Massachusetts as Horace Mann looked back on his decade of service to the state board of education. In his final annual report he sounded even more radical than the workingmen as he candidly described the evils of a burgeoning capitalism and forecast that the common schools would soften or at least counteract the excesses of the new industrialists in his state. He said that

> vast and overshadowing private fortunes are among the greatest dangers to which the happiness of the people of a republic can be subjected. Such fortunes would create a feudalism of a new kind, but one more oppressive and unrelenting than that of the middle ages. . . .
>
> Now surely nothing but universal education can counterwork this tendency to the domination of capital and servility of labor. If one class possesses all the wealth and the education, while the residue of society is ignorant and poor, it matters not by what name the relation between them may be called: the latter, in fact and in truth, will be the servile dependents and subjects of the former. But, if education be equably diffused, it will draw property after it by the strongest of all attractions. . . .
>
> Education, then, beyond all other devices of human origin, is the great equalizer of the conditions of men, the balance-wheel of the social machinery.[13]

Mann's hope that universal education would prevent poverty and obliterate class and economic distinctions did not materialize. But he did come closer to stating the principal aspirations and convictions of the vast majority of the people in the United States than did another publication in 1848. In their *Communist Manifesto* Marx and Engels arrived at quite a different prescription for abolishing the exploitation of labor by capital. Mann was, of course, no revolutionary, but he *was* a meliorist who believed that the evils brought on by a capitalist drive to modernization could be moderated by various kinds of social reform, the premier one being universal education. In this respect he reflected, and indeed helped mightily to formulate, the predominant educational views of the major political parties in the mid-1800 period.

Common Agreements / This view of education was an integral part of the political philosophy of both the Democrats and Whigs, as Rush Welter has so thoroughly documented.[14] Both parties agreed that the United States should try to live up to the basic principles of the founders of the Republic. Each party argued, of course, that *it* was more loyal to those principles than its competitor, but nowhere did either try to repudiate the principles. The

Democrats made much more of the demands for equal rights, but they did not openly argue for wiping out all social or economic distinctions; rather they urged the abolition of the distinctions that would give *political* privileges, and thus power, to the few over the many. Their hostility to aristocrats had rather more of a political than an economic context. In other words, social classes were not so fixed that they could not be remedied by an all-out guarantee of equal rights within the republican political system.

Thus, Democrats put great emphasis upon extending the suffrage to all men, without much ado about qualifications of residence or property or religion or whatever, and of course ignoring race and sex. They applied this belief in minimal special qualifications to executives and the judiciary as well as to legislators and electors. As in the Revolutionary era, liberty meant the suffrage, which would protect the people against the probably hostile government "out there." So the best chance for liberty to work would be in local governments. Democrats therefore tended to be suspicious, if not hostile, as we have seen, to the common school revival if it were to become primarily a *state* matter, but nevertheless they often pushed the idea in their own states as well as in Whig states.

For their part, the Whigs more or less reluctantly went along with the Democrats' calls for equal rights except, of course, if it meant dividing up and distributing property or wealth equally. They were more likely to accept a hierarchical structure of society as desirable as well as inevitable, and to be in favor of an active beneficent government as long as it was run primarily by the specially qualified, that is, the well-born, the well-situated, and the well-educated. Whereas the Democrats looked upon the suffrage as the best guarantor of liberty, the Whigs viewed property as indispensable to liberty. Thus they turned enthusiastically to the constitutional revisionism of the 1830s to 1850s as an opportunity to impose the same system of checks and balances upon the states that the federalists had adopted in forming the national government. Interestingly enough, the Democrats joined in these constitutional "reforms" in order to protect and secure the legislative policies that they had already won in the states. As the Whigs would use checks and balances to keep the governments from responding too easily to the whims of the *electorate*, so the Democrats approved checks and balances as a hedge against a too autocratic or paternalistic *administration*.

The upshot was that underneath their differences of rationale, both political parties agreed that free, universal, and common schools were politically necessary.

The Civic Role of Public Schools

Despite the great amount of public discussion about common schooling as a bulwark of republican institutions, there was relatively little explicit controversy over the kind of civic education that would best serve the general purposes so widely agreed upon. The degree of political inculcation must largely be inferred from the textbooks that were used. In the middle half of the nineteenth century the political values inculcated by the civic education program of the schools did not change substantially from those celebrated in the Republic's first 50 years. In the textbooks of the day, the rosy hues of those values became even more golden. To the resplendent values of liberty, equality, patriotism, and a benevolent Christian morality were now added the middle-class virtues (especially of New England) of hard work, honesty, and integrity; the rewards of individual effort; and obedience to legitimate authority.

The predominant tone of the school textbooks of the nineteenth century was a combination of Federalist, Whig, and conservative pronouncements in which

> contemporary problems are conspicuously absent, and reform movements which would have profound social or political effects are either ignored or derided. While Jeffersonian and Jacksonian democracy agitated the adult world, the child was taught the necessity of class distinctions. Nor are Jefferson and Jackson ever ranked as heroes; . . . in the schools Hamilton and Daniel Webster governed the minds of the children.[15]

Horace Mann on Political Education / No advocate was more eloquent than Horace Mann himself on what he candidly called "political education." Summing up his conclusions on 12 years as secretary of the State Board of Education in Massachusetts in 1848, Mann began with the assumptions of the founders that citizens of a republic must "understand something of the true nature of government under which they live." But, caught in the swirl of contesting forces caused in Massachusetts by the immigration of Irish and Germans of Roman Catholic faith and by the changes in urban life as a result of the industrial factory system, Mann knew all too well that if the "tempest of political strife were to be let loose upon our Common Schools, they would be overwhelmed with sudden ruin." He recognized that many would object to *any* study of political matters in the schools because the constitution was subject to different readings:

> If parents find that their children are indoctrinated into what they call political heresies, will they not withdraw them from the school; and, if they withdraw them from the school, will they not resist all appropriations to support a school from which they derive no benefit?[16]

Mann could not admit that the public schools should avoid political education altogether, nor could he risk the destruction of the public schools by urging them to become "theatres for party politics." His solution was similar to that which he proposed for religious controversies: the schools should teach the common elements that all agreed to, but should skip over the controversial issues. In his words,

> those articles in the creed of republicanism, which are accepted by all, believed in by all, and which form the common basis of our political faith,

shall be taught to all. But when the teacher, in the course of his lessons or lectures on the fundamental law, arrives at a controverted text, he is either to read it without comment or remark; or, at most, he is only to say that the passage is the subject of disputation, and that the schoolroom is neither the tribunal to adjudicate, nor the forum to discuss it. . . . political proselytism is no function of the school; but that all indoctrination into matters of controversy between hostile political parties is to be elsewhere sought for, and elsewhere imparted.[17]

Mann was so intent upon getting common schools established for an ever-wider range of the potential school population that he would not risk the failure of the common school idea by introducing political controversy into the subject matter. Thus, the political curriculums of the emerging public schools were largely oriented toward a civic program that initiated the poor, the foreigner, and the working class children into the political community by literacy in English; by didactic moral injunctions; by patriotic readers and histories; and by lessons that stressed memory and recitation of the structural forms of the constitutional order.

Industrial Urbanization: The Magnet of the City

When we move from political ideology, which is a vital aspect of public decision making, to the everyday arenas where people live and work and jostle each other, perspectives often change. One arena is no more "real" than the other, but they often pull in such different directions or they confront each other so traumatically that something must be done: a person might negotiate and compromise, or consign to separate compartments, or ignore as long as possible, or fight. All these modes of action happened in the middle period. The confrontations and tensions were especially acute in the streets and alleys of the booming cities. In more academic terms, rapid urbanization put to an extremely severe test the inherited political ideas and values that had been formulated in a predominantly rural and agrarian age. And one of the severest tests was faced when the time came to design a common school system that embraced both what the political ideology said it *should* be and what the teeming cities determined it *could* be.

Effects of Too Rapid Urbanization

First, a few reminders. The United States in the middle decades of the nineteenth century was not only a land of vast open spaces and frontiers; it was also rapidly becoming a land of cities, growing at a faster rate than at any other time in its history. In 1820 less than 8 percent of U.S. inhabitants lived in urban centers (700,000 of 9 million); by 1870, 25 percent (10 of 40 million) lived in centers of 2,500 or more. While the total population increased fourfold, the urban population increased nearly 15 times between 1820 and 1870. But even more significant for the management and control of local public schools was the increase in the number of larger cities. In 1820 there were 13 U.S. cities with over a 10,000 population; only three of these were over 50,000, and one over 100,000. By 1870 there were 168 cities with over 10,000, of which 25 were over 50,000 and 14 over 100,000. Nearly 20 percent of all U.S. citizens lived in places having 10,000 or more residents.

This rapid growth of the number of mid-sized and large-sized cities meant that the speed of the modernization process was almost overwhelming, especially in the eastern and middle western sections of the country. The westward movement, at least as far as the Mississippi, was toward the inland cities located at transportation centers on rivers, lakes, and crossroads as well as to the farmlands of the valleys and plains. Opening up the frontier was as much a process of citifying as it was a settling of open land. Richard C. Wade calls the towns and cities the "spearheads of the frontier."[18] Charles N. Glaab and A. T. Brown revised Turner's thesis that the frontier gave the United States its distinctive character by arguing that "American expansion was largely a function of urban expansion, and . . . the civilization which pushed the edge of the wilderness toward the Pacific drew most of its impulses and took most of its direction from the cities."[19]

Recognition of the citified character of U.S. society serves to help explain the spread of literacy, books, magazines, printing presses, libraries, literary societies, and the whole panoply of an urban way of life over a vast continent-wide country in a fairly short time. Schools and colleges quickly took their place among the most common and visible signs of the spread of a common culture that served to bind the seemingly isolated "island communities" together.

But the most predominant signs of the urban modernization process were the factories, the mills, the grain elevators, the steamboat docks, the railroad yards, the stockyards, and the shops and stores where the implements and objects of mechanical mass production were centralized. And, above all, there was the human side of industrial urbanization—the slums and ghettos where masses of human beings huddled together in congested, filthy, disease-ridden squalor. Peasants from overseas and ruralites from agrarian United States poured into the cities in search of the new life, and instead so often found themselves living in a degradation of health, morals, and human dignity. As in England, the cities were not prepared for the speed or the size of the influx. For a time, voluntary and philanthropic organizations tried to cope with the clangor and crunch, the grime and crime, the poverty and deprivation that the booming cities brought on. But the problems soon became so overpowering that much more comprehensive and organized efforts were soon seen to be necessary.

Solutions by Government Intervention

To alleviate these problems of urbanized populations, government was the obvious answer, and in an era when there was so little central government, city governments had to try to cope. In this effort they were almost overwhelmed by the staggering problem of simply providing the basic conditions of survival. The tasks of organizing such elemental matters as making available fresh water, disposing of sewage, lighting the streets, putting out fires, and preventing crime soon made it clear that in crowded cities such tasks could not be left to individual effort, or to families, or even to voluntary organizations. Organized, regular, consistent, reliable, specialized, and coordinated efforts were required. This required bureaucracies in which a group of people devoted their efforts and time to carrying out particular, assigned, and recognized tasks. Thus water departments, sewage departments, and police departments were organized, and eventually fire departments and transportation facilities became public or under public control. The schools were no exception. They, too, had to become bureaucratic or be decimated. Both extremes occurred.

Effect of Bureaucratization on Schools / The best general description of the way the modernization of cities engulfed the schools and the way the schools tried to respond is by David B. Tyack. There are several other excellent studies of particular cities to which I shall refer, but Tyack's is the most evenly balanced and most vivid picture of the total process to be described in a single volume. Tyack makes it clear that "the pressure of numbers was a main reason for the bureaucratization that gradually replaced the older decentralized village pattern of schooling."[20] In the 1840s three teachers in one Chicago school struggled to handle over 500 pupils in one year and over 800 the next. And they were "expected to instruct all those children in ungraded classrooms, with no uniform texts." In 1850, 21 teachers had to deal with 1,900 pupils in the whole city of Chicago; in 1860, 123 teachers tried to deal with 14,000 pupils in the city schools. Even without a handy computer one can figure out that the average class size per teacher moved up in a decade from 90 to well over 110. What should Chicago or any other large city do under the circumstances?

Under such circumstances what *could* a teacher do with 100 children whose ages ranged from 5 or 6 to 13 or 14, whose former schooling ranged from none to several years, whose mother tongue might include several languages besides English, and who probably did not have any textbooks of their own? The rural idyll of a little one-room schoolhouse had become a nightmare; as for the image of Mark Hopkins on one end of a log and one student on the other end—here was the original impossible dream. What teacher would not prefer almost any other arrangement to the prospect of trying to hear 100 different pupils recite individually while the other 99 did something else—the usual pattern of an ungraded village school? What teacher would not prefer graded classrooms where the children were a bit more alike in their academic attainments and where the cumulative effect of a sequentially organized curriculum could be ascertained and tested? What teacher would not welcome a bit more quiet and order—and discipline—in a class composed of upwards of 100 pupils? Assuming that most teachers *would prefer* such conditions, would they simply make life easier for the teacher or would they also make for better learning—and behavior—among the pupils?

Few teachers were accustomed to asking the pupils what *they* preferred, and few school board members or administrators would ask teachers what *they* preferred, but it soon became clear what the educational reformers preferred. Faced with the onrush of such large numbers, the schoolmen set out to build large-scale systems in the cities. They argued for—and instituted —graded schools so that children could be divided into classes according to their age or achievement. They argued for graded curricula in which the content of specific subjects was to be taught in specified order in each grade. They argued for what was obvious—if the class size was to be smaller, there had to be more teachers, which would cost more money—and they argued for what was not at all obvious to many taxpayers, namely, that the teachers should be better trained in special institutions designed for the purpose of teacher training (normal schools).

They argued that a large city system with many schools and teachers could not be run efficiently by the direct management of a large number of ward committees. In the 1850s Boston had 190 lay trustees who supervised the elementary schools of the city; in 1860 Philadelphia's 92 schools had 24 ward boards whose members hired teachers, built schools, and supervised the curricula. So the reformers argued that running a school system of hundreds of teachers and thousands of pupils required full-time professional administrators to deal with the public boards of education on one side and with the teachers on the other. This meant principals in the schools and a superintendent (with a staff) at the head—in other words, a professional bureaucracy.

The Need for an Urban Discipline

Just as bureaucracy placed emphasis upon order and system in the organization and control of large systems, it also stressed order and system in the conduct of individual schools and classrooms. To many teachers and principals, this also implied insistence on order, compliance, and obedience for their own sake, anything that would make life tolerable for teachers. But to discerning educational leaders, the fundamental reason for order and system was to aid the young to be able to cope with the new industrial and urban society that was threatening to inundate this country. One of the most discerning of the educators to stress this point was William T. Harris, first as superintendent of schools in St. Louis, then as U.S. Commissioner of Education, and, throughout the latter part of the nineteenth century, as the leading philosopher of education in the United States.

Harris often spoke and wrote about the need for inculcating in the young an "urban discipline." For Harris this meant the development of moral conduct appropriate to an urban civilization, the essence of which was self-discipline—"the habitual practice of obedience to principle." In his annual report for 1871 he put it this way:

> The discipline of our Public Schools, wherein punctuality and regularity are enforced and the pupils are continually taught to *suppress mere self-will* and inclination, is the best school of morality. Self-control is the basis of all moral virtues, and industriousness and studious habits are the highest qualities we can form in our children.[21]

Over and over again Harris returned to the theme that large city schools must be conducted differently from one-room rural schools, not simply for the obvious reasons of maintaining classroom order, but also for the fundamental reason that children must learn how to live in close association with others in the modern urbanizing society of the future rather than in the traditional isolated agrarian societies of the past.

Confusion Over the Meaning of Discipline / Harris' insights, a product of the boisterous tensions of the modernizing process itself, have been borne out by recent historical scholarship; that is, that the fundamental social changes with which the schools had to reckon were relevant to the transition from an agrarian to an industrial-urbanizing society. Herbert G. Gutman sums up the process whereby the social habits of successive waves of tradition-oriented people came into conflict with the demands of a new modernizing society. The source of the tension resulted from

> the fact that the American working class was continually altered in its composition by infusions, from within and without the nation, of peasants, farmers, skilled artisans, and casual day laborers who brought into industrial society ways of work and other habits and values not associated with industrial necessities and the industrial ethos.[22]

Harris and many other educational reformers urged the public schools to aid in this modernizing process, which they saw as inevitable. Harris himself *opposed* the idea that the schools should become an agency for training workers for U.S. industry in the occupational or technical skills required in the factories. In this he was on the losing side, as we shall see in Chapter 8 on vocationalism in the schools. And he could not prevent practicing schoolmen from translating his philosophical justifications for an *urban* discipline into the overt practices of a strict *classroom* discipline. Whereas Harris talked about obedience to moral principle, the administrators stressed obedience to the school principal.

Note the change in tone from Harris' annual reports to a statement that he formulated with Duane Doty, superintendent of Detroit, and which was eventually signed by some 80 administrators in colleges and school systems:

> In order to compensate for lack of family-nurture, the school is obliged to lay more stress upon discipline and to make far more prominent the moral phase of education. It is obliged to train the pupil into habits of prompt obedience to his teachers and the practices of self-control in its various forms, in order that he may be prepared for a life wherein there is little police restraint on the part of constituted authorities.[23]

It is easy to see how teachers could quickly translate "obedience to principle" into punctuality, regularity, attention, and silence. But it is fair to point out that the sections that followed this widely circulated statement stressed Harris' other strong points on modernization: that "initiation into the means of association with one's fellowmen, the world of humanity" required a great stress on learning to read so that the pupils could begin as early as possible the processes of *self*-learning and "the practical method of conducting investigations for the purpose of verification and of original discovery."

The St. Louis Experience

Whatever the interpretation of the meaning of an urban discipline, it is clear that it was intended to apply to *all* children in a free, universal, and common school. Harris and his predecessors in St. Louis worked relentlessly to get all classes of children into the public schools, an effort that became an established fact by the end of the Civil War period. Selwyn Troen's careful statistical analysis of the social backgrounds of children makes this clear. At the elementary school level, ages 6 to 12, the children of unskilled and skilled laborers attended in as high a proportion as did the children of well-to-do parents, but they did drop out with greater frequency after that time. Therefore, at the higher levels, the more affluent economic classes made more use of the public schools than did the working classes:

> It is now clear that schooling was nearly universal during the mid-century, with about 90 per cent of all children between eight and eleven in school and the great majority in public schools. The efforts expended by public and nonpublic institutions to reach the mass of the city's children and to create generations of literate individuals were successful.[24]

But to achieve this, the schoolmen had to convince the middle and upper classes to send their children to the public schools rather than to private schools. Once the fee system was abolished in order to remove the taint of pauperism and charity so that poor children were attracted to the public schools, then the educators had to laud the values that a common school contributed to the general welfare, thus assuring that the quality of education would be improved and would attract the middle classes. The "urban discipline" might have been imposed upon the working classes in separate schools designed especially for them, but the idea of the *common* school serving all classes won out and in fact was well established in St. Louis by 1880:

> Thus, in mid-nineteenth century, young children attended as popular and democratic an educational system as the nation ever possessed. . . . The ideal of the common school where children from all segments of society would have a common experience was approximated.[25]

It may be, as Troen remarked, that St. Louis had come closer to realizing a free, universal, common school system than most other cities of the middle period, but the ideal, if not the practice, was spreading. In looking more broadly at the development of urban education, Tyack comes to this conclusion concerning the urban schools of the nineteenth century:

> To assert that the schools served a modernizing function for workers is not to imply that the schoolroom was a necessary anteroom to the factory— . . . nor is it to claim that educators were attempting to create a class-biased system to teach workers their place. On the contrary, most school leaders of the nineteenth century asserted that class-consciousness was wrong and that the common school should combat group divisiveness of all kinds—class, ethnic, religious, and political.[26]

Compulsory Education

As we shall see in Chapter 5, the school reformers were by no means able to prevent group divisiveness through the agency of the common schools, but they did begin to see their role in connection with another aspect of the industrializing and urbanizing process. This had to do with child labor, which had increased dramatically with the upsurge of the factory system in the cities. Child labor was intimately connected with poverty, and poverty in crowded tenements was seen to be associated with a frightful increase in crime. So, it was not long before another characteristic of common schools was thought necessary. Schools might be free but free education was of little use if children were in factories instead of in school. And they would not be common or universal if the poor could not or would not attend. Therefore, it began to be argued that elementary schooling ought to be compulsory, as Robert Coram had urged a half-century earlier. First the cities and then the states began to assert the power of government to take precedence over the rights of parents to send their children to the factories instead of to school.

The cities and states had passed all sorts of laws requiring the apprenticeship of poor children whose parents were dependent upon the public for support or provision for their maintenance in almshouses or orphan asylums. As the numbers of poor children rapidly increased in the cities of the early nineteenth century, swelled largely by the influx of poor immigrants from Ireland and Germany especially, attention was focused more and more upon providing some sort of schooling for them—and often of seeing to it that the children actually got to school.

In the 1820s, Boston was one of the first cities to appoint a truant officer to oversee the "idle, vagrant, and vicious children" on the streets of the city and to try to get the truants back into school, or get them a job, or commit them to the House of Reformation for Juvenile Offenders. One of the main causes of truancy was, of course, child labor in the burgeoning factories of the New England towns. So harsh and cruel were the working conditions that in 1836 Massachusetts passed a law prohibiting the employment of children under 15 years of age unless they had attended a school for three months during the prior year.

After years of effort by Horace Mann and others, in 1842 the legislature went so far as to prohibit the labor of children under 12 for more than 10 hours a day. And Mann estimated that even with this cautious legislation some 40 percent of working-class children had no schooling at all. With the upswing in immigration the problem became ever more acute until in 1850 the Massachusetts legislature authorized the towns to take more positive action toward compulsory attendance at school and finally passed in 1852 the first compulsory attendance law applying to a state as a whole. This law required children from 8 to 14 to attend a public school for at least three months a year (with at least six weeks consecutively), imposed fines on parents who failed to comply, and allowed certain exemptions.

Mixed Motivations for Compulsory Attendance / The reasons for moving to compulsory education were complicated and mixed. They included on one hand a benevolent or paternal humanitarianism that was aimed at protecting the poor and the immigrant from exploitation by greedy manufacturers, helping them to improve themselves; and there was the belief that civic education for political self-government should be a prime function of the schools, aimed at all classes and cultural groups in society in common. On the other hand, there were doubtless many in the more affluent or comfortable classes who reacted in revulsion against what they considered to be the uncouth habits, ignorance, and loose morals of the lower class, rural, and village peoples who had crowded into the cities; and there was undoubtedly a religious motive on the part of native-born Protestants to try to prevent the spread of what they considered not only "foreign" language cultures but an alien Roman Catholic religion.

Whatever the mix of motivations or reasons or rationalizations, the prevailing view came to be that a *common* schooling amid the diversity of religions, languages, ethnic and national backgrounds, and socioeconomic classes would be advantageous to achieving a sound and durable political community. When this could not be achieved by persuasion, the educational and social reformers of the mid-1800s turned to compulsory attendance laws. So, between 1836 and 1854 the New England states and Pennsylvania passed laws requiring certain periods of school attendance for *working* children. The ages affected ranged from those under 12 to those under 15; the length of schooling ranged from 11 weeks to 4 months; usually there was no provision for enforcement.

When it became clear that this kind of legislation was not going to do the job, the child labor abolitionists and the school reformers turned to the task of requiring *all* children to attend school. After the Civil War the movement for compulsory attendance laws applying to all children picked up momentum. In the 1870s, 14 states enacted laws; in the 1880s, another ten. Despite indifferent enforcement, the principle had been established. Though the civic motive remained strong, compulsory attendance was rationalized primarily as a counteraction to the exploitation and dislocations arising from the urban and industrial conditions of modernization. Four of the ingredients of public schooling were now on center stage: elementary schools were rapidly becoming free, universal, common, and compulsory. A fifth, consisting of several aspects of secularization, was now in the wings.

Secularization

The term "secularization" is not used here in a simple restrictive sense to imply that doctrinal religious teachings were banished from the public schools and that nonreligious materials were substituted. That, to be sure, did gradually happen in many different places for very complex reasons (as described in Chapter 5), but at this point the term is used in a much more subtle and pervasive meaning. I am referring to the fact that the whole cultural tone of modern societies became more analytical, rational, and empirical as they adopted or were affected by the methods of science in its broadest problem-solving sense.

Along with the other signs of modernization mentioned in this chapter, U.S. society and U.S. education during the middle decades of the nineteenth century, became more scientific, more practical, more differentiated and diversified, more technical, and more professional. These trends first became more obvious at the secondary and higher levels of education than at the elementary level, and they accelerated with far greater speed in the late nineteenth and twentieth centuries. However, the beginnings of these changes are worthy of note here for comparative purposes as the modernizing forces gathered momentum in the realms of knowledge and culture as well as in political and economic development. Their combined impact served to modify, if not radically alter, the traditional religious-moral assumptions and civic-literacy goals upon which the common school was originally based.

A New Attitude Toward Children

One of the most important aspects of the impact of secularization was upon the family. Children became freer and more independent as changes in attitudes toward children were accompanied by the decline of the traditional hierarchical family and the rise of the modern household.

Of course this new freedom for children was appalling to many ministers, social critics, and guardians of tradition, as well as to teachers and foreign observers. Manuals on child rearing, sermons, and the press were full of laments and calls for restoration of obedience, piety, and discipline in the family as well as in the schools. And the teachers and school reformers, often caught in the middle, were themselves divided over how the schools should respond to the changes in family life. Should teachers try to emulate the traditional patriarchal head of the family and act as "supreme earthly legislators" over the children, as proposed by Herman Humphrey, president of Amherst College, or should they try to rear the innocent children on the principle of affection by considering their feelings as they guided their behavior, as proposed by the feminist reformer Lydia Child?[27]

Learner-Oriented Ideal / School reformers like Horace Mann, Samuel R. Hall, Edward Sheldon, and William T. Harris were likely to respond on the side of reasonableness, affection, and motivation rather than to rely exclusively upon unreasoning obedience and harsh discipline. One of the most celebrated of the conflicts within the profession was that between Horace Mann and a group of 31 Boston schoolmasters. Mann came back from a a tour of Europe to write glowingly about the new instructional methods in Prussian schools based upon the use of objects, sense experience, play, and activity, and using a discipline based upon love and affection rather than fear and the rod.

To this the Boston schoolmasters retorted that authority, not love, must be the backbone of the tie between student and teacher. Duty must come before affection, and devotion to duty must be reinforced by fear and by wise punishment, including corporal punishment and physical coercion if necessary.[28] Mann, of course, replied with some of his most outraged rhetoric.[29] Though the controversies between professionals found ready outlet in the press, the trend in Mann's favor was quietly being supported by parents and laymen in town after town across the state. Note the annual reports from school committees whose members represented parents and adults concerned about the methods of public schools as well as the welfare of their children. From the town of Tewksbury for the year 1842–1843 came a laconic comment typical of other school committees:

> One of our teachers used no corporal punishment, and his was the best regulated school in the town. Another spent a portion of almost every day in punishing some of the scholars; and his was the worst regulated and most unprofitable school in town.[30]

The school committee of Roxbury probably summed up the predominant public outlook in reporting that

> Corporal punishment is not, and cannot be, absolutely prohibited in our schools. . . . The rules of our board allow it only as a last resort. . . . We must not take the rod out of the teachers' hands, but we may hope that they will never have the disposition, and very seldom feel the necessity, to take it into their hands. . . .
>
> In all our schools we want to hear words of encouragement, tones of kindness. We would see the authority tempered, not relaxed, by love; firmness fortified by mildness; heart answering to heart; mind pouring itself into mind genially; the common routine of labor and learning become a labor of love; and all the intercourse between the teacher and the taught, full of the tokens of mutual interest, affection and respect.[31]

Needless to say, this lofty goal so eloquently penned into the usually dull rhetoric of an annual school report was not to be quickly or universally achieved. Nevertheless, it was a sure sign of the movement away from a traditional hierarchical view of family and of school governance in the direction of a modern secular reliance upon reason and concern for the learner as well as for the knowledge to be achieved.

Such goals, to be sure, had been expressed by modern-minded European educators like Pestalozzi and Froebel in Switzerland and Germany, who had been impressed by the liberal ideas of the early nineteenth century. They were echoed by some U.S. educators like Carter and Hall, who argued that teachers should be trained with learner-oriented pedagogy explicitly in mind. As early as 1823, Samuel R. Hall had begun a private normal school in Concord, Vermont, and by 1829 had published his *Lectures on School-Keeping*. Devoted to the common district schools as a meeting ground for the wealthy and for the poor, Hall held out the hope that a teacher could not only teach the rudiments of knowledge in a much more effective way than simply by drill and rote, but could also be a humane, moral, and civic exemplar for the young as well as their friend and mentor:

> In the general management of a school, it is important to keep in mind always the great object for which it is designed. That object is, to prepare children to be happy; and to be useful to themselves and others—to teach them how to acquire knowledge and to apply it. . . . Endeavour to adopt such a course as shall render the school *pleasant* to those who compose it. If children are brought to associate with the school, a variety of agreeable objects, they will be led to think of study as a pleasure, and delight in it. . . . Let the teacher of a school wear a smiling countenance—let him appear happy, and desirous of making others so, and he will hardly fail of seeing smiling faces and contented looks around him.[32]

Teacher-Oriented Practice / Despite the models envisioned by the Carters, the Halls, the Manns, and the parents of the school committee of Roxbury, Massachusetts, it will come as no great surprise that the average teacher could not, or at least did not, very often live up to the goals. As the Roxbury report recognized, the union of discipline and gentleness was indeed a very high and a very rare attainment. Much more common was what Barbara Finkelstein calls "pedagogy as intrusion." In an extensive survey of primary source materials related to early teaching methods in the 1820–1880 period, she has demonstrated that most teachers actually behaved not so much as the friendly guide and counselor as they did the authoritative conveyor of the knowledge, manners, and morals most highly approved by the dominant society.[33] And they did it in a "rigid and highly controlling manner." Teachers almost everywhere pressured students to learn the value of conformity to law and regulations, and stressed obedience and submission to authority.[34] The rural sections of the country were slower to abandon corporal punishment than their colleagues in the cities, but by the end of the period were beginning to do so by substituting social and psychological pressure for physical coercion.

So here we have it—reformers preaching a learner-oriented pedagogy and teachers practicing an achievement-oriented pedagogy. The increasing tension between the two perspectives of teaching marked the secularizing aspect of the modernization process, and the debate really began on a large scale in the middle years of the nineteenth century. It was to become even more heated in the coming Progressive years.

The Achievement Goal

Though the modernization of pedagogical methods was slow in coming, the expansion of the curriculum was somewhat more rapid as the secularization of knowledge itself began to accelerate. Literacy in reading, writing, and arithmetic continued to be the core of the common school, but many reformers insisted that preparation in the "common branches" should also include spelling, geography, history, civil government, the U.S. Constitution, nature study, physical training, drawing, and music.

Furthermore, the argument went, it was not just that the new subjects were necessary for a more complete life in a rapidly modernizing society, but that all these common school studies would be more "practical" and useful in everyday life. Writing ought to help a person to write legibly, to produce a clear personal or business letter, a promissory note, or a receipt. Arithmetic ought to aid the farmer, or mechanic, or business man to keep accurate accounts. Sporadic proposals for the teaching of agriculture, gardening, mechanic arts, and manual labor were made in this period though they did not greatly affect the common schools. The real drive for vocational and technical education was to come later and was to be directed largely at post-primary schools. Meanwhile, drawing came into the curriculum of some of the common schools of the cities. This seemed to respond to a learner-oriented pedagogy designed to develop the coordination of eye, hand, and mind, and at the same time satisfied the achievement-oriented requirements of captains of commerce and industry by developing the practical capabilities of youngsters in mechanical drawing.

The most famous name in the textbook litany of achievement was that of William Holmes McGuffey. His graded readers dominated the field for nearly a hundred years from the 1830s onward. His selections of modern English literature, extolling the ideals of achievement, certainly advanced the modernization process by instilling the ideals of hard work, thrift, punctuality, modesty, propriety, contentment, and conformity. In the United States of the 1800s, these values were consonant with middle-class virtues, but they were also applicable to the modernization process avidly promoted by imperialist Japan in the late nineteenth century and by communist Russia and China in the twentieth century.

Even before children were taught to read in the primary grades, the secularization trend had affected them in the preschool years. As early as the 1850s, kindergartens were established in St. Louis, Milwaukee, and in other cities where German migrants had adopted the ideas of Friedrich Froebel. In the early 1870s, William T. Harris and Susan Blow persuaded the St. Louis board of education to incorporate kindergartens into the public school system for three- and four-year-olds.[35] Whatever the religious and moral underpinnings that justified the kindergarten, its activities were concentrated on playlike manipulation of objects, and on coloring, drawing, music, modeling, weaving, and manual skills. Harris saw these skills as a means by which the school could enable the child (especially the poor child of the city slums) to cope more effectively with the new urban way of life, which had done so much to demoralize the traditional family.

The Public High School

By the end of the middle decades of the 1800s the trend toward secularization was even more marked in the secondary schools than at the elementary level. This was marked by the remarkable expansion of private academies, which sprang up rapidly under the impulse of a booming economy and a second Great Awakening of religious revivalism in the early nineteenth century. The academies appealed to the growing middle classes who wanted an education that was more practical than that provided by the colonial Latin grammar schools, and who believed that a boarding school could offer a more protected and moral/religious environment than would be provided in the booming urban centers. By 1860 there were well over 6,000 private academies enrolling more than a quarter of a million young people—some for males, some for females, and even some coeducational. The curriculums of these academies tried to combine the advantages of the college-preparatory classics with a wider range of more modern and secular studies ranging across the romance languages, the useful sciences, commercial arts, and the fine or performing arts. The private academies dominated secondary education until the Civil War, but then began to decline.

A More Practical Education / Meanwhile, the public high school, a formidable competitor, was gathering strength. Like many competitors, the newcomer had to beat the leaders at their own game as well as offer additional attractions. No wonder, then, that many· of the early high schools tried to provide the traditional college preparatory studies in the classics as well as more modern and scientific subjects. True, the very earliest attempt in Boston to establish an English Classical School in 1821 did propose to omit the classics and foreign languages in favor of English and a great deal of applied as well as theoretical mathematics, along with some history, geography, science, and philosophy. But by 1827, when a high school law was passed in Massachusetts, the schoolmaster in towns of 4,000 population was expected to be able to teach Latin, Greek, history, rhetoric, and logic, as well as history, bookkeeping, geometry, surveying, and algebra.

Despite the arguments that a more practical advanced education should be provided at public expense, there was no great push to establish public high schools until later in the century. By 1860 there were only about 300 high schools in the entire country, and 100 of these were in Massachusetts alone, signifying a very great popular demand. But even in that state only about two-thirds of the towns obeyed the state law. The school reformers often had a hard time convincing the people that they ought to add to their tax burdens in order to provide a free education beyond the common school. Henry Barnard argued in 1838 that high schools would give girls as well as boys a more practical education in the useful arts that would prepare both sexes for the everyday business of life.[36]

The different social roles for boys and girls envisioned by Barnard will not be lost on modern readers, but even so an appeal to open up public education to girls beyond the common school was still a radical enough proposal to alienate many property owners, especially in the rural districts and in the less affluent classes. Barnard and the other reformers also emphasized the argument that public high schools, by equalizing the opportunities for a good education, would have a beneficial effect on the whole community by bringing education to all classes and bringing all classes together. Both rich and poor would profit.

At first, neither the poor nor the rich always responded with alacrity to such an appeal. In fact, Michael B. Katz has portrayed at some length the details of the opposition to the public high school in Beverly, Massachusetts, by the workingmen of the town, who voted to abolish it in 1860.[37] Katz points out that those in the least prestigious occupations (fishermen, farmers, shoemakers, and laborers) were solidly opposed to the high school. The vote of the artisans and businessmen was split, largely on the basis of whether or not they had children who would benefit. By and large, those of wealth and prestige were in favor of the high school. Antagonism toward the industrial owners, the repression of wages, strikes, and unemployment undoubtedly played a part in the attitudes of the workingmen. They felt that the privileged classes were somehow ganging up on them to support an institution that would not be as useful to them as the reformers claimed.

Nor did the rich always respond favorably to the proposals for a public high school in which their children would mingle with the poor. Some groups tried to stave off the secularizing trend of the high schools by founding exclusive denominational schools like St. Paul's in Concord, New Hampshire, in 1855. Others argued that privately endowed schools could maintain the standards of quality and freedom even better than could the public high schools because the mass of voters who elected school boards were too often swayed by passion, prejudice, and jealousy of the aristocrats.[38]

The Legal Base Secured / But the defense of the private school as the predominant instrument of secondary education gradually became a lost cause. The educational reformers were a persuasive lot and soon picked up strong support from political sources. For example, George S. Boutwell, a "free soil" Democratic governor of Massachusetts and later a Radical Republican congressman and senator, argued for the common school. He contended that the public high school was superior to the privately endowed academies primarily because it dealt with all the people and was supported by all the people "without any reference to social, pecuniary, political, or religious distinctions, so that every person may have a preliminary education sufficient for the ordinary business of life."[39] Boutwell even argued ingeniously that common public high schools would not only open up opportunities for the poor, but would also enable the rich parent to provide the means for developing self-reliance among his children, who would otherwise have no such chance in the pampered, sheltered environment of a private academy.

The middle classes were probably more receptive to such an appeal than were the rich, but the movement to popularize the public high school lost impetus and was not to be accelerated among all classes until after the Civil War. At that time the legal obstacles were soon cleared away, and later in the century a more fundamental reform in the matter of a directly practical and vocationally oriented curriculum helped break down the reluctance of the working classes to send their children to the public high schools. (See Chap 8.) The middle classes were indeed the first beneficiaries of the public high schools, but if the votes and attitudes of the Beverly workingmen had continued to prevail, the opportunities for secondary and college education among the vast majority of U.S. young people would have been even longer delayed and more sharply curtailed.

Court cases were brought in many states to test the legality of tax support for public high schools. The narrow issue was whether the taxing powers of the school boards were restricted to "common schools" of the primary grade levels or whether they extended to levies for the support of high schools as well. A conclusive test arose in Kalamazoo, Michigan, where certain citizens brought suit to restrain the local school board on the grounds that secondary education, usually conceived to consist of the classical and foreign languages (and thus not practical or necessary for all), was an accomplishment for the few rather than for the many, and thus should be paid for privately by those who could afford it.

The Supreme Court of Michigan, in a decision written by Justice Thomas M. Cooley in 1874, held that the whole history of education in Michigan—from its beginnings in the Ordinance of 1787 to its Constitution of 1850—pointed to the conclusion that the state did have the right "to furnish a liberal education to the youth of the state in schools brought within the reach of all classes."[40] Furthermore, the decision stated, this could include a classical education if the people so declared. It was clear that primary schools and a university were state obligations to be supported by public funds, and it would be absurd to suppose that the state could not provide secondary schools as a means of transition from one to the other at public expense.

The Common School Remarkable to Europeans

In this and in other cases the line was definitely drawn between the United States and the European systems of education. In the latter, common schools at state expense were maintained for the common people, but secondary education was reserved for private schools, which were attended by those who could pay the fees and the tuitions, namely, the more well-to-do classes. By contrast, the value claims of the democratic political community in the United States so modified the modernization drive that a dual system of education based primarily upon wealth and social class was avoided. Even though more students of the affluent classes than of lower and middle classes attended the public high schools during the formative period in the middle decades, the system eventually opened up to a very wide spectrum of the population, far exceeding anything achieved by other modernizing countries of the world. Foreign visitors to this country found the educational opportunities available to be a matter of considerable remark. The distance that the public school system had come during the middle years can be gauged from the praise heaped upon its success by an English visitor in 1875. Francis Adams may have been overly enthusiastic, but his comparison of the system with that of his own country was nevertheless very complimentary:

> This widespread popular regard which constitutes the propelling power, appears to be chiefly due to two features—government by the people, and ownership by the people. It is a vast proprietary scheme, in which every citizen has a share. . . .

If the elementary schools of England were free, and the course of study raised above its present pauper level, a large proportion of the middle classes would be glad to send their children to them, in preference to the inefficient private schools. There would then be no reason why the elementary schools of our large towns should not rival those of the great American cities, the results of which, in the absence of compulsion, must be regarded as very admirable.[41]

We know that there were great elements of comparative truth in this picture of U.S. schools in 1875, but we also know that it did not apply everywhere nor equally to all groups. The public school may indeed have been the palladium of the republic, but it had many imperfections. It was far from the genuine unitary system that the rosy picture of its admirers portrayed. Not only the gaps among social classes hindered the development of an integrative system, but even more powerful were the segmental and pluralistic forces based on religion, ethnicity, race, and locality. To these disjunctions we now turn.

Notes

1. De Witt Clinton, quoted in Rush Welter, ed., *American Writings on Popular Education: The Nineteenth Century* (Indianapolis: Bobbs-Merrill, 1971), pp. 24–26.
2. Clinton Rossiter, *The American Quest, 1790–1860: An Emerging Nation in Search of Identity, Unity, and Modernity* (New York: Harcourt, 1971), p. 200.
3. Rossiter, p. 141.
4. Rossiter, pp. 142–143.
5. Welter, *American Writings*, p. 82.
6. Welter, *American Writings*, p. 91.
7. Michael B. Katz, ed., *School Reform: Past and Present* (Boston: Little, Brown, 1971), pp. 284–286.
8. John E. Coons, William H. Clune III, and Stephen D. Sugarman, *Private Wealth and Public Education* (Cambridge, Mass.: The Belknap Press of Harvard University Press, 1970), pp. 14–15.
9. Katz, *School Reform*, p. 286.
10. Robert H. Bremner, ed., *Children and Youth in America: A Documentary History*, Vol. I: 1600–1865 (Cambridge, Mass.: Harvard University Press, 1970), pp. 455–457.
11. Michael B. Katz, *The Irony of Early School Reform: Educational Innovation in Mid-Nineteenth Century Massachusetts* (Cambridge, Mass.: Harvard University Press, 1968), p. 218.
12. Rena L. Vassar, ed., *Social History of American Education*, Vol. I: Colonial Times to 1880 (Chicago: Rand McNally, 1965), pp. 174–175.
13. Vassar, pp. 230–234.
14. Rush Welter, *The Mind of America, 1820–1860* (New York: Columbia University Press, 1975), pp. 292–293.

15. Ruth Miller Elson, *Guardians of Tradition: American Schoolbooks of the Nineteenth Century* (Lincoln: University of Nebraska Press, 1964), p. 340.
16. Lawrence A. Cremin, ed., *The Republic and the School: Horace Mann on the Education of Free Men* (New York: Teachers College, Columbia University, 1957), p. 95.
17. Cremin, p. 97.
18. Richard C. Wade, quoted in Alexander B. Callow, Jr., ed., *American Urban History* (New York: Oxford, 1969), p. 99.
19. Charles N. Glaab and A. Theodore Brown, *A History of Urban America* (New York: Macmillan, 1967), p. 51.
20. David B. Tyack, *The One Best System: A History of American Urban Education* (Cambridge, Mass.: Harvard University Press, 1974), pp. 38–39.
21. William T. Harris, quoted in Selwyn K. Troen, *The Public and the Schools: Shaping the St. Louis System, 1838–1920* (Columbia: University of Missouri Press, 1975), p. 47.
22. Herbert G. Gutman, "Work, Culture, and Society in Industrializing America, 1815–1919," *American Historical Review*, June 1973, 78 (3):541. See also his *Work, Culture, and Society in Industrializing America* (New York: Knopf, 1976).
23. Bremner, pp. 1436–1437.
24. Troen, p. 128.
25. Troen, p. 140.
26. Tyack, *The One Best System*, p. 73.
27. Bremner, pp. 350–355.
28. Association of Masters of the Public Schools, *Remarks on the Seventh Annual Report of the Hon. Horace Mann* (Boston: Little, Brown, 1844).
29. Horace Mann, *Reply to the "Remarks"* . . . (Boston, 1844), pp. 130–131.
30. *Seventh Annual Report of the Massachusetts Board of Education* (Boston: Dutton and Wentworth), 1844. See the reports from the various Massachusetts towns in the Appendix.
31. *Seventh Annual Report*, appendix.
32. Samuel R. Hall, *Lectures on School-Keeping* (Boston: Richardson, Lord, and Holbrook, 1829), p. 75.
33. Barbara Finkelstein, *Governing the Young: Teacher Behavior in American Primary Schools, 1820–1880*. Unpublished doctoral dissertation, Teachers College, Columbia University, 1970.
34. Barbara Finkelstein, "Pedagogy as Intrusion: Teaching Values in Popular Primary Schools in Nineteenth-Century America," *History of Childhood Quarterly: The Journal of Psychohistory*, 1975, 2(3):368–369. See also Finkelstein, "The Moral Dimensions of Pedagogy," *American Studies*, Fall 1974, pp. 79–89.
35. For details, see Troen, chapter 5.
36. Bremner, Vol. II, p. 1386.
37. Katz, *The Irony of Early School Reform*, Part I. Diane Ravitch has

pointed out some considerable methodological shortcomings in Katz. See her "The Revisionists Revised," *National Academy of Education Proceedings*, 1977, 4:35–42.

38. Katz, *School Reform*, pp. 222–235.
39. John Hardin Best and Robert T. Sidwell, *The American Legacy of Learning: Readings in the History of Education* (Philadelphia: Lippincott, 1967), pp. 202–206.
40. Bremner, p. 1391. For a more complete text of the decision, see Daniel Calhoun, *The Educating of Americans: A Documentary History* (Boston: Houghton Mifflin, 1967), pp. 298–304.
41. David B. Tyack, ed., *Turning Points in American Educational History* (Waltham, Mass.: Blaisdell, 1967), pp. 171–177. See also the commentaries by Thomas Hamilton, Alexis de Tocqueville, James Fraser, Anthony John Mundella, and Ferdinand Eduard Buisson, in Stewart E. Fraser and William W. Brickman, eds., *A History of International and Comparative Education: Nineteenth-Century Documents* (Glenview, Ill.: Scott, Foresman, 1968).

5 Segmental Pluralisms:
Religious and Ethnic

Religious Diversity

At least three elements in the religious complex of the United States made the development of a common public school system a sensitive and unstable matter in the mid-1800s. The first element was the consolidation of the legal basis for the separation of church and state. The second was the rivalry among Protestant sects, and the third was the effect of increasing numbers of immigrant adherents to Roman Catholicism. It was not surprising that the result was political and educational discord.

Constitutional Separation of Church and State

First, the Constitution's principle of separation of church and state, as defined in the First Amendment, was adopted in new state constitutions and became more firmly fixed in the organic laws of the original 13 states. This principle affirmed the free exercise of religion without imposition by the state of doctrinal belief or mode of worship, and guaranteed the right of taxpayers to be free of levies that would support religious institutions or teachings (that is, freedom from "an establishment of religion"). Just what this principle should mean with respect to religious instruction in the public schools and the use of public funds for religious schools had yet to be worked out, though it had seemed clear enough to Jefferson and Madison in their fateful fight in the 1780s over the bill for religious freedom in Virginia.[1]

The state constitutions in the antebellum years commonly followed the

114

wording of the 1776 constitutions of Pennsylvania, North Carolina, New Jersey, or the Virginia Statute for Religious Freedom of 1786. The constitutions of Iowa, Utah, South Carolina, and Louisiana adopted the wording of the First Amendment. By the 1830s and 1840s some constitutions began to prohibit the use of public monies for the benefit of any religious societies or schools. By the end of Reconstruction, the constitutional principle as developed in the states was well formulated. In 1868, Thomas M. Cooley, the judge who later wrote the Kalamazoo (Michigan, 1874) decision and who taught constitutional law at the University of Michigan, summarized those things that were not lawful under the state constitutions: No law could be passed that called for compulsory support of religious instruction by taxation, compulsory attendance at religious worship, or restraints on the expression of religious belief.[2]

Nondenominational Solutions

The second element was the reassertion of Protestant evangelicalism, which swept the country during the opening decades of the nineteenth century, and which had two quite different results. On one hand, it strengthened each of the many Protestant denominations so that never again would it be possible for a single Protestant establishment to exert control over all the others on a statewide or national basis. The very rivalry that existed among Protestant sects of differing national origin was in fact an incentive that drew them toward endorsing the First Amendment freedoms of religion throughout the states and stimulated the spread of state laws and constitutions in the early decades. It was this Amendment that guaranteed each sect an individual autonomy.

On the other hand, the Protestant denominations that had fought each other so bitterly in the eighteenth and early nineteenth centuries tended to draw together on a common ground to face what they considered the threat of a third element in American religious diversity, the arrival of large numbers of Roman Catholic immigrants from Ireland and Germany in the antebellum years. The Roman Catholic Church was not new to America, but the rapid influx of so many new adherents made it strong enough to assert itself much more aggressively and even to engage in direct combat with the Protestant majority who had been quarreling among themselves and splitting off in all directions. For example, some of the liberal doctrines of Unitarianism had appeared to be scarcely Christian to fundamentalists, whose insistence in turn upon a literal interpretation of the words of the Bible was to liberals a denial of the basic tenets of human reason. In this context, Catholic leaders began to make a bold bid for leadership on the basis of offering an authoritative dogma that would insure doctrinal security among a medley of dissenting sectarian creeds.

The more effective the Catholic offensive became in the hands of an

Orestes Brownson or a Father Isaac Hecker, both converts from Protestantism to Catholicism, the more the Protestants drew together. Especially was this true when Catholics argued that a democratic republic could be safe only when led by people who found authoritative religious and moral guidance in a church that was the infallible custodian of God's eternal truth. When the offensive was led by such aggressive and militant Irish immigrants as Bishop John Joseph Hughes, the antagonism aroused soon consolidated the opposition so that the ensuing conflict appeared to be a crusade of native Protestants protecting American liberty against subversion by foreign Catholics.

When nationalistic patriotism was joined with religious prejudice, the result was bitter controversy and even violence. All sorts of secret societies were formed, such as the Order of United Americans, Sons of the Sires, and the Supreme Order of the Star Bangled Banner. Protestant editors like William G. Brownlow publicly condemned Catholicism as a threat to all that was fine and decent in American life, and anti-Catholicism broke out as a political movement when the Native American Party (also called Know-Nothings) was formed in the 1850s to defeat Catholic candidates at the polls. All this sometimes led to outright mob violence, stonings, and the burning of churches.

Recrimination was the order of the day on both sides as Catholicism became associated in Protestant minds with "foreignism," "un-Americanism," and "popery." They especially resented the unfamiliar sacraments, rituals, miracles, saints, relics, a different version of the Bible, and the use of Latin as well as the claim of the Catholic Church to be the only true church of Christ and therefore entitled to authoritative interpretation of God's word to all true believers. Nothing could arouse Protestants more than to be told that the individual or "the people" were to have no voice in religious or ecclesiastical affairs, but that they were only to learn and obey. Nothing infuriated Catholics more than to be told that their language, their poverty, their newcomer status, their lack of education and manners, and their subservience to a clerical hierarchy made them unfit to be good Americans or to associate with their "betters," who arrogantly claimed to know what was good for their manners and morals.

So the confrontations inevitably affected the idea and practice of public education. Protestants could quarrel among themselves, split, and set up their own religious schools, but when faced with what they took to be an alien voice of authority, they tended to draw together and confront what they believed to be the common enemy. This approach to "nondenominationalism" was transferred to public schooling. The splintering of education along religious lines, which had characterized the eighteenth century, had been slowed down by the impact of the Revolutionary goals for national and republican unity; it was further slowed by the bid for Catholic power in the antebellum years. More and more Protestant groups began to cooperate in their efforts to establish nonsectarian common public schools and to oppose the diversion of public funds to Catholic parochial schools. To their surprise, chagrin, and sometimes fury, they found that their "nonsectarianism" was viewed by Catholics as exceedingly sectarian. The common-school reformers sometimes found that their proposals for nonsectarian religious instruction in the public schools also met with opposition from the more fundamentalist Protestant leaders. This was the unhappy experience of Horace Mann in Massachusetts.

As a result of the pushes and pulls of these three aspects of religious pluralism, the adherents of the common school had to weave their path through the political value claims of religious freedom, the moral and religious claims of a dominant Protestant majority, and the claims for religious freedom and for financial justice by an increasingly aggressive Catholic minority. Common school advocates had to steer a course that would recognize freedom of religious conscience and yet somehow satisfy both majority and minority demands, or lose the battle to a pluralism that could lead to a resurgence of private Protestant schools on one side and the growth of a massive Catholic parochial school system on the other.

Either or both solutions would spell the doom of the Revolutionary dream of a republican education and thus threaten the goal of achieving a stable republican polity through a common school system. Indeed, free and universal education *could* be achieved by splitting up the reservoir of public tax funds among the private and religious groups, as was done in some European states. But this departure from the common school ideal could then lead to the separatisms, which *in extremis* could lead to the pluralistic "disjunctivitis," which might threaten the very life of the polity. The most dramatic, or at least the best publicized, cases took place in Massachusetts and New York in the antebellum years.

It must be remembered that by far the most common assumption among the people of the United States at that time was that morality and religion were closely if not inextricably linked. It did not occur to many that morality could be inculcated without some kind of religious sanction or authority, and most assumed that religion to be Christianity. Almost by definition, infidels like Mohammedans would be counted as immoral. Now the troubling question was: Did morality rest upon a particular *kind* of Christianity? This was not so troubling when each Christian denomination conducted its own schools. But now that statesmen and educators alike were arguing that a common school was essential for political community, what religious doctrines could be taught in a common school? If the tenets of one general faith (Protestantism or Catholicism) were introduced, the rights of conscience of other children, now protected in the constitutional order, would be violated. If the tenets of a particular Protestant denomination were introduced, schools supported by public funds would be teaching a specific religion, and this too would be a violation of the constitutional prohibition of an establishment of religion. On both counts the constitutional separation of church and state would be endangered. What to do?

Horace Mann and Protestants in Massachusetts

For a dozen years Horace Mann and the State Board of Education in Massachusetts thought they had found an answer. Basically, they proposed that the schools should instill morality by teaching those elements of Christianity that were common to both major faiths and to all sects. And where were the common elements of Christianity to be found? In the Bible, of course. The Bible was given by God to man, while sectarian doctrines were created by man. Therefore, there could be no danger or offense in the reading of the Bible by the teacher and by the pupils as long as there was no intervention or comment by the teacher.

Mann was trying to defend himself and the Board for their advocacy of nonsectarian religious instruction, for they had been berated and bombarded for years by conservative Protestant ministers who objected vigorously, and sometimes vitriolically, to simple reading of passages from the Bible as too little and too insipid. The Reverend E. A. Newton argued that a book on religion, as on politics or morals, that had no sectarian views would contain no distinct views of any kind, and thus would encourage doubt and skepticism. The Reverend Mathew Hale Smith in his *The Ark of God on a New Cart* argued that simple Bible reading of selected passages would actually stimulate irreligion, crime, and intemperance because, in effect, morality would decline whenever the religion was watered down to nondenominational or neutral tenets. Unless the *entire* Bible was read and believed as the inspired word of God, the reading of mere selections would make the common schools a counterpoise to the sectarian religious instruction that should go on in the home. Reverend Smith was ready and eager to remove from the State Board all those who held Unitarian views, and then divide the public funds among the people of each district who would have the right to make their schools as religious as they pleased. If they could not agree, then they could withdraw their allotted proportion of public funds for their own sectarian schools. Thus, he urged Protestants to adopt a system of parochial schools and to demand a kind of voucher system for their support, arguing that

> the church of every denomination is called upon to do its duty, which is nothing more or less than to teach the people Christianity, and if this cannot otherwise be done thoroughly and effectually, as we are persuaded it cannot, than by having a school in connection with every congregation, then it is the duty of the church to enter upon the plan, and prosecute it with all her energy.[3]

The trend among Protestants, however, was against Reverend Smith. With few exceptions the major Protestant denominations turned more and more to the idea of a nonsectarian common school. This was sometimes the result of weariness with sectarian ideological disputes, sometimes in recognition of the added expense of independent denominational effort, sometimes of the need for counteraction against the Catholic threat, and sometimes of a genuine belief in the priority of political community as the goal of training in common citizenship. On the frontier, it was also a matter of the necessity for cooperative effort among many small struggling denominations to achieve a better quality of education than each could provide by its own independent efforts. Timothy Smith has well documented these efforts at community interdenominational cooperation in promoting the nondenominational school in Illinois and Wisconsin as typical of the Middle West,[4] and David Tyack has done the same for Oregon.[5]

The Developing Protestant Consensus

One of the best examples of the developing Protestant nondenominational consensus was expressed by Horace Bushnell, the liberal Congregational minister in Hartford, Connecticut. He was indeed resisting Roman Catholic attacks upon the common school, but he was also expressing the positive role of the common schools in forging a common sense of political community among the immigrants and native-born, among Catholics and Protestants alike. Speaking in a widely publicized sermon in 1853, when Catholic groups in most cities were campaigning for public funds for their schools, Bushnell took his stand. He described how the purely Puritan school had given way to the Protestant school because of the intermingling of Methodists, Unitarians, Episcopalians, and others. Although he agreed that the bonds of Protestantism in the schools must be loosened, he objected to making education wholly secular. He urged, nevertheless, that they become so broadly Christian that Catholics could join in and help make the common schools genuinely common to *all* classes, sects, and denominations. The only way to make common schools common was to have them established by law, supported at public expense, and organized and superintended by public authority, thus assuring that

> the common school is, in fact, an integral part of the civil order. It is no eleemosynary institution, erected outside of the state, but is itself a part of the public law, as truly so as the legislatures and judicial courts. The schoolhouses are public property, the district committees are civil officers, the teachers are as truly functionaries of the law as the constables, prison-keepers, inspectors and coroners. . . . an application against common schools, is so far an application for the dismemberment and reorganization of the civil order of the state. . . .
>
> Common schools are nurseries of a free republic, private schools of factions, cabals, agrarian laws and contests of force. Therefore, I say, we must have common schools; they are American, indispensable to our Ameri-

can constitutions, and must not be yielded for any consideration smaller than the price of our liberties.[6]

So, Bushnell pleaded with Catholics to join in with the common schools, become genuine Americans, and not wall themselves up in ghettos. In lieu of that, he said, it would be better to go back to the countries where different religious groups were segregated by the laws themselves. An even worse danger would be the establishment of ghetto schools in the United States, for which the state would pay the costs of all manner of religious instruction. To make the common schools palatable to Catholics and Protestants alike, Bushnell proposed that the Bible in the Protestant or Douay version be optional, scripture lessons be compiled from both versions by agreement, special religious periods be conducted by clergy or teachers chosen by the parents, and a common catechism of Christian *morality* be taught to all rather than articles of *faith*. Thus, this common Christian public school could become the means by which

> we may be gradually melted into one homogeneous people. . . . a means of cementing the generations to come in a closer unity, and a more truly catholic peace; that, as being fellow-citizens with each other, under the state, in the ingenuous days of youth and youthful discipline, they may learn how also to be no more strangers and foreigners, but fellow-citizens with the saints and of the household of God.[7]

But Bushnell's plea for reconciliation and assimilation did not meet universal acceptance. It did appeal to a great number of Protestants, but it did *not* appeal to some Protestants, nor to most Catholics. The Protestant dissenters were divided. Some believed that using the King James version of the Bible was perfectly all right, as long as those who objected were excused from its reading. The Massachusetts Supreme Court upheld such a ruling by the school committee of Woburn in 1866. The court held that reading the Bible without comment was not sectarian, and thus it was within the competence of the school committee to require it on behalf of the "principles of piety and justice and a sacred regard for truth." Public schools in many parts of the country began to bow to this majority Protestant attitude, but it came increasingly under fire from Catholics. Two celebrated cases illustrate the reasons and the reasoning: one was in New York City, the other in Cincinnati.

Protestants versus Catholics in New York City

In 1826 when the Free School Society in New York City became the Public School Society, it was authorized to educate *all* children, not just all *poor* children. The schools of the Society, following the nonsectarian ideal, based their moral instruction on the common elements of Protestant Christianity and required the reading of the Bible without comment.

This was the situation, then, in the 1830s when the increasing Catholic population of New York City injected a new note. In 1834 Bishop John

Dubois complained that the school books used by the Public School Society were obviously sectarian Protestant in quality and requested that such books be reviewed by him to make sure that all sectarianism and aspersions toward Catholics be omitted. The Society's trustees agreed to confer on this matter and to remove any objectionable material, but the process was never completed.

The situation came to the point of real conflict in the school controversy of 1840–1842.[8] Catholics, instigated by Bishop John Joseph Hughes and encouraged by public statements of Governor William H. Seward, a Protestant Whig who was eager to attract Irish Democratic votes, began a concerted campaign against the sectarianism of the Society's public schools. Catholics precipitated a crucial struggle when they asked the city council for a share of the public school funds to support their own parochial schools. At hearings before the city council in October 1840, Bishop Hughes argued that the public schools, being Protestant, violated the rights of conscience of Catholics and that their moral instruction was based upon the common elements of *Protestant* Christianity only. He therefore concluded that the only way to insure the equal rights of conscience to Catholics was to grant them a share of the public funds for their own schools.

In his reply to Bishop Hughes, the counsel for the Public School Society, Theodore Sedgewick, argued that the state could properly support a purely secular English education in the basic skills and a moral education based upon fundamental principles about which there was no dispute among Christians, but it could not support religious instruction based upon the specific doctrines of any of the several sects. In essence, the Protestants were saying that "nonsectarian" religious instruction was acceptable to them in public common schools. The Catholic request was turned down. Catholics, however, protested that the only arrangement acceptable to them was a distribution of public funds to aid them in supporting their own Catholic schools conducted apart from the common schools.

In the following two years Catholics carried their fight against the Public School Society to the state legislature, charging that it had obtained an unfair monopoly of public school funds. In the state election of 1842, much of the campaigning was on the school issue. Catholics formed a separate political organization, endorsed several candidates already nominated, and also nominated some candidates on their own ticket for the Assembly and for the Senate. Counterattacks were, of course, made upon the Catholics, who were charged with trying to take the Bible out of the public schools and thus make the public schools godless.

The State Steps In / As a result of this storm of religious conflict, a law was passed by the state legislature to incorporate New York City into the state's common school system. New York City was authorized to form a board of education and to establish a city system of ward schools to supplement the schools of the Public School Society and those of several approved religious or charitable agencies. This Act of 1842, however, included a provision that no public funds should go to any of these schools if they taught sectarian religious doctrines.

The political result of the school controversy was scarcely satisfactory to either Protestants or Catholics. The Public School Society lost out to a city system, and Catholics did not share in the public funds. The decision reached, on the one hand, took out of the public schools all sectarian instruction, and on the other hand denied public funds to parochial schools. This, of course, did not settle the question permanently, but logic made increasingly clear that complete separation was the only practicable way to resolve the conflict between church and state in the matter of controlling education.

Further steps were taken in this direction before the Civil War when a state law of 1848 authorized a Catholic orphan asylum in Brooklyn to share in the public school funds and was declared unconstitutional in a court decision of 1851. The grounds were that the revenue of the common school fund must be used for common schools only (Article 9 of the New York State constitution) and that an orphanage conducted by a church was not a common school.

In 1853 an important decision of the New York State superintendent of schools, Henry Stephens Randall, ruled that prayers could not be required as a part of the school exercises, and where the King James version of the Bible was read in the schools, Catholic children could not be required to be present or to memorize parts of it:

> The government not relying on the ability or willingness of every part of the State to maintain efficient schools for the education of the young, by voluntary contributions, and recognizing the imperative necessity of universal education for the maintenance of our civil and political institutions, organized a general common school system. . . . The common schools were thus clearly made a government institution. To introduce into them, or permit to be introduced into them, a course of religious instruction conformable to the views of any religious denomination, would be tantamount to the adoption of a government religion—a step contrary to the Constitution, and equally at variance with the policy of a free government and the wishes of the people. . . . In view of the above facts, the position was early, distinctly, and almost universally taken by our statesmen, legislators, and prominent friends of education—men of the warmest religious zeal and belonging to every sect—that *religious education must be banished from the common schools and consigned to the family and church.*[9]

This remarkable statement reveals the thinking that inevitably led to a more complete secularization in education. Superintendent Randall was obviously a deeply religious man and indeed felt that the Bible may be rightfully taught in the public schools, but he was firm in his belief that it should not be used to violate the conscience of Catholic children and parents. He took severe action against the teacher whose punishment of a Catholic child for refusing to memorize passages from the Bible precipitated the decision. Decisions such as his inevitably led religious people of all Protestant faiths to the conclusion, however reluctantly, that the common school must be "common and neutral ground" with respect to religious instruction and that public funds must not be divided among the religious sects.

On the other hand, Bishop Hughes—undoubtedly gaining satisfaction from the political defeat he administered to the Public School Society in the 1840s, but still smarting under his own failure to obtain public funds and unhappy over the persisting derogation of Catholicism in the Protestant-oriented public schools—pressed harder than ever to establish a system of Catholic parochial schools. His fellow bishops in many parts of the country carried on similar campaigns when they failed to gain access to state funds. Episcopalians in Massachusetts and Germans in the Middle West sometimes joined in the effort to share the public monies. Robert Cross and Vincent Lannie have documented how Catholics were reluctant to accommodate themselves to the nonsectarian consensus that led so many Protestants eventually to support public schools. (See Recommended Readings.)

Catholics tried for two decades to get Protestant public schools to adapt themselves to Catholic objections, but even goodwill on the part of Protestant advocates of the public schools did not seem to be enough, and the goodwill was not widespread. Protestants were often exasperated, too, when they did make the effort to reduce the nondenominational approach only to find they were then subjected to the Catholic charge that they had made the public schools godless and irreligious. Catholics for their part seldom believed that nondenominational instruction was a satisfactory accommodation to their demands; they rejected the compromise and always objected to the use of the Protestant Bible. When courts in Massachusetts, Maine, and other states upheld Bible reading, their worst fears were realized. By the 1850s, positions on both sides were hardening. Constitutions in state after state prohibited public funds for parochial schools.

The Trend from Nonsectarian to Secular

Meanwhile, more and more Protestants began to accept, however reluctantly, that the common schools after all ought to become genuinely secular and not simply nondenominational. A few Protestant ministers began to make the point that religion, even simply reading the Bible without comment, was no business of the state and thus should not be permitted in state schools because of the offense to non-Christian citizens. For example, a Presbyterian minister in Brooklyn, Reverend Samuel T. Spear, spoke out forthrightly that the Constitution had not established a Christian government but a *republican* government, one in which all men, not just Christians, enjoyed equal rights of conscience, and therefore the schools should not compromise these rights by religious instruction.[10]

The Cincinnati Case / Gradually, the courts began to pick up this secular view of the Constitution as it applied to Bible reading. An important decision was handed down by the Supreme Court of Ohio in 1872 when the board of education in Cincinnati resolved that "religious instruction and the reading of religious books, including the Holy Bible, are prohibited in the common schools of Cincinnati."[11] A group of taxpayers successfully brought action in the Superior Court of Cincinnati to enjoin the board of education from carrying out its resolution. When the case was appealed, the Ohio Supreme Court unanimously upheld the board of education in a notable ruling that religious instruction was unconstitutional in the public schools of Ohio, and concluded its decision by referring to the principles held by Madison:

> The principles here expressed are not new. . . . They are as old as Madison, and were his favorite opinions. Madison, who had more to do with framing the constitution of the United States than any other man, and whose purity of life and orthodoxy of religious belief no one questions, himself says: "Religion is not within the purview of human government."[12]

When the court emphasized the religious neutrality of a government based upon *human* experience, it defined a *secular* basis for public education, a basis specifically not antireligious or irreligious, but a basis upon which the several religions then might build their own activities free of government interference. But it was to be nearly a hundred years before the Supreme Court of the United States took a similar position.

A National Movement / Meanwhile, prohibition of the use of public funds for sectarian schools was more quickly and more widely adopted. Building upon the start that had already been made prior to the Civil War, the movement gained great headway after 1865. One of the reasons for this acceleration was that the Roman Catholic Church had redoubled its efforts to secure a share of public funds for supporting its parochial schools. These, in turn, were met with equal efforts of other groups to counter the pressure. These struggles took place on the national level as well as among states. Action was so widespread and in general so uniform in intent, despite differences of wording in constitutions and statutes, that details cannot possibly be recited here.

As the controversy began to heighten after the Civil War, the state of Illinois led off with the provision in its new constitution of 1870, which sharply closed the door on the use of public funds "for any church or sectarian purpose" as follows:

> Neither the general assembly nor any county, city, town, township, school district or other public corporation shall ever make any appropriation or pay from any public fund whatever, anything in aid of any church or sectarian purpose, or to help support or sustain any school, academy, seminary, college, university or other literary or scientific institution, controlled by any

church or sectarian denomination whatever; nor shall any grant or donation of land, money or other personal property ever be made by the State or any such public corporation to any church or for any sectarian purpose.[13]

Some of the states did not act so conclusively as did Illinois, but virtually all states included some constitutional provision to prohibit tax funds for sectarian purposes.

The final point to be made is to note the repercussions of this movement on the national political scene. As the campaign for public funds for parochial schools took on national proportions, it also took on political form, for often the local and state Democratic parties became allied with the Catholic point of view, or at least were not hostile. This meant that the Republican Party was not slow in taking the opposite stand. President Grant brought the issue into the national political arena in his speech to the Army of the Tennessee in Des Moines, Iowa, in September 1875:

> Let us all labor to add all needful guarantees for the security of free thought, free speech, a free press, pure morals, unfettered religious sentiments, and of equal rights and privileges to all men, irrespective of nationality, color, or religion. Encourage free schools, and resolve that not one dollar appropriated for their support shall be appropriated to the support of any sectarian schools. Resolve that neither the State nor the nation, nor both combined, shall support institutions of learning other than those sufficient to afford every child growing up in the land the opportunity of a good common-school education, unmixed with sectarian, pagan, or atheistical dogmas. Leave the matter of religion to the family altar, the church, and the private school, supported entirely by private contributions. Keep the church and the state for ever separated.[14]

As a corollary to this speech, Grant recommended specifically in his annual message to Congress on December 7, 1875, that an amendment to the Constitution be adopted that would specifically prohibit any public funds for the direct or indirect aid of any religious sect and prohibit the teaching in public schools of any "religious, atheistic, or pagan tenets." James G. Blaine, as leader of the House, thereupon introduced a resolution to amend the Constitution by adding to the clauses of the First Amendment a specific and detailed statement that no funds of the United States, any state, territory, district, or municipality shall be used for the support of any school or other institution

> under the control of any religious or anti-religious sect, organization or denomination, or wherein the particular creed or tenets of any religious or anti-religious sect, organization, or denomination shall be taught. . . . This article shall not be construed to prohibit the reading of the Bible in any school or institution. . . .[15]

On August 4, 1876, this resolution was passed by a large majority of the House. The section permitting Bible reading identified the Protestant inspiration of the resolution, and the large number of abstentions in the voting revealed the difficulties many members of the House had in deciding a religious issue that had become so entangled in politics. The reference to "anti-religious" sects must have raised many questions concerning how a religious sect could be defined as antireligious. The national election of 1876 was in full swing at this time, and the Republican national convention inserted in its platform the following plank:

> The public school system of the several States is the bulwark of the American Republic; and with a view to its security and permanence, we recommend an amendment to the Constitution of the United States forbidding the application of any public funds or property for the benefit of any school or institution under sectarian control.[16]

The partisan, sectional, and sectarian character of Blaine's amendment was still more clearly revealed when the Senate voted on the resolution; 27 Republicans favored, 16 Democrats against, and 27 senators not voting. The measure was lost because a two-thirds vote was required.

Despite the failure in the Senate to gain concurrence for the Blaine resolution, the Congress nevertheless required that all new states (those admitted to the Union after 1876) must adopt an irrevocable ordinance that not only guaranteed religious freedom but also required the states to include a constitutional provision

> for the establishment and maintenance of a system of public schools, which shall be open to all the children of said State and free from sectarian control; . . .[17]

By passing this legislation, Congress recognized that the majority opinion of the country was in favor of common school systems based upon separation of church and state, and the adoption of the bill was an endorsement by the federal government of that movement.

Ethnic Separatism

The trend toward secular education was not simply a matter of difference over religious doctrine or theological interpretation of morality. Important as these doctrinal matters were, the whole matter was far more complicated. The struggle in the middle decades was also permeated with ethnic differences, fears, and hostility. Stimulated by the reassertion of ethnic minority claims in the 1960s and 1970s, much recent historical scholarship has been reexploring the role of ethnicity in the American past and reinterpreting the earlier historical studies of immigration and immigrant life in the United States. Leonard Dinnerstein and David M. Reimers define ethnic group as "a group with shared culture and sense of identity based on religion, race, or nationality."[18] This is substantially the same definition as that given a decade earlier by Milton M. Gordon.[19]

Sources of Ethnic Differences

What made the lot of public education so difficult in the antebellum years was that it had to face for the first time on a massive scale the confrontation of groups that were different in both religion *and* nationality, rather than simply religion *or* nationality. Up until the 1830s, Englishmen had been split into Congregationalists, Anglicans, Methodists, Baptists, Quakers, and the like, but they were all English in language and cultural background. Meanwhile, Scotch Presbyterians, English Puritans, Dutch or German Reformed, and French Huguenots had a common Calvinist theological background, despite their language and national differences. There was thus a kind of cohesive Protestantism that cut across the national lines. But now, with the large and rapid influx of Irish Catholics and German Catholics, differences of religion became more firmly linked with differences of nationality, language, recency of arrival, poverty, occupational skills, rural background, and lower-class behavior patterns.

Countries of Immigrant Origin / On the numerical side, the flow of people to the United States was part of a vast migration of peoples that the world had seldom seen before. In the 150 years between 1800 and 1950, some 60 million persons moved from their native lands to other places. Roughly two-thirds came to the United States alone. This meant that the problems raised by enormous numbers of newcomers in a tremendous variety were unmatched anywhere else in the world—and all in a relatively short period of time. During the middle decades of the nineteenth century, the numbers coming to the United States began to increase greatly, with some nine million arriving in those 50 years. One peak was reached just before the Civil War in the period 1846–1855; the other, after the Civil War in the decade 1866–1875. Table 1 lists the number of immigrants in the several decades.

TABLE 2

Immigrants to the United States from All Countries* by Decades (rounded to thousands)

1826–1835		355,000
1836–1845		777,000
1846–1855		3,031,000
1856–1865		1,652,000
1866–1875		3,240,000
	Total	9,055,000

* Compiled from *Historical Statistics of the United States, from Colonial Times to 1957* (Washington, D.C.: Government Printing Office, 1957).

In the decades just before the Civil War the largest numbers came from Ireland and Germany; just after the War, newcomers from England and Scandinavia joined the Irish and German. (After 1876 the vast majority of immigrants came from eastern and southern Europe; see Chapter 9.) The predominant reason why most immigrants came to the United States was the deteriorating economic conditions affecting peasant and farming populations in Europe, as the agricultural and industrial transformation attendant upon modernization took place. Added to this and intertwined with it were reasons of religious prejudice, social class discrimination, and political reaction. In any case, a large proportion of the three million Irish who emigrated in the middle decades were poor or destitute peasants affected by the famines; and the early immigrants of the three million Germans arriving in this country came from the rural and agricultural regions of southern and western Germany.

Conditions at home were not the only reason for emigrating, of course; there were also the enticements and attractions of a booming and expanding United States. Most states of the West, to encourage immigration, set up bureaus to supplement the recruiting efforts of the railroads and steamship lines. The Irish largely remained in the port cities; many Germans hoped to transform Missouri, Texas, and Wisconsin into virtual German colonies; and Scandinavians were attracted to the farming regions of the Middle West. The most obvious and serious problems arose in the biggest cities as a result of the overcrowding, squalor, disease, and crime. By 1870, New York City's 950,000 people included 200,000 Irish immigrants and 150,000 German, roughly a third of the total; of St. Louis' 300,000, the Germans made up 60,000 and the Irish 30,000, again nearly a third; Chicago's 300,000 had 50,000 Germans and 40,000 Irish; Boston's 250,000 had nearly 60,000 Irish; and Cincinnati's 200,000 had 50,000 Germans.

Growth of Nativism / Not surprisingly, the "settlers" of the United States and their descendants, who had been in this country much longer, were often alarmed and angered by this "invasion." Intolerance, discrimination, and suspicion of the foreigners' personal habits, religion, poverty, and language were obvious reactions. This phenomenon of nativism began in the 1830s, grew into a major force in the 1840s, and reached its peak in the 1850s with the political organization of the American Party, or Know-Nothings, which captured control of several state governments and elected many Congressmen in the northeastern and border states. In his classic study of American nativism, John Higham located the ideological core of nativism in a growing sense of nationalism:

> Nativism . . . should be defined as intense opposition to an internal minority on the ground of its foreign (i.e., "Un-American") connections. Specific nativistic antagonisms may, and do, vary widely in response to the changing character of minority irritants and the shifting conditions of the day; but through each separate hostility runs the connecting, energizing

force of modern nationalism. While drawing on much broader cultural antipathies and ethnocentric judgments, nativism translates them into a zeal to
destroy the enemies of a distinctively American way of life.[20]

Higham identifies three ingredients of American nativism that had originated
before the Civil War. By far the most important and most virulent was the
complex of anti-Catholic feelings and beliefs that stemmed from the Protestant Reformation and the religious wars of the sixteenth and seventeenth
centuries. This could easily be inflamed into fear that the Pope's agents, now
present in massive numbers, were out to subvert the U.S. institutions of political liberty and popular consent. A second and sometimes quite paradoxical
theme was an antiradical fear that European insurgents, like those who failed
in the revolutions of 1848, would try to subvert the established political or
economic order of the United States. The third was an ever-present belief of
Anglo-Saxons that they were superior to all the other "races" of Europe.
This, of course, could only regenerate and exacerbate the deeply held resent-
ments by the Irish against English rule and oppression in the "old country."

Ethnicity and the Public Schools

All these factors meant that the newcomers tended to draw together, to
live together, and to reinforce one another to preserve their sense of identity.
If the Anglo-Saxon descendants retained a sense of superiority over Celtic
Irishmen, the Irish Catholics also retained their age-old grievances and were
militantly eager to pay back the Protestant Anglo's for having won their traditional privileges. But the Irish were desperately handicapped economically
because of their rural peasant backgrounds, which had not provided them
with even agricultural skills, let alone the commercial or professional skills
of an urban middle class. Because they could not compete for skilled jobs,
they clustered in what were almost separate and isolated ghettos. No wonder
they responded to political appeals that urged them to fight for parochial
schools rather than submit to an Anglo-Protestant domination of the public
schools.

If anything, the ethnic factor played an even larger part than religion
in the Irish determination to establish and maintain parochial schools. Just
as the public schools were turned to by Anglo-Protestants to achieve an
American nationalism, so did Irish Catholics turn to parochial schools to
preserve Irish nationalism. German Catholics also sought this nationalistic
distinction for building and expanding their parochial schools, for pride in
German nationality centered very largely in the German language and
literature.

The pulls toward segmentation were countered by pushes toward cohesion, so that the religious, the ethnic, the linguistic factors were extremely
difficult to separate out. In one sense there was more flexibility to the religious
factor because many of the battles over the separation of church and state
had been fought before the Catholics contended for recognition. Thus, the

freedom of different religious groups to conduct their own schools at their own expense was fairly firmly fixed in the constitutional order and in the ideology of the people of the United States. But there still remained a great resistance by native Americans to the establishment of foreign "colonies" in separate geographic entities or states, and thus great resistance to the perpetuation of foreign language schools. Because of this, the immigrant groups were more likely to use the religious freedom argument for establishing parochial schools than the ethnic solidarity or national language argument. Paradoxically, as things eventually turned out, Italian Catholics would sometimes prefer the public schools to Irish Catholic parochial schools, or French-Canadians in Vermont might prefer to send their children to *public* schools, where they could learn French, rather than to an Irish parochial school where they could not. But it is fruitless to try to separate the religious from the ethnic factors except in particular cases and situations.

In general, however, in the middle decades of the nineteenth century the religious issue in relation to public education was more crucial than the ethnic differences. That is, despite the onrush of the "old immigration" and the variety of peoples and religions involved, they were still mostly North and West Europeans coming from countries that were leading the modernization process. The ethnic problem, and thus the Americanization task of the public schools, was not nearly so severe as it became in the late nineteenth and early twentieth centuries when the flood tide of "new immigration" swept into the United States from the less modern and more rural, agrarian, and traditional societies of eastern and southern Europe. The demands for cultural assimilation became ever more insistent in the later period, but their origins were clearly present before the Civil War.

The promotion of the common school was caught in this religious-ethnic turmoil, as we have seen. There were extremists on both sides, those who demanded that all foreign immigrants conform to American ideals of the common school, and those who demanded that there be complete freedom for cultural and linguistic separatism, with pluralistic schools supported at public expense. But after the Civil War the ethnic rivalries became less intense in the decade of the 1870s. The enormous industrial and geographic expansion, which required vast armies of manpower, stimulated immigration again and was encouraged by business and government. The nativism of the 1850s was largely muted—or at least was quiescent—and faith in the almost unlimited capacity of the nation to absorb and assimilate was widespread during the 1870s. A democratic and cosmopolitan faith in assimilation was reasserted, and this meant that public education, stripped of its religious biases, could become a prime agent in the process. At one extreme, the generous and enlightened spirit of the populace could view the public school as the proper agency for bringing to fruition the value claims of political democracy; at the other extreme, the narrow-minded and unenlightened nativist could see in the public school a tool to impose conformity on the ignorant and possibly dangerous alien.

Assimilation Through Anglo Conformity

In other words, the public school became the focus of interplay and conflict for purposes that stemmed from a wide variety of motivations. On one hand, there was the demand that the schools become a prime agency for bringing foreign children under the blanket of Anglo conformity. A good example of this was the speech by Calvin Stowe in 1836 to the Western Literary Institute. First, there was the danger posed by the immigrants:

> Let us now be reminded that unless we educate our immigrants, they will be our ruin. It is no longer a mere question of benevolence, of duty, or of enlightened self interest, but the intellectual and religious training of our foreign population has become essential to our own safety; we are prompted to it by the instinct of self-preservation.[21]

Then, there was the need to develop national unity in a large country beset with pluralistic segments:

> It is not merely from the ignorant and vicious foreigner that danger is to be apprehended. To sustain an extended republic like our own, there must be a *national* feeling, a national assimilation; and nothing could be more fatal to our prospects of future national prosperity, than to have our population become a congeries of clans, congregating without coalescing, and condemned to contiguity without sympathy.[22]

Next, this unity was to be achieved on the basis of Anglo-Americanism:

> It is altogether essential to our national strength and peace, if not even to our national existence, that the foreigners who settle on our soil, should cease to be Europeans and become Americans; and as our national language is English, and as our literature, our manners, and our institutions are of English origin, and the whole foundation of our society English, it is essential that they become substantially Anglo-Americans.[23]

And, finally, the guarantor of such Anglo-American cohesion, inevitably, was to be the public school. With a distinctly American attachment to the *common* school, Stowe argued for bringing *all* children together—the wealthy, the poor, the native American, the immigrant, the affluent, and the destitute:

> The public schools should be our best schools, and possess a character sufficiently elevated to secure the patronage of the influential and the wealthy, that all the children of our republic may be educated together. This would be our strongest national aegis, the surest palladium of our country.[24]

The preference of the majority of U.S. citizens might have been to try to impose Anglo conformity upon the foreigners by herding them into *separate* schools. In fact, this was proposed and even tried in various parts of the country, but the general consensus was that the United States should reject the assumptions of the European common schools, which segregated working-class people from the middle and upper classes. Rather, the overall direction was to try to absorb the various ethnic groups into the mainstream of U.S.

life by persuading them and eventually, through compulsory attendance laws, requiring them to attend schools with all others.[25]

Assimilation Through Democratic Cosmopolitanism

There was no doubt that the Anglo-conformity motivation was strong, but it is also true that a generous, democratic, and cosmopolitan view of assimilation leading to a new Americanism was also a strong motivating force in mobilizing the public schools to tackle the problem of ethnic segmentation. One cannot discount the importance of such spokesmen for the "new America" as Ralph Waldo Emerson, Walt Whitman, and Herman Melville. While they did not use the term "melting pot" in its later (and lately criticized) connotations, they had a vision of the enrichment that could come from a broadly tolerant view of welcome to ethnic variety. Higham makes the point exceedingly well when he describes the "age of confidence" following the Civil War:

> "E pluribus unum" expressed the essence of America's cosmopolitan faith—a conviction that this new land would bring unity out of diversity as a matter of course. Intellectually, this conviction was rooted in Christian and democratic values. Along with the parochialisms, the fanaticisms, and the xenophobias that Christianity has nourished, it has had another, perhaps more important, side. The ancient Christian doctrine of the brotherhood of man proclaimed the ultimate similarities between all peoples and their capacity for dwelling together in unity. The democratic values enshrined in the Declaration of Independence postulated an equal opportunity for all to share in the fullness of American life. Both Christian universalism and democratic equalitarianism had withstood the nativist ferment of the ante-bellum period.[26]

The Pluralistic Public School / Translation of the ideal of fusion of many peoples into Melville's "one federal whole" posed an almost insuperable problem for teachers in the public schools. It was so much easier for the poorly trained classroom teacher simply to preach and practice Anglo conformity. But the broader and more liberal goal of assimilation was being set for teachers whether they could achieve it or not. One version was presented before the American Institute of Instruction in 1849 by Benjamin Larabee, president of Middlebury College:

> Shall these adopted citizens become a part of the body politic, and firm supporters of liberal institutions, or will they prove to our republic what the Goths and Huns were to the Roman Empire? The answer to this depends in a great degree upon the wisdom and fidelity of our teachers and associated influences. They have a two-fold duty to perform in regard to this class of our population. On the one hand they must act the part of master-builders, and by degrees mould these unprepared and uncongenial elements into the form and character which the peculiar nature of the edifice demands, and in due time the youth especially may become intelligent, enterprising and liberal-minded supporters of free institutions. On the other hand, our instruc-

tors must prepare our native population for the suitable reception and treatment of these strangers, must teach them to lay aside prejudices and animosi-
ties, to meet the newcomers in the spirit of kindness and benevolence, and
to enlist their sympathies and good-will on the side of liberty, humanity and
truth.[27]

Larabee not only stressed the value claims of the democratic political
community as one of the building blocks in public education, which was difficult enough for the "master builder" teachers to achieve, but he also hit upon
a pluralistic theme that received even less attention from teachers—that is,
recognizing that democratic and liberal assimilation was a two-way process.
The "natives" must adapt to the foreigners and the foreigners must adapt to
the receiving institutions. This is a lesson that educators have taken a long
time to learn. Nevertheless, there were some examples of flexibility even in
the mid-1800s. In fact, there were early attempts to establish bilingual schools
within the public system as well as, of course, in the parochial schools, which
stressed instruction in a non-English language.

Bilingual Public Schools / The most successful groups in gaining attention for
their language were the Germans, who rapidly achieved political as well as
economic power in several major cities. In Cincinnati, bilingual schools were
organized as early as the 1840s. Children learned both English and German
in the early grades, and in the later grades sometimes received instruction on
alternate days in English and in German. In 1865 San Francisco established
"cosmopolitan schools" that taught in French and German as well as in
English. Tyack reports that between 1854 and 1877, eight midwestern and
western states passed laws providing that local boards could, upon request of
a certain number of petitioners, require the teaching of German in the elementary schools.[28]

Probably the most interesting development was in St. Louis. Troen
describes this at length.[29] As early as 1864 German lobbyists convinced the
board of education to offer German instruction in the public primary schools.
It was not long before non-German children were also taking the courses.
Superintendent William T. Harris encouraged this development on the dual
grounds that the teaching of German could make the German-speaking children feel more at home and less alienated, while it also would help the Anglo-
American children to appreciate the customs and traditions as well as the
language of the German newcomers. This was not only a generous approach
to the problem of assimilation, but was also a canny political move to try to
counteract the rapid growth of private parochial schools conducted by both
Catholic Germans and Lutheran Germans. In the 1830s and 1840s the Catholics had pushed rapidly ahead in establishing their own schools.

By 1850 there were roughly as many students in St. Louis parochial
schools as in public schools, but after 1850 the proportion in public schools
rapidly gained, and by 1880 only about 20 percent were attending parochial

schools. This was due to several developments: the responsiveness of the public schools, the continued use of foreign-born teachers in the parochial schools even while assimilation was proceeding outside the schools, and the distinction the public school educators tried to make between the values of ethnicity and the values of religion. By admitting German language teaching into the public schools, the school people decreased the chances of alienation even though the public schools remained nondenominational or even secular. Harris was able to speak persuasively on behalf of a secular morality, and his arguments began to appeal to more and more Protestants as they were faced with intransigent demands that morality must be based upon religion—the Catholic religion—and that therefore public funds must be allocated to the Catholic schools. Catholic political efforts to achieve a voucher plan were defeated in the legislature in 1870.

Harris was reasonably successful in converting the Germans to the public schools. Troen estimates that four of five German children were in separate schools in 1860, but that by 1880 four of five attended public schools. But the kind of accommodation that followed closely upon the Civil War was not to last. The German language had been the only one to receive recognition. As political rivalries grew between Republican Germans and Democratic Irish, the Irish began to ask that Gaelic be taught. A full-scale political battle over the public school curriculum eventually took German out of the schools when the Democrats consolidated their power in the late 1880s. So the fate of pluralistic languages in the common schools was similar to that of pluralistic religions. When competition among them threatened to split apart the whole enterprise, the political process led to a kind of uneasy accommodation that stressed commonalities rather than differences. As a result, the overall commitment to a common public education rather than to a series of separate ethnic/religious schools gained strength in St. Louis.

The Trend—Ethnic—But Not Racial—Assimilation

Superintendent Harris' cosmopolitan doctrines of assimilation as applied to education struck a responsive note in the public temper, described by Higham as "the age of confidence."[30]

Elsewhere, the idea of the common public school became fairly well established in much of the country north of St. Louis during the 1860s and 1870s. But the going was not smooth. While nativism was being held in check, it had not been expurgated from U.S. life, and movements against Catholics and Democrats sprang up again, spurred by Republicans in the Grant period. But this was all fairly mild compared to earlier and later manifestations.

Yes, the public schools survived the nativist turmoils of the middle decades, and indeed promoted the cause of political community and cosmopolitan assimilation as well as Anglo-conformity assimilation. How successful one goal could have been without the other is a matter of historical debate, and which one dominated the ideals and practices of the schoolroom is even harder to determine. But that both were present in some degree is reasonably clear.

What is undeniable is that the democratic and cosmopolitan goals of political community were least honored when it came to black slaves prior to the Civil War and to black freedmen after the Civil War. It was not that a dedicated band of blacks and whites did not try to apply the principles to the education of blacks. But by 1876 the cause of national community was almost swamped by the resurgence of regional and racial segmentalism. True, religious and ethnic segmentation was somewhat held in check. Thus, a disjunctive pathology of pluralism had been held off during the middle decades in that public schooling was *not* broken up into segments that would serve the particular demands of specific religious and white ethnic groups.

But, even though the public educational system was not divided up among religious and ethnic segments, it *was* divided according to race. While the public system in the North was able to strengthen itself during the quiescent ethnic periods of the 1860s and 1870s, the public system in the South (and, to a lesser degree, in the North) was being carved up along racial lines. The result was indeed a disease of the body politic, a "disjunctivitis" from which it has not yet fully recovered. Crucial battles were fought and lost by the end of the middle period. It was not until the 1950s that the patient began to recover. But the road to recovery was constantly blocked by resurgences of religious, ethnic, and racial viruses which Part IV will demonstrate.

Notes

1. See R. Freeman Butts, *The American Tradition in Religion and Education* (Boston: Beacon Press, 1950).
2. T. M. Cooley, *A Treatise on the Constitutional Limitations*, Vol. II (Boston: Little, Brown, 1927), Chap. XIII, pp. 966–969.
3. *The Bible, the Rod, and Religion in Common Schools* (Boston: Redding, 1847), p. 54.
4. Timothy L. Smith, "Protestant Schooling and American Nationality, 1800–1850," *The Journal of American History*, March 1967, 53(4).
5. David Tyack, "The Kingdom of God and the Common School," *Harvard Educational Review*, 1966, 36(4).
6. Rush Welter, ed., *American Writings on Popular Education: The Nineteenth Century* (Indianapolis: Bobbs-Merrill, 1971), pp. 181, 183.
7. Welter, p. 199.
8. For documents relating to this controversy, see Welter, pp. 97–120. For an excellent full discussion, see Diane Ravitch, *The Great School Wars, New York City, 1805–1973* (New York: Basic Books, 1974), pp. 3–79.

9. Henry Stephens Randall, *Decision of the State Superintendent of Common Schools* . . . (Albany, N.Y.: Department of Common Schools, Oct. 27, 1853), pp. 5–8.

10. Samuel T. Spear, *The Bible in Public Schools* (New York: William C. Martin, 1870).

11. *Board of Education* v. *Minor*, 23 Ohio 211 (1872), p. 211.

12. *Bd. of Ed.* v. *Minor*, pp. 253–254.

13. Illinois Constitution of 1870, Article 8, Section 3.

14. Ulysses Grant, quoted in *Catholic World,* January 1876, 22:434–435.

15. U.S. Congress, House, Res. 1, *Congressional Record*, 44th Cong., 1st sess., 1876, 4, pt. 6, p. 5453.

16. Carl Zolman, *Church and School in the American Law* (St. Louis, Mo.: Concordia Publishing House, 1918), p. 8.

17. F. N. Thompson, *The Federal and State Constitutions* (Washington, D.C.: Government Printing Office, 1909), p. 2964.

18. Leonard Dinnerstein and David M. Reimers, *Ethnic Americans: A History of Immigration and Assimilation* (New York: Dodd, Mead, 1975), p. xiii.

19. Milton M. Gordon, *Assimilation in American Life: The Role of Race, Religion, and National Origins* (New York: Oxford, 1964), pp. 27–28.

20. John Higham, *Strangers in the Land: Patterns of American Nativism, 1860–1925* (New York: Atheneum, 1974; © 1955), p. 4.

21. Quoted in David B. Tyack, ed., *Turning Points in American Educational History* (Waltham, Mass.: Blaisdell, 1967), p. 149.

22. Tyack, p. 149.

23. Tyack, p. 149.

24. Tyack, p. 150.

25. For the ins and outs of the efforts to establish separate schools for the poor and the immigrant in Boston, see Stanley K. Schultz, *The Culture Factory; Boston Public Schools, 1789–1860* (New York: Basic Books, 1974) Chaps. 9–11; and for New York, see Diane Ravitch, *The Great School Wars: New York City, 1805–1973* (New York: Basic Books, 1974), Chaps. 3–10.

26. Higham, p. 20.

27. Robert H. Bremner, ed., *Children and Youth in America: A Documentary History*, Vol. I: 1600–1865 (Cambridge, Mass.: Harvard University Press, 1970), pp. 457–458.

28. See David B. Tyack, *The One Best System: A History of American Urban Education* (Cambridge, Mass.: Harvard University Press, 1974), pp. 104–109.

29. Selwyn K. Troen, *The Public and the Schools: Shaping the St. Louis System, 1838–1920* (Columbia: University of Missouri Press, 1975), Chaps. 2 and 3.

30. Higham, pp. 33–34.

6 Disjunctive Pluralisms:
Racial and Regional

Racial Segregation

What is sometimes forgotten is that legal segregation of the races with regard to schooling was in origin a creation of the free states of the North more than of the slave states of the South. While the southern states were *prohibiting* the education of black slaves in the antebellum years, the northern states were, by custom or by law, *separating* children into white schools and black schools. This is not to say that there was little difference in the two regions before the Civil War, but it *does* say that a kind of racism in both sections viewed blacks as inferior to whites. The basic difference was that the dominant view of whites in the North was that black inferiority did not justify slavery, but that it did justify customs and even laws that kept blacks separate from whites in school, whereas the view of the dominant white group in the South was that blacks did not require schooling at all. This was indeed a significant difference. Though both sections believed that blacks should be brought under social control by whites, the northern states came to believe that blacks should have some of the personal liberties and rights of free men. These rights would still permit, at first, laws that required separation in the schools; that is, schooling could be separate without violating equal rights. This kind of social control was affirmed in northern laws and courts many times, whereas the southern states could not admit of either liberty or equality for black slaves. While slavery exerted an inclusive kind of social control over black slaves, "free" blacks could be granted a certain degree of liberty, but not full equality.

De Facto *Segregation in the North*

Thus, the antebellum period was marked by the growing conflict between two different systems of law existing in what was founded as a federal union of states. In the North, slavery had been abolished by law or was being abolished; in the South, it was firmly entrenched in the law and defended. The "irrepressible conflict" not only revolved around the issue of extending slavery to the western territories, but also around the conflict between slave-owners' rights to their slaves as property and the blacks' rights to liberty as persons. In the South, the laws viewed the slaves' personal rights as inferior to the property rights of the owner; in the North, the states increasingly passed laws between the 1820s and 1850s guaranteeing the personal liberty of blacks as well as of whites.

Personal Liberty Laws / Conflict arose between the states themselves over those personal liberty laws of the northern states that guaranteed the right of blacks to move about, to change their situation, to gain the right of a fair trial by jury, to testify against whites as well as blacks, and to be protected against kidnapping, being reduced to slavery, or being returned by law or by force to a slave state from which they had escaped. Thomas D. Morris argues that the basic legal problem was

> to decide whether mere residence on free soil made a man free, or whether those states were bound to give judicial recognition to the status created by the laws of the slave states. If the American states had been completely independent sovereigns, this question would have been governed wholly by principles derived from international law, or by treaty.[1]

After a period of compromise and adjustment between the states in the 1820s and 1830s, all the states of the North moved decisively during the next two decades to strengthen their personal-liberty laws related to habeas corpus, trial by jury, and protection against kidnapping and legal return of fugitives. This was done amid growing abolitionist sentiment and political action in the North, countered by hardening resolve on the part of the South to exert *its* states' rights over slaves escaping to northern jurisdictions. And the halls of Congress rang with debates about the rights of states to interpose their authority over federal laws and the rights of the federal government to interpose *its* authority over the laws of the southern states. The upshot, of course, was that interposition was eventually decided adversely against the southern states and the Civil War was fought. The aftermath of the war brought the passage of the Thirteenth Amendment whereby the federal government prohibited slavery in the states, and the adoption of the Fourteenth Amendment, which extended the principles of the personal-liberty laws in the northern states to the actions of all states. It was almost another hundred years, however, before those principles were applied to the question of segregated schools.

Public Education for Blacks—But Segregated / The northern states did not move unanimously or enthusiastically to provide public education for blacks prior to the Civil War, but they *had* taken some action. Litwack sums up the early situation:

> Although some white schools admitted Negroes, especially before 1820, most northern states either excluded them altogether or established separate schools for them. . . .
>
> The means employed to exclude Negroes from the public schools varied only slightly from state to state. In New England, local school committees usually assigned Negro children to separate institutions, regardless of the district in which they resided. Pennsylvania and Ohio, although extending their public school privileges to all children, required district school directors to establish separate facilities for Negro students whenever twenty or more could be accommodated. The New York legislature authorized any school district, upon the approval of a town's school commissioners, to provide for segregation. The newer states frequently excluded Negroes from all public education, but by 1850, most of them had consented to segregated instruction. In the absence of legal restrictions, custom and popular prejudice often excluded Negro children from the schools.[2]

Gradually, however, the states of the North began to make broader and broader provision for black children in their public education systems.[3] But the process of bringing them into the *common* public school system was slower in law and still slower in practice. It took the combined efforts of blacks—who established their own schools and then lobbied for admission to public systems—and of philanthropic, religious, and antislavery societies, which established *their own* schools for blacks and then worked for their admission to public education. The renewed abolition movement of the 1830s pushed the process along despite community protests and opposition like that which forced Prudence Crandall to close her school for black girls in Canterbury, Connecticut, and prevented the opening of a manual labor institute for blacks in New Haven.

Campaigns for Desegregated Schools / In the face of such opposition, even in states with the most active abolitionist movements, many blacks were willing to settle for public support and public schooling, even though it had to be in separate schools. But after the 1830s the movement for integrated schooling gained momentum among black spokesmen, and white abolitionists also came to believe that separate schools were bound to be unequal and unfair. During the 1840s and 1850s a growing barrage of petitions, public appeals in the press by such leaders as Frederick Douglass, black convention resolutions, and court cases was aimed at doing away with segregated schools. For example, by the mid-1840s, several towns in Massachusetts had desegregated their schools: Salem, New Bedford, Worcester, Lowell, and Nantucket. When the abolitionists' guns were finally leveled on Boston, the basic pro-and-con arguments were plainly set forth in a precedent-setting case. The issue went as high as the Supreme Court of Massachusetts, where the integrationists lost the court battle that preceded winning the legal war in that state.

In 1846 a group of 86 black citizens petitioned the Primary School Committee of Boston to abolish the separate schools for blacks. They argued that

> the establishment of exclusive schools for our children is a great injury to us, and deprives us of those equal privileges and advantages in the public schools to which we are entitled as citizens. These separate schools cost more and do less for the children than other schools, since all experience teaches that where a small and despised class are shut out from the common benefit of any public institution of learning and confined to separate schools, few or none interest themselves about the schools,—neglect ensues, abuses creep in, the standard of scholarship degenerates, and the teachers and the scholars are soon considered and of course become an inferior class. . . . the establishment of separate schools for our children is believed to be unlawful, and it is felt to be if not in intention, in fact, insulting. If, as seems to be admitted, you are violating our rights, we simply ask you to cease doing so.
>
> We therefore earnestly request that such exclusive schools be abolished, and that our children be allowed to attend the Primary Schools established in the respective Districts in which we live.[4]

The Primary School Committee rejected the petition by a vote of 59 to 16, simply saying that they had the right under the law to "distribute, assign, and classify, all children belonging to the schools in the City, according to their best judgement." They argued on the racial grounds that colored children had a "peculiar physical, mental, and moral structure" that required an educational treatment different from that for white children. This meant to the Committee that black children would learn better in a special environment appropriate to their needs. Besides, few blacks were inconvenienced by attending special schools, and if these schools were abolished, far fewer blacks would attend at all, since most black as well as white parents preferred the established system. The Committee concluded:

> As, then, there is no statute, nor decision of the civil Courts, against classifying children in schools according to a distinction in races, color, or mental and physical peculiarities, the Committee believes that we have the right to classify on these principles; nor do they believe, that, by so doing, we defeat the intent, or violate the spirit, of the law, the Constitution, or the invaluable common-school system established by our fathers; nor in any way infringe the rights of the colored child, or degrade the colored people. These schools were established for their special benefit: for the same reason we would have them vigorously sustained. No man, colored or white, who understands their real value to the colored people, would seek their destruction.[5]

Charles Sumner and the Roberts Case / The Primary School Committee was wrong, however. Some very determined men, both black and white, did seek the destruction of the segregated schools, and on the very ground that the Committee had overlooked in their argument: Separate schooling could *not* be a consistent part of a *common* school. So, after a great deal of petitioning and public discussion, Benjamin Roberts took the Boston school committee to court in 1849 for not admitting his daughter Sarah to the neighborhood school nearest her home, but requiring her to attend the special colored school, which necessitated her walking past five elementary schools to get to the one to which she was assigned. Charles Sumner, who was retained as Roberts' lawyer, was just beginning a long and notable career as an abolitionist and advocate of equal rights.

Sumner argued that the school committee was violating the guarantees of the Massachusetts Constitution that all men, without distinction of color or race, are equal before the law. He said that the public schools were founded to serve all persons equally and therefore separation according to race was a violation of equality. In terms that anticipated the Brown decision of a hundred years later, Sumner defined the meaning of a common public school:

> I conclude . . . that there is but one kind of public school established by the laws of Massachusetts. This is the general Public School, free to all the inhabitants. There is nothing in these laws establishing any exclusive or separate school for any particular class, whether rich or poor, whether Catholic or Protestant, whether white or black. In the eye of the law there is but *one* class, in which all interests, opinions, conditions and colors commingle in harmony—excluding none, comprehending all.[6]

Sumner hammered away at the school committee's argument that the separate schools for blacks had provided them with an education equivalent to the schools for whites. He argued that separate could not be equal because

> the matters taught in the two schools may be precisely the same; but a school, exclusively devoted to one class, must differ essentially, in its spirit and character, from that public school known to the law, where all classes meet together in equality. It is mockery to call it an equivalent. . . .
> The law contemplates not only that they shall all be taught, but that they shall be taught *all together*. They are not only to receive equal quantities of knowledge, but all are to receive it in the same way. All are to approach together the same fountain. . . . since according to our institutions, all classes meet without distinction of color, in the performance of civil duties, so should they all meet, without distinction of color, in the school, beginning there those relations of equality which our Constitution and laws promise to all.[7]

Sumner's argument that equality called for a common and uniform treatment of all classes should be remembered when public schools are being condemned for trying to impose uniformity upon different ethnic groups or social classes. One of the perennial dilemmas facing the educator is how to treat difference differentially but not unequally. The Supreme Court of Massachusetts was unmoved by Sumner's eloquent and constitutional arguments. Based on a unanimous opinion, Chief Justice Lemuel Shaw ruled that differential treatment on the basis of race by assignment of black children to separate schools did not violate the principle of equal rights guaranteed by the Massachusetts constitution. The committee's right to classify children on the basis of race did not violate their equal rights before the law. In the public schools of Massachusetts, separate *could* be equal.

Desegregation by Legislation / Failing in their appeal to the courts to desegregate schools, black and white integrationists turned to the political process, and within a half-dozen years the Massachusetts legislature enacted the 1855 law prohibiting segregation by race, color, or religious opinion in the public schools of the commonwealth. The law did not wipe out prejudice and discrimination by fiat, as Justice Shaw said it would not, but it overruled his decision and pointed in the direction that the northern states would eventually take after the Civil War. The ironic twist is that once the doctrine of "separate but equal" was embedded in the case law of the northern courts in 1849, the remedy for segregated schools had to be found in legislation, passed at a time when the states of the South were legislating *on behalf of* school segregation. It was thereafter, more than a hundred years later, that the *federal courts* rediscovered Sumner's arguments and declared the laws of segregation unconstitutional.

Similar legislation followed in other states, but it took time. Connecticut outlawed segregation in public schools in 1868 and again in 1872; Iowa in 1872; Minnesota and New York in 1873; and Michigan and Illinois in 1874. Indiana and Ohio delayed longer because state courts ruled that the Fourteenth Amendment did not apply. The Supreme Court of Ohio in 1871 ruled that boards of education did have the right to classify students on the basis of color:

> Equality of rights does not involve the necessity of educating white and colored persons in the same school, any more than it does that of educating children of both sexes in the same school, or that different grades of scholars must be kept in the same school. Any classification which preserves substantially equal school advantages is not prohibited by either the state or federal constitutions, nor would it contravene the provisions of either.[8]

The court could see no inequality in the process of classification and assignment. After all, white children were told where they were to go, just as black children were told where *they* were to go. So why should black children or their parents complain? Both races were being treated equally by the officials in charge. But even where the courts upheld segregation in the North, the states eventually moved to desegregate schools by legislation. By 1880, 18 northern states had passed civil rights laws that in effect wiped out the racial school-segregation laws that they had passed earlier in the nineteenth century. True, these laws were not always well enforced. The big cities more stubbornly resisted integration than did smaller communities, but the direction in which northern states were moving was radically different from that of the South. Segregated schools were enforced in Virginia and Tennessee in 1870, North Carolina in 1876, Georgia in 1877, and Louisiana in 1877.

A Special Curriculum for Blacks? / Even before the Civil War another problem began to agitate black educators in addition to the problem of gaining access to schooling. This was what *kind* of education would be best for black students, once they did get to school. The dominant theme was that education ought to be *practical* so that black children could become self-reliant, get jobs, and advance themselves and their race. In 1853 Frederick Douglass put it very bluntly: "Learn trades or starve":

> Now, colored men, what do you mean to do, for you must do something? The American Colonization Society tells you to go to Liberia. Mr. Bibbs tells you to go to Canada. Others tell you to go to school. We tell you to go to work; and to work you must go or die. . . .
> If the alternative were presented to us of learning a trade or getting an education, we would learn the trade, for the reason, that with the trade we could get the education, while with the education we could not get the trade. What we, as a people, need most, is the means for our own elevation.[9]

Douglass was reflecting a popular educational proposal of the day in a time of booming economic activity and plentiful jobs for whites. This economic argument for "industrial education" for blacks became much more controversial in the following decades, when slavery had been abolished in law but the "black codes" of the South were enforcing segregation upon free blacks in many realms of life as a substitute for the social control that slavery had exerted over the blacks.

Legal Segregation in the South

Under slavery the southern slaveholders did not need to keep Negroes separate in order to control them. White and black children could play together, even be taught together, in a society where the social roles were so explicitly spelled out. But when the Civil War was over and the Thirteenth Amendment abolishing slavery went into effect in 1865, the white southerners quickly adopted the Jim Crow type of law that had originated in the free states of the North in order to maintain by law the distinctions of superiority and inferiority that had prevailed under slavery by custom. Radical Republicans in Congress reacted by passing the Civil Rights Act of 1866 to enforce the Thirteenth Amendment prohibition of slavery, and to give blacks equal rights with whites in making and enforcing contracts. Little did they suspect that a hundred years later the Supreme Court would rule in 1976 that the Act also forbade private schools from excluding blacks because of their race. (See page 00.)

Black Codes / During the relative autonomy of the years of presidential reconstruction from 1865 to 1867, the southern states moved rapidly into the breach and passed a series of laws known as "black codes," enforcing segregation in social and economic life and especially in education, both public and private. Every effort was made to salvage as much of the traditional way of life as possible, despite the Confederates' political and military defeat. There was little disposition among white landowners to extend public education benefits to lower-class whites, much less to freed blacks. Some, indeed, thought that freedmen might be taught the rudiments so that they would adopt a moral Christian way of life, but others felt an education would simply make blacks more dangerous than ever. And few wanted to tax themselves for lower-class white children, let alone blacks.

Political or economic freedom did not convince the majority that blacks were equal in intellect or intelligence. Hadn't the scientists, biologists, and anthropologists of England, Europe, and the United States found a hierarchy of races that always put whites at the top and blacks at the bottom?[10] Why, then, try to educate those who were clearly incapable of academic learning? The white politicians of 1866 in the South saw little reason to depart from the views expressed in *De Bow's Review* in 1856. In an article presumably written by J. H. Thornwell, an advocate of reform for white public education in South Carolina, the racist view was candidly stated:

> Fortunately for us. . . . The great mass of coarse and unintellectual labor which the necessities of the country require, is performed by a race not only especially fitted for its performance, but especially unfitted and disqualified for that mental improvement which is generally understood by the term education. . . . In establishing, then, a system of education for a slave State, there are two principles which may be placed as the foundations upon which to build:
>   1. That the state is *not* required to provide education for the great bulk of its laboring class.
>   2. That it *is* required to afford that degree of education to every one of its white citizens which will enable him intelligently and actively to control and direct the slave labor of the State.[11]

Until 1867 the attitudes reflected here were often applied to freedmen who were no longer legally slaves. Where there was not active exclusion of Negroes from public schools by law or by constitution, as in Florida (1866), Georgia (1866), Texas (1866), Arkansas (1867), there was silence or indifference or exclusion by custom. And there was widespread antagonism, hostility, and even violence displayed toward the invading Yankee schoolmarm teachers who went to the South to teach the Negroes in special schools established under religious, philanthropic, or governmental auspices from the North.

Even before President Lincoln's Emancipation Proclamation of 1863, which freed three million slaves in the Confederate States, several northern religious and philanthropic organizations had begun to mobilize to bring schooling to the blacks of the South. As early as 1861 the American Missionary Association (predominantly Congregational, Methodist, and Baptist) began to send teachers to regions controlled by the Union armies in

Virginia, South Carolina, and Tennessee. By 1864 there were more than 500 teachers (mostly young women) in the South under the auspices of the Association, which also founded Berea, Hampton, Fisk, LeMoyne, Talladega, Straight, and Tougaloo colleges.

In 1865 several secular agencies for the education of freedmen joined together to form the American Freedmen's Aid Union, but the most effective agency was established by Congress, also in 1865, to coordinate and promote the efforts. During the five years of its existence, the Freedmen's Bureau established several thousand schools, enrolling between 150,000 and 250,000 black pupils. The Bureau provided the buildings and the private associations provided the teachers: 1,000 in 1867, 3,000 in 1868, and 10,000 in 1869. Added to all this was the money poured in by several philanthropic foundations for establishing and maintaining separate schools for Negroes in the South. The Peabody Fund was among the earliest of these; its chief executive, Barnas Sears, was convinced that separate schools for blacks would avoid the head-on collision that was bound to come with the demand for integrated (mixed) schools in the South.

Congressional Reconstruction / By 1867 the Radical Republican members of Congress were ready to react to the black codes of the southern states. Beginning with the Reconstruction Act of 1867, the so-called Congressional or Radical Republican period of reconstruction lasted for a decade until Union troops were finally withdrawn in 1877. During this time the Fourteenth (1868) and Fifteenth (1870) Amendments were adopted, and the Civil Rights Act of 1875 was passed (subsequently declared by the Supreme Court to be unconstitutional). These were key elements in the Radical Republican attempt to force the southern states to give equal rights to the black freedmen. Ultimately, though not at the time, the Fourteenth Amendment was to be the principal constitutional element in the eventual desegregation of schools. The key sentence of that amendment reads as follows:

> No state shall make or enforce any law which shall abridge the privileges or immunities of citizens of the United States; nor shall any state deprive any person of life, liberty, or property without due process of law; nor deny to any person within its jurisdiction the equal protection of the laws.

Many people in both North and South were uncertain as to just what the Fourteenth Amendment would mean for black education in the South. It is certain that most blacks and their white allies from the North, who were elected to state constitutional conventions and subsequently to state legislatures under the universal suffrage requirements of the Reconstruction Act, did campaign for public school systems that would be free and open to blacks. But when the southern legislatures were elected, they generally skirted the issue. Perhaps they were fearful that a too obvious return to separate schools or denial of schools for blacks at public expense would bring into play the

Fourteenth Amendment, which all confederate states had been required to ratify as a condition for reentry to the Union under the Reconstruction Act.

Resistance to Mixed Schools / Most blacks would probably have preferred mixed schools along the lines that some of the northern states in New England and the Middle West were finally establishing. But the results were largely disappointing to the advocates of mixed schools. Some of the state constitutional provisions under Reconstruction turned out to be very vague about establishing free universal education for blacks and especially vague about outlawing segregated schools or mandating integrated or mixed schools. Two states were, however, explicit. South Carolina's constitution of 1868 stipulated that all public schools supported by public funds should be free and open to all without regard to race or color. And Louisiana's constitution of 1868 specifically provided that there should be no separate schools established exclusively for any race.[12]

Whatever the legal formulas, it was soon clear that mixed schools had little chance of success in the climate of the Radical Reconstruction era. The final withdrawal of federal troops from the last of the military districts into which the South had been divided by the Reconstruction Act signalized the "Compromise of 1877," whereby the Radical Republicans would give up efforts to control the southern states from Washington and rely upon their party's control of the South through Negro suffrage. With this there was no chance for integrated schools in the South for the foreseeable future. Conservative Democrats had begun to regain political control as early as 1869 and 1870 in the upper South (Virginia, Tennessee, and North Carolina) and finally completed the process in South Carolina, Florida, and Louisiana in 1877.

As all this happened, the hostility to mixed schools became more open; and eventually during the 1880s and 1890s, all 17 states of the former Confederacy rebuilt and strengthened their black codes, which enforced segregated schools by legislative act or constitutional requirement, or both. And the powerful support of the Peabody Fund under Barnas Sears was added to the pattern of segregation in private schools for blacks as well as in the state systems of teacher training, which the fund helped to support. Sears argued that insistence upon mixed schools would destroy the public school systems in the South. Similarly, the threat to the planter aristocracy, which derived from the doctrine of equality implicit in the public school, was contained in such arguments as those of "Civis," a nom-de-plume for a writer in *The Southern Planter and Farmer* in 1877:

> I am a friend of the Negro, but a friend to him in his proper place of subordination. . . . I well understand the peculiar qualities of the race, and they are exactly such as fit them for menial offices and subordinate positions, and of necessity disqualify them for the higher walks of life, and particularly for the great functions of citizenship. . . .

> The public school system recognizes the doctrine of Negro equality, and professes to prepare him for the highest functions of life, the duties of political sovereignty. If he is, by congenital inferiority, not competent to such functions, the attempt to prepare him for them is a manifest absurdity. . . . Having shown . . . that the public school, even without reference to the question of races, is utterly indefensible, both as a matter of morals and of policy, I oppose it in its application to the Negro race . . . because it is an assertion, in the most dangerous form, of the hideous doctrine of Negro equality.[13]

Gains for Black Education / The presence of such views in high as well as low places in the Reconstruction South meant that what gains were made for the education of black children would have to come initially from the federal government and philanthropic sources outside the South and would then be absorbed by the efforts of blacks and their allies in the Reconstruction era. Vaughn sums up the gains of Reconstruction education as follows:

> The struggle for black education in the South during Reconstruction produced many achievements. Black schools, either illegal or severely circumscribed before 1860, became viable institutions. Whereas less than 10 percent of the black population was literate by 1860, within a decade that figure had increased to over 25 percent as a result of massive efforts by the Freedmen's Bureau and private benevolent associations. Southern blacks confounded their most severe critics and proved to be highly educable, at times to a degree embarrassing to local whites. Blacks trained in bureau-association schools provided most of the dedicated teachers for black schools when the majority of Yankee instructors returned home after 1870.[14]

The contributions of government and philanthropic societies were not inconsiderable accomplishments, given the mood and temper of the times following one of the most bitterly fought civil wars of all modern history. While the racist views of "Civis" continued to attract a large following, the more genuinely civic aspirations of proponents for a democratic political community were also widespread in the North. For example, the Unitarian minister of Boston, Edward Everett Hale, expressed the hope that the working-class whites of the South could be educated in the principles of liberal democracy as well as the blacks. As secretary of the Soldiers' Memorial Society of Massachusetts, Hale wrote that the Society

> regards the education of the South as the only satisfactory solution of the problem of Reconstruction, as, in fact, the key to the whole social and political position. When the laboring population of the South is elevated into equal intelligence with that of the North, it will begin to feel that the interests and hopes of both sections are identical. Union will become real, peace and prosperity permanent.
> . . . By educating these poor whites we make them our friends by showing them that we are theirs. . . . This new democracy which we are waking into life will hereafter rule the State. None can fail to see the immense political importance of using all possible means to train this new power so that it shall be a beneficent one. Every school is a centre of political as well as

intellectual and social force. Every teacher is an apostle of republican freedom.[15]

The Defeat of Reconstruction / While this idealism went far in the North, it was exactly the fear that Yankee teachers *were* political apostles of republican freedom that agitated the South. Christian missionaries to black slaves or even to black freedmen were one thing; *political* missionaries from any northerners to any southerners were quite another. A fascinating exchange of letters took place in 1867 between Anna Gardner, a Yankee schoolmarm from Nantucket who was teaching black children in Charlottesville, Virginia, and the editor of the *Chronicle*, who wrote:

> The impression among the white residents of Charlottesville is, that your instruction of the colored people who attend your school contemplates something more than the communication of ordinary knowledge implied in teaching them to read, write, cypher, etc. The idea prevails that you instruct them in politics and sociology; that you come among us not merely as an ordinary school teacher, but as a political missionary; that you communicate to the colored people ideas of social equality with the whites. With your first object we sympathize; the second, we regard as mischievous, and as only tending to disturb the good feeling between the two races.[16]

Miss Gardner replied, pointedly and firmly:

> I teach in school and out, so far as my influence extends, the fundamental principles of "politics" and "sociology," viz.: "Whatsoever ye would that men should do to you, do ye even so unto them."
> Yours on behalf of truth and justice.[17]

Miss Gardner may have had justice on her side, but she was far from home and soon returned there, and the good people of Charlottesville, in the shadow of Jefferson's Monticello, won the "political" battle on behalf of disjunctive segregation in education. In other words, regional localism prevailed in the control of public education in the South over the value claims of a wider national political community. This conflict was waged in the Reconstruction period, not only in thousands of local communities throughout the South, but also in bitter political contests in the halls of Congress in Washington.

The Power of Localism

One thing the Civil War and Reconstruction accomplished was to make education a subject of intense national debate in the press; in professional organizations; in boards of education; in state legislatures; in any number of reform, religious, and philanthropic societies; and in the halls of Congress itself. For the first time during the hundred years of its history, the legislative branch of the federal government fought and wrangled over what its role, specifically of Congress, ought to be in promoting education in the states. In the Revolutionary era the Northwest Ordinance went through the Continental Congress almost unnoticed, the debates at the Constitutional Convention scarcely mentioned education, the early Congress passed over successive presidential pleas for a national university, and Congress all but ignored the clamor of the states for common school systems during the Jacksonian era. True, Congress had been lavish in making grants of public land to the states, not only the 16th-section sales, but also swamp lands, salt lands, and even surplus cash from the Surplus Revenue Deposit Act of 1836. Many states used some of such income for their school funds. And, true also, Congress passed the Morrill Act of 1862 to grant public lands to the states to support agricultural and mechanical colleges. But it took the Reconstruction period to revive the idea that perhaps the United States ought to have a *national* system of education in which the Congress should have some authority in defining its character and purposes. Nothing like this had been heard since the post-Revolutionary era, and even then nothing so drastic had been proposed.

The prime issue was whether Congress ought to be able to prohibit segregated public schools in the several states. Behind this, of course, was the issue as to whether U.S. Negroes were to be admitted to full citizenship rights under the mandate of the federal government or whether the states were to be free to decide for themselves. Was the constitutional order of the nation to prevail, or were the localist and segmental rights of the several states to prevail? The Thirteenth, Fourteenth, and Fifteenth Amendments pointed one way. The upshot of a 10-year campaign for Congress to outlaw segregated schools pointed another way. The presidency was silent, the courts stood on the sidelines, and the Congress ultimately decided under the pressures of regional localism that it would leave the matter to the states. This meant that by 1876 the political community of the United States was almost fatally divided on the issue; the northern states went one way and the southern states another, and they were not to meet again until the courts began to take an active stand 75 years later.

Radical Republicans and Federal Reconstruction in Education

The issue came to a head in Congress under the hammer of equalitarian drives by the Radical Republicans and under the prime leadership of Charles Sumner with the aid of such men as Henry Wilson and George F. Hoar of Massachusetts, John A. Bingham, John Sherman, and James Garfield of Ohio, Justin Morrill of Maine, Levi P. Morton of Indiana, Richard Yates of Illinois, Austin Blair of Michigan, Samuel Pomeroy of Kansas, Theodore Frelinghausen of New Jersey, and George F. Edmunds of Vermont. The Fourteenth Amendment was to become their principal achievement in attempting to purge racial caste from U.S. society and politics. They certainly intended the amendment to be a broad constitutional attack upon state legislation that sought to preserve class distinctions based upon color or race. It is not clear that the framers intended specifically for it to prohibit segregated schools as such, but it is clear that Sumner himself could well have intended it to do so, given his prior position on the Roberts case in Massachusetts in 1849 and his support of the Civil Rights legislation that was eventually passed in 1875 after his death. This latter was the key, and losing, battle.

The "Sumner phalanx" tried to enforce a prohibition against segregated schools in several different ways. They tried to impose "conditions subsequent" on the readmission to the Union of the southern states, which would prohibit the states from ever amending their constitutions so as to permit segregated schools. But there were strong constitutional objections to this procedure on the grounds that this would create a class of unequal states in the Union. Nevertheless, the Congress attached such "conditions subsequent" to the readmission of Virginia, Mississippi, and Texas. Despite this, however, the Radicals did nothing when the Virginia legislature almost immediately in 1870 established a system of segregated schools. Though the Radicals "won" the votes, they were not strong enough to bring the recalcitrant states to heel, nor could they even summon the necessary votes against conservative Democrats and moderate Republicans to outlaw segregated schools by legislation in Washington, D.C.

The Quest for Federal Authority / This "Sumner phalanx" also tried to achieve their objective through sponsoring bills on federal aid to education. Bills to give general subsidies to primary and secondary schools in the states were introduced in almost every session of Congress during the Reconstruction period. One of the early bills would have gone much farther than simply giving federal aid to the states. In February 1870, Representative George F. Hoar of Massachusetts introduced into the House a bill to establish a national system of education:

> The purpose of this bill, by which it is for the first time sought to compel by national authority the establishment of a thorough and efficient system of public instruction throughout the whole country, is not to supersede, but to stimulate, compel, and supplement action by the States.[18]

Hoar argued that the states of the South were dismantling their public school systems so rapidly that illiteracy among the younger generation in the coming decade would rise to something like 75 percent. And, he said, this was being done at a time when the Fourteenth and Fifteenth Amendments had just declared the right of every citizen to take part in the administration of government. It was only right and proper, therefore, that the federal government should take the initiative to see that the expanded citizenry be properly prepared for their duties. So, the Hoar bill proposed that whenever any state slipped below a declared minimal standard, the President would be empowered to declare it a "delinquent state," and appoint a state superintendent of national schools for that state. The Secretary of the Interior would appoint federal inspectors for each school division, and a local superintendent of national schools in each local school district. These several authorities would be empowered to build schools, supply textbooks, and appoint teachers. In summing up his proposals, Representative Hoar said:

> the purpose of this bill is simply to establish by national authority a common-school system which shall instruct all children of school age in the ordinary knowledge of reading, writing, and arithmetic in those States which fail or refuse to make such provision by State authority. It does not propose to meddle with or disturb the existing condition of things in any State where a competent common-school system now exists, or where, within a reasonable time hereafter, such a school system may be established by State authority.[19]

Opposition to Federal Control / The Hoar bill never came to a vote in either house of Congress. One can almost still hear the howls of anguish that such a "harsh" proposal brought forth from the conservative Democratic South. But the opposition from professional educators of the North was almost as strong. The spirit of localism emanated from all sections of the country when it was faced with the specter of federal control of education from Washington. The state superintendent of schools of Pennsylvania, James P. Wickersham, led the attack before the National Education Association convention in 1871. He argued that such a "national system of compulsory education" was contrary (1) to the uniform practices whereby education has been left to the states for a century, (2) to the views of the founding fathers, (3) to constitutional precedent, and (4) to sound republican political philosophy, which keeps government as close as possible to the people.

Wickersham acknowledged the backwardness of education in the South and agreed that it had been a great blunder to readmit the southern states without requiring their constitutions to provide for universal education. But what was done was done. All states were now equals. The solution was *not* to put education in the hands of the federal government. The solution was for the federal government to provide the money and let the states improve matters. Federal aid, but not federal control, became the goal of the teaching profession. The National Education Association (NEA) agreed heartily and passed a resolution favoring federal aid to the South. Localism won the day and the battles in Congress shifted from a "national system" to plans to provide federal aid to the states with federal directives stipulating its use.

In the furor over North–South relations and black–white segregation, a little noted section of Hoar's bill read that "no books shall be used in any of the national schools, nor shall any instruction be given therein, calculated to favor the peculiar tenets of any religious sect." So, now, three of the four major segmental pluralisms were involved: religion as well as race and localism. *The Catholic World* entered the fray to condemn the Hoar bill, and contended that it was a great design to "suppress Catholic education, gradually extinguish Catholicity in the country, and to form one homogeneous American people after the New England Evangelical type." The federal government had no business in public education, which should be a local and state concern. But, if a national system should go the way of public support for parochial schools, presumably Catholics could live with it, since "we could manage to get along with national denominational schools as well as others could."[20]

But the Radical Republicans did not give up, even in the face of sectional, religious, and Democratic opposition. They kept up a drumfire of proposals for federal aid. In 1872 a bill proposed by Legrand Perce, a black representative from Mississippi, would have appropriated the proceeds of public land sales to the states, provided they established mixed schools. After a long and bitter debate, the House passed the bill 117 to 98, but it died in Senate committee. In 1879 a Senate bill introduced by Ambrose E. Burnside of Rhode Island passed the Senate, but died in the House. The fact was that the Radical Republicans could not muster enough political support to push through a federal aid bill. Middle-of-the-road and conservative Republicans were too often willing to side with Democrats to defeat mixed school proposals. Segmental pluralism was to defeat general federal aid to education for about 90 years.

School Desegregation in the Civil Rights Bill / The last hurrah for the Radicals' efforts to overcome segregated school systems centered in their efforts to pass a strong Civil Rights bill in Congress. For nearly ten years, Sumner and his colleagues introduced bill after bill prohibiting segregation on the basis of race, color, or previous condition of servitude in public accommodations—restaurants, hotels, theaters, railroads, and schools. Although a basic question was whether the Fourteenth Amendment prohibited such discrimination by private persons or solely by state governments, this issue did not come up directly in the early bills. It proved to be crucial later on.

Much debate was spent on whether the broad interpretation of the "privileges and immunities" clause of the Amendment gave Congress the power to prohibit segregated schools. The Radicals argued that it did; the conservatives that it did not. Then the "equal protection" clause was appealed to by the Radicals, and the conservatives argued that enforcement would destroy the public school system. It was here in 1874 that Barnas Sears of the Peabody Fund lobbied hard in Washington against a civil rights bill that contained a mixed school provision. The Senate passed such a bill in 1874, but the House would not go along until the school clause was dropped. The southern Democrats and the northern conservatives together were too strong, and an equivocal stand by Representative Richard Cain, a black congressman from South Carolina, let some middle-of-the-roaders off the hook. So, the Civil Rights Act of 1875 was passed after the controversial section on segregated schools was dropped. (This happened again in 1957.) Even so, the Supreme Court in 1883 declared the law to be unconstitutional, ruling that it tried to regulate rights between private citizens, whereas the Fourteenth Amendment simply gave a federal guarantee against *state* encroachment on those civil rights adhering to citizens.

The Radical Failure / The integration of schools by congressional action was a dead issue. Decisions on segregation were to be left to the states. The political process had shown that pluralistic localism was more powerful than federalism. The conservatives won the ten-year battle of Reconstruction against segregated schools. Sumner had lost in Massachusetts in 1849. Later, he won on the Fourteenth Amendment, but his followers lost again in the Civil Rights Act. The end of Reconstruction spelled the doom of the common school ideal in the South. Not even Sumner's ideological eloquence in 1872 could win the day for the common school, although he pleaded

> how impossible it is for a separate school to be the equivalent of the common school. . . . The indignity offered to the colored child is worse than any compulsory exposure, and here not only the child suffers, but the race to which he belongs is blasted and the whole community is hardened in wrong.
>
> The separate school wants the first requisite of the common school, inasmuch as it is not open equally to all . . . such a school is not republican in character. Therefore it is not a preparation for the duties of life. The child is not trained in the way he should go; for he is trained under the ban of inequality. How can he grow up to the stature of equal citizenship? He is pinched and dwarfed while the stigma of color is stamped upon him. . . .
>
> Nor is separation without evil to the whites. . . . Better even than knowledge is a kindly nature and the sentiment of equality . . . but the school itself must practice the lesson. . . . How precious the example which teaches that all are equal in rights. But this can be only where all commingle in the common school as in common citizenship.[21]

As the Reconstruction era came to a close, the "sentiment of equality" could not win in the Congress of the United States. Congress decided that it would not intervene in the matter, but would leave it to the courts. The courts decided that *they* would not construe the power of the federal judiciary broadly enough to intervene in the civil rights affairs of the states. And the presidency looked the other way throughout. Again, the federal effort turned out to be too feeble in the face of powerful segmental localisms.

The Struggle for a Federal Office of Education

Even where the virulent sentiments of race, or religion, or ethnicity were not the central issue, belief in education as a state, local, or private matter remained strong. A good example is the history of the effort to establish a federal office of education. Donald Warren's full-scale study of the founding years makes the strength of localism amply evident.[22] Warren argues persuasively that the idea of creating a national agency to promote education was an integral part of the general movement to create common public school systems in the middle decades of the nineteenth century. It reflected at once a continuation of revolutionary idealism devoted to creating a republican nation, a belief in equalitarianism, the faith in education as a means to social reform, *and* a belief that *systems* of education—efficient, thorough, and dependable—were necessary to carry out the goals in an expanding, booming, heterogeneous nation.

It also reflected the value claims of a democratic political community as expressed by public school reformers who began to focus more upon equality than upon liberty as they confronted the growing pluralisms that seemed to spring up in every quarter. And above all, the confrontations of North and South made still more difficult the federal effort to guarantee (or enforce, as Warren puts it) equality of educational access and curriculum all over the country. This effort was in direct opposition to the localism practiced by those states and regions that claimed the liberty to decide for themselves whether or not to segregate schools and thus to impose inequality within their own jurisdictions. This was the prime political setting in which efforts were made in the mid-1860s to establish a federal office of education.

The Revolutionary dreamers had touched only lightly upon a specific federal role (aside from the plans for a national university in Washington, D.C.). The Radical Republicans and their predecessors had tried over a period of several decades to work out specific plans in practice, but their hope that federal intervention could guarantee common schools, equality, and efficiency foundered in the tempest of Reconstruction. The reformers had to compromise on a much less effective office than some had hoped for. In one sense, though, it is surprising that any federal office of education was adopted and survived considering the suspicion of federal control kept alive by the many pluralistic and local loyalties that surrounded education. Again, liberty of local choice won out over the claims of equality to be guaranteed by federal enforcement.

The Background / As early as 1829 Congressman Joseph Richardson of Massachusetts had proposed that the House of Representatives should establish a Committee on Education to carry out the founders' vision of a republican education through federal effort as implied by the general welfare clause of the Constitution. His proposal was quickly squelched by a 3 to 1 vote—education was a state affair, not federal! In 1837 proposals for increasing federal support for education from the sale of public lands never came to a vote. In 1839 Charles Brooks, a Unitarian minister and school reformer in Massachusetts, began his nearly three decades of effort to produce a plan for a national system of common schools whose curricula would be supervised by a centralized agency that would assure equality in backward states as well as in the more progressive ones. Though such a proposal left most educators aghast, they nevertheless were beginning to form nationwide professional associations to maintain communication, promote public education on a statewide basis, and counteract the growing segmentation of society along racial, ethnic, and religious lines. Warren sums up the interrelation of the state and national reform movements of the day:

> drives for state and national school agencies originated from similar circumstances, attempted to realize similar goals, on different levels, of course, and confronted the same opposition, often from the same opponents. Both campaigns emerged at approximately the same time, during the early years of the common school movement, amid schoolmen's growing recognition that their crusade cut across local and regional achievements. Infused with passion by nationalistic goals and the grail of administrative orderliness, both sought the establishment of government bureaus modeled upon the presumed reform effectiveness of collecting and disseminating school data.[23]

As we have seen, about half the states had established state systems of schools by 1860. The problem of achieving equality produced a persistent tension in local communities that did not want county or state officials to interfere with their schools, and in state or regional agencies that rejected federal directives. Yet the dilemma was always there. How could equality be achieved unless *all* the schools of a state, or a region, or the nation had a common and uniform standard of instruction? The reformers (mostly Whigs and Radical Republicans) were likely to opt for equality, which meant to them that poor schools had to be brought up to a uniform or common standard of quality. Opponents (mostly Democrats) opted for liberty of choice by local, regional, state, racial, or ethnic groups, no matter what happened to equality.

In the 1840s the tempo for national action began to pick up. Resolutions of a Convention of the Friends of Education were sent by Horace Mann to Congress in 1849 requesting creation of a bureau of education to gather information about public education across the country. In the 1850s Henry Barnard presented plans for Congress to establish a federal "agent for education" who would be an expert (that is, Barnard himself) in writing reports, planning conferences, and gathering and publishing information. But even such modest and bland proposals had little chance in the heightening sectional temper of the times preliminary to the Civil War. For a while, more positive plans might have had a chance in the two or three years following the war, but the Reconstruction Act and the three amendments to it, the Freedmen's Bureau, and the battles over segregated school legislation monopolized the major efforts of the Radical Republicans.

A Modest Federal Agency Created / Several types of plans were proposed in the post-war period. Brooks, the Massachusetts reformer, reappeared with his "strong" plan for a national system of schools with a cabinet-level officer heading a federal bureau that would guarantee equality of education for freedmen, immigrants, and all citizens. Barnard reappeared with his plans for a bureau to conduct research and exert leadership by scholarship. And Emerson White, with support from the National Association of School Superintendents, proposed a bureau whose prime purpose would be to persuade or induce states to maintain efficient and thorough systems, largely by the collection and dissemination of school statistics and comparative studies of school laws, conditions, finances, and achievements.

In 1865–1866 the school superintendents began a concerted lobbying campaign for a moderate plan that would suggest and recommend rather than exert pressure upon the states by the federal government. Brooks, Barnard, and White all joined in, but, as Warren comments, they softened their differences and glossed over the many real problems that were agitating the halls of Congress and the state legislatures:

> On . . . the nature of the crisis to be resolved by school reform; the meaning and urgency of equal educational opportunity and its role in reconstruction; the mode of educational enforcement required to meet the crisis; and the priority of black education among postwar goals—on issues such as these, educators' seeming unity, along with their zeal would shortly wilt.[24]

The disparity of views among reformers ranged from a "hard line" approach to "soft." Ignatius Donnelly, Radical Republican from Minnesota, introduced a bill asking the Joint Committee on Reconstruction to consider establishing in Washington

> a national bureau of education, whose duty it shall be to enforce education, without regard to race or color, upon the population of all such States as shall fall below a standard to be established by Congress, and to inquire whether such a bureau should not be made an essential and permanent part of any system of reconstruction.[25]

As Warren says, Donnelly's bill followed the "logic of guaranteed common school opportunities" and dared to speak of "enforcing education" in the states. The House approved overwhelmingly, but there is no record that the Joint Committee on Reconstruction ever gave it any consideration. Shortly thereafter, Congressman James A. Garfield introduced a "soft" bill embodying Emerson White's proposals. After some complicated maneuvering, but actually attracting very little attention, it was passed and signed by President Andrew Johnson on March 2, 1867, creating a Department of Education

> for the purpose of collecting such statistics and facts as shall show the condition and progress of education in the several States and Territories, and of diffusing such information respecting the organization and management of schools and school systems, and methods of teaching, as shall aid the people of the United States in the establishment and maintenance of efficient school systems, and otherwise promote the cause of education throughout the country.[26]

Gone was any reference to race or color, to equality, to justice, or even to "republican institutions." All that remained were "statistics," "information," and "efficient systems of education." The most inflammatory words were possibly "promote the cause of education throughout the country." But the emphasis upon the other cautious terms must have wiped out any lingering fears about "enforcing equality" in education. Such was the modest beginning of an office that was to be dispensing billions of dollars a hundred years later in the cause of reducing inequality in education and enforcing affirmative action on behalf of equality.

A Victory for Localism / Yet, there must have been those among the supporters who quietly hoped that the new department would become the forerunner of an active federal agency and not remain simply a data gatherer. Unfortunately for such views, the first commissioner, Henry Barnard, was far more a scholarly data gatherer and reporter than he was an activist. Above all, he was a poor administrator and handily alienated so many Congressmen that the attempts to abolish the department or cut its tiny appropriation became endemic during his three years from 1867 to 1870. But, when he was not reappointed, Barnard began to argue that the ineffective Department of Education, now reduced to a Bureau, should have more authority to put pressure on state agencies to improve themselves.

Barnard's successor, General John Eaton, had worked as a Radical Republican in the army and in the Freedmen's Bureau to improve the education of blacks. His first act was to draw up an impressive list of activities that were not appropriate for a federal agency to undertake and those that were. In addressing the National Teachers Association in 1871, he argued that the federal office should, of course, not violate the Constitution or decrease local or individual effort, but when it came to the things that the government *may* do, the list was much longer: everything necessary to promote education for Washington, D.C., the territories, the Indians, and international relations, and to hold the states to account for their use of federal funds. He then ended up with a remarkable statement:

> 10. The Government may take, as has been established, by legislative and executive action, and by the decision of the courts, such exceptional action as exceptional circumstances may require, (a), for the public welfare, (b), for the assurance of a Republican form of government, (c), for the protection of the liberty of those lately slaves, (d), for the security of their citizenship, (e), for the free exercise of the right to vote, (f), for the equality of all men before the law, and (g), for the fitting of any citizen for any responsibility the nation may impose on him.[27]

The references to the preamble and amendments to the Constitution were unmistakable, but he found that to keep his little Bureau alive, he had to trim his sails to the declining zeal for reconstruction. So, he settled largely for the informational purposes that Barnard had pursued. The dream of a federally guaranteed equality of education faded before the political realities of pluralism, localism, and a persistent racism. The dream was barely recognizable in "a forgettable federal agency" that became a kind of information branch for the National Education Association. As Warren says, the Bureau of Education "left the traditional localism of American public education virtually intact. . . . By the end of Eaton's term it was clear that in the crucial matter of educational policy, the South and the past were winning the Civil War."[28] This conclusion seemed to apply for most of a hundred years. Then, in the 1950s, 1960s, and 1970s, latter-day reformers found that the legacy of the Reconstruction was still embedded in federal law, in the Constitution, and in the federal bureaucracy. The Supreme Court turned to the Civil Rights Act of 1866 and to the Fourteenth Amendment as authority to declare segregation in the schools to be unlawful. A reform-minded President and Congress of the "Great Society" approved and legislated massive federal aid to be disbursed by the Office of Education to compensate for the inequality of educational opportunity throughout the country—a heritage that the Reconstruction reformers had failed to obliterate. How *that* war on inequality was progressing is the subject of Chapter 11.

Notes

1. Thomas D. Morris, *Free Men All: The Personal Liberty Laws of the North, 1780–1861* (Baltimore: Johns Hopkins University Press, 1974), p. 13.
2. Leon F. Litwack, *North of Slavery: The Negro in the Free States, 1790–1860* (Chicago: University of Chicago Press, 1961), pp. 114–115.
3. For useful selections from state laws in Connecticut, Ohio, New York, and Massachusetts, see Robert H. Bremner, ed., *Children and Youth in America: A Documentary History* (Cambridge, Mass.: Harvard University Press, 1970), Vol. I, pp. 513–547.
4. Bremner, p. 528.
5. Bremner, p. 529.
6. Bremner, p. 531.
7. Bremner, pp. 533–534.
8. Earle H. West, *The Black American and Education* (Columbus, Ohio: Merrill, 1972), pp. 77–78.
9. West, p. 51.
10. See, for example, Charles H. Lyons, *To Wash an Aethiop White: British Ideas About Black African Educability, 1530–1960* (New York: Teachers College Press, 1975), Chaps. 3 and 4.
11. Rush Welter, ed., *American Writings on Popular Education: The Nineteenth Century* (Indianapolis, Ind.: Bobbs-Merrill, 1971), pp. 204–205.
12. For an excellent overall study of black education during Reconstruction, see William Preston Vaughn, *Schools for All: The Blacks and Public Education in the South, 1865–1877* (Lexington: University Press of Kentucky, 1974).

13. West, pp. 92–93.
14. Vaughn, p. 158.
15. Bremner, Vol. II, pp. 1163–1164.
16. Bremner, p. 1171.
17. Bremner, p. 1172.
18. *Congressional Globe*, 41st Cong., 2d sess., 1870.
19. *Congressional Globe*, 41st Cong., 3d sess., 1871, p. 1042.
20. "Unification and Education," *Catholic World*, 1871, 13:1–14.
21. Bremner, Vol. II, p. 1189.
22. Donald R. Warren, *To Enforce Education: A History of the Founding Years of the United States Office of Education* (Detroit: Wayne State University Press, 1974).
23. Warren, p. 44.
24. Warren, p. 75.
25. Warren, p. 78.
26. Warren, p. 204.
27. Daniel Calhoun, ed., *The Educating of Americans: A Documentary History* (Boston: Houghton Mifflin, 1969), pp. 344–345.
28. Warren, p. 173.

part III
The Burden
of Modernization

1876-1926

Introduction

If one were to look backward from the vantage point of the nation's centennial celebration in 1876, what generalizations could be made about the educational structure that had been so far assembled as a result of the interactions of value claims made by the democratic political community, the modernization process, and segmental pluralism? For one thing, the first tier of a public education system had been pretty solidly built in the northern and western states, a system intended to provide a minimum of common schooling for the vast majority of white children. In this respect the claims of a democratic political community and the political aspects of modernization had supported each other in the many ways described in Chapter 4. The idea of free universal education at the elementary level was widely accepted and deeply embedded in the laws and practices of most of the states. Important strides toward making elementary education compulsory, secular, and common (for native whites and many immigrant whites) had also been made in the northern cities and states. Racial and local segmental pluralism continued to produce segregated schools for blacks and whites in the South (where it produced any public schools at all) and continued to exist, though in lessening force, in many parts of the North.

On the other hand, secondary education remained predominantly in the hands of private academies, and higher education was dominated by private colleges and universities. In this respect the forces of pluralism, drawing upon the voluntary efforts of religious, philanthropic, and local groups, were widely assumed to serve adequately the democratic ideals of liberty and the public good, while the common schools served the goals of equality and popular consent. The forces of modernization had touched secondary and higher education only lightly in comparison with what was to come. Resistance to public secondary education in the form of the free high school was strong in many parts of the country, especially outside New England and in the South. Efforts to modernize the college and university programs by making them more secular, scientific, practical, and diversified met with only indifferent and sporadic success until after the Civil War. An elitist conception of gentlemanly higher education designed to prepare special talent for the professions and the public service infused the precincts of the leading colleges of the East. It was also suffused through the scores of struggling denominational colleges that dotted the nation's landscapes and that tried to emulate the classical and disciplinary goals of a traditional liberal education as proclaimed by the Yale Faculty Report of 1828.[1]

If at that time one could look forward a half-century from 1876, what would one see? Most impressive would be the dramatically rapid, and sometimes confused and chaotic, expansion involved in the building of the second and third tiers of public education. By 1926 the public high schools had all but overwhelmed the private academies. The state universities and colleges

162

were pulling abreast of the private institutions in numbers of students and in quality of education, and were beginning to surpass them in technical, practical, diversified, and applied scientific fields. The forces at work here had predominately emanated from the modernization process led by industrial urbanization, secularization, the centralizing and mobilizing power of state and federal governments, and increasing citizen participation in the political process.

Modernization Triumphant

In the 50 years straddling the nineteenth and twentieth centuries, American public education took on its definitive "modern" characteristics. Along with other rapidly modernizing institutions of government, business, industry, and labor, it assumed the bureaucratic aspects of large-scale organization in general. It became more secular and scientific, more practical and vocational, more differentiated and diversified, and more torn by tension between achievement-oriented pedagogy and learner-oriented pedagogy.

The pluralistic segments were still at work, as we shall see, but the overall impact of the combined modernization trends was, if anything, more powerful in shaping the ultimate direction in which public education took during the half-century whose early decades have often been called the "Gilded Age" and whose later decades have usually been called the "Progressive Era." In other words, educators were challenged more acutely than ever by insistent, imperative, and imperious demands to reorder systems of public education that would not only respond to the booming and often irrepressible economic modernization impelled by industrial capitalism, but would at the same time cope humanely with the bewildering variety of ethnic, linguistic, and cultural pluralisms swept in on the massive flood tide of immigration. In the process, the value claims of a democratic political community were almost drowned out, especially in the Gilded Age, by the raucous voices and sometimes malignant practices of the new business and industrial order. Although the goals of these enterprises were wrapped in the folds of liberty and the public good, the ideal of popular consent was submerged, and entrepreneurs seldom spoke of equality except as a dangerous tool of foreign or agrarian radicals.

So, in striving to understand this exceedingly important and formative period in American public education, no simple causal explanation will do. What was built in the 50 years beginning with the collapse of Civil War Reconstruction and ending with the collapse of Progressivism was not simply a result of conflict between socioeconomic classes, though that was present, or the victory of bureaucratic middle-class values, though they were present, or nativistic Americanizers imposing their values on foreign immigrants, though they too were clearly evident. Rather, the period should be viewed as the recurring and various attempts of public groups and educators to cope with the forces of modernization on one side and the forces of pluralism on the other, while at the same time preserving (at least in name) some of the democratic values that were regularly celebrated on the Fourth of July. By and large, modernization was the winning contender during this period, and it was no easy burden for the educators or the American public to bear.

The emergence of a modern United States was so complicated and so rapid that it has long prompted a vast amount of historical research, and it has been the especial subject of intensive scrutiny by historians of education in recent years. It is impossible to summarize this research here, but a few guideposts can serve to help those who would trace the development of public education and find their way through the maze of events that seems to lead in all directions or nowhere.

In the Gilded Age. The first thing to be said is that the weight of recent historical judgment about the Gilded Age (especially the 1880s and 1890s) is that the development of institutions and processes like education was the result of the interactions of many social and political groups. Changes did not occur solely because capitalists exploited the working class, or because corrupt politicians and greedy businessmen took advantage of embattled farmers and laborers. Walter T. K. Nugent points out that recent historians have more often assumed the basic motivations in politics to be sectional, religious, or ethnic interests rather than those of social class or economic self-interest.[2] For example, Paul Kleppner finds that voting behavior in the Gilded Age was more related to religious, ethnic, and group variables than to the straight-line values of economic class.[3] This was especially true of voting behavior on such reform issues as public school laws, women's suffrage, and prohibition. And Herbert G. Gutman has impressively documented the complicated interactions of the successive waves of immigrants who persistently resisted and in turn helped reshape the work habits and culture sought by individual employers.[4] Such findings support the framework of analysis being presented here.

In the Progressive Era. Even more important in giving broad and deep underpinnings to the emphasis upon the modernization process is the weight of recent historical research on the Progressive Era, summarized by Robert H. Wiebe who is himself one of the major contributors to the scholarship of that period. The essence of Wiebe's point is that the first two decades of the twentieth century can best be viewed as the modernization of America.[5]

Wiebe recognizes that the concept *modern* is as elusive as it is important, but he argues that it serves to distinguish an urban-industrial type of society from a traditional type of society wherever it may be found. Even though there is wide difference among American historians over its details, modernization remains the principal overarching framework of historians whose outlook ranges from conservative to new left, in that

> there is approximate agreement that its components are found somewhere in these categories: the mechanization of production and distribution; the im-

personality of social relations, including large bureaucratic organizations and centralized power; the development of mass communication with increasing uniformity of attitudes; and the secularization of popular thought, accompanied by a greater discipline to the clock and calendar and by a rising faith in scientific solutions to human problems. . . . Modern, in the sense of this paragraph, still dominates our national life.[6]

Wiebe concludes his analysis with the following comment:

The total effect of scholarship on the progressive era, therefore, is to confirm a critical transition, with historians debating the sources and timing of change but not the overarching framework of modernization.[7]

Contrary Burdens Laid Upon the Schools

As one seeks to understand the fundamental meaning of public education from 1876 to 1926, it is the "overarching framework of modernization" that should be kept in mind. Today, different groups and individuals view its workings and its results with different attitudes. Some view it with distaste, as basically a malevolent influence imposing uniformity and conformity in cultural life—something to be exorcised somehow from contemporary society. Others view it as a basically benevolent force in achieving a higher standard of living for the many as well as for the few. Some believe that public education responded too readily to modernization and thus became dehumanized, as did other institutions of family, church, and community. Still other individuals believe that educators responded too timidly, too slowly, and too conservatively in meeting the basic requirements of a modern industrial and secular society. And, to a degree, this same range of attitudes was found among the educators and the public critics who were themselves parties of the Gilded and Progressive ages. Regardless of the breadth and depth of the ongoing arguments of those times, we can touch upon only a few of their salient features here.

It is very difficult to try to line up those who were for or against modernization in general, or pluralism in general, or democratic values in general. Too many alliances on particular educational issues found their interests crossing the demarcation lines of these three elements, and therefore bonds of alliance were subject to change or realignment in different times and places. It is more useful to consider the major educational trends of the 50-year period in two overall kinds of categories and then try to identify what elements in the triform building blocks seemed to support or stand athwart the flow of change. Several aspects of modernization, of democratic political values, and of pluralism contributed to a greater *coherence* in education, whereas several other aspects of this triform stimulated *differentiation*. How these conflicting characteristics affected education is the subject discussed in the three chapters of this Part II. But first a few preliminary words are in order so that the issues debated can be clearly distinguished.

Pushes to coherence. The interplay of political democracy, modernization, and pluralism forced educators and public alike to figure out appropriate ways for education to cope with the resulting tensions. In endeavoring to do so, one general type of response was to try to give greater coherence to the entire educational enterprise; that is, to find ways to unify it, to connect the parts, and to enable it to stick together logically and consistently according to some common principle or relationship. Of all the various measures taken to achieve order and congruity, or "fit," to the nation's diverse, complex, chaotic, educational efforts, three kinds of "pushes" emerged: to build "thorough and efficient systems" of education at state and local levels of government; to standardize the curriculum, especially of the new, burgeoning secondary schools; and to make "social efficiency" the prime goal of public education. (These are the topics of Chapter 7.) In all these efforts to achieve greater coherence, a variety of motivations were at work, and all precipitated sharp differences of opinion as to just what ingredients would best bring about the desired coherence.

Pulls to differentiation. Against these pushes toward coherence were some old and some new pulls to differentiate the educational system: to diversify it to meet the different needs of different groups of children who were pouring into the schools, to loosen it up, to make it more flexible, and in general to give special attention to differences of many kinds. Again, three "pulls" to differentiate came to be most persistent and influential. Chapter 8 deals with the pull to adapt academic content and pedagogical method to "individual differences" of the learners and the pull to develop new vocational education programs adapted to the occupational destinies of different persons and groups. Chapter 9 deals with the pulls to treat different ethnic, cultural, and racial groups differently. Again, the motivations for differentiation ranged from the humanitarian and the generous to the self-seeking and self-serving. Each position had its variety of opinions about the kind of educational program that would best serve the desired differentiation—ranging from empirical, objective, and scientific psychology to racist, ethnic, or intellectual tracking.

The problem faced by public education in the Gilded and Progressive ages was the public's demands that it not only try to solve many social problems, but also that it should accomplish so many diametrically opposed social changes. Because it was pushed and pulled in so many directions, it is remarkable that it retained any identity at all as a distinctive social institution. Somehow the public school system had to reconcile the polarities in U.S. life which it had inherited from the conflict between democratic political value claims and unstable pluralisms of the past, and do it under the new and almost unbearable burdens of a rampant and aggressive modernization process.

Notes

1. For details see R. Freeman Butts, *The College Charts Its Course* (New York: McGraw-Hill, 1939; Arno reprint edition, 1971).
2. William H. Cartwright and Richard L. Watson, Jr., eds., *The Reinterpretation of American History and Culture* (Washington, D.C.: National Council for the Social Studies, 1973), pp. 380–381.
3. Paul Kleppner, *The Cross of Culture: A Social Analysis of Midwestern Politics, 1850–1900* (New York: Free Press, 1970).
4. Herbert G. Gutman, *Work, Culture, and Society in Industrializing America* (New York: Knopf, 1976).
5. Cartwright and Watson, pp. 425–426.
6. Cartwright and Watson, p. 426.
7. Cartwright and Watson, p. 439.

7 Push Toward Coherence:
Efficiency and Discipline

In the years from the end of Civil War reconstruction to the mid-1920s, modernization in general seemed to obscure the ideals of political community and pluralism in educational thought and practice. Too, the industrializing and urbanizing aspects of the modernization process under the constant drumming of laissez-faire capitalism seemed to take precedence over all other elements of social change. The growth of industry, railroads, banking, and business enterprises was phenomenal, and the shift from rural to urban centers fundamentally changed the demographic contours of the United States. In 1870, less than one-third of the U.S. population lived in urban settlements; by 1920, more than one-half did so. In 1870, the small town was the characteristic community, with approximately 25 cities over 50,000 and 14 over 100,000. Fifty years later there were 184 cities over 50,000, 68 over 100,000, and 12 over 500,000. With the growth of giant corporations and monopolies that spanned the continent and beyond, many people began to lose confidence in the abilities of discrete local communities to solve their problems of health, sanitation, housing, safety, poverty, crime, drunkenness, corruption, exploitation—*and* schooling.

Protest and Reform in the Gilded Age

In the last quarter of the nineteenth century the ever-burgeoning question was what to do about the excessively rapid and drastic changes in lifestyle brought about by mass production, mass cities, mass laboring force,

169

and mass education. "Reform" became the battle cry of all the organizations that attracted the worried, the anxious, the fearful, the angry, the resentful, the humanitarian, and the altruistic. The scapegoat selected as the cause of the time of troubles varied, of course, with the plight and perspective of the blamer. But there was a pervasive conviction among the many protest groups that great corporate monopolies and business interests were stifling opportunity for economic improvement of ordinary people, an opportunity that had been part of the American Dream for decades. And the public schools were caught up in the protest and reform movements of the period as they had been in the prior half-century. Whatever the class or social or political orientation of a particular group, it was likely to proclaim its support for some aspect of public education. This somewhat strengthened the case for public schools, but it also helped to separate their supporters and disperse their efforts and effects.

Populism

During the 1880s and 1890s the more conservative craft-labor unions, such as the American Federaltion of Labor (A.F. of L.), generally sought to accommodate themselves to the growth of industrial capitalism by accepting a working-class role in society. They thus favored more specific vocational education in the schools, but they still held to the ideal that public education was the bulwark of republican institutions. More radical groups like the Labor Reformers of the 1860s and 1870s, and especially the Knights of Labor of the 1880s, put less reliance on formal schooling, even opposing the high school as an upper-class institution; but nevertheless they favored compulsory attendance at elementary school, federal aid to education, and prohibition of child labor. After the bitter and violent strikes in the 1880s virtually destroyed the radical Knights of Labor, the A.F. of L. and the railroad brotherhoods dominated the labor movement by the turn of the century. These unions strongly supported public education but largely for the economic advantages that vocational education would give to working people.

Resentment against big business and big industry also brought a tremendous surge of protest from farmers. They, too, had their more radical and less radical wings. The National Grange, organized in 1867, strongly supported public education, echoed the claims of the common school movement, advocated compulsory attendance laws, and argued for a more vocationally oriented program of studies, including the new agricultural and mechanical colleges built with the aid of the Morrill land grant subsidies legislated by Congress in 1862.

In the 1880s a much more militant and more politically minded group appeared, the Farmers' Alliances. As with other radical groups they believed more in direct political action than in the slower methods of formal education. Their platforms endorsed regulation of railroads, banking, credit, and currency, but they also urged technical and agricultural education in the schools. Both the Grange and the Alliances fed the "agrarianism" that so frightened conservative business groups because it demanded a much more active government to promote farmers' interests and to bring corporate activity under government control through state action.

Populism became an increasingly strong political force in the early 1890s in several of the states as well as on the national scene. The conflict reached a crescendo in the national election of 1896 when conservatives rallied around the Republican McKinley to defeat populist Democrat Bryan. Despite a Sherman antitrust law or an interstate commerce commission, the growth of industrial urbanism was not to be curtailed or even slowed very much by radical political effort.

Middle-Class Liberalism

Meanwhile, middle-class spokesmen of both liberal and conservative persuasions were also greatly disturbed by the constrictive impact of industrial corporations upon U.S. economic freedom and the corrupting influences of urban politics upon government. Their claims and solutions were extremely varied and so diverse that the ins-and-outs of their reform proposals cannot be described or analyzed here.[1] Those committed to a minimal laissez-faire state did not argue for aggressive collective political action by special interest groups, but called for greater leadership by well-educated persons committed to scholarship, specialized expertise, democratic values, and independence of thought. Men like E. L. Godkin, editor of the *Nation* for 30 years, and the eminent presidents of Harvard, Charles W. Eliot and A. Lawrence Lowell, were typical proponents of this branch of liberalism. The basic determinant of their movement was a strong belief that civil service reform was necessary to replace the corrupt practices of party bosses. They believed that patronage must be replaced by a merit system so that government would be staffed predominantly by persons who had the knowledge and the character to promote democratic welfare rather than greedy self-interest. The objectives of the National Civil Service Reform League typified this approach. The whole idea was posited upon the importance of education (especially higher education) in molding the skills and talents needed for public service.

Many other points of view were trumpeted through the 1880s and 1890s. Their followers ranged from those who stressed the need for a reassertion of Christian devotion to social justice and the amelioration of poverty and inequality—like the Social Gospel of Washington Gladden or Lyman Abbott, or Utopian radicals like Henry George or Edward Bellamy who hoped for comprehensive social reform—to social evolutionists like William Graham Sumner of Yale, who based his views on Darwin and Spencer, and argued that the development of the "natural" social structure would lead to progress and human betterment if only it were free of interference by government. None of these views put primary emphasis upon public education as a major force in remedying the evils associated with modernization. Sumner did acknowledge that universal public education was a necessary exception to the desirable operation of a laissez-faire society. People must be educated, he said, so that they will realize the importance of keeping the social evolutionary process free from the harmful restrictions that might be imposed by an activist government.

Just the opposite views' came from another and more optimistic branch of the evolutionary school of thought, which was exemplified by Lester Frank Ward of the University of Chicago. Ward argued that public schools organized and supported by the state should have a central role in preparing citizens to engage in the deliberate control over social evolution for the purpose of creating a more rational, humane, and just society. Whereas Sumner had assumed that inequalities inevitably required a hierarchical social system, Ward put his faith in public education as an "equalizer":

> Universal education is the power which is destined to overthrow every species of hierarchy. It is destined to remove all artificial inequality and leave the natural inequalities to find their true level. With the artificial inequalities of caste, rank, title, blood, birth, race, color, sex, etc., will fall nearly all the oppression, abuse, prejudice, enmity and injustice that humanity is now subject to. It is true there will still be room for passion to rage, and strife to continue, but it will be between equals, it will be between individuals, it will be isolated and sporadic; not, as now, general, organized, systematic.[2]

Ward's optimistic prediction that all this *would* come about was not to be realized, but his view reflected an undercurrent of faith in public education which stemmed from the Revolutionary dream and continued into the twentieth century.

Meanwhile, the various reform-minded protests that blossomed in the 1880s and 1890s were destined to be cut off before they could come into full bloom. The conservative power centers in the cities and in industry mobilized political forces that beat back the reformers. They spoke, as the reformers did, in terms of individualism, liberty, and unity but their "individualism" meant the right of businessmen to increased profits, "liberty" meant the unrestricted rights of property, and "unity" meant the enforcement of law and order. Andrew Carnegie's *The Gospel of Wealth*, along with works by John Fiske and Sumner, set the tone of argument.

The catalogue of middle-class virtues, preached over and over in millions of copies of the McGuffey readers and Horatio Alger novels, stressed faith in equal opportunity, reward for merit and hard work, and faith in social progress under a government of limited power. A great many people in all classes of U.S. society saw enough reality in their surroundings and conditions to sustain their belief in the values of these virtues. This, combined with strenuous organized actions by conservative business leaders to put down overt signs of protest, served to quell much of the populist reform movement by 1900. Employers' associations were formed to combat farmer and labor organizations, the liberal press, and pulpit. Commerce and industry appealed to Congress for tariff protection against foreign competitors and to the courts for injunction protection against workers' strikes. They were rewarded with police and even army intervention to keep law and order in the face of such drastic occurrences as the Haymarket riot in 1886, Coxey's "army" of the poor, and the Pullman strike of 1894. And, above all, leaders of business and industry were able to organize politically around the Republican Party so effectively that in the crucial test of 1896 they were able to turn back the Democrats, who had harbored much of the populist discontent.

After 1896, populism declined, Jim Crow revived, agrarian movements were on the run, reform efforts for women's suffrage and temperance dropped in popularity, and anti-immigrant and Protestant fundamentalist movements were on the rise. The efforts of the various reform groups to achieve some sort of reconciliation among the forces of modernization, democracy, and pluralism seemed to have achieved little. Indeed, their failures seemed to enhance the dominance of industrial capitalism in the modernization process, and to breed ever more virulent strains of pluralism in the forms of racism, nativism, anti-Catholicism, and anti-Semitism. It was in this period at the turn of the twentieth century that a public sense of crisis spawned the mobilizing ideology and political movement of Progressivism. It was supported not only by activist political parties in the several states but also by a newly generated middle class. The political significance of Progressivism for public education was its emphasis on the advantages to be achieved by perfecting "thorough and efficient systems" of public schools.

The Search for Structural
Coherence in the Progressive Era

The Lure of "Thorough and Efficient" Systems of Schools

Much of the concern for "system" in schooling originated, as we have seen, in Revolutionary proposals and the common school movement of the first century of the republic, and the idea was further reinforced by the later Reconstruction goals of equality. For example, the phrase "thorough and efficient system" of education was embedded in the 1875 amendment to the Constitution of New Jersey, of which Article VIII, Section 4, paragraph 1, reads:

> The legislature shall provide for the maintenance and support of a thorough and efficient system of free public schools for the instruction of all children in the State between the ages of five and eighteen years.

Two points should be noted here.

First, a hundred years *after* this amendment was adopted, a radical transformation in the support of New Jersey public schools was initiated by a decision of the New Jersey Supreme Court in 1973 which declared the local property tax system to be unconstitutional because it violated the 1875 amendment in that it produced such unequal amounts of money throughout the various school districts. In *Robinson* v. *Cahill*, the Court said ". . . we do not doubt that an equal educational opportunity for children was precisely in mind."[3]

Second, the emphasis on thoroughness and efficiency was made long before the specific Progressive era and grew out of the concern for equality. What the Progressives faced was how to achieve equality in a population faced by the modernization, the pluralisms, and the democratic values that seemed to be working against each other.

While the new Progressive movement grappled with this problem, most states became increasingly concerned with efficiency in education. A recent compilation reveals that all but two or three states specifically mandated in their constitutions that the legislature should provide for "free," "public," or "common" schools; and at least 36 states specifically used words denoting a "system" that would be "thorough," "efficient," "uniform," "general," "complete," or "statewide."[4] Here the value claims for equality in the political community and the modernization thrust toward management of large-scale organization were working together, a link that was still more closely forged by the new middle class that proved to be the nucleus of the Progressive movement.

Progressives and the New Professionals / In its broader sense, "Progressivism" was not simply a label for a reform group within the Republican Party; it was also a term descriptive of the cooperative efforts made by like-minded spokesmen among organized labor, organized farmers, organized business, and the organizing professions. As a matter of fact, Progressivism was not confined to either major party. Above all, it was the *professionals* who were of special importance in developing the bureaucracies that eventually reshaped the direction of organized education.

There were two broad categories of professionals: those whose prime concerns rested in the service occupations, such as medicine, law, education, social work, journalism, public administration, and architecture; and those whose concerns were in the productive occupations of business, industry, labor, and agriculture.[5] Both categories recognized a common need to devise social and political structures that would better cope with the onrush of industrial urbanism and transcend the disintegration of local and isolated communities by achieving greater coherence among the diversifying parts of a modernizing social order. The professionals argued that the necessary social reform to cope with modernization could best be achieved under the guidance of experts who had acquired appropriate scientific knowledge through specialized academic training. To promote and protect this expertise, rigorous standards of admission to the profession should be required and proficiency in practice recognized by publicly authorized credentials. Thus selected and trained, the expert would then be equipped to promote both governmental efficiency and the public welfare through strong professional associations and a humane bureaucratic type of organization in government.

Thus, the new professional middle class began to formulate a new set of loyalties that would transcend local community and segmental pluralisms that had so dominated much of the nineteenth century. On behalf of reform, they played up the need for more active, affirmative, and aggressive roles by city, state, and federal governments in regulating the wide-ranging corporations; and, conversely, they played down the importance of economic and social class lines, religious and ethnic segmentation, and partisan political identification. However, they underestimated the strength of pluralistic values. Because most professionals were largely urban-oriented, they often incurred the wrath of rural folk. And since they were predominantly White Anglo-Saxon Protestants (WASPs), they incurred the resentment of the ethnic poor. Moreover, as middle-class professionals, they were scorned by the wealthy class and successful entrepreneurs.

Despite such unpopularity, the new professional middle class continued over the next two decades to work ardently for "progressive" reforms in the major institutions of U.S. life. In Wiebe's terms, this is how the progressive middle class tried to cope with modernization up to World War I:

> By contrast to the personal, informal ways of the community, the new scheme was derived from the regulative, hierarchical needs of urban-industrial life. . . . It assigned far greater power to government—in particular to a variety of flexible administrative devices—and it encouraged the centralization of authority.[6]

The mode of attack was centered in effective organization:

> A bureaucratic orientation now defined a basic part of the nation's discourse. The values of continuity and regularity, functionality and rationality, administration and management set the form of problems and outlined their alternative solutions.[7]

As members of the new urban professional class accelerated their efforts to reform various social institutions, they often turned to educators for assistance and called upon them to aid in effecting reform. Consequently, professional educators sought to cope with modernization in much the same way that professionals in other fields did.

Two Kinds of Progressives / By 1905 a fairly clear divergence was taking place among the *business-oriented progressives*, who were speaking more and more of "social control" and "social efficiency," and those *welfare-oriented progressives* who were speaking more of "social service." Professionals in education began to do likewise in the first decades of the twentieth century.

While both types of progressives believed in introducing order and efficiency into the management of social affairs and relying upon the scientific knowledge of experts, their goals and orientations were quite different. Wiebe describes the difference this way:

> One explained process through human consent and human welfare: adjust interactions according to the wishes and needs of the people involved. That spirit informed significant sections of urban reform, social work, and progressive education, and even a portion of scientific management. The second construed process in terms of economy: regulate society's movements to produce maximum returns for a minimum outlay of time and effort; to get, in other words, the most for your money. Touching almost every area, this view appealed particularly to business, labor, and agricultural organizations, and to a large majority of professional administrators.[8]

Both the business-oriented and welfare-oriented progressives believed that they must go beyond the utopian, idealistic protests of earlier reforms and reduce grand theory to manageable actions and procedures. Thus they believed in better organization—in essence, bureaucratic structure. Some welfare progressives argued and worked for streamlining government through an efficient civil service, secret ballot, direct election of senators, direct primaries, initiative, recall, and referendum (a reliance upon that part of modernization having to do with mass participation and that part of the democratic process having to do with popular consent). Others focused on the slums and child labor. Welfare-progressive educators carried over similar democratic notions into various proposals for school reform, as we shall see.

Business-Oriented Progressives in School Organization

However, a different group of professional educators, especially school administrators backed by new middle-class members of boards of education, took on the coloration of the business-oriented progressives and concentrated on streamlining school organization and administration. They adopted variations of the bureaucratic techniques that were being injected into the administration of city, state, and federal governments, business, industry, and labor. School administrators were likely to argue for "efficiency as economy"; other educators, especially philosophers, social workers, and teachers, spoke up for "efficiency as social service."

In any case, those schoolmen who adopted most vigorously the themes of "efficiency as economy" took two major roads: One was the effort to transform the jumble of school governance into genuinely "thorough and efficient systems" of organization (dealt with briefly here); the other was to reorganize the instruction of the schools along the lines of "social efficiency" (dealt with in subsequent sections of this chapter).

Fortunately, we now have available a growing body of historical scholarship giving the details of the movement toward large-scale organization, a sure sign of modernization. Much of this took place first in urban schools, especially in the larger cities, where the demands to accommodate large numbers of students required drastic changes in the usual ways of organizing and administering schools. It became readily apparent that thousands upon thousands of children could not be cared for by a "village" system of school committees consisting of elected or appointed citizens who served on a part-time basis with no remuneration. So, the development of bureaucratic organization that had begun in the middle of the nineteenth century was accelerated to a high-speed velocity in the Progressive era.[9]

Centralization of Control: Reform of the Ward System / The bureaucratic modernization of urban schools took several forms, each dependent on the particular political process that developed in different cities. But, in general, the trend was (1) to concentrate more policy decision making in a central board of education, rather than leave it dispersed among many local boards, and then (2) to delegate the power to *initiate* policy proposals for budgets, buildings, appointment of teachers, and curriculum to a professional administrator, who in turn could develop a larger and larger staff to carry out the policies. This model of administrative organization began to appear noticeably among the major cities in the latter half of the nineteenth century. It spread rapidly after 1890, and mushroomed in rural as well as urban communities between 1900 and 1920. In practically every way, it duplicated the structure being developed in almost all large-scale organizations of the day: business corporations, universities and colleges, professional associations, labor organizations, and city governments.

The early city systems of education had reflected small town and rural arrangements in which a local community elected a school board whose members ran the schools in their spare time. Their duties were to appoint teachers, select textbooks, decide where schools should be located, fix teachers' salaries, and determine how much taxes should be raised. As the city systems grew in size and cities were divided into wards for electing city officials, the wards commonly became the school board districts. When immigrant groups poured into the cities, especially from the 1880s onward, the wards became centers of ethnic concentration so that elected officials represented their ethnic constituencies. This had the merit of "keeping the schools close to the people of the local community" so that they could reflect the wishes of the people, but the danger was that the schools could easily become the special province of local political bosses. In fact, they *did* become patronage bases of ward leaders, whose wishes could determine whose daughter was appointed as teacher, or whose brother or cousin would become janitor, or who would be awarded the contract for school buildings, repair, maintenance, and supplies.

The usual arrangement from the 1850s on had been for the central boards of education of the large cities to be made up of representatives of the local wards, either elected or appointed. This meant that as the cities grew and the number of wards grew, the size of the central boards of education grew; some boards had as many as 25 to 30 members. The trend in the 1870s to 1890s was to reduce the representation by wards and to reduce board size by having their members elected at large or appointed by public officials such as mayors or judges. This centralization process, begun in the period from 1850 to 1890, was accompanied by the increase in delegation of functions to a full-time superintendent of schools, functions that had been carried out by subcommittees of the board of education itself.

The movement toward educational centralization was accelerated by sensational exposures in the press (in the Lincoln Steffens' muckraking genre of the day) of corruption and cronyism in the management of schools by local political bosses. With Jacob Riis and Joseph Mayer Rice leading the way, welfare-progressive reformers of a humanitarian bent were persuaded that the welfare of the children would be served by the "clean government" processes being proposed as other municipal and state reforms. Progressive reformers of an economy/business orientation were persuaded that the solution was to reduce the power of local political bosses by replacing the larger boards with smaller boards composed of more public-spirited citizens who would be elected at large or be appointed. Moreover, political cronyism would be eliminated by giving more power to professional administrators, who would establish a civil service type of personnel selection based on the criteria of merit and training, rather than on the kinship or personal relation criteria that evidently prevailed.

Questions about Progressive Reforms / The tendency of earlier historians of education was to laud unreservedly this movement in school governance as "progressive" in the best sense. It has been the tendency of more recent historians of education to regard this movement as a part of the imposition of social controls by an elite WASP upper class on the new working-class ethnics and to deprive them of their legitimate rights to control their own schools as they wished. Recent historians are so impressed by the rigidities, the obstacles to change, the ponderous and inhumane red tape, and the alleged racism of some contemporary school bureaucracies that they tend to blame the progressives of the early decades of this century for loosing such a monster upon the schools. (See Bibliographical Notes.) The final judgment, if there ever is to be one, will almost surely be somewhere between the older simplistic optimism and the newer simplistic pessimism in relation to bureaucracy and efficiency.

Few will deny the presence of corruption and inefficiency in the ward or local community control of schools in the big cities of the 1890s. And few will deny that the reformers came largely from the new professional middle class that spearheaded progressive reforms of many kinds at all levels of government and society. Their motives were obviously mixed—as were the motives of the ethnic-minded political bosses. But the questions about historical judgment are exceedingly difficult to answer. No simplistic amount of historical praise or blame of the Progressive era will do. Nagging questions persist. Was the loss of community control too high a price to pay for reducing corruption? Was the rise of professionalized expert management too high a price to pay for solving the problem of how to provide mass education to a whole population and for improving the quality of teaching through merit appointment and greater efficiency? Could corruption and inefficiency have been reduced without bureaucratization? Could diverse ethnic values have been brought into the process more constructively while at the same time improving the educative process? When settlement workers and teachers alike gave lessons in cleanliness and bathing to dirty immigrant children, were they simply imposing alien middle-class values on the working-class poor, or were they trying to improve the social and educational level of the impoverished prisoners of the urban ghetto?

These questions can certainly be debated, but the fact remains that the centralizing of school organization and professionalizing of school administration did sweep the country as a result of the political processes of the Progressive era. City after city and state after state made the decision to modernize their systems and make them more thorough and efficient. They claimed that only in this way could they achieve the goals of equality in the face of the crime, the corruption, the ugliness, and the poverty that accompanied industrialization and urbanization. So, they adopted and adapted that other facet of modernization which had been so important in promoting the technology behind industry—namely, science and the scientific method as applied to management.

The Spread of Business Efficiency in Schools / Some educators were indeed caught up in admiration for business management techniques of efficiency as proclaimed by Frederick W. Taylor and others around 1910. These techniques involved the careful planning that any engineering process requires, the standardization and specialization of tasks that the new industrial production lines were beginning to utilize, careful analyses of specific jobs to be done, and incentives for workers to increase their productivity. The image that a school could become as efficient as a well-run factory became a hopeful promise to hard-pressed school administrators. They listened attentively to the new breed of professors of educational administration who began to teach at the more prestigious institutions of professional education. Among these were Ellwood P. Cubberley at Stanford, George D. Strayer at Teachers College, Columbia University, Paul Hanus at Harvard, Franklin Bobbitt at Chicago, W. W. Charters at Ohio State, and Edward C. Elliott at Wisconsin.

The idea of a more activist government to achieve social reform and humanitarian welfare by means of a more effective civil service and bureaucracy was certainly a progressive ideal and offered a promising solution. But the professors of educational administration were scarcely noted for their devotion to democratic, humanitarian reform. They were likely to be conservative in politics, and they were certain to be devoted to business-oriented scientific management techniques and to the application of scientific methods to the study of educational organization and administration. It was not surprising, then, that they turned to the newly developing scientific studies of human psychology, aptitude and intelligence testing, and objective measurements of achievement in various school subjects like reading and arithmetic. These were the new techniques that could be and were used to collect masses of data about pupils and teachers, to conduct large-scale surveys of city school systems, to build record systems upon which evaluation of the quantity and quality of the educational systems could be based.

Bureaucratic Reform and the Political Process / The push toward greater coherence in the structure of educational systems was more a matter of political pulling and hauling than of a steady uniform trend, but there were common elements. In summarizing the developments in New York, Philadelphia, St. Louis, and San Francisco, Tyack has this to say:

> Running through these episodes is a common theme with some local variations. In each case, the proponents of reform were members of highly educated civic elites who believed that structural reforms were necessary to create efficient, rational, and "non-political" school bureaucracies. The opponents of centralization tended to be those who had a political or occupational stake in the system or who viewed the reformers as snobbish intruders. In New York and San Francisco, in particular, the centralizers managed to alienate a large proportion of teachers by their publicity and tactics. In all of the cities, some lower class or middle class ethnic groups such as the Irish spoke out against the "aristocratic" premises of the reformers.[10]

Though the reforms were often undertaken in the name of keeping politics out of the schools, the reformers won when they were able to master the art of politics, and they lost when their opponents did so. In *The Great School Wars*, a study of New York City schools, Diane Ravitch paints the broad canvass with vivid details, and dramatically portrays the swings of political rough-and-tumble politics. The progressive reformers were able to combat the notorious and corrupt hold of Boss Tweed and Tammany over the schools under the local ward system by setting up an independent board of education, but the struggle went on and on for the entire half-century from the 1870s to the 1920s. Ravitch summarizes:

> [In the 1890s] the public schools were once again plunged into controversy as school reformers demanded modernization, centralization, and professionalization of the system. The reformers crusaded to eliminate local lay boards and to replace them with a strong centralized bureaucracy. Centralization was initially construed as a means of reforming the schools by getting the politicians out of education and putting educational experts in charge. But, as usual, more was involved than educational reform. The reformers

were white Protestants reasserting their dominance over the city's educational system, seeking to shape the rude immigrant masses to their own image. In the pursuit of assimilation and Americanization, alien languages and cultures were disregarded, even disparaged.[11]

But Ravitch makes it clear in her study that through the ups and downs of reform efforts, the net result of the political process over the half-century was the trend toward centralization. When Tammany returned to power in New York City, and when Democrats ousted Republicans in the state, the bureaucracy was not destroyed and the cumbersome ward system was not restored. Ethnic minorities quickly learned how to move into the bureaucracy alongside the WASPs. The modernization process was moving toward coherence and was steadily permeating the structural organization of education.

The Search for Social and National Cohesion

Compulsory Attendance

Another sign of the push toward coherence to overcome purely voluntary or haphazard interest in schooling was the nationwide adoption of compulsory attendance laws. It was in this period that the political process in state after state led to something like a national *legal* consensus, though opposition of particular groups was often widespread and bitter. Here, again, the motivations for compulsory attendance were mixed. They grew primarily out of the conjunction of two major drives that coincided in the late nineteenth and early twentieth centuries. These were the drive toward Americanization and the drive to abolish child labor. First, a few words about the spread of the idea and practice of compulsory attendance.

David Tyack argues that there were two major phases in the development of compulsory school attendance laws. He designates the first period (from 1850 to 1890) as the symbolic stage, and the second (from 1890 to the 1920s and 1930s) as the bureaucratic stage.[12] Tyack speaks of the first period as the "symbolic" stage because school attendance in many of the states was already very high, even before the laws were passed, and because they were seldom very carefully enforced until after the 1890s. However, the passage of so many state laws following the Civil War and Reconstruction reflected very strong political feelings that national political cohesion should be strengthened by increasing the common bonds of political community through education, especially in the face of the cultural pluralisms represented by a vast increase of foreign population through immigration. In any case, in the 1870s, 14 states enacted laws; in the 1880s, another 10 states. By 1900, 30 states had laws; in the first decade of the 1900s, another 10 states; and by 1918 all states had some sort of compulsory attendance law. The southern states, by and large, were the later ones to do so; Mississippi was last.

The Effect of State Legislation / The laws varied considerably in their details, and up to 1890 or 1900 the enforcement ranged from lax to indifferent to nonexistent. In many cases there were not even enough schools or teachers available to take care of the children who did try to attend. In most cases the blame was attributed to the negligence of parents. The U.S. Commissioner's Annual Report for 1888–1889 was a dismal recital of lack of enforcement by state after state. Of all the county superintendents in Kansas, 70 percent reported that the state law was "inoperative, deficient, or a dead letter," largely because the people were unwilling to report to the proper authorities the instances of their neighbors' noncompliance. Especially lax was enforcement in the western plains states.

In the first quarter of the twentieth century, however, the states began to organize themselves more effectively in an effort to administer and enforce their laws. This was part of the larger administrative reform movement associated with the political Progressivism that surged throughout the country— an increasing centralization of education in state hands that paralleled the centralization movement in the cities. Elaborate techniques were instituted to enforce attendance: school census data, child accounting records, school social workers, financial aid based on average daily attendance, and the like.

In the words of Michael S. Katz:

> Between 1900 and 1930, compulsory schooling laws were transformed in many states from symbolic "dead letters" into reasonably effective statutes. . . . As a legal rule, compulsory schooling was transformed from a relatively simple statute requiring a fixed period of school attendance into a complex network of interrelated legal rules. This network of rules involved not only requiring school attendance but also hiring truant officers, defining their responsibilities, establishing and supporting truant schools, delegating jurisdictive power, and dealing with a host of child labor regulations. These child labor regulations often established school attendance as a prerequisite for younger children's employment and made employment for other categories of youth impossible during the period of their schooling.[13]

By 1920 more than 85 percent of those required to go to school were actually attending. By 1920, 31 states required attendance to age 16; one, to 17; and five, to 18. Only eight states, mostly in the South, held the compulsory age of attendance to 14.

In any case, the period from 1890 to 1930 saw a massive effort to get youth into high school, whereas in prior years the emphasis had been on elementary schooling. In Katz's terms, a monumental shift took young persons from a career of work to a career of schooling. A new high school was opened on the average of more than one a day for 30 years; enrollments increased over 800 percent while the total population increased only 68 percent; and the proportion of youth aged 14 to 17 enrolled in public high schools went from 1 percent in 1880 to 47 percent in 1930. This tremendous shift was, of course, not due solely to the enforcement of state attendance laws upon recalcitrant parents. It reflected as well a growing social and cultural consensus that more education for more children was basically good for the children, for society, and for the political community.

By the early 1920s, then, there was widespread agreement in legislation, in judicial review, and in public opinion that the state had legitimate authority to require all parents and guardians to see to it that the children under their control or supervision attended a state-approved school. This was in line with the expansion of other state commitments to protect the health, care, and welfare of poor, dependent, and delinquent children. Compulsory attendance laws reflected the primacy of the state's interest in preparing an educated citizenry as well as the primacy of the child's right to an education despite neglect or indifference on the part of some parents.

Assimilation through Americanization / A few paragraphs earlier I stated that compulsory attendance requirements were an amalgam of the drive *for* Americanization and the campaign *against* child labor. In a limited sense, the term "Americanization" might better be reserved for the period after 1900, for up to that time—as John Higham points out—there was a predominant feeling that foreign immigrants *could* be assimilated in the ordinary processes of a free society: "cohesion developed without coercion."[14] On the other hand, the 1880s and the 1890s saw a resurgence of nativism that formed a background for the Americanizing campaigns that flourished during World War I and its aftermath. The nativist revival of the 1880s coalesced around antiradical and anti-Catholic prejudices more than around antiracial discrimination. Both prejudices fed a nationalistic aggressiveness that burst forth in the nativist movements of the mid-1880s.

In this period of national xenophobia, the recruits to a whole panoply of openly patriotic organizations (and secretly anti-Catholic societies) found it easy to make the public school a patriotic symbol. They were attracted to the programs of the Grand Army of the Republic and later to the American Protective Association. They helped to provide the political support for the compulsory attendance laws that sprouted in the 1870s to the 1890s. But there was also support from those who held humanitarian and basic democratic instincts that persisted in relying on education in the common schools to bring immigrants into the democratic political community as partners. These more cosmopolitan and sympathetic views toward immigrants were dominant in the early decades of the twentieth-century Americanization movement when urban progressives, taking their cue from the settlement-house movement (see Chaps. 8 and 9), tried to achieve action on the national as well as on the state level "to promote their assimilation, education, and advancement."

However, it was not the predominant practice of the schools to try to adjust to immigrant culture; they simply tried to teach the immigrant youth the same things they taught to other students. With the return of conservatism following the decline of Progressivism in the 1920s, the coarser and cruder elements of nativist Americanization came to prevail in some quarters. It took the form of legislation during and after World War I to require English as the medium of instruction in private as well as in public schools, to out-law the teaching of foreign languages in any schools, and even to require all children to attend *public* schools rather than the private schools that were suspected of teaching alien, and thus probably subversive, doctrines. These movements will be discussed in Chapter 9.

Meanwhile, educators became more and more inclined to support compulsory attendance laws and, as usual, for a number of mixed reasons. Some advocates argued in the vein of the Revolutionary goal of education for republican citizenship, harking back to Robert Coram or to Horace Mann or to Charles Sumner. This effort of educators to create good citizens was now seen as all the more important because the diversity that the nation's founders had worried about could scarcely have been imagined to occur in such quantity or variety. Other advocates distorted the generous nationalism of the democratic political community (values of liberty, equality, and popular consent) into the narrow nativistic fears and antagonisms mentioned above. They interpreted "Americanism" as a collective expression of their own image and urged compulsory attendance legislation to make sure that the aliens gave up their undemocratic, illiberal, authoritarian habits as well as their foreign languages and customs in favor of Anglo-American majority views.

Increasing Emphasis on Nationalism

Educational cohesion was seen in achieving not only common attendance but also common civic values in the curriculum. In the 50 years straddling the turn of the twentieth century, the rhetoric of basic values characterizing the political community did not change radically, but significant adjustments of emphasis in the schools responded to the rapid social transformations occurring in the half-century of modernization. The earlier stress on love of a "grand, free country" became a more shrill and passionate devotion to a "*great* and powerful nation." The doctrines of manifest destiny, winning of the West, overseas empire, and "making the world safe for democracy" led to exaltation of the United States as *the* superior nation of the world imbued with the mission to lead all others and thus deserving—*no*, demanding—a loyalty to "my country, right or wrong."

The Spanish-American War and World War I also added a nationalistic and even militaristic fervor to civic education, but the massive immigration that characterized almost the whole period contributed an additional flavor. The influx of immigrants seemed to many conservatives and liberals alike a basic threat to the commitments of the democratic political community, to the stability of the constitutional order, and to the functioning of governing authorities. To substantiate these claims, they could point to ghettos in the cities, crime in the streets, bloody strikes in the factories, corruption in local governments, and spreading of socialist, communist, and revolutionary doctrines by radical groups.

This lurking fear of the alien and foreigner, which was almost ever present, was inflamed by the millions upon millions of immigrants who poured in from southern and eastern Europe and Asia. While civic education programs and textbooks attributed this influx to the search for liberty and equality, they also began to turn more and more to Americanization programs that not only stressed didactic praise of the historic values of the United States, but also demanded outward signs of loyalty and social cohesion. Stress upon the public pledge of allegiance, salutes to the flag, loyalty oaths, patriotic songs and marching, required instruction in English, and attacks upon foreign-language teaching in the schools now were added to the more traditional and conservative content of the textbooks.

A third shift in emphasis in the political-value commitments was the more prominent role given to the image of the self-made man, the self-reliant individual who had shifted from pioneering in the West to pioneering in the development of the industrial, urban, business system that was modernizing the United States so rapidly and thrusting the country's producing and consuming capacity ahead of all other nations of the world in such a short time. The political virtue of this image was, of course, that it had all happened under auspices of a free enterprise system self-regulated and free of government controls.

The school textbooks surely did give a coherent picture of nationalistic values, but it was a one-sided and incomplete recital. They not only portrayed a common image of what it was to be an American, but it was almost always an idealized middle-class version. Tyack admirably sums up what he calls the "conservative persuasion" of the textbooks of the era:

> In an urban and industrial society, whose agriculture was fast being mechanized and aimed at a world market, the schoolbooks painted a sentimental picture of rural bliss. In a period of great stress on the family, they drew a cloying picture of home sweet home. In times of industrial violence they ignored the condition of labor and described unions as the evil plots of foreigners, anarchists, and Communists. In the midst of unparalleled political corruption they portrayed statesmen of stainless steel. The Negro appeared infrequently in the texts, and then usually in the guise of Sambo. People of other nations often appeared as foils to illustrate the superior virtue of Americans. A pervasive Protestantism colored the readers and downgraded other religions either openly or by implication. A pluralistic, expansive society undergoing great intellectual, social, economic, and political change, was reduced in the textbooks, as Ruth Elson has observed, to a "fantasy made up by adults as a guide for their children, but inhabited by no one outside the pages of schoolbooks."[15]

Child Labor Reform

While the conservative persuasion may have painted a picture of unrelieved goodness in U.S. life, the welfare-oriented progressives knew better. Faced with the grim realities of industrial modernization, they sought quite a different road to national coherence. This was their genuinely humanitarian response to the evils of child labor. While some middle-class conservatives wanted compulsory attendance in order to impose upon immigrants their glorified ideology of what it meant to be an "American," other middle-class advocates of compulsory attendance were militantly concerned about child labor in the sweatshops of the cities and wanted to coerce reluctant owners and employers of the capitalist class to give up the cruel exploitation of children for their own selfish profit. These reformers found that they were not politically strong enough to pass laws directly prohibiting child labor, but they could circumvent this hurdle by separating employees from employers through compulsory school attendance laws. Therefore, if they could place the children in school by law, the children would obviously not be in the factories.

The campaign of the reformers reflected a whole new conception of the function of families in a modernizing United States and the legal status of children. The first six parts of Volume II of the documentary history of *Children and Youth in America*, edited by Robert H. Bremner, give an excellent account of the conditions surrounding family life, the settlement house movement, the legal status of children, care of dependent children, and juvenile delinquency, as well as child labor. The introduction to the section on child labor contains the following statement:

> In retrospect much of the history of modern American reform can be written in terms of the struggle to curb child labor. The movement held the attention of Americans from the 1880's to the 1930's.[16]

Spread of State Legislation / Though reform movements aimed at child labor in New England had begun before the Civil War, it was not until the end of the century that the movement took on a national character. This developed largely because the amount of child labor was rapidly increasing after the Civil War as a result of rapid industrialization. In 1870 about one child of every eight was at work; by 1900, it was one of six, totaling about 1,750,000 children. Of these, 60 percent were on farms and 40 percent in factories (about half of these were immigrant children). One-third of all workers in southern mills were children. The effort directed toward child labor laws before the Civil War had been largely intended to mitigate pauperism and crime by requiring some schooling for working children. But the effort after the War was aimed more directly at the welfare of the children, to protect their health and welfare and prevent their exploitation.

By 1899, 28 states had passed some sort of child labor legislation as "part of a general protest against exploitation of the working class, industrial hazards, and involuntary poverty. . . . Accounts of the 'slaughter of innocents,' 'child slavery,' and 'cannibalism' in American factories pricked the conscience of the middle class."[17] Between 1902 and 1909, 43 states passed significant legislation restricting child labor.

Organized protest movements boomed in cities and states across the nation; opposition to child labor became "an organized crusade":

> Social workers, political economists, constitutional lawyers, and disinterested industrialists came together in tightly-organized state committees supported by consumers' leagues and women's clubs. In true Progressive spirit the reformers relied on exposure to arouse the public conscience, and on the leadership of informed citizen's groups to point the way to corrective legislation and effective enforcement.[18]

Here was another example of that new professional middle class at work. In 1904 the National Child Labor Committee was formed with Felix Adler, professor of ethics at Columbia, as chairman, and such leading lights of the social settlement field as Florence Kelley, Lillian Wald, and Jane Addams as active members. Until 1914 the Committee worked for national coherence by trying to get the states to pass uniform laws containing a minimum age of 14 for work in factories and 16 for work in the mines, documentation of age, a maximum of eight hours a day, and prohibition of night work.

Failure of National Legislation / But no state achieved all these standards, enforcement was still lax, and farm labor, the street trades, domestic service, and sweatshops still escaped regulation. So, the Committee resorted to federal legislation. The Keating-Owen bill, passed by Congress in 1916, was the climax of the Progressive reform movement, but it was declared unconstitutional in 1918 as an unwarranted invasion by Congress of the rights reserved to the states. The alternative was a Constitutional amendment, but efforts to accomplish this died in the states, a casualty of the conservative and segmental pluralistic resurgence of the middle 1920s. This defeat is counted as the Progressive's worst failure in the search for national coherence.

Meanwhile, much of the drive to eliminate child labor found an outlet in the effort to establish certain mandatory educational requirements before children could be employed, or to compel continuing education while they were at work. Sometimes this included the ability to read and write English. Most often a certain grade level had to be completed before a child could be employed. By 1930, 38 states had some sort of educational requirement, 31 states required the completion of a specified school grade, and the age of compulsory attendance gradually was moving up, all of which also restricted child labor. In fact, the argument for compulsory school attendance was seen as the most effective means of enforcing child labor standards. It perhaps was best stated by Florence Kelley of Hull House in Chicago, the Henry Street Settlement in New York, and the Children's Bureau in Washington:

The best child-labor law is a compulsory education law covering forty weeks of the year and requiring consecutive attendance of all children to the age of fourteen years. It is never certain that children are not at work if they are out of school. In order to keep the children, however, it is not enough to compel attendance,—the schools must be modified and adapted to meet the needs of the recent immigrants in the North and of the poor whites in the South, affording instruction which appeals to the parents as worth having, in lieu of the wages which the children are forbidden to earn, and appeals to the children as interesting and attractive. These requirements are so insufficiently met in the great manufacturing centres of the North, that truancy is in several of them, at present, an insoluble problem. No system of child-labor legislation can be regarded as effective which does not face and deal with these facts.[19]

Once children were taken out of the factories and sent to school, the question was what to teach them. Florence Kelley's call to adapt the curriculum and teaching in the schools to the needs of immigrants went largely unheeded. The search for coherence was always more insistent among public school educators than the calls for diversity based on cultural pluralism. So impressed were most educators by the practice of *in*coherence in the curriculums that they were often preoccupied with repeated efforts to find a common rationale in the school program.

The Search for Academic Coherence

The efforts to achieve academic coherence dispersed in three different directions: mental discipline, social efficiency, and civic responsibility to democracy. Toward the end of the nineteenth century the purposes of education as well as the curriculums of the schools had become so scattered and fragmented that these three diverse programs for curriculum reform had the common objective of imposing some order, uniformity, and consistency upon the educational enterprise, although they took quite different directions to achieve this purpose. The dissonant voices of academic discipline and social efficiency created such a clamor that the political purpose to develop civic responsibility, which harked back to the Revolutionary era, was almost submerged in the tumult except when its ideals were distorted in a raucous call for "Americanization."

The Call for Mental Discipline: The Committee of Ten

One of the principal ways in which the academic profession responded to the influx of new kinds of students with a wider range of abilities or interests or aspirations was to reassert ever more emphatically the intellectual value of academic training as the prime purpose of secondary and higher education.

The landmark document linking the secondary schools and the colleges together in support of this view was the now famous report of the Committee of Ten on Secondary School Studies of the National Education Association, published in 1893. The influential "Big Three" in this enterprise were Nicholas Murray Butler of Columbia University, who was chairman of the conference that proposed the basic idea, Charles William Eliot of Harvard University, who chaired the Committee, and William T. Harris, U.S. Commissioner of Education, who drew up the ideal high school curriculum.

While admitting that the high school had become a terminal institution for most of its students, the Committee argued that four years of "strong and effective mental training" would be the best preparation for both those going on to college and those going directly into practical life. The subjects best suited for both purposes turned out to be the usual academic subjects, the traditional (Latin, Greek, and mathematics) as well as the "modern" (English, French, German, history, and the sciences).

The "reform" in this proposal was that not all students were required to take exactly the same courses. They could elect from among four curriculums or courses of study, ranging from the more traditional to the more modern, in each of which all the subjects would be prescribed. The classical course required three foreign languages (Latin, Greek, and one modern); the Latin-Scientific course required two foreign languages (one modern); the Modern Language course required two foreign languages (both modern); and the English course required only one foreign language (either ancient or modern). The student could thus be graduated from high school or admitted to college without Latin or Greek, but not without at least one foreign language. In 1899 the same general outlook dominated the report of the Committee on College Entrance Requirements, which recommended that certain "constants" be required of all college entrants: four units in foreign languages, two in mathematics, two in English, one in history, and one in science, leaving six electives.

These reports did have a standardizing effect and thus were fairly effective means of achieving coherence, albeit with relatively little regard for the impact of modernization upon the value claims of the political community or the growing pluralism of U.S. society. Perhaps this should have been expected of the Committee of Ten, since it included five college presidents, a college professor, a philosopher-turned-administrator, two headmasters of prestigious schools, and a principal of a city public high school—all in 1893. Despite all the talk about reforming curriculum to meet modern needs, the college-oriented committee and their nine appointed conferences on specific subject fields argued for the coherence of academic scholarship and mental discipline.

In their view, the secondary schools were not primarily intended to prepare for college, for only an insignificant percentage of high school graduates would go on to higher education. At the same time they believed that only a small proportion of all children would be able to profit from continuing education up to 18 years of age or would have parents who could afford to support them in school for so long a period. So, they concluded, the main purpose of secondary education was to prepare this minority "for the duties of life."

As it happened, the same subjects that best prepared for college also best prepared for the duties of life. Therefore, no distinction should be made between the "insignificant percentage" who were bound for college or a technical school and those going to neither:

> every subject which is taught at all in a secondary school should be taught in the same way and to the same extent to every pupil so long as he pursues it, no matter what the probable destination of the pupil may be, or at what point his education is to cease. . . . the allotment of time and the method of instruction in a given school should be the same year by year. Not that all the pupils should pursue every subject for the same number of years; but so long as they do pursue it, they should all be treated alike.[20]

As for those few who *do* go to college, the disciplinary object is the same:

> Every youth who entered college would have spent four years in studying a few subjects thoroughly; and, on the theory that all the subjects are to be considered equivalent in educational rank for the purposes of admission to college, it would make no difference which subjects he had chosen from the programme—he would have had four years of strong and effective mental training.[21]

It is clear why colleges would be pleased if this kind of academic coherence could be imposed on high schools and why academic teachers in high schools would feel more secure in their calling.

But the Committee of Ten was quite wrong in its assumptions about the clientele of high schools. They were soon to be overwhelmed by vast numbers of youth. Between 1890 and 1930 the secondary school enrollment leaped from 360,000 to nearly 5 million—from 7 percent of the group aged 14 to 17 years to more than 50 percent of that age group, no longer an "insignificant percentage." This meant that an increasing number of educators and the public began to array themselves against a purely academic and disciplinary emphasis in school and college.

The Call for Social Efficiency

A strong and vocal group began to demand that the secondary schools become more efficient in preparing students for the real everyday life, especially the majority that would not go on to college. Since the high school had to take care of such youth, and indeed *ought* to take care of them, the high school purposes and curriculum should embrace much more than the usual college-preparatory subjects. In 1900 the special objects of attack were not only Latin and Greek and foreign language in general, but also all academic subjects that did not directly serve some social purpose. For several decades the all-embracing popular term that was coined to counteract arguments for academic discipline was "social efficiency."[22]

The early advocates of social efficiency have not had a very good press from historians of education in recent years. This is because of their overly enthusiastic acceptance of business ideals of management efficiency and their belief that education ought to perform the function of social control on behalf of the values of the predominantly business society in a modernizing nation. Much of the intellectual framework for the theory of social control was distilled from a conjunction of free enterprise ideology and the newly developing field of sociology fathered by William Graham Sumner at Yale and E. A. Ross at Stanford. Much of the enthusiasm for applying the ideas to public education originated with David Snedden, one of Ross's students at Stanford and later a professor at Teachers College, who became Commissioner of Education in Massachusetts.

Sociologists have long argued not only that schools *do* follow the dictates of society, but that they *should* do so. By substituting the technical term "socialization" for the earlier term "social control," modern sociologists have given more sophistication to the concept, but have scarcely placed less emphasis upon the importance of individuals picking up by "manifest learning" or by "latent absorption" the dominant values of the group to which they belong.

Some of the most widely publicized examples of "efficiency as economy" were the four reports issued between 1915 and 1919 by the Committee on Economy of Time in Education, appointed by the Department of Superintendence of the National Education Association. Lawrence A. Cremin rightly points out that the Committee's "efficiency as economy" approach was actually socially conservative and not socially progressive or reformist in that

> the Committee had ended by defining the goals of education in terms of life as it was, and hence by proposing a curriculum that would accommodate youngsters to existing conditions with little emphasis upon improving them. This was hardly the progressive or Deweyan ideal, however much it was construed as such in some circles. It was utilitarian and antiformalist, to be sure, but with conservative overtones that ultimately set it apart from its sources in the earlier progressive movement.[23]

The primary purpose of education for social control, then, was not to acquire knowledge as such or simply to develop academic power; it was to prepare the individual for his role in an urban, industrializing, and capitalist society as it really existed. This often assumed that since people differ in talents, abilities, interests, and aptitudes, they should be prepared for the different social roles for which they seemed to be fitted.

These pronouncements all sounded quite logical to those educators who were not particularly enamored of the academic subjects but were aware that most of their "nonacademically" minded students would not be going to college. So, the call was for each school subject to justify itself on the basis of how directly useful it was to the daily life of students in their activities in their homes, in their jobs in factory or office or farm, in their duties as citizens, and in their leisure or recreational activities. Indeed, Franklin Bobbitt and W. W. Charters almost turned the problem around in the 1920s by *starting* with a detailed analysis of the major adult "activities of life" and then classifying those activities as the subjects of the curriculum. This was a clear adaptation to education of the "job analysis" technique of scientific management.

The social efficiency view led to arguments that students should be classified according to their presumed futures and assigned to appropriately differentiated curriculums, namely, college-preparatory, vocational, or general. *This* deduction assumed that cognitive development was *not* so important for the majority as it was for the fewer college-bound students. Elements of the social efficiency idea are found later in the ill-fated movement called "Life Adjustment," which sought in the 1940s and early 1950s to concentrate on the 60 percent of youth who were not destined to go to college (20%) or be trained in vocational schools for the skilled trades (20%). This earlier emphasis upon social efficiency also had curious similarity to the stress in the 1960s upon compiling detailed lists of specific objectives in the service of accountability, management by objectives, and competency-based teacher education.

The Call for Civic Responsibility to Democracy

There was another side to the call for social efficiency. The desire to prepare students for civic responsibility in a democratic society was quite at odds with the notion of efficiency as social control and as conformity to the predominant values of a middle-class and business-managed social order. The sociology of Albion Small and Lester Frank Ward, the philosophy of John Dewey, the "new" history of James Harvey Robinson and Charles A. Beard, all contributed to a socially progressive intellectual framework for testing the usefulness of school subjects by the extent to which they contributed to a genuinely democratic social order. This framework reflected the humanitarian or welfare progressive strain of "efficiency as social service," and, as such, it conflicted with the other major avenues to curricular coherence. It opposed "efficiency as economy" on political and social grounds, and it opposed mental discipline and academic standardization on pedagogical grounds.

These conflicting political values began to reveal themselves in various approaches to civic education in the schools, as educators responded in different ways to the ebullient modernization of the U.S. polity and economy. Despite the Committee of Ten's predictions, educators had to face the problem of what to do about the massive increases in school enrollments brought about by a growing consensus that education was a prime means to get ahead in American society, aided and abetted by compulsory attendance laws aimed at abolishing the evils of child labor and achieving the benefits of national assimilation.

Academic History as Discipline / The problems of creating cohesion in civic education were especially acute at the secondary-school level, where educators had to cope with a new and diverse noncollege-bound majority. The response of academically minded educators in the 1880s and 1890s had been to emphasize and stiffen the study of history (and thus reduce the emphasis on the study of civil government) by introducing more rigorous scholarly knowledge into the history texts and courses. In the early 1890s such proposals made by the Madison Conference on History, Civil Government, and Political Economy became a part of the overall reexamination of the entire secondary school curriculum undertaken by the Committee of Ten in 1893.

The main assumption of the Committee of Ten was, as we have seen, that all courses in high school should provide the same strong mental discipline for the noncollege-bound majority as for the college-bound minority. Thus, the primary objective in teaching history was not to develop good citizenship or patriotism, but to teach high school students to think like historians. For two to three decades the academic orientation of the Committee of Ten dominated curriculum thinking and curriculum making in the civic education programs of the secondary schools, as it did in other subject fields. In history the emphasis was upon the use of primary sources to develop in pupils a historic sense and to train them in the search for historical materials, the weighing of evidence, and the drawing of conclusions. In the effort to get children to think like historians, it was hoped that the flamboyant nationalistic and patriotic history of the preceding century would be modified. In 1899 a Committee of Seven of the American Historical Association urged the use of primary sources as supplementary to textbooks. Both the *History Teachers Magazine* (founded in 1909) and the work of Henry Johnson at Teachers College, Columbia University, contributed to the new movement that stressed historical problem solving and reasoned judgment in a laboratory or workshop setting.

Meanwhile, the study of civil government had an upsurge in the early 1900s as new ideas about civic education began to appear among progressives in political science, economics, and sociology. In 1916 a committee of the American Political Science Association, reflecting the Progressive reform movements of the day, argued that standard courses in civil government should be reorganized. Instead of starting with the study of the U.S. Constitution or a description of the formal and structural organization of government, and then proceeding to a similar study of state constitutions and governments, the procedure should be reversed. The committee endorsed the study of "community civics," assuming that political affairs nearest to home were the most important and should be considered first. The progressively-inspired Municipal League promoted this idea.

The Seven Cardinal Principles / In the long run, however, the rising movement to make citizenship education the special province of the "social studies" was probably more influential, for it came to pervade the elementary as well as the secondary school. This movement took place under the auspices of the NEA's Commission on the Reorganization of Secondary Education, whose final report, *Cardinal Principles of Secondary Education*, was published in 1918.

First let us review what the seven cardinal principles stated. Their succinctness has made them a reference point for over a half century: health, command of fundamental processes, worthy home membership, vocation, citizenship, worthy use of leisure, and ethical character. They have been repeated until they are trite, and they have been derided for a tone of middle-class puritanism connoted by the repetition of the word "worthy" and the didactic redundance of "ethical" and "character."

But take away the out-of-style adjectives, and we are still talking about them today, for all of our more sophisticated terminology. Health, vocation, citizenship, and leisure are still perfectly good words and are very much in the forefront of educational discussion. Substitute "cognitive skills" for "fundamental processes," "family influence" for "home membership," and the "teaching of values" for "ethical character," and *they*, too, are very much with us.

What the seven *Cardinal Principles* did was to shift the emphasis in schooling away from preoccupation with the academic and intellectual disciplines and to broaden the social role of education almost beyond recognition. The "constants" were now to be thought of in terms of the common social needs and activities required of all individuals, rather than subject matters to be mastered. Variation and differentiation appropriate to differing individuals could be served in connection with vocation and leisure, but the goals of cohesion should be achieved by common studies having to do with health, family, knowledge-acquiring skills, and democratic citizenship.

Citizenship the Task of Social Studies / From 1912 to 1916 a subcommittee on social studies was at work preparing its report for the overall Commission. James Harvey Robinson of Columbia was a member of this committee, which was dominated by high school teachers and administrators. Again reflecting the Progressive views of reform, the committee brought citizenship explicitly to the forefront as a social responsibility of the secondary school. In a preliminary statement in 1913, Thomas Jesse Jones, the chairman of the committee and formerly a teacher at Hampton Institute, revealed the social-reform intent to make civics much more than a study of government:

> Good citizenship should be the aim of social studies in the high school. While the administration and instruction throughout the school should contribute to the social welfare of the community, it is maintained that social studies have direct responsibility in this field. Facts, conditions, theories, and

activities that do not contribute rather directly to the appreciation of methods of human betterment have no claim. Under the test the old civics, almost exclusively a study of Government machinery, must give way to the new civics, a study of all manner of social efforts to improve mankind. It is not so important that the pupil know how the President is elected as that he shall understand the duties of the health officer in his community. The time formerly spent in the effort to understand the process of passing a law over the President's veto is now to be more profitably used in the observation of the vocational resources of the community. In line with this emphasis the committee recommends that social studies in the high school shall include such topics as the following: Community health, housing and homes, public recreation, good roads, community education, poverty, and the care of the poor, crime and reform, family income, savings banks and life insurance, human rights versus property rights, impulsive action of mobs, the selfish conservatism of tradition, and public utilities.[24]

Broadening the Concept of Social Studies / In the final report of the committee, the term "social studies" was used to include not only history, civics, and government, but also those concepts of sociology and economics that related directly to the organization of society and man as a member of social groups. History still held a major place in the course proposals for grades 7 to 12, but a "problem approach" was to infuse the whole program. Civics was proposed for the junior high school years as well as a new course in "problems of democracy" for the twelfth grade. While the commission's final report in 1918 helped make citizenship one of the cardinal goals of secondary education, especially of the social studies, and while it tended to reduce emphasis upon abstract academic material in favor of live problems, it also tended to reduce the *political* concerns of civic education in favor of social, economic, and practical personal problems. Note the withdrawal from "constitutional questions" in the pursuit of good citizenship:

> Too frequently, however, does mere information, conventional in value and remote in its bearing, make up the content of the social studies. History should so treat the growth of institutions that their present value may be appreciated. Geography should show the interdependence of men while it shows their common dependence on nature. Civics should concern itself less with constitutional questions and remote governmental functions and should direct attention to social agencies close at hand and to the informal activities of daily life that regard and seek the common good. Such agencies as child welfare organizations and consumers' leagues afford specific opportunities for the expression of civic qualities by the older pupils.[25]

Even the skills of civic participation began to be touched upon as social studies teachers were urged to adopt the new stress of progressive education on projects, units, and activities in the classroom in order to promote the habits and outlooks appropriate to a democracy. The *Cardinal Principles* found valuable

> the assignment of projects and problems to groups of pupils for cooperative solution and the socialized recitation whereby the class as a whole develops

a sense of collective responsibility. Both of these devices give training in collective thinking. Moreover, the democratic organization and administration of the school itself, as well as the cooperative relations of pupil and teacher, pupil and pupil, and teacher and teacher, are indispensable.[26]

While this approval of the study of problems and "socialized recitation" in the classrooms may seem to be a modest proposal to modern teachers, it by no means swept the profession off its feet. Teaching by the book, lecturing, note taking, questions and answers, recitation, memorizing, essay writing, and examination passing continued to be the prime methods used in history and civics classrooms. And venturing out into the community was still more radical, especially if a zealous civics teacher actually ran up against the local politicians. In this case, however, the study of "remote governmental functions" could actually be conducted more freely and would avoid treading on local political toes. At least the *idea* of participation could now take its place alongside the inculcation of values and political knowledge as the main ingredients of a civic program in the schools. And the way was being prepared for teachers to distinguish and compare the stated values of the political community with the actual performance of governmental authorities. The stress on critical thinking, scholarly sources of knowledge, and first-hand study of the actual functioning of government, at least at the municipal level of community civics, laid the foundation for a more realistic study of the political process.

No Simple Solution / Above all, it was recognized that the high schools had to deal with a very different kind of population from that of the secondary schools of the first hundred years of the Republic, that is, the noncollege-oriented students. Assimilation of vast numbers of foreign immigrants, both youthful and adult, nearly engulfed the schools and exhausted their energies. Teaching English and the rudimentary structure of government were the easiest ways to cope with the demands. For all the protestations of the Progressives, the national committees, and the teachers of teachers, the courses in U.S. history, civics, and civil government—which might be engrossing to adult immigrants—did not appeal to millions of high school students who were not college-bound. They were often bored by the repetitive cycles of social studies, second only to English and physical education in total time allotments of the usual curriculum: "communities" in the third and fourth grades, civics in the ninth and twelfth grades, American history in the fifth, eighth, and eleventh grades, with geography, state history, and European or world history sandwiched in, probably in the seventh and tenth grades.

Regardless of the efforts to achieve curricular coherence as a means to realize greater political and social cohesion, the outcome was often disappointing to educators and public alike. Further disagreement arose from conflicts among adherents devoted to academic discipline, to social "efficiency as economy," and to social responsibility in a democratic society. And all these approaches were likely to be suspect by those who favored the rising demands for differentiating the school program according to the needs of different individuals. This tension between the goal of social efficiency (whether for social control or for democratic responsibility) and the call for individual development continued to agitate educators and the public throughout the twentieth century. Indicative of the complex nature of the problem was the fact that John Dewey could be arrayed on both sides of the dilemma. On behalf of civic education for social responsibility, Dewey could say:

> Our famous, brief definition of democracy, as "government of the people, for the people, and by the people," gives perhaps the best clew to what is involved in a democratic society. Responsibility for the conduct of society and government rests on every member of society. Therefore, every one must receive a training that will enable him to meet his responsibility, giving him just ideas of the condition and needs of the people collectively, and developing those qualities which will insure his doing a fair share of the work of the government.[27]

While this statement reflected the value claims of the democratic political community, other statements by Dewey, as we shall see in the next chapter, were applauded by the child-centered wing of twentieth-century progressive education. Thus he became a kind of patron saint appealed to on behalf of individual differentiation as well as democratic community.

Notes

1. For details see especially Rush Welter, *Popular Education and Democratic Thought in America* (New York: Columbia University Press, 1962), pp. 141–244; and Robert H. Wiebe, *The Search for Order, 1877–1920* (New York: Hill and Wang, 1967), pp. 1–110.
2. Quoted in Clarence J. Karier, ed., *Shaping the Educational State, 1900 to the Present* (New York: Free Press, 1975), p. 146.
3. *Robinson* v. *Cahill*, 62 N.J. 473, 303 A 2d. 273 (1973).
4. U.S. Department of Health, Education and Welfare, Office of Education, *State Constitutional Provisions and Selected Legal Materials Relating to Public School Finance* (Washington, D.C.: Government Printing Office, 1973), p. 6.
5. Wiebe, *Search for Order*, Chap. 5.
6. Wiebe, p. xiv.
7. Wiebe, p. 295.
8. Wiebe, pp. 154–155.
9. The general development in the cities has been described in a number of recent studies. See the Bibliographical Notes for Chapter 7.
10. David B. Tyack, *The One Best System: A History of American Urban Education* (Cambridge, Mass.: Harvard University Press, 1974), p. 148.
11. Diane Ravitch, *The Great School Wars, New York City, 1805–1915:*

A History of the Public Schools as Battlefield of Social Change (New York: Basic Books, 1974), p. xiv.

12. David B. Tyack, "Ways of Seeing: An Essay on the History of Compulsory Schooling." Unpublished manuscript, 1976.
13. Michael S. Katz, *A History of Compulsory Education Laws* (Bloomington, Ind.: Phi Delta Kappa, 1976), p. 21, a "fastback" monograph No. 75.
14. John Higham, *Strangers in the Land: Patterns of American Nativism, 1860–1925* (New York: Atheneum, 1974), p. 235.
15. David B. Tyack, ed., *Turning Points in American Educational History* (Waltham, Mass.: Blaisdell, 1967), p. 184. For sample quotations from texts see also Ruth Miller Elson, *Guardians of Tradition: American Schoolbooks in the Nineteenth Century* (Lincoln: University of Nebraska Press, 1964).
16. Robert H. Bremner, ed., *Children and Youth in America: A Documentary History* (New York: Random House, 1974), p. 601.
17. Bremner, pp. 601–602.
18. Bremner, p. 601.
19. Bremner, p. 670.
20. Report of Committee of Ten, quoted in Alexander S. Rippa, ed., *Educational Ideas in America: A Documentary History* (New York: McKay, 1969), p. 466.
21. Rippa, p. 470.
22. For the details of "social efficiency" as an academic movement, see Edward A. Krug, *The Shaping of the American High School* (New York: Harper & Row, 1964).
23. Lawrence A. Cremin, *The Transformation of the School: Progressivism in American Education, 1876–1957* (New York: Knopf, 1961), p. 196.
24. Thomas Jesse Jones, quoted in Daniel Calhoun, ed., *The Educating of Americans: A Documentary History* (Boston: Houghton Mifflin, 1969), p. 495.
25. National Education Association, Commission on the Reorganization of Secondary Education, *Cardinal Principles of Secondary Education,* U.S. Bureau of Education Bulletin No. 35 (Washington, D.C.: Government Printing Office, 1918), p. 14.
26. NEA, p. 14.
27. John and Evelyn Dewey, *Schools of Tomorrow* (New York: Dutton, 1919), p. 303.

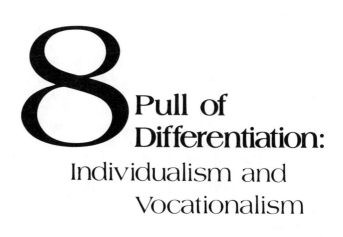

8 Pull of Differentiation:
Individualism and Vocationalism

The beginning of Chapter 7 suggested the generalization that the Gilded and Progressive eras should be interpreted in the light of various attempts made by public groups and educators to cope with the forces of modernization on one side and the forces of pluralism on the other side while trying to preserve, at least in name, the democratic values of the overall political community. It was concluded that, by and large, the winning contender was modernization, and that education pushed, or *was* pushed, toward greater coherence in organization and curriculum as a result of the interplay of modernization, pluralism, and democratic community. While the generalization holds for this period in U.S. history, the pulls toward differentiation began to accelerate and, as a result of tremendous tugs generated by a bewildering diversity of segmented pluralisms, gained strength through most of the middle decades of the twentieth century.

Many kinds of centrifugal pulls were exerted on the schools to try to get them to pay special attention to the enormously different kinds of clientele who were flooding into public educational institutions. Of these, three became the most persistent, complicated, and often contradictory. First, there was the growing refrain to pay attention to individual differences, to focus upon the unique characteristics of children, their stages of development, and the differences among them. This led to a child-centered pedagogy or learner-oriented curriculums whose prime goals were to break out of the crust of academic uniformity imposed by the disciplines of knowledge or by social efficiency, and to promote the self-fulfillment of individuals.

There was, secondly, the rising demand for schools to break out of the academic lockstep in order to face the dual economic realities of a modern industrial society that needed skilled and trained workers and the needs of vast numbers of persons who were ill equipped to earn their living in a modern society unless especially trained to do so. Thus, a second call for differentiation was for vocational training adapted to the different occupations that students might enter, and in which they could earn a livelihood. This plea for differential programs of study in the schools appealed not only to the industrial and business employers who would profit from better trained workers; it also appealed to masses of migrants who poured into the cities from the rural and agricultural regions of the United States as well as from foreign countries. Vocational education was seen as vitally necessary to personal welfare as well as to social welfare.

Third, there was the constant urging by the diverse pluralisms to provide them with educational programs that would keep alive their group differences, whether based upon ethnicity, language, race, religion, sex, or locality. This set of pluralistic pulls (to be dealt with in Chapter 9) is probably more complicated and more difficult to sort out than any other because there were not only differences within groups but also conflicts among them. Some ethnic groups were more determined to preserve their distinctive cultures, while others were more ready to assimilate; within groups there were differences among older and younger generations, between middle and working classes. Some religious groups were more determined than others to hold on to their religious schools and therefore opposed public schools or secular schools of any kind. Blacks responded differently from Indians, and some black leaders were more intent on gaining an industrial type of vocational education, even if it meant an inferior opportunity for higher education. And women were divided as to their need or desire to have available to them a differentiated woman's education or to compete in a man's world with a man's education. Then there were the regional and local differences, which continued to play an enormous role in the kind and degree of educational opportunity provided for their citizens, whether on a coherent or differentiated basis, whether integrated or segregated, whether academic or vocational.

Just as there were mixed motivations and mixed advantages in the pushes toward coherence and unity, so were there mixed motivations and advantages in the various pulls for differentiation. Innovations made for the best of reasons sometimes had a way of working to the disadvantage of some individuals and groups as well as of the democratic community itself. Greater attention to individual differences in ability or vocational destiny might serve to loosen up the academic lockstep and make school more lively and vital, but if it was based upon assumptions about the inevitable inequality and inferiority of some groups compared with others, the doctrine of individual differences could become a shackle for some while it was an invitation to self-fulfillment for others. Similarly, the freedom of ethnic or religious or racial groups to preserve their distinctive cultural heritages in isolation from the dominant trends in society might enhance the traditional loyalties of an older generation, but it might deprive the younger generation of the opportunity to participate in the larger community upon which the welfare of all so much depended.

The Call for Individual Differentiation

Around the turn of the twentieth century a growing chorus of voices complained about the uniformity, rigidity, and irrelevance of the teaching in the elementary schools of that day. Joseph Mayer Rice's muckraking articles for the *Forum* in the early 1890s set the fashion for public criticism of the public schools. After Rice had visited schools for six months in 36 cities, he lambasted most classroom teachers for their deadly dull methods that brought about miserable results. He attributed much of the fault to the political appointment of unqualified teachers by party bosses, and to poor training and supervision of those who pretended professional qualifications. Cremin sums up the subjects of Rice's findings as "political hacks hiring untrained teachers who blindly led their innocent charges in singsong drill, rote repetition, and meaningless verbiage."[1] The remedy was, of course, to release the child from oppressive teachers and inject interesting, enlivening options to encourage the active development of the individual child.

Two decades later it was the turn of secondary schools to undergo similar public criticism—incidentally just two decades after the Committee of Ten had thought it had imposed some coherence upon the chaos of the high school curriculum. Not only did publicists like Randolph Bourne protest the formality and the uniformity of the classrooms; leading educators also had long been exhorting teachers to free the child and promote his individual development.

Learner-Oriented Progressive Theory

In 1902 John Dewey himself noted that 50 years of educational theory, from Horace Mann in the 1830s and 1840s to the 1880s and 1890s, had been "on the side of progress, of what is known as reform." Who could better sum up the essence of learner-oriented pedagogy than Dewey did in 1902 in his *The Educational Situation*?

> The supremacy of self-activity, the symmetrical development of all the powers, the priority of character to information, the necessity of putting the real before the symbol, the concrete before the abstract, the necessity of following the order of nature and not the order of human convention—all these ideas, at the outset so revolutionary, have filtered into the pedagogic consciousness and become the commonplace of pedagogic writing and of the gatherings where teachers meet for inspiration and admonition.[2]

Cannily, Dewey remarked that while the reformer had won the field of theory, the conservative still held the classroom field of practice. Despite the injection of "object teaching" into the normal schools, patterned after the model of Edward Sheldon's at Oswego, New York, or of Francis Parker's in Cook County, Illinois, Dewey observed that most teachers taught by the book, not by the "objects" of nature or of human contrivance:

> The conservative was still there. He was there not only as a teacher in the schoolroom, but he was there in the board of education; he was there because he was still in the heart and mind of the parent; because he still possessed and controlled the intellectual and moral standards and expectations of the community. We began to learn that an educational reform is but one phase of a general social modification.[3]

Colonel Francis Parker / The interrelation of social reform and educational reform was one of the most important tenets of progressive educational doctrine. Even so, it was a principle that many "child-centered" progressive educators overlooked. They could look back to the "New Departure" in the schools of Quincy, Massachusetts, under the stimulation of Colonel Francis W. Parker as superintendent between 1875 and 1880, and over and over again find sustenance for their belief that the prime objective of schooling was development of the individual. As he wrote in 1882 in his "Notes of Talks on Teaching," Parker put stress on the "teaching of things, and not words alone," but he also put constant stress on the active child's spontaneity, joy, and happiness in learning:

> One great reason why we continue unnatural teaching [in the primary school], may be found in the fact, that the strongest tendencies and impulses of beautiful child-nature are utterly ignored. Every child loves nature: the birds, flowers, and beasts are a source of exhaustless curiosity and wonder. Carry this love into the school-room, bring the child closer and closer to the thought of God and His creatures, and that implanted desire to know more and more of His works, will never cease. . . . The child has a strong desire to express his thoughts in the concrete, by recreating the forms that come into his mind. He makes mud-pies, hills and valleys, fences, and houses, with childish glee. Carry this same impelling tendency into the school-room; lay the foundation of the grand science of geometry, by moulding in clay. Next to the child's love for making forms, comes the joy he finds in drawing; a child loves to draw, as well as if not better, than he loves to talk. Continue this love, by putting crayon or pencil in his hand as soon as he enters school, and give him free room to express all he can.[4]

By 1891 Parker also talked about the public school as "a tremendous force for the upbuilding of democracy" in which children of all classes, nationalities, sects, rich and poor alike, boys and girls alike, could be taught together from kindergarten to university. He criticized the indifference of the "most intelligent people" toward the public schools as well as that of the "pot-house politicians" and "spoilmongers" who thought of the schools only as sources of their patronage:

The common school can be made the best school, in every respect, in the world. . . . A school should be a model home, a complete community and embryonic democracy. How? you ask. Again I answer, by putting into every schoolroom an educated, cultured, trained, devoted, child-loving teacher, a teacher imbued with a knowledge of the science of education, and a zealous, enthusiastic applicant of its principles.[5]

Where could the schools find such teachers? Naturally, Parker looked toward the Cook County Normal School, where he became head in 1883, and toward the University of Chicago, where John Dewey began his work in education.

John Dewey / Although Parker had pioneered the movement, it was John Dewey who became the leading light of the child-centered progressives as well as of the social reform progressives. Dewey wrote so much and so cogently in the decade between his founding of the experimental school at the University of Chicago in 1896 and the publication of his fully developed philosophy of education in *Democracy and Education* (1916) that he could easily be quoted on both sides of the relationship between the individual and society. In his early descriptions of the curriculum of his university school, Dewey did not sound so radical. To be sure, he would require manual training of all (boys and girls alike took courses in cooking, sewing, and carpentry), and that was radical enough, but his other two main studies were more traditional: history and literature were to be started at a very early period to give the child insight into social life, and science was to arouse the child's spirit of curiosity and investigation, train the powers of observation, and instill a practical sense of methods of inquiry. What *was* radical was that the formal subjects of reading, writing, spelling, and numbers, and the technical side of history and geography were to be regarded as instruments or tools, not as isolated things in themselves. All this was scarcely radically child-centered, but when Dewey began to speak more theoretically and forcefully *against* traditional education, he began to sound more child-centered, as he did in one of his lectures on *The School and Society* in 1889.

In a climate of progressive reform on behalf of the child in the early decades of the century it was fairly easy for enthusiasts to pick out and emphasize such statements as Dewey's admittedly exaggerated contrast between traditional education and the new education:

Now the change which is coming into our education is the shifting of the center of gravity. It is a change, a revolution, not unlike that introduced by Copernicus when the astronomical center shifted from the earth to the sun. In this case the child becomes the sun about which the appliances of education revolve; he is the center about which they are organized. . . . In this [ideal] school the life of the child becomes the all-controlling aim. All the media necessary to further the growth of the child center there. Learning?— certainly, but living primarily, and learning through and in relation to this living.[6]

What was sometimes not recognized—then or now—is that Dewey's main contribution to educational thought and practice was to insist that individuality was developed only in a "congenial" (and he meant democratic) social environment. But as the attack on formal subjects grew and as the specialties of child study and educational psychology gained greater attention, it became harder and harder for the educational practitioner to keep the individual and society in finely attuned balance. The extremists on social efficiency or academic discipline somehow lost the individual; and extremists on the individual somehow lost the society.

Conservative Influence of Educational Psychologists

It is true that the early calls for greater individual development were couched in terms that applied to the younger child and to the elementary school more than they did to the secondary school or college. But, nevertheless, the child study movement often associated with G. Stanley Hall did move into the field of adolescence, and the psychological testing movement led by Lewis M. Terman of Stanford, Edward L. Thorndike of Teachers College, and Frank N. Freeman of Chicago soon embraced youth and adults as well as children.

In the early decades of the century the idea of individual differences, closely linked with the idea of individual development, received strong support in educational theory and practice from the psychological testing community, the child development psychologists, and the guidance counseling movement as well as from progressive critics of the goals of academic discipline and social efficiency. This was the avant-garde thinking of the day. Recent historical revisionism, however, has begun to question whether the end result of the psychological and testing movements was really to release the child for individual development or whether in reality the testing led to predicting, sorting, and tracking of students according to social class or racial grouping.

Middle-Class Bias / Clarence Karier finds nativism, racism, elitism, and social-class bias in the underlying assumptions of many testers, who then claimed that their test results proved the inferiority of non-whites and of immigrants in the society of their day, and in general showed a strong correlation between social class and native intelligence.[7] Testers seemed to assume that if there were differences among individuals, there must be inequality. If one purpose of schooling was to help each individual make the most of his abilities and interests, another purpose must be to help the less able child adjust to the realities of inequality.

There is, however, a different explanation of the reasons why some of the early educational psychologists (particularly E. L. Thorndike) were more conservative than progressive. When Robert Church faced the question as to why educational psychology, after Dewey's and Hall's early psychological studies, rejected the social reform elements that characterized the "new education" prior to 1905, he came up with a different answer. Church studied the publications of the *Journal of Educational Psychology* from 1905 to 1920 and found very little concern with education's social role at a time when progressive social reform dominated the political and intellectual atmosphere. He concluded that this avoidance must have been deliberate and not simply a matter of indifference.

Church also found that most psychologists publishing in the *Journal* did not question the basic academic purpose of schooling, and thus concentrated on techniques of better teaching of the academic subjects. Their stress on individual mental differences encouraged schoolmen "to demand that schools repudiate their customary formalism in order to serve different children in different ways." In contrast, the progressive social reformers believed that the very purposes and content of the school should be broadened in order to enable different children to cope more fully with a changing society. The experimental educational psychologists had little hope that human nature or society was malleable enough to warrant such optimism.

Striving for Academic Respectability / While psychologists like Thorndike may have been economically and politically conservative in their social backgrounds, Church believes there were underlying professional and academic reasons why the influential psychologists eschewed a social reform role for education. He finds much of the reason in the marginal position that educational psychology held in relation to "pure psychology." Put it this way: Psychologists were trying hard in the early years of the twentieth century to make their subject as much a science as physics. Thus, pure psychology must be as rigorous, experimental, objective, and as "hard" as physics. Therefore, as Wilhelm Wundt argued, it must not appear to be "applied." So, if *educational* psychology was to avoid the contempt of the purists, it must be as rigorous as scientific psychology itself and must not appear to be too practical or too applicable to classroom practice.

Although Thorndike and his followers did turn to practical classroom problems, as was appropriate for psychologists at Teachers College, I myself saw at first hand for many years the urge of Teachers College professors to display their expertise as pure scientists so that they would not be regarded as inferior in scholarship to their Columbia University counterparts. Though many were subjected to the contempt of the Columbia graduate faculties, Thorndike clearly was highly regarded in the field of psychology, probably higher than most of his Columbia colleagues. This push to make the field of educational psychology academically respectable in imitation of pure psychology surely did divert psychologists from the social reform movements of the day and prompted them to divorce themselves from "amateurs" in educational thought who were less rigorous in their methods and possibly more popular in their appeal. Strong reliance upon statistics and quantitative methods, suspicion of "social psychology" in contrast to "experimental psychology," a stimulus-response conception of learning as conditioning that stressed the passive role of the student, all tended to build a gap between psychology and the progressive vision of the school as social service.

The Ambiguity of "Progressive" in Progressive Education

Thus, educational psychology broke away from its social reform impetus to be found in William James and Dewey, and became profoundly conservative in its acceptance of the social order and its search for "norms" that describe *what was* rather than *what should be*. And, as some of the anthropological and sociological scientists of the day assumed a hierarchy of races and proclaimed the inferiority of the colored races, so did their assumptions concerning race carry over to some educational psychologists. These latter had a strong influence on the pull to individual development based upon study of individual differences, but they departed sharply from those aspects of progressive education considered to be a part of social service, social welfare, and social reform. In the view of reform-minded progressive educators, the experimental educational psychologists and their testing programs had the potential for a profoundly conservative impact upon U.S. education. Accepted uncritically by guidance counselors, administrators, and teachers, the aptitude and achievement tests did serve to channel students with the greatest social disadvantages into programs that demanded less academic achievement. How this circular tracking dilemma could be resolved provided a continuing bone of educational contention. To lump conservative-minded psychologists in the category of "the liberal progressive tradition" does little to enlighten or resolve the question.

Sometimes Social Reform / The reform impulse in the "new education" that grew out of the social progressivism of the 1890s and early 1900s was diluted and diminished in still another way—a curious reversal of meaning that has plagued American education ever since. To Dewey, the "new education" was always an interactive process between individual and society, a democratic society was the only one in which individual self-fulfillment could be achieved, and the school had the responsibility to prepare individuals for participation in and through social situations. Aiding individuals to develop their full potential was a means to social as well as individual development. Therefore, the reform of the school was a necessary ingredient of *social* reform.

The social settlement movement shared to a large degree this genuine outlook of Progressivism in the 1900s. Kindergartens were adopted by the reformers to help the slum poor improve their sense of cooperation, observation, and active participation through all the enriched materials and activities that characterized the movement. And they even provided nourishing meals and hygienic attention as well as play. For a couple of decades the linkage between social reform and settlement houses, kindergartens, and public schools was very close.

Following World War I, however, the reform progressivism withered in politics, in economics, and in education. Yet the term, "progressive," was picked up and promoted by a new group of well-to-do school "reformers" whose prime concern was individual development divorced from social reform. "Progressive education" moved from the urban public schools dealing largely with working-class children into private schools and affluent suburban public schools. Patricia Albjerg Graham admirably sums up the shift:

> Prewar educational progressivism was a movement essentially continuous with the social and political progressivism that flourished in the last quarter of the nineteenth century. It had for a major object the expansion of public school facilities and curriculum offerings with a view to accommodating the children of the working class, removing obstacles from their path of entry into full participation in American life. Postwar progressive education bloomed in private schools and, . . . its reforms from first to last appealed primarily to the middle and upper middle class.[8]

Graham's analysis reminds us that the term "progressive education" is a tricky one. It has been used for nearly a hundred years in all sorts of ways, as glowing panacea by some and as the depths of chaotic degradation by others. At this point the important thing is to recognize that its meaning changed over time and in different hands. If the term is to be used carefully in historical discourse, both time and basic orientation should be made clear. One step toward accuracy (but an awkward one, to be sure) would be always to distinguish between "child-centered progressive education" and "social reform progressive education." Even this does not always help to explain John Dewey's position. Indeed, if it were not that he was appealed to so often by both orientations, the confusion would be reduced. Better still, it would have been easier if the same term had not been applied to and adopted by both sides, but untidiness has always been a characteristic of education in this country.

More Often Child-Centered / In any case, the promoters of individual development as a prime goal, if not *the* prime goal, of education in the period after World War I were the well-to-do ladies and gentlemen who started private progressive schools in Cambridge, Massachusetts; Greenwich Village, New York; Baltimore; Philadelphia; Dayton, Ohio; and Chevy Chase, Maryland. A few affluent suburban centers like Winnetka, Illinois, public schools also were attracted to the child-centered approach. Stimulated by the momentum from the child-study movement personified by Arnold Gesell at Yale, the new child-centered progressives resonated to such dicta about the primary school child as these:

> Order, system, detail, and prescription have replaced spontaneity,

grace, initiative, and investigation. The spirit of childhood languishes, and in its place stalk the stern figures of propriety and formalism. . . .

It is the boast of schools that everything goes like clockwork. Such formalistic uniformity and concerted action are foreign to the grace, spontaneity, and individuality of childhood. Children who grow up under such systematized direction are denied the very essence of mental growth, which depends upon original, constructive effort. . . . Nature endowed the six-year-old with an impulse to investigate, pry into, and discover. Some primary schools are veritable tombs of deadened curiosity and initiative. . . . Too much formalism in childhood kills spontaneity and interest.[9]

Such eloquent appeals to the natural laws of child development in 1912 echoed the words of Francis Parker, spoken 30 years earlier, but now they were reinforced by the science of child psychology and empirical observations in Yale's Clinic for Child Development. The slums, the foreign immigrants, the poverty, the crime, the grime of the city streets and public schools seemed far removed from the "spontaneity," "grace," "instinctive impulses," "creativity," "eagerness," and "initiative" of Gesell's six-year-olds. And the country day schools, the city private schools, and the public schools of the affluent suburbs were included in this pristine world.

The Progressive Education Association / No wonder that when the Progressive Education Association was organized in 1919, its guiding principles smacked little of social reform but concentrated almost all its purposes on individual development. The organizers formulated their guiding principles in these terms:

> The aim of Progressive Education is the freest and fullest development of the individual, based upon the scientific study of his mental, physical, spiritual, and social characteristics and needs. . . .
> 1. Freedom to Develop Naturally. . . .
> 2. Interest the Motive of All Work. . . .
> 3. The Teacher a Guide, Not a Task-Master. . . .
> 4. Scientific Study of Pupil Development. . . .
> 5. Greater Attention to All That Affects the Child's Physical Development. . . .
> 6. Co-operation Between School and Home to Meet the Needs of Child-Life. . . .
> 7. The Progressive School a Leader in Educational Movements. . . .[10]

These principles, published continuously in the association's magazine *Progressive Education* after it began in 1924, became the epitome of the call for individual development. They were taught in hundreds of classrooms in schools of education, from Teachers College and Harvard in the East to Chicago and Ohio State in the Midwest and on to Stanford in California. They became indelibly connected in the public and professional mind with "progressive education." But just how much they changed the character of public education in the thousands upon thousands of schools across the country is hard to say. Recurrent criticisms from both ends of the ideological spectrum

contended either that public schools were monotonous monopolies of conformity or that they were too soft on intellectual skills, which probably meant
that the extreme child-centered approach had had relatively little effect. What
is more certain is that by the mid-1920s a different kind of differentiation
aimed at training for specialized occupations had come to have enormous
effect.

The Call for Vocational
Differentiation

Perhaps the most obvious way in which the curriculum and goals of
U.S. education responded to the onrush of modernization was the impetus
toward studies that had direct practical usefulness in a work life. Within the
processes of modernization the industrial urbanization was most prominent,
and within the "practical" studies the vocational courses drew the most public
attention. Organized interest groups and organized educators responded in
different ways, but both tried to come to terms with the forces that historian
Samuel P. Hays sums up under the term industrialism as

> the expansion of economic relationships from personal contacts within a
> village community to impersonal forces in the nation and the entire world;
> the standardization of life accompanying the standardization of goods and of
> methods of production; increasing specialization in occupations with the
> resulting dependence of people upon each other to satisfy their wants; a feel-
> ing of insecurity as men faced vast and rapidly changing economic forces
> that they could not control; the decline of interest in non-material affairs and
> the rise of the acquisition of material wealth as the major goal in life. These
> intangible innovations deeply affected the American people; here lay the real
> human drama of the new age.[11]

Hays' interpretation of the major theme of U.S. history in the late nineteenth and early twentieth centuries illuminates the drive for vocationalism
in the schools during that general period. He argues that the stark conflict
between economic or social classes, as portrayed in Populist or Progressive
rhetoric, is not the only way to interpret the era. It was far more complicated than that. In Hays' words,

> the social, economic, and political movements of those thirty years [1885–
> 1914] reveal something more fundamental and more varied than an attempt
> by the dispossessed to curb the wealthy. They comprised a reaction not
> against the corporation alone but also against industrialism and the many
> ways in which it affected the lives of Americans. The people of that era
> sought to do much more than simply to control corporations; they attempted
> to cope with industrial change in all its ramifications. . . . A simple interpre-
> tation of the discontented poor struggling against the happy rich does vio-
> lence to the complexity of industrial innovation and the variety of human
> striving that occurred in response to it.[12]

The rise of the vocational education movement fits this general interpretation of U.S. history in the Populist/Progressive era. Workers and farmers were concerned about making their education more useful in their jobs; and businessmen and industrialists were interested in better-trained employees. Social workers were interested in helping the poor and the immigrants to improve the quality of their urban life; and the poor and the immigrant sought to acquire the skills required in industrial jobs. Too, reform-minded educators wanted to broaden and enliven a stultifying academic or literary curriculum with practical activities that would enhance both the learning of the students and the participation of citizens in building a democratic society. Only in this way, they claimed, could the nation survive the inroads of industrial corporatism on individual and group freedoms in politics and education as well as in the economy.

So it was that, despite widely differing motivations, a coalition of organized groups outside of professional education as well as within was able to muster sufficient political clout to achieve direct federal aid to the public school systems of the United States for the first time in American history. The passage of the Smith-Hughes vocational education act in 1917 culminated two decades of organized effort to promote vocational education through state and federal support. After nearly a half-century of ideological debate, the values of manual training, industrial education, and vocational studies gained a place alongside the values of a general, liberal education in secondary school and colleges.[13]

The Manual Training Movement

From the mid-1870s to the mid-1890s the major response of educators to industrialism had been expressed in the manual training movement in the North and "industrial education" for blacks in the South. The two principal proponents of manual training in the schools were university leaders concerned with the training of engineers to meet the new industrial needs of the age. John D. Runkle was president of the Massachusetts Institute of Technology, and Calvin M. Woodward was professor of applied mechanics and dean of the Polytechnic Institute at Washington University in St. Louis. Their stated concern was primarily to achieve a better balance between mental culture and manual skill in the public school curriculum. The argument for manual training was basically that the school curriculum overemphasized literary studies for the majority of pupils who were flooding into the schools. Many of these students no longer had the advantages of the home training in mechanical skills that the farms and village communities had earlier provided. Thus, the public schools should respond to the industrialism of the country by giving all boys a firsthand acquaintance with the tools, the materials, and the discipline of mechanical drawing, woodworking, and metalworking, and by giving all girls an acquaintance with the cooking and sewing skills of home economics. This would be good pedagogy and of course would increase the skills the boys would eventually need when they were ready for jobs in the industrial world.

In the academic climate of the day (remember the Committee of Ten's academic orientation), advocates of manual training could not adopt as their prime argument the importance of job-oriented preparation specifically and directly for the skilled trades. Therefore, they stressed a pedagogical reform objective by arguing that most students would be more interested and thus more eager to learn when the studies were less bookish and more appealing to eye and hand. Nevertheless, the practical values in promoting better skill training in technical studies for the prospective worker and for the prospective employer were never far below the surface. Despite the stress on the pedagogical effects of reform, the basic implication was not lost on prospective employers, who eagerly supported the introduction of mechanical drawing and manual training into the schools.

Labor unions and educators were not so sure of the benefits to be realized. Labor had sought to counteract the power of industrialists over employment and employees by keeping control over entry to apprenticeship for the trades. They feared that manual training in the schools might be a device to circumvent this control or that the establishment of separate manual training courses or specialized manual training high schools would lead to dual school systems designed to keep the working classes in a subordinate social and economic position, as in Europe. But the objections of labor were ambivalent because manual training did have an immediate appeal to working-class children whose family or ethnic traditions had not given high priority to literary or intellectual study. Labor eventually came around, as we shall see.

William T. Harris / The educators themselves were a bigger stumbling block. There was, of course, the mine-run of academic-minded teachers to whom education and schooling were in essence the study of books. But there were also those who genuinely believed that the distinctive thing about schooling was its power to develop the mind and thus give the best preparation for coping with a changing world that was threatening to engulf society. Outstanding among such spokesmen was William T. Harris. As superintendent of schools in St. Louis, his opposition to board member Calvin Woodward temporarily prevented the introduction of manual training into the St. Louis schools. Later, as U.S. Commissioner, Harris battled the expansion of manual training throughout the country.[14]

Harris contended that the introduction of differentiated manual training courses would dilute the common school curriculum, appeal only to those not interested in the traditional academic programs, and thus divide still further the less intellectually inclined from the more advantaged students. He argued that manual training would *not* provide the kind of intellectual discipline needed in the modern world, which the vast majority of children could acquire if they tried and if the schools genuinely helped them to try. In contemporary terms, Harris thought that manual training was a cop-out of the schools, a retreat from their appointed cultural and intellectual tasks in a democratic yet modern world.

But Harris was to lose the battle in St. Louis. Upon his departure from St. Louis, a Manual Training School was established in 1880 and the idea and practice spread through many of the cities of the country. Ironically, however, both Harris *and* Woodward were to lose their war. Both were overtaken by the tide of vocational education that swept in after 1900. The academic curriculum was not preserved from contamination by manual training, nor were separate manual training schools to become the major response of U.S. public education to industrialism in the early 1920s.

Debates over Industrial Education in the South

Meanwhile, a very interesting and very important variation on the manual training scheme was going on in the South from the 1870s to the 1890s with regard to education of blacks. (For the setting in which this debate went on, see Chapter 9.) The question concerned the kind of education most appropriate for the blacks, in view of the failure of Reconstruction to achieve equal social and political rights and integrated public school systems in the South. The prevailing view of most black and white supporters of improved education for blacks accepted the harsh fact that education had to accommodate itself to the realities of inequality in the economic as well as the social and political worlds.

Hampton, Tuskegee, and Booker T. Washington / General Samuel Chapman Armstrong, founder of Hampton Institute, argued from a humanitarian but paternalistic attitude of white superiority that the racial differences as well as the economic disabilities of Negroes required a special kind of education. They could improve themselves only by great effort to learn the skills and values offered by "industrial education." These would prepare them for the only kinds of jobs that would be available to them in a segregated society—skilled trades on farms and in the cities—if bulwarked by Puritan virtues of hard work, frugality, thrift, and honesty.

In 1901, Hampton Institute not only had an academic department that taught the usual secondary school subjects—especially English, arithmetic, history, and geography—but also a manual training school where the "book side is subordinated to the work side" in woodworking, metalmaking, cooking, and sewing. These subjects were followed by a wide variety of courses in such specific trades as blacksmithing, wheelwrighting, carpentry, painting, bricklaying, glass setting, shoemaking, harness making, and mechanical drawing.[15]

Booker T. Washington generally promoted these same views of his mentor Armstrong when he founded Tuskegee Institute. As the leading black spokesman for "industrial education" of the period, he was able to attract large sums of money from northern philanthropic foundations (Rockefeller, Peabody, Slater, Jeannes, and Rosenwald) for such a differentiated education, and to obtain the acquiescence of Southerners to the buildup of black educational facilities to provide such an education. Differentiated education for blacks thus meant not only a disjunction between two separate systems, but also acknowledgment that blacks would be served best by a practical vocational type of education, rather than by an advanced academic type of education. From the practical viewpoint,

> thirty-six industries are taught the young men and women [at Tuskegee]. These are: Agriculture; Basketry; Blacksmithing; Bee-keeping; Brick-masonry; Plastering; Brick-making; Carpentry; Carriage Trimming; Cooking; Dairying; Architectural, Freehand, and Mechanical Drawing; Dressmaking; Electrical and Steam Engineering; Founding; Harness-making; Housekeeping; Horticulture; Canning; Plain Sewing; Laundering; Machinery; Mattress-making; Millinery; Nurse Training; Painting; Sourmilling; Shoemaking; Printing; Stock-raising; Tailoring; Tinning; and Wheelwrighting.[16]

Here, curiously, Harris was again in the battle on the side that today would be considered liberal, while in his contest with Woodward he would be considered conservative. But he was making the same argument. He protested such undue emphasis on vocational education for blacks as he had protested manual training for whites. The difference was that one case smacked of race inequality and the other smacked of class inequality. Harris believed that black leadership needed the same kind of rigorous and intellectual education that white leadership did. He went a little far in saying a classical education was the appropriate college education for both, but he was convinced that it was the liberal academic subjects that would enable black leaders to bring their fellows out of slavery into a modern industrial society. Some black intellectuals were expressing views quite similar to those of Harris. Alexander Crummel, noted minister in Washington, D.C., spoke of the blacks' need for civilization and higher mental and spiritual values; and R.S. Livinggood, president of Sam Houston College, spoke out strongly for the classical college course as the builder of discipline and character.[17]

W. E. B. Du Bois / This was substantially the view that W. E. B. Du Bois expressed after 1900 when he began to attack Booker T. Washington for accepting a segregated second-class citizenship and for promulgating a second-class type of education. On behalf of his fellow blacks, he pressed vigorously for an intellectually rigorous education that would prepare a black leadership in the push to break out of the bonds of inequality and segregation, and which would produce enough black professionals and teachers to make up the "talented tenth" required of any civilized modern society.

Du Bois agreed it was all right, as Washington argued, to put brains and skills into common occupations and to dignify common labor, but there was far more to education for free blacks than being prepared to go into the farms, sawmills, factories, and mines. Such "industrial education" would never equip blacks to achieve genuine freedom or equality. He advocated manual training and trade teaching for black boys as well as white. But that was not enough:

> I insist that the object of all true education is not to make men carpenters, it is to make carpenters men; there are two means of making the carpenter a man, each equally important: the first is to give the group and the community in which he works, liberally trained teachers and leaders to teach him and his family what life means; the second is to give him sufficient intelligence and technical skill to make him an efficient workman; the first object demands the Negro college and college-bred men, but enough to leaven the lump, to inspire the masses, to raise the Talented Tenth to leadership; the second object demands a good system of common schools, well-taught, conveniently located and properly equipped.[18]

Here, Du Bois was talking more like the liberal reformers among the progressives than like the efficiency-minded modernizers. He had not criticized "industrial" education before 1900, but, like white humanitarian reformers, he began to worry about the single-minded intentions of businessmen whose aristocratic assumptions presumed a hierarchically stratified society, and Du Bois knew better than most what group was assumed to remain at the bottom. If the humanitarian reform groups that had formed industrial education associations to promote special public high schools for manual training in Boston, New York, Philadelphia, Baltimore, and elsewhere had won the day in combining liberal and vocational studies. Du Bois and others might have continued support for them. But when new forces got into the act and began to turn an educational reform movement into a class-oriented and economically one-sided campaign, that seemed to be too much, and the blacks deserted.

The Victory of Vocational Education

The progressive reformers had organized the Industrial Education Association in 1887 and the Public Education Association in New York in 1895. The organizers were from the professional middle-class groups of social workers, editors, clergymen, university professors, and educators who were fighting for so many other social welfare reforms together. But they were soon forced to take another tack when the depression of 1893–1894 introduced a new demand for vocational training. As imports and exports fluctuated, many industrialists were prompted to reexamine their situation in the world, and decided that they must take more aggressive action to compete in foreign markets. As their first action they formed the National Association of Manufacturers (NAM) in 1895 and soon began to argue that steps should be taken to improve the vocational training of employees. They found U.S. schools deficient in this regard, and they saw efficient German technical schools helping to make German industrial prowess the best in the world. The NAM appointed a Committee on Industrial Education whose reports of 1905 and 1912 set the tone for aggressive vocationalism in American schools.[19]

Enter the NAM / In general the NAM came out strongly for the kind of trade school found in Germany. True, the sprinkling of technical and manual training schools already established in the United States had helped, but a massive effort was necessary to make trade training available for the vast majority of American children who were going to do the work of the United States. This would provide much greater opportunity and better jobs for poor children (and it would in the process break the stranglehold of unions on an outmoded apprenticeship system). There were three types of children, and they needed three kinds of schools. The first group included the relatively few (perhaps 1 in 30) abstract-minded students for whom the usual literary school was all right. The second group was made up of concrete- or hand-minded children who dropped out after the sixth or seventh grade. These represented about half of all children, the ones most neglected by the public schools. For those between 14 and 16 years of age, continuation trade schools should be established on the model of German post-primary schools.

The third group, composed of those who stood between the abstract-minded and the hand-minded, should have the opportunity to sample highly developed prevocational and manual training courses in the upper grades of the regular elementary schools. To make sure that such vocational courses would be really practical, they should be under the control of separate boards of vocational education whose members were practical businessmen and practical educators rather than regular school personnel. Thus, differentiation would apply to organization and control of vocational education as well as to curriculum. Differentiation would be achieved by different courses in regular schools or in specialized trade schools separated from the common school system. These specialized schools could be run by private corporations or, if under public auspices, should be separated from the regular public schools. Such proposals by the NAM were sure to be criticized by labor and by some educators.

Labor's Reaction / Though the earlier trade unions had been able to persuade several state legislatures to pass apprenticeship laws that gave the unions control over the written indentures required before a youth could go to work, by 1900 it became clear to the American Federation of Labor (AFL) as well as to the NAM that the traditional apprenticeship system was no longer appropriate to the specialized jobs of the factory system. Faced with the NAM's clamor for separate trade schools under corporate or private auspices, which labor viewed as a union-breaking scab activity, the AFL adopted a stand that public schools take on the task of trade-skill training, a proposal initiated by the Massachusetts Commission on Industrial Education and the National Society for the Promotion of Industrial Education. Formed in 1906, both organizations were, in a sense, the successors to the progressive humanitarian reform associations of the 1890s, but they differed in that their membership was a coalition of businessmen and industrialists as well as settlement-house reformers and educators.

It soon became apparent, however, that the social efficiency wing of educators rather than the humanitarian wing would be in charge. Nevertheless, the AFL, after its committee reported in 1910 and 1915, joined the coalition in favor of vocational education under public auspices. This was in line with the earlier success of the farm lobbyists, who had received labor support in persuading Congress to pass the Smith-Lever Act in 1914. This Act provided for county agricultural agents to help improve farm life by disseminating knowledge of agriculture and home economics. Now it was the turn of the farm organizations to support labor in achieving federal aid for vocational education in the public schools.

The AFL joined in the campaign for vocational education, but opposed the idea of separate trade schools, or continuation schools, or separate administration. Labor leaders were suspicious of the NAM's motives, and constantly held out for the common school ideal in order to prevent the working class from being segregated in second-class schools, as in Europe. They wanted better vocational training to improve the workers' standard of living, but they also wanted to retain the advantages of social mobility made possible by the general liberal education obtainable in the common public school system. The AFL Report of 1915 was especially insistent on this point and reacted strongly against efforts in Illinois in 1913 to set up a State Board for Industrial Education apart from the regular state board of education:

> Perhaps the most vicious element threatening to divert the movement of industrial education in our public schools from our American ideals of democracy in education, is the continuous effort made by the commercial interests to place industrial education under the direction of a distinctive board of management, separate from the board of administration governing the general education of the children. . . . Vocational school courses should at all times be under the guidance and control of school authorities having control of the general education of the children. The unit system of administration is best adapted to educating our children properly for their future guidance as citizens and as workers.[20]

The AFL was obviously impressed by the social welfare wing of progressive educational reformers, and rejected the efficiency wing that had teamed up with the businessmen and industrialists to eventually win the campaign that led to the Smith-Hughes Act of 1917. A significant and influential factor in the passage of the Smith-Hughes Act was the authorization by Congress, and the appointment by President Wilson, of the Commission on National Aid to Vocational Education. The Commission's report of 1914 very largely followed the line of the NAM reports in stressing the economic need for vocational education as a prime means for conservation of natural resources, prevention of the waste of human labor, increase of the wage-earning power of laborers, a wise investment for capital, and a stimulus of national prosperity.[21]

Result: The Smith-Hughes Act / Thus, a coalition of business, farm, labor, and reform groups managed the political feat of federal aid to public education. The Smith-Hughes Act of 1917 called for the federal government to cooperate with the states in the promotion of vocational education in agriculture, home economics, and the trades and industry. Federal funds were to be matched dollar for dollar, as in the Smith-Lever Act, and such funds were to be used (1) to pay the salaries of agricultural teachers in the proportion that the rural population of a state bore to the total rural population of the nation; (2) to pay the salaries of teachers of home economics as well as trade and industrial education in the proportion that a state's urban population bore to the total urban population of the nation; and (3) to help the states prepare teachers of these subjects in the proportion that the state's total population bore to the total population of the country. A Federal Board of Vocational Education and comparable state boards were authorized to administer the funds and to supervise and evaluate the programs designed for students over 14 years of age in public schools below college grade.

Smith-Hughes was a victory for the social efficiency vocationalists, and there was little joy among the social reform educators. Though they had come together in the early industrial education associations, their divergent concerns were apparent almost from the beginning. David Snedden, Charles Prosser, and George D. Strayer symbolized the social efficiency vocationalists; John Dewey, Jane Addams, and the NEA Commission on the Reorganization of Secondary Education represented the claims of the democratic common school in the effort to cope with industrial modernization. In the decade leading up to Smith-Hughes, the differences between the two approaches became greater and more acute.

Ideological Debate over Vocational Education

As early as the report of the Massachusetts Commission on Industrial Education in 1906, the differences between the social welfare and social efficiency reformers began to appear. All could pretty well agree that the elementary and secondary schools were too literary and academic, and that manual training was potentially a good antidote if it became more practical and occupationally oriented instead of too formalistic and "disciplinary." All could agree that too many children at age 12 and 13 of *all* social classes were dropping out of school because of lack of interest in the curriculum and that "industrial" courses would be attractive to them. But when it came to setting up separate trade schools under separate administration, the humanitarian democrats balked. Jane Addams objected, John Dewey objected, and eventually the majority of secondary school people reaffirmed the values of common schooling at the secondary level as well as at the elementary level.

But despite the objections, the National Society for the Promotion of Industrial Education—closer to the mood of business, industry, farm, labor —and its political allies won out in the federal legislation. With the backing of President Theodore Roosevelt, and then of Wilson, the Smith-Hughes legislation was passed on the eve of U.S. participation in World War I.

All kinds of organizations came out in support of industrial or vocational education, but the educational profession itself was deeply split. This was not simply the old-line academic traditionalists versus the "practicalists" and the "vocationalists." Even more significant was the split among the "reformers" themselves. The root of this split had to do with assumptions about the class character of U.S. society. Vocationalists were likely to assume that there were well-defined layers in society, that these were not likely to change radically, that industrial education would be especially appropriate for the lower layers, and that making industrial education more easily available to the lower layers was the democratic thing to do.

Charles W. Eliot on a Class Society / As early as the 1890s, Charles W. Eliot of Harvard expressed the widely held view of vocationalists that equality and freedom were incompatible in a democracy:

> The freedom and social mobility which characterize the democratic state permit, and even bring about, striking inequalities of condition; and if the surface of democratic society should be levelled off any day, inequalities would reappear on the morrow, unless individual freedom and social mobility should be destroyed. The children of a democratic society should, therefore, be taught at school, with the utmost explicitness, and with vivid illustrations, that inequalities of condition are a necessary result of freedom; but that through all inequalities should flow the constant sense of essential unity in aim and spirit.[22]

As he approached his retirement as president of Harvard in 1909, Eliot made more explicit the relation of the layers of society to vocational education. In the *School Review* in 1909, Eliot pointed to "four layers in civilized society which are indispensable, and, so far as we can see, eternal."

> Those layers are four in number and of very different thickness: The upper one is very thin; it consists of the managing, leading, guiding class— the intellectual discoverers, the inventors, the organizers, and the managers and their chief assistants. Next comes an absolutely indispensable and much more numerous class, namely, the highly trained hand-workers, that is, the men who are always going to get their living by skilled manual labor. . . . The next layer, indispensable and thick, is the commercial class, the layer

which is employed in buying, selling, and distributing. Lastly, there is the thick and fundamental layer engaged in household work, agriculture, mining, quarrying, and forestry work. . . . These four layers are indispensable to the progress of modern democratic society, as of every older form of industrial and political organization; and our school systems must be so reorganized that they shall serve all four of the social layers or sets of workers, and serve them with intelligence, and with keen appreciation of the several ends in view.[23]

This platonic model of a class society was enough to ruffle the democratic reformers, but Eliot had been even more provocative the year before in a speech to the National Society for the Promotion of Industrial Education. At that time, he not only proposed the introduction of trade schools for the several skilled trades separate from existing public schools, but also argued that it was up to the elementary school teachers to sort out the children and guide them into the appropriate schools according to their probable destinies, that is, their special layers.

Eliot's proposal for classifying children really did arouse the hackles of the democratic reformers, and although he later backed away from sorting by the elementary teachers, the social efficiency reformers plugged hard for the new testing procedures to be used as an aid to the coming new profession of vocational guidance. Snedden, Prosser, and Strayer were successful in advancing the cause, and strong support from industry as well as from educators led to the separate organization of the National Vocational Guidance Association. At first, it, too, attracted some humanitarian progressives like Ida Tarbell, who vigorously argued for including the "domestic industries" in industrial education in order to dignify and elevate the role of women in modern society.

A Divided NEA / The National Education Association found itself divided on the issue of vocationalism, but it finally joined the NAM and the AFL in support of greater attention to industrial education in the schools. The 1910 report of its Committee on the Place of Industries in Public Education recognized the need for a radical educational response to modern complex and highly specialized industrialization:

> The social aim of education and the psychological needs of childhood alike require that industrial (manual-constructive) activities form an important part of school occupations.
> (a) In the elementary schools, such occupations are necessary to provide concreteness of motive and meaning. . . .
> (b) In intermediate schools, industrial occupations are an important element in the wide range of experience necessary for the proper testing of children's aptitudes as a basis for subsequent choice of specific pursuits either in vocations or in higher schools.
> (c) In secondary schools, industrial occupations properly furnish the central and dominant factor in the education of those pupils who make final choice of an industrial vocation. Vocational purpose is the distinguishing

work of the "technical" high school as distinct from the "Manual Training" high school.[24]

The tip-off of NEA's capitulation was the reference to industrial occupations as furnishing the "central and dominant factor" in secondary education for those whose probable destinies were the industrial vocations. This was to be a bone of contention between two major committees appointed by the NEA in subsequent years. The Committee on Vocational Education and Vocational Guidance (1912) followed the vocationalist efficiency lines of Prosser and Snedden and of the National Society for the Promotion of Industrial Education. The Commission on the Reorganization of Secondary Education (1913) followed the more democratic humanitarian line of social progressives to be developed in its *Cardinal Principles of Secondary Education* of 1918. Clarence D. Kingsley, inspector of high schools in Massachusetts, was the prime author, surprisingly progressive in view of his professional association with Snedden. But, after all, his reviewing committee included William H. Kilpatrick and Thomas H. Briggs of Teachers College, Alexander Inglis of Harvard, Charles Hughes Johnston of Illinois, Henry Neumann of the Ethical Culture School, and Otis W. Caldwell of the Lincoln School of Teachers College. While Edward Krug finds no direct influence on *Cardinal Principles* from John Dewey, the point of view and general orientation were quite compatible.[25]

The Cardinal Principles / The Commission did endorse vocational education as one of the seven cardinal principles, but it rejected the notion that there should be separate trade schools in the public education system and endorsed the comprehensive or cosmopolitan high school as the basic institution of secondary education. Thus, vocational training should come into the high school as differentiated courses or alternative curriculums, but not as a differentiated institution, as was the case in most of the other modernizing countries of the world. The Commission called for the common school ideal to apply to the secondary school and to preserve the goal of a common curriculum for social and civic responsibility, no matter what specialization might result from different vocational goals. The hope was that the secondary school would continue to be a unifying force, despite the pluralisms in society, and develop the common knowledge and values of political democracy.

The strong support for commonality was based upon the belief that the time was ripe for compulsory universal secondary education to age 16. This would suit the modern times much as universal, free common schooling had represented the goal of the early nineteenth century. All this was coupled with the hint that a vastly expanded higher education would be possible if *all* courses in the comprehensive high school, vocational as well as academic, were to be so shaped that they could lead on to higher education. Arthur Wirth sums up the *Cardinal Principles*:

The keynote of the Report was a contention that the high school should abandon its traditional attachment to the colleges and become a secondary extension of the elementary common school. Its programs should meet the "real life" needs of all youths rather than cater to the minority that was college-bound.

America's high schools should be rededicated to the old ideal of equalizing opportunities and of instilling common loyalties and commitments in young Americans from all backgrounds. The Report was an example of the progressive yearning to sustain values of democracy and community under conditions of corporatism and megalopolitan living.[26]

Thus, the issues were not easy to solve or simple to define. There was the question as to whether vocational education should be a separate function, organized by the state or by private industry apart from the public school system. There was the question as to whether it should be conducted as part of the comprehensive high school or in separate, specialized technical or vocational high schools. There was rivalry between the NAM, which pressed for specialized and (if need be) separate institutions of vocational training, and the AFL, which was ever alert to the possibilities that vocational education could become an inferior education, designed to keep labor in its place, if it were separated into a track different from academic education.

Some educators were willing to follow the model of Germany because they believed that a separate system of vocational schools for the working classes—quite specialized and nonacademic, and thus leading to a job but *not* to the university—must have been the basis for the rapid and efficient industrialization of Germany. But, in the words of Arthur Wirth, the majority did not agree:

> For most educators, however, such a medicine was too strong to swallow. For one thing, it seemed outrageously at odds with the common school ideal, with its promise of producing socially mobile, self-reliant, involved citizens rather than compliant hired hands.
>
> The move then was toward compromise, one which would reconcile the conflicting desires for efficiency and economic welfare with those for self-realization and democratic citizenship.[27]

Threat of a Dual System in Illinois / Reconciliation or compromise was not the password in the early stages of the struggle. In fact, a fairly clear showdown occurred in Illinois in the years 1912 to 1915. Efficiency-minded educators and leaders of the industrial community proposed a bill in the legislature to establish a separate system of industrial schools for all children who left public school at age 14, one that would be tailored to the industrial needs of the local community. This was introduced by Edwin G. Cooley, a former superintendent of Chicago schools, who worked closely with Prosser and Snedden. The AFL, settlement house leaders, and democratically minded educators bitterly resisted the bill when it was introduced in 1914. The tenor of the debate is illustrated by an article Dewey wrote for *School Review* in

1912, in which he observed how general academic education was being revitalized by the introduction of manual and social activities and by its recognition of responsibility to prepare *all* youth for citizenship, including a useful calling. Therefore, he said, the proposal in Illinois to *segregate* the vocational school pupils would destroy both gains:

> It is inconceivable that those who have loved and served our American common school system will, whatever the defects of this system, stand idly by and see such a blow aimed at it. . . . It is truly extraordinary that just at a time when even partisan politics are taking a definitely progressive turn, such a reactionary measure as the institution of trade and commercial schools under separate auspices should be proposed. . . .
>
> Those who believe in the continued separate existence of what they are pleased to call the "lower classes" or the "laboring classes" would naturally rejoice to have schools in which these "classes" would be segregated. And some employers of labor would doubtless rejoice to have schools supported by public taxation supply them with additional food for their mills. All others should be united against every proposition, in whatever form advanced, to separate training of employees from training for citizenship, training of intelligence and character from training for narrow industrial efficiency.[28]

The contrast between efficiency-as-economy and democratic responsibility could not be more clearly drawn. Someone must have been listening to these and similar arguments, for the Cooley bill in Illinois was defeated in 1915. The problem and the debate, however, were far from over.

John Dewey on a Unitary Public School System / While some of the extreme advocates of social efficiency, as exemplified in the NAM approach, might have been willing to accept a stratified-class social order as normal and normative, John Dewey returned again and again to the danger that separating academic and vocational studies would perpetuate class distinctions. In 1915 Dewey and his daughter put it this way in *Schools of Tommorow*:

> It is fatal for a democracy to permit the formation of fixed classes. Differences of wealth, the existence of large masses of unskilled laborers, contempt for work with the hands, inability to secure the training which enables one to forge ahead in life, all operate to produce classes, and to widen the gulf between them. Statesmen and legislation can do something to combat these evil forces. Wise philanthropy can do something. But the only fundamental agency for good is the public school system. . . .
>
> There must not be one system for the children of parents who have more leisure and another for the children of those who are wage-earners. The physical separation forced by such a scheme. . . . brings about a division of mental and moral habits, ideals and outlook. . . . A division of the public school system into one part which pursues traditional methods, with incidental improvements, and another which deals with those who are to go into manual labor means a plan of social predestination totally foreign to the spirit of a democracy.
>
> The democracy which proclaims equality of opportunity as its ideal requires an education in which learning and social application, ideas and

practice, work and recognition of the meaning of what is done, are united from the beginning and for all.[29]

Few statements come closer than Dewey's to bringing the goals of academic discipline, social responsibility, and individual development into some sort of congeniality with the goal of vocational competence, but he continued to call upon educators to try to hold off the purely trade-skill approach to vocational education and to try to make it contribute to general educational reform. He picked up the currently popular term "industrial intelligence" and tried to give it a much broader social and civic meaning:

> It will be recognized that, for this purpose, a broad acquaintance with science and skill in the laboratory control of materials and processes is more important than skill in trade operations. . . . such a conception of industrial education will prize freedom more than docility; initiative more than automatic skill; insight and understanding more than capacity to recite lessons or to execute tasks under the direction of others.[30]

The Compromise: Differentiated Courses, Not Schools

But Dewey's concepts were difficult to get across or to put into practice. The plain fact was that teaching of skills was easier than teaching "understanding," whether in learning to read or learning to run a machine. The upshot of the struggle over differentiation according to vocation was that the political process produced substantial changes in school organization. Curriculums *were* differentiated and proliferated; students did flock to the vocational or nonacademic courses; and testing, ability grouping, and vocational guidance were all involved in differentiation, but separate public systems of trade schools were not generally established. A compromise *was* reached through a differentiation of courses within the comprehensive high school rather than outside it. Indeed, the rapid adoption of the *junior* high school was a product of the larger drives for vocational differentiation.

Wirth sums up the political process as follows:

> In actuality, public education repudiated both the educational approach recommended by John Dewey and the policies of social efficiency urged by Snedden and Prosser. The nation produced as a compromise the comprehensive secondary school which promised both to preserve the egalitarian values of the common school tradition and to satisfy the skill requirements of industrialism. The actual performance of the schools demonstrated the strength of the pressures of the technocratic system. The use of ability tracks and differentiated courses tended to reflect and preserve the social class ordering of society. Prosser's kind of vocationalism isolated vocational training from academic courses. Imaginative integrations of liberal with vocational studies which might have served to enliven each were not effected. Students in "voced." tended to move in a world separate from classmates headed for the university.[31]

Technology and the Youth Labor Market / While we may argue the merits of the debate and lament the losses on one side or other of vocationalism,

Selwyn Troen reminds us that technological developments adopted by business and industry in the early twentieth century had a determining influence that neither side could overlook.[32] The manual training movement of the last two decades of the nineteenth century had been devised by educators to entice adolescent youth to stay in school instead of going to the beckoning jobs in factory or office. But in the first two decades of the twentieth century, vast numbers of those jobs for unskilled youth disappeared. Thousands of cash girls and cash boys in department stores were no longer needed when the pneumatic tube and later the cash register took their place. Thousands of Western Union messengers were not needed when the telephone became commonplace. Stock clerks, delivery boys, wrappers, markers, and dozens of others were put out of jobs by machines.

Now, the boy or girl who found school uninteresting might drop out, but would find no job to go to, only unemployment. An increasing number of employers just did not have much use for children under 16 or for unskilled labor of many kinds. Thus, the child who formerly could get a job and some income after finishing the fifth or sixth grade could no longer expect much more than temporary, poorly paid work and had little chance to acquire the necessary skills as he or she advanced beyond the age of 12 or 13. George Strayer's survey of 318 cities in 1911 showed that the public schools lost half of their students between ages 13 and 15 (the junior high school years). Strayer argued that the "democratic way" was to provide separate trade schools for those who had to work and those who could go to college. This would have meant giving up the common school ideal for a European type of disjunctive system.

The United States was not receptive to the European system. It pioneered, instead, something new among modernizing nations. It tried to provide schooling for all youth to age 16 or so, using the principle of both push and pull: child labor laws to pull children out of the factories that still hired them, compulsory attendance laws to push the children off the streets and into the schools, and manual training courses or vocational skill courses to pull them to studies that would attract them to stay in school longer. Troen reported that in St. Louis the high school population increased fivefold between 1900 and 1920; and by 1920 more than three-fourths of high school students were enrolled in "general," "manual training," or "commercial" courses. Troen believes that the attractiveness of the new courses plus the decline of opportunity for employment sparked the vast increases in secondary school enrollment.

The Uniqueness of the U.S. School System

It has become fashionable to denigrate the motivation of compulsory education as an invasion of freedom, and of vocationalism as a perpetuation of class structure in the United States. There is some evidence to substantiate each argument. But the opportunities provided by an almost universal secondary schooling may, in the long run, turn out to be a fundamentally formative element in social change that cannot yet be fully assessed. Like democracy itself, the compromises between coherence and differentiation that American public education has devised may be the worst arrangement so far conceived —except for all those other systems. The question is, how successful have we been? In rejecting the European systems that deliberately and openly separated the schools for the masses from the schools for the classes, the United States made a radical departure from established Continental practice, one that some European countries are belatedly trying to emulate. In comparing actual to ideal practice, many investigators now charge that we have had in fact a tracking system that has channeled the lower-class children into vocational courses. Thus, we have perpetuated the very class system that Dewey and social progressives hoped to prevent.

We must always compare the reality with the ideal so that we can identify areas in which improvements must be made. But we might also compare occasionally this country's reality with the reality in countries where the class system and disjunctive differentiated educational systems have produced an even tighter fit of hand-in-glove. Recent European educators' move to modernize by reforming their educational systems in ways similar to those of the United States in the early twentieth century represents their various attempts to close the gap between the growing demands of a democratic ideal and the modernizing reality of differentiation.[33]

While the United States was responding in the late nineteenth and early twentieth centuries to the divergent pushes toward coherence and the pulls toward differentiation by reaching the accommodations between democratic community and modernizing demands that we have just described, the European countries responded less quickly to democratization and more directly to differentiation—whether according to social class, vocation, or academic ability. In Europe primary schools for the many were rigidly distinguished from secondary schools for the few; technical and trade schools proliferated in their specialization and in their separation from the academic secondary schools; formal hierarchies of stratification and prestige among these different kinds of schools far exceeded the informal but far less rigid hierarchies that marked most U.S. educational systems; selection for admission to general secondary education and to higher education was extremely restricted. It was not until after World War II that the march to secondary education in Europe approximated some of the progress made in the United States two or three decades earlier. This resulted in increasing pressure in the late 1960s to open up the access to European universities, again representing a delayed reaction time of several decades compared to that in the United States.

Few will argue that European systems have been more overtly and candidly based on class distinctions than those of the United States, a result in large part of recurring pressure for public schools to live up to the historic democratic value claims of freedom and equality. At the same time, European educational systems did not have to deal—at least until recently—with the large and complex ethnic and racial problems that plagued the United States. On the other hand, in its self-congratulation about the relative lack of class bias in its educational structures, its openness of access to secondary and higher education, and its flexibility of academic and vocational offerings, the United States has often not faced up to its own rigidities based on ethnicity and race—at least until recently. The successes and failures of U.S. public schools in coping with these problems to the mid-1920s are dealt with in the next chapter.

Notes

1. Lawrence A. Cremin, *The Transformation of the School* (New York: Knopf, 1961), p. 5.
2. John Dewey, quoted in Robert H. Bremner, ed., *Children and Youth in America: A Documentary History*, Vol. II: 1866–1932 (Cambridge, Mass.: Harvard University Press, 1971), p. 1134.
3. Bremner, p. 1135.
4. Francis Parker, quoted in Alexander S. Rippa, ed., *Educational Ideas in America: A Documentary History* (New York: McKay, 1969), pp. 303–304.
5. Rippa, p. 309.
6. Bremner, p. 1119.
7. See, for comparison, Clarence J. Karier, ed., *Shaping the American Educational State, 1900 to the Present* (New York: Free Press, 1975), Chap. 5; or Karier, "Testing for Order and Control in the Corporate Liberal State," *Educational* Theory, Spring 1972, 22:159–190; and Robert L. Church, "Educational Psychology and Social Reform in the Progressive Era," *History of Education Quarterly*, Winter 1971, 11(4): 390–401.
8. Patricia Albjerg Graham, *Progressive Education: From Academy to Academe; a History of the Progressive Education Association* (New York: Teachers College Press, 1967), pp. 11–12.
9. Bremner, pp. 1123–1125.
10. Cremin, pp. 240–245.
11. Samuel P. Hays, *The Response to Industrialism, 1885–1914* (Chicago: University of Chicago Press, 1957), p. 4.
12. Hays, pp. 188–189.
13. For a comprehensive analysis, see Arthur G. Wirth, *Education in the Technological Society: The Vocational-Liberal Studies Controversy in the Early Twentieth Century* (Scranton, Pa.: Industrial Textbook Co., 1972).

     For a briefer analysis and a series of related documents, see Marvin

Lazerson and Norton W. Grubb, eds., *American Education and Vocationalism: A Documentary History, 1870–1970* (New York: Teachers College Press, 1974).

14. For an excellent description of Woodward versus Harris in St. Louis, see Selwyn K. Troen, *The Public and the Schools: Shaping the St. Louis System, 1838–1920* (Columbia: University of Missouri Press, 1975).

15. Quoted in Earle H. West, *The Black American and Education* (Columbus, Ohio: Merrill Publishing Co., 1972), p. 114.

16. Daniel Calhoun, ed., *The Educating of Americans: A Documentary History* (Boston: Houghton Mifflin, 1969), p. 348.

17. West, pp. 105–110.

18. Rena L. Vassar, ed., *Social History of American Education*. Vol. II: *1860 to the Present* (Chicago: Rand McNally, 1965), p. 72.

19. Lazerson and Grubb, p. 88.

20. Lazerson and Grubb, pp. 113–114.

21. Lazerson and Grubb, pp. 116–132.

22. Charles W. Eliot, quoted in Henry J. Perkinson, ed., *Two Hundred Years of American Educational Thought* (New York: McKay, 1976), pp. 170–171.

23. Eliot, quoted in Bremner, II, p. 1114.

24. Quoted in Lazerson and Grubb, pp. 83–84.

25. See Edward A. Krug, *The Shaping of the American High School* (New York: Harper & Row, 1964), Chap. 15.

26. Arthur G. Wirth, *Education in the Technological Society: The Vocational-Liberal Studies Controversy in the Early Twentieth Century* (Scranton, Pa.: Intext Educational Publishers, 1971), p. 125.

27. Wirth, p. 123.

28. Dewey, quoted in Bremner, pp. 1418–1419.

29. Bremner, pp. 1126–1129.

30. Dewey, quoted in Wirth, p. 217.

31. Wirth, p. 222.

32. Selwyn K. Troen, "The Discovery of the Adolescent by American Educational Reformers, 1900–1920: An Economic Perspective," in Lawrence Stone, ed., *Schooling and Society* (Baltimore: The Johns Hopkins Press, 1976).

33. For a brief analysis of these developments and a bibliography, see R. Freeman Butts, *The Education of the West: A Formative Chapter in the History of Civilization* (New York: McGraw-Hill, 1973), Chap. 11. For details, see Raymond Poignant, *Education and Development in Western Europe, the United States, and the U.S.S.R.: A Comparative Study* (New York: Teachers College Press, 1969).

9 Pathologies of Pluralism: Nativism and Racism

As noted at the end of the preceding chapter, in comparing their public educational system with those of Europe, Americans have commonly pointed with some justifiable pride to its unitary, single-track or ladder character as more democratic than the European two-track or dual system. There is, of course, considerable truth to the generalization. European school systems grew up as social class systems: primary schools for the working classes leading to the skilled and unskilled occupations, and secondary schools for the middle and upper classes leading to the universities, the higher technical schools, and the professional and managerial occupations. The two systems were parallel to each other, with relatively little chance for crossing over from one to the other. The inbred separation was perpetuated by training teachers for primary schools in institutions separate from those training secondary school teachers. I have called this disjointedness or separatism the disease of "disjunctivitis" which afflicted all major European systems in the eighteenth and nineteenth centuries and was carried around the world by the Western empires in the nineteenth and twentieth centuries.[1]

In contrast, the American system much more easily led students from the elementary school to the secondary school and on to the post-secondary and higher educational institutions. No selective examinations were required for a child to pass from the primary school to the secondary school. Primary schools were not reserved for the working classes. Everyone was expected, even required, to go on to a secondary school. Teachers were trained for both types of institutions in most colleges and university departments of education.

There have been, of course, financial, regional, and social barriers that produced differentiated dropout patterns in rural-urban, poor-rich sectors of U.S. society. But, by and large, the system has not been based upon academic barriers that acted as occupational or professional dead ends which barred a primary school product from ever attending a university because he or she had been barred from attending a secondary school on the basis of an examination at age 11 or 12.

While this general analysis has large elements of truth in it, the fact remains that the U.S. system has harbored a far more deadly strain of the disjunctivitis virus than the European systems themselves. United States disjunctivitis has been based upon racial or ethnic discrimination even more than upon social class or academic attainment. It has too often been judged as simply a minor fault in this country's ideal of universal, free education. It can no longer be overlooked and must be recognized as a disease that could have fatal consequences for the very existence of American society if not alleviated and cured. Its consequences have extended far beyond the percentage of the population that is black, or the smaller racial groups made up of American Indians, or peoples who have come from East Asia and the Pacific islands.* It affected as well the larger minority groups of Spanish-speakers from Puerto Rico to Mexico. And in the end it was a virus that affected equally the white majority in whose outlooks and attitudes the depredation of the disease of racial segregation continued to fester as denials of the very ideals of equality, freedom, and justice which the United States claimed as its contribution to Western and world civilization.

Flood Tide of Immigration

While the interplay between democratic values and the modernization process in the United States may have paralleled to some extent similar processes in certain western European countries, the push and pull of the racial and ethnic pluralisms in the United States were vastly different from those in western Europe. In the 50 years from 1876 to 1926, approximately 27 million immigrants came to the United States. This "new" immigration equaled well over half the total population of the country in 1875 (some 45 million), and it was three times the volume of the "old" immigration that occurred during the prior 50 years from 1826 to 1876 (some 9 million). The extent of the increased pressure can be gauged by the fact that well over 9 million immigrants arrived in the single decade of 1906–1915, and around 4 million in each of the other decades, until the sharp decline that occurred after the

* The 1970 Census, in round figures, listed 178,000,000 Americans as white, 22,600,000 as black, 800,000 American Indian, 600,000 Japanese, 435,000 Chinese, 340,000 Filipino, and 720,000 "other" (including Korean, Hawaiian, Aleut, Eskimo, Malayan, and Polynesian).

restrictive legislation of the 1920s. While the western European countries also experienced in-migration from other parts of Europe during this half-century, it was nothing like the numbers that arrived in the United States. Rather, the western European countries continued to lose large numbers of their citizens to the United States in the years 1876–1926.

From the 1880s on, however, the vast majority of immigrants into the United States came from the less modern and more agrarian societies of central, eastern, and southern Europe. The influx of 40 million immigrants over a period of a century thus helped to account for the total population growth of the United States from 12 million in 1826, to 45 million in 1876, to nearly 120 million in 1926. The familiar phrase that "America is a nation of immigrants" was more than ever a reality.

The U.S. Census figures for 1870 show approximately 40 million total population. Of these, in rough figures, 5½ million were classified as foreign-born whites, 5½ million as native-born whites of foreign or mixed parentage (second generation), and 5½ million Negroes and other nonwhites, for a total of 16½ million (about 41 percent of the total). This left 23½ million as "native-born whites" (59%), of whom a large proportion was, of course, made up of descendants of those 9 million immigrants who had come to the United States in the 50 years before 1870, mostly Irish, German, and Scandinavian from northern and western Europe.

Thus, in 1870, persons who had come from northern and western Europe comprised the vast majority of the American white population.

TABLE 3

The "New" Immigration to the United States 1876–1926

	From All Countries	From Central, Eastern, and Southern Europe*	Percent of Total Immigration
1876–1885	4,000,000	463,000	16
1886–1895	4,400,000	1,635,000	37
1896–1905	5,400,000	3,707,000	69
1906–1915	9,400,000	6,528,000	69
1916–1925	3,900,000	1,361,000	35
Total	27,100,000	13,694,000	51

* Central Europe = Poland, Czechoslovakia, Yugoslavia, Hungary, Austria
  Eastern Europe = Russia, Baltic States, Rumania, Bulgaria, Turkey (in Europe)
  Southern Europe = Italy, Greece, Portugal, Spain, Albania
  Source: Compiled from *Historical Statistics of the United States, from Colonial Times to 1957* (Washington, D.C.: U.S. Government Printing Office, 1957)

Then, when the immigration inflow reached its peak in the years from 1890 to 1920, the largest numbers came from central, eastern, and southern Europe, a total of more than 11 million people, or about two-thirds of the total from all countries. For example, in the year 1882, which saw the largest number of immigrants in any one year of the nineteenth century, 32 percent came from Germany and only 4 percent from Italy, 4 percent from central Europe, and 2 percent from Russia. Twenty-five years later, in 1907, the highest year of immigration in the twentieth century, only 3 percent came from Germany in comparison to 22 percent from eastern Europe.

The three largest groups of the "new" immigrants in the twentieth century were Italians, East European Jews, and Poles, followed by large numbers of Russians, Ukrainians, Slovenes, Slovaks, Croatians, Serbs, Bulgarians, Hungarians, Czechs, Rumanians, Greeks, and Portuguese as well as Armenians and Syrians from Asia Minor. Two-thirds of the new immigrants settled in the Northeast (New England, New York, New Jersey, and Pennsylvania). The large cities were the principal magnets: New York, Philadelphia, Baltimore, Pittsburgh, Buffalo, Cleveland, Detroit, Milwaukee, St. Louis, and San Francisco.

Fifty years later in 1920, the year in which immigration quotas were fixed by law, the numbers and the proportions* of the most recent immigrants and the children of immigrants reached approximately 35 percent of the total population as follows:

	Number	Percent	Cumulative Percent
Foreign-born whites	14,000,000	13	
Native-born whites of foreign or mixed parentage	23,000,000	22	35
Other native-born whites	58,500,000		55
Negroes and other nonwhites	11,000,000		10
Total	106,000,000		100

The distribution of the first and second generations of this "new immigration" according to the regions of national origin was approximately as shown in Table 4, according to the Census of 1920.

The Johnson-Reed Act of 1924 marked the imposition of general restrictions upon immigration according to quotas of national origin. The presi-

---

* The tabulations in this and the following tables were compiled from *Historical Statistics of the United States, from Colonial Times to 1957* (Washington, D.C.: U.S. Government Printing Office, 1957.)

TABLE 4
Countries of Immigrant Origin (as of 1920)

	Foreign-born	Native-born of Foreign or Mixed Parentage	Total	Percent
North and western Europe	5,516,000	13,618,000	19,134,000	52
Central and eastern Europe	4,449,000	4,867,000	9,316,000	25
Southern and other Europe	1,917,000	2,077,000	3,994,000	11
Asia	238,000	176,000	414,000	01
Canada	1,138,000	1,841,000	2,979,000	08
Latin America	589,000	304,000	893,000	02
Other	74,000	——	74,000	+
	13,921,000	22,883,000	36,804,000	
Percent of Total population	13	22	35	

dential commission established by the Act estimated that the contours of the American white population in 1920 encompassed persons descended from

Colonial stock	41,300,000	44%
Post-Colonial stock	53,500,000	56%
	94,800,000	100%

Figuring that three-fourths of the white colonial stock were of British origin and 65 percent of the post-colonial stock were from northern and western Europe, the general distribution of the white population was estimated to be something like this, as of 1920:

	Northern and Western Europe	All Others
Colonial Stock		
75% British	31,000,000	——
25% non-British	10,000,000	——
Post-Colonial Stock		
65% northern & western Europe	35,000,000	——
35% all others	——	18,500,000
	76,300,000	18,500,000
Percent of total	80	20

In the five years from 1926 to 1930, immigration continued at a fairly high rate (almost 1,500,000), but in the five years from 1931 to 1935 the total dropped to a little over 200,000 as the restrictive quotas of the Johnson-Reed Act of 1924 took effect in 1929, giving huge preference to the peoples of northern and western Europe. Thus, of an annual immigration limited to 150,000 persons, approximately 125,000 entry permits were allocated to the countries of northern and western Europe (somewhat over 80 percent).

Nativist Drives To Assimilate European Immigrants

The problems arising from this change in the immigrant population were many: There were vast numbers of immigrants to be accommodated in a short time; their cultural characteristics changed drastically and dramatically from what they had been; an enormous variety of languages and customs was introduced; the tensions of segmental pluralism were multiplied many times over; and many "natives" as well as "aliens" found the adjustment traumatic. This led to renewed nativist movements and attacks upon the newcomers by the oldtimers. Old-line British descendants heaped contempt upon many immigrants, and old-line Irish and Germans sometimes looked with contempt upon "micks" and "Plattdeutschers," the common derogatory terms at that time. Some newcomers found it difficult to accommodate to other newcomers as well as to the strangers they found already here. Polish and Italian Catholics did not like Irish Catholics, who monopolized the Catholic hierarchy. German Jews looked down upon Russian and Rumanian Jews. Urbanized northern Italians could not abide southern peasant Italians. Virtually all whites in California looked down upon Chinese, because of their working-class status, and disliked Japanese because of their superior adaptability and speed in moving into the middle class. Greek and Italian labor agents exploited their newly arrived compatriots as efficiently as old-line industrial employers might do.

All these generalizations are too broad and are subject to exceptions and modifications. They are intended simply to indicate that pluralism produced an infinitely complicated social situation with which the public schools were forced to deal. With so many differences flooding into the public schools, what were the schools to do? Should the public schools ignore all differences and treat all ethnic groups the same? There would be a certain kind of equality involved in such uniform treatment. Or should they try to treat each group differently, and all individuals within the groups differently? If so, what should be the basis of differentiation? According to language? If equality were to be served, this would mean giving instruction in each of the many mother tongues spoken among the immigrants. Would it mean keeping alive all the foreign languages represented in a particular local community, or just the language of the majority in each community? Differentiate according to religion? There had already been three hundred years of experience with religion in the schools, and it had just about been decided that religion was not the business of public schools. Differentiate on the basis of "cultural heritage?" Surely, more could have been done to acknowledge the distinctive art, music, drama, and literature of different cultural groups. But the public schools were not noted for their close attention to the creative arts of *any* culture except in connection with the study of languages.

Faced by these monumental problems, the public schools did not try very hard to accommodate themselves to the pluralistic values of their new immigrants. And when they did, they were likely to run into other problems with the minority groups. Troen reports how the rising Irish politicians in St. Louis argued that if German were to be taught in the public schools, then Gaelic should also be added to the curriculum.[2] And as the *Globe-Democrat* editorialized, why not French and Hebrew, and all the other languages as well? In answering its own question, the newspaper concluded that this solution would be so costly that the simplest way would be to eliminate German. This was reminiscent of the solution to religion in the curriculum, also a volatile political question. Meanwhile, before the Democratic Irish were able to outvote the Republican Germans on the St. Louis school board, and thus able to abolish German in 1887, the St. Louis public schools were acknowledged to have been a potent force in the amalgamation of the city's foreign population. Troen points out that in 1860 St. Louis had the highest proportion of foreign-born whites of any major city in the United States, that is, 60 percent of the entire population was foreign-born, mostly from Germany. In 1880, a generation later, 94 percent of the white school-age children had been born in the United States, while 75 percent of their fathers were foreign-born (nearly half in Germany and more than 15 percent in Ireland). A similar situation could be found in city after city. It was estimated that in 1909 nearly 60 percent of students in the schools of 37 of the larger cities of the United States were either immigrants or children of immigrants.

The Push Toward Anglo Conformity

Solutions to such problems seemed impossible, and the schools approached the matter of assimilation with a set of attitudes like those displayed by the adult population. These attitudes ranged from the harsh, crude, racist demand of Anglo nativists that the new immigrants must conform now or go back where they came from, to the more reasonable and sympathetic expectation that all newcomers could still be assimilated into the infinitely expansive melting pot of the country, or perhaps even that their various cultures could be preserved and could contribute to a genuinely pluralistic and flexible democratic culture. Since Anglo conformity turned out to be the dominant mood from the turn of the twentieth century onward, the public schools reflected this attitude. The more generous assimilation proposed by progressive and humanitarian reformers in the 1890s generally was overcome by the growing nativist tenor of the early 1900s. While the number of immigrants from northern and western Europe remained high in the 1870s and 1880s, Anglo conformists could still believe that most immigrants were "somewhat like us." But when the tide turned from the 1890s onward to Poles, Russians, Slavs, Italians, Hispanics, and Asians, the hue and cry for conformity became louder and more shrill.

Victory of Restrictive Legislation / Indeed, the legal attack upon free immigration policies began as early as 1875 when Congress passed the first restrictive legislation, prohibiting prostitutes and alien convicts from entering. Thus began a 50-year period that ended with general restrictions and quotas upon all comers. The campaigns against immigrants took all manner of forms, from organizations devoted to propaganda and politics and violence to the infinite informal networks of prejudice and discrimination. In 1882 the virulent hostility to Chinese laborers resulted in the Chinese Exclusion Act, and at the same time Congress excluded lunatics, idiots, and persons likely to become public charges, irrespective of nationality or ethnic origin. California went much further than the federal law on Chinese, and excluded Japanese as well. The San Francisco board of education segregated all Oriental children, although they were only a tiny fraction of the public school enrollment.

In the late 1880s the antipathy toward Catholics, especially the Irish, took organized form in the American Protective Association (APA), which campaigned for immigration restriction and used compulsory attendance at the public schools wherever possible as a weapon against Catholic schools. While the APA was especially strong among working-class Protestants in the West, the Immigration Restriction League was formed by the upper-class elite in Boston, especially to campaign for a literacy test as a tool for restricting immigration, obviously aimed at southern and eastern Europeans. Backed by the Republican Party, such a law was passed by Congress in 1896, but was vetoed by Grover Cleveland. Three more literacy test laws were passed by Congress, vetoed once by William Howard Taft and twice by Woodrow Wilson, but finally prevailing over Wilson's veto in 1917. Meanwhile, Congress established a joint Commission on Immigration in 1907. The Commission issued a 42-volume report in 1911 suggesting restrictive legislation based upon the percentage of persons from each ethnic group already in the United States, again obviously aimed at the southern and eastern Europeans.

The "Americanization" Movement / As World War I approached, the campaign to limit immigration turned especially against the Germans, abetted by Theodore Roosevelt himself, but was broadened to include an aggressive movement for quick and complete "Americanization" of all foreign elements. The Americanization movement reflected the extremes of Anglo-conformist assimilation, calling upon immigrants to renounce their native cultures and attachments in favor of the dominant "American" (that is, middle-class white Protestant) culture as well as to affirm overt loyalty to U.S. political institutions. This started a nationwide campaign to teach English, U.S. history, and civics to adult foreigners through industrial and community programs and to install such requirements in the public schools. Before World War I patriotic groups took the lead: Daughters of the American Revolution, Sons of the American Revolution, Society of Colonial Dames, and the North American Civic League for Immigrants. After that war the American Legion was especially active in promoting the patriotic and antiradical themes of Americanization; and the Ku Klux Klan spread its umbrella of antipathies toward radicals and liquor to cover blacks, Catholics, liberals, Jews, and immigrants. The Klan's obverse campaign was for compulsory Bible reading in the public schools as a bulwark for its basically nativist Protestant orientation.

Campaigns by extremists were sometimes joined by more moderate Anglo conformists who believed that some sort of control should be exerted over immigration so that the assimilation process would have a better chance to work. As a result, the restrictive immigration laws of the 1920s were passed.[3]

The Role of Public Education in Assimilation

Public education naturally reflected these pushes to cohesion and pulls to differentiation that threatened to split apart the American political community in the early decades of the twentieth century. The gentle comprehensiveness of a Francis Parker, echoing the common school ideal, was about to be shattered. In a talk to teachers at the Chautauqua Assembly, New York, in 1891 Parker said:

> The public school in a republic means that in their early life children of all classes, of all nationalities, of all sects, of rich and poor alike, children of both sexes, shall work together under the highest and best conditions in one community for from eight to twelve years.[4]

How different was the attitude of Ellwood P. Cubberley in 1909, echoing from the idyll of the Stanford campus after two decades of massive immigration and nativist and racist agitation:

> These southern and eastern Europeans are of a very different type from the north Europeans who preceded them. Illiterate, docile, lacking in self-reliance and initiative, and not possessing the Anglo-Teutonic conceptions of law, order, and government, their coming has served to dilute tremendously our native stock, and to corrupt our civic life. . . . Our task is to break up these groups or settlements, to assimilate and amalgamate these people as a part of our American race, and to implant in their children, so far as can be done, the Anglo-Saxon conception of righteousness, law and order, and popular government, and to awaken in them a reverence for our democratic

institutions and for those things in our national life which we as a people hold to be of abiding worth.[5]

This oft-quoted passage reveals the dominant view of educators that the purpose of the public school was indeed to impose the prevailing core culture of America upon the non-northern and non-western European immigrants. In other words, differentiation should *not* be made by public schools on behalf of ethnic cultural differences. Depending upon what view one takes of the assimilation process, this approach of the public schools may be regarded as either highly successful or dismally unsuccessful.

From an Anglo-conformist point of view the schools were highly successful in bringing millions of foreigners into U.S. life with amazingly little disruption and comparatively little open conflict, if we compare the process with the later tribal or ethnic conflicts that tore apart India, Pakistan, and other countries of the Middle East, Africa, and Asia. From the point of view of cultural pluralism, the schools failed to give the respect and attention to diverse national cultures that would have prevented deep-seated alienation between new and old groups, and between older and younger generations.

By and large, the public schools saw their main job as assimilation of immigrants to the dominant culture. Francesco Cordasco argues that the school saw its role essentially as one of "enforced assimilation" and seldom developed a policy to meet the special needs of the immigrant child.[6] Indeed, Cordasco points out that a few educational reformers in New York, like Julia Richman as a district superintendent, did form many special classes for immigrant children to give particular help in learning English, depending upon their age and fluency. Needless to say, the easiest way to differentiate further was to guide the immigrant children to manual training and industrial education tracks. Little or no effort was made to change the course of study in regular academic classes.[7]

Mary Antin on the Values of Assimilation / The irony was that this kind of education leading to rapid assimilation was exactly what some immigrants most wanted. A striking example is the well-known reflection of Mary Antin, a Russian Jewish girl who came to the United States in 1894 and whose elder sister had to work, instead of going to school, to enable the poverty-stricken family to survive:

> Education was free. That subject my father had written about repeatedly, as comprising his chief hope for us children, the essence of American opportunity, the treasure that no thief could touch, not even misfortune or poverty. It was the one thing that he was able to promise us when he sent for us; surer, safer than bread or shelter. On our second day I was thrilled with the realization of what this freedom of education meant. A little girl from across the alley came and offered to conduct us to school. . . . This child, who had never seen us till yesterday, who could not pronounce our names, who was not much better dressed than we, was able to offer us the freedom of the schools of Boston! No application made, no questions asked,

no examinations, no rulings, exclusions; no machinations, no fees. The doors
stood open for every one of us. The smallest child could show us the way. . . .
    The apex of my civic pride and personal contentment was reached on
the bright September morning when I entered the public school. . . . the
importance of the day was a hundred times magnified, on account of the
years I had waited, the road I had come, and the conscious ambitions I
entertained.[8]

And, furthermore, Mary Antin found sympathetic teachers who helped speed
the process of assimilation by individualized instruction:

    Miss Nixon made a special class of us, and aided us so skillfully and
earnestly in our endeavors to "see-a-cat," and "hear-a-dog-bark," and "look-
at-the-hen" that we turned over page after page of the ravishing history,
eager to find out how the common world looked, smelled, and tasted in the
strange speech. The teacher knew just when to let us help each other out with
a word in our own tongue,—it happened that we were all Jews,—and so,
working all together, we actually covered more ground in a lesson than the
native classes, composed entirely of the little tots.[9]

It is clear that Mary Antin became a devoted Anglo conformist, seeking
eagerly, as so many of the younger generation of immigrants did, to assimilate
as quickly as possible by learning the language and customs of the new land.
She was glad to be acculturated so quickly, but she also recognized that the
price of eager and quick Anglo conformity was likely to be an assault upon
the security provided by the traditional family:

    My parents knew only that they desired us to be like American chil-
dren; and seeing how their neighbors gave their children boundless liberty,
they turned us also loose, never doubting but that the American way was the
best way. . . . The result was that laxity of domestic organization, that inver-
sion of normal relations which makes for friction, and which sometimes ends
in breaking up a family that was formerly united and happy.
    This sad process of disintegration of home life may be observed in
almost any immigrant family of our class and with our traditions and aspirations. It is part of the process of Americanization; an upheaval preceding the
state of repose. It is the cross that the first and second generations must bear,
an involuntary sacrifice for the sake of the future generations.[10]

Mary Antin and millions of other aspiring immigrants were more or less willing to pay the price of Anglo conformity, or acculturation. Millions of older
Americans, however, did not see that such assimilation was any particular
hardship on the newcomer and, if they did, they assumed it was a necessary
sacrifice on behalf of a greater America.
    Organized political action to break the "shackles of ancestral bondage"
of immigrant cultures resulted in legislation to put the force of state law
behind the drive for Anglo conformity in the 1890s and later in the Americanization movement of the World War I era. Sometimes the Anglo assimila-
tors were surprised at the strong reaction when immigrant populations were
powerful enough to object. When the Republican-controlled Wisconsin legislature passed the Bennett Law in 1889, requiring that all children in the state

receive elementary instruction in English, the German community reacted so vigorously that the Republican governor was defeated in 1890 and the state went Democratic in 1892. The Anglicists argued that a knowledge of English would aid the German child to succeed in America; the Germans cried that the law was a tyrannical violation of parents' rights to educate their children as they saw fit.[11] By 1898 a compromise of sorts was struck when the legislature prescribed that all district schools must teach American history, the constitutions of the United States and of Wisconsin along with the 3 R's, the medium of instruction must be English, and any foreign language might be taught to such pupils as desired it—but not for more than one hour a day!

John Dewey and Jane Addams on the Values of Cultural Pluralism / As the calls for Anglo conformity became more strident, some educators of the more humanitarian progressive persuasion began to urge that the ethnic heritage of immigrants was far from an "ancestral bondage," but rather should be honored and utilized in a generous and sympathetic process of assimilation. This view, later to be called "cultural pluralism," was formulated principally by progressive-minded reformers in education and in social settlement work. In addressing the NEA in 1902, John Dewey reflected the views emanating from Jane Addams' Hull House:

> The power of the public schools to assimilate different races to our own institutions, through the education given to the younger generation, is doubtless one of the most remarkable exhibitions of vitality that the world has ever seen.
> But, after all, it leaves the older generation still untouched; and . . . in some respects the children are too rapidly . . . denationalized. They lose the positive and conservative value of their own native traditions, their own native music, art, and literature. They do not get complete initiation into the customs of their new country, and so are frequently left floating and unstable between the two. They even learn to despise the dress, bearing, habits, language, and beliefs of their parents—many of which have more substance and worth than the superficial putting-on of the newly adopted habits.[12]

A few years later, Jane Addams herself, who obviously influenced Dewey, told the NEA in 1908 that while the public school is the "great savior of the immigrant district," it must be indicted for widening the gulf between parents and children. Instead, she said,

> the schools ought to do more to connect these children with the best things of the past, to make them realize something of the beauty and charm of the language, the history, and the traditions which their parents represent. . . . In short, it is the business of the school to give to each child the beginnings of a culture so wide and deep and universal that he can interpret his own parents and countrymen by a standard which is world-wide and not provincial. . . .
> If the body of teachers in our great cities could take hold of the immigrant colonies, could bring out of them their handicrafts and occupations, their traditions, their folk songs and folk lore, the beautiful stories which

every immigrant colony is ready to tell and translate; could get the children to bring these things into school as the material from which culture is made and the material upon which culture is based, they would discover by comparison that which they give them now is a poor meretricious and vulgar thing. Give these children a chance to utilize the historic and industrial material which they see about them and they will begin to have a sense of ease in America, a first consciousness of being at home.[13]

Teachers thus could hear if they would but listen to the ideals of what was later to be called "cultural pluralism" or "multicultural education," and some undoubtedly tried to put them into practice. But World War I was approaching, and as the Americanization rhetoric began to heat up the educational atmosphere, these goals of pluralism were likely to be smothered by the "uncultivated" drive to ethnocentric conformity. To be sure, the sentimental goal of assimilation of different ethnic strains through intermarriage caught the public fancy in 1908 through Israel Zangwill's popular play, *The Melting Pot*, but this solution was not generally adopted. There were indeed a large number of intermarriages across ethnic lines, but they seemed to be mostly concentrated within the major religious groupings of Protestant, Catholic, and Jewish.[14] Besides, intermarriage was something that the elementary schools could not directly have done very much about, but they could have done much more about cultural pluralism.

Building upon such liberal ideas as those of Dewey and Addams, a number of other scholars and publicists began to argue against the harsh imperatives of Anglo-Americanism. Horace Kallen and Isaac Berkson from the academic world and Norman Hapgood and Randolph Bourne from the literary world argued that the communal and cultural traditions of the varied ethnic groups *ought* to be preserved and cultivated, and not be submerged or annihilated by the dominant cultural patterns of Americanism.[15] The values of group identity could be promoted by ethnic churches, newspapers, mutual aid societies, recreation groups, marriage, and informal friendship cliques and circles. Much of this would happen inevitably, but it should be seen as a positive contribution to American life as a whole and not as a threat. The early cultural pluralists also believed in the public schools as a common experience to promote the integration of immigrants into citizenship and economic affairs. The distinction between *political* and *cultural* was sometimes slurred over by both the Anglo conformists and the cultural pluralists. This was done even when cultural pluralism was rediscovered later on in the twentieth century (see Chapter 12).

Meanwhile, despite the efforts of progressive reformers to combat both the extremes of Anglo conformity on one side and of the amalgamating melting pot on the other, the trends were against them. Throughout the prewar and postwar periods Dewey argued against both the "anonymous and drilled homogeneity" of Anglo conformity and the disappearance of ethnic variety implied by the melting-pot metaphor.[16] In a study of schooling of immigrants in 1920, Frank Thompson, superintendent of schools in Boston, urged that persuasion rather than compulsion should be used in getting immigrants to learn English, to adopt American customs, and become naturalized citizens. He also urged the development of bilingual schools, which would instill the "new allegiance without relinquishing old associations," as the most effective institution to promote citizenship.[17] But the "compulsionists" seemed to be winning.

The Popularity of Americanization Legislation / As might be expected, campaigns at the state level were more successful than at the federal level. The Senate passed a bill in 1919 for the compulsory teaching of English to illiterates, but it died in a House committee. On the other hand, campaigns for the compulsory use of English in the schools at the state level were extremely successful. Between 1917 and 1921 some 30 states passed laws requiring all instruction in the public schools, and often in private schools as well, to be given in the English language. Several states went even further and prohibited the teaching of foreign languages in elementary schools. These moves, however, were slowed down when the Supreme Court decided in *Meyer* v. *Nebraska* (1923) that such laws passed in Nebraska, Iowa, and Ohio were unconstitutional.

These Anglo-conformist tendencies even spilled over to the attempt to compel all children to attend a *public* school. An Oregon law of 1922 saw such requirements as a safeguard for the teaching of citizenship, the prevention of juvenile delinquency, and the diminution of religious prejudice to be achieved in a common school rather than in separate private or parochial schools. However, the U.S. Supreme Court ruled the Oregon law unconstitutional in *Pierce* v. *Society of Sisters* in 1925. Since the decisions in *Meyer* and in *Pierce* heralded the new search for freedom in the mid-twentieth century and put a brake upon the excesses of the Americanization movement, they will be discussed in Chapter 10.

Decisive Role of Public Schools / Whatever one may think about the desirability of assimilation, its slowness or its speed, there is considerable agreement that the public schools of the United States played a large, if not a decisive, role in the process. Milton M. Gordon, a discerning sociologist and student of the entire process, puts it this way:

> This brings us to the children of the uprooted. Here is where the acculturation process has been overwhelmingly triumphant. . . . in whatever contest ensued between the behavior models of the parents' culture and those of the general American society, the latter pressed upon the new generation's sensibilities by the public school system and the mass media of communication, there is no question as to which would be the winner.[18]

Gordon's conclusion that urbanization and the modernization process were aiding and abetting the assimilation process and thus working against the perpetuation of segmental pluralisms is supported by recent historians of the assimilation process who make much the same point that Gordon does about its imperative march.

As Dinnerstein and Reimers survey the past and look to the future they argue that the public schools were one of the factors that tended to lessen the differences among peoples of different backgrounds:

> The twentieth-century development of a public school system was certainly another key factor in breaking down ethnicity. The immigrants' descendants were being instructed in Anglo-American values. . . . The forces undermining ethnicity—mass education, social mobility, and an American culture—are strong determinants that no group in the past has been able to withstand indefinitely.[19]

Other scholars have argued that it was not the oppression of Americanization laws nor of the public schools but the very openness, general tolerance, and high absorptive qualities of American culture, including that of the public schools, which speeded assimilation. For example, a German student of assimilation in various countries wrote that

> the achievements of the Anglo-American society and the possibilities for individual achievements and advancements which this society offered were so attractive that the descendants of the aliens sooner or later voluntarily integrated themselves into this society.[20]

Responses of European Immigrants to Public Education

In view of the "inevitability" of assimilation, as of modernization, the question arises as to how the various immigrants responded to the role of the public school. We know that the response of individuals varied. We know that there was opposition to compulsory attendance laws, to the requirement of English as a medium of instruction, and to the denigration of native cultures by insensitive teachers. We know that some recent writers have levied blame upon the public schools for their pressurized Americanization tactics. But the weight of historical evidence so far points to the receptiveness and even eagerness with which large numbers of immigrants responded to the opportunities offered by the public schools. Their faith in the public schools as a major means for advancement in their adopted society was equal to and often greater than that of older Americans. What recent scholarship emphasizes is that there were basic group differences among the immigrant nationalities which helped to mold their differing attitudes towards schooling and the expected benefits to be derived from it.

Immigrant Commitment to Public Schooling

David Tyack summarizes some of the earlier scholarship on the subject of immigrant commitment to education.[21] As early as 1909, Leonard Ayres' study showed that literacy and school attendance among white immigrant children and second-generation children were higher than that of native whites (due largely to the low figures in southern states), and that attendance of immigrants' children in most northern cities was also higher:

> Although they feared losing their children through Americanization, the great mass of immigrant parents also saw schooling as a doorway to new opportunities. John Daniels, a sociologist who traveled all over the nation studying biculturism, wrote in 1920 that "if you ask ten immigrants who have been in America long enough to rear families what American institution is most effective in making the immigrant part and parcel of American life, nine will reply "the public school."[22]

This faith in education induced large numbers of immigrant children to become teachers and thus help to Americanize still younger descendants of immigrants.

Three recent investigators have thrown a great deal of light on the way the immigrants responded to public education. Timothy Smith has shown that attendance of children of foreign parentage was as high as, or higher than, those of native-born parents, and that second-generation teachers were common in the public schools. Also, ethnic associations, churches, and newspapers displayed a great commitment to public education and urged their newly arrived countrymen to attend school for three major purposes: to enable them to earn a better living, to enable the agrarian-oriented newcomer to cope with an urban and industrial (that is, a modern) way of life, and to achieve a responsible U.S. citizenship while maintaining a sense of national identity with the homeland. So, these organizations urged and even helped the foreign-born to learn English, and they encouraged enrollment in the new vocational classes. Many immigrant parents sought money, education, and respectability as eagerly as any Puritan brought up on the work ethic; and many experienced little of the generational conflict or alienation between parent and child, which has become a favorite theme among historians and sociologists. Leading ethnic editors and societies worked for compulsory attendance compliance among their compatriots as avidly as did any Anglo assimilationist. As Smith says:

> Quite as much as any coercion from compulsory education acts or any pressures from professional Americanizers, the immigrant's own hopes for his children account for the immense success of the public school system, particularly at the secondary level, in drawing the mass of working-class children into its embrace. By their presence, and by their commitment to these several ambitions, the first generation of immigrant children prompted educators, in administrative offices as well as classrooms, to a thousand pragmatic experiments geared to the interests and the needs of their students. . . . [This] con-

tributed heavily to the national consensus about progressive reform in both school and society which has dominated American social ideals throughout the 20th century.[23]

Factors Affecting Immigrant Achievement in School / Smith's analysis is a persuasive refutation of arguments that the public schools were simply an agency for imposing unwanted cultural values upon docile or resentful but helpless newcomers. No matter what the answer as to the desirability of assimilation might be, another question was how well the immigrants did in the schools. Here the judgment so far seems to be that some immigrant groups did exceptionally well, even better than native-born, and others did rather poorly. David Cohen makes the point:

> Children whose parents emigrated from England, Scotland, Wales, Germany, and Scandinavia seem to have generally performed about as well at school as native whites; certainly their average performance never dropped much below that level. The children of Jewish immigrants typically achieved at or above the average for native whites. It was central and southern European non-Jewish immigrants—and to a lesser extent, the Irish—who experienced really serious difficulty in school. On any index of educational attainment (whether it was retardation, achievement scores, IQ, or retention), children from these nationalities were a good deal worse off than native urban whites.[24]

An interesting interpretation of the reasons for these differences is Cohen's conjecture that they were not simply the result of differences in culture and motivation but were related to the degree of urbanization from which they came, that is, the more urban (and I would say, the more modern) the background, the higher the achievement in schooling in the United States. Rural (and traditional) Poles and southern Italians ranked lower than urbanized Germans and Jews. And even more interesting, the Jews who came from urban or modernized sectors surpassed Jews who came from traditional societies; that is, the modernized German Jewish children were less retarded than the more traditional or rural Russian Jews, Rumanian Jews, and Polish Jews, in that order.

A more extensive and more recent study by Michael R. Olneck and Marvin Lazerson carries the analysis of school achievement still further.[25] In general, they found that children of foreign parentage were somewhat, but only negligibly, disadvantaged in comparison to those of native-born parents with regard to school attendance and retardation, but this was not a substantial difference at the elementary level. There was greater disadvantage in starting and completing high school. The great difference was between the nationality groups themselves, and especially so in entrance to and completion of high school. Olneck and Lazerson marshal a great deal of data to show that the children from northern and western Europe (English, Swedish, German, Irish, and German Jews) continued in school longer than did those from eastern and southern Europe (Russian Jews, southern Italians, and

Poles). The attendance of girls compared with that of boys followed a similar nationality pattern. These nationality differences seemed to persist over the 30-year period from 1900 to 1930.

Olneck and Lazerson made a special comparative study of Russian Jews and southern Italians and found that the Jewish children outperformed the Italian children on measures of retardation, retention, and standardized tests. The researchers argue that such differences were not merely a function of economic income, social class, occupational status of fathers, English language familiarity, age of school entrance, or length of father's residence in the United States. Although these were important matters, still more important were the group cultural values that the immigrants brought with them and which helped to shape their responses to American institutions and the public school.

Russian Jewish culture placed high value on learning and study, agility with words, belief that education would lead to advancement, all contributing to the emphasis by parents on their children's achievement. Southern Italian culture, in contrast, was suspicious of schooling, teachers, and officials of the state and the church, who were often viewed as exploiters. It thus emphasized the family and kinship groups as the basis of collective and communal life; filial obligation to family and parents was more important than filial success. Since schooling and education had elitist and alien connotations for most Italian peasant families, schooling was not viewed as a ladder to success. So Italian parents did not put pressure on their children to stay in school or to excel, as so many Jewish parents did. In a word, the values of the Jewish culture were closely attuned to the achievement syndrome of modernization, while the Italian culture preserved much of the ascriptive values of a traditional society. In the booming modernization of the early twentieth century, the Jewish culture adapted more readily to the requirements of public education.

Immigrant Adaptability and Upward Social Mobility

Whatever the connection between education and social mobility, a subject which deserves and is receiving more and more attention, it is apparent that the ethnic groups that took advantage of or adapted to the public school system also moved up the social and economic ladder more successfully and quickly.[26] Of the "old immigrant" groups, the Germans and the Scandinavians prospered economically sooner than did the Irish. Of the "new immigrants" the Jews moved up spectacularly, even when beginning at low economic levels, and Greeks did well in both school and economy, but Italians and Slavs, who usually began farther behind, tended to stay farther behind in both educational and economic achievement.

One can generalize about the parallel relationship between mobility and education, but much more historical research needs to be done concerning the qualitative role that education played. Some of the more recent historical studies of occupational achievement are beginning to show that there was much more upward movement, even from the lowest levels, than it has been popular for sociologists of stratification to admit.

Ethnic and Religious Disparities / One of the most significant of such studies is that of Boston by Stephan Thernstrom, in which he himself reverses his earlier pessimistic review of the little mobility he found in Newburyport, Massachusetts.[27]

In studying the fortunes of nearly 8,000 males in Boston from 1880 to 1970, Thernstrom found that indeed those who started higher up in the occupational structure had distinct advantages over those who started lower down, but there was also a surprising amount of movement from unskilled to skilled labor and from skilled jobs to lower white-collar levels:

> The occupational structure of Boston, in sum, was remarkably fluid in one sense of the term, offering significant opportunities for self-advancement to a very substantial proportion of the men who started work in menial manual jobs. . . . Neither those who boasted that America was a land of endless opportunity nor their critics who insisted that the deck was stacked against the poor man were entirely correct; the two groups, it seems, had seen different facets of the same complex social society.[28]

Though to a Horatio Alger the glass was half-full and to a radical revisionist the glass was half-empty, it is clear that the glass was fuller for those immigrants who took advantage of the public educational system. True, again, the newcomers were disadvantaged with respect to the Yankees, but this gap was narrowed as time passed and the initial advantages diminished. The disparity between the new ethnic immigrant groups themselves was even more striking: Irish and Italians had less schooling and lagged behind; and the British and Russian Jews had more schooling and forged ahead.

Thernstrom found that the amount of schooling was an important factor here and that religious as well as ethnic backgrounds were involved. He speculated that the Protestant and Jewish immigrants had a further advantage because they attended public schools rather than congregating in Catholic parochial schools:

> Large numbers of Boston's Irish and Italian Catholics attended parochial schools, and one wonders how effective these institutions were in providing the kind of training that was conducive to occupational success. . . . What this may have meant is that the parochial system, although it offered the security of the familiar, muted rather than heightened aspirations and fostered a sense of alienation from the larger society.[29]

It was indeed a difficult decision for immigrant parents to make—whether to send their children to the public school and risk alienation from the old-world ethnic community, or to send them to a parochial school and risk alienation from the modern American community of the future. Whether or not such decisions were made with deliberate attention to alternatives, Protestant and Jewish immigrants tended to opt for the public schools rather more often than did Catholic parents.

The Classlessness of Opportunity / Of even greater interest is Thernstrom's suggestion that Boston's patterns of mobility represented not simply a unique urban case "but rather were products of forces that operated in much the same way throughout American society in the nineteenth and twentieth centuries."[30] The most striking finding was that children of unskilled manual laborers and semiskilled workers were not trapped permanently in a "culture of poverty," but had as good prospects of moving into nonmanual occupations as did the sons of skilled craftsmen.[31]

Thernstrom agrees that there were rigidities in the occupational structure that perpetuated inequality, but the strength or height of the barriers should not be overestimated:

> The social system was more fluid than could be seen at any one moment. The middle class and particularly its high white-collar stratum, was relatively successful in transferring status from father to son, but upward mobility both from blue-collar to white-collar callings and from low-ranked to high-ranked manual jobs was quite common. If Horatio Alger's novels were designed to illustrate the possibility not of rags-to-riches but of rags-to-respectability, as I take them to have been, they do not offer wildly misleading estimates of the prospects of mobility open to Americans. . . .
>
> It is true that the climb up the class ladder was harder for men of foreign stock than for Yankees, and harder for some immigrant groups than for others. But part of the explanation, at least, was not simple prejudice or even passive structural discrimination but objective differences in qualifications to perform demanding occupational tasks. And all of the major immigrant groups, however dismal their plight when they first arrived, experienced substantial upward mobility in subsequent years. The only group that could be considered a truly permanent proletariat was the blacks, and even they have found new opportunities for advancement in recent years.[32]

So, an argument might be made that too much differentiation of educational programs for immigrants would have imposed even greater handicaps upon them. When differentiation was voluntary, as in the case of religious parochial schools or early dropping out, it was one thing; when it was enforced against the will of the group, as in the case of blacks, it was quite another thing. Those immigrant groups who were willing to achieve the qualifications "to perform demanding occupational tasks" moved into a more desirable occupational status; those whose culture saw less value in such qualifications and those who were denied access to the educational programs appropriate to them were the most disadvantaged.

Racist Differentiation Imposed
Upon Non-European Minorities

While European ethnic immigrants, whatever their disadvantages, were gradually improving their lot between 1876 and 1926, as Thernstrom's study shows, the same was not nearly so true of Mexican Americans and black Americans, whose educational opportunities were even more severely limited. Patently segregated systems were imposed on them in the South and Southwest, and severe discrimination met those who poured into the North and West between 1900 and 1920 in the hopes that they could better themselves. If many European immigrants wished for more differentiation from the public schools to take account of their distinctive cultures, Mexicans and blacks could have wished for less of the enforced differentiation that effectively kept them out of the mainstream of political, economic, and social life of the nation. Despite the admitted failures to do all they could for the European immigrant ethnics, the public schools did fairly well for them compared with their failure when barriers of racism were set up for the education of Mexicans in *de facto* segregated schools and for blacks and American Indians in *de jure* segregated schools.

Pervasive Discrimination Against Mexican-Americans

There were some parallels between the situation of the new European immigrants who poured into the cities of the North and Midwest and the plight of the Mexicans in the Southwest, but there were also great differences. The Spanish-speaking peoples of Texas, New Mexico, Arizona, Colorado, and California were there long before the Anglos came. For nearly three hundred years, they were there under Spanish rule and for a quarter-century under Mexican rule before the United States took over in 1848. From then on, the Anglo-Americans arrived by the thousands from a rapidly modernizing nation to exploit a basically rural, traditional society that had changed little since the sixteenth century. The Anglos grabbed the land, disregarded the Treaty of Guadaloupe Hidalgo (1848), which had guaranteed the rights of U.S. citizens to those Mexicans who chose to stay, and generally acted like the emissaries of the colonial powers that were taking over vast territories and the peoples of Africa and Asia at the same time in the late nineteenth century.

The general judgment is that the Anglo-American colonizers, by and large, ran roughshod over the Mexican-Americans whose homeland the Southwest had been for several centuries. The Anglos understood little of the ancient Spanish and Indian cultures that had often joined to form the culture of Mexican-Americans, or Chicanos (as they were at first disparagingly called), and the Anglos seemed to care little whether they ever did understand it. Confident in the superiority of their own institutions and culture, and indifferent or hostile to the Spanish and Indian inheritance, the Anglos quite naturally imported their own institutions, as colonialists did throughout the underdeveloped world. The adventurers and exploiters showed the arrogance and brutality of their kind: More Mexican-Americans were lynched in the Southwest between 1865 and 1920 than were blacks in the Southeast, a comparison of no credit to either section. Deprived of land and property rights, never gaining full political rights, despised for their language and lack of modern skills, the Mexican-Americans found themselves at the bottom of the economic, political, and social ladder. In fact, there seemed to be no ladder to climb in what approached a caste society, albeit not a slave society. Mexican-Americans rapidly became a minority of second-class citizens, not to say outcasts, in what had been their homeland. They were the manual laborers, the subsistence farmers, the tenants, the ranch hands, and the migratory workers for Anglo owners and employers.

The story was, of course, not as unrelieved as this may appear. There were missionaries, teachers, and others of good will who sought to convert, aid, uplift, and improve the lot of the Chicanos. One of the outstanding Roman Catholic emissaries was Jean Baptiste Lamy, who built missions and schools and eventually became Archbishop in Sante Fe. Public schools, which were established in the territories and in the states along the models of the public schools in the rest of the nation, generally paid little attention to the Spanish culture, sought to teach English to replace the Spanish language, usually prohibited the use of Spanish in the classrooms and on the playgrounds, and found it desirable to separate the Chicano children from the Anglos. Though the southwestern states did not go the full legal route of requiring segregated schools by constitution or by law, the practice of segregation became customary: separate schools, separate classes, poorer buildings and facilities, fewer well-trained teachers, smaller budgets. The discrimination, prejudice, and segregation were particularly evident in Texas and southern California. These were heightened after 1900 when the flow across the border, both legal and illegal, increased markedly with the onset in 1910 of the unrest that finally led to the Mexican revolution of 1920.

Mexicans had earlier begun to arrive in larger numbers to take the jobs on railroads, farms, and mines that became available when the Chinese were excluded in 1882 and the Japanese restricted in 1907. Before the Mexican revolution, the influx was largely made up of temporary workers, mostly male, seeking the better wages that the United States could provide, which sometimes amounted to five times the level available in Mexico. After the Mexican revolution, more and more Mexicans stayed on in the United States, and when the restrictive laws on European immigration were passed in the 1920s, the Southwestern agricultural growers persuaded Congress to exempt Mexicans. The Census records show that nearly 700,000 came across the border between 1909 and 1930, perhaps as many again illegally.

Barriers to Assimilation / The educational situation was particularly complicated, curiously, by the fact that the vast majority of the Mexican immigrants shared a common Spanish language and culture, in contrast to the great variety of European languages and cultures in the cities of the East and the North. Many of the European immigrants, as we have seen, especially from northern and western Europe, were eager for an American education. But the large number of Mexicans of peasant and peon background had no such positive attitude toward the value of schooling, viewing it as southern Italians did, as a luxury for the elite. Finding such large Spanish-speaking communities so long established and so rigidly circumscribed within the *barrio*, the newcomers saw even less reason to learn English than did those who poured into the polyglot northern cities. Thus, the process of assimilation was slower, and the disadvantaged economic status was maintained longer.

The corpus of teachers and administrators included no large number of Spanish-speaking immigrant stock comparable to the contingent of European immigrants in northern city schools. The predominantly Anglo teachers seemed particularly prejudiced or hostile to the unfamiliar Spanish Mexican ways. The Mexican-American parents were even less likely to see the benefits of urging their children to acquire an education, especially as it was likely to undermine their traditional beliefs and religion and culture. Besides, many came to the United States with the thought that the sojourn was to be only temporary. For all these reasons the public schools were not destined to aid very rapidly the assimilation or the advancement of the Mexican-Americans who remained, fairly forgotten on the national scene as compared with other highly visible ethnic groups who became active in national as well as urban politics before World War II.

In addition to the inhibiting cultural influences, the great influx of Mexicans came at just the time when the Americanization and nativist campaigns were at their peak in the years prior to and following World War I. Thus, they received the brunt of the antipathies that had been building up from the 1890s with respect to the new immigrants from Europe. The ambivalence between Anglo employers who welcomed Mexicans for their cheap labor and those Anglo workers who resented their competition caused further difficulties. This was often shared by the older and better educated Mexicans who had been able over time to move into preferred economic and social positions.

Yet, public schools *were* established, Mexican-American children *did* go to them, and ever so gradually a few began to make their way into positions of leadership. Occasionally, an optimistic note would be sounded, even before World War I, atypical as it may now seem. In 1916 Alvin Johnson, who was to become president of the New School for Social Research, wrote for the *New Republic* an enthusiastic account of at least one outstanding public school educator:

Mr. W. G. Knox of San Antonio . . . is a devoted educator, an excellent representative of the American schoolman, our best national contribution to civilization. Since boyhood he has known the Mexicans and liked them, and for the last sixteen years he has taught them in the Navarro public school, of which he is head. Mexicans are not segregated in the public schools of San Antonio, but the Navarro school is in the Mexican quarter, and of its twelve hundred pupils, more or less, ninety per cent are Mexican. . . . Mr. Knox knows of no characteristic intellectual differences between Mexican and American children. . . . the Mexican children make as rapid progress through the grades as American. In writing, drawing, and music they are better than the American; in mathematics, as good, in English they are inferior. . . . Here is a people well endowed intellectually, eager to learn, capable of artistic expression, with an emotional life intense, but wholesome, with extremely vital family institutions, and apparently with enough cooperative instinct to manage the practical affairs of life without the capacity for individual accumulation necessary for survival in a race like our own, unsocial, unkind.[33]

Obviously, there were other educators like Mr. Knox and there were other voices like that of Alvin Johnson's, but they were in the minority, and the majority was not listening. It took another quarter of a century or more before the consciousness and the conscience of the nation began to stir under the proddings of a new generation of Anglo liberals and especially of new Chicano leadership that emerged around and after World War II.

Legal Segregation of Blacks

More obvious in the national politics and in the national consciousness of the period was the largest body of depressed citizens, the people of darkest color—the blacks. The failure of Reconstruction to achieve a uniform national policy of integrative schools through action of the federal government meant that the promise of desegregation of education in the South went unfulfilled for nearly a hundred years. White southerners began to regain political control in their states in the early 1870s, a process they liked to refer to as a "redemption" that saved the South from the alien rule of the North. When President Rutherford B. Hayes signalized the end of Reconstruction by removing the last of the federal troops from the South in 1877, it may have seemed like redemption to white southerners, but it seemed like the same old repression to blacks, for it meant a renewed and still harsher inequality for them.

Jim Crow Athwart Assimilation / All 17 of the southern states and Washington, D.C. reinstituted new and more severe black codes, regulating association among the races in public places, conveyances, theaters, and hotels, and relegating Negroes to an inferior status in all cases, including, of course, segregated schools. So, by 1880, the southern states had achieved in practice segregated schools for blacks (though the constitutions in some states were not changed until the 1890s), while most northern states were deciding in favor of legally integrated schools, either by legislative action or judicial decision. A nation half-integrated and half-segregated led to an insidious racial disjunctivitis on a national scale, a disease that was to continue to undermine the social health of both halves.

The Supreme Court had forecast its eventual support for redemption when it declared the Civil Rights Act of 1875 to be unconstitutional on the grounds that the federal government could not protect private citizens from discrimination against each other on the basis of race or color, and that states could be held in check only with respect to *civil* rights (like voting) and not *social* rights (like frequenting restaurants and hotels). When it came to matters of legal separation, the test was to be equality, not integration.

Efforts to break down the Jim Crow laws in transportation and education were met by decisions of state and federal courts upholding the principle that segregation was legal as long as *equal* facilities for both races were maintained. This doctrine went back at least as far as the Roberts school case in Boston in 1849, when the supreme court of Massachusetts decided that Boston could maintain a segregated school system. The "separate but equal" doctrine was firmly incorporated in *Plessy* v. *Ferguson* in 1896 when the United States Supreme Court upheld the right of railroads to segregate passengers according to race as long as equal facilities were provided.[34] The Plessy case, setting a seal of approval upon the power of states to deal with civil rights free from federal intervention, provided the legal precedent for segregated public schools until the middle of the twentieth century. In 1899 the case of *Cumming* v. *Board of Education* applied the separate but equal doctrine to public schools.[35]

Separate and Unequal Schooling / As the nineteenth century turned into the twentieth century, the American dream of equality turned into a nightmare of repression. The goals of 60 years of postbellum education for blacks in the South could be summed up under the heading of three R's as follows:

Reconstruction (1860s–1870s): integrated and equal schools
Redemption (1870s–1890s):   separate but equal schools
Repression (1890s–1920s):   separate but unequal schools

The disjunctive racist disease was running its course with ever more devastating effects. Generations of black children were being taught what it meant to be inferior and were learning the lessons perforce. Generations of white children were being taught what it meant to be a superior race and were learning the lessons only too well. In the South as a whole, expenditures that had been approximately in the proportion of $3.00 per head for whites and $2.00 for blacks in the 1870s became by 1930 a proportion of $7.00 for whites and $2.00 for blacks. No matter what the laws said or what the courts said, the practice was clearly not only separate but also unequal.[36]

Despite the efforts of some forward-looking southerners and humanitarian northerners, the black schools continued to be a disgrace in a democratic nation, a massive roadblock in the way of democratic modernity. White teachers received little enough in salaries; black teachers received a pittance, averaging $1,500 a year in some states. In 1910 no rural black school included an eighth grade; no black school provided as much as two years of high school. Elementary schools operated about four months a year, taught by teachers with an eighth-grade education. By 1900, compulsory attendance laws were not to be found in any southern state. Less than half of all children in the South actually attended schools, and only one of every 70 who started the first grade ever reached the eighth grade. The modern trend toward universal, free, and compulsory education was being thwarted by the forces of social, political, and educational racism.

Once it was clear that the Reconstruction ideal of integrated and equal education was unattainable under the political conditions of redemption, and once it was equally clear that even the redemptive ideal of separate but equal education was not going to be honored by white majorities in the southern states, those concerned with black education, both northern and southern, white and black, had to decide what to do under the repressive practices of separate and unequal education. During the 50 years of repression, the predominant response of the promoters of black education was to accept the conditions under which Southern white majorities would permit black education at all and then to persuade them to support it. This attitude of accommodation or compromise has been termed the "great detour" by Henry Allen Bullock of Texas Southern University in his prize-winning historical study of black education.[37]

Booker T. Washington echoed the sentiments of accommodation publicly for many years, becoming the symbol of the moderate and reasonable Negro leader who was willing to eschew the radical Reconstruction doctrine of equality and integration, and was ready to work to expand educational opportunities for blacks under the segregated system. This meant, as we have seen, a strong emphasis upon useful industrial education as the prime means to economic sufficiency for black workers and a stress upon the value of the dignity of labor as the means to proving merit and achievement as the principal road to economic efficiency in a segregated social, economic, and political system.

The merits of this educational response to repression have been vigorously debated in recent years, much to the discredit of Booker T. Washington and his supporters for acceding so wholeheartedly to the castelike system of legal and customary segregation. Whatever else may be said, it is a fact that enormous amounts of northern money poured into the South from a number of new philanthropic foundations. School attendance increased rapidly from around 30 percent of black children (age 5 to 19) in 1910 to 60 percent by 1930; literacy (age 10 and over) moved up from around 19 percent in 1870 to 84 percent in 1930; and an educated black leadership was being trained in the segregated black colleges.

The spearhead of the separate black education movement was the Conference for Education in the South, first convened in 1898 at Capon Springs, West Virginia, which led to the policy activities of the Southern Education Conference and the financial activities of the General Education Board.[38] In a matter of two decades the Conference persuaded the South to support universal public education for whites and to provide widespread special education in rural, manual, and industrial trades for blacks. Not only did Rockefeller money pour into the General Education Board to aid Negro education in the South, but several other foundations turned special attention to the problem. Prominent among these were the funds built by George Peabody, John F. Slater, Anna T. Jeannes, and Julius Rosenwald.

In the early decades of the twentieth century the dominant tone of compromising moderation reflected by Washington and philanthropic foundation executives like Barnas Sears of the Peabody Fund began to be challenged by a rising note of protest against the failures of the "great detour" that was supposed to lead from the paths of inequality to the highway of equality by going through the swamps and byways of segregated education. To be sure, more black children were in schools, and literacy was rising, but inequality was not giving way: black school terms were shorter than those for whites, school attendance was smaller (largely because of a tenant farm system), less money was spent on black schools, teachers' salaries were lower, buildings, equipment, and facilities were inferior, industrial education was really artisan training for a decaying traditional agricultural way of life and not the technical training needed for a modern industrial and urban way of life, and almost everywhere the black institutions were qualitatively second- and third-rate compared with those for whites. The Negro elementary schools seemed to be performing much the same function as that of the disjunctive primary schools of Europe—perpetuating a lower class, if not a caste system, for the maintenance of a traditional class society.

But recent research by Horace Mann Bond reveals a remarkable cluster of black high schools able to maintain high academic standards that produced a steady flow of black graduates to colleges and graduate schools.[39] Among these were the Dunbar High School in Washington, D.C., Douglass in Baltimore, and McDonough in New Orleans. This kind of evidence documents the little-publicized vitality of devotion to education on the part of black communities and seems to justify in large part the views of Du Bois, Harris, and the devotees of Northern missionary education that academic achievement was an essential formative influence in the creation of a people's cultural and political leadership. The experience of the newly independent nations of Africa provides an interesting parallel.[40]

Segregated Assimilation for American Indians

While the graph of black and white racism in U.S. education was rising and falling in the century following the Civil War, a variant of the same disease, a red-and-white strain, was infecting another whole sector of American life. Less immediately and directly in the forefront of the consciousness of most citizens, the educational plight of the American Indian was no less poignant in its impact upon the spirit and outlook of a whole people. Because the Indians were far less numerous than the blacks, were farther removed from the major centers of population, and had blocked so painfully the trails to the open lands of western settlements, concern for the welfare of the Indian was less prevalent and less pronounced than for the freed blacks. And because their dealings were largely with the federal government itself and their sense of common identity so weakly developed, the Indians' efforts at self-help were either less efficacious or longer-delayed than those of the blacks.

Segregation in Social Life / In the years following the end of the Civil War, the Plains Indians continued to resist the encroachment of settlers upon the lands west of the Mississippi, which they believed were rightfully theirs and which had been assigned to them by treaty after treaty with the federal government. However, by 1890, when effective military resistance had ended, most Indians had been pushed back within reservations defined by the federal government and for which the government took formal responsibility.

As the Indians tried to survive on the reservations, their plight attracted the attention of religious humanitarians, who preached the need for Christianizing and civilizing the Indians, as they had done for blacks in the United States and for Africans and Asians in their own homelands. They even persuaded President Ulysses S. Grant to assign the reservations to the several denominations, which ran them virtually as their own private religious domains.

In 1887 a new policy was enunciated in the General Allotment Act, or Dawes Act. Viewing the reservations as unwarranted prisons for the Indians, the Act's sponsors sought to free the Indians from their constrictions so that they could more quickly drop their tribal ways and become civilized. They argued that the best way to assimilate Indians into modern American life was to make them into citizen farmers by breaking up the common tribal lands of the reservations and allotting separate plots to individual Indians who could gain full title after 25 years. The trouble was that many Indians did not want to become farmers or did not know how to farm. In any case, white promoters managed to deprive the Indians of most of their lands. A total of 138 million acres of Indian lands in 1887 had dwindled under the Dawes Act to 48 million in 1932.

Reprehensible as the economic treatment of Indians was, the massive deprivation of the Indians' sense of dignity and self-respect was even worse. Prey on one side to the sordid and mercenary dealings of private entrepreneurs as well as by bureaucratic hirelings in the Indian Service, and enveloped on the other hand by the self-righteous and self-serving piety of zealous missionaries, the Indians could take little hope from the education they had been promised. By and large, they were subjected to an education whose main purpose was to assimilate them into American life by inducing them to give up their Indianness and accept the teachers' values of white, Christian, middle-class Americanism. To the end of the 1920s, this was the prime goal of educational effort.[41]

Attempted Assimilation by Segregated Schools / Three principal types of special schools undertook the task. Mission schools run by Catholic and Protestant denominations under contract with the government dominated the 1870s and 1880s. They concentrated on the three R's, some vocational and agricultural education, and of course religion. They often were taught in the Indians' languages as the best way to lead them to conversion. This subsidy of sectarian education by government was one of the outstanding violations of the doctrine of separation of church and state, which was gaining ground in the rest of the country. In 1917 these arrangements for operating Indian mission schools at government expense were ended.

In the 1880s and 1890s, government day schools run by the Bureau of Indian Affairs on the reservations began to outdistance the mission schools in number and influence. These schools did not continue the bilingual approach and the Indians were universally taught in English in order to speed up assimilation through the learning of non-Indian knowledge, skills, and values. In addition to the government-reservation day schools, a number of boarding schools were established off the reservations with support from the Bureau of Indian Affairs (some eight of them by 1887). Many educators felt that the quickest and most efficient way to transform the Indian child into an American was to remove him from his tribal setting, give him strict (even military) discipline, combine work with study, and saturate him with English language and civilized customs. The most influential of these schools was at Carlisle, Pennsylvania, founded in 1879 by General Richard Henry Pratt. In principle, Pratt was an aggressive and unrelenting assimilationist, devoted to the transformation of his wards but hardly in a compassionate way: "Kill the Indian, and save the Man" was the epitome of his educational goal,[42] helping the child to vanish as an Indian and reappear as an American:

> The goal was to provide a maximum of rapid coercive assimilation into white society. It was designed to separate a child from his reservation and family, strip him of his tribal lore and mores, force the complete abandonment of his native language, and prepare him in such way that he would never return to his people.[43]

In the early decades of the twentieth century the spirit of progressive reform that began to appear in so many aspects of American life found expression in the rise of Pan-Indianism, an effort to find a common identity that transcended tribes and led to a future in which the Indian could find pride in his Indianness and still come to terms with the modernizing Western civilization of the United States.[44] However wanting in other respects they may have been, the boarding schools, especially at Carlisle and Hampton, had made it possible for a cadre of young Indians to receive an education in English that enabled them to communicate with one another and to exert leadership in the kind of intellectual association and national organization that eventually could promote fundamental change in the Indian condition. An important force in developing a reform ideology was the Society of American Indians, founded in 1911, whose middle-class and professional leadership, pride of race, and commitment to democratic political methods paralleled those of the National Association for the Advancement of Colored People. Each in its own way symbolized the spearhead of movement that led to the search for freedom and for equality for the minority races in the decades to come.

Notes

1. R. Freeman Butts, "Teacher Education and Modernization," in George Z. F. Bereday, ed., *Essays on World Education* (New York: Oxford University Press, 1969), pp. 111–123.
2. Selwyn K. Troen, *The Public and the Schools: Shaping the St. Louis System, 1838–1920* (Columbia: University of Missouri Press, 1975), pp. 57–58.
3. Leonard Dinnerstein and David M. Reimers, *Ethnic Americans: A History of Immigration and Assimilation* (New York: Dodd Mead, 1975), p. 72.
4. Francis Parker, quoted in S. Alexander Rippa, ed., *Educational Ideas in America: A Documentary History* (New York: McKay, 1969), p. 307.
5. Ellwood P. Cubberley, *Changing Conceptions of Education* (Boston: Houghton Mifflin, 1909), pp. 15–16.
6. Francesco Cordasco, "The Children of Immigrants in Schools," in William W. Brickman and Stanley Lehrer, eds., *Education and the Many Faces of the Disadvantaged: Cultural and Historical Perspectives* (New York: Wiley, 1972), pp. 199–200.
7. Brickman and Lehrer, p. 204.
8. Mary Antin, quoted in David B. Tyack, ed., *Turning Points in American Educational History* (Waltham, Mass.: Blaisdell, 1967), pp. 235–236.
9. Antin, quoted in Theodore Rawson Crane, ed., *The Dimensions of American Education* (Reading, Mass.: Addison-Wesley, 1974), pp. 101–102.
10. Tyack, *Turning Points*, p. 238.

11. See Rush Welter, ed., *American Writings on Popular Education: The Nineteenth Century* (Indianapolis: Bobbs-Merrill, 1971), pp. 382–388.
12. John Dewey, quoted in J. Christopher Eisele, "John Dewey and the Immigrants," *History of Education Quarterly*, Spring 1975, 15(1):69–70. This whole article is an effective refutation of recent radical revisionist charges that Dewey was actually illiberal toward immigrants.
13. Jane Addams, quoted in Daniel Calhoun, ed., *The Educating of Americans: A Documentary History* (Boston: Houghton Mifflin, 1969), pp. 421–423.
14. Milton M. Gordon, *Assimilation in American Life: The Role of Race, Religion, and National Origins* (New York: Oxford University Press, 1964), pp. 121–131.
15. Gordon, pp. 132–159.
16. For details, see Eisele, pp. 71–80.
17. Robert H. Bremner, ed., *Children and Youth in America: A Documentary History;* Vol. II: 1866–1932 (Cambridge, Mass.: Harvard University Press, 1971), p. 1328.
18. Gordon, pp. 107–108.
19. Dinnerstein and Reimers, p. 55.
20. Quoted in Diane Ravitch, "On the History of Minority Group Education in the United States," *Teachers College Record*, December 1976 78(2):219.
21. David B. Tyack, *The One Best System: A History of American Urban Education* (Cambridge, Mass.: Harvard University Press, 1974), pp. 229–255.
22. Tyack, p. 241.
23. Timothy Smith, "Immigrant Social Aspirations and American Education, 1880–1930," *American Quarterly*, Fall 1969, 21(3):542–543.
24. David K. Cohen, "Immigrants and the Schools," *Review of Educational Research*, February 1970, 40(1):24.
25. Michael R. Olneck and Marvin Lazerson, "The School Achievement of Immigrant Children, 1900–1930," *History of Education Quarterly*, Winter 1974, 14(4):453–482.
26. For a convenient summary see Dinnerstein and Reimers, pp. 117–138.
27. Stephan Thernstrom, *The Other Bostonians: Poverty and Progress in the American Metropolis, 1880–1970* (Cambridge, Mass.: Harvard University Press, 1973). Quotations by permission of the copyright holders, The President and Fellows of Harvard College.
28. Thernstrom, pp. 74–75.
29. Thernstrom, p. 174. But see Andrew Greeley, who argues that the most successful ethnics went to parochial schools: "The Ethnic Miracle," *The Public Interest*, Fall 1976, 45:29.
30. Thernstrom, p. 220.
31. Thernstrom, pp. 249–250.
32. Thernstrom, pp. 257–258.
33. Alvin Johnson, quoted in Wayne Moquin, ed., *A Documentary History of the Mexican Americans* (New York: Praeger, 1971), pp. 261–263.
34. *Plessy v. Ferguson*, 163 U.S. 537 (1896).

35. *Cumming* v. *County Board of Education,* 175 U.S. 528 (1899).
36. For a full documentation of the effects of racism in the establishing of public segregated schools in North Carolina, Virginia, South Carolina, and Georgia, see Louis R. Harlan, *Separate and Unequal: Public School Campaigns and Racism in the Southern Seaboard States, 1901–1915* (Chapel Hill, N.C.: University of North Carolina Press, 1958). Atheneum edition, 1968.
37. Henry Alden Bullock, *A History of Negro Education in the South from 1619 to the Present* (Cambridge, Mass.: Harvard University Press, 1967).
38. Bullock, Chap. 4.
39. Horace Mann Bond, *Black American Scholars: A Study of Their Beginnings* (Detroit, Mich.: Balamp, 1972).
40. R. Freeman Butts, *The Education of the West* (New York: McGraw-Hill, 1973), Chaps. 14–15.
41. Margaret Szasz, *Education and the American Indian* (Albuquerque, N. M.: University of New Mexico Press, 1974), chap. 2.
42. Richard Henry Pratt, *Battlefield and Classroom: Four Decades with the American Indian, 1867–1904* (New Haven, Conn.: Yale University Press, 1964).
43. Special Subcommittee on Indian Education, U.S. Senate Committee on Labor and Public Welfare, *Indian Education: A National Tragedy—A National Challenge* (Washington, D.C.: U.S. Government Printing Office, 1969), pp. 147–148.
44. Hazel W. Hertzberg, *The Search for an American Indian Identity: Modern Pan-Indian Movements* (Syracuse, N.Y.: Syracuse University Press, 1971).

part IV
The Trichotomy
of Reform

1926-1976

Introduction

Alternative Ways To View Recent History

One way to look at the history of American public schooling in the middle decades of the twentieth century would be to divide it chronologically and neatly into periods coinciding with the succession of political administrations. First came the 12 Harding/Coolidge/Hoover years of Republican "Normalcy" (1920–1932), followed by the 20 Democratic years of Roosevelt's New Deal and Truman's Fair Deal (1932–1952). Then came the alternation of eight-year periods: the Eisenhower years of Republican accommodation at home and cold war abroad (1952–1960); the Kennedy/Johnson years of vigorous Democratic movement in the New Frontier and Great Society (1960–1968); and, finally, the Nixon/Ford years of Republican conservatism at home and détente abroad (1968–1976).

There is great temptation to see the Republican years as periods of stand-pattism, encouragement of private enterprise, slowing down of governmental activism, and relative inattention to the problems of public education. In the same vein we might view the Democratic years as periods of social and economic reform involving the more active role of government (especially the federal government) in promoting the welfare, security, health, and public education of the vast majority of ordinary citizens. And there would be a great deal of truth in such an analysis, as the subsequent chapters will reveal. But such a picture would be too simple. There were Republican Congresses with Democratic presidents and Democratic Congresses with Republican presidents. There were conservative coalitions that crossed the party lines in Congress; there were Supreme Court majorities that sometimes slowed down the economic reform efforts of a Roosevelt or a Truman, but at other times they relentlessly pushed ahead on broadening civil rights despite the foot-dragging of an Eisenhower or a Nixon. And there were particular local conditions and coalitions in dozens of states, hundreds of cities, and thousands of school districts. All this made for an enormously complicated picture in an enterprise that involved a fourth to a third of the entire population.

Another way to explain and describe the history of American public education in the middle 50 years of the twentieth century would be to relate it to the succession of major domestic and international events that made fundamental economic, political, and social impacts upon the lives of millions of Americans: the Great Depression, World War II, nuclear threat to civilization itself, cold-war rivalries with the Soviet Union, hot-war entanglements in Korea and Vietnam, the civil rights movement with attendant riots in the cities, student rebellions on the campuses, stubborn recession, inflation and unemployment, and the constitutional crisis surrounding Watergate. These, again, are indispensable to a full understanding of the complexities of the half-century of breathtaking changes that overtook the people of the

262

United States and their public schools. But to sort these out in a few pages might lead to oversimplified generalizations that would be misleading.

A third possibility would be to focus more directly upon educational or pedagogical trends that marked the period. Here could be traced the fortunes of progressive education in the 1920s and 1930s, the reactions against child-centered education ranging from the social frontier proposals in the 1930s and 1940s to demands for greater intellectual discipline in the 1940s and 1950s, the massive curriculum development projects of the 1950s and 1960s, and then the spate of critics who pilloried the public schools for their grim and joyless repression of the interests and creativity of most children. Here, we could carry forward the continuing tensions among the four major purposes identified in earlier chapters:

1. The call for greater emphasis upon academic studies and intellectual discipline erupted recurrently: "essentialism" in the 1920s; intellectualism in the 1930s and 1940s; the new math, the new science, the new social studies in the 1950s and 1960s; the stress on a national assessment of school achievement, the decline of achievement test scores, and "back to the basics" in the 1960s and 1970s.

2. The call for greater attention to development of the individual's talents went from the "project method" and intelligence testing of the 1920s, to the "child-centered" emphasis of progressive education of the 1930s and 1940s, to the "romantic reformers" of the 1960s, to the national commissions on youth and secondary education of the 1970s.

3. The call for vocational competence was heard time and time again in demands for training in the technical skills needed in both World War I and World War II, and in jobs for unemployed youth in the New Deal's Civilian Conservation Corps and National Youth Administration during and after the 1929 depression. Alarms incited by Sputnik in 1957 emphasized the need for scientific and technical studies; and vocational training was re-emphasized by the influx of rural youth to the cities of the 1950s, by the war on poverty of the 1960s, and by the new stress on career education of the 1970s.

4. The call for social efficiency was expanded to include students in programs of "common learnings" and "life adjustment" of the 1940s, and "behavior modification" and psychological "intervention" in the 1950s and 1960s. It also included teachers and administrators in the demand for accountability, management by objectives (MBO), and competency-based teacher education (CBTE) in the 1960s and 1970s.

To continue the analysis and interpretation of the fortunes of these four key purposes would be valuable and illuminating. It would lead into the recurring "reforms" that were heralded every few years, sometimes without realizing what the fortunes of earlier reforms had been. Each period produced surveys, studies, reports, critiques, and recommendations galore, each concentrating mostly on a version of one of the four purposes for reemphasis by an era or a school system that had neglected or forgotten them, or which had vacillated so long that rapidly changing circumstances had left them behind. Such a historical analysis is particularly useful when it applies to the formative phases of public education during the nineteenth and early twentieth centuries.

Three Quests for Purpose

As I view the recent history of public education, three still more crucial issues have appeared with increasing urgency and frequency. Almost as soon as the basic institutional frameworks of public education had been hammered out under the driving blows of modernization, as described in Part III, the tensions between the forces of pluralism and the value claims of the democratic political system began to raise fundamental questions about the very idea of public education and its role in American society. As early as the 1920s, but with ever-increasing insistency during the ensuing 50-year period, three other purposes of public education were highlighted. These underlay the more narrow pedagogical or curricular purposes that had to do with academic discipline, learner-oriented methods, vocational preparation, or social skills, but they were also issues basic to the most fundamental purposes and cherished ideals of American society: the search for freedom, the search for equality, and the search for the common good.

As we have seen in earlier chapters, these three purposes were not new goals for public education. They had been stated at the outset of national existence and they had been called to witness recurrently in the course of 150 years, but they had been almost smothered in practice during the frenzied years of growth and development of the late nineteenth and early twentieth centuries. Now, as the United States faced wars, depressions, and internal conflicts and dissensions, the fundamental meaning and purposes of public education in a modern, democratic, pluralistic society kept coming to the fore as the public and the profession grappled with the often conflicting claims of liberty, equality, and community. Probing and deciding what the public schools should be doing on behalf of these values raised the most fundamental questions of public policy, political practice, and constitutional order.

I find that the most illuminating and valuable way to think about the latest 50 years of our public school history is to approach it through these three basic quests for reform. They provide, I believe, the most important framework for thinking about and interpreting the historic trends of the past half-century. They reveal the historical complexities and paradoxes, the interplay of social, political, and economic forces with education, the conflicts among groups and ideologies, and the persistent, insistent, unending claims made upon public education to do this, to do that, not to do this, and not to do that.

The Trichotomy of Educational Goals / Each of the three major quests for reform has within itself a series of complicated, interweaving, and overlapping elements that tend to branch off from the other two in different directions. In other words, these three values often conflict and negate or minimize each other, sometimes with devastating effect upon the body politic. The trouble is that each one of the three-way cuts or parts (hence "trichotomy"), when viewed by itself, seems to some observers to be the primary goal for public education. Still more troublesome is the fact that public schools are often expected to accomplish all three goals at the same time. This, to say the least, raises appalling problems of priorities. No wonder that the temptation was often to say simply that public schools should stick to the basic three R's, even when this plausible solution was made impossible by insistent demands for additional "R's." Most often the additional "R's" pointed to **R**eligion, or civic **R**esponsibility, or human **R**esource development, or **R**ationality, or social **R**eform of some of the basic ills of society. Less often they called for **R**econstruction of the social order or indeed **R**evolution itself.

Attacks upon the Idea of Public Education

The crowning irony of the recent half-century is that as the nation approached its bicentennial celebration, one of the oldest and apparently firmest articles of faith in the American public creed was being called into question. Not solely was it argued that public education was not performing as well as it had in the past, or as well as it might, but that the very idea itself had outworn its usefulness.

As the 1920s opened, there had developed a very wide consensus that public education expressed the values of *free, universal, secular, compulsory, common schooling.* When put together, these six words pretty well summed up the major elements in the framework of belief about American public education. In the course of the following 50 years, every word in the phrase came under critical and sometimes bitter attack.

"Free?" For generations, "free" simply meant that all children could go to public schools without paying rate bills, fees, or tuition. Schools were free because they were tax-supported, publicly controlled, open to all. Today, it is argued, free education means that public funds should be distributed to parents through vouchers or tax credits or scholarships so that they may choose any kind of school they wish: public, private, parochial, or proprietary. And, of course, "free schools" have come to mean to some people any kind of school that is *not* under public control. The so-called "free school movement" has been basically animated by antipublic school forces.

"Universal?" It meant simply that *all* children could and should go to school, preferably on a regular full-time basis. Originally, it meant three or four years of primary schooling for younger children; then it came to mean that virtually all young people should go to or through high school. Now we hear that high school is unsuitable for large numbers of youth, or simply that they do not want to be there. So, they should be encouraged to stop-in or stop-out, or indeed it might even be better for some of them to drop out and go to work or engage in some kind of more constructive activity than simply going to school.

"Secular?" As the period opened, the vast majority of children were sent to public schools on the assumption that they would not be required to learn particular religious doctrines that would be offensive to their parents. True, schools in homogeneously Protestant communities winked at the observance of nondenominational Protestant practices, but if compared to the sectarian teachings of a hundred years earlier, most schools were "secular"; that is, their main emphasis was not religious. But throughout the 50-year period, persistent efforts were made to find some way to get around the constitutional mandate for separation of church and state. The dockets of hundreds of state and federal courts were jammed with litigation over the role of religion as the fourth "R."

"Compulsory?" By the 1920s, it was believed, and still is by the vast majority of the public, that for the sake of the child and of the society the state should *require* children to attend school, not leave it to chance, neglect, indifference, or avarice. Today, there is a rising tide of doubt about the very idea of compulsory education. This has become a noticeable phenomenon of the early 1970s. One of its most remarkable aspects is that educators, academics, and educational critics seem more doubtful of the values of compulsory attendance than does the public itself. This is a curious reversal from the days when educators, especially in the 1890 to 1920 period, led campaigns to convince the public that compulsory attendance laws were needed to protect the child from the exploitation of child labor.

"Common?" A hundred years of effort led to the belief that it was good for children from the whole range of social, cultural, and economic backgrounds to go to school together. It was believed that this common schooling amid the diversities of religions, ethnic backgrounds, and socioeconomic classes would help achieve an enduring political community based upon freedom, justice, and equality. Now we hear that homogeneous separate schools are better for different ethnic, racial, religious, linguistic, or cultural groups. The rationalization for separate schools may be a sophisticated argument on behalf of a philosophy of cultural pluralism; or it may be a euphemism for ethnic purity sublimated in the term "neighborhood school"; or it may be a blatant or latent racism involved in the term "forced busing."

"Schooling?" Throughout the world for more than three hundred years the institution known as the school has been increasingly looked upon as a prime agent for socializing the young into the knowledge, the values, and the skills needed for adult life in a modern society and a national political community. In fact, the more modern the society, the more it has relied upon formal schooling rather than the informal agencies of education that are characteristic of traditional societies. Now we hear from some social scientists that schooling is not all that important for cognitive achievement or for economic income in comparison to the influence of family, social class, occupation, or pure luck. While the "deschooling" movement does not seem as popular as it was in the 1960s, the tendency to play down the values of schooling, especially of *public* schooling, has elevated the educative value of all *other* agencies of society that presumably can do a better job of education than the school can—or does: the family, the church, TV, business, labor, neighborhood, and voluntary associations of many kinds.

Current Status of the Search for Purpose

Fundamental criticism of the several terms of public education—"free, universal, secular, compulsory, common schooling"—highlights some of the most basic issues concerning the goals of education in U.S. society. It raises questions concerning freedom, and the respective rights of parents, children, and teachers in the educative process. It raises questions concerning justice and equality, and the respective rights of minorities and the disadvantaged in achieving equal educational opportunity. It raises questions concerning the authority of the state and the public school to require education for citizenship in a democratic political community. In fact, the answers given to such questions will have a bearing upon the very future of U.S. political institutions.

As I view the search for purpose in this country's education over the past half-century, I would sum it up this way: Freedom in education has generally been enhanced; equality has been pursued with some success, especially since 1965; but the sense of community has been diminished. Compared with a half-century ago, the freedom of parents, children, and teachers, as expressed in terms of civil rights, is surely more protected by the courts and by the laws today than it was then. The opportunity for education today is more open and available to minority groups than it was 50 years ago, largely through the efforts of government and the political process. But, belief that the prime goal of public education is to promote a sense of civic community and obligation for the public good has markedly decreased. The decline in faith in public education is partly cause and partly result of a diminished sense of community in the nation as a whole. The reasons for these generalizations form the basis of discussion in this Part IV.

Although each chapter in this part focuses on a central theme that runs throughout the 50-year period from the 1920s to the 1970s, there is a reason for the order in which they are treated. The search for freedom (Chapter 10) reached particular prominence in the early decades of the period when parents, minority religious groups, and teachers sought relief from what they considered to be unwarranted coercion by corporate capitalists, by government officials and legislators, or by nativists and religious bigots.

Then, in the middle decades of the period, the search for equality (Chapter 11) was given greatest attention as government was importuned to take steps to redress the economic, political, and social handicaps imposed upon minority racial and ethnic ·groups by galloping urbanization, pervasive racism, class distinctions, discriminating practices, and legal segregation.

In the search for freedom and equality, contending forces often moved from the educational forums of professional and public debate or local school board meetings into the broader arenas of the political and judicial process. One of the most significant features of the history of public education in the period since the 1920s has been the massive resort to law, legislation, and especially to the courts (what some have called the penchant for litigiousness). Nothing like it had ever been seen before in the 200 years of the nation's history. Organized interest groups and beleaguered minorities sought redress in legislative halls and in state and federal courts on behalf of their constitutional rights to freedom and equality. The court cases, especially, defined the cutting edges where the rights and interests of different groups clashed and where critical issues were defined at a fundamental legal and constitutional level. The decisions often had direct impact upon classroom practice as well as educational policy. This remarkable tendency to resort to the law and to the courts is the reason why Chapters 10 and 11 rely so heavily upon discussion of major precedent-setting and landmark cases in which the clash of ideologies was paramount, not simply a legal nicety. In Philip Kurland's words:

> The Supreme Court of the United States is really the schoolmaster of the Republic, and if it cannot command, it can at least educate the American people about what they need to do to improve the educational systems of the country.[1]

In the mid-1970s there were signs that the Supreme Court was backing away from its role as "schoolmaster of the Republic," but the search for freedom and equality cannot be understood without studying the Court's efforts to educate the American people during most of this period.[2]

Toward the end of the 1960s, the cohesive glue of national unity and political community began to weaken in the face of an unpopular war, immorality in business and politics, and resurgence of religious and ethnic loyalties. The period closed with widespread feelings of alienation and distrust of governmental institutions, erosion of the sense of the legitimacy of all major U.S. institutions, and a corresponding crisis of confidence in the legitimacy and moral authority of public education. All this led to a renewed search for the meaning of community in relation to education (Chapter 12).

Notes

1. Philip Kurland, "Equal Educational Opportunity or the Limits of Constitutional Jurisprudence Undefined," in Charles U. Daly, ed., *The Quality of Inequality* (Chicago: University of Chicago Press, 1968), p. 65.
2. See Betsy Levin, *The Courts as Educational Policymakers and Their Impact on Federal Programs* (Santa Monica, Calif.: Rand, 1977); and David L. Kirp, "Law, Politics, and Equal Educational Opportunity: The Limits of Judicial Involvement," *Harvard Educational Review*, May 1977, 47(2).117–137.

10 The Search for Freedom

Throughout the course of the middle decades of the twentieth century, recurrent waves of national chauvinism, nativism, business assertiveness, and religious authoritarianism swept through state legislatures and the Congress. In various guises these forces sought to impose majoritarian demands for conformity and orthodoxy in political, economic, or religious outlooks upon U.S. public schools. They were especially successful in war times and postwar times. But they also succeeded in provoking countervailing movements for protecting the civil liberties of parents, children, and teachers, and in reasserting the values of personal and group liberty, diversity, pluralism, difference, and dissent.

The search for freedom made education an especially fertile battleground on several fronts, beginning in the early 1920s, accelerating during and after World War II, and continuing right through to the 1970s. The public schools became a major arena of conflict among the rights claimed by contending groups. Parents claimed certain inalienable personal rights on behalf of themselves and their children as compared to those of the state; civil liberty groups claimed specific rights on behalf of teachers and children against the authority of church or state or school. The difficulty in such conflicts was that there was often no easy distinction between rights and wrongs; rather, the conflict was between one legitimate right and another legitimate right.

Most people would agree that a certain amount of freedom for parents and for teachers is desirable, but the arguments arose over the scope and limits of freedom for one group in relation to the freedoms of others and in

271

relation to the legitimate authority of state and school on behalf of the public good. Two aspects of the search for freedom appeared in many different forms as various controversies embroiled the public schools:

1. The first aspect I call the search for education's role in protecting *private* freedoms; that is, those that inhere in the individual and therefore may not be invaded or denied by the state. In the most general terms, freedom was sought for parents and their children on the grounds that every human being has the right, and should have the opportunity and the ability, to live one's own life in dignity and security. Further, he or she is entitled to seek one's self-fulfillment or self-realization as a person and as a member of a chosen cultural or religious group without arbitrary constraint on action or coercion of belief by the state or by other community pressures. Most often, appeal was made to the free exercise of religion guaranteed by the First Amendment of the Constitution (and as applied by the Fourteenth Amendment to the states) as a protection against coercion of belief or action by school or governmental authorities. As we shall see, this line of argument led in several different, and sometimes surprising, directions. In general, it followed the line of argument often used on behalf of freedom from constraint in one's use of private property, security of person and possessions, privacy, and movement in general.

2. The second aspect of freedom was the search for education's role in guaranteeing *public* freedoms; that is, those that inhere in the welfare of the democratic political community and which the liberal state is obligated actively to safeguard, protect, and promote whether threatened by a majority or minority in the community. Again, in general terms, freedom was sought for teachers and their students on the grounds that every person in his or her capacity as a teacher, learner, and citizen had the right and should have the opportunity to speak, to read, to teach, to learn, to discuss, and to publish without arbitrary constraint on action or coercion of belief by the state or by other pressures. Most often, appeal for academic freedom of teachers and students was made to the First and Fifth amendments (as applied to the states by the Fourteenth) as a guarantee that both teachers and students would thus be enabled or empowered to make deliberate choices among real alternatives and to carry out freely chosen purposes on the basis of reason, scholarship, and valid and reliable knowledge.

This latter approach to freedom of speech and expression in public education stressed its public nature, that is, its indispensability for the maintenance and improvement of a democratic political community. As we shall see, *this* search for educational freedom not only ran into powerful opposition from persons and groups who saw in it dangers to the established social and economic order, but it also sometimes ran into the claims for the private freedom by parents to direct and control the education of their children. As so often was the case, the public school found itself caught in the middle.

Private Freedoms

In the half-century between the middle 1920s and the middle 1970s, the most common and persistent controversies arising over the private freedoms of parents to guide and direct the education of their children had to do with the conflict between private religious beliefs and the authority of the state to promote the public good. This involved such matters as the right to attend private schools, opposition to the requirement of salutes to the flag and recitation of the pledge of allegiance, and opposition to compulsory attendance laws. Toward the end of the period the claims for freedom of choice for parents to decide what kind of education their children should receive went beyond religious arguments to include the inherent advantages of all kinds of "alternatives" to public schools: free enterprise in the establishment of schools, vouchers to aid parents to send children to the schools of their choice, and in general the liberation of parents from governmental restraints and children from school restraints. Eventually, the rights of children themselves to freedoms of due process were exerted against the authoritative discipline of parents and schools.

Rights of Parents versus Authority of the State

By the early 1920s there was widespread agreement in legislation, in judicial review, and in public opinion that the state had a legitimate authority to require all parents and guardians to see to it that the children under their control or supervision received a certain amount of schooling in state-approved institutions. By 1976 the most common age limits were from 7 to 16, with a wide latitude for exemptions; all states except one had some sort of compulsory attendance law. Three states revoked these laws in the effort to avoid the ruling in the racial desegregation decision of the Supreme Court in the *Brown* case of 1954: Virginia and South Carolina subsequently reinstated theirs; Mississippi left it to the discretion of the legislature.

Resistance to compulsion in education, leading to innumerable court cases, arose not only from compulsory attendance laws but also from the requirement to make public expression of loyalty to the nation, both of which were resisted as infringements upon the private rights of freedom of religious beliefs. Most of the issues were raised by two celebrated cases in the early 1920s, two celebrated cases in the early 1940s, and a celebrated case in the early 1970s. All five cases occurred in war or post-war periods and all had religious overtones.

Meyer v. Nebraska / Between 1917 and 1921 some 30 states had passed laws requiring all instruction in the public schools to be given in the English language. This was obviously a reflection of the patriotic fervor engendered by World War I and a heightening of nativistic nationalism incurred by the massive foreign immigration of prior decades. In 1919 Nebraska passed a law prohibiting the teaching of any subject in a private, denominational, parochial, or public school in any language except English, and prohibiting the teaching of foreign languages to any child who had not completed the eighth grade. In 1923 the Supreme Court ruled in *Meyer* v. *Nebraska* on cases brought from Iowa, Nebraska, and Ohio that the law was unconstitutional under the due process clause of the Fourteenth Amendment, which protected the liberty of teachers to make contracts to engage in the common occupations of life (Meyer was a teacher of German in a Lutheran school) and the liberty of parents to educate their children as they saw fit (by sending them to private or religious schools that gave instruction in a foreign language).

The Supreme Court ruled that the state has the power to compel the attendance of children at *some* school and to make reasonable regulations for *all* schools, including the giving of instruction in English, and that it can prescribe a curriculum for institutions that it supports. But, the Court said, a state cannot unreasonably interfere with the religious and private rights of parents to seek the kind of education they desire for their children:

> Without doubt, it [liberty as guaranteed by the Fourteenth Amendment] denotes not merely freedom from bodily restraint, but also the right of the individual to contract, to engage in any of the common occupations of life, to acquire useful knowledge, to marry, establish a home and bring up children, to worship God according to the dictates of one's own conscience, and, generally, to enjoy those privileges long recognized at common law as essential to the orderly pursuit of happiness by free men. . . .
>
> The established doctrine is that this liberty may not be interfered with, under the guise of protecting the public interest, by legislative action which is arbitrary or without reasonable relation to some purpose within the competency of the state to effect. Determination by the legislature of what constitutes proper exercise of police power is not final or conclusive, but is subject to supervision by the courts. . . .
>
> Evidently the legislature [of Nebraska] has attempted materially to interfere with the calling of modern-language teachers, with the opportunities of pupils to acquire knowledge, and with the power of parents to control the education of their own. . . .
>
> That the state may do much, go very far, indeed, in order to improve the quality of its citizens, physically, and mentally, and morally, is clear; but the individual has certain fundamental rights which must be respected.[1]

So, *Meyer* was an early attempt by the Court to define the line between the rights of parents to freedom of choice and the authority of the state to promote the public welfare. It should be noted that Justices Oliver Wendell Holmes and George Sutherland dissented in the *Meyer* case on the grounds that the state *did* have the right to take appropriate measures to maintain the common welfare through education as a means of preserving political unity.

Pierce v. Society of Sisters / The Supreme Court soon had another occasion to be even more precise in defining the line between the liberty of parents and the authority of the state. In 1922 the state of Oregon passed by initiative and by a very narrow margin (105,000 to 103,000) a compulsory attendance law requiring, with certain exceptions, that all normal children between the ages of 8 and 16 must attend a *public* school, or that any who attend a private school must obtain the permission of, and be examined by, the county superintendent of schools. Fearful that the law would seriously harm or destroy parochial schools, a Roman Catholic teaching order brought suit to have the law declared unconstitutional, which the Supreme Court unanimously did in its landmark decision of *Pierce* v. *Society of Sisters* in 1925.

Those who favored the law argued that the requirements of citizenship justified the state's using its authority to assure that all potential citizens be given appropriate preparation for their responsibilities; that the increase in juvenile delinquency had followed upon an increase in enrollments in *non*-public schools; that attendance at a common school would tend to prevent religious hostility and prejudice; and that instruction in U.S. government and institutions for immigrant children could best be given in common public schools where children of all classes and creeds were being taught together. The crowning argument was that loyalty to the United States could best be taught in public schools, and that if the law were declared unconstitutional the state would have no means of prohibiting the teaching of subversive doctrines by bolsheviks, syndicalists, or communists in private schools.

To some persons these were perfectly legitimate arguments for preserving public schools as the palladium of the republic, serving the public good, and striving to overcome the divisiveness of parochial schools for particular religious groups and of the private academies for the well-to-do. To others they masked a nativist Protestant hostility to Roman Catholics and foreign immigrants, a fear fanned in the Oregon case by the propaganda and lobbying of the Ku Klux Klan.[2] The law did not take effect in Oregon because it was nullified by the courts; and similar laws did not pass when they were proposed in a few other states. But it gave the Supreme Court the opportunity to outline more explicitly the balance between the rights of parents and the authority of the state in the field of education. The decision became a charter granting privileges that allowed private schools to exist alongside the public schools and permitted parents to have a certain freedom of choice with regard to the kind of education they would seek for their children.

Although the Supreme Court ruled that the Oregan law was unconstitutional under the Fourteenth Amendment's protection of liberty and property under due process of law it did affirm that the state could certainly regulate all schools and could compel parents to send their children to *some* school. Nevertheless, the state could not deprive parents unreasonably of the liberty to send their children to a private or religious school, as long as such a school was not inherently harmful to the child or to the state, and as long as it met reasonable standards set by the state with regard to curriculums and qualifications of teachers:

No question is raised concerning the power of the State reasonably to regulate all schools, to inspect, supervise and examine them, their teachers and pupils; to require that all children of proper age attend some school, that teachers shall be of good moral character and patriotic disposition, that certain studies plainly essential to good citizenhip must be taught, and that nothing be taught which is manifestly inimical to the public welfare.

The inevitable practical result of enforcing the Act under consideration would be the destruction of appellees' primary schools, and perhaps all other private primary schools for normal children within the state of Oregon. These parties are engaged in a kind of undertaking not inherently harmful, but long regarded as useful and meritorious. . . .

Under the doctrine of *Meyer* v. *Nebraska* . . . we think it entirely plain that the Act of 1922 unreasonably interferes with the liberty of parents and guardians to direct the upbringing and education of children under their control. As often heretofore pointed out, rights guaranteed by the Constitution may not be abridged by legislation which has no reasonable relation to some purpose within the competency of the State. The fundamental theory of liberty upon which all governments in this Union repose excludes any general power of the State to standardize its children by forcing them to accept instruction from public teachers only. The child is not the mere creature of the State; those who nurture him and direct his destiny have the right, coupled with the high duty, to recognize and prepare him for additional obligations.[3]

It should be noted that both *Meyer* and *Pierce* were decided under the due process clause of the Fourteenth Amendment: to wit, "no state shall deprive any person of life, liberty, or property without due process of law." The liberty of parents to guide the education of their children is a constitutional right, but that right is always hedged by the legitimate authority of the state to legislate reasonably upon matters essential to its welfare and within its competency.

Variations on Meyer and Pierce / The doctrines of *Meyer* and *Pierce* have been referred to in a great number of cases since those decisions were handed down. The Supreme Court carried them forward and applied them to the territory of Hawaii, which since 1920 had tried to limit the scores of foreign-language schools that had been established to teach in Korean, Chinese, and especially in Japanese. In 1925 the territorial government, through legislative enactment and regulations of the department of education, moved to limit the attendance at such foreign-language schools to those who were enrolled in public schools or approved private schools, or who had finished the eighth grade, or who were 14 years of age. It also reserved the right to designate the textbooks that the foreign-language school should use in its primary grades. The Supreme Court struck down this attempt in a 1927 decision, which said in part that

the School Act and the measures adopted thereunder go far beyond mere regulation of privately supported schools, where children obtain instruction deemed valuable by their parents and which is not obviously in conflict with any public interest. They . . . deny both owners and patrons reasonable choice and discretion in respect of teachers, curriculum and text-books. Enforcement of the Act probably would destroy most, if not all, of them; and, certainly, it would deprive parents of fair opportunity to procure for their children instruction which they think important and we cannot say is harmful. The Japanese parent has the right to direct the education of his own child without unreasonable restrictions; the Constitution protects him as well as those who speak another tongue.[4]

It should perhaps be noted here that while the Supreme Court in the 1920s was assiduously protecting the freedom of parents to make educational choices to attend private schools, it was not so concerned about the equal rights of minority parents to send their children to common public schools. In a case involving Chinese parents in Mississippi who wanted their child to attend the white schools rather than the black schools, which were segregated by law, the Supreme Court in 1927 (the same year as the Japanese case in Hawaii) ruled that the state of Mississippi *could* prohibit the Chinese child from attending the white schools under the "separate but equal doctrine" of *Plessy* v. *Ferguson*.[5] In other words, a state cannot force parents to attend a public school, nor can it abolish private schools, but it *may*, at its discretion, segregate children according to race as a valid exercise of legislative power. The Supreme Court was upholding the due process clause protecting "liberty and property" in the Fourteenth Amendment. It was more than 25 years before it interpreted the "equal protection" clause of the Fourteenth Amendment to mean that separate segregated schools were unequal. Liberty stood first before equality in the eyes of the Supreme Court of the 1920s.

Freedom of Religious Belief versus Public Profession of Loyalty

Minersville v. Gobitis / Just as *Meyer* and *Pierce* were debated in the aftermath of World War I passions, so were two other cases heard and decided in the heat of World War II. In 1940 the issue was raised by a ruling of the Minersville, Pennsylvania, board of education that all teachers and students in the public schools take part in a daily pledge of allegiance and salute to the flag. This was protested by parents named Gobitis, who were members of Jehovah's Witnesses, on the grounds that the requirement violated their rights to free exercise of religion under the First Amendment. Their religious belief, based upon a literal version of Exodus 20:4,5, prohibits worship of any "image," which they considered the flag to be. While this case dealt with compulsory flag salute and not directly with compulsory attendance at public school, it fundamentally raised in Justice Felix Frankfurter's words "the conflicting claims of liberty and authority. . . . [W]hen the liberty invoked is liberty of conscience, and the authority is authority to safeguard the nation's fellowship, judicial conscience is put to its severest test."

The majority opinion, written by Justice Frankfurter, upheld the flag salute rule as a legitimate exercise of state authority; the lone dissent was by Justice Harlan Fiske Stone. One of the key points made by Frankfurter was as follows:

> The ultimate foundation of a free society is the binding tie of cohesive sentiment. Such sentiment is fostered by all those agencies of the mind and spirit which may serve to gather up the traditions of a people, transmit them from generation to generation, and thereby create that continuity of a treasured common life which constitutes a civilization. . . .
>
> A society which is dedicated to the preservation of these ultimate values of civilization may in self-protection utilize the educational process for inculcating those almost unconscious feelings which bind men together in a comprehending loyalty, whatever may be the lesser differences and difficulties. That is to say, the process may be utilized so long as men's right to believe as they please, to win others to their way of belief, and their right to assemble in their chosen places of worship for the devotional ceremonies of their faith, are fully respected.[6]

Because the flag "summarizes" these values of cohesive sentiment, Justice Frankfurter held for the court that legislatures and boards of education should be permitted by the courts to compel a pledge of allegiance to the flag. In his dissent Justice Stone held that it is the function of the courts to try to arrive at a reasonable accommodation between the interests of liberty and the interests of government. His sense of accommodation was that the state should not try to coerce affirmation of *belief* contrary to religious conviction but could and should achieve feelings of cohesion by requiring *study* and *instruction* in civil liberties:

> So here, even if we believe that such compulsions will contribute to national unity, there are other ways to teach loyalty and patriotism which are the sources of national unity, than by compelling the pupil to affirm that which he does not believe and by commanding a form of affirmance which violates his religious convictions. Without recourse to such compulsion the state is free to compel attendance at school and require teaching by instruction and study of all in our history and in the structure and organization of our government, including the guaranties of civil liberty which tend to inspire patriotism and love of country.[7]

West Virginia v. Barnett / A short three years later, Justice Stone had become Chief Justice and his *Gobitis* dissent became in effect the Court's ruling when it reversed the *Gobitis* decision in *West Virginia State Board of Education* v. *Barnett* in a 6:3 decision written by Justice Jackson and now supported by three "liberal" members who had changed their opinions: Hugo L. Black, Frank Murphy, and William O. Douglas.[8] The argument was in essence that the First Amendment prohibited the compulsion to declare a belief, but that the schools *could* require the study and teaching of civic matters—namely, by persuasion and example but not by imposition of any ideological discipline nor by a compulsion that "invades the sphere of intellect and spirit." As might be expected, Justice Frankfurter wrote a long and impassioned dissent. Both cases deserve study in their full texts.

Religious Freedom versus Compulsory Attendance

The tension between freedom of religious belief and the authority of the state took a different turn in the closing days of the Vietnam War. Whereas the earlier confrontation had been between the search for freedom of religious belief against the pledge of allegiance and salute to the flag as specific requirements of school practice on behalf of loyalty, in the 1970s the opposition of minority religious groups turned against the very idea of a compulsory attendance requirement by the state, charging that it violated certain personal freedoms. In fact, this opposition set off a flood tide of doubt about the validity of compulsory education and the legitimacy of public education itself.

In its September 1972 issue, the *Phi Delta Kappan* reported Gallup findings that 73 percent of the public were in favor of compulsory attendance at high school, whereas only 56 percent of professional educators agreed. More of the public (61 percent) would require attendance beyond age 16 than would the educators (35 percent). In 1974 a survey by the Children's Defense Fund reported 93.6 percent of parents favored compulsory attendance, a view especially strong among the poor,[9] and a 1976 Gallup poll found that 69 percent of public school parents still approved of compulsory attendance beyond 14, as did 73 percent of parochial school parents.

Wisconsin v. Yoder / Regardless of public sentiment, the courts, some lawyers, and some educators had growing doubts. In May 1972, the U.S. Supreme Court upheld the Wisconsin Supreme Court decision of 1971, which ruled that Old Order Amish parents were not required to obey Wisconsin's compulsory attendance laws by sending their children to school to age 16. The reasoning in *Wisconsin* v. *Yoder* was that the First Amendment protected the free exercise of the parents' religious views. In this case, the parents contended that an elementary education was sufficient to prepare children for their separated rural and traditional way of life. In their view, a high school education in modern and secular values would be detrimental to the way of life of the Amish community, which, their religious convictions commanded, should be conducted apart from worldly concerns. The Court held that the Amish religious beliefs had been genuinely and conscientiously held for centuries and thus took precedence over the undoubted right of the state to require school attendance to age 16.

Chief Justice Warren E. Burger conceded that:

> There is no doubt as to the power of a State having a high responsibility for education of its citizens, to impose reasonable regulations for the

control and duration of basic education. . . . Providing public schools ranks at the very apex of the function of a State. Yet even this paramount responsibility was, in *Pierce*, made to yield to the right of parents to provide equivalent education in a privately operated system.[10]

The Court's opinion was that the state's interest in universal compulsory education beyond elementary school was not of such magnitude, nor was it so compelling, as to overbalance the Amish legitimate claims to the free exercise of religion:

> Thus, a state's interest in universal education, however highly we rank it, is not totally free from a balancing process when it impinges on other fundamental rights and interests, such as those specifically protected by the Free Exercise Clause of the First Amendment and the traditional interest of parents with respect to the religious upbringing of their children so long as they, in the words of *Pierce*, "prepare [them] for additional obligations."[11]

The Court thus leaned toward the superiority of parents' private rights and interests in the education of their children over the rights of the state to require universal education, which Jefferson had claimed was "a bulwark of a free people against tyranny." To be sure, the state could reasonably and constitutionally require education to age 16 in some public or private schools, but not when it conflicted with genuine religious beliefs that deny its importance, provided always that:

> The duty to prepare the child for "additional obligations," referred to by the Court, must be read to include the inculcation of moral standards, religious beliefs and elements of good citizenship.[12]

Justice Douglas on Children's Rights / In effect, the Court accepted the notion that the requirements for citizenship education in the modern world can be satisfied by an elementary school education that normally ends at age 14. The Court did not believe that one or two years of further schooling would make that much difference in preparing for good citizenship, but it did accept Amish arguments that the two additional years *would* do irreparable damage to their religious way of life. Interestingly, in a partial dissent, Justice Douglas went so far as to argue that while the *parents'* rights had been served by the decision, the *children* themselves should have had more to say about whether *they* wished to go to high school:

> It is the future of the student, not the future of the parents, that is imperilled by today's decision. If a parent keeps his child out of school beyond the grade school, then the child will be forever barred from entry into the new and amazing world of diversity that we have today. The child may decide that that is the preferred course, or he may rebel. It is the student's judgment, not his parent's, that is essential if we are to give full meaning to what we have said about the Bill of Rights and of the right of students to be masters of their own destiny. If he is harnessed to the Amish way of life by those in authority over him and if his education is truncated, his entire life may be stunted and deformed. The child, therefore, should be given an

opportunity to be heard before the State gives the exemption which we honor today.[13]

These words on behalf of children's rights breathe much of the humanitarian reform spirit that motivated the earlier arguments on behalf of compulsory attendance at school—a compulsion on behalf of students that could enable *them* to achieve more freedom of choice than might be open to them by upholding the parents' rights to the free exercise of *their* religion.

Widening Debate over Compulsory Education

The arguments pro and con compulsory education waxed noticeably following the *Yoder* decision. Some educators rose to support it. One of the more powerful defenses was the article by Robert M. Hutchins on "The Schools Must Stay." Hutchins argued that the essential purpose of universal, free, compulsory education is to form independent, self-governing members of a self-governing community. And he, like the Amish, also appealed to the First Amendment:

> The basic commitment is that of the First Amendment which lays it down that Congress shall make no law abridging the freedom of speech. This provision means that every American is encouraged to express himself on public questions—or on any other subject. The notion is that of a self-governing community of self-governing citizens locked in argument. This was the kind of community the founders wanted. They could not hope to have one of this kind without an educated people. They had to have citizens who could think, and think for themselves.
>
> Is this a sufficient basis for a political community? I think it is when combined with universal citizenship and universal suffrage. Does it justify compulsory schooling in institutions supported and controlled by the state? I think it does.
>
> Every child must be given the chance to become the kind of citizen the First Amendment demands. The obligation is too important to be left to parents. The community must compel them to allow their children to have this opportunity either by offering the education itself or through institutions it approves.[14]

Gerald M. Reagan of Ohio State University argued in *Educational Studies* for Spring 1973, that the greatest benefit from abolishing compulsory schooling would go to those who would ordinarily be schooled to a relatively high level and thus be enabled to maintain or even increase their advantages over the unschooled. He said that the greatest harm would adhere to those who were already educationally disadvantaged and who would be most likely to drop out and thus widen the gap in the level of formal schooling between them and their more fortunate peers.[15]

On the other hand, the complaints against compulsory schooling have rapidly grown in number, volume, and effectiveness. The December 1973 issue of the *Phi Delta Kappan* contained a symposium in which several contributors argued that compulsory attendance laws are outdated.

Research lawyers like John E. Coons, Stephen D. Sugarman, and William H. Clune have argued for greater freedom for parents to send their children to schools of their choice—with aid of public funds or vouchers.[16] Advocates of a sophisticated philosophy of cultural pluralism called for release from the compulsion of attendance laws so that a "hundred cultural flowers may bloom." Proponents of a revived ethnicity found a suffocating cultural conformity omnipresent in a common school to which all children are expected or required to go.[17] Radical critics argued that compulsory attendance laws bolster a public school system devoted to maintaining the middle-class values of an exploiting capitalist establishment. And opponents of court-ordered busing, of whatever political hue, perceived that weakening of compulsory attendance laws would also weaken the drive toward desegregation in the schools and would probably impair the whole force of the civil rights movement.

In its report of 1973, the National Commission on the Reform of Secondary Education, headed by B. Frank Brown and supported by the Kettering Foundation, proposed that the school-leaving age be lowered to age 14.[18] Its argument rested on several grounds: (1) The rising tide of crime and violence in the schools means that the high schools are not serving vast numbers of youth who do not want to be there, and thus secondary schools can no longer be custodial or incarcerating institutions; (2) youths mature earlier than they did when the laws were passed; (3) youth and children have been extended constitutional rights on which the laws infringe and which validate the claim that compulsory education over age 14 is an unconstitutional violation of liberty; (4) education is not a fundamental right protected by the Constitution, as stipulated in *Rodriguez* (see page 242); (5) a job can "educate" as well as, or better than, the schools can; and (6) students can acquire all the fundamentals they need by age 14 or grade 8, and thus they should have the right to say "No more." In sum, according to these facts, the reasons for a prolonged education no longer exist. Youth should be given the alternative of going to work (by amending child labor laws) or of rendering social service in the community on the basis of one month of service in exchange for one year of free public education. Public service might be conducted in CCC camps for ecology and conservation for recalcitrant youth, or in optional community-based learning centers at public expense for all.

Similar to this proposal, although somewhat at odds with it, was the proposal made by a Task Force on Secondary Schools and adopted by the board of directors of the National Association of Secondary School Principals in the report *This We Believe* (1975). Free compulsory education should be provided for all youth until one of two conditions is met: (1) the high school diploma is earned, or (2) the age of majority is reached at the eighteenth birthday. This does *not* mean compulsory *schooling* alone; it includes all educational programs organized and sponsored by the school both on the campus and in the community. So, the report would not lower the age limits; it would even extend them, but a wide variety of work and service experiences would be offered along with academic study.[19] These and similar proposals heightened the tempo of debate in the late 1970s as more states were urged to change their laws; by mid-1975, the states of Florida, California, and Virginia had already begun to take action.

Private Freedoms versus Public Education

Private Sovereignty Superior to Public Sovereignty / Meanwhile, the effort to justify and expand parents' rights in the education of their children took on new theoretical dimensions as it became the subject of intensified legal research and action. Two examples will illustrate. The Childhood and Government project, under the leadership of John E. Coons at the School of Law at Berkeley, is studying the relative degrees of authority and responsibility to be allocated to parents and the state for education of children. This involves the use of vouchers, tuition grants, tax credits, attacks upon compulsory attendance laws, and a whole range of alternatives for parental choice that raise serious questions about the traditional role and authority of public education itself.

Coons distinguishes between "private sovereigns" over the life, welfare, and education of children (principally the family) and "public sovereigns" (the public schools, social workers, juvenile courts).[20] He clearly opts for the priority of parents and the "amateur" circle of family, or family-like clusters of intimate associates, taking precedence over the professional and bureaucratic sovereigns of the public. This exemplifies the principle of "subsidiarity," defined as the presumption that the power to choose among acceptable social options should be kept as close as possible to the individual whose interests are at stake. And it should be lodged with those most likely to provide effective protection of the individual's interests, most accessible to his voice, and knowing best and caring most about his welfare.

Coons argues not only against the overweening authority of public sovereigns, but also against the radical libertarians who would go to the extremes of rejecting all forms of control over children and allowing complete freedom and self-direction of the child, summed up as "kids lib." The sovereign should be the parent:

> Children are small, weak, and inexperienced; adults are big, strong, and shrewd. One may liberate children from the law of man, but the law of nature is beyond repeal. There is no way to send an 8-year-old child out of the sovereignty of the parent and into a world of liberty. He will be projected instead into a new sovereignty of one kind or another. . . . Children—at least small children—will not be liberated; they will be dominated. And none of this is altered by providing "open schools" and permissive child rearing.[21]

Development of the autonomy of the child is best left to the family, despite its autocratic traditions, for it is the sovereign that cares most about the child's welfare and development. It can do this better than any large-scale institution. Thus the family is the ultimate reservoir and source for private liberty and is its protector against the authority of the state. This view stands in the tradition of *Pierce* v. *Society of Sisters*.

Public Schools Unconstitutional / A second example has even more extreme implications for public education. Stephen Aarons, assistant professor of legal studies at the University of Massachusetts, argues that the *Pierce* case decision, properly interpreted, would find that it was not only unconstitutional to require children to attend public schools instead of private schools, but that the very institution of public education itself was an unconstitutional violation of private rights and freedoms under the First Amendment.[22] Aarons' thesis is a complicated legal argument that cannot be explored at length here, but it is significant because it carries to extreme lengths an analysis of the doctrine of private rights which he finds enshrined in the First Amendment. I happen to believe that he reads the First Amendment incorrectly, but this is not the place to debate that issue.

Aarons' argument runs something like this: The holding of all beliefs and values is protected by the First Amendment's guarantee of the "right of individual consciousness to be free of government coercion." All schooling is inevitably an agency for influencing the formation of beliefs and values. Since public schools shape beliefs and values on behalf of government, by their very nature they violate the core of meaning of the First Amendment. Therefore, public schools inherently violate the First Amendment and are unconstitutional. Schools, in Aarons' words, should be "separated from the state."

Legal Ambiguities / Aarons argues that separation of schools and state is the conclusion to which the *Pierce* case would lead if it had been decided on the basis of the First Amendment instead of under the due process clause of the Fourteenth Amendment. As it is, Aarons argues, the *Pierce* case had in itself many ambiguities, which have been multiplied each time it has been cited in a wide variety of cases that have also been ambiguous. One of the reasons for this ambiguity is that the Supreme Court has tried to assume that public schooling can be neutral with respect to religious beliefs (protected by the free exercise clause of the First Amendment) and has argued that secular education is neutral with respect to beliefs and values in general. This was its mistake, for all education is value-laden. Thus it must remain in the hands of parents to decide, free from imposition by public education—which is inevitably controlled by political majorities who inevitably coerce some minorities on behalf of state-sponsored socialization, which in turn is bound to violate private values of some parents. This conflict is fairly easily demonstrated when the values are religious, but Aarons argues that a much broader doctrine should prevail, and that

> any conflict between public schooling and a family's basic and sincerely held values interferes with the family's First Amendment rights.[23]

Because the parental right of educational choice and freedom from compulsory value inculcation are central to the First Amendment, Aarons concludes that since "families and individuals should hold the preponderance of power in overseeing the transmission of values to their children"[24] there should be a fundamental restructuring of educational systems. In effect, such restructuring would reduce government regulation of private schools, reduce or abolish compulsory attendance laws, and probably do away with public educational institutions themselves:

> The specific application of this principle to education is that any state-constructed school system must maintain a neutral position toward parents' educational choice whenever values or beliefs are at stake. If schools are value-inculcating agencies, that fact raises serious constitutional questions about how a state can maintain a sufficiently neutral posture toward values while supporting a system of public education.[25] . . . Some extensive restructuring of compulsory education may be constitutionally required and publicly acceptable.
>
> This restructuring would enjoin the government from abridging the right of educational choice, a right which would affirm more than the parents' ability to choose *against* a public school; it would affirm their right to have the child attend a school which reflected family values.[26]

To accomplish this, Aarons says,

> the First Amendment may require changing the economic and political structure of compulsory schooling to separate school and state, just as the First Amendment requires separation of church and state.[27]

Aarons concludes his article by references to John Stuart Mill's view that state-sponsored education established a despotism over the mind, and to Ivan Illich's reference to the public school as the established church of secular times. These references indicate his devotion to private freedoms. What influence such views may have on public policy in the final quarter of the twentieth century is not for the historian to predict. What is clear, however, is that widespread adoption of such views could well mean the abolition of a public school system because they play up the role of private freedoms but neglect the constitutional tradition of *public* freedoms. These ideals have affirmed over and over again not only the importance of keeping the state clear of imposing religious beliefs, but also the importance of the state's maintaining a system of public schools as a prime agency for promoting public freedoms and public rights. To this part of the search for freedom in education we now turn.

Public Freedom: Separation of Church and State

The search for the role that public education should play in promoting public freedom took two major forms in the middle decades of the twentieth century. One had to do, once again, with certain aspects of the relation of church and state, and the other had to do with academic freedom for teachers and learners. The extent of the public interest and the role of the First Amendment were paramount in both forms.

The problem of the role of education and religion as related to the public interest centered around two exceedingly controversial issues: the use of public funds to aid religious schools, and the promotion of religious instruction within the public school system. In the simplest of terms, the argument for the first was deduced from the *Pierce* doctrine: If parents have a private *right* to send their children to religious and private schools to meet the compulsory attendance requirements of the state, then distributive justice requires that the state provide parents with public funds to enable them to do what they have the private right to do. The objection to such claim invoked the establishment clause of the First Amendment ("Congress shall make no law respecting an establishment of religion . . ."), arguing that such use of tax funds would violate a taxpayer's public right to be free of any taxation that involves the state in promoting religion, his own or anyone else's. The essential meaning of the phrase "separation of church and state" as a shorthand description of the First Amendment was debated long and heatedly in hundreds of court cases.

The second issue over religion also involved an entanglement of private and public freedoms. Many religious groups argued that it was appropriate public policy for public schools to promote religious instruction because religion was the foundation of public morality and good government. Therefore, some kind of deliberate religious instruction should be required in the public schools as the fourth "R," whether by released time for separate classes in denominational teachings, or by common Bible reading, or by common nondenominational prayers and other observances. Those who opposed such practices appealed not only to the First Amendment's establishment clause, but also to its free exercise clause ("or prohibiting the free exercise thereof").

Both issues assumed extraordinarily great force about the same time in the late 1940s. They illustrated as few other issues did the continuing vitality and diversity as well as the rancorous divisiveness of religious pluralism as it affected the public schools. In the conflict of educational ideas in the 1920s, the religious issue was incidental to the broader struggle between private and public education. But in the 1930s and 1940s the religious element of the issue came to the forefront. The basic question was, "Shall public funds be used for the support of religious schools, and, if so, for what purposes?"

Public Funds for Religious Schools?

As we have seen in the earlier chapters of this book, the struggle between church and state has had a long history. By and large, the American people had moved away from direct public support for religious schools and had generally agreed that the best interests of the nation and of religion alike would be served if public funds were not granted to religious schools. This was one of the generally accepted interpretations of the principle of separation of church and state at the end of the nineteenth century. Now, however, the whole question of that meaning was reopened, and at mid-century several well-defined positions were stated.

Direct Aid / First, it was argued that public funds should be granted to religious and parochial schools as a recognition of their role in serving the public welfare and in meeting the requirements of compulsory attendance laws on a level of equality with the public schools. The most outspoken advocates of this position were the leaders and members of the Roman Catholic Church. They argued that, as a matter of distributive justice, the parochial schools should share with public schools in tax funds, for it was unfair to tax Catholic parents for the public schools and then expect them also to pay for their Catholic schools, which in private conscience they believed were needed for their children. They also said that constitutional provisions for the separation of church and state permitted "cooperation" between church and state, as long as the state aided all religious schools equally without showing preference for any one religion or denomination over others. Finally, they argued that the only thing the First Amendment prohibits is the granting of privileges to one church that are not granted to others.

Child Benefit: The Cochran Case / A second general position on this issue held that *direct* aid for the support of religious schools by public funds was contrary to good policy and to the constitutional separation of church and state, but it was nevertheless justifiable for the state to use public funds for *indirect* aid to the parochial schools. This could be achieved under the "child benefit" theory that public funds for certain auxiliary services to parochial school children were aiding the child to take advantage of the welfare services of the state and were not aiding the school itself. Thus, the state could not give financial aid to pay salaries of teachers or build buildings or help maintain parochial schools, but it *could* use public funds to pay for transportation of children to parochial schools, give them free textbooks, pay for health and medical services, and furnish free school lunches. The United States Supreme Court affirmed this doctrine as early as 1930 in the *Cochran* case when it permitted free textbooks in Louisiana, and again in 1947 in the *Everson* case, which was concerned with free bus transportation for parochial school children in New Jersey.

The *Cochran* case appealed to the Fourteenth Amendment in challenging a Louisiana law, arguing that taxation for the purchase of texts for use in private sectarian schools constituted a taking of private property for a private purpose without due process of law. The Louisiana Supreme Court upheld the law, however, on the premise that the books benefited the children and therefore benefited the state rather than the religious school. Chief Justice

Charles Evans Hughes agreed with the Louisiana Supreme Court that the law served a public purpose rather than a private purpose:

> Viewing the statute as having the effect thus attributed to it, we can not doubt that the taxing power of the state is exerted for a public purpose. The legislation does not segregate private schools, or their pupils, as beneficiaries or attempt to interfere with any matters of exclusively private concern. Its interest is education broadly; its method, comprehensive. Individual interests are aided only as the common interest is safeguarded.[28]

Note that the *Cochran* case was decided under the Fourteenth Amendment's due process protection of "life, liberty, and property," as had been true also in *Meyer* and in *Pierce*.

Following World War II, however, the issue took quite a different form as religious groups, Protestant as well as Catholic, began to step up their drive to gain public funds for "auxiliary services" or for indirect aid under the child benefit theory established by *Cochran*. Now it was not only free textbooks, but free health and medical services, free lunches, and especially free bus transportation to be provided for parochial school children as well as public school children. The Fourteenth Amendment's protection of liberty for parents to send their children to private schools and its protection of property for private schools now ran into a different opposition. Opponents of aid to religious schools, whether direct or indirect, turned to the First Amendment and to its establishment clause to protect taxpayers in their right to be free from taxation by the state for religious purposes. They argued that *Cochran* had not seen the essentially *religious* ingredient of public aid, which is what should bring it under the ban of the First Amendment rather than the Fourteenth.

Indirect Aid: Everson v. Board of Education / The landmark case involved the use of tax funds to pay for free bus transportation in New Jersey to enable Catholic children to attend parochial schools (*Everson* v. *Board of Education*). By 1950 almost half of the states (22) had taken some action to permit public funds for free busing of parochial school children. State courts in eight states had ruled *against* the practice and a bare majority of states did not permit it. Thus, the country was flooded with disputes and court cases during the 1940s and 1950s. The *Everson* case in 1947 settled what the establishment clause of the First Amendment meant in principle, but the 5:4 decision reflected the sharp divisions as to what it meant for *practice* in the case of indirect aid for auxiliary services.

The majority opinion written by Justice Hugo Black defined the first sentence of the First Amendment as follows:

> The "establishment of religion" clause of the First Amendment means at least this: Neither a state nor the Federal Government can set up a church. Neither can pass laws which aid one religion, aid all religions, or prefer one religion over another. Neither can force nor influence a person to go to or

to remain away from church against his will or force him to profess a belief or disbelief in any religion. No person can be punished for entertaining or professing religious beliefs or disbeliefs, for church attendance or non-attendance. No tax in any amount, large or small, can be levied to support any religious activities or institutions, whatever they may be called, or whatever form they may adopt to teach or practice religion. Neither a state nor the Federal Government can, openly or secretly, participate in the affairs of any religious organizations or groups, and *vice versa.* In the words of Jefferson, the clause against establishment of religion by law was intended to erect "a wall of separation between church and state."[29]

This paragraph, the whole opinion, and accompanying dissents are worthy of the closest study by anyone who would understand the historical meaning of the public aspects of religious freedom for public education. For the following 30 years the *Everson* case was cited and argued over in possibly more court cases than any other having to do with religion and education. One reason was that while the entire Court could agree to the principles as stated in the preceding quotation, the majority of five justices argued that free bus transportation in New Jersey came under the heading of proper use of the state's police power in providing general public welfare *for the benefit of the child,* and—echoing *Cochran*—was not an aid to the religious school, and was thus not prohibited by the First Amendment. A state could prohibit such use of public funds if it wished, but it was not required to do so under the majority's interpretation.

The minority, following powerful dissents by Justices Wiley Rutledge and Robert H. Jackson, argued that public funds for busing certainly do substantially aid the children to obtain religious instruction at taxpayers' expense and represent precisely the kind of exaction that the Amendment was originally designed to prevent:

> It was to create a complete and permanent separation of the spheres of religious activity and civil authority by comprehensively forbidding every form of public aid or support for religion. . . . The prohibition broadly forbids state support, financial or other, of religion in any guise, form or degree. It outlaws all use of public funds for religious purposes.[30]

Rutledge specifically criticized *Cochran* and the majority in *Everson* for casting their decision on the police power argument and thus ignoring the religious factor, which thus left out the one vital element in the case:

> This is not therefore just a little case over bus fares. In paraphrase of Madison, distant as it may be in its present form from a complete establishment of religion, it differs from it only in degree; and is the first step in that direction.[31]

In a separate dissenting opinion, Justice Jackson also put the matter in a way that highlighted the difference between private and public freedoms:

> The prohibition against establishment of religion cannot be circumvented by a subsidy, bonus or reimbursement of expense to individuals for

receiving religious instruction and indoctrination. . . . I agree that this Court has left, and always should leave to each state, great latitude in deciding for itself, in the light of its own conditions, what shall be public purposes in its scheme of things. It may socialize utilities and economic enterprises and make taxpayers' business out of what conventionally has been private business. It may make public business of individual welfare, health, education, entertainment or security. But it cannot make public business of religious worship or instruction, or of attendance at religious institutions of any character. . . . we cannot have it both ways. Religious teachings cannot be a private affair when the state seeks to impose regulations which infringe on it indirectly, and a public affair when it comes to taxing citizens of one faith to aid another, or those of no faith to aid all. . . . If the state may aid these religious schools, it may therefore regulate them.[32]

Many Protestants joined many Catholics in support of the belief that the separation of church and state did not prohibit certain kinds of aid to the parochial schools or to the children who attend parochial schools,[33] but most explicit and most persistent in their demands for "auxiliary services" or indirect aid to parochial schools were Roman Catholic leaders. In his controversy with Mrs. Eleanor Roosevelt in July 1949, Francis Cardinal Spellman of New York insisted that he merely wanted public aid for health and transportation benefits and the distribution of nonreligious textbooks to children in parochial schools as a recognition of justice for the parochial schools. Further, he did not seek or expect funds for parochial school construction, maintenance, or teaching services. In a series of articles on federal aid to education, beginning in *America* on January 7, 1950, Father Robert C. Hartnett made the same claim, but many critics felt that the *ultimate* goal of many Catholic leaders was full public support of Catholic schools. The history of the next 25 years pretty well proved this to be the case.

Year after year the statements of Catholic bishops in the United States edged closer and closer to demands for full support. Their efforts were strengthened by the pronouncement from Rome on July 5, 1977, in which the Vatican appealed to the national states around the world to provide subsidies for Catholic schools. The appeal was contained in a major document entitled "The Catholic School" issued by the Sacred Congregation for Catholic Education. This could provide timely doctrinal and political support for hard-pressed American Catholic educators who had seen their five and a half million students in 13,000 schools dwindle to three and a half million students in 10,000 schools between 1965 and 1975.

No Aid: The Public School Position / Alarmed at the prospect of government subsidies, the third general position on this issue, stated simply, is not only that direct aid from public funds to religious schools is unconstitutional but also that *indirect* aid in the form of "auxiliary services" is also unconstitutional. Aid to parochial school children for free transportation, free textbooks, and free health and medical services is a form of indirect aid to the religious schools, and thus unsound and unwise as public policy, for these beginnings could eventually lead to direct aid and a reversal of 175 years of American effort to separate church from state. Aiding all religions or churches equally is just as unconstitutional and unwise as aid to one church in preference to others. The history of separation of church and state in the United States shows that multiple establishment of religion was outlawed as well as single establishment.[34]

The proponents of this third position pointed to the minority opinion in *Everson* as the constitutional basis for adhering to complete separation rather than cooperation between church and state. They felt that the majority had stated the *principle* of separation correctly, but had not applied it correctly in practice. Many Protestant groups, most Jewish groups, and most educational and civil liberties groups adhered to this position.

After considerable debate, the largest organization of U.S. educators came to a similar conclusion as a matter of policy. Virtually identical resolutions were adopted at their annual conventions in 1950, 1951, and 1952 by the National Education Association and its most powerful affiliate, the American Association of School Administrators:

> We believe the American tradition of separation of church and state should be vigorously and zealously safeguarded. We respect the right of groups, including religious denominations, to maintain their own schools so long as such schools meet the educational, health, and safety standards defined by the states in which they are located. We believe that these schools should be financed entirely by their supporters. We therefore oppose all efforts to devote public funds to either the direct or indirect support of these schools.[35]

Continuing Campaigns for Public Funds

Thus, the lines were drawn on a very complicated and controversial issue that was fought out in the political arena for the next two decades, for the *Everson* case had not settled the issue of public support for religious-oriented education. During the 1950s and 1960s almost every conceivable variation of practice and of legal effort was dreamed up in order to try to circumvent the basic principle. In the course of 30 years, however, the use of tax funds for direct aid to private and religious schools at the elementary and secondary level was increasingly rebuffed by the federal courts, while it was more and more allowed at the college and university level.

At the Federal Level / Federal legislation itself was a major factor in this trend. The School Lunch Act of 1948 authorized federal funds for school lunches in parochial schools even if state law or regulation prohibited the use of state funds for that purpose The pattern of the G.I. Bill of 1944 was followed in the National Defense Education Act of 1958, which permitted students to use their scholarships at private religious institutions as well as public. In addition, the National Science Foundation began to make unrestricted grants directly to private colleges and universities, and then the Higher Education Facilities Act of 1963 and the Higher Education Act of 1965 began to pour money into private church-related institutions for nonreligious purposes.

At the lower levels of education the main breakthrough came with the passage of the Elementary and Secondary Education Act of 1965. Title II recognized in effect the child-benefit principle of *Cochran* and *Everson* when it authorized federal funds to be used for school libraries, textbooks, and instructional materials for private as well as public schools, with the provision that no such aid be used for religious instruction and the materials remain in the legal ownership of public authorities. This recognition of *indirect* aid for parochial schools was one of the main compromises that made massive federal aid to education finally possible. The main stumbling block had been for decades the political opposition to federal aid unless it included aid to parochial schools.

Success had seemed within sight when a federal aid bill was passed by the Senate in 1948 and again in 1949, but in both cases it died in the House of Representatives amid wide public clamor over the religious issue. Especially bitter was the public response in 1949 when charges of bigotry were leveled at Mrs. Eleanor Roosevelt by Cardinal Spellman for her stand against aid to parochial schools. Similar charges were made in 1950 against Representative Graham A. Barden of North Carolina for his efforts to gain support for a bill that would give federal aid *only* to public schools and would rule out transportation and health services for parochial schools. Federal aid to education had become a bitter political issue at both the national and state levels.

At the State Level / Gradually, however, the acrimonious antagonisms of the late 1940s and 1950s were sufficiently moderated to permit passage of federal aid to education as a part of the Great Society social reforms of the mid-1960s. By then, 36 of the 50 states had enacted some variation of indirect aid to church-related schools. Emboldened by these successes on indirect aid, but frustrated by a succession of defeats during the 1960s with regard to religious instruction in public schools (to be described shortly), aggressive religious forces and their political allies turned to state legislation to try to achieve more direct aid to religious schools. But this time the popular terminology became the "purchase of services" for the private schools, to be procured with public funds. A New York law of 1965 required local school boards to lend textbooks free of charge to all students in the district, whether they attended private or public schools. The U.S. Supreme Court in 1968 upheld this law as being in line with *Everson's* majority opinion that such lending was simply a benefit to the child and not to the school.[36] Significantly, Justices Black and Douglas, who had been in the majority in *Everson* 20 years earlier, dissented on the ground that books were not the same as buses, even though sectarian religious books were not permissible.

Pleased by this success, private and parochial school proponents began campaigning for a wide variety of "freedom of choice" plans, whereby parents would be given tax credits or vouchers out of public tax funds, which they could use to defray the expenses of educating their children either at public or private schools of their choice. (Note that white parents in the South could benefit from such a plan by using public funds to send their children to free private schools for whites only.) The argument here was that parents were entitled to public support for the education of their children, and they should be free to decide the kind of school to which they would send their children with such support.

Seeing the success of direct aid to private higher institutions from federal and state funds (New York State began to give all private colleges and universities a money grant for each degree granted), the private school forces turned openly to seek direct aid. Pennsylvania led the way in 1968 with a law that would use public funds to pay part of the salaries of private school teachers in certain nonreligious subjects: modern languages, mathematics, physical sciences, and physical education. In 1969, Connecticut and Rhode Island followed suit; seven other states turned down similar proposals; and 22 were still debating. These laws for "purchase of services" were immediately tested in the courts.

The Constitutional Tests / In June 1971, the Supreme Court declared in two 8:1 decisions that the Pennsylvania and Rhode Island laws were unconstitutional because the state aid given to church-related schools violated the First Amendment's guarantee of the separation of church and state. In a succinct historical statement going back to the *Everson* case, Chief Justice Warren E. Burger summed up the cumulative criteria developed by the court over many years to test the constitutionality of laws on this subject: "First, the statute must have a secular legislative purpose; second, its principal or primary effect must be one that neither advances nor inhibits religion; finally, the statute must not foster an excessive Government entanglement with religion."[37]

Of particular importance was the warning that granting direct public support for the teaching process would produce a divisive political potential far exceeding that from support of indirect nonideological services like bus transportation or lunches. It looked as though another watershed had been reached by which a three- to four-decade trend toward aid for church-related elementary and secondary schools would be halted. Whether the court's decision would diminish or increase the political divisiveness remained to be seen. The New York State legislature went right ahead to pass laws in 1971 and 1972 that would provide $33 million a year for "secular educational services for pupils in nonpublic schools." As expected, a federal court promptly declared the laws unconstitutional and, even more promptly, Governor Nelson

Rockefeller and legislators swore they would find some way to aid the parochial schools with state funds.

The culmination seemed to come in 1973 when the Supreme Court invalidated a whole series of laws and practices in several states that had sought to get closer to direct aid for parochial schools. Perhaps the most important were the New York cases, in which four kinds of aid were struck down: reimbursement from public funds for tuition paid by parents (whose annual taxable income was less than $5,000) to send their children to nonpublic schools; tax deductions from state income tax for costs of sending children to nonpublic schools (for parents whose annual taxable income was over $5,000 but less than $25,000); reimbursement to nonpublic schools for part of the expenses of maintenance and repair of school facilities and equipment; and similar reimbursement for part of the costs of record-keeping and testing required by the state.[38]

At the same time the Court invalidated a Pennsylvania statute that was designed to reimburse all parents (not just low-income parents) for part of their tuition costs for children in private schools[39] and prohibited Mississippi from providing free textbooks for private academies that discriminated in their admission policies on the basis of race.[40] The net result was to strengthen the principle that tax funds could not be used either directly or indirectly for educational purposes that have a direct and immediate effect of advancing religion, even though the primary intent of the legislation was to promote secular general welfare and was within the police power of the state.

The Court began to recognize that government aid to individuals which advances religion is no more constitutionally allowable than direct aid to religious institutions (the basic argument of the minority in *Everson*). It also recognized the danger that such legislation would lead to ever-increasing political divisiveness, since small successes would encourage aggressive religious factions to seek ever-larger tuition grants and eventually *complete subsidization* of all religious schools on the ground that such action is necessary if the state is to equalize fully the position of parents who elect such schools —a result wholly in violation of the Establishment clause.[41]

Preservation of the political community and education's role in that purpose was a prime reason for the Court to delimit the public support for religious segmental pluralism in order to preserve the values of public freedom guaranteed by the establishment clause of the First Amendment. What all this meant for the future was by no means clear. Just when it seemed that the Court would not repudiate the line of reasoning that led from *Everson* to the 1973 decisions, the Supreme Court ruled on June 24, 1977, in an Ohio case that states could use public funds to pay for therapeutic, remedial, and guidance counseling services for parochial school children on the condition that such services were rendered in "neutral" places, that is, off the parochial school premises. Also, purely diagnostic and testing services could be provided to the parochial schools if such services were provided to the public schools. On the other hand, public funds could not be used to finance field trips for parochial school children or to purchase such instructional aids as wall charts and projectors (even though secular textbooks had long been approved). The key principle seemed to be that aid was permissible if the parochial school children were not isolated or insulated from the public school children and if the aid was not so extensive that it amounted to an establishment of religion, that is, it must pass the constitutional tests mentioned on page 00. But the justices split five different ways on the several legal points at issue. Jefferson's high and impregnable wall of separation between church and state was becoming more than ever a serpentine affair.

Religious Instruction in the Public Schools

The other side of the problem of defining the role of public education in the search for public freedom in religion has to do with the efforts to enlarge the attention to religious instruction in the public schools themselves. By the end of the nineteenth century the general principle had been established that sectarian religious instruction should not be promoted by the public schools if freedom of religious conscience and the separation of church and state were to be preserved. But after World War I, and especially after World War II, the demands grew for some sort of religious instruction to be given in public schools. The public schools were labeled as "godless" and "secularist," and it was charged that the neglect of religion had promoted not only indifference to religion but also active irreligion, both of which contributed to a decline of moral and spiritual values, which in turn led to positive juvenile delinquency.

States and communities kept trying throughout the 1940s and 1950s to overcome in some way the principle that public schools ought to be secular and should *not* promote religious instruction if they were to protect and cherish the public freedom, which was the only genuine guarantee for the privilege of religious pluralism and diversity. By the early 1960s, the Supreme Court decisions had pretty well blunted the major arguments of these drives.

Two general points of view received considerable attention. One view, promoted largely by Protestants and Catholics, urged a revival of sectarian religious instruction, notably through a released-time plan whereby public school children could be released from their regular school work for a certain period of time each week in order to receive special instruction from teachers of their own particular religious faith. A second view, promoted almost exclusively by Protestants, urged more attention to nonsectarian religious instruction through such requirements as daily reading of selected passages of the Bible or reciting of nonsectarian prayers. Opposition was expressed to both of these forms of instruction as threats to the principle of separation of church and state and infringements upon religious freedom.

Released Time / The spread of released-time programs led to a whole series of court cases. One New York court prohibited the practice in Mount Vernon in 1925; another New York court permitted it in White Plains in 1927. State courts permitted it in California and in Illinois in 1947. When the Illinois case was appealed, the U.S. Supreme Court ruled in 1948 that the released-time plan in Champaign, Illinois, was unconstitutional because it violated the First Amendment and was in effect "an establishment of religion":

> The foregoing facts . . . show the use of tax-supported property for religious instruction and the close cooperation between the school authorities and the religious council in promoting religious education. The operation of the State's compulsory education system thus assists and is integrated with the program of religious instruction carried on by separate religious sects. Pupils compelled by law to go to school for secular education are released in part from their legal duty upon the condition that they attend religious classes. This is beyond all question a utilization of the tax-established and tax-supported public school system to aid religious groups to spread their faith. And it falls squarely under the ban of the First Amendment (made applicable to the States by the Fourteenth) as we interpreted it in *Everson* v. *Board of Education*.[42]

The religious classes in Champaign were taught by religious teachers and held inside the public school buildings; it thus remained uncertain as to whether a plan in which children left the school buildings and went to their own churches would likewise be unconstitutional. A court in St. Louis in 1948 held that such a plan would be unconstitutional under the McCollum decision, whereas courts in New York in the same year held that the New York plan was enough different to be permissible because the children left the school buildings.

The New York case was taken to the Supreme Court and was decided in April 1952.[43] By a 6:3 decision, the Supreme Court decided that the New York system was unlike the Champaign plan, and was therefore permissible because the schools did not aid the religious groups to promote their religious instruction in school buildings and did not spend public funds for the purpose. The majority opinion, written by Justice William O. Douglas, argued that no coercion was exerted in the New York plan, but that the plan would be unconstitutional if coercion were present. The majority opinion reaffirmed the *Everson* and the *McCollum* principle of separation of church and state, but it stated that government and religion need not be unfriendly or hostile to each other. They can "cooperate" to the extent that students are enabled by the schools to take part in religious instruction offered by the churches.

The minority of three justices (Robert H. Jackson, Hugo L. Black, and Felix Frankfurter) argued that there was no essential difference between the New York plan and the Champaign plan, and that therefore the New York plan was unconstitutional because it violated the separation of church and state by using the power of the state to secure the attendance of children at religious classes. The dissenters made it clear that they would have little objection to allowing *all* children to leave school to go to religious classes if their parents so chose, but that the refusal of religious groups to accept this "dismissal plan" was evidence that they really wanted the compulsion of the school system to work in their favor.

Bible Reading / The campaign for released time, however, faded in the 1950s. Instead, the efforts of religious-minded groups during the next decade turned more vigorously to Bible reading and prayers as means of promoting religious values through the public schools. Persuaded by Protestant groups, at least 12 states enacted laws requiring that passages from the Bible be read in the public schools. In at least 25 other states, Bible reading was permitted by legislation, by court decision, by rulings of attorney generals or state education departments, or by local custom. Despite the fact that 12 states had constitutional provisions prohibiting sectarian instruction in the public schools and 24 states had similar laws, most states have ruled by court decisions that Bible reading is *not* sectarian instruction and is thus permissible. But at least six state courts ruled that the Bible *is* a sectarian document in the eyes of Catholics, Jews, and nonbelievers, and is thus unconstitutional. These latter states included Wisconsin, Illinois, Ohio, Louisiana, South Dakota, and Washington. Many of the cases on Bible reading have been brought on behalf of Roman Catholic and Jewish plaintiffs, who argued that the King James version of the Bible was actually Protestant sectarianism, and thus should be prohibited because it violated the religious conscience of Catholics and Jews.

Roman Catholics have long argued that reading of the Bible by a non-Catholic without comment is in effect a Protestant use of the Bible, to say nothing of the fact that the King James version is not the authorized Roman Catholic version. Jews have also long objected to Bible reading because it does not hold the same place in their religion that it does for Christians, and they oppose all sectarian religious practices, observances, and festivals in the public schools.

Nonsectarian Prayers / Typical of other demands that the public schools recognize some sort of nonsectarian religious instruction or observance in the public schools was the proposal in November 1951 by the New York State Board of Regents urging that a nonsectarian prayer be recited in the public schools.[44] The regents argued that public acknowledgment of dependence upon God would be one of the best methods of achieving security against the dangers of those difficult days. Similarly, the International Council of Religious Education had been urging that faith in God and the teachings of a theistic religion should be promoted in the public schools. This would amount to a common core of religious faith that could be agreed upon by all major religions and thus taught in the public schools. Proposals such as these were opposed by many religious as well as educational groups on the grounds that they would use the public schools to promote religion, a violation of the principle of separation of church and state as defined in the *Everson* and the *McCollum* cases.

A decade later, two Supreme Court decisions pretty well decided the matter. In the heat of the aftermath of the *McCollum* case, the New York State Board of Regents had not only urged local boards of education to institute nonsectarian prayers in the public schools, but the Board itself also formulated and approved such a prayer. But in the *Engel* case, the U.S. Supreme Court found in 1962 that such a prayer was "a religious activity" promulgated by public authorities and wholly inconsistent with the establishment clause of the First Amendment.[45] A particularly interesting sidelight of this decision was the fact that the three living former presidents of the United States (all Protestants) deplored the decision, while President John F. Kennedy, a Catholic, urged that the Court be obeyed.

A year later in Pennsylvania and Maryland cases, the Supreme Court similarly found that the compulsory recitation of the Lord's Prayer and daily reading from the Bible was an unconstitutional invasion of religious liberty by an agency of the government.[46] Although these cases seemed to settle the legal question, the hue and cry did not lie down for quite a while, fanned as it was by calls for impeachment of the Supreme Court justices. In fact, a strong movement urged an amendment to the Constitution specifically to permit Bible reading and religious prayers in the public schools. The proposed Becker amendment in 1964 was finally sidetracked, but not before the major public controversy that ensued threatened to rival in intensity the furor over the *Brown* desegregation case in 1954.

From the mid-1960s onward, the organized effort to link religion and public education more closely was directed away from the effort to inject more religious instruction in the public schools and toward public support for sectarian schools, as we have seen. The intensity of the religious rancor of the 1950s and 1960s gradually moderated, the ecumenical movement of better feeling among Christians was symbolized by the second Vatican Council called by Pope John XXIII in 1962, the fiscal crises hit parochial schools harder and harder, and the public school establishment was being belabored year after year for its failures in urban and ghetto education. But it soon became apparent that the problem of religious freedom and public education had by no means disappeared. By the beginning of the 1970s the barometers of public opinion indicated that more and more of the population was turning again to religion. The Gallup poll saw 1976 as the start of a new religious revival in which religious schools by fundamentalist Protestant sects were rapidly multiplying and Catholic parochial schools were taking on a new burst of life. The question was how far religious pluralism would go in weakening public education.

Public Freedom: Teaching
and Learning

One of the most ambiguous questions concerning education and freedom was how vigorously the educational profession itself would act with regard to the role that public education ought to play in the search for public freedoms guaranteed by the First Amendment. The freedom of the teaching profession itself was often at stake, especially in the wake of World War II. The profession has long been caught in the crossfire of efforts to limit or to expand both the private and civil rights of teachers and their public freedom of discussion and expression in the classroom. In documenting the variety of efforts to force teachers to stay within the bounds of conservative thought and practice as defined by religious, political, and economic majorities, Howard K. Beale pointed out that teachers in the 1920s and 1930s were always more free to express conservative views than to air liberal or radical views.[47] International, sectional, patriotic, economic, political, and religious ideas were the views most thoroughly subjected to restriction by powerful elements in the community. But the teachers' personal conduct outside the classroom probably got more of them into trouble than did their views inside the classroom: theater-going, smoking, drinking, immodest dress, and sexual indiscretion were sure to invite censure, especially in rural areas, small towns, and the border and southern states.

Since World War II, greater personal freedom has been granted teachers as their civil rights gained greater protection through the vigorous action of professional organizations and the courts. Such matters are still troublesome in spotty areas throughout the country, but the whole trend of greater freedom in dress and grooming codes, private habits of smoking and drinking, marriage, divorce, and sex relations has weakened the special restrictions that made teachers for so long second-class citizens.

Meiklejohn on Education and the First Amendment

Gains were also made during the middle half of the twentieth century in the achievement of public freedoms for the teaching profession, but not without tremendous controversy and trauma, especially during the post-World War II period when the "cold war" was at its height. By public freedom of teachers I mean, as stated earlier, the untrammeled right, opportunity, and power to teach, to discuss, to express ideas, to criticize, and to disseminate knowledge, without coercion or undue pressure from government, business, or labor, from patriotic, ethnic, or special interest groups, or from parents themselves. Alexander Meiklejohn, an outstanding teacher and philosopher at the University of Wisconsin and spokesman for civil liberties, argued for several decades that this public freedom for education rested upon the First Amendment, that education had a special responsibility to promote that freedom as the very foundation of the public well-being in the exercise of self-government, and that

> a primary task of American education is to arouse and to cultivate, in all members of the body politic, a desire to understand what our national plan of government is. . . . a challenge to all of us, as citizens, to study the Constitution. That constitution derives whatever validity, whatever meaning, it has, not from its acceptance by our forefathers one hundred and sixty years ago, but from its acceptance by us, now. Clearly, however, we cannot, in any valid sense, "accept" the Constitution unless we know what it says. And, for that reason, every loyal citizen of the nation must join with his fellows in the attempt to interpret, in principle and in action, that provision of the Constitution [the First Amendment] which is rightly regarded as its most vital assertion, its most significant contribution to political wisdom.[48]

Further, Meiklejohn said:

> When men decide to be self-governed, to take control of their behavior, the search for truth is not merely one of a number of interests which may be "balanced," on equal terms, against one another. In that enterprise, the attempt to know and to understand has a unique status, a unique authority, to which all other activities are subordinated.[49]

Therefore,

> the protection of public discussion in our nation takes on an ever-increasing importance as the nation succeeds in so educating and informing its people that, in mind and will, they are able to think and act as self-governing citizens. And this means that far deeper and more significant than the demand for freedom of speech is the demand for education, for the freeing of minds. These are not different demands. The one is a negative and external form of the other. We shall not understand the First Amendment unless we see that underlying it is the purpose that all the citizens of our self-governing society shall be "equally" educated.[50]

Clearly, Meiklejohn's view of education as the very foundation of public freedom was not everywhere accepted in practice, but it did gradually gain wider acceptance as the century wore on. In the post-World War II period, four kinds of efforts were made to shield students and society from the dangers assumed to emerge from the ideas or actions of unorthodox teachers. Teachers were required to subscribe to special oaths of loyalty to the government; legal measures were taken to discover and oust teachers who belonged to the Communist Party or other subversive organizations; restrictions were put upon freedom of teaching, of writing, and of speech by teachers in their classrooms or on the campus; and measures were taken to restrict the political activity of teachers outside the classroom. Such efforts were on the increase from World War I and reached their peak in the McCarthyism of the 1950s.

As early as 1938 the House UnAmerican Activities Committee was formed under Representative Martin Dies of Texas and made permanent under John Rankin of Mississippi, first to fight the New Deal and then to ferret out disloyal citizens in schools, colleges, the churches, and the press. In 1940 the Smith Act was passed under reactionary pressures to make "teaching" or advocating the overthrow of the government unlawful. And in the 1940s and early 1950s the House Committee, with its fervor stoked by J. Parnell Thomas of New Jersey and Richard M. Nixon of California, drew up blacklists and searched for Communists in the churches, schools, and Hollywood until Senator Joseph R. McCarthy took over the center of the stage in the campaigns to ferret out real or imaginary subversives.

Loyalty Oaths

One of the most common measures designed to keep the teaching profession clear of alleged subversive teachers was the passage of state laws requiring teachers to take special loyalty oaths. By 1952 a total of 30 states had enacted such legislation. So extensive had this movement become that most of the influential teachers' organizations had taken stands against such laws, including the National Education Association, the American Association of University Professors, and the American Federation of Teachers. These and other professional organizations were supported in their views by the American Civil Liberties Union and other organizations concerned with academic freedom in a democratic society.

Opposition to special loyalty oaths for teachers rested on two practical grounds: They discriminated against teachers and gave them less than the civil right of freedom of speech accorded to all other citizens; and they were useless and ineffective in their purpose because no genuinely subversive person would hesitate to sign such an oath. Loyalty oaths were thus deemed an affront to loyal teachers and ineffective in discovering disloyal ones.

But opposition to loyalty oaths also rested on basically constitutional grounds. On December 15, 1952, the U.S. Supreme Court declared an Oklahoma oath law for teachers to be unconstitutional, a violation of freedom of thought, action, and association as guaranteed by the First and Fourteenth Amendments.[51] The majority opinion in *Wieman* v. *Updegraff* stressed the view that membership in an illegal organization may be innocent association, and therefore the loyalty oath should not be the basis for penalizing those who were simply nonactive members of alleged subversive organizations. But a concurring opinion by Justices Frankfurter and Black went still further to argue that teachers have a special obligation to *promote* freedom of thought:

> That our democracy ultimately rests on public opinion is a platitude of speech but not a commonplace of action. Public opinion is the ultimate reliance of our society only if it be disciplined and responsible. It can be disciplined and responsible only if habits of open-mindedness and of critical inquiry are acquired in the formative years of our citizens. The process of education has naturally enough been the basis of hope for the perdurance of our democracy on the part of all our great leaders from Thomas Jefferson onwards.

To regard teachers—in our entire educational system, from the primary grades to the university—as the priests of our democracy is therefore not to indulge in hyperbole. It is the special task of teachers to foster those habits of open-mindedness and critical inquiry which alone make for responsible citizens, who, in turn, make possible an enlightened and effective public opinion. . . . They must have freedom of responsible inquiry, by thought and action, into the meaning of social and economic ideas, into the checkered history of social and economic dogma. They must be free to sift evanescent doctrine, qualified by time and circumstance, from the restless, enduring process of extending the bounds of understanding and wisdom, to assure which the freedoms of thought, of speech, of inquiry, of worship are guaranteed by the Constitution of the United States against infraction by National or State Government.[52]

Communist Party Membership

Granted that teachers had a special responsibility to promote freedom of thought, the most difficult question for the profession and for the courts to decide was the source of the greatest threats to academic freedom. Did it come from the conspiritorial Communists in the United States who followed a party line dictated by the Communist Party of the Soviet Union? Or from those reactionaries in communities or government who would impose on teachers and students conformity to their own peculiar brand of orthodoxy of thought and belief? My own interpretation as stated in the early 1950s was that the threats to freedom in public schools came more from the latter than from the former. In fact, the threats to freedom of teachers came from at least three sources: the attempted tyranny of government officials; the attempted tyranny of coercive majorities in the community; and the attempted tyranny of despotic minorities in the community.[53] In an unpublished lecture given at Teachers College, Columbia University, in the summer of 1953 I characterized the atmosphere of the day as follows:

> The threats to freedom have been unmistakable for some time, but now the character of the attacks upon freedom are more clear than ever. They have increased in scope and intensity to the place where suspicion, fear, timidity, and caution have become the dominant atmosphere of many of our schools and colleges. The morale of teachers is reported to be at a new low, as indeed it is in many government agencies. Attacks upon the schools by individuals and by organized groups have increased, but since the election of President Eisenhower the center of the stage has been held by the investigations and hearings conducted by three legislative committees of Congress, the Senate Permanent Subcommittee on Investigations under Senator Joseph R. McCarthy, the Senate Internal Security Subcommittee under Senator William E. Jenner, and the House Committee on Un-American Activities under Representative Harold H. Velde.
>
> In their search for Communists and "Communist thinkers" and "controversial writers" these committees have taken for their field of investigation not only the schools and colleges but also the churches, radio, TV and the movies, the press, the agencies of information of the government, and

the overseas libraries. Note that these are all critical agencies concerned with the dissemination of ideas, knowledge, beliefs, and information. They are the ones where the problem of freedom is most acute and the values of freedom are most precious. One thing the past year has made clear. Teachers in schools and colleges are in the same boat with clergymen, librarians, authors, publishers, newspapermen, composers, artists, scientists, and all others to whom freedom of ideas and freedom of spirit are the very life-blood of existence. An attack upon one is an attack upon all.

I argued that educators must oppose all threats to their freedom from whatever source they came and that reactionary witch hunts were as subversive of free institutions as Communist conspiracies. Indeed, in the atmosphere of the McCarthy era they were *more* dangerous to the schools, because they were more powerful in government offices, legislatures, boards of education, and the community. After all, at the height of the Communist movement among students, probably in the year 1939, the American Student Union claimed 12,000 paid-up members—out of 30,000,000 students. Even the most prejudiced claims about the numbers of teachers who belonged to the Communist Party ranged from 1,500 to 3,500 out of a half million teachers.[54] True, the Communists captured control of the New York City local of the American Federation of Teachers in 1935, precipitating a furious struggle for several years until they lost control in 1939 and the AFT ousted Communist-controlled locals in 1941.

The general furor continued during the postwar period, fired up by the onset of the cold war, and reached its peak in the late 1940s and early 1950s. The hottest issue arose over whether membership in the Communist Party was prima facie evidence that a person was not free to think for himself or herself and was therefore not fit to be a teacher. Was mere membership in the Party sufficient reason to justify dismissal from the teaching profession?

Meiklejohn versus Hook / One view, typified by Alexander Meiklejohn, held that scholarship and competence are the only grounds for judging the worth of a teacher and that each person should be judged solely on the merits of his or her work in the classroom. The basic test of fitness of a teacher is devotion to freedom of inquiry and to the honest and scholarly pursuit of truth, and competence in the development of critical intelligence among his or her students through the teaching and learning process. If membership in the Communist Party prevents a person from genuine devotion to these goals and actual practice of them, then such a person is not fit to teach. But the test is competence, not membership. And the judgment of competence is to be made by one's peers, not by outside inquisitors. Dismissal solely on the basis of membership is a violation of academic freedom. This view was, by and large, the official position of the American Association of University Professors and the Academic Freedom Committee of the American Civil Liberties Union. It should be noted that it was more likely that college professors would hold this view because the tradition of academic freedom was much stronger in the institutions of higher education than in public schools.

The other view, and probably the majority view among teachers in elementary and secondary schools, was typified by Sidney Hook, New York University philosopher.[55] Hook and Meiklejohn took part in a head-on debate on this issue in *The New York Times*.[56] Hook argued that there were no innocent members in the Communist Party; their membership meant that they accepted its discipline and therefore could not think for themselves. Since committed Party members were not free to investigate freely or speak critically, they were not competent to be teachers. Hook believed that he had documented over and over, from Communist documents themselves, that the Communist Party was a conspiracy and that loyal membership incapacitated a teacher from freedom of inquiry and thus from fitness to teach. In a recent restatement of his long-held position Hook puts it this way:

> . . . I make abundantly clear that a teacher has a right to profess any heresy in any field, *including communism and fascism*, and that the academic community is under the intellectual and moral obligation to defend his or her right to do so.
>
> I asserted, on the other hand, that present membership in *any* organization which issues instructions to its members to indoctrinate in the classroom for a party line or which dictates in advance the conclusions of research in accordance with a party line constitutes a violation of the professional ethics of teaching and scientific inquiry. Such membership warrants not automatic dismissal, but the presumption of unfitness, final judgment to be made by autonomous faculty bodies in complete independence of any agency of the state.[57]

For some two decades the profession, the legislatures, the public, and finally the Supreme Court debated the issue whether teachers who belonged to the Communist Party would be permitted to teach in the nation's schools and colleges.

Position of Professional Associations / After considerable discussion over a period of years, the National Education Association came to the conclusion that members of the Communist Party should not be permitted to be teachers or members of the NEA. At its convention in July 1949, the NEA delegates confirmed the position taken by the Educational Policies Commission in its statement on international tensions:

> *Members of the Communist Party of the United States should not be employed as teachers.*
>
> Such membership, in the opinion of the Educational Policies Commission, involves adherence to doctrines and discipline completely inconsistent with the principles of freedom on which American education depends. Such membership, and the accompanying surrender of intellectual integrity, render an individual unfit to discharge the duties of a teacher in this country.[58]

The American Federation of Teachers (AFT) was more divided in its outlook. In 1948 its National Commission on Educational Reconstruction decided that the conspiratorial and disciplinary nature of the Communist Party did not permit its members the freedom and intellectual integrity required of teachers in a free and democratic society. Membership in the Party is a form of action that repudiates freedom and scholarship; thus to prohibit such members from holding teaching positions is not to find them merely guilty of association but guilty of a definite act of disloyalty.

In August 1949, however, the convention of the AFT subscribed to a different position. The majority report of its Committee on Civil and Professional Rights of Teachers declared that membership in an organization or in a legal political party is not in and of itself sufficient grounds for the dismissal of a teacher. The federation had been one of the first to outlaw Communist as well as Fascist party members from its own membership, but its convention was not disposed to apply this principle to all teachers. The grounds for dismissal should be individual competence rather than membership in an organization as such, and wherever Communist teachers violated the rights of students to learn in an atmosphere of freedom and impartiality, their competence is affected and dismissal should be on those grounds. But by August 1952 the AFT convention changed its mind and decided that party membership *was* grounds for dismissal from teaching, just as it was grounds for exclusion from the AFT.

On the other hand, a consistent policy was maintained by the American Association of University Professors (AAUP), which upheld the doctrine that individual competence should be the determining factor rather than guilt by association, and continued to reaffirm its 1940 Statement of Principles on academic freedom. These were interpreted in such way that party membership as such was not automatically grounds for dismissal.[59] In April 1952 the Academic Freedom Committee of the American Civil Liberties Union issued a statement on academic freedom and responsibility in which it aligned itself with the position of the AAUP.

Thus, the profession was divided about membership in the Communist Party as a disqualifier of teachers, but it was united in opposing repressive witch-hunts and stringent limitations on genuine academic freedom intended to rout out subversive teachers. Much fear was expressed that the definition of "subversive" would be so broadened that it could include any kind of criticism or genuine intellectual inquiry that might offend anyone.

Feinberg Law Upheld—and Then Reversed / Considerable controversy was waged, for example, over the Feinberg law passed by the New York State Legislature in April 1949. It authorized the state Board of Regents to draw up a list of organizations which it believed to be subversive, and then to make regulations whereby membership in such organizations would be prima facie evidence of disqualification for holding a teaching position in the public schools of the state. Subversive groups were defined as those that "advocate, advise, teach, or embrace the doctrine that the Government of the United States, or of any state, or of any political sub-division thereof, shall be overthrown or overturned by force, violence or any unlawful means." The Board of Regents drew up regulations whereby boards of education and school administrators were empowered to conduct continuing investigations of all school personnel and to prefer charges against those for whom evidence justified dismissal. Passage of the Feinberg law was fought by the American Federation of Teachers, and it was later opposed by the Committee on Academic Freedom and Tenure of the National Education Association in its report of 1952.

The Feinberg law was declared unconstitutional by a district court in Albany in November 1949. Following this, its constitutionality was upheld by the New York Court of Appeals in November 1950 and also by the U.S. Supreme Court by a 6:3 decision in March 1952.[60] The arguments of the majority and minority in *Adler* v. *Board of Education* represent excellent statements of the conflicting views among educators. Stressing the right of the state to protect its schools, Justice Sherman Minton stated the case for the majority in upholding the Feinberg law:

> A teacher works in a sensitive area in a schoolroom. There he shapes the attitude of young minds toward the society in which they live. In this, the state has a vital concern. It must preserve the integrity of the schools. That the school authorities have the right and the duty to screen the officials, teachers, and employees as to their fitness to maintain the integrity of the schools as a part of ordered society, cannot be doubted. One's associates, past and present, as well as one's conduct, may properly be considered in determining fitness and loyalty. . . . we know of no rule, constitutional or otherwise, that prevents the state, when determining the fitness and loyalty of such persons, from considering the organizations and persons with whom they associate.[61]

In contrast, stressing the rights and values of academic freedom, Justice William O. Douglas stated the case against the Feinberg law:

> The present law proceeds on a principle repugnant to our society— guilt by association. A teacher is disqualified because of her membership in an organization found to be "subversive." The finding as to the "subversive" character of the organization is made in a proceeding to which the teacher is not a party and in which it is not clear that she may even be heard. . . . The mere fact of membership in the organization raises a prima facie case of her own guilt. . . .
> The [Feinberg] law inevitably turns the school system into a spying project. Regular loyalty reports on the teachers must be made out. The principals become detectives; the students, the parents, the community become informers. Ears are cocked for tell-tale signs of disloyalty. The prejudices of the community come into play in searching out the disloyal. This is not the usual type of supervision which checks a teacher's competency; it is a system which searches for hidden meanings in a teacher's utterances. . . .
> What happens under this law is typical of what happens in a police state. Teachers are under constant surveillance; their pasts are combed for

signs of disloyalty; their utterances are watched for clues of dangerous thoughts. A pall is cast over the classrooms. There can be no real academic freedom in that environment. Where suspicion fills the air and holds scholars in line for fear of their jobs, there can be no exercise of the free intellect. Supineness and dogmatism take the place of inquiry. A "party line"—as dangerous as the "party line" of the Communists—lays hold. It is the "party line" of the orthodox view, of the conventional thought, of the accepted approach. . . .

This, I think, is what happens when a censor looks over a teacher's shoulder. This system of spying and surveillance with its accompanying reports and trials cannot go hand in hand with academic freedom. It produces standardized thought, not the pursuit of truth. Yet it was the pursuit of truth which the First Amendment was designed to protect. A system which directly or inevitably has that effect is alien to our system and should be struck down. Its survival is a real threat to our way of life. . . . The Framers knew the danger of dogmatism; they also knew the strength that comes when the mind is free, when ideas may be pursued wherever they lead.[62]

In the course of the 1950s, several other Supreme Court cases reflected the majority view in *Adler*[63] with a continuing refrain of dissent from Justices Black, Douglas, and then Chief Justice Earl Warren. In 1959 the Court ruled that the First Amendment does not protect a teacher from Congressional investigation.[64] But then, in 1960, the Court ruled that an Arkansas law requiring teachers as a condition of employment to reveal all their affiliations with associations and organizations had gone too far and had violated the First Amendment.[65] Finally the Court, after 15 years of constitutional doctrine that had emerged following 1952 (especially under the Warren Court), specifically reversed the *Adler* majority decision and in effect moved toward the Douglas dissent when it ruled that mere membership in an alleged subversive organization or guilt by association could not constitutionally be grounds for a teacher's dismissal.[66] On the other hand, clear and unambiguous requirements for simple oaths to uphold the Constitution and professional standards have consistently been sustained by the Court as matters within the cognizance of government and do not violate the public freedom of teachers.

Freedom of Teachers To Teach

One final point remains to be made. By and large, the trend of court cases in recent years has tended to reinforce the view that teachers have the same rights of political activity that all other citizens have.[67] But, most important of all, teachers' freedom of expression has gained considerably since the 1920s. They are now protected by law in the right to speak out on controversial issues, including criticism of the schoolboard and administration, both outside and inside the classroom:

> The courts . . . have given us some guidelines that show the enormous gains made by teachers in the cause of freedom of speech in the schools. As a general rule, the teacher's use of controversial material or language will be

protected by the First Amendment unless it can be shown that it is irrelevant to her teaching objective, inappropriate to the age and maturity of her students, or disruptive of school discipline.[68]

It is clear, however, that practice does not always follow the law and that, in a segmented pluralistic society, there will always be controversial issues that only the fearless and dedicated teacher will openly discuss. Tradition-bound parents will continue to censor books and censure teachers for introducing ideas and matters that violate their sense of religious or sexual propriety (as in the controversy in Kanawha County, West Virginia in the 1970's), and conservative politicians will continue to try to control the scholarship that guides curriculum development projects (as in the furor over the anthropological details of family and sex life in traditional societies as described in "Man As a Course of Study"). It took 50 years, for example, for the religious/secular issue over the teaching of evolution to be somewhat resolved.

The fundamentalist revivals of the 1920s led to the introduction of bills in at least 20 states, all designed to prevent the teaching of the theory of evolution in the public schools because it conflicted with the Biblical versions of the creation of the world and the origins of mankind. Tennessee's "monkey law," passed in 1925, became the most famous of these, mainly because of the dramatic trial of a high school science teacher, John Thomas Scopes, in which William Jennings Bryan duelled with Clarence Darrow. Forty-two years later, Tennessee repealed its law in 1967, leaving only the laws of Mississippi and Arkansas still on the books.

Finally, in 1968, the Arkansas law was declared unconstitutional because, in the words of the state's lower court, it "tended to hinder the quest for knowledge, restrict the freedom to learn, restrain the freedom to teach."[69] Reciting precedents that ranged from *Everson* and *McCollum* to *Engel*, *Abington*, and *Keyishian*, the Court declared that the state could not make it unlawful to teach the "theory or doctrine that mankind ascended or descended from a lower order of animals." The grounds were that

> the law must be stricken because of its conflict with the constitutional prohibition of state laws respecting an establishment of religion or prohibiting the exercise thereof. The overriding fact is that Arkansas' law selects from the body of knowledge a particular segment which it proscribes for the sole reason that it is deemed to conflict with a particular religious doctrine; that is, with a particular interpretation of the Book of Genesis by a particular religious group.
>
> The State's undoubted right to prescribe the curriculum for its public schools does not carry with it the right to prohibit, on pain of criminal penalty, the teaching of a scientific theory or doctrine where that prohibition is based upon reasons that violate the First Amendment. It is much too late to argue that the State may impose upon the teachers in its schools any conditions that it chooses, however restrictive they may be of constitutional guarantees.[70]

If one expected that such a clear ruling by the nation's highest court would settle the matter of practice in all the nation's schools, then this history of 50 years will not have been understood. In the same year that the *Epperson* case was decided, some members of the State Board of Education in California began to demand that textbooks adopted in the state must equally treat the Biblical account of creation as a counter-theory to that of evolution. Since then, resolutions have been passed and debates have arisen periodically over whether evolution is just one theory among many, as conservative religionists argued, or whether it was the only adequate explanation for life's origin, as the National Academy of Science and 19 California Nobel Laureate scientists argued. In 1973 Tennessee passed a new textbook law requiring school textbooks to give equal emphasis to all accounts.

Children's Rights to Due Process

The search for freedom, and public education's role in it, had both private and personal as well as public aspects, but it was often difficult to distinguish the two. Indeed, they were often interrelated, one leading to the other. A unique example of this interrelationship arose in the drive for "children's rights," which mushroomed with extraordinary speed in the late 1960s and early 1970s. A survey of 24 states by the *New York Times* in October 1976 revealed that cities in all those states had active legal groups working for children's rights. It was predicted that, within the decade, aggressive advocacy groups would make this a major concern of federal courts and of the Supreme Court in their effort to gain for children the same kind of individual rights granted to adults and both protected by the Constitution:

> What they hope to do is establish that a child has a right to a safe, stable home, to a reasonable education, to due process of law and to freedom from abuse and neglect. They hope, in other words, to provide that adults and institutions have obligations to the young as well as powers over them.[71]

The landmark case was decided in 1967 when the Supreme Court ruled that children in juvenile courts must be given the same procedural rights that adults have with regard to notice of the charges and the right to a lawyer, to confront and cross-examine witnesses, and to adequate warning of privileges against self-incrimination. This case had to do with a 15-year-old boy who had been sentenced to an industrial school in Arizona without such protection.[72]

During the course of the following decade the children's advocates gathered momentum both in research and in court action. One of the most active research organizations has been the Children's Defense Fund of the Washington Research Project, and among the scores of legal groups the American Civil Liberties Union has been prominent. State legislatures and the Congress have been prodded to take action, notably by the Federal Juvenile Justice and Delinquency Act, sponsored by Senator Birch Bayh and passed in 1974, and the Education of All Handicapped Children Act of 1975. In the October term of 1976 the Supreme Court agreed to review at least five cases concerned with the constitutional rights of children. For example, the State of Pennsylvania was charged with violating the due process provisions of the Fourteenth Amendment by committing four children to mental hospitals with the consent of their parents but against the will of the children. These and other cases may serve to raise questions concerning the rights of parents to make decisions for their children in the field of education, rights sustained all the way back to *Pierce* in 1925.[73] The effort is being made to ascertain in what respects children's interests may be defined as independent of those of the parents and to what extent they may be asserted competently by children themselves.

Goss v. Lopez / The drive to achieve more protection of due process for children's private rights in the juvenile justice system was quickly directed at schools as well. The key case here was *Goss* v. *Lopez*, which involved nine high school students in Columbus, Ohio, who had been suspended (during racial demonstrations and unrest in 1971) for up to 10 days without a hearing, as permitted under Ohio law. The students charged that the law was unconstitutional under the Fourteeenth Amendment because it deprived them without due process of their property (the right to an education) and of their liberty (by harming their record in school without a hearing).[74] In January 1975, the Court declared by a 5:4 decision that the law was unconstitutional, and ruled that students in high school are to be granted due process in suspensions. This must include oral or written notice of the charges of misconduct, an explanation of the charges, and a statement of the evidence against them. Students must be given an opportunity to present their side of the story before suspension from school for 10 days or less.

A minority of four justices, all appointed by President Nixon, dissented, arguing that the decision was an unwarranted intrusion of the federal courts into what was the proper arena of authority for state legislatures and educational officials, that is, school discipline. But the Court majority went right ahead a month later to rule in an Arkansas case that school board members and educational officials who discipline students unfairly and without due process by claiming ignorance of students' constitutional rights may be liable for damages. The majority argued that school officials must know the basic unquestioned constitutional rights of students. The same Nixon minority argued that this was too harsh a standard for laymen who serve as school board members and who are generally immune from civil suits for their good-faith actions as public officials. When the character of the Court became more conservative with the retirement of Justice Douglas, the new "Burger majority" began to draw back from children's rights, or so it seemed, when the Court decided in April 1977 that paddling of children in public schools was not a "cruel and unusual punishment" under the Eighth Amendment.[75]

The Right to Privacy / The outreach of the federal government on behalf of private rights and freedoms was being pushed ahead, not only by the courts but also by acts of Congress. The most notable, as it turned out, controversial legislation was the Family Educational Rights and Privacy Act of 1974, sponsored by Senator James Buckley, Conservative Republican of New York, and promoted most actively by the National Citizens' Committee in Education. In a reaction to the revelations of Watergate and the unrest of the prior decade, the Congress aimed at "opening up institutions," making them more accountable, and protecting the privacy of individuals. The Act denies funds to any school that prevents parents of children under 18, and students themselves over 18, from having access to any or all school records for inspection or review. School records may not be released to others without written consent except to school officials and to certain federal or state officials in connection with application for financial aid. The primary intent of the law is to prevent abuses whereby careless or incorrect entries in the files are damaging to a student's further education or career, and to prevent releasing files to banks, credit agencies, police departments, and the like without the knowledge of the students or their parents. However, many college and university associations, led by the American Council on Education, protested vigorously that there were many ambiguities in the law and that confidential recommendations would no longer be useful if the writers knew that the students could read them. As a result, a long process of rewriting the regulations in the Department of Health, Education, and Welfare led to their effective date being June 1976, with still further review to take place during 1976–1977.

Freedom of Students To Learn/Tinker v. Des Moines

While the most publicity and outward controversy took place over the notable efforts to achieve constitutional protection of due process under the Fourteenth Amendment for students' private rights, the most important and most difficult in the long run may be the effort to put into practice the *public* right to freedom of learning for students to match the public freedom of teaching for teachers. But definite gains in constitutional law have been made here, too. The landmark case was *Tinker* v. *Des Moines* in 1969, in which the protection of the First Amendment was at stake.[76] The case began in 1965 when some Quaker children attended school in Des Moines wearing black armbands to protest the government's war policy in Vietnam. The students were suspended from school, even though they had acted quietly and had not disrupted the school discipline, and had not infringed upon the rights of others.

The Court's decision, written by Justice Abe Fortas, found that wearing the armbands was a symbolic act of expression that came under the protection of the free speech clause of the First Amendment:

> First Amendment rights, applied in light of the special characteristics of the school environment, are available to teachers and students. It can hardly be argued that either students or teachers shed their constitutional rights to freedom of speech or expression at the schoolhouse gate.[77]

Citing precedent after precedent as far back as *Meyer* and *Pierce* and up to *Keyishian* and *Epperson*, Justice Fortas argued that not only do states have comprehensive authority to prescribe and control school conduct, but they must exercise it in ways consistent with fundamental constitutional safeguards. So, where there is no finding of substantial interference with appropriate discipline, or material interruption with classwork, or invasion of the rights of others, there must be freedom of expression for students as well as teachers:

> In our system, state-operated schools may not be enclaves of totalitarianism. School officials do not possess absolute authority over their students. Students in school as well as out of school are "persons" under our Constitution. They are possessed of fundamental rights which the State must respect, just as they themselves must respect their obligations to the State. In our system, students may not be regarded as closed-circuit recipients of only that which the State chooses to communicate. They may not be confined to the expression of those sentiments that are officially approved. In the absence of a specific showing of constitutionally valid reasons to regulate their speech, students are entitled to freedom of expression of their views.[78]

While the *Tinker* v. *Des Moines* case represented a great gain for public freedom of teaching and learning, it was still not obvious to the general public or even to the whole educational profession that the First Amendment was at the very heart of public freedom and that its validity and authority, in Meiklejohn's words, were "to be found, not in the separate demands of independent individuals, each fighting for his own rights and interests, but in the concerted wisdom and action of a political community."[79]

The Rising Tension between Freedom and Equality

In sum, though the search for freedom as a prime goal of public education was generally enhanced from the 1920's to the 1970's, it was the *private* freedoms that dominated the scene as the period closed. To the claims for the personal rights of parents, or the personal rights of children, or the personal rights of teachers were added the insistent voices of the several cultural and ethnic pluralisms seeking not only private freedoms but also equality. It seemed as though the *public* freedoms, so essential to the health of the democratic political community, would shrink into the background of public consciousness. Or, perhaps, it was simply that the gathering movement to achieve *equality* of rights for minorities commanded greater political power and thus reduced the focus on public freedoms.

This meant that the role of government and of governmental institutions, like public education, came to be hotly debated in a new context. On behalf of protecting private freedoms, it was argued, government and public education should be kept to a minimum so that they could not invade private rights; the revelation of the intrusions upon privacy by governmental intelligence agencies during the Vietnam era was shocking and disheartening. On the other hand, the government and public education were being asked to be more aggressively positive on behalf of achieving equality for one disadvantaged group after another; so, a stronger—not weaker—government and public education were required to ensure compliance, if necessary, to prevent the discrimination that often occurred when individuals or groups practiced freedom of choice in schooling or neighborhoods.

This cross-cutting of purposes often led to a weakening of the historic faith in public education as a remedy or as a reform potion for the ills of society. The more successful the schools were in fostering the private freedoms of some, the less successful they might become in ensuring the equal rights of others—and vice versa. This dilemma found the public schools once again in the middle. If they tried to do what they were asked to do by the more powerful special interest groups, they were open to attack from others whose rights might be affected adversely. Therefore, fundamental purposes would have to be clarified and priorities set. Somehow, both freedom and equality had to be served. It is the search for the latter that we shall review in Chapter 11.

Notes

1. *Meyer* v. *Nebraska*, 262 U.S. 390((1923).
2. For the Klan's role in the Oregon case, see David B. Tyack, "The Perils of Pluralism: The Background of the Pierce Case," *American Historical Review*, October 1968, 74:74–94.
3. *Pierce* v. *Society of Sisters*, 268 U.S. 510 (1925), pp. 534–535.
4. *Farrington* v. *Tokushige et al.*, 273 U.S. 284 (1927), 47 Sup. Ct.
5. *Gong Lum* v. *Rice*, 275 U.S. 78.
6. *Minersville* v. *Gobitis*, 310 U.S. 586 (1940).
7. *Minersville* v. *Gobitis*.
8. *West Virginia* v. *Barnette*, 319 U.S. 624 (1943).
9. Washington Research Project, Children's Defense Fund, *Children Out of School in America* (Cambridge, Mass.: 1974), p. 55.
10. *Wisconsin* v. *Yoder*, 406 U.S. 213 (1972).

11. *Wisconsin* v. *Yoder*, p. 214.
12. *Wisconsin* v. *Yoder*, p. 233.
13. *Wisconsin* v. *Yoder*, p. ?.
14. Robert M. Hutchins, "The Schools Must Stay," *The Century Magazine,* Jan/Feb. 1973, p. 16.
15. Gerald M. Reagan, *Educational Studies*, Spring, 1973.
16. John E. Coons, Stephen D. Sugarman, and William H. Clune, *Private Wealth and Public Education* (Cambridge, Mass.: Harvard University Press, 1970).
17. For discussion of cultural pluralism and ethnicity, see Chapter 12.
18. The National Commission on the Reform of Secondary Education, *The Reform of Secondary Education: A Report to the Public and the Profession* (New York: McGraw-Hill, 1973).
19. National Association of Secondary School Principals, *This We Believe* (Washington, D.C.: NASSP, 1975).
20. John E. Coons, "Law and the Sovereigns of Childhood," *Phi Delta Kappan*, September 1976, 58(1):19–24.
21. Coons, p. 22.
22. Stephen Aarons, "The Separation of School and State: *Pierce* Reconsidered," *Harvard Educational Review*, February 1976, 46(1):76–104.
23. Aarons, p. 84.
24. Aarons, p. 90.
25. Aarons, p. 97.
26. Aarons, pp. 98–99.
27. Aarons, p. 104.
28. *Cochran* v. *Louisiana State Board of Education*, 281 U.S. 370 (1930), p. 375.
29. *Everson* v. *Board of Education*, 330 U.S. 1 (1947), pp. 15–16.
30. *Everson* v. *Board of Education*, pp. 29–33.
31. *Everson* v. *Board of Education*, p. 57.
32. *Everson* v. *Board of Education*, pp. 24–28.
33. See "Statement on Church and State," *Christianity and Crisis*, July 5, 1948, 8(12):2. See also letter of the National Council of the Churches of Christ in the U.S.A., *New York Times*, December 13, 1952. See *Social Action*, November 15, 1948, 14(9):35–36. See also "The Public Schools and Protestant Faith," *Social Action*, December 1952, 19(3).
34. See R. Freeman Butts, *The American Tradition in Religion and Education* (Boston: Beacon Press, 1950) for the details of the meaning of "multiple establishment" (that is, public aid to all religions equally).
35. *School Administrator*, Journal of the American Association of School Administrators, April 1950, p. 2.
36. *Board of Education of Central School District #1* v. *Allen*, 392 U.S. 236 (1968).
37. *Lemon* v. *Kurtzman*, 403 U.S. 602 (1971). See also *Early* v. *DiCenso*, 403 U.S. 602 (1971).
38. *Committee on Public Education and Religious Liberty* (PEARL) v. *Nyquist*, 413, U.S. 756 (1973); and *Levitt* v. *Committee on Public Education and Religious Liberty*, 413 U.S. 756 (1973).

39. *Sloan* v. *Lemon*, 413 U.S. 756 (1973).
40. *Norwood* v. *Harrison*, 413 U.S. 756 (1973).
41. *PEARL* v. *Nyquist*, footnote. 38.
42. *McCollum* v. *Board of Education*, 330 U.S. 203 (1948), pp. 209–210.
43. *Zorach and Gluck* v. *Board of Education*, 343 U.S. 306 (1952).
44. See *New York Times*, December 1, 1951. By January 1953, only 300 of 3,000 school districts in the state had followed the regents' proposal. See *New York Times*, January 16, 1953.
45. *Engel* v. *Vitale*, 370 U.S. 421 (1962).
46. *Abington Township District School* v. *Schempp*, 374 U.S. 203 (1963).
47. Howard K. Beale, *A History of Freedom of Teaching in American Schools* (New York: Scribner's, 1941). Reprinted by Octagon Books, 1968 and 1974.
48. Alexander Meiklejohn, *Political Freedom: The Constitutional Powers of the People* (New York: Harper & Row, 1960), pp. 3–4.
49. Meiklejohn, pp. 59–60.
50. Meiklejohn, p. 86.
51. *Wieman* v. *Updegraff*, 344 U.S. 183 (1952).
52. *Wieman* v. *Updegraff*. Quoted in Robert H. Bremner, ed., *Children and Youth in America: A Documentary History; Vol. III: 1933–1973* (Cambridge: Harvard University Press, 1974), p. 1745.
53. R. Freeman Butts, "Freedom and Responsibility in American Education," *Teachers College Record*, December 1952, 54(3):117–124.
54. Robert W. Iversen, *The Communists and the Schools* (New York: Harcourt, Brace, 1959), pp. 361–362.
55. Sidney Hook, *Heresy-Yes; Conspiracy-No!*, (New York. Day, 1953).
56. *The New York Times Magazine*, February 27, 1949; and March 27, 1949.
57. Sidney Hook, "Letter to the Editor," *The Chronicle of Higher Education*, May 23, 1977, p. 11.
58. National Education Association, Educational Policies Commission, *American Education and International Tensions* (Washington, D.C.: The Commission, 1949), pp. 39–40.
59. American Association of University Professors, *Bulletin*, Spring 1950, pp. 41–43.
60. *Adler* v. *Board of Education*, 342 U.S. 485.
61. *Adler* v. *Board of Education*.
62. *Adler* v. *Board of Education*.
63. *Beilan* v. *Board of Education*, 357 U.S. 399 (1958).
64. *Barenblatt* v. *United States*, 360 U.S. 109 (1959).
65. *Shelton* v. *Tucker*, 364 U.S. 479 (1960).
66. *Keyishian* v. *Board of Regents*, 385, U.S. 589 (1967).
67. See David Schimmel and Louis Fischer, *The Civil Rights of Teachers* (New York: Harper & Row, 1975) Chap. 8.
68. Schimmel and Fischer, p. 149.
69. *Epperson* v. *Arkansas*, 393 U.S. 97 (1968). Quoted in Bremner, p. 1904.
70. Bremner, p. 1905.

71. Barbara Campbell, "Children's Rights Drive Is Centered in Courtroom," *New York Times*, October 31, 1976.
72. *In re Gault*, 387 U.S. 1 (1967).
73. For convenient summaries of the various aspects of personal rights of children, see Bibliographical Notes, page 000.
74. *Goss* v. *Lopez*, Sup. Ct. No. 73-898, p. 4181. The minority were Chief Justice Warren E. Burger and Associate Justices Harry A. Blackmun, William H. Rehnquist, and Lewis F. Powell.
75. *Ingraham* v. *Wright*, 45 U.S.L.W. 4364 (April 19, 1977). Also cited as Sup. Ct., No. 76-6527 (1977).
76. *Tinker* v. *Des Moines*, 393 U.S. 503 (1969).
77. *Tinker* v. *Des Moines*, p. 506.
78. *Tinker* v. *Des Moines*, p. 511.
79. Alexander Meiklejohn, *Education Between Two Worlds* (New York: Harper & Row, 1942), p. 217.

11 The Search for Equality

We come now to another great wave of reform that swept U.S. education in the middle of the twentieth century, a reform intended to put into practice, at long last, a second article of faith in the "American Dream"—equality. We have seen how the role of education in the search for the values of freedom was largely instigated by the oppressive political attacks upon schools, by overweening nativism directed at foreigners, by war-induced patriotism aimed at dissidents, by political and corporate conformity alarmed by radicalism, and by religious fundamentalism bent on imposing various orthodoxies upon teachers and students. Accepted in principle but long denied in practice, the equality expressed in the nation's creed began to gain more attention as a major reform movement in which education would be the "open sesame" to its success. In essence, this meant the reform of the education system itself, for only in this way could equality of educational opportunity for minorities be realized, and only in this way could the poor, women, and the handicapped be compensated by enabling them to overcome economic, political, and social disadvantages, and to cope with pervasive racism, discrimination, and segregation.

From a modest beginning during the reform era of the New Deal of the 1930s and 1940s, the search for equality gained so great a momentum that it engaged much of the public and professional attention in the 1950s and 1960s. By the end of the 1970s, substantial gains had been made, but the results were mixed and judgments of progress were always circumscribed by the level of optimism or pessimism of the beholders, who often could not decide whether the reservoir was half-full or half-empty, or whether the direction was forward or backward. And judgments were also affected by an individual's definition of the term "equality" when applied to education and what he or she considered as education's role in society.

The search for equality, which took over the center of the educational stage in the 1960s, was spearheaded by liberal and minority civil rights organizations concerned with gaining equal rights for minority racial and ethnic groups who were often termed "disadvantaged," joined later by women's rights organizations. Together they carried the fight for equal rights, first to the courts and then to the legislatures and government agencies which were eventually persuaded to use their powers to enlist the nation's educational institutions in the movement.

Expanding Access to Secondary and Higher Institutions

The first thing to remember when judging the search for equality of opportunity through education is the great extent to which education has been made available to an increasing percentage of the American people. The most remarkable historical fact of the past 50 years, especially in comparison with other countries, is the tremendous increase in the number of children and youth who have attended school and college for lengthened periods of time. From the mid-1920s to the mid-1970s the total population approximately doubled from about a hundred million to more than two hundred million. During the same period, the attendance at all schools and colleges, public and private, tripled from something like 20 million to nearly 60 million: approximately 35 million in elementary schools, 15 million in high schools, and 10 million in colleges and universities.

Growth of Attendance

The most striking figures showing the extent of access to formal education were not in the elementary schools, which had reached nearly universal attendance in the 1920s (around 97 percent of all children aged 6 to 13). The most remarkable aspect of the march to formal schools and colleges was the increase at the secondary and post-secondary levels where enrollments increased at a startling rate, eventually embracing a very high proportion of the school age population, far exceeding that of most other nations of the world. Secondary school enrollments, which stood at about 5 million at the end of the 1920s (about 50 percent of the youth aged 14 to 17) jumped to about 15 million by the mid-1970s (approaching 95 percent of that age group).[1] This came close to universal secondary schooling, bringing much satisfaction to many citizens, but causing consternation among those who observed the increasing tide of violence, crime, and unemployment that enveloped a growing number of youth in the 1970s.

By 1975 approximately 80 percent of all American youth between the ages of 25 and 29 had completed four or more years of high school (but only 71 percent of nonwhites). This worked out to be 60 percent of all adults over age 24 having four years or more of secondary schooling (but only 44 percent of nonwhites). So, even though the statistics showed very high attendance averages, compared with those of the rest of the world, they also revealed persistent inequalities among the races. In other words, while the median number of years of schooling completed by all American adults over age 25 had reached 10 years by the early 1950s, the educational disadvantage of nonwhites was revealed by the fact that their median number of years of schooling was nearly three years less than that of the total adult population.

As a result of the search for equality, however, gains were undoubtedly made over the next 20 years. By 1974 the median number of grades completed for all persons over age 25 had increased to more than 12 years and for nonwhites to 11 (now only one year behind). And for persons aged 25 to 29, the gap was even narrower; 12.8 years for whites and 12.5 years for nonwhites. The quantity of educational attendance at elementary and secondary schools had almost equalized among the races, according to the Census figures. A closer look revealed, however, that large numbers of poor and nonwhite (as many as one or two million) children were either out of school and unrecorded or were extremely irregular in attendance, with high absenteeism in large urban centers.[2]

What may in the long run be even more significant was the expansion of access to colleges and universities (or, as the terminology of the 1970s would have it, "postsecondary" institutions). This increase was the result not only of nearly universal attendance at secondary institutions but also of the increasing number who *completed* high school (a jump from around 30 percent of 17-year-olds who graduated in 1930 to 75 percent by mid-1970s). So, with over 90 percent of high-school-age youth attending high school and 75 percent graduating, the pressure on colleges was bound to increase. In 1925 about 10 percent of the college-age population (17 to 21) was attending college, but 50 years later more than 50 percent was doing so. In actual numbers this meant an increase from about a half-million students in the 1920s to 10 million in the mid-1970s, a twentyfold increase in 50 years.

Such statistics may not excite the imagination of those to whom universal education is commonplace, but the historical implications were momentous. While some observers may not believe that more education for more people is necessarily a good thing, the trend was unmistakable in all modernizing nations of the world. It was just earlier and more rapid in the United States. In 1900 an elementary education was the accepted requirement for general admission to adult life in a rapidly modernizing America. By 1930 a secondary education was virtually a necessity, and by 1980 it could very well become the completion of two or four years of post-secondary education.

Comparison of United States and European Systems / In the comparatively short period of nearly 15 years from 1960 to 1974, the percentage of all adults over age 25 who had completed four or more years of college had nearly doubled (from 7.7 percent to 13.3 percent). The percentages of non-whites went from 3.5 percent to 8 percent. But for the younger adults between ages 25 and 29, the percentage with four or more years of college jumped from 11 percent to nearly 21 percent (from 5.4 percent to 11 percent for nonwhites). Whether such gains would continue could not be predicted with confidence, but the statistics were clear and the comparison with other modernizing countries was significant.

In 1950 the proportion of young people in Western Europe and Russia who finished a secondary school course entitling them to attend a post-secondary institution was about 5 percent, whereas it was 50 percent in the United States. Some 10 years later the trend was evident. In all cases the proportion in Western Europe had jumped to 8 to 15 percent, while it had increased to 30 percent in the Soviet Union and to 70 percent in the United States. Similarly, in the early 1960s, the western European countries were admitting about 5 to 10 percent of the relevant age groups to higher educational institutions, while the Soviet Union was admitting around 16 percent and the United States 35 percent. And the proportion of the age group graduating from an institution of higher education with a first degree was around 4 to 5 percent in Western Europe, 8 percent in the Soviet Union, and 20 percent in the United States.[3]

The Greater Demands of Modernization / Quantity of education was, of course, not the only question with regard to equality of opportunity. Much of the controversy of the recent period has had to do with quality. It was one thing to assert that the literacy of the U.S. population was over 98 percent. This was cause for congratulation when compared with underdeveloped nations, whose literacy rate was anywhere from 10 to 30 percent. But it was also true that simply being able to write one's name and read a third-grade reader might make a person literate, but it did not necessarily qualify that person for effective functioning in a modern industrial society.

In the 1920s, simple literacy may have been sufficient for unskilled laborers who as recently as 1945 held as many as 30 percent of the jobs in a labor force that presumably required only a minimum of simple or inert literacy. But by the 1970s the proportion of unskilled jobs had dropped to 5 or 10 percent, and minimal literacy was no longer sufficient for the vast number of jobs. Even more important, the need was for a fully functional and active literate capability to enable a citizen to keep up with, and partici-pate in, the political, social, and cultural activities of a complex modern society. Thus, lack of the basic skills of reading, writing, and arithmetic was a constant source of controversy. But it became ever more clear that special handicaps devolved upon those whose length of schooling or access to school-ing had been limited by inequalities imposed by racial, ethnic, or economic deprivation. While white literacy approximated 99 percent, nonwhite literacy was less than 90 percent. A larger proportion of nonwhite workers was thus handicapped at the very basic levels of admission to skilled jobs, let alone participation in the political and cultural life of citizenship even if racial discrimination did not operate at higher levels. And when unskilled jobs tended to decline, literacy became ever more important.

Disparities in Availability

Despite the enormous expansion in educational attendance throughout the system, drastic inequalities continued to exist in the quality and amount of education available in various regions of the nation. The more highly industrialized and richer states spent more on education and thus provided better opportunities for their citizens. By 1970 several states were spending only one-half to one-third as much per pupil as other states were spending. The poorer states, mostly in the South, had to exert greater effort than the richer states to maintain even the one-half relationship.

It was clear, too, that within the states, the urban and industrial areas were more advantageously situated than the rural and farming regions. As long as local units provided the bulk of school support, those units with greater wealth could spend more money on their schools. Likewise, great inequalities existed in the provision of educational opportunities for black and other minority children as compared with those for white children. In the early decades of the century in the southern states, the average expenditure per black child was about one-fourth to one-half what it was for each white child. Thus, in general, the inequality was enormous, either because some communities simply did not have enough money to provide decent education or because they did not wish to spend equal amounts for all groups in the population, or both.

Attempts to equalize these differences took several forms. Within the states, equalization funds were set up to distribute state aid to the local communities on a basis that would help the poorer districts. Forward-looking states adopted the general principle that the entire wealth of the state should be tapped to serve the entire population of the state. Various kinds of formulas were developed to give state aid to communities commensurate with their need and ability to raise funds for schools, the number of children to be educated, and their willingness to tax themselves as fully as possible for the support of schools.

Early Equalization Efforts / Many states set out to consolidate local rural districts into larger units in order to provide more efficient schools at less cost. By pooling their resources on a county basis, local districts could provide fewer but better schools, served by school buses and manned by better-paid and better-trained teachers. The consolidation movement met vigorous opposition from many partisans of localism who supported local and decentralized control and who feared that the county or state would usurp their rights. But the trend toward consolidation made steady headway despite this continuing opposition. Through the middle decades of the twentieth century the 120,000 local school systems of 1940 had been consolidated into 16,000 in 1976; and the 10 percent of pupils transported by bus in 1934 had become more than 50 percent by 1974.

In general, the states were willing, even eager, to receive financial aid from the federal government, but they were reluctant to have the federal government extend its control over the state systems. Nevertheless, the federal government's role began to increase, and state financing began to overtake local financing sources. In 1930 the total funds expended for public elementary and secondary schools was something like $2.5 billion, with about 83 percent coming from local property taxes and about 17 percent from state sources, with a negligible amount from the federal government except for vocational education. By the 1970s the local funds had dropped to little more than 50 percent and the state proportion had jumped to more than 40 percent, with the federal contribution hovering around 7 to 8 percent of a total that approximated $8.5 billion.

Undoubtedly, great educational gains were made by the vast development of elaborate state machinery for the control and support of public schools. The unifying tasks of raising standards and equalizing educational opportunity have often been promoted far beyond what could have been achieved for a state as a whole under the varying conditions of local autonomy represented by hundreds of small school districts; and equalization funds for providing state aid to poor districts and requiring richer but reluctant districts to put forth greater effort to raise their school taxes (and thereby decrease their share of aid) have generally been to the good. The great increase in the proportion of school support that has come from state funds to the poorer districts is the result of this redistribution.

Continuing Inequalities / There was, however, a serious debit area in state support of public schools because some states were not able to meet the accepted standard for a satisfactory minimum education for all their children. This inequality was caused by great differences of wealth between the states, as well as the efforts to remedy the inequities.[4] At mid-century, several states had more than an annual income of $12,000 for each child of school age, whereas other states had less than $5,000 income. In general, the poorer states put forth even more effort than the wealthy states; that is, they spent a higher proportion of their incomes on education, but, despite this, their expenditure per pupil was only one-fourth as much per pupil each year as other states spent. It was clear that the southern states had less resources with which to provide education for their children. Their problems were complicated further by the larger proportion of children in those states to be educated and by the added cost of attempting to maintain two separate school systems for blacks and whites. This meant that teachers' salaries were, on the average, lower in many southern states than elsewhere; that the salaries of black teachers were lower than those of white teachers; and that twice as much was spent on the average for each white pupil as for each black pupil. All of these factors showed wide inequality among the states and within some states.

Effects of Migration / The inequality of ability or willingness to support schools was further brought home by the realization that migration and mobility of people from one state to another had rapidly increased in recent years. In the decade of the 1930s there was more migration than in any previous decade, mostly stimulated by the economic depression. In the 1940s the migration was even greater, largely as a result of the movements of people to engage in war work. From 1940 to 1947, some 13 million people moved from one state to another. The states with the largest net gains were those of the West, and the states with the largest net losses were those of the South. By 1940 it was estimated that nearly one-third of the total population of the United States lived in states other than the one of their origin. Significantly enough, the states with the highest number of children sent the largest number of people to other states. The trend from rural regions to cities was also marked.

All this added up to the fact that the kind of education provided by one state was of concern to other states because of the constant migration. People who had received a poor education as children were likely to migrate to states where they would have received a better education if they had been born and lived there from the beginning. The facts of inequality and of mobility highlighted the debits of the system of state support of education and stressed the need for general federal aid, which could help the states to equalize their educational facilities. In addition, it could protect the wealthier states and the whole nation from the dangers of inadequate education, for poor education for some anywhere was a threat to all everywhere. But it took several decades of contentious debate and controversy for the argument to affect the political process on behalf of federal aid to public education.

The Federal Government and Equality of Opportunity

During the 1920s and 1930s the issue of general federal aid to education was relatively quiescent. Significant gains for grants to special forms of education had been achieved under the Democratic administration of President Woodrow Wilson through the Smith-Lever Act of 1914 for agricultural extension service and the Smith-Hughes Act of 1917 to aid vocational education. But the drive for federal aid to improve education generally throughout the states gained little headway under the Republican administrations of the 1920s.

The dominant view of both the Democratic and Republican parties in the 1920s and 1930s was that education was largely a matter for state and local control. This followed the traditional view that decentralized control and support of education was the democratic American way. The Republican Party platforms maintained this view throughout the 1930s and 1940s, either by omitting mention of the problem of federal aid entirely or making very vague statements in favor of equality of educational opportunity and freedom of the states.

The Democratic Party, however, gradually began to change its stand. In the election years of 1944, 1948, and 1952 the Democratic platform explicitly came out for federal aid to education, to be administered by the states without federal control. President Truman actively urged Congress to pass a federal-aid-to-education bill and also federal aid for scholarships. Amounts for these purposes were included in his proposed budgets of the late 1940s and early 1950s. Thus, the two major parties had made a complete reversal of policy from the 1870s and 1880s, when the Republican Party was the strong advocate of federal aid to education.

The Battles for Federal Aid

Meanwhile, several professional education organizations and advisory commissions to the president began to recommend more forcefully in the late 1930s and 1940s the need for federal aid to education. They deplored centralization of *control* of education by the federal government and pointed to its dangers, but they just as vigorously asserted that the federal government should participate in *support* of education in the states in order to equalize educational opportunity among the population. Prevailing control of education should be at local and state levels, but the federal government should aid the states to achieve a minimum level of quality of education, and aid should be granted according to wealth, ability to tax, and need of the several states for help.

With the policy clearly stated, the problem then became one of putting the policy into practice by persuading Congress to pass a federal aid bill. The details of this struggle cannot be told here, but two points were clear: The struggle increased in intensity and in public debate in the late 1940s and 1950s; and the main stumbling blocks were the issues over whether or not federal funds should be available for parochial school children in any form, and whether or not southern states should be required to allocate equitable proportions to their segregated schools for whites and blacks. Some bills required funds to go to parochial schools; others would prohibit such use. But no bill could pass both houses of Congress.[5]

Despite the failure to pass major federal aid legislation in the 1950s, all three branches of the federal government began to play larger and larger roles in the conduct of education, regardless of the fact that the school systems themselves were largely under state and local control. We have seen how federal courts, for example, began to play a larger part in saying what states could and could not do about the questions of freedom in their own educational systems (as pointed out in Chapter 10). When it came to achieving equal educational facilities for blacks, the federal courts were the initial and key instrument, as we shall see presently.

It seems clear that danger to the national security and threats to its welfare were the prime motivations in stimulating the federal government to take action when it did. The early federal programs for vocational education began in the World War I period; a second spurt of federal activity took place in the depression years of the early 1930s; other bursts of federal activity followed the World War II period of the 1940s, the "cold-war" period of the 1950s, and the civil rights movements of the 1960s.

ESEA

The most important piece of federal legislation aimed at reducing inequality in the field of education was The Elementary and Secondary Education Act of 1965. This brilliant piece of political action overcame the longstanding roadblocks that had impeded federal aid to general education for nearly a hundred years. Key personalities in the achievement were Francis Keppel, who had been brought from the deanship of Harvard University's School of Education to be Commissioner of Education; John Gardner who had come from the Carnegie Corporation to be Secretary of Health, Education, and Welfare; and President Lyndon B. Johnson, whose strong support for the bill did indeed justify his oft-stated desire to become known as America's "education president."

The bill turned out to have something for most interested parties. It recognized the growing need to give special attention to the poor of the urban ghettos and the rural slums; this meant special attention to blacks, Puerto Ricans, Mexican-Americans, and other minority ethnic groups. So, Title I of the Act provided funds to states and localities to improve schooling for educationally deprived children (83 percent of the total), using a quantitative formula based upon child population, family poverty, and the need of the local district for funds. In this way most of the 18,000 school districts in the United States at that time were entitled to some aid.

The Act also recognized the political need to provide something for parochial schools, so Title II made it possible for school library resources, textbooks, and other instructional materials to go to private as well as to public schools, with the caveat that no such aids should be used for religious instruction and all materials continued to be owned by public authorities. The child-benefit theory had won the day over heated opposition. By this time, many groups were ready to gloss over the question of separation of church and state, which had agitated the country for some three hundred years, in order to get the benefits of massive federal support for education. This issue was not finally decided by any means, but a major breakthrough was made from which there would be greater and greater difficulty in turning back.

The more direct purpose, however, was to put the federal government squarely on the record in behalf of the search for equality that was agitating the American educational and political communities in the mid-twentieth century. The most pervasive and fundamental problem centered on dismantling the segregated school systems established by law (*de jure*) in the southern states and practiced in fact (*de facto*) by states of the North and West. In addition, there were four other problems, all interrelated with the mainline problem of desegregation, which permeated the search for equality. These problems had to do with the drive to equalize financial support for public school systems, the role of schooling in reducing economic inequality, compensatory education for the disadvantaged minorities and the poor, and affirmative action on behalf of minorities and women.

Dismantling the Dual Systems of Public Schools

By the 1930s, leaders of the black community and their white allies began a concerted drive to achieve the original ideals of equality and freedom envisioned in the Declaration of Independence and the American Revolution and to realize the goals of equal and integrative education that had been sought under Reconstruction after the Civil War. The promise of equality had been held out for 150 years, only to be withdrawn when it came close to integrated education. A determined band of black and white Americans felt that the time for implementation of the promised equal rights was long overdue—in voting, in jobs, in housing, in the access to public facilities, and especially in public education.

Agitation for breaking down the system of segregated black schools and colleges, where they existed, paralleled somewhat the general state of race relations in the country. After World War I, the new freedom found by many blacks in war work led to violent reactions in many parts of the country. The revived Ku Klux Klan reached its height of power in the 1920s, and it looked for a while as though few gains could be made. Then, with the rise in liberal social consciousness that developed in the depression years—an increasing awareness of the sorry plight of millions of black Americans, the spectacle of racial persecution exhibited by German Nazism and Italian Fascism in the 1930s, and finally the call for achievement of better democratic relations that accompanied World War II—notable gains began to appear in the 1940s. Leadership, initiated by President and Mrs. Franklin D. Roosevelt in the New Deal attack upon discrimination in employment, was carried considerably further by President Harry S Truman when he appointed the President's Committee on Civil Rights. The far-seeing report issued by this committee in 1947 contained a sweeping indictment of segregation and discrimination based on race, color, creed, or national origin. Upon the basis of this report, *To Secure These Rights*, President Truman formulated a comprehensive civil rights program, which he urged upon Congress and which became one of the most controversial political issues in the elections of 1948 and the 1950s.

The report of the President's Committee urged that civil rights legislation be enacted on a broad front both by Congress and by the several states. Among its recommendations to achieve civil rights and equality of opportunity was legislation to prohibit segregation and discrimination in education on the basis of race, color, creed, or national origin. Although Congress did not act on Truman's full legislative program, some gains were made in housing and voting rights. When Truman ordered the integration of the armed forces in 1948, a Democratic president had finally placed the Office of the President on the side of the search for equality. No wonder that the majority of blacks shifted their political loyalties from the party of Sumner and Lincoln to the party of Roosevelt and Truman.

Spurred by this general program and the attendant arousal of public opinion, efforts were redoubled to try to break down the walls of segregated education in the South. Two major frontal attacks were made, one through legislation and one through court cases to require public educational institutions to admit blacks. In general, more progress was made through court decisions than by legislation until the advent of the Great Society of the 1960s. Sparked by the National Association for the Advancement of Colored People (NAACP), the Urban League, the Southern Regional Council, and other groups, several states of the South began to equalize salaries for black and white teachers, but the main drive of the NAACP was carried out in court cases to gain admittance of blacks to the graduate and professional schools of the higher institutions in the South, based on the guarantee of the Fourteenth Amendment that all citizens shall be entitled to equal protection of the law.

Appeal to the Federal Courts

As early as 1938 the Supreme Court in the *Gaines* case required the University of Missouri to provide a black student with a law school education equal to that for whites.[6] But this did not touch the "separate but equal" doctrine; it meant that segregation was still possible. More influential were two unanimous Supreme Court decisions in July 1950. In the *Sweatt* case, the University of Texas was required to admit a black to its law school and could not make him attend a separate, segregated institution because it was far from equal in quality to the University of Texas Law School.[7] In the *McLaurin* case the University of Oklahoma was prohibited from requiring a Negro graduate student in the School of Education to be set apart in the classrooms, library, cafeteria, or other facilities of the university.[8] Thus, the Supreme Court made it clear that southern states must provide *equal* educational opportunities for blacks in their state institutions, but it did not face squarely the "separate but equal" doctrine and did not say flatly that *any* legal separation or segregation was thereby automatically a denial of equality.

Encouraged by the gains made against segregation in higher education, efforts were turned directly upon the segregated school systems at the elementary and secondary level. The NAACP lawyers were now convinced that they could successfully attack the "separate but equal" doctrine that still held sway in the 17 southern states and the District of Columbia.[9]

Brown v. Board of Education / The legal and constitutional breakthrough took place on May 17, 1954, when the Supreme Court did indeed reverse the *Plessy* doctrine that "separate but equal" facilities could be constitutional.[10] The Court held that segregated schools in and of themselves denied black children the equal protection of the laws and were thus abhorrent to the Constitution even though physical facilities and tangible factors like salaries and buildings might be equal. In words that resounded in literally dozens of federal court rooms for the next 20 years, Chief Justice Earl Warren handed down the decision of a unanimous court:

> Today, education is perhaps the most important function of state and local governments. Compulsory school attendance laws and the great expenditures for education both demonstrate our recognition of the importance of education to our democratic society. It is required in the performance of our basic public responsibilities, even service in the armed forces. It is the very foundation of good citizenship. Today it is a principal instrument in awakening the child to cultural values, in preparing him for later professional training, and in helping him to adjust normally to his environment. In these days, it is doubtful that any child may reasonably be expected to succeed in life if he is denied the opportunity of an education. Such an opportunity, where the state has undertaken to provide it, is a rgiht which must be made available to all on equal terms.
>
> We come then to the question presented: Does segregation of children in public schools solely on the basis of race, even though the physical facilities and other "tangible" factors may be equal, deprive children of the minority groups of equal educational opportunities? We believe that it does. . . .
>
> To separate them [minority children] from others of similar age and qualifications solely because of their race generates a feeling of inferiority as to their status in the community that may affect their hearts and minds in a way unlikely ever to be undone. . . .
>
> We conclude that in the field of public education the doctrine of "separate but equal" has no place. Separate educational facilities are inher-

ently unequal. Therefore, we hold that the plaintiffs and others similarly situated for whom the actions have been brought are, by reason of the segregation complained of, deprived of the equal protection of the laws guaranteed by the Fourteenth Amendment.[11]

The words spoken by Warren in the *Brown* decision are quoted as a reminder that the court's emphasis was upon equality of educational *opportunity* and that such opportunity must be on equal terms. It stressed the notion of equal *rights*, which is the basic sense in which the founders of the Republic thought of equality in education. The founders did not suggest that public education would produce an equality of *condition* or equality of *results*. They did envision education in common schools where rich and poor were instructed together, but they did not assume that the rich and poor would thereby turn out to have equal incomes. They did not foresee a leveled economic society, but they did reject a deferential society in which some people had the right to rule and others the obligations to obey. One might say they accepted a differential society but opposed a deferential society.

It is important to note, as James S. Coleman does, the difference between inequality of *result*, in which different persons acquire differential distribution of income, and inequality of *access* to those positions that award higher income or bestow other social rewards. Equality of access has been the principal goal of those who have argued for a common public school system, from the founding of the Republic through the common school revival of the nineteenth century to the desegregation and open access movements of the twentieth century. This is at the heart of the many court cases that appeared all over the South in the two decades following *Brown*, and of the court cases that mushroomed in the second decade all over the North. Though the Court applied both concepts in *Brown*, the fundamental question that dominated scores of desegregation cases had to do with the constitutional imperatives of equal civil and educational *rights*. They did not assume that a common education would produce equality of academic results or correct the *economic* inequalities that characterized different children as they began their schooling.

Ready compliance to the *Brown* decision was achieved in orderly desegregation in some of the North-South border states, but the problem was by no means fully settled. Even though the Court's decision was a great and historic policy statement, reaffirming the best of the American tradition of commitment to equality of educational opportunity, it met with open defiance in many parts of the South. The prejudices inculcated over two hundred years could not be easily or quickly changed.

The Broader Civil Rights Movement

From the mid-1950s to the present, the confrontation over civil rights spilled from the courts to the campuses, the schools, the restaurants, the buses, the streets, and the countryside of the South. Both blacks and whites promised "massive resistance." Blacks fought back with nonviolent resistance to the repression of segregation. Whites resorted to legal resistance, and occasionally to violent demonstration, against what they claimed to be an invasion of the rights of the states by the federal government. Hundreds of White Citizens Councils were formed, 101 Southern Congressmen signed a manifesto pledging to reverse the school desegregation decision, and the Ku Klux Klan made yet another appearance.

From amid the conflicting factions, Martin Luther King emerged as the leader of the nonviolent mass civil rights movement that was impressed on the national consciousness by the Montgomery bus boycott in 1955 and which swelled in power and effect until its culmination in the march on Selma in 1965. Violence broke over the campuses and school as crowds of white resistors, as well as state officials, opposed the entrance of black students to the educational institutions. Finally, President Eisenhower sent federal troops to Little Rock in 1957 to enforce the Supreme Court's orders in a genuine showdown of federal and state power.

Subsequently, the Warren Supreme Court held in *Cooper* v. *Aaron* that neither delay by the legislature, the governor, or the local board of education, nor threats of mob violence, tension, bedlam, chaos, and turmoil in the schools could nullify the lower federal court's order for Little Rock to desegregate its schools.[12] Public school officials were state officials and they had the duty to uphold the constitutional rights of black children as defined in *Brown*. Such rights cannot be nullified openly by state officials, nor can they be nullified indirectly by evasive schemes or delaying tactics. The intrepretation of the Fourteenth Amendment enunciated by the Supreme Court in the *Brown* case was the supreme law of the land and was binding upon the states. No state official could war against the Constitution without violating his solemn oath to support it, and any state support of segregated schools violated the constitutional command for equal protection under the laws.

Progress in Desegregation of Southern Schools / In the early 1960s the tempo of desegregation picked up, but so did the violent resistance. From 1963 on, demonstrations erupted in the northern ghettos, and riots in the cities during the summers of 1966 and 1967 surpassed all previous violence in the South. After the assassination of Martin Luther King in 1968, there were riots in 125 U.S. cities, and the impatience, the frustration, and the anger welled up over the whole country. For a time, it seemed that racial conflict would be fought in the streets and the jails rather than in the courts or in Congress.

But the legal confrontation on matters of education continued into the 1960s with slow but noticeable success. In fact, by the end of the decade, the educative effect of the law in persuading white public opinion to accept desegregation in the South turned out to be remarkably significant. A decade that had begun with the governors of Alabama, Mississippi, and Georgia "standing in the school house door" to bar the entrance of black children ended with the governor of Virginia escorting his own 13-year-old daughter to the John F. Kennedy high school in Richmond, which opened in September 1970 with 70 percent black children and 30 percent white.

The year 1964 was a turning point in the progress of legal desegregation, a full ten years after the Supreme Court's major decision. Now Congress finally got into the act. The progress in Congress seemed to have been excruciatingly slow in the view of those civil rights reformers who thought the Supreme Court had settled the matter in 1954. The Senate filibuster against its legal implementation seemed invincible, but finally the first halting step in 75 years led to the Civil Rights Act of 1957, which, reminiscent of the Civil Rights Act of 1875, struggled through only after the deletion of school desegregation provisions. But the momentum of the push toward full equality continued to build up under pressure from President Lyndon Johnson and from the emergence of new and more aggressive civil rights organizations: the Southern Christian Leadership Conference, the Student Nonviolent Coordinating Committee, and the Congress for Racial Equality, as well as a more activist stance by the NAACP and the National Urban League. The momentous march on Washington, led by Martin Luther King in 1963, provided a powerful impetus to a racial breakthrough, which was realized when the continuing filibuster was finally broken and the Civil Rights Act of 1964 was passed.

The Civil Rights Act of 1964 / This Civil Rights Act now put all three branches of the federal government behind the drive for black equality in education. Title IV authorized the Justice Department to initiate law suits on behalf of individuals to compel compliance with desegregation in the schools and to give assistance to school districts in desegregation. Title VI put financial teeth into the operation by authorizing the withholding of federal funds from state or local agencies, including school districts, that continued to discriminate. This last provision turned out to be especially significant when the passage of the Elementary and Secondary School Act of 1965 poured new federal funds into the nation's schools for disadvantaged children, most of whom belonged to black or ethnic minorities. The consensus was building overwhelmingly on the side of the federal authority against states' rights. The 450 resolutions, legislative acts, and other actions of the southern states to slow down or erode desegregation were slowly but surely nullified by federal courts. Of especial significance was the decision of the Supreme Court in 1964 that abolishing public schools in Prince Edward County, Virginia, to avoid integration was unconstitutional, as was the payment of tuition grants to white private schools that were set up after the public schools were closed.[13] The Supreme Court also struck down another favorite device known as "freedom of choice," which presumably permitted parents to choose the school their children would attend.[14] The burden to desegregate rested upon the responsibility of each school board to come forward with a genuine, realistic, and quickly effective plan for virtual desegregation. The burden to cope with a dual system must not be placed upon parents.

In the course of the next half-dozen years, the pace of desegregation in the South picked up remarkably, despite the foot-dragging and guerrilla warfare of delay and opposition. Ten years after the Supreme Court's decision, only 1.2 percent of the nearly three million black students in the 11 states of the deep South in 1965 attended school with white students. In 1971 it was 39 percent, and practically all of the slow-moving school districts in the old South had submitted plans to desegregate. But the Supreme Court had become increasingly impatient with the delay. In October 1969, it changed its 1954 command to desegregate schools "with all deliberate speed" to "end segregation at once."[15]

As the decade of the 1960s ended, it became clear that the *fact* of separation was outlasting the *outlawing* of legal segregation. The most active scene of action shifted from the *de jure* segregation of the South to the *de facto* segregation of the northern urban centers. As might be expected, some courts said the schools themselves could not do anything about *de facto* segregation when it resulted from residential patterns that produced all white or all black neighborhoods, but other courts said that if neighborhood schools proved to be segregated, then they must be modified or abandoned. The most common method of modification was to transport children by bus from one school to another, to achieve proportions in all schools that approximated the racial proportion in the school district or community as a whole.

The Great "Busing" Debate

In April 1971, in what became known as the first busing case, the Supreme Court decided that southern school districts could constitutionally assign pupils to schools in such a way as to achieve a racial balance that corrected a previously segregated system. This could be done by altering attendance zones or by transporting pupils from one zone to another. In *Swann* v. *Charlotte–Mecklenburg*, the Supreme Court summed up its 15-year history of segregation cases by saying that "the constant theme and thrust of every holding from *Brown I* to date is that state-enforced separation of races in public schools is discrimination that violates the equal protection clause [of the Fourteenth Amendment]. The remedy commanded was to dismantle the dual school system."[16] This decision nailed down the lid on the constitutional question: The South *had to replace* its legal dual system with a legal unitary or integrative system. The decision did not touch the *de facto* question in the northern and western states where the percentage of blacks in majority white schools as late as 1973 remained at around 28 percent, whereas in the South it was more than 46 percent.

Meanwhile, an especially explosive political issue was in the making as the percentage of blacks in large northern cities who attended majority white schools was actually declining. Thus, neighborhood segregation in northern city schools was increasing at the same time that the South was making substantial headway toward desegregation. A curious ambivalence surrounded the problem of school busing. The Supreme Court said busing was a constructive way to attain desegregation, while the President of the United States instructed the Justice Department to draw up a constitutional amendment to nullify the Court's action. In 1971, there were nearly 20 million public school children transported every day by state-aided busing (42 percent of the total). In addition to this vast number of public school children who were regularly bused, there were millions of Catholic parents who also desired to have their children transported by bus (if financed by public funds) so their children could acquire religious instruction in Catholic parochial schools. Conversely, there were apparently millions of white parents who did *not* want their children to be transported by bus to public schools outside their neighborhood in order to achieve racially integrated schooling, but they had not seemed to mind the busing that had long preserved segregated schools.

The complex of racial feelings and politics was symbolized by a Gallup poll in 1975 which revealed that a majority of the public favored desegregation of schools, but 75% opposed busing.

Though the extremes of militant resistance to busing began to die down in the middle of the 1970s, the drumbeat of court cases continued apace. In *Keyes* v. *Denver*, the Supreme Court defined the distinction between *de jure* and *de facto* segregation in a northern city.[17] It found that where the school board *intentionally* took actions that resulted in segregation, the result was *de jure*, even though no law had been passed by the legislature or other legislative body. So, if it could be proved that such intentions were at work in gerrymandering school-attendance districts, or in setting up segregatory feeder systems of lower schools to upper schools, or in assigning staff on a racial basis, such actions were unconstitutional and must be corrected. Indeed, if such intentions were proved to be operative in one part of the school system, this was *prima facie* evidence of *de jure* segregation throughout the system, unless the school board could convincingly demonstrate otherwise.

Metropolitanizing School Districts

The *Keyes* decision put the pressure upon the northern cities as *Brown* had put it on the southern states. But just when most of the loopholes were about to be closed, the liberal character of the Supreme Court began to change from what it had been under Chief Justice Earl Warren. It began to take on a more conservative aspect under the growing number of justices appointed by President Nixon, with Warren Earl Burger as Chief Justice. One key example had to do with the plan of "metropolitanizing" school districts. For example, in Richmond, Virginia, in 1972 the federal district judge, Robert R. Herhige, Jr., ordered the merging of the Richmond school district (about 70 percent black) with those of two surrounding counties (about 90 percent white) to form one metropolitan school district, which would be about two-thirds white and one-third black. The argument was that education was a state function, that all school district lines were more or less arbitrary, and that state action and local district action had long contributed to segregation by creating artificial school districts. Thus, the state should now take action to desegregate. A metropolitan school district would have the same advantages that metropolitan water or sewer districts have by serving the whole people of a region. When appealed to the Supreme Court, however, the Court divided 4:4; this decision in *Bradley* v. *State Board of Education* had the effect of leaving the district lines as they were, and thus countermanded the district judge's orders to create a metropolitan district.[18]

Milliken v. Bradley / More crucial, however, was the Court's decision in a Detroit case where a federal district judge and the U.S. Court of Appeals had ruled that a metropolitan solution (including busing) to Detroit's segregated schools was both proper and essential to correct the *de jure* segregation found in Detroit's largely black public schools. But in a decision that was almost unparalleled in rancor and bitterness, the Supreme Court split 5:4 in reversing the ruling of the lower federal courts.[19] Chief Justice Burger, speaking for the majority, argued that the federal courts had no business entering the case unless segregative intent was proved in the suburbs as well as in the city, or unless one district had taken actions that promoted segregation in the other districts.

In long and vigorous dissents, Justices Douglas, White, Brennan, and especially Marshall, castigated the majority, arguing that ruling against a metropolitan solution would return the blacks in U.S. society to the separate but equal days of *Plessy* v. *Ferguson*. Just 20 years after he had pleaded the *Brown* case on behalf of the black children before the Supreme Court in 1954, Justice Marshall accused the Court majority of "following the election returns," alluding to the fact that President Nixon had played on public antipathy toward busing as a political ploy in the election of 1972, had refused to allow federal funds to be used for carrying out court-ordered busing, and had proposed legislation by Congress to limit busing.

By the end of 1976 it was not clear whether *Milliken* v. *Bradley* heralded an about-face by the Court after more than 20 years of attack upon segregation, or whether it was a sign of a kind of compromise and accommodation. In any case, the Detroit schools opened quietly in the fall of 1976 with a moderate amount of busing in the effort to prevent further white flight to the suburbs. The NAACP denounced the plan, but political leaders, both black and white, urged compliance.

Morgan v. Hennigan / In the case of Boston, which was wracked with violence by antibusing forces for several years when whites protested court-ordered busing, the Supreme Court refused in January 1977 to review Judge W. Arthur Garrity's decision of 1974. Garrity had found massive factual evidence that the school board in Boston had for years deliberately and intentionally increased racial segregation by its policies of locating new school buildings, drawing attendance district lines, pupil assignments and feeder patterns, "open enrollment" or freedom of choice, and teacher assignments according to racial population of schools.[20] Antibusing militants had urged a Supreme Court review in the hopes that its more recently conservative stance would lead it to rebuke Judge Garrity for his insistence upon busing and his placing the school system in federal court receivership until the board complied with his meticulously drawn orders. But the Supreme Court somewhat encouraged civil rights groups in January 1977 by its refusal to review the U.S. Court of Appeals' decision, which had upheld Judge Garrity's ruling. At about the same time, however, the Supreme Court did agree to review broad desegregation plans for the Dayton, Ohio, and Indianapolis school systems that had been ordered by the district federal courts. With scores of cases still on the dockets of federal courts all over the country, the final determinations were by no means absolutely settled.

No Segregation in Private Schools

Meanwhile, the Supreme Court closed one more loophole that segregationists had used to evade public school desegregation. Several cases were brought before the Court in which private schools argued that they had the right to deny admission to blacks on the grounds that the school authorities had constitutional rights to freedom of association and privacy under the First Amendment and parents had freedom of choice under the Fourteenth Amendment. The Court, however, in a decision written by Justice Potter Stewart, applied to the private schools an article of the Civil Rights Act of 1866, still in force, which granted blacks equal rights with whites to make and enforce contracts. Thus, black parents had a right to contract with private schools for the education of their children, and the schools could not deny them that right solely on the basis of race. So, while white parents do have freedom of educational choice to send their children to private schools under the doctrines of *Meyer, Pierce*, and *Yoder*, the private schools do not have the right to deny black children admission on the basis of race, since

> it may be assumed that parents have a First Amendment right to send their children to educational institutions that promote the belief that racial segre-

gation is desirable, and that the children have an equal right to attend such institutions. But it does not follow that the practice of excluding racial minorities from such institutions is also protected by the same principle.

The Court has repeatedly stressed that while parents have a constitutional righat to send their children to private schools and a constitutional right to select private schools that offer specialized instruction, they have no constitutional right to provide their children with private school education unfettered by reasonable Government regulation.[21]

Although this case probably had little practical effect, it was an important statement of principle that reasonable governmental regulations on behalf of equality would weigh heavily against parental private freedoms in the education of their children.

The Outlook for Black Desegregation in the 1970s

While the final word on two decades of desegregation effort for blacks had not been heard, there was cautious optimism in the fall of 1976 as the new school year opened. The election had sent to the White House the first president from the Deep South since the Civil War, and he promptly sent his nine-year-old daughter to a mostly black public school in Washington, D.C., the first President to send a child to a public school since Theodore Roosevelt did so early in the century. James Earl Carter, the former governor of Georgia, whose predecessors had been such violent opponents of desegregation for nearly 20 years, was elected with massive support from southern blacks who obviously believed that he would speed the new day to come in race relations.

President Carter's policies could not be predicted so early in his administration, but even before the November election of 1976 and the defeat of President Gerald Ford there were signs that the days of the greatest violence had ceased. Louisville's second year of busing opened with relative quiet, as did Boston's third year. Communities like Cleveland, facing desegregation, were actively trying to head off opposition; the steam had gone out of Nixon and Ford proposals for federal legislation or a constitutional amendment to prevent enforcement of court-ordered busing; and state boards of education were beginning to exert more pressure upon local boards to take positive action without waiting for the federal courts to take the initiative. Cases were still pending, however, in such strategic cities as Milwaukee, St. Louis, Dayton, Omaha, Detroit, Kansas City, Indianapolis, Los Angeles, Chicago, and New York.

By the end of its term in June 1977 the constitutional stance of the Burger Supreme Court looked something like this: For segregation in schools to be declared unconstitutional it must be shown that it was the result of deliberate and intentional action by government agencies, including, of course, boards of education and administrators. This probably meant that court-ordered desegregation need not go beyond what was necessary to redress the segregation resulting from intentional government policies. It also meant that a district once desegregated need take no further action to prevent resegregation caused by housing patterns or white flight to the suburbs. But in the Dayton case in June 1977 the Court reaffirmed the authority of federal courts to order city-wide desegregation, including city-wide busing, if the factual findings of segregation warranted it. This seemed to be in accordance with and not a retreat from the *Keyes* v. *Denver* decision. Metropolitan solutions, however, which include inner city and suburbs (as disapproved for Detroit in *Milliken* v. *Bradley*) would not normally be required as an overall solution, although metropolitan busing could be an acceptable remedy and might even be necessary in special cases.

A significant expansion of the role of federal courts was approved by the Supreme Court in the Detroit case of June 1977, when it ruled that federal courts could require school districts to provide compensatory programs for children who had been disadvantaged by being required to attend segregated schools in the past. This could include special remedial courses in reading and speaking, testing, guidance, and teacher training in order to help children overcome the speech habits, attitudes, and conduct bred in enforced cultural and educational isolation. This was a rather remarkable extension (by unanimous decision) of the meaning of desegregation to include recompense for past injuries caused by segregation. It remained to be seen how far the American people would go in approving inconvenience or sacrifice on the part of the more advantaged children (who had not discriminated against anyone) in order to assist less advantaged children (whose parents *had* been discriminated against) to have an equal opportunity to get a better education.

If the mood of Congress in the summer of 1977 was any indication, such approval was not to be forthcoming very soon. Both the House and the Senate attached amendments to the appropriations bill that would prohibit the Carter administration from carrying out its intention to withhold funds from districts that refused to merge or pair schools in order to achieve desegregation if such merger required busing. (Pairing consists of combining the facilities, faculties, and students of a mostly black school and a mostly white school, so that instead of both schools offering all grades from kindergarten through grades six or eight one school would provide the early years and the other the later years for the merged student body. Some busing is usually required to make the pairing work.)

Thus matters stood the year after the bicentennial. The Burger Court had seemed to slow down but not reverse the role of federal courts in desegregation of public schools, and it did not limit them as much as civil rights leaders at first had feared. The Carter White House certainly promised to reverse the Nixon/Ford slow-down on desegregation and busing, but in its first year it had not moved as actively as some had hoped. And Congress seemed to be the most reluctant of the three branches of the federal government to push ahead with desegregation, a significant departure from the

Great Society days of the mid-1960s. The hope of civil rights liberals was that in the long run the Congress would not emasculate the legislative heritage of the Great Society nor counteract the constitutional precedents set by the federal courts over nearly a quarter of a century.

For the first time, even the U.S. Commission on Civil Rights was somewhat optimistic after a year-long survey and assessment of the progress of desegregation.[22] Its most important conclusion in its report of August 1976 was that desegregation works, despite stubborn and even violent opposition. Where community leadership and school officials led the way, desegregation could be implemented smoothly, race relations could improve, and minority student achievement could rise. The greatest problems remained in the largest districts. The Commission severely criticized President Ford for his proposed bill to narrow the meaning of illegal segregation and to restrict the scope of remedies available to the courts. The Commission stated its belief that desegregation had not lowered, but had rather improved, the quality of education in the schools and that it was not the principal cause of the flight of whites to the suburbs. But, even if it did, it had no effect on the constitutional right to equality of educational opportunity, which had primacy.

Ups and Downs for American Indian Education

Other items on the agenda of the search for equality of educational opportunity for minority groups gained higher priority in the wake of the agitation and the gains made by and for blacks. Indeed, the goals for a revived and improved education for American Indians antedated the major drives for equality in black education. The climate of attitude toward Indian education began to change as early as the 1920s. In 1924, when the Snyder Act conferred citizenship upon all Indians, attention was drawn to the shortcomings in the administration of Indian affairs, including Indian education. The key goals were outlined in 1928 in a large-scale series of surveys conducted by a team of investigators of the Brookings Institution under the direction of Lewis Meriam as part of a reassessment of the administration of Indian affairs. Sponsored by Herbert Hoover's Secretary of the Interior, Ray Lyman Wilbur, the report urged doing away with the regimented, uniform, and alien white curriculum in favor of a more indigenous curriculum conducted in the more individualized setting of community-centered schools.

When reform became the official policy of the New Deal and the Indian Reorganization Act of 1934 (Wheeler-Howard Act) was passed, the administration of Indian Affairs was put in the hands of John Collier as commissioner. Self-government of tribes was promoted, revival of Indian culture was encouraged, and educational facilities were improved. Assimilation was still the ultimate goal, but it was now to be accomplished by retaining and enlivening such elements of their traditional culture as the Indians themselves wished to retain. Two directors of education in the Indian Bureau from 1930 to 1952, who reflected the liberal and progressive approaches of the day, focused upon the school as a means of community development as well as meeting the needs of individual children.[23] Both W. Carson Ryan and Willard Beatty were active in the Progressive Education Association and served as its president at various times.

Although major gains were made during the New Deal, a major setback occurred under the Eisenhower administration when a resolution of Congress in 1953 declared its intention to terminate federal relations with Indians as soon as possible in order to speed assimilation. This meant that tribal lands would no longer be tax-exempt and the tribes themselves would be dismanted under land allotment plans. Despite the reversal and dismay it caused, this policy was never carried through, and the 1960s saw a rapid upswing in attention to Indian affairs.

The Kennedy administration reaffirmed the Collier policies under Phileo Nash in 1961, and the American Indian Chicago Conference of 90 tribal groups declared that education was the key to the salvation of the Indian people. In July 1970, President Nixon formally renounced the 1953 policy of forced termination and reaffirmed the integrity and right to existence of all Indian tribes and Alaskan native governments. Not only must the relationship between the government and the Indian communities not be abridged without the consent of the Indians, but the communities must be given control over the federally funded programs of education, including membership on school boards.

The decade of the 1960s was a period of extraordinarily rapid growth in Indian education. The National Study of American Indian Education, conducted by Robert J. Havighurst of the University of Chicago for the Office of Education, detailed the growth as well as some of the problems. Indian children in 1970 were predominantly in public schools (63 percent), with 31 percent in government schools conducted by the Bureau of Indian Affairs (half in boarding schools and half in day schools), and 6 percent in mission schools. The report recommended that the boarding schools be eliminated for elementary school-age children, but possibly continued for such isolated communities as the Navaho and Alaskans. The most striking expansions in the decade of the 1960s were the growth of the Indian population in urban centers (30 percent in 1960; 38 percent in 1970) and the proportion of young people going through secondary school and on to college: 55 percent of the age group finished high school; 20 percent entered college, and another 10 percent entered other types of post-high-school institutions; and 5 percent graduated from four-year colleges.[24] These were relatively high proportions of attendance in comparison with other U.S. low-income groups.

But the attendance figures, of course, did not solve the problems of education for Indians. If anything, they simply brought them into the mainstream of educational problems: rural-oriented youth transferred to an urban environment that was more alien and hostile than the reservation and more contemptuous of poor vocational skills; a curriculum that paid little attention to the Indian heritage; teachers who had little training, understanding, or appreciation of the special need for respect and dignity of a people who were being asked to move skillfully between the traditional culture of a tribal folk society and a modern urban civilization, and be able to find values in both.

Slow Gains for the Spanish-Speaking Minority

A third minority group whose treatment by the dominant American majority produced a debilitating educational discrimination consisted of those whose mother tongue was Spanish. Standing in numbers in 1970 between the 23 million black Americans and the 800,000 American Indians were the 10 million Americans with Spanish surnames. (And some predictions were that by the 1980s they would outnumber blacks.) Only the Indians had been on the North American continent longer than the Spanish-speaking peoples (sometimes referred to as "La Raza," the people), but the latter's plight in educational discrimination was the latest to come to national consciousness in the United States. Despite the presence of Spanish-speaking peoples for more than four hundred years within what is now the continental United States, their confrontation with the dominant English-speaking Americans was only a little more than 150 years old, and for most of that time it was largely a regional matter of the American Southwest (principally the states of Texas, New Mexico, Arizona, Colorado, and California).

Despite the historical inadequacies and failures of the public school system, it did eventually open up opportunity for a leadership to emerge, determined to achieve for La Raza the full promise of American citizenship: the civil and political rights being demanded by blacks and Indians, greater educational opportunity, a better economic deal, and (above all) a greater respect, pride, and dignity to be accorded to their heritage, language, history, and culture as a people. From 1940 onward the reawakening accelerated, fed not only by a new aggressiveness among Mexican-Americans in the Southwest, but by the influx of newcomers from Puerto Rico, Cuba, and Central America (800,000 Puerto Ricans moved to the mainland in a matter of three decades). By the late 1960s, more than 80 percent of all persons with Spanish surnames were living in cities, and 70 percent lived in three states: New York, Texas, and California. The problems of La Raza were no longer regional, but national. The urbanization that characterized all of the country, and which was exacerbating the plight of all minority city dwellers, now encompassed La Raza, and brought the same problems: inferior education, segregated housing patterns, a constricted ghetto life, low-paying jobs or no jobs, and cultural deprivation, all complicated (even more than for blacks) by the fact that their mother tongue was usually viewed as a foreign language in an Anglicized society.

While the legal battles over unequal and separate education for La Raza have not been so spectacular as in the case of the black codes, nevertheless there has been a certain parallel. Beginning about the same time as the black desegregation campaigns, court cases were brought in the 1940s by Mexican-American parents who claimed that even if there were no *legal* separation, there was *de facto* segregation by school board regulation, usage, and custom.[25] The courts found for the parents, but—as was so often the case elsewhere—practice was harder to change than law. As late as 1970 a federal judge ruled that Corpus Christi, Texas, was actually operating a dual school system for Mexican-Americans, and ordered the board of education to submit a plan for desegregation as provided in the *Brown* case.[26]

Thus, the educational rights of the two largest identifiable minorities were linked in a common cause, the cause of stamping out discriminations that produced major imbalances in school attendance, school achievement, and school satisfaction. When the average number of years of schooling in California was 12 for Anglos, 10 for blacks, and eight for Mexican-Americans, discrimination was still rampant. The imbalances in attendance, teaching staffs, school board memberships, and administrative staffs were documented for Mexican-Americans as well as for blacks by the U.S. Commission on Civil Rights. (See Bibliographical Notes, p. 417). What was far more difficult to document in human terms in the history of education was the decivilization of La Raza and the attempts, sometimes successful and sometimes disastrous, to reeducate a people nourished in a traditional civilization but determined to live in a modern one.

It is more than symbolic that just as the *Brown* case in 1954 which set off massive integration of southern schools was brought to court on behalf of black children, so was a major case in 1971 brought on behalf of Mexican-American children in the schools of east Los Angeles. Both cases appealed to the "equal protection of the laws" as guaranteed by the Fourteenth Amendment. Both were aimed at curing different forms of inequality. On August 30, 1971, the California State Supreme Court decided in *Serrano* v. *Priest* that the state's system of financing public schools through local property taxes invidiously discriminated against poor children because it made the quality of education provided in local schools dependent upon the wealth of the local school district in which they happened to live. The court said: "By our holding today we further the cherished idea of American education that in a democratic society free public schools shall make available to all children equally the abundant gifts of learning. This was the credo of Horace Mann, which has been the heritage and the inspiration of this country."[27]

Equalizing Financial Support of Public Schools

Serrano/Unequal Property Taxes Unconstitutional

The decision on state financing of public education in California struck like a bombshell at a time when the Nixon administration was busily shifting back to the states the responsibility for supporting education and trying to reverse the major federal responsibility for school aid that had grown so greatly and so quickly in the Great Society programs of Lyndon Johnson. One significance of the *Serrano* decision was that it did not refer so much to race as to the poor, declaring that the right to an education is a "fundamental interest" which cannot be conditioned on wealth. It held that a public school financing system that relied heavily on local property taxes, and thus caused substantial inequities among individual school districts in the amount of revenue available per pupil, discriminated against the poor and violated the equal protection clause of the Fourteenth Amendment. Especially important, in view of what happened later in a case in Texas (*San Antonio Independent School District* v. *Rodriquez*) the California Supreme Court held that the equal protection provisions in the California State constitution were substantially equivalent to the equal protection clause of the Fourteenth Amendment.

The Court found in *Serrano* that indeed there was wide disparity among California school districts in the assessed valuation of property which could be taxed within the districts for school purposes, ranging from as low as $103 per unit of average daily attendance of elementary school children to as much as $952,156, a ratio of nearly 1:10,000. This, of course, meant a vast difference in the amount of funds that could be produced and vast differences in the tax rates that could be levied. So, despite the equalization efforts through state aid, great differentials remained in the revenues available to different districts and consequently to their level of expenditures. This inability of various school districts to finance education equally had long been known to school finance experts, but until *Serrano* this fact had not been declared unconstitutional: Classification by wealth, whether of individuals or districts, was as unconstitutionally discriminating as classification by race.

The *Serrano* decision could have been even more revolutionary if its argument that education was a fundamental interest had been later upheld by the U.S. Supreme Court in *Rodriquez*. It had long been clear that persons could not be classified according to wealth when exercising such fundamental rights as voting or rights of defendants in criminal cases. What *Serrano* tried to do was make education a fundamental right that could not be conditioned on the wealth of individuals or of school districts. *Serrano* declared, following *Brown*, that education played an indispensable role in the modern industrial society, helping the individual's chances for success in life and uniquely influencing the child's development as a citizen. The court even went so far as to say that the citizen's right to an education might be even more important than the right to a court-appointed lawyer in a criminal trial, and surely education was an indispensable factor in meaningful voting.

As a result of the shock waves that swept through the country in the two years after *Serrano*, more than 50 suits were filed in federal and state courts in more than 30 states attacking local property taxes as the chief support for public schools because they resulted in unequal educational opportunities for the children of the several states. Federal courts in Texas and Minnesota struck down the property tax on the grounds that it violated the Fourteenth Amendment; in 1973 the New Jersey State Supreme Court declared that sole reliance on the local property tax violated the state constitution; and the Supreme Court of Connecticut did the same in 1977.

Meanwhile, as many as 20 other states passed laws making major changes in school financing. A national reassessment of the entire financing of public education was under way that could lead to fundamental changes not only in racial and ethnic relations, but also in public financing, taxpaying, housing, welfare, and social patterns in general. If the local property taxes in separate districts were unconstitutional, then the states would have to take over. Furthermore, if the disparity among states was as real as among districts (and it was), and if education was to be construed as a fundamental interest under the federal constitution, then perhaps the Constitution should be interpreted as requiring full-scale federal financing of public education in order to achieve equality of educational opportunity throughout the 50 states of the union. Why should the school expenditures in Alabama, or Mississippi, or Kentucky, or Tennessee be only $800 per child while it was over $2,000 per child in Alaska and New York? Wasn't *that* kind of wealth disparity between states just as unconstitutional as disparity *within* the states? But such dreams were quickly to be dispelled, at least for a while.

Rodriquez/*Property Taxes* Not *Unconstitutional*

In 1973 the U.S. Supreme Court in a 5:4 decision reversed a Texas federal district court and held that the Texas system of local property taxation for school finance, though not producing equality among districts, did not discriminate against any definable category of "poor" people, nor did it result in the absolute deprivation of education for a particular disadvantaged class.[28] This ruling in *San Antonio School District* v. *Rodriquez*, written by Associate Justice Lewis F. Powell, was not too surprising in view of the fact that the majority of five were all Republicans (four appointed by Richard Nixon) and the minority of four all Democrats, the liberal wing of the Court. What was even more depressing to educational liberals throughout the country was the ruling that education, though one of the most important "services" performed by the states, was *not* recognized as a fundamental right specified by the U.S. Constitution. Even if some small quantum of education *could* be shown to be necessary for the exercise of other constitutionally protected rights, it had not been proved that Texas failed to provide that minimum.

So, *Rodriquez* ruled that the Texas system of property taxation did not violate the equal protection clause of the Fourteenth Amendment [as the California State Supreme Court had said it did in California]. Local taxation did assure a basic education for all, and it did encourage local participation in education at the district level. Since educational experts like Christopher

Jencks and James S. Coleman disagreed about the relationship between expenditures and quality of education, the federal judiciary should not intervene in local affairs with inflexible constitutional requirements. The Texas system of school finance through local property taxes could stand.

Justice Powell took 60 pages to outline the majority opinion; the minority took 76 pages to dissent. The latter argued that education was indeed a fundamental right protected by the Constitution because, as Justice Brennan put it, "there can be no doubt that education is inextricably linked to the right to participate in the electoral process and to the rights of free speech and association guaranteed by the First Amendment."[29] He pointed out that "fundamentality" was a function of education's importance in carrying out those rights that *are* specified in the Constitution. Here, as with the dissents by Justices White, Douglas, and Marshall, was the voice of the Warren court, now in the minority on the Burger court. Justice Marshall dwelt at great length on the "nexus" between education and other constitutional rights, especially in preparing citizens for participation in the open and democratic political process. In dissenting, he said: "The majority's decision represents an abrupt departure from the mainstream of recent state and federal court decisions concerning the unconstitutionality of state educational financial schemes dependent upon taxable wealth."

It seemed to many that the Burger court was intent here in *Rodriquez* on slowing down the search for equality of educational opportunity for the poor through reforming state financing in Texas. The decision foreshadowed the slowdown of metropolitan plans for desegregation of the races in the Detroit case two years later.

Property Taxes Struck Down under State Constitutions

By the narrowest possible margin, the Supreme Court had failed to apply the Fourteenth Amnedment to the search for equal financing of educational opportunity. But the states were not without *their* constitutions, which included bills of rights modeled upon the federal constitution and which included provisions for public education modeled upon the educational reforms of the nineteenth century. After the Supreme Court's decision in *Rodriquez* ruled out the Fourteenth Amendment, the California Supreme Court reviewed the *Serrano* case. Five years after its first decision, it declared on the last day of 1976 that the legislature had failed to live up to its earlier ruling, but still had to do so—and do it by 1980. This time, the justification was not the Fourteenth Amendment, but the California State constitution, which guaranteed equal protection of the laws in the spirit of the Fourteenth Amendment. Thus, even though *Rodriquez* kept the U.S. Supreme Court out of the political process, the California Supreme Court put itself directly into it; by September 1977 an equalization law had been passed.

Three years to comply seemed too short a time to California legislators, who had already had five years to plan while *Serrano* was being retried. But New Jersey had given them a kind of preview of what to expect, if they had been noticing. In January 1972 a State Superior Court judge, Theodore I. Botter, had ruled that New Jersey's system of property taxes had resulted in such educational inequalities that they violated the equal protection provisions of the state and federal constitutions as well as the educational provisions of the New Jersey state constitution. He gave the legislature a year to come up with an acceptable plan.[30] The case was, of course, appealed, but in 1973 (just two weeks after *Rodriquez*) the New Jersey Supreme Court, though rejecting Judge Botter's ruling on the federal constitution, upheld him on the New Jersey constitution. The court affirmed that the system of local property taxes discriminated against the poorer districts and thus violated the command of the 1875 amendment of the New Jersey constitution, which says:

> The Legislature shall provide for the maintenance and support of a thorough and efficient system of free public schools for the instruction of all children in the state between the ages of 5 and 18.

The court declared:

> A system of instruction in any district of the state which is not thorough and efficient falls short of the constitutional command. Whatever the reason for the violation, the obligation is the state's no rectify.[31]

This seemed to support Republican Governor William T. Cahill's efforts to persuade the legislature to pass a state income tax as an equalizing measure, but the legislature was reluctant and even refused Democratic Governor Brendan T. Byrne's similar efforts. Finally, the State Supreme Court had to threaten in the summer of 1976 to take over the entire public school system and shut it down until the legislature came up with a plan. Ever so reluctantly, and only after five years of judicial intervention in the political process, did the legislature finally accede; a state income tax law was passed, and New Jersey's public school system continued to function.

Schooling and Economic Inequality

Whatever all this activity on the state financial front might come to mean, it was clear that the state and federal courts assumed that a determined effort to equalize the financial support for the public schools of a state would mean a more equal educational opportunity for the children who lived in the poorer and less affluent districts. In simplest terms, more money for the schools in poorer districts would mean better education for the children who attended them. This had been an assumption behind educational reformers' efforts for 50 years. It had became apparent as early as the 1920s that children's educational achievement was lower in those areas where financial support was consistently and markedly lower. These areas included the poorer states of the South as compared with those of the North, the rural sections in comparison with urban areas of states wherever they were located, and the regions where blacks and other minority children were relegated to segregated schools, whether *de jure* or *de facto*; in fact, achievement was low wherever the disparity of financial support was evident.

Ironically, however, just as the courts began to be more and more insistent that legislatures equalize financial support of schools in order to conform to constitutional mandates for equality of opportunity and to achieve one of the historic purposes of public education, some social science investigators began to question the very assumption that more money and more equal financing would make any substantial difference in children's achievement in school. Compensatory education as a device to help the disadvantaged minority child was not accepted as very valuable in improving achievement and the role of education in helping minority children to overcome economic handicaps began to be questioned. For about a decade, some social science investigators argued so vehemently about the extent of children's achievement on the basis of the results of their performance as measured by objective tests that they forgot about the constitutional rights of the children involved. In some cases the way the researchers reframed the issues about equality served to becloud the constitutional issues that had concerned the civil rights groups and that the courts were in general protecting.

Equality of Opportunity versus Equality of Condition

The essence of the reframing of the issues surrounding the search for equality lay in the difference between equality of *opportunity* (or access) and equality of *condition* (or results). The extensive quotations from the federal and state court cases that have been presented here clearly show that the legal and constitutional meaning propounded by the courts has concentrated on the *right* to equality of opportunity or access; that is, no legal or financial barriers should be allowed to prevent individuals or groups from obtaining an education. Thus, equality of educational opportunity should stand on the same constitutional basis as equality of political rights and civil rights. No person should be denied *access* to educational institutions (any more than to polling booths) on account of race, religion, ethnic background, economic or social status, or sex. This was the basic intent of the *Brown* decision and the subsequent cases having to do with desegregation and equal protection of the laws.

In contrast, equality of *condition* or of *results* seemed to imply that all persons should be required or expected to have the *same amount* of wealth or power, or in the case of education, the same amount of knowledge or information. Most welfare societies have come to believe that there should be a *minimal* economic level guaranteed to all persons, but only the most egalitarian or utopian societies have sought to ensure that everyone should have the same income, or the same wealth, or the same knowledge; that is, that all people should be at the same level of wealth, or power, or knowledge, or of any other social good. To insist upon equality of condition would mean that there could be no significant differences in any of these categories.

The argument has thus been made by radical egalitarians in recent years that compensatory education for disadvantaged children cannot enable them to become equal in economic condition with children who started out with more advantages, nor can it enable them to attain equal results on academic achievement tests. By taking off from the seminal but much criticized work of James S. Coleman of Chicago[32] and reframing the question in a way that ignored the constitutional issues, a series of New Left social scientists found, not surprisingly, that the advantage of special attention for poor children in school for relatively short periods of time could not overcome the longer and larger disadvantages represented by lower family income and occupation, lower educational attainment of parents, and lower aspirations for educational achievement. Among those who seemed to find that school did not make much difference in narrowing the economic gap between rich and poor were Christopher Jencks and his colleagues at Harvard, Martin Carnoy and Henry M. Levin at Stanford, and Samuel Bowles and Herbert Gintis at the University of Massachusetts. (See Bibliographical Notes, p. 00.)

The researchers as well as many others who came out of the political disenchantment of the 1960s with a foreshortened view of the role that education could play in social change began to argue that schooling could not equalize academic performance between the well-endowed and poorly endowed children, nor could it equalize their economic incomes. They professed that it was just such claims that had been made by the "liberal" educational reformers of the Great Society era. Their radical views that education could only perpetuate the capitalist system and could *not* lead to equality of condition or equality of results, thus fit neatly with the radical historical revisionists who were claiming the same thing about the school reformers of the nineteenth and early twentieth centuries (see pages 00–00).

Historic Meaning / But neither the history nor the consensus of social science researchers would support this revised meaning of equality by changing it from *opportunity* to *condition*. The founders of the Republic certainly thought of equality of *rights* when they spoke of equality in education. They did not argue that public education would produce an equality of economic condition. They did want a common education where rich and poor went to school together, but they did not assume that thereby all would be equally rich nor that all would be equally poor. Likewise, it was inequality of *access* to free common public education that the reformers of the nineteenth century attacked. They indeed believed that access to education would help the poor to rise out of poverty and perhaps even become "respectable," as Thernstrom put it, but in addition to education it would take hard work, thrift, prudence, and moral character.

Even the workingmen of the 1830s did not visualize an equally leveled society; they spoke of education as providing the "means of equal knowledge." And while Horace Mann used the phrase, "education . . . is the great equalizer of the conditions of men" he meant that it could give to each man the *means* to prevent poverty and to move up into the "cultivated class." Reducing the social and political distinctions and privileges between the richer and poorer classes was the prime goal of public education historically, but the nineteenth century reformers of education had not reckoned sufficiently with the power of legal segregation in the South and the power of the prejudices and discriminations of white racism in the North to produce an enduring inequality in housing, income, employment, and unionism as well as in schooling and thus to set up rigid bars to equal access to the mainstream of American life.

To break these barriers was the goal of the social reform efforts of the civil rights movement of the 1950s and 1960s, a goal stressed in the "war on poverty" and the other instrumentalities of the Great Society. Education became a means to aid the poor to rise above poverty and stay above the *minimum* deemed necessary for a decent life in a modern society. It did not pretend to make all incomes equal. It proposed compensatory programs like Head Start and special help for poor and minority children so that they could move up from where they were and overcome somewhat their own disadvantageous start. Few reformers or educators argued that the school could *create* the equality of condition in which all children would achieve the same scores on I.Q. tests, or mathematics tests, or reading tests, or science tests. Raise the level of the lowest, yes; reduce the gap, perhaps; but make all equal in achievement, no.

Schooling and Academic Achievement

Rampant controversy and debate exploded in the 1970s over the question as to what difference the schools could make in reducing the gaps in academic achievement between the initially advantaged and the initially disadvantaged children. The principal stokers of the controversy after Coleman's original surveys of the 1960s were Christopher Jencks and his colleagues at Harvard.[33] The furor broke over their book almost immediately upon publication. Jencks was understood to be claiming that schools cannot make as much difference in cognitive achievement as family characteristics and social class do; success in school did not make much difference in the eventual economic status or occupational achievement of adults; school reforms in curriculum, instruction, teachers' qualifications, or amount of money spent did not make much difference in the achievement of pupils as measured by objective tests. What did make a difference in adult life were racial discrimination, family background, and luck. The schools should thus concentrate on making children happy, giving them the basics, and permitting all kinds of alternatives that a voucher system would make possible. If the people wanted to achieve economic equality, they should do so directly through political socialism because they would not be able to do so through such a marginal institution as the schools.

The Jencks Controversy

The course of the debate cannot be followed here; the record is much too voluminous, the arguments too involved, and the evidence marshaled on all sides too contradictory. (See Bibliographical Notes, p. 00.) Jencks was often severely criticized on methodological grounds or on ideological grounds, and many contradictory studies showed that the schools did indeed make a difference: They *had* enduring effects, they *were* related to economic status in the long run; and the quantity and length of schooling and the quality of teachers and instruction *did* have a measurable effect. (See Bibliographical Notes, p. 00.) But the response of black educators was also most interesting. In their view, inequality of income was *not* the prime goal of education. Kenneth Clark believes that

> it is difficult to comprehend why or how a group of social scientists who are experienced in educational research could publicly define the primary function of education almost exclusively in terms of economic reward. Unfortunately, nowhere does the Jencks report seriously discuss the educational goals of social sensitivity, respect for justice, and acceptance of differences among human beings. And Jencks and his associates missed, or deliberately ignored, the chance to define as important the need of our educational system to reinforce in children their potential for empathy and dignity.[34]

A statement signed by ten black social scientists and educators made a similar point in criticizing Jencks:

> Income cannot buy societal appreciation of individual worth, or group cohesion, or community, in a society that is characterized by racism, materialism, and inhumanity. Jenck's repudiation of schooling as an instrument of social improvement is valid only if one accepts income as the end toward which we strive.[35]

Professor Coleman himself, though commending Jencks for his technical expertise, pointed to the basic fault that

> there is now, with the existence of a large amount of sociological research on inequality of opportunity and inequality of result, and with the resurgence of interest among moral philosophers in inequality, as manifested in John Rawls's work, the possibility of serious examination of social ideals and social reality in this area. Jencks's book could have begun that examination. Its

failure to do so is . . . the lack of attention to the deeper questions of moral philosophy surrounding the existence of inequality in society.[36]

Note the phrases:

> "social sensitivity"
> "respect for justice"
> "group cohesion, or community"
> "social ideals and social reality"
> "moral philosophy"

Ignoring these values and stressing only the equality of economic condition or the results of tests led the "inequality" social scientists to a downgrading of the historical goal of public schools, which was to help all students to achieve a greater equality of opportunity, or access, as a basic matter of equal rights.

Compensatory Education

Much of the struggle over desegregation had to do with dismantling the *de jure* dual system in which white students were required by law to attend white schools and black students to attend black schools. One of the aspects of *de facto* segregation that the Commission on Civil Rights criticized most severely, however, was "ability grouping" within the schools where black and white students attended the same schools together. The problem was much more than simply the physical enrollment of blacks and whites in schools together. Before 1977 the Supreme Court did not deal very fully with this issue of the quality of education provided in desegregated schools, but lower federal courts did.

Hobson v. Hansen/*Tracking Unconstitutional*

One of the most important of such cases was decided in 1967 by Judge J. Skelly Wright with regard to the segregated schools of Washington, D.C., in a remarkable decision dealing as much with educational policy as with constitutional law. After exhaustive hearings and testimony, Judge Wright declared that the version of ability grouping known as the tracking system was unconstitutional, as were also the District's policies regarding neighborhood schools and the assignment of pupils and teachers on a racially segregated basis:

> The track system as used in the District's public schools is a form of ability grouping in which students are divided in separate, self-contained curricula or tracks ranging from "Basic" for the slow student to "Honors" for the gifted.
> The aptitude tests used to assign children to the various tracks are standardized primarily on white middle class children. Since these tests do

not relate to the Negro and disadvantaged child, track assignment based on such tests relegates Negro and disadvantaged children to the lower tracks from which, because of the reduced curricula and the absence of adequate remedial and compensatory education, as well as continued inappropriate testing, the chance of escape is remote.

Education in the lower tracks is geared to what Dr. Hansen, the creator of the track system, calls the "blue collar" student. Thus such children, so stigmatized by inappropriate aptitude testing procedures, are denied equal opportunity to obtain the white collar education available to the white and more affluent children.[37]

Judge Wright particularly castigated the superintendent and board of education for trying to wrap themselves in the historical mantle of Horace Mann as they defended the neighborhood schools. He gave them a short lesson in the history of education, as follows, saying that the

defendants' appropriation of Horace Mann as the supposed architect of today's neighborhood school policy is singularly unjust. For Mann believed that public schools were at the source of democratic enterprise; his faith, like that of his fellow reformers, was that the public school, by drawing into the close association of the classroom students from every social, economic and cultural background, would serve as an object lesson in equality and brotherhood and undermine the social class divisions which he and his colleagues felt were inimical to democracy. If there is a characteristically American philosophy of public school education, this is its apparent substance.

The democratizing relevance of public school education, so intense a concern for the founders of our public schools, has lost none of its urgency in the intervening century, if only because society now is finally beginning to contemplate the assimilation of the Negro, hitherto systematically excluded from participation in our political life and from the abundance of our economy.[38]

Of special importance in Judge Wright's decision was his linking of minority students and poverty. Throughout, he argued that the unconstitutionality of the track system had to do with discrimination against the poor on behalf of the affluent as well as discrimination against the black on behalf of the white. In both cases the segregation of the tracking system made more necessary than ever special efforts at compensatory education, for

almost cynically, many Negro students are either denied or have limited access to the very kinds of programs the track system makes a virtual necessity: kindergartens; Honors programs for the fast-developing Negro students; and remedial and compensatory education programs that will bring the disadvantaged students back into the mainstream of education. Lacking these facilities, the student continues hampered by his cultural handicaps and continues to appear to be of lower ability than he really is.[39]

Significance of ESEA

As a result of such decisions as that of Judge Wright, and more generally of the civil rights movement and the resurgence of liberal political reform in the Kennedy and Johnson administrations of the 1960s, the schools began to hear the historic message that clarified their prime purpose. It was their duty not only to dismantle the dual system of segregated schools, but also to take special positive steps to promote equality of educational opportunity by concentrating upon compensatory programs for low-income, and thus "educationally deprived," children. The message was clear in the Elementary and Secondary Education Act (ESEA) of 1964, and it was made doubly clear when they began to receive large amounts of money from the federal government.[40] So much has been said and criticized about the intentions of the reformers of the 1960s that it is well to repeat the basic purpose as set forth in the Act itself:

> An Act to strengthen and improve educational quality and educational opportunities in the Nation's elementary and secondary schools. . . . In recognition of the special educational needs of children of low-income families and the impact that concentrations of low-income families have on the ability of local educational agencies to support adequate educational programs, the Congress hereby declares it to be the policy of the United States to provide financial assistance . . . to local educational agencies serving areas with large concentrations of low-income families to expand and improve their educational programs by various means (including preschool programs) which contribute particularly to meeting the special educational needs of educationally deprived children.[41]

Much debate has centered upon whether the ESEA was successful or not. In the early years of the 1970s the pullback in federal activism represented by the Nixon administration and the radical analysis embodied in the Jencks study led to easy and flat statements that the liberal reforms of the 1960s had failed. But by the mid-1970s the mood of researchers and policymakers began to change somewhat. For example, in an issue of *The Public Interest* in 1974 devoted to "The Great Society: Lessons for the Future," Ralph Tyler, one of the country's most respected social science evaluators, pointed out that increasing numbers of studies conducted by the states, the Office of Education, and others were pointing to the same conclusion:

> There has been a steady increase in the number of Title I programs that are reproducing measurable improvements in the educational achievements of disadvantaged children, although there are still many programs that appear to be ineffective.[42]

Significantly, Tyler pointed out that the Coleman and Jencks studies used data that had been derived *before* the ESEA began to function and before schools became greatly concerned with the learning problems of disadvantaged children. Even more significantly, he argued that the Coleman and Jencks studies were interested primarily in *differences* among children rather than the *level* of what they had learned:

> The standard tests used were norm-referenced tests. In building these tests,

questions that most children could answer correctly were eliminated, but questions which only about half the children could answer correctly were retained. This was done to spread the scores as widely as possible so that children could be arranged on a scale from highest to lowest. The purpose of norm-referenced tests is to sort students, not to assess what they have learned. It happens that many of the items that are effective in sharply sorting students are those that are not emphasized in a majority of schools.[43]

In general, Tyler argued that the compensatory efforts of the 1960s had selected the right problems to be attacked and that substantial gains had been made, but that too many ESEA programs had not reckoned sufficiently with the complexity of the problems of learning by disadvantaged children. They had not considered the amount of extra money necessary to make real differences (only about $150 per year went to supplementary programs per disadvantaged student), or the length of time required (too many programs were one-shot, short-term affairs, whereas they should have involved sequences of instruction over three to four years).

Another sign of the change of mood by 1975 was the review by Samuel Halperin, Assistant Commissioner of Education in the Office of Education from 1964–1966 and Deputy Assistant Secretary for legislation in the Department of Health, Education, and Welfare from 1966–1969. As he looked back at the decade from the vantage point of the Institute for Educational Leadership of The George Washington University, Halperin found several enduring legacies of ESEA.[44] It had broken a century-old log jam on federal aid to education, principally by defusing the public versus parochial school issues, and thus had legitimized a federal role in education. It had focused on the special educational needs of disadvantaged children, so that by 1974 the Stanford Research Institute was reporting that most districts in most states were achieving a month's gain or more in reading achievement for each month of participation in Title I programs.

Halperin said further that ESEA had fueled other movements toward equality of educational opportunity, and had become a rallying point for the special needs of out-of-school youth, the handicapped, the bilingual, the preschool child, those needing day care and better nutrition. Most importantly, it had sparked the movement to reform state school finance systems, as displayed in *Serrano* and *Rodriquez*, and had promoted parental and community participation in school affairs, public-nonpublic school cooperation, scholarly research and evaluation, and improvement of state departments of education. Despite mistakes, overeagerness in some quarters, and indifference in others, Halperin was convinced that ESEA had a number of impressive achievements to its credit even in its first decade, which passed almost unnoticed in 1975. But at the end of 1976 with a president who rode into office with the support of minorities and Joseph Califano as Secretary of Health, Education, and Welfare, who had been a prime initiator of Lyndon Johnson's Great Society programs of the 1960s, the future of ESEA seemed to take on a new light.

Evaluation of Compensatory Education

But Halperin's judgment that ESEA was alive and well could still have its setbacks even though the political climate in Washington has become more favorable than it had been in the preceding eight years, for the mind-set of a great many scholars and critics has become hardened over that time. The difficulties of arriving at hard-data evaluations of massive governmental programs over a short period of time are immense. (See Bibliographical Notes, p. 418.) The mind-set formed by the academic climate of the late 1960s could continue to lead many educators and critics to condemn compensatory education as a failure, and thus generalize that the liberal educational reforms of the 1960s and of the Great Society were failures.

In 1976, this outlook attracted a wide range of advocates. There were the radicals who kept saying that the liberal reforms were failures because they simply propped up a stumbling and halting capitalist educational establishment. There were the conservatives who were pleased to find that large doses of federal aid were judged to be useless, since that meant to them that funds could be cut back and (without saying it) the search for equality of the lower classes could be slowed. Some disappointed minority leaders, who felt that the programs had gone too slowly or had still been infused with attitudes smacking of earlier Anglo-conformity, criticized compensatory education because it implied that the child was at fault and did not acknowledge that the schools were remiss for not paying enough attention to the minority cultures. The very term "disadvantaged" or "deprived" became an affront to the minority child. Even a generous attempt to assist the *"educationally* deprived" could be interpreted as an arrogant gesture toward a *"culturally* deprived" minority child. To those having a newly aroused ethnic consciousness, this was an insult to their culture. Such views complicated the search for equality, which had seemed such a clear-cut objective a decade earlier. (See Bibliographical Notes, pp.419–420.)

What might settle the issue was convincing evidence that compensatory education had worked and was continuing to work. Tangible evidence of this nature began to appear at the end of 1976. The National Assessment of Educational Progress reported that the reading skills of 9-year-olds had improved significantly between 1971 and 1975, while the 13- and 17-year-olds were holding their own.[45] This began to dull the mournful litany that compensatory education had failed. Even more potentially significant was the news that the most dramatic increases in reading tests in the early 1970s had been made by black nine-year-olds who had been the major recipients of federally funded compensatory education under ESEA. Though black children were still below white as a total group, the gap in academic achievement between the advantaged and the disadvantaged was significantly narrowing. If the trend continued, it could lead to the conclusion that special programs at the elementary school level were paying off and that special efforts ought to be made at the intermediate and secondary levels as well.

And, most significantly, it might mean that the Jencks study would have to be amended to show that schooling can and does indeed make a difference.

Benjamin S. Bloom of the University of Chicago argued this point positively by marshalling data to show that systematic and individualized instruction in schools *could* overcome the handicaps of homes, neighborhoods, and socioeconomic status for 80 percent of children, and bring them up to the level usually reached by only 20 percent.[46]

Affirmative Action

In the third quarter of the twentieth century, as we have often noted, the search for equality increasingly ran headlong into the search for freedom. "Freedom" said that individuals and local communities should have a wide range of choice and action in running their own affairs without interference or coercion by the federal government. "Equality" said that government was the prime agency to achieve justice for minorities and that "freedom" did not include the right to discriminate against minorities or the poor on the basis of race, color, ethnic origin, religion, or sex. We have seen how this conflict between the rights of freedom of some and the rights of equality for others shook the foundations of public education as the government undertook to dismantle segregated school systems and grant justice to minorities.

The search for equality was eventually broadened to include the physically handicapped along with the other disadvantaged groups. The Rehabilitation Act, passed in 1973 but not put into effect until June of 1977, applies to schools and colleges as well as to hospitals and other institutions receiving HEW funds. It prohibits discrimination against the handicapped in employment and requires educational institutions to make reasonable accommodations in their facilities (doorways, ramps, elevators, toilets, and the like). It mandates free education in public schools as well as adherence to "mainstreaming," that is, providing instruction for the handicapped in regular classrooms with other students whenever possible rather than separating them into classrooms of their own.

One final point here. Not only did federal legislation require affirmative action in the search for equality, the federal courts did not simply say what the states and local boards of education and educational officials could *not* do; they moved positively and actively to tell public school authorities what they *must* do to dismantle the system and promote equality of educational opportunity. States and local school boards *must* take *affirmative action* against discrimination and segregation.

Equality for Women

Affirmative action began to apply not only to the *assignment* of teachers and students already *in* a school system but also to the *admission* of pupils and the *employment* of teachers. "Affirmative action" as a term came to be applied particularly to the conditions for employment of teachers, their salary scales and promotion. In the 1960s and 1970s a whole battery of federal and state laws was passed to require equal pay and equal services. Amendments to the Civil Rights Act of 1964 and Title IX of the Education Amendments of 1972 (taking effect in July 1975) specifically applied to affirmative action for women. Title IX, proposed by Representative Edith Green of Oregon, applied to all public school systems as well as most post-secondary institutions:

> No person in the United States shall, on the basis of sex, be excluded from participation in, be denied the benefits of, or be subjected to discrimination under any program or activity receiving federal financial assistance.[47]

There was much controversy over the guidelines eventually issued by HEW (after much frustrating delay) concerning what the law meant for such single-sex activities as facilities for and participation in athletic programs and sports, fraternities and sororities, Boy Scouts and Girl Scouts as separate organizations, sex education classes, scholarships, and even separate schools for boys and for girls. Problems cropped up throughout the educational system as consciousness was raised concerning all kinds of sex discrimination against women, ranging from blatant discrimination in lower salaries and the pitifully few administrative positions held by women to the more subtle biases portraying the traditional role model of girls and women described in textbooks. (See Bibliographical Notes, p. 419.) The National Education Association and many civil rights women's groups like the National Organization for Women argued that the law should require school boards to screen textbooks for their sexist discriminatory features. This, of course, ran into counterclaims by publishers, who protested that their First Amendment rights to freedom of the press would be violated by such censorship laws or rules.

The Women's Rights Movement / By the end of 1976 the equal rights movement for women still showed mixed results after a hectic decade of political agitation during which significant gains were made in legislation and in the courts. These gains were reflected by equal pay for equal work, equal access to financial credit, and equal access to education. In 1977, for the first time in history, there were more women than men enrolled in U.S. colleges and universities. But these gains appeared to be too little and too late to those genuinely concerned with the whole range of equal rights for women in the broad spectrum of social affairs: the job market; roles in family life; property rights; access to high-level positions in the professions, business, labor, politics and government; fringe benefits; pregnancy leaves; inheritance rights; and the like. At the end of 1977 the Equal Rights Amendment (ERA) had still not been ratified by 15 states; at least three more were needed for adoption. As Patricia Sexton points out in one of the most useful summaries of the role of women in education, the women's movement ranged from the most activist and politicized feminists to those who felt privileged but would like some moderate reforms, with possibly the majority of women in the middle.[48]

As Sexton also points out, the women's movement had little impact on public elementary and secondary schools until the end of 1976. The most active arena was in higher educational institutions that sponsored research and courses in women's studies and offered an expanding series of programs of continuing education for adult women interested in careers or creative personal development. Women's studies for undergraduates, begun in 1970 at San Diego State College, had proliferated by 1973 to more than 1,200 courses across the country, few of which, however, were directed at the education of teachers.

In January 1977, five hundred women met in San Francisco to form the National Women's Studies Association. The purpose of the organization is to strengthen the rapidly growing movement, which at that time was represented in some 300 colleges and universities. Of these a hundred offered majors or minors for the bachelor's degree, a dozen offered the master's degree, and three offered doctoral programs. One of the announced aims of the new organization is to lobby for the support of women's studies in elementary and secondary schools. If this should be successful, it could mean an extremely significant change in the role of public education in the search for equality.

Women and the Public Schools / While there was much dispute over the value of women's studies, there was little dispute over the fact that there had been more discrimination (obvious and subtle) in the running of American public schools than was usually recognized. This is likely to be documented more and more as much needed research on women's education is pushed forward. Yet, in comparison with other countries, the U.S. public schools did historically open up jobs for women in the teaching profession, an opportunity seldom available anywhere else in the world until very recently. Although Sexton documented the many ways in which full equality has not been achieved for girls and women in public education, and indicated the distances still to go, the schools still received a passing mark from her for their contributions to the search for equality, albeit mostly in elementary education, less in secondary education, and least in higher education:

> As employers, they [public schools] have provided many desirable jobs for women. In offering role models to the young, they have supplied many living examples of successful career women, the teachers themselves. In their role as interpreter of an ostensibly democratic and meritocratic ideology, they have taught the value of equal opportunity and, in the early years at least, they have treated females perhaps more equitably than have other social institutions. . . .

Modern elementary and secondary schools have played a special role in the education of female children. Despite some conspicuous problems, females are probably treated in a more egalitarian way in schools than in other institutions, including religious, familial, economic, and political institutions. In the modern school, females and males attend classes together, and in approximately the same, rather than token, numbers. They compete on an equal footing and they pursue essentially the same courses of study. The sex-segregated public school, while it thrives in some other societies, has almost vanished in the United States. Virtually nowhere in the adult working world or in adult organizations is so little sex segregation present.[49]

"Reverse Discrimination" against White Males?

In general, affirmative-action requirements of the federal government having to do with admission of students and employment policies caused more of a stir in colleges and universities than in public schools. One of the knottiest problems was the question of "reverse discrimination," occasioned in 1971 by the refusal of the University of Washington Law School to admit a white applicant who charged that he was denied admission because of preferential treatment and reservation of quotas for less-qualified minority students. He claimed that this constituted denial to him of the equal protection of the laws under the Fourteenth Amendment.[50] A lower court ordered him admitted, the Washington Supreme Court reversed the lower court, and the U.S. Supreme Court in April, 1974 declared the case moot on the grounds that no matter what it decided, the student would graduate in June, having finished the law school course while the courts were trying the case. The majority of five consisted of those appointed by Republican presidents; the minority of liberals protested that the constitutional issue should have been decided.

The Bakke Case / As 1977 ended, it looked as though the constitutional issue would be decided on a case in California, where the supreme court of that state had ruled 6:1, in September 1976, that the University of California's policy of giving disadvantaged minorities preferential treatment in admissions to its medical school at Davis was unconstitutional:

> Regardless of its historical origin, the equal protection clause by its literal terms applies to "any person," and its lofty purpose, to secure equality of treatment to all, is incompatible with the premise that some races may be afforded a higher degree of protection against unequal treatment than others.[51]

The case was similar to that in Washington. Allan Bakke, a white applicant, charged that he had been denied admission because he was white, even though he was more highly qualified than some minority students who were admitted. The U.S. Supreme Court, in November 1976, declared that it was willing to decide the case if the University of California wished to appeal. The University finally decided to do so, even though certain civil rights leaders were concerned that the outlook of the Supreme Court was such that it might stop the whole affirmative action approach if it decided that "reverse dis-crimination" on behalf of minorities was just as unconstitutional as discrim-ination against them. In October 1977 the Supreme Court heard the case, and the University of California having asked Archibald Cox of Harvard, the Watergate special prosecutor, to represent it before the Supreme Court.

It was unlikely that a single Supreme Court decision could nullify a decade of achievements in legislation and in jurisprudence. But it *would* be a monumental irony if a Supreme Court that had started to blaze the path to equality under a Republican administration in the 1950s and which sustained that drive during another Republican regime from 1968 onward should begin to dismantle the nexus of governmental structure *for* equality just as a new Democratic administration came to power with the overwhelming support of the very minorities who had benefited by the Court's earlier decisions—decisions that were made before the complexion of the Court changed as a result of appointments made by a president who resigned in disgrace to avoid impeachment.

Even if the Supreme Court were to uphold the California Supreme Court in its decision and thereby slow down affirmative action on admissions to public professional schools, the effect on public elementary and secondary education would be uncertain and hardly predictable. The more certain result would be that in an unforeseen and curious way the attack upon the basic premises of public education itself would be rekindled by certain conflicting aspects of the search for freedom and the search for equality. The proposi-tion was bound to revive that freedom of choice was the prime goal for individuals and that equality for groups could best be achieved in separate schools that would serve their particular needs. The search for freedom and the search for equality led in their different ways to a series of crossroads in the search for community, the ultimate objective of the nation's founders. The problem now was how to plan a junction at those crossroads where freedom and equality could both contribute to a cohesive democratic community.

The Bakke case is much more than a legal matter, more even than a matter of constitutional rights. It symbolizes a conflict of basic values at the deepest levels of moral and political philosophy. It raises the most funda-mental questions regarding what holds a political community together. Is it force, or law, or day-to-day government, or even the constitutional regime itself? The answer must be found in the nature of the pervasive sense of political community and the commitments that bind a people together in a common sense of belongingness and identity. Is there such a thing as obli-gation to the public good that transcends loyalty to one's ethnic, racial, or cultural group? If so, what creates and nourishes it? And what specifically is the role of public schooling in that process? (See Chapter 12, Note 52.)

In its broadest reaches the Bakke question is this: Is there an over-arching sense of community—or if not, can it be created—that will lead the American people to decide that the opportunity for education open to most majority persons (freedom) should be reduced somewhat in order to increase the educational opportunity for some minority persons (equality) whose group identity has long made them subjects of discrimination? Is there an obligation for a just political community to remedy past injustices to minorities? One's reading of the history will largely determine one's answer to that question.

In a lengthy editorial on June 19, 1977, *The New York Times* defined the issue this way:

> Wise and generous people disagree profoundly about these questions. And many grow anxious on the threshold of this case. They say we must not fight evil with evil, discrimination with "reverse discrimination." They say the entire society will suffer if it compromises standards of merit in education or employment and holds back competent people to promote the fortunes of the "less qualified." They say an America only recently liberated from official racism must require its institutions to be color-blind, to judge individuals without reference to race or ethnic origin.
>
> Others argue, with equal passion, that there can be no remedy for inherited damage without transferring some opportunity from the advantaged majority to injured minorities. They say we cannot proclaim equal rights and expect to achieve them without helping minorities to exercise those rights. They say the damage will endure if policy ignores the handicaps currently inherent in some racial and ethnic status—that color must be relevant today if it is to be irrelevant tomorrow.

After stating the issues, *The Times* came out for the second position, arguing that it is in the national interest for Bakke to lose his case in the Supreme Court. Two weeks later *The Times* reported on its editorial page of July 3, 1977, that the letters from its readers had disagreed with its position in a ratio of 15 to 1. Apparently the public was not convinced. But on September 19 *The Chronicle of Higher Education* reported that 41 briefs had been filed with the Supreme Court supporting the position of the University of California against 16 for Bakke.

The University of California argument opens with the words:

> The outcome of this controversy will decide for future decades whether blacks, Chicanos, and other insular minorities are to have meaningful access to higher education and real opportunities to enter the learned professions, or are to be penalized indefinitely by the disadvantages flowing from previous pervasive discrimination. . . . There is, literally, no substitute for the use of race as a factor in admissions if professional schools are to admit more than an isolated few applicants from minority groups long subjected to hostile and pervasive discrimination.[52]

The "pervasive discrimination" to which the University of California refers includes, of course, the history of inequalities in schooling which this chapter has discussed. Admission to professional schools at the highest levels is only the tip of the educational iceberg. The elementary and secondary schools are just as surely involved. What is their contribution to the search for a just community that will embrace both freedom and equaliy? This is the subject of Chapter 12.

Notes

1. For a summary of recent statistics, see articles by W. Vance Grant in successive issues of *American Education* (especially October 1975).
2. See Children's Defense Fund of the Washington Research Project, *Children Out of School in America* (Cambridge, Mass.: Children's Defense Fund, 1975.)
3. For details see Raymond Poignant, *Education and Development in Western Europe, the United States, and the U.S.S.R.: A Comparative Study* (New York: Teachers College Press, 1969).
4. For details of educational inequality in the states see Bibliographical Notes, p. 417.
5. For details see R. Freeman Butts and Lawrence A. Cremin, *A History of Education in American Culture* (New York: Holt, Rinehart and Winston, 1953).
6. *Missouri ex rel. Gaines v. Canada*, 305 U.S. 337 (1938).
7. *Sweatt v. Painter*, 339 U.S. 629 (1950).
8. *McLaurin v. Oklahoma State Regents for Higher Education*, 339 U.S. 637 (1950).
9. For a fascinating description and analysis of the events and court cases leading to the landmark decision in 1954, see Richard Kluger, *Simple Justice: The History of Brown v. Board of Education and Black America's Struggle for Equality* (New York: Knopf, 1976).
10. *Brown v. Board of Education of Topeka*, 347 U.S. 483 (1954).
11. *Brown v. Board of Education*, 493, 495.
12. *Cooper v. Aaron*, 358 U.S. 1 (1958).
13. *Griffin v. Prince Edward County School Board*, 377 U.S. 218 (1964).
14. *Green v. County School Board of New Kent*, 391 U.S. 430 (1968).
15. *Alexander et al., v. Holmes County (Mississippi) School Board*, 396 U.S. 19, (1969).
16. *Swann v. Charlotte-Mecklenburg (North Carolina) Board of Education*, 402 U.S. 1 (1971).
17. *Keyes v. School District #1, Denver*, 413 U.S. 189 (1973).
18. *Bradley v. State Board of Education of Virginia*, 412 U.S. 92 (1973).
19. *Milliken v. Bradley*, 418 U.S. 717 (1974).
20. *Morgan v. Hennigan*, 379 F. Supp. 410 (D. Mass. 1974).
21. *Runyon v. McCrary*, 96 S. Ct. 2586 (June 25, 1976).
22. A Report of the United States Commission on Civil Rights, *Fulfilling the Letter and Spirit of the Law: Desegregation in the Nation's Public Schools*, August 1976, p. 312.
23. For an excellent historical account of this and later periods, see Margaret Szasz, *Education and the American Indian: The Road to Self-Determination, 1928–1973* (Albuquerque: University of New Mexico Press, 1974).
24. The National Study of American Indian Education, Robert J. Havighurst, Director, *The Education of Indian Children and Youth, Summary Report and Recommendations* (Minneapolis: University of Min-

nesota Center for Urban and Regional Affairs, December 1970), pp. 43–46.

25. See *Mendez* v. *Westminster School District of Orange County (California)* 64 F. Supp. 544, affirmed 161 F. 2nd 744 (9th Cir. 1947); *Delgado* v. *The Bastrop Independent School District*, Civ. No. 388 (D.C.W.D. Texas 1948).

26. *Cisneros* v. *Corpus Christi Independent School District*, Civ. No. 68-C-95 (D.C.S.D. Tex. Corpus Christi Div. 1970).

27. *John Serrano, Jr., et al.* v. *Ivy Baker Priest*, 96 Cal., Rptr., 601, (August 30, 1971).

28. *San Antonio Independent School District* v. *Rodriquez*, 411 U.S. 1 (1973).

29. *San Antonio School District* v. *Rodriquez* p. 63.

30. *Robinson* v. *Cahill*, 289 Atlantic Reporter, 2nd Series, 569.

31. *Robinson* v. *Cahill*.

32. James S. Coleman, et al., *Equality of Educational Opportunity* (Washington, D.C.: Government Printing Office, 1966).

33. Christopher Jencks, et al., *Inequality: A Reassessment of the Effect of Family and Schooling in America* (New York: Basic Books, 1972).

34. Kenneth B. Clark, "Social Policy, Power, and Social Science Research," *Harvard Educational Review*, February 1973, 43(1):119.

35. Ronald Edwards et al., "A Black Response to Christopher Jenck's Inequality and Certain Issues," *Harvard Educational Review*, February 1973, 43(1):83.

36. Coleman, "Equality of Opportunity and Equality of Results," *Harvard Educational Review*, February 1973, 43(1):137.

37. *Hobson* v. *Hansen*, 269 F. Supp. 401 (1967), at pp. 406–407.

38. *Hobson* v. *Hansen*, p. 505.

39. *Hobson* v. *Hansen*, p. 514.

40. For the politics involved in the early years see Stephen K. Bailey and Edith K. Mosher, *ESEA; The Office of Education Administers a Law* (Syracuse, N.Y.: Syracuse University Press, 1968).

41. Quoted in Robert H. Bremner, *Children and Youth in America.* Vol. III, p. 1806. See this source for several analyses of the titles of the act.

42. Ralph W. Tyler, "The Federal Role in Education," *The Public Interest*, Winter 1974, p. 170.

43. Tyler, p. 170.

44. Samuel Halperin, "ESEA Ten Years Later," *Educational Researcher*, September 1975. (A similar series in *Phi Delta Kappan*, November 1975).

45. See National Assessment of Educational Progress, *Newsletter*, October 1976; and Peggy Gardner, "The Good News in Reading," *American Education*, December 1976, pp. 14–17.

46. Benjamin S. Bloom, *Human Characteristics and School Learning.* New York: McGraw-Hill, 1976.

47. See Patricia Sexton, *Women in Education* (Bloomington, Ind.. Phi Delta Kappa, 1976), p. 137.

48. Sexton, p. 149.

49. Sexton, pp. 4–5.
50. *De Funis* v. *Odegaard*, 40 S. Ct. Rpts, L Ed 2d.
51. *Bakke* v. *Regents of the University of California*, SF 2331 (Super. Ct. #31287).
52. Brief for the Petitioner, *Regents of the University of California* v. *Allan Bakke*, Supreme Court, October Term, 1977, No. 76–811, pp. 13–14. Because of the deadlines for the publication of this book and the timing of the arguments before the Supreme Court, it has not been possible to discuss adequately the substantive issues in the Bakke case here. Much controversy arose over the meaning of "quotas" and the extent to which race may be taken into account in affirmative action to achieve greater equality of educational opportunity for historically disadvantaged groups. Oceana Publications, Dobbs Ferry, New York, has announced plans to publish in four volumes some time in 1978 the complete record of court decisions and the more than 58 *amicus curiae* briefs. This will make possible a thoroughgoing study of a case that has been more widely discussed and is viewed as more significant than any other civil rights case on education since Brown in 1954.

The Search for Community

The Historic Goal of Political Community: E Pluribus Unum

In this final chapter we return to the theme that has threaded this history of education in the United States since its beginning—the continuing search for the role that public education should play in building a sense of community among all the American people. This theme involves two principal questions: What kind of authority should be the basis for the common undertakings of the new nation; and what kind of education could best serve to legitimize, maintain, and improve that community? We have seen that the founders of the Republic rejected military power, religious sanction, and the inherited prerogatives of kinship or hierarchical social class as the bases for the authority of the new American community. They proclaimed instead that the democratic *political* community was to be the binding element of social cohesion and that this political community was to be based upon liberty, equality, and justice. And they decided that the most appropriate means of education to achieve and preserve such a political community was through *public* education, oriented toward public purposes rather than through private education devoted to military, religious, ethnic, or social-class preferments.

Vision of the Founders

We have seen that the founders viewed the American Revolution itself and the kind of education needed in the new republic primarily in *political* terms

364

rather than in terms of academic achievement, social class, individual fulfillment, or occupational preparation. Thus, they declared public education to be the bulwark of liberty, equality, and the public good, goals that took precedence over the rewards of knowledge, of social class, of individual effort, or of occupation. Over and over again, the founders and their followers asserted their faith that the welfare of the Republic rested upon an educated citizenry and that public schools had the primary purpose of educating that citizenry in the values, the knowledge, and the obligations required of everyone in a democratic republican society.

Jefferson, as did so many of the founders, thought of "liberty" very largely in terms of widespread political participation; thus public education should prepare the citizenry for such participation. The view of the revolutionary generation that literacy and some study of history and civil government would be a sufficient education for the citizenry may seem to us as overly simple, but the point is that whatever the public school did was to be justified on political grounds. Equality also had strong political connotations. *All* citizens needed a common political education in republican principles, rich and poor alike, North and South, city and country, farmer and artisan. And education for the public good nearly always carried moral as well as religious connotations (given the widespread assumption that Christianity provided the basis of morality despite sectarian differences). But, again, the point is that education was expected to develop sentiments that served the public welfare, sentiments that were superior to motives of individual or personal or family preferment. And the new republic was to be the object of affection, loyalty, and patriotic devotion that dominated self-serving and parochial interests.

We have also seen how, as early as the beginning of the nineteenth century, the Revolutionary fervor for education to stress *Unum* began to give way to the forces of *Pluribus*. The Revolutionists' purposeful civic goals for education continued to be stated and often to be served as the years passed. But by 1900 they had become muted and dispersed under the burdens of an exhuberant and aggressive modernization process that turned the streams of life from rural to urban centers, from agrarian to industrial processes, from devotion to the public good to aspirations of individual enterprise and economic advancement. The ideals of liberty and equality found expression in the common school movements of the early nineteenth century, but they were increasingly strained by massive immigration from Europe and Asia, and they were simply denied by the slavery of blacks and the restrictive penalties laid upon Indians. In the middle of the nineteenth century, the political *Unum* of the federal government survived the Civil War, and the subsequent Reconstruction laid the groundwork for educational *Unum* on a national level. But these efforts proved to be short-lived in the face of increasing social, economic, ethnic, religious, and racial *Pluribus*.

The Asymmetries of Community/Pluralism and Civism

We have tried to indicate how public education for the past century has been pulled and hauled by the divergent forces seeking cohesion on one side and differentiation on the other. This tug of war may be described as the tension between the realms of the public and the private (as Robert Wiebe does), or between inclusiveness and exclusiveness (as Nathan Glazer does), or between integrationists and pluralists (as John Higham does). In all cases, the arguments pointed to a significant shift in the 1960s. Wiebe argues that the 1960s revealed a national style, which was sectarian not pragmatic, that looked for boundaries that divided people, not common ground that bound them together; thus, a major casualty was the dream of moderation, accommodation, and cohesion.[1] Glazer points to the ideal of the inclusiveness that welcomed immigrants and differences of national style, and seemed to be winning—up to the 1880s and 1890s—until the exclusiveness of the nativist attacks on foreigners gained ascendancy and set up obstacles to free immigration in the 1920s. He argues that the exclusive mentality was beginning to be dismantled in the reforms of the 1930s and increasingly so in the 1960s, when (he might have said) a startling new ethnic exclusiveness set in.[2] Higham describes vividly the long persistent dilemma posed on one hand by integrationists in our history who stressed the equality of individuals, majority rule, the elimination of cultural boundaries, a unifying ideology and cohesion around the American creed of the past or the visions of a Great Society in the future. On the other hand, he says, there were the pluralists who sought to maintain cultural boundaries, who looked to the little communities of the past, who found cohesion in the heritage of distinctive memories, and who stressed the equality of groups and their minority rights.[3]

Any one of the preceding interpretations would be a useful basis for analysis of the search for community, but there is the danger that the values and virtues of community might be seen as wholly on one side, on the side of the public, or inclusiveness, or integration. Such an assumption would be far too easy to explain a complex and often ambiguous history. The way I like to put it is that almost all persons seek some sort of community or communities to which they can feel attached and at home. The question here is, rather, what sort of community should provide the authority for public education, and to what sort of community should the goals of public education most appropriately lend legitimacy? I believe it is clear from the history of public schooling that public education once had powerful moral as well as legal authority behind it. Until almost yesterday, the public school was a well-fixed article in the American public creed, commanding powerful moral authority as a national unifier, liberator, and equalizer.

At various times in the past the public school has drawn upon the political authority residing in the ideals of the founders of the Republic, the religious authority of nondenominational Protestantism, the moral virtues and work ethic of middle-class ideology, the academic authority of literacy and of knowledge in an education-oriented society, the cohesive authority of assimilator and Americanizer in an immigrant-flooded society, and the socializing authority as an agent of progressive reform in a rapidly modernizing and industrializing society. But for a decade or more in the 1960s and 1970s, the erosion of the legitimacy of some of the major institutions in U.S. society began to affect the "deauthorization" of the public school as well; that is, its moral authority to act as a guide or leader in social affairs has been seriously questioned and weakened. At the end of the Republic's two-hundredth year, the value of public education was being attacked from several quarters, and the American people were engaged in searching anew for the basis of legitimate authority upon which their education should rest in the future. The question became: What sort of community could most appropriately give legitimacy to the goals of education in general, and to public education in particular? There were two principal kinds of reply. One said that authority should rest with a number of pluralistic communities; the other said that authority should be vested in the overall political or civic community. In oversimplified but useful terms, the two approaches could be identified as pluralism and civism.

Pluralism sought moral authority and legitimacy for education in the many diverse communities that serve to bind individuals and groups together on the basis of religious, racial, ethnic, linguistic, cultural, or local cohesion and unity. Pluralists saw such positive values in diversity and variety of pluralistic associations that they considered them to be the essence of community around which education and schooling should cluster. Some pluralists were exceedingly critical of public education for being so comformist in outlook and practice, recommending that public schools should emphasize ethnic studies, multicultural studies, bilingual studies, and reflect in general the enormous diversity of their cultural communities. Other pluralists saw no special authority in public education at all, viewing it as no more legitimate or authoritative than private schools or any number of other educative agencies such as the family, churches, and voluntary associations of all kinds. Still others viewed public education as positively *illegitimate* because of its historic connection with an exploitative, capitalist, corporate, and liberal state.

By contrast, civism (or citizenism) sought the principal authority and legitimacy for public education in the democratic civic or political community.[4] "Civicists" argued that public education had a special responsibility for being a positive force in promoting the values, the knowledge, and the skills of participation required for maintaining and improving the democratic political community and for strengthening the freedom, the equality, the justice, and the popular consent promised by the Declaration of Independence, the Constitution, and the Bill of Rights. For these values to provide protection for the diversity of pluralist associations, they must be held in common by all pluralisms; otherwise, privatism, contention, and conflict might threaten the welfare of any but the most powerful groups in the society.

The "New Pluralism"

Despite the origins of the term "cultural pluralism" in the early decades of the twentieth century, the term was not in widespread professional or popular usage until it had a rather sudden and vital rebirth in the 1960s. For a decade or so thereafter it became exceedingly popular in the hands of a number of different critics as well as friends of public education. Only three examples can be mentioned: representatives of the new ethnicity, of a neo-conservative as well as a new-left political philosophy, and a variety of critics in educational philosophy and in educational policy who espoused pluralism, both from within and outside the educational establishment.

The New Ethnicity

Heartened by the success of blacks in the civil rights movement of the 1960s, but frustrated by the indications that similar forms of discrimination continued to apply to the descendants of white immigrants, a new and some-times fierce pride in ethnic traditions appeared in both the professional and popular literature, and especially reappeared as a lively political force in the elections of the 1960s and 1970s. Books and articles by Michael Novak formerly on the staff of the Rockefeller Foundation, Nathan Glazer and Daniel Patrick Moynihan at Harvard, and Father Andrew Greeley, director of the Center for the Study of Pluralism at the University of Chicago, became well-known names.[5]

The new ethnicity is defined by Michael Novak as

> a movement of self-knowledge on the part of members of the third and fourth generation of southern and eastern European immigrants in the United States. In a broader sense, the new ethnicity includes a renewed self-consciousness on the part of other generations and other ethnic groups: the Irish, the Norwegians and Swedes, the Germans, the Chinese and Japanese, and others.[6]

Novak argues for the introduction of ethnic studies into the public school curriculum:

> With even modest adjustments in courses in history, literature, and the social sciences, material can be introduced that illuminates inherited patterns of family life, values, and preferences. The purpose for introducing multi-cultural materials is neither chauvinistic nor propagandistic but realistic. Education ought to illuminate what is happening in the self of each child.[7]

From views and sentiments like those of Novak have arisen the demand for ethnic heritage studies and multicultural studies in the public schools. But another approach arising from the new ethnicity was the argument that "ethnic" schools would be better than common public schools. Andrew Greeley implies this when he argues that an "ethnic miracle" has been achieved by some of the immigrant groups in rising out of poverty, hatred, and discrimination by their own efforts and in spite of the public schools.[8] In fact, their own parochial schools aided Irish Catholics, Italians, and Poles to achieve financial success and middle-class status in a matter of a few decades from their arrival in the United States. The public high school did not assist in this process because the immigrants' financial success came *before* they began to flock to schools. It was their family life, their hard work, their ambition, their courage, their work ethic, and their sacrifice. They were given no favors and no help, but they *were* given personal freedom and the chance to turn their hard work into economic progress. Greeley also argues that Catholic students in parochial schools were more tolerant and less racist than those Catholics who attended public schools.[9]

The hint for social policy in all this was that public funds should go to aid ethnic schools, which have been so important in the "ethnic miracle" of the past, assuming that

> *one might take it as a tentative hypothesis that the school is a rather poor institution for facilitating the upward mobility of minority groups—until they first acquire some kind of rough income parity.* The naive American faith that equality of education produces equality of income seems to have been stood on its head in the case of the ethnics. For them, better income meant more effective education.
>
> Nor did the public schools play the critical "Americanization" role that such educators as Dr. James B. Conant expected them to play in the 1940s and 1950s. Even taking into account parents' education and income, the most successful of the ethnics—educationally, occupationally, and economically—went to parochial schools, and they did so at a time when the schools were even more crowded than they are today, staffed by even less adequately trained teachers, and administered by an even smaller educational bureaucracy than the very small one that somehow manages to keep the parochial schools going today. Again: a social hint: Maybe what matters about schools for a minority group is, as my colleague Professor William McCready has remarked, that they are "our" schools (whoever "we" may be).[10]

Neo-Conservative Political Philosophy

A second fountainhead of the new pluralism sprang from a variety of political analyses in the fields of moral and political philosophy in which fundamental questions were being raised concerning the future of the institution of public education itself, and in broader terms, of the whole range of institutions that made up liberal democratic government in the United States.

It seemed clear that during the early 1970s there was a growing conservative reaction against the educational and social reform efforts of the 1960s.

One could cite the more obvious political and economic policies of the Nixon/Ford presidencies, designed to withdraw from or roll back the social, humanitarian policies of the New Frontier and Great Society programs, the cutbacks in financial support, the retreat from desegregation, the exploitation of the busing issue, the veto after veto of welfare and education bills. But even more significant in the long run, perhaps, was the resurgence of a neoconservative stance in the intellectual and academic community, which presented a new and persuasive element of the climate in which educational debates take place. One could cite Robert Nisbet of Columbia in historical sociology, Robert Nozick of Harvard in political philosophy, Milton Friedman of Chicago in economics, and Nathan Glazer of Harvard in education and social structure. Theirs was a call for the reassertion of the values of private freedoms, individual rights, the free-market mechanism, the minimal state, the free play of voluntary groups, mutual aid associations, and reinforcement of pluralistic racial and social groupings of all kinds.

Along with the positive values to be associated with freedom for the "hundred flowers to bloom" went an attack upon the overweening welfare state, the inquisitional and repressive measures of the bureaucracies, the leviathan mentality, and in general a disenchantment with the liberal welfare state and its policies. The neoconservatism now added its voice to the radical attacks upon the public schools and supported efforts to "reform" them by the use of vouchers, tax credits, free schools, alternative schools, or other measures designed to loosen up or escape from the alleged monolithic monopoly of public schools and their authoritarian, bureaucratic machines that imposed welfare-state values through compulsory education.

One example of the new conservatism, a most elegant and persuasive one, is by Robert Nisbet of Columbia:

> I believe the single most remarkable fact at the present time in the West is neither technological nor economic, but *political*: the waning of the historic political community, the widening sense of the obsolescence of politics as civilized pursuit, even as a habit of mind. By political community I mean more than the legal state. I have in mind the whole fabric of rights, liberties, participations, and protections that has been even above industrialism, I think, the dominant element of modernity in the West. . . .
>
> Once political government in the United States signified some degree of austerity of life, of commitment to the public weal, of a willingness to forego most of life's luxuries in the name of service that was for a long time closely akin to what one found in the ranks of clergy and teachers. . . .
>
> We are witnessing . . . a gathering revolt . . . against the whole structure of wealth, privilege, and power that the contemporary democratic state has come to represent. What we are also witnessing, and this tragically, is rising opposition to the central values of the political community as we have known them for the better part of the past two centuries: freedom, rights, due process, privacy, and welfare.[11]

Nisbet's prescriptions for the restoration of authority are to recover the central values of social and cultural pluralism rather than political cohesion, and to revive the prestige of the private good as contrasted to the public good. In briefest terms, Nisbet defines four central values of pluralism. As correctly interpreted: (1) It preserves functional autonomy of major social institutions (avoiding intrusion of the state into the spheres of school, university, family, and religion); (2) it decentralizes power into as many hands as possible; (3) it recognizes that hierarchy and stratification of function and role are unavoidable and honorable and to be preserved from intrusion by the arbitrary power of regulatory agencies in the "name of a vain and vapid equality"; and (4) it relies as much as possible upon informal custom, folkway, spontaneous tradition—sanctioned habits of mind—rather than formal law, ordinance, or administrative regulation.

Thus, Nisbet argues for the renascence in education of pluralism, privatism, kinship, localism, and voluntary association. For example, with regard to kinship, it was a great mistake in the democratic dogma to think that political institutions, like the public school, could do better than the family in the realm of education. With regard to localism, the opposition to busing springs from pride of attachment to neighborhood rather than from racism. Regarding voluntary association, the prime agents of human accomplishment are the intimate, free, relevant, and spontaneous associations of self-help and mutual aid, the best illustration of such laissez-faire phenomena being Milton Friedman's proposal for educational vouchers. In other words, private schools under the auspices of churches, labor unions, cooperatives, neighborhoods, and families have been notably less expensive and more efficient than public schools:

> From what labyrinths of bureaucracy we would be saved in the grim worlds of social workers and educational administrators had there been instituted in the beginning a system [of education] whereby a natural, already existing social group—the household—would be the means of distributing public funds for welfare and for education.[12]

In the concluding paragraphs of his book, Nisbet argues that it all comes down to the way we conceive the nature of citizenship. And Nisbet clearly prefers the medieval version, in which the essence of citizenship was the urban man's freedom from the exactions of obedience to the feudal countryside, but the citizen was still bound by the loyalties and obligations of kinship, occupation, and religion. In early modern times, citizenship was allied to the national state by ties of a broad patriotism that were vastly stronger than the parochial patriotisms. For a time, in the United States, the citizen was bounded by a hierarchy of local, state, and regional authorities, but the Civil War and World War I largely overcame the loyalties to neighborhood and region by the tides of war fervor, totalitarian enthusiasms, and melting-pot assimilation. Today we see the twilight of this centralized conception of citizenship:

> If there is to be a citizenship in the useful and creative sense of that word, it must have its footings in the groups, associations, and localities in

which we actually spend our lives—not in the abstract and now bankrupt ideal of *patrie*, as conceived by the Jacobins and their descendants.[13]

If the signposts of the future are the upthrusts of ethnicity, localism, regionalism, religion, and kinship, it should be pointed out that this is exactly what we had two hundred years ago when the founders of the American commonwealth sought to overcome those very pluralistic elements in the framing of a political community and a constitutional order whose motto became *E Pluribis Unum*. Nisbet's notions of private education, based upon those same elements of traditional pluralism, were exactly the characteristics of the schools and colleges of the colonial period before the founders and their successors sought to replace them by proposing a public education that would be universal, free, common, and eventually secular and compulsory.

Neo-Radical Proposals for Pluralism

Now conservative intellectuals joined radicals in questioning the unifying value of public education. For more than a decade the major attacks on the public schools, which accused them of being authoritarian bureaucratic machines imposing the wrong values upon helpless minorities through compulsory education, had come from the *radical* sector of the academic and professional community rather than from the conservative. This had been inspired not only by radical romantic critics like Paul Goodman, Jonathan Kozol, Herbert Kohl, and Ivan Illich, but also by radical revisionists in the history of education, like Michael B. Katz, Clarence Karier, Paul Violas, Joel Spring, and Marvin Lazerson, and by radical social scientists like Christopher Jencks, Samuel Bowles, Herbert Gintis, Martin Carnoy, and Henry Levin.[14]

The radical view of the public schools as instruments of capitalist oppression on behalf of the privileged upper classes ranges from the anarchist libertarian view of Joel Spring and the romantics (that the public schools were hopeless and might as well be abolished in order for the freedom of stateless anarchy to prevail) to the more "neutral" views of Katz (that they should be stripped of their value teaching and reduced to the three Rs so that they could not do too much damage with their racist, materialistc, exploitative, capitalistic, class-biased teachers). However, the remedy of both Spring and Katz was to return to small, informal groups, abolish compulsory attendance, root out bureaucracy, and give power to teachers, students, and citizens of the community rather than to administrators.[15] The neo-radical remedies closely paralleled Nisbet's neo-conservative views.

Romantic Critics / A third source of the new pluralism focused critical attention directly on the policies of public education. One line of reasoning, often summed up under the heading of the "romantic critics," led to the conclusion that the public school system could not be reclaimed and should be replaced by voluntary efforts of many kinds. Another line of argument led to the proposals for all sorts of "alternatives" to loosen up and introduce flexibility into the public system itself. These two refrains became dominant themes of the educational discussions of the 1960s and 1970s

One of the best and most insightful short summaries of the romantic critics has been written by Henry J. Perkinson, historian of education at New York University.[16] He identifies and discusses briefly a dozen of the most widely read critics of the public schools, whose dominant theme was that the prime fault of the public schools was that they followed too closely the needs and demands of the national community and thereby neglected or even destroyed the natural needs and creative impulses of children. In place of large, uniform, authoritarian, bureaucratized schools, the critics proposed smaller, more intimate, more humane kinds of schools that deliberately tried to meet the needs of the learner and of the local community.

Paul Goodman spoke of an underlying philosophy of community more than most of the others. He referred to the community as the prime educative agency in terms of Aristotle's Greek polis, which aided human nature to develop to its fullest. He found that modern American society was no longer promoting human growth, but was stifling it, and the public schools were primarily concentration camps designed to socialize the young to the dominant economic and social values of an aggrandizing society. So, the walls of the schools should be crumbled so that the young could learn from the community in decentralized informal contact with all the plural educative agencies of the society.

Edgar Z. Friedenberg took up the refrain that U.S. society was stamping out the individuality and the individual differences that should be honored and cultivated through an educational freedom and release of creativity rather than an imposition of the economic motivations of a capitalist society. Children should be allowed to go to any kind of school that would enable each one to develop an individuality and identity of his or her own. "Community" was to be seen in highly subjective terms as the individual seeks the meaning of his or her own life in relation to the meaning of other peoples' lives.

Following the general strictures of Goodman and Friedenberg in the early 1960s, the next stage was, as Perkinson points out, a series of personal exposés by teachers of the actual conditions under which they had to work in the public schools:

> On the basis of their experiences they located the true roots of what was wrong with American education in the curriculum, or in the teaching methods, or in the classroom structure and climate, or in the bureaucratic system itself. In book after book of careful scrutiny and scathing analyses they laid bare the institutionalized authoritarianism that obstructed learning and psychologically damaged the children in American schools.[17]

Among such critics were John Holt, Neil Postman, Charles Weingartner,

Herbert Kohl (in Harlem), Jonathan Kozol (in Boston), and George Dennison (in New York). Holt stressed that the child should learn whatever he chose from a smorgasbord of learning possibilities; Kohl's "open classroom" encouraged students to talk and question, and teachers to care and listen; Dennison's "free" school was divorced entirely from the public system, and the community to be served was the school, the children, and the parents themselves. Alan Graubard found some 350 such "free" schools in 1972, enrolling about one-tenth of 1 percent of the school children and—too often in Graubard's mind—having a too narrow provincial and nonpolitical view of the community they sought to serve. Interestingly enough, Graubard found only two or three years later that "radical school reform isn't really interesting any more" and "nothing really big seems potential in educational reform activities."[18]

The ultimate logic of the romantic movement was reached by Ivan Illich and Everett Reimer in their view that all schools were essentially and inevitably authoritarian, seeking to impose the dominant values of a competitive capitalistic consumer society upon the young. The only nonviolent way to overthrow such a technologically oriented society was to do away with the schools as an institution and restore learning to individual learners who would seek out persons who had something to teach them. "Educational networks" and "learning webs" would replace institutionalized schools and professional teachers, and public funds would go directly to the learners to enable them to find their education wherever and whenever they would. The first amendment of a new bill of rights for a humanistic society would be "The State shall make no laws with respect to the establishment of education."

Perkinson accurately summed up the movement:

> One after another the romantic critics have uncovered layers of authoritarianism in our educational arrangements. To a man they reject imposition and advocate a child-oriented or learner-centered education. The smorgasbord curriculum of John Holt, the inquiry method of Postman and Weingartner, the open classroom of Herbert Kohl, the free school of George Dennison, the learning web of Ivan Illich—all point to an educational process where people learn what, how, and when they like.[19]

The embrace of pluralism by educators could scarcely go further. The search for community centered upon idealized goals of humanistic togetherness; and the concern specifically for political community was scarcely in evidence except for a minor refrain of somehow removing the evils of a capitalist system. The second kind of educational pluralism, that which emanated from within the establishment and focused upon reform of the public schools in the direction of greater "alternatives," reflected much of the orientation if not the fire and outrage of the romantics. Philosophers of education, educational policy advisers, national commissions, federal programs, and national association projects began to echo, if not incorporate, the pluralistic criticisms that had reverberated through the press and other mass media for over a decade.

Philosophy of Education and Cultural Pluralism

Philosophy of education—which had been socially oriented to the ideals of democracy as well as to individual development in the spirit of John Dewey's pragmatism and experimentalism through most of the period from the late 1920s to the early 1950s—began to concentrate on the linguistic analysis of philosophical problems in much of the 1950s and early 1960s. Then in the mid 60s it began to rediscover the individualistic and pluralistic side of Dewey's philosophy, and especially that of Horace Kallen, generally conceded to be the father of the term "cultural pluralism." (See Bibliographical Notes, p. 00.)

The essence of the idea of cultural pluralism is that primary human associations are the most basic communities, consisting of natural affinities and sentiments. The individual can most readily develop the potentials of his personality and self-fulfillment in and through such associations. A genuine pluralist society will thus honor and encourage the diversity of the natural primary groups based upon kinship, language, religion, culture, and locality. Education should therefore recognize and encourage such diverse loyalties as the essential ingredients of both democracy and personal development. Obviously, this revival of the philosophy of cultural pluralism complemented nicely the rise of the new ethnicity and a nonauthoritarian political philosophy, whether stemming from conservative or liberal or radical sources.

Itzkoff's "New" Public Education / Some philosophers and practitioners of education moved on to argue that public schools should stress the pluralistic character of American society through multicultural studies. Others followed an argument that led them to a purely pluralist view of education, which found a greatly reduced role, or none at all, for public education as it had been historically developed. One of the most forthright of such philosophies is that of Seymour Itzkoff of Smith College, whose book *A New Public Education* found a large place for private voluntary effort and little for a public governmental role in education. His view of "public education" is so "new" that it really means private education.

Calling to witness Horace Kallen, John Dewey, Thomas Green, and George Dennison, Itzkoff argues that the local autonomous cultural community is the natural context and authority for education. In opposition to the call for basic changes in the social structures recommended by radical revisionists, he argues that the social and educational system *could* be reformed by a gradual shift to voluntarism and eventually to a full-voucher system. In this way the stagnant, bureaucratized, politicized public system could be given over to those who would be the ultimate beneficiaries; and parents and children would have maximum opportunity to realize their value commitments in a wholly voluntary system of community-based schooling.

Itzkoff concludes that the legitimacy of the public school and the moral authority it once had are irretrievably lost, confounded at least in part by the new stress on an aggressive equality by fiat, forced integration, affirmative action, and proliferation of quotas enforced by the intercession of government:

> The traumas that the schools have recently undergone have arisen precisely because of our waning confidence in the school. The moral consensus that undergirded the public school for so many decades has dissolved. And in its absence the state schools have fallen prey to a host of political locusts. Drained of its integrity, public education has become an automatic target for every new political grab. This has caused many thoughtful people to abandon hope for the public school as a functioning national institution in its traditional moral as well as skill-training role.[20]

In place of the *common* public school should arise a pluralism of voluntary schools around which individuals with similar values, social concerns, and cultural ideals would cluster. Itzkoff prefers unregulated vouchers so that the greatest kind of differentiation (except racial) could lead to schools based on special interests, special talents, special cultural and ethnic orientations, and specialized admission policies:

> Free choice is the key, the right to be taught by whom one chooses, and the right to teach only those one feels will benefit from one's skills.[21]

The Rush to Alternatives

As the year of the nation's bicentennial celebration came to a close, it was still too early to record the denouement of the public school that Itzkoff proposed, but prominent voices on the policy scene were giving notice that its role and importance should be viewed as greatly curtailed.

Sizer on a Smorgasbord of Schools / One such policy was taken at the end of 1976 by Theodore R. Sizer, dean of the Harvard Graduate School of Education from 1964 to 1972, who argued for a pluralism of educational institutions as the best solution for the future. He acknowledged that he had been particularly influenced by Lawrence A. Cremin's *Public Education*, David B. Tyack's *One Best System*, Nathan Glazer's *Affirmative Discrimination*, and Glazer and Moynihan's *Ethnicity*. Sizer's policy proposals are threshold. The first is: Do not simply reassert that the public schools are the one best system; because

> the sooner those responsible for public education recognize that nonpublic schools, the so-called deschooling movement, the alternative education movement, and the advocates of neighborhood community schools all in their several ways represent a new reality in American educational politics, so much the better for the children. It is no surprise that efforts at a national unified teachers union have lost momentum and the political interest for increased federal involvement in the "improvement" of education has slowed. Disaggregation is a policy with new adherents. One need only look at the growing edge of the curricula of teacher training institutions to see the interest in alternatives and in the special educational needs of special groups,

increasingly ethnic as well as racial groups. The *common* school, the single institution built around a common American creed, never was and clearly never will be.[22]

A second pluralistic injunction from Sizer rests on Cremin's argument that the part that *schools* can play in the education of children is limited. In fact, he goes so far as to acknowledge that Cremin's message on ecology and configurations will serve to bury the public school:

> Cremin would include, along with the school, the church, the family and the ethnic group. *The times are ready for a new kind of pluralism in schooling*, a pluralism which relates the schools with other institutions in carefully contrived and thoughtfully constructed ways. Cremin's "Public Education" drives the final nail in the coffin of the late-nineteenth century nativist creation of a "one best system." The sooner that the educational establishment at large recognizes this, the better (again) for the children.[23]

Sizer is apparently not worried about the segregative aspects of alternative schools. He believes that the "thread of nationhood" and social cohesion would be adequately served by the much more powerful mass media. He is apparently willing to leave the common thread to Walter Cronkite, Harry Reasoner, and Ann Landers. His third proposal is that youngsters could well divide their time between different kinds of schools—ethnic schools, community schools, regional schools, even "national" schools. So, his final message is that there should be multiple opportunities for all children and parents to choose among complementary institutions, a smorgasbord of schools.

The Varieties of Alternatives

"Alternatives" became one of the most popular terms in the educational lexicon of the 1970s. It has been applied to all sorts of undertakings. Vernon Smith, Robert Barr, and Daniel Burke compiled a useful summary of meanings and practices up to 1976,[24] which range from full-fledged efforts based on a well-thought-out program like that of the Parkway Schools in Philadelphia to almost any kind of improvisation that would take disruptive youth off the hands of embattled and harassed public school administrators. Smith, Barr, and Burke estimated that there were some 5,000 alternative public schools in operation in 1976 with a total enrollment of about one million, or approximately 2 percent of the total elementary and secondary school enrollment in the United States. This meant that about 10 percent of families have some choice in about one-fourth of 15,000 school districts. Relatively few communities seem to be trying to offer options to every family, notable exceptions being Berkeley, Grand Rapids, and Minneapolis.[25] The authors point out that the alternative of private school attendance had long been possible, but that enrollment in nonpublic schools had dropped to less than 10 percent by 1970; thus, if genuine full-scale choice of alternatives was to become available, it would have to come within the public school system.

Encouragement for alternatives came from a number of influential sources during the 1970s: the Ford Foundation; several national commissions on secondary education; and such state commissions as the Fleischman Commission in New York, the California Commission for Reform of Intermediate and Secondary Education (RISE), the North Central Association; and special efforts on a city-wide basis in Evanston, Houston, Pasadena, and Louisville as well as Berkeley, Philadelphia, Grand Rapids, Minneapolis, and St. Paul.

Stimulated by the critics, by the restlessness of the public, and especially by the unrest of the 1960s on college and high school campuses, the surge to find new ways to capture the interest and attention of disaffected or bored youth found expression in the findings of several national commissions of the 1970s. These included the Panel on Youth of the President's Science Advisory Committee, chaired by James S. Coleman; the National Commission on the Reform of Secondary Education and Task Force '74, headed by B. Frank Brown; and the Office of Education National Panel on High Schools and Adolescent Education, chaired by John Henry Martin.[26]

Bilingual Education

The federal government was also responding to the special interests of particular target groups in society and was thus receptive to the call for alternatives. This was shown not only by the massive programs of the Elementary and Secondary Education Act of 1965, but also in a number of other programs sponsored by special legislation. The Teacher Corps was enacted as a special title of the Higher Education Act of 1965 to encourage colleges and universities to give special preparation to student teachers from disadvantaged areas and who, after training, would instruct students in areas having large concentrations of low-income families. By 1971, 60 percent of Teacher Corps interns had come from nonwhite ethnic minorities, and by 1976 the Teacher Corps was deliberately promoting bilingual and multicultural education, training for alternative school designs, and cultural pluralism.[27]

In 1968 the ESEA was amended in Title VII, creating the Bilingual Education Act to give federal aid to local school districts to enable them to meet the special needs of children of "limited English-speaking ability."[28] The 1970 Census reported about 33 million people (16 percent of the total U.S. population) who spoke a first language other than English. Designed for some three million children from non-English-speaking homes, aged 3 to 18 years, the guidelines to the Bilingual Education Act drawn up in 1967 stressed the need for English instruction:

> The concern is for children in this target group to develop greater competence in English, to become more proficient in the use of two languages, and to profit from increased educational opportunity. . . .

> Bilingual education is instruction in two languages and the use of those
> *two languages* as mediums of instruction for any part or of all of the school
> curriculum. Study of the history and culture associated with a student's
> mother tongue is considered an integral part of *bilingual education.*[29]

Though there has been considerable controversy as to whether the bilingual
education programs should be primarily transitional to better English or
should be designed to maintain a bilingual facility throughout life, the pluralist character of its impact is clear. By the end of 1976 the U.S. Office of
Education estimated that there were federally aided programs in 41 states,
serving 165,000 children in 68 languages (of which 40 were native American,
or Indian, languages).

In 1974 the Supreme Court decided that a school system's failure to
provide special language instruction for children whose mother tongue was
not English denied them equal opportunity to participate in public educational
programs, a violation of the Civil Rights Act of 1964. In San Francisco,
children of Chinese ancestry had brought a class suit to require the public
schools to design special programs for them. In *Lau* v. *Nichols*, Justice
Douglas spoke for the court in finding that California had to take special
affirmative action to enable the Chinese-speaking children to profit from their
school experience; simply providing the same texts and curriculum to all
children was not equality of treatment.[30]

Multicultural Programs

The Supreme Court's action on bilingual education came on the heels
of strong ethnic pressure upon Congress in 1973, which finally passed the
Ethnic Heritage Studies Act. Advocates of the Act repeatedly denounced the
melting-pot themes and argued on the basis of cultural pluralism that the
Congress should promote studies to highlight the strength and desirability of
the variety of ethnic traditions that were preserved in U.S. society and should
be preserved in education. Some of these programs ran into controversial
political opposition, which charged that the program risked the dangers of
ethnic separatism and segregation. In any case, separate ethnic studies for
particular groups seemed to be declining in the mid-1970s in favor of "multicultural studies" that not only would stress the variety and differences of the
pluralist society, but also would seek mutual study and mutual respect among
the several groups. The major professional associations adopted multicultural
education with enthusiasm.

An example of the enthusiastic reception of multicultural education and
of a philosophy of cultural pluralism was the action of the American Association of Colleges for Teacher Education (AACTE), which appointed its
Multicultural Education Commission in February 1971 and officially adopted
its statement entitled "No One Model American" at its Board meeting in
November 1972. The statement indicates its strong attachment to the philoso-

phy of cultural pluralism and urged all institutions of teacher education to promulgate it.[31]

Horace Kallen on Cultural Pluralism

The AACTE statement reveals its obvious desire to promote the values of pluralistic communities, but it makes virtually no reference to the common elements that would bind the different groups together. In this respect, the AACTE and many other enthusiastic adopters of multicultural education had forgotten or ignored a major tenet that Horace Kallen, the father of cultural pluralism, always insisted upon: The fundamental principles of *political* democracy must underlie the diversities of *cultural* pluralism. Kallen had always claimed that it was only upon this foundation that

> the outlines of a possibly great and truly democratic commonwealth become discernible. Its form would be that of the federal republic; its substance a democracy of nationalities, cooperating voluntarily and autonomously through common institutions in the enterprise of self-realization through the perfection of men according to their kind. The common language of the commonwealth, the language of its great tradition, would be English, but each nationality would have for its emotional and involuntary life its own peculiar dialect or speech, its own individual and inevitable esthetic and intellectual forms. The political and economic life of the commonwealth is a single unit and serves as the foundation and background for the realization of the distinctive individuality of each *nation* that composes it and of the pooling of these in a harmony above them all. Thus, "American civilization" may come to mean the perfection of the cooperative harmonies of "European civilization"—the waste, the squalor and the distress of Europe being eliminated—a multiplicilty in a unity, an orchestration of mankind.[32]

When Kallen identified the "common institutions" fundamental to the political commonwealth, he always gave primacy to the public schools. He was opposed to separate schools for separate cultural groups except as supplementary and voluntary additions to the public schools, which he urged all to attend. He opposed the injection of pluralistic religion into the public schools, and he opposed public support for private or ethnic schools. When in 1956 he defined the elements of the "American Bible" which summed up the common creed of all Americans, he included not only the Declaration of Independence, the Constitution, and the great credos of Washington, Jefferson, Madison, Lincoln, Wilson, Holmes, Brandeis, F. D. Roosevelt, Truman, and the Supreme Court on separation of church and state, but also Horace Mann's Twelfth Annual Report to the Massachusetts Board of Education.[33]

Kallen's faith in the political commonwealth of democracy, and in the common public school as a bulwark for the maintenance and flourishing of the cultural pluralisms that must cooperate in its support, could qualify him as an advocate of civism as well as of pluralism. The same could be said of John Dewey. Though it was popular to call upon Dewey as well as Kallen in support of pluralism, as Cremin and Itzkoff and others have done, it is also true that Dewey's *political* philosophy stressed the importance of the meaning of "the public" as the key to the building of a Great Community that would transcend as well as embrace the smaller face-to-face communities so important in nourishing pluralism.

The New Civism

John Dewey on the Meaning of the Public

In the 1920s the excessively individualistic and pluralistic character of U.S. society led John Dewey to be concerned about recapturing the meaning of "the public," just as the nativist drive for assimilation led Horace Kallen to be concerned about revitalizing the meaning of ethnic pluralism. In his lectures at Kenyon College in 1926, just 50 years before the 1976 bicentennial year, Dewey expressed his concern about the search for conditions under which the Great Society could become the Great Community. Modern science, technology, and industrialization had created a Great Society characterized by large-scale associated or joint activity and aggregated collective action, but what was needed was a Great Community that was not simply physical and organic, but which was characterized by a communal life that was morally, emotionally, intellectually, and consciously sustained. No amount of merely aggregated collective action in itself constituted a community. Dewey found the essence of community in the generic social sense of democracy nourished by intelligence and education:

> The clear consciousness of a communal life, in all its implications, constitutes the idea of democracy. . . . Fraternity, liberty and equality isolated from communal life are hopeless abstractions. Their separate assertion leads to mushy sentimentalism or else to extravagant and fanatical violence which in the end defeats its own aims.[34]

Single-minded stress upon individual liberty would end in dissolution or anarchy; singular stress on equality would lead to mechanical identity or mediocrity. The two must be brought together in the dynamic relationship of community. And the means of doing this was to be through the revivifying and vitalizing of an organized, articulate "Public." His meaning of "Public" went something like this: Human acts have consequences upon others; perception of these consequences leads to subsequent effort to control action so as to secure some consequences and not others. Consequences of actions are of two kinds: Those that affect only the persons directly engaged in a transaction are private; those that affect others beyond those immediately concerned are public. The effort to regulate these indirect consequences and care for the welfare of others is the realm of the "Public," that is,

> the line between private and public is to be drawn on the basis of the extent

and scope of the consequences of acts which are so important as to need control, whether by inhibition or by promotion. We distinguish private and public buildings, private and public schools, private paths and public highways, private assets and public funds, private persons and public officials. It is our thesis that in this distinction we find the key to the nature and office of the state. . . . The public consists of all those who are affected by the indirect consequences of transactions to such an extent that it is deemed necessary to have those consequences systematically cared for. Officials are those who look out for and take care of the interests thus affected.[35]

Significantly, Dewey argued that this supervision and regulation of the consequences of actions by individuals and by groups cannot be effected by the primary groups themselves. It is just such consequences that call the public into being. The public organized to conduct these affairs through officials is the state. When the association known as the public takes on the task of regulating the conjoint actions of individuals and groups, the public becomes a political state or political community. And among the major characteristics of a state or political community are not only a temporal or geographic location and organized political institutions like legislatures and courts, but also a special care for children and other dependents who are looked upon as peculiarly its wards:

In the degree, then, that a certain measure of instruction and training is deemed to have significant consequences for the social body, rules are laid down affecting the action of parents in relation to their children, and those who are not parents are taxed—Herbert Spencer to the contrary notwithstanding—to maintain schools.[36]

The Citizen as Officer of the Public / The significance of a representative democracy, in contrast to an autocracy, is that every citizen-voter is an "officer of the public," a representative of the public as much as a senator or a sheriff is. So, every citizen has a dual capacity: as a private person and as an officer of the public. The essential meaning of a representative democracy is to organize its affairs in such a way that the public good dominates the private interest. Herein lies the significance of public schools in contrast to private schools—to develop the "officer of the public" role in all individuals and thus to aid them to enhance their political roles on behalf of the public good:

Rarely can a person sink himself in his political function; the best which most men attain to is the domination by the public weal of their other desires. What is meant by "representative" government is that the public is definitely organized with the intent to secure this dominance. The dual capacity of every officer of the public leads to conflict in individuals between their genuinely political aims and acts and those which they possess in their non-political roles. When the public adopts special measures to see to it that the conflict is minimized and that the representative function overrides the private one, political institutions are termed representative.[37]

Although Dewey assuredly stressed at the end of his book the importance of restoring local communities to vitality after their disintegration caused by the conforming inroads of modernizing technology and industrialization attendant upon the Great Society, he also argued that while the Great Community cannot possess all the qualities of the local community, "It will do its final work in ordering the relations and enriching the experience of local associations."[38]

This concern by Dewey for a search for political community and its application to the role of public schooling was reflected in the recurrent calls for "education for democracy," which infused the thought of social frontiersmen and social reconstructionists from the 1930s to the 1950s. But the mood of democratic social reform and the search for a community of persuasion went out of style among philosophers of education during the late 1950s and early 1960s, as it did among academic philosophers themselves. Meanwhile, calls for political community were expressed in a variety of proposals for reform of civic education in the public schools.

The Civic Role of Public Education

In general, it can be said that the urge to promote or improve the civic role of public education not only accelerated in times of crisis and rapid social change, but also took on special urgency in the minds of two quite different kinds of persons who saw the need for greater cohesion and unity to be particularly acute. There were the liberals, who saw the need to mobilize disparate groups on behalf of pressing new social or political or economic reforms. The reformers of the New Deal, the New Frontier, and the Great Society saw themselves in the role of reformers similar to that in the Revolutionary, Jacksonian, and Progressive eras. Then, there were the conservatives who saw the need for social cohesion to stem the tide of change and to rally the people round their version of the authentic tradition of the American way of life in order to stave off threats from "alien" sources, such as the massive immigration in the early and later nineteenth century, militant radical movements, hot wars, and cold wars. Sometimes the rhetoric of liberals and conservatives sounded remarkably similar, but more often they contended for pride of place as being upholders of the authentic American creed and thus claimed legitimate authority for programs of civic education that would achieve the values of political community as they saw them.

The outpouring of proposals and projects to create more effective civic education programs during the period from 1926 to 1976 would take volumes to relate. The variations of detail are multitudinous, yet there was often a repetitiveness and similarity in the lists of goals and objectives set forth by one commission after another. After the brutal realities and disillusionments of Vietnam and Watergate, some of the earlier statements seem blatantly and grimly superpatriotic, while others exude the bland optimism of a Pollyanna mentality. All that can be done here is to suggest the range of political outlooks that seemed to motivate some of the major approaches to civic education.

In the wake of World War I, citizenship education programs in the schools, the textbooks—and the teachers themselves—were subjected to almost constant campaigns led by conservative civic and patriotic organizations whose views today seem particularly narrow-minded and defensively patriotic in their antiforeign, antipacifist, anti-immigrant, antiradical outlooks. In the 1920s the American Legion led the campaigns to get Congress and the state legislatures to require civic instruction, flag salutes, military training, and loyalty oaths. The dominant mood of civic education in the 1920s was to "rally round the flag," extoll the merits and successes, and say nothing derogatory about the greatest country on earth. Of course other nations were doing the same thing in their programs of civic education, which has been so well documented in the ten volumes produced between 1929 and 1933 under the leadership of Charles E. Merriam, professor of political science at Chicago.[39]

The Social Frontiersmen

In contrast, the 1930s witnessed a social reformist outlook sparked by the economic depression, the New Deal, and the onset of totalitarianism in the world. One of the most impressive examples of educational response was the Commission on the Social Studies of the American Historical Association (AHA), which was funded by the Carnegie Foundation for five years from January 1929 to December 1933, and which issued 17 volumes between 1932 and 1937. The dominant tone of the most widely read volumes (such as those by Charles A. Beard, George S. Counts, Bessie L. Pierce, Jesse H. Newlon, and Merle Curti) was set by the *Conclusions and Recommendations of the Commission* (1934): The age of individualism and laissez-faire in economics and government was closing, and a new collectivism requiring social planning and governmental regulation was emerging.

The marshaled arguments struck notes remarkably familiar to those of the 1970s: deprivation in the midst of plenty, inequality in income, spreading unemployment, wasted natural resources, rising crime and violence, subordination of public welfare to private interest, and international struggle for raw materials. A particular curriculum was not promulgated, but the intention was clear that this view of life and the political/economic framework of reference should guide specific curriculum making for civic education programs. The clear implication was that youth should be inculcated with the values of economic collectivity and interdependence in place of economic individualism, while at the same time promoting personal individualism and cultural freedom.

Like-minded proposals were flooding from the pens of George S. Counts, John Dewey, Harold Rugg, William H. Kilpatrick, John L. Childs,

R. Bruce Raup, and other social frontiersmen at Teachers College and else-where. Take, for example, the spring of 1932. On February 18, George Counts addressed the Progressive Education Association on the theme, "Dare Progressive Education Be Progressive?" Two days later he addressed the National Education Association's National Council on Education on "Free-dom, Culture, Social Planning, and Leadership." Three days after that he addressed the NEA Department of Superintendence on "Education through Indoctrination." By April the three speeches were issued together in printed form, and became perhaps the most widely discussed pamphlet in the history of American education, *Dare the School Build a New Social Order?* Many were impressed by his prophetic and portentous call to the profession:

> In their own lives teachers must bridge the gap between school and society and play some part in the fashioning of those great common purposes which should bind the two together. . . .
> If the schools are to be really effective, they must become the centers for the building, not merely for the contemplation, of our civilization. This does not mean that we should endeavor to promote particular reforms through the educational system. We should, however, give to our children a vision of the possibilities which lie ahead and endeavor to enlist their loyalties and enthusiasms in the realization of the vision. Also, our social institutions and practices, all of them, should be critically examined in the light of such a vision.[40]

Meanwhile, the Commission on the Social Studies in the Schools issued its first official publication in 1932, *A Charter for the Social Sciences in the Schools*, drafted by Charles A. Beard. In 1933 several colleagues at Teachers College (William H. Kilpatrick, John L. Childs, and R. Bruce Raup) joined with others in writing *The Educational Frontier*. Then, in 1934, came Counts' *Social Foundations of Education*, the *Conclusions and Recommendations* of the AHA Commission on the Social Studies, and the first issue of *The Social Frontier*, a magazine whose first editor was Counts. In summing up *The Social Frontier's* editorial stand, Counts explicitly accepted the point of view of the *Conclusions and Recommendations* of the AHA Commission on the Social Studies:

> In a word, for the American people the age of individualism in econ-omy is closing, and an age of collectivism is opening. Here is the central and dominating reality in the present epoch. . . .
> In the years and decades immediately ahead, the American people will be called upon to undertake arduous, hazardous, and crucial tasks of social reconstruction. . . . [making] decisions concerning the incidence of economic and political power, the distribution of wealth and income, the relations of classes, races, and nationalities, and the ends for which men and women are to live. . . . In particular, they must choose whether the great tradition of democracy is to pass away with the individualistic economy to which it has been linked historically or is it to undergo the transformation necessary for survival in an age of close economic interdependence.[41]

This was the nub of the question for Counts and for others: Could the liberal freedoms of cultural and political democracy be maintained and strengthened while at the same time public controls and economic planning were exerted to achieve the close integration required of a modern industrial, technological, and urban-based economy?

The Educational Policies Commission

Naturally, these social frontiersmen set the public and the profession on their ears and elicited vigorous and shrill counterattacks, especially from the major patriotic organizations. While there was much trepidation among major professional organizations, they responded on the whole positively as far as giving renewed attention to civic education was concerned. The National Education Association and the American Association of School Administrators jointly sponsored the Educational Policies Commission in 1935, enlisting Counts' membership along with that of several more conservative administrators. The pronouncements of the Educational Policies Commission softened the economic views of the reconstructionists, but they did emphasize over and over again the need for education for democracy.

In 1938, when *The Purposes of Education in American Democracy* was produced (written by William H. Carr, executive secretary) listing four objectives, "civic responsibility" was retained as the fourth (in addition to self-realization, human relationship, economic efficiency). The stated objectives of civic responsibility do not sound particularly daring today, and there was little emphasis upon liberty or equality or due process, but for all the bland language there was scope for realistic civic studies if teachers or communities had the stomach for them. Among those suggested were:

> Social Justice. The educated citizen is sensitive to the disparities of human circumstance.
> Social Activity. The educated citizen acts to correct unsatisfactory conditions.
> Social Understanding. The educated citizen seeks to understand social structures and social processes.
> Critical Judgment. The educated citizen has defenses against propaganda.
> Tolerance. The educated citizen respects honest differences of opinion.
> Conservation. The educated citizen has a regard for the nation's resources.
> Social Applications of Science. The educated citizen measures scientific advance by its contribution to the general welfare.
> World Citizenship. The educated citizen is a cooperating member of the world community.
> Law Observance. The educated citizen respects the law.
> Economic Literacy. The educated citizen is economically literate.
> Political Citizenship. The educated citizen accepts his civic duties.
> Devotion to Democracy. The educated citizen acts upon an unswerving loyalty to democratic ideals.[42]

The consensual effort to make civic education more realistic, while at the same time *not* embracing the extremes of radical-sounding reconstructionism or reactionary radical baiting, led civic educators to the generally agreed-upon ideals of democracy, as Horace Mann had proposed, and to community activities that would involve students in participation but not controversy. World War II, which intercepted this movement by its emphasis on mobilizing the schools for the war effort, served to reassert the values of patriotism as the basis for political unity.

Following World War II, the idea of special projects in civic education again was revived as a means of mobilizing school systems of cities or states into giving special attention to citizenship education.

The Concept of "Good Citizenship" in the 1950s

In the 1950s, education for good citizenship became an imperative in many school systems all over the country. Its primary objective was to infuse the social studies with the idea and to highlight the fact that the schools were *not* radical and *not* subversive, but were supporting the basic principles of *political* democracy and the basic *economic* values of the free enterprise system. This was a response to the "cold war" crusade against Communism in the world and a kind of defense against the onslaughts of McCarthyism at home. The hope was, obviously, that children could be taught the values of consensus on these matters, reflecting the spirit of accommodation and goodwill epitomized by the Eisenhower presidency.

A general theme was that the schools should develop the knowledge, the attitudes, the problem-solving ability, and the skills of working with others for the general welfare. Furthermore, the conception of citizenship should not be limited to a narrow view of legal relationship to government. Rather, echoing the *Cardinal Principles* of 40 years earlier, social studies teachers were urged to adopt a much broader concept of citizenship education, one that would include "all the mutually helpful social relationships with others which democracy assumes should be characteristic of human life and living." Programs of social studies tended either to adopt some version of the popular core curriculum that mushroomed in the 1950s or to concentrate on specific courses in "problems of democracy," which often drifted off to "problems of democratic living" involving the behavior and psychology of adolescents, their personal problems, marriage and family problems, vocational interests, and personal values. As the social reconstructionists stressed the economic side of civic education, so the broad social conception of citizenship often became so broad and so social that it embraced almost all conceivable aspects of a social studies approach. In the process, it watered down or neglected the basic *political* questions of power, influence, and decision making.

The "New Social Studies" of the 1960s

In the 1960s a curious coincidence of forces tended toward a general relaxation of explicit calls for more and better civic education. Both the "new social studies movement" and the rise of student unrest and activism undercut patriotism as an argument for civic education. Responding to the successes of the "new math" and the "new science"—stimulated by Sputnik and funded so generously by NDEA, the National Science Foundation, and the private foundations—the "new social studies" took on the patterns of the social science disciplines by stressing cognitive analysis, systematic acquisition of sequential and organized knowledge, conceptual analysis, "inquiry learning," "discovery method," and in general, thinking like a social scientist.

It was clear that the revived disciplinary approach to knowledge tended not only to belittle "soft," diffuse, and superficial programs of social studies in the schools, but also to downgrade explicit citizenship education as a proper goal of the school curriculum.

Political scientists were likely to argue that citizens were shaped by the total process of political socialization outside the school. Actually, they contended, democracy (like all big governments) must rest upon the expert knowledge of specialists, which cannot be fathomed by the average citizen, and, besides, political science is a very complicated, intellectual discipline about political behavior, not a set of maxims about good citizenship. Caught in the middle by such disciplinary views at one extreme and by the raucous "non-negotiable" demands for "relevance now" from militant student activists at the other extreme, the traditional programs of civic education seemed pointless, irresolute, and outmoded.

But many of the new curriculum development projects of the late 1960s and early 1970s were more realistic, more sophisticated, more analytical and skeptical, and more attuned to the claims for equality of the unincorporated minorities and their struggles for civil rights than was the civic education of the 1950s. Some of these curriculum projects tried to avoid both the naive, unrealistic, and romanticized image of political life which the schools had often portrayed, as well as the narrow, partisan, one-sided lines that were so commonly favored by conservative or radical groups in the local communities.

In any case, the experiences of the Vietnam War, the campus unrest with its attendant change in values, and the constitutional crisis swirling around the Watergate struggles pointed in two directions: an increased cynicism and alienation with regard to political affairs; and a marked revival of concern for deliberate education in the public schools that would help to bring closer to realization the historic value claims of the democratic political community.

Political Alienation and Lack of Political Knowledge

Almost all the polls and observers since the early 1970s continued to document the decline of respect for the legitimacy and moral authority of the political system. The percentage of voter turnout dropped steadily in each election from 1960 to 1976, when only 53 percent voted and when the proportion was especially low among people under 30, the poor, the less well-educated, and blue-collar workers. It was estimated that two-thirds of those between the ages of 18 and 21 did not vote, and over half of those between 21 and 29 did not vote. Though there was not the massive failure to vote in 1976 that some had predicted, there was nevertheless evident a widespread sense of powerlessness among voters and even more so among nonvoters.[43]

And what of college-age youth? A Yankelovich survey of the changing values of youth published in 1974 found the years from 1967 to 1973 to be a period of startling shifts in values and beliefs that marked the end of one era and the beginning of a new one.[44] What was labeled the "New Values" of a minority of college students in 1967 had spread to the entire youth generation by 1973. The surveyors called attention especially to the trend of "deauthorization"—that is, the marked rise since 1969 in the values assigned to privatism and preoccupation with self—and a corresponding lessening of respect for established institutions as guides for moral behavior and a decline in values assigned to constituted authority, obligation to others, and patriotism. This applied to noncollege youth as well as to college students.

Especially discouraging was the evidence from surveys that high school and college students felt they had little obligation to take part in the political system. Alexander Astin's survey reported in *The Chronicle of Higher Education* for January 13, 1975, revealed an apparent "political withdrawal." Only one-fourth to one-third of college freshmen in 1974 believed that "participating in community action programs," or "keeping up with political affairs," or "influencing social values" was essential or that any of these were very important objectives for them as persons. And only 12 to 15 percent thought that "influencing the political structure" was essential or very important. These were students who entered college only a month after the House Judiciary Committee voted for impeachment and the subsequent resignation of Richard Nixon.

And what of prospective teachers? The Study Commission at the University of Nebraska reported in October 1974 that of all teacher candidates in all subjects, only 2.6 percent felt that it was essential for them to influence the political structure, and 10.8 percent that it was very important to do so.[45] Prospective teachers were only a few percentage points below all undergraduates; and potential secondary school teachers were only slightly higher.

These attitudes should not be particularly surprising to those who had followed the reports of surveys of political knowledge achieved by high school students. The National Assessment of Educational Progress (NAEP) has documented in great detail the status of political knowledge among 13-year-olds and 17-year-olds. The fairly flat conclusion showed by test surveys of citizenship made in 1969–1970 and of social studies in 1971–1972 was that "young Americans lack knowledge of the fundamentals of politics and civil rights."[46] A preliminary report on the second round of achievement tests conducted in the school year 1975–1976 found little cause for encouragement.[47]

One of the most important findings of the NAEP was that the political knowledge (as revealed by tests) of students who were poor or black, who had less well-educated parents, and who lived in inner cities or in rural communities or in the southeastern states, lagged behind the level of achievement in the rest of the country. Put another way, the students from the more affluent communities and educationally advantaged school systems had more knowledge and better prospects of influencing political decisions. Such findings led to renewed efforts to improve the civic role of public schools and especially the civic knowledge disseminated by them. This was stimulated not only by the findings with respect to the *results* of civic education programs, but also by criticism of the teaching, content, and methods of courses in civics and government.

The shortcomings of most civic education in the schools were aptly appraised by the Committee on PreCollegiate Education of the American Political Science Association in 1971:

> [It] transmits a naive, unrealistic, and romanticized image of political life which confuses the ideals of democracy with the realities of politics. . . .
>
> In summary, the majority of civics and government curriculum materials currently in use at all grade levels either completely ignore or inadequately treat not only such traditionally important political science concepts as freedom, sovereignty, consensus, authority, class, compromise, and power but also newer concepts such as role, socialization, culture, system, decision making, etc.[48]

New Approaches to Civic Education in the 1970s

On the positive side, there was in the 1970s an upsurge of efforts to focus the civic instruction of the schools upon problems of civil rights of ethnic minorities, women, and youth, the basic concepts of law and justice, the Constitution and Bill of Rights, and the moral and civic values appropriate to a democratic political community. The scope and variety of the new civic education approaches are analyzed in a 1977 report of the National Task Force on Citizenship Education under the aegis of the Danforth Foundation and the Kettering Foundation.[49]

Law-related Education / Two aspects of the renewal of interest in civic education for political community seemed especially promising. In the 1970s, projects classified as "law-related education" began snowballing under the assiduous sponsorship of several new organizations and old foundations that were encouraging the joint efforts of social science scholars, practicing teachers, and representatives of the legal, justice, and education professions. Several of these projects are described in a 1975 publication of the Constitutional Rights Foundations. Norman Gross and Charles White, staff members of the Special Committee on Youth Education for Citizenship of the American Bar Association, summarize the rapid development as follows:

In 1971, statewide programs were being organized or were under headway in only six states. Now [1975], 26 states have at least incipient statewide projects. In 1971, no more than 150 law-related education projects were active in the schools. Today, there are almost 400. In 1971, only seven summer teacher-training institutes were held. Last summer, 26 such institutes were offered. . . .

Curriculum materials have multiplied dramatically in the past decade . . . 500 books and pamphlets suitable for classroom use . . . 400 films, filmstrips, and tapes.[50]

Especially impressive is the project on Law in a Free Society, conducted under the direction of Charles Quigley in Santa Monica, California. This includes lesson plans, case books, course outlines, and teachers' guides and multimedia instructional materials covering eight basic concepts that should pervade a comprehensive curriculum in civic education from kindergarten through the twelfth grade. Four concepts stress civism (authority, justice, participation, and responsibility), and four stress pluralism (freedom, privacy, diversity, and property). The project claims that these are the fundamental ideas necessary for the understanding of a free polity and should be the core of study in civic education. Such concepts could fruitfully bring to life the values, the knowledge, and the practice in real-life experiences that must go together in an efficacious civic education.

Education for Moral Development / Another pedagogical movement that gained widespread attention among professionals as well as the public relates to a renewed interest in the "teaching of values." Of special significance for civic education is the work pioneered by Lawrence Kohlberg at Harvard and applied to civic education programs in schools in Cambridge and Brookline, Massachusetts under the direction of Kohlberg and Ralph Mosher of Boston University; and in the Pittsburgh area under the direction of Edwin Fenton of Carnegie-Mellon.[51] The work, based on a theory of six stages of moral/cognitive development, caused considerable stir in psychological and philosophical as well as educational circles.

In the first two stages of the Kohlberg theory, people are found to think and act on the traditional bases of fear of punishment, desire for reward, or exchange of favors. In the middle two stages, they think and act on the conventional bases devoted to maintaining the political and social order by meeting the expectations held out for them or duties imposed upon them by authorities for the sake of the good of the order. In the upper two stages, people think and act on the basis of moral principles genuinely accepted by the individual rather than on the basis of simply conforming to the authority of the group. Stage 5 is the level of the social contract and human rights (for example, the Declaration of Independence and the U.S. Constitution); and stage 6 is based upon universal ethical principles pertaining to liberty, equality, and justice. The Kohlberg theory and experimentation over several years postulate that the most effective teaching of values can be undertaken by direct confrontation of moral decisions in open discussions between teachers and students; and that such a process, conducted in the school setting of a just community, will move students from the lower levels to the higher stages of development.

The Kohlberg approach also means that if the vast *majority* of American youths are ever to reach the higher stages, then a civic education should include the deliberate effort to develop a civic morality among all elementary and high school students—not simply "clarifying one's values," not simply acquiring a breadth of political knowledge, not simply acquaintance with the history and structure of government in the past. If the United States is to continue to have mass elementary and secondary education devoted to a democratic political community, there should be a common civic core to it, and the schools should give priority to their civic task.

What Underpinnings for Public Education in the Future?

It was clear that didactic moral instruction and outward expressions of patriotism through pledges of allegiance, loyalty oaths, or flag salutes had lost their *raison d'être* among academics. The danger of attempts to use the schools for self-serving patriotism, manipulative propaganda, or partisan politicization was well known. Yet civicists like Robert M. Hutchins argued that the schools must promote, somehow, a strengthened sense of the importance of civic morality and political integrity—a revitalized civism devoted to the political values of constitutional self-government.[52] It also became evident to civic-minded public school educators that a revival of an appropriate civic role for public education was inevitably linked with the vitality of the public schools themselves as a major force in American life.[53] Could they serve the values of the political community devoted to freedom, and equality, and justice, and still serve the values of the several pluralistic communities? Could they serve such values if weakened and diminished? Had that constant drumbeat of attack upon the idea as well as the practices of public schools so undermined faith in them that they could not be a vital force in revitalizing the very future of the liberal democratic political institutions which had nurtured them and which they had originally been designed to serve? In the mid-1970s, the evidence was ambiguous.

Whether the search for public education's role in achieving civic community could be made compatible with the search for pluralistic communities was one of the major questions as the third century of the Republic began. Much depended upon the realities of the political process undertaken in dozens of states and hundreds of school districts as well as in the Congress and the federal courts. But, in the long run, it also depended upon the leadership of the profession in its relationships with the public. Here the contrast was remarkable. The child-centered school of the Progressive era was alive and well in the profession's preoccupation with personalized learning, individualized instruction, and alternatives, while parents clamored for "back to the basics." Neither seemed to pay much attention to the need for a new civism. The judgment of many observers was that the lesson of Watergate called for the reassertion of the moral authority and leadership of educators imbued with a sense of civic community and justice. Such views sprang on the one hand from the deepest aspirations of many in the pluralisitc minorities, and on the other hand from one of the most sophisticated moral philosophies of the day. I note just two examples, one from politics and one from philosophy.

Barbara Jordan on a National Community / When Barbara Jordan, a black woman, was chosen in July 1976 to be the keynote speaker at the Democratic National Convention, what was her message?

> A nation is formed by the willingness of each of us to share in the responsibility for upholding the common good. . . .
> Let there be no illusions about the difficulty of forming this national Community. A spirit of harmony can only survive if each of us remembers, when bitterness and self-interest seem to prevail, that we share a common destiny.
> I have confidence that we can form a national community.[54]

John Rawls on a Public Sense of Justice / And what philosophical rationale might undergird such a national community? John Rawls, moral philosopher at Harvard, argues that it is a *public sense of justice* that produces a well-ordered society in which everyone accepts and knows that the others accept the same principles of justice. This means that the members of a well-ordered society should have a strong and normally effective desire to act as the principles of justice require. In response to the diversity of the pluralists' many communities, Rawls finds that it is only through a shared sense of justice that they can satisfactorily live together in political community:

> If men's inclination to self-interest makes their vigilance against one another necessary, their public sense of justice makes their secure association together possible. Among individuals with disparate aims and purposes a shared conception of justice establishes the bonds of civic friendship; the general desire for justice limits the pursuit of other ends. One may think of a public conception of justice as constituting the fundamental charter of a well-ordered human association.[55]

What a public sense of justice does is to establish the claims of what is *right* as prior to the claims of what is *good*, as defined by different individuals and different groups as they formulate their plans of life which promise to satisfy their particular rational desires. The principles of what is *right* and what is *just* put limits and impose restrictions on what are the reasonable conceptions of one's good as it is may affect others. A just social system defines the boundaries within which individuals and pluralistic communities must develop their aims and desires. Rawls defines two principles of justice that determine these boundaries, and it is to be noted that the first principle has prior importance over the second in that it *must* be satisfied before moving on to the second. The first principle of justice is the principle of equal liberties of citizenship. The second has to do with the regulation of social and economic advantages on behalf of equality.

The first principle is stated as follows:

> Each person is to have an equal right to the most extensive total system of equal basic liberties compatible with a similar system of liberty for all.[56]

What are the equal liberties of citizenship? They bear close resemblance to the American constitutional order based upon the Bill of Rights:

> The basic liberties of citizens are, roughly speaking, political liberty (the right to vote and to be eligible for public office) together with freedom of speech and assembly; liberty of conscience and freedom of thought; freedom of the person along with the right to hold (personal) property; and freedom from arbitrary arrest and seizure as defined by the concept of the rule of law. These liberties are all required to be equal by the first principle, since citizens of a just society are to have the same basic rights.[57]

After the citizenship principle of equal political liberties is satisfied, then the second principle of justice may be activated:

> Social and economic inequalities are to be arranged so that they are both:
> (a) to the greatest benefit of the least advantaged. . . . and
> (b) attached to offices and positions open to all under conditions of fair equality of opportunity.[58]

Once the *political* principle of justice is satisfied, then a just society will move on to distribute income and wealth equitably, and to satisfy a design of organization that makes use of differences in authority and responsibility:

> While the distribution of wealth and income need not be equal, it must be to everyone's advantage, and at the same time, positions of authority and offices of command must be accessible to all. One applies the second principle by holding positions open, and then, subject to this constraint, arranges social and economic inequalities so that everyone benefits.[59]

The total position elaborated in great detail by Rawls cannot even be hinted at here, and it has been powerfully criticized by some philosophers and social scientists. Nevertheless, it is clear that his position points to the priority of the common civic community based upon the citizenship principle of justice as the prime authority for public education. This is in extreme contrast to the pluralistic views of a Nozick or a Nisbet. Like Nisbet and Nozick, however, Rawls has not elaborated a full-scale philosophy of education based upon his underlying political and moral philosophy, as Dewey did. This remains for the philosophers of education to do if they decide to turn once again to restore a profound political and moral base for public education. It was already clear by 1976 that there was some affinity between Rawls' view and that of Kohlberg, and Kohlberg claimed to be in the tradition of Dewey. But the search for a comprehensive role for public education in civic community was still open-ended.

It might just be that recapturing a sense of legitimacy and of moral authority for public education might rest upon the success with which the educational profession could make effective what so many of the American people had hoped from it for two hundred years—a priority in purpose for the vigorous promotion of the basic values of the American civic community: liberty *and* equality *and* justice. It might just be, too, that not only was the fuure of public education at stake, but also the existence of the democratic political community itself.

Notes

1. Robert H. Wiebe, *The Segmented Society* (New York: Oxford, 1975), pp. 8–9 and 168 ff.
2. Nathan Glazer, *Affirmative Discrimination* (New York: Basic Books, 1975), pp. 12–20.
3. John Higham, "Another American Dilemma," *The Center Magazine,* July/August 1974, 7(4):67–74.
4. Though not found very often in current usage, I derive the word "civicist" from civics (the study of government) as "physicist" is derived from "physics." In fact, however, the words "civism," "civicism," and "citizenism" are perfectly good but seldom used English words, included in both Webster's unabridged dictionary (second and third editions) and the Oxford English Dictionary. "Civism" is taken from the French *civisme* (taken in turn from the Latin *civis*, meaning "citizen") which the French coined to refer to the devotion or well-affected disposition toward the new nation they established in their own Revolution of 1789. According to the Oxford English Dictionary, the word "civism" refers generally to the "citizen principle" as envisioned in the ancient Greek and Roman republics, especially imputing the tradition of self-sacrifice for the public good. It came, then, by extension to mean in general the "principles of good citizenship in a republic." Civism connotes the need for building a sense of cohesion that will bind citizens together into a viable political community. "Civicism" is defined in *Webster's (Second) New International Dictionary of the English Language* as "principles of civil government" and "devotion, adherence, or conformity, to civic principles or to the duties and rights belonging to civic government." "Civicism" in Webster's Third Edition is "devotion to civic interests and causes: civic-mindedness." "Civism" in both editions is: "the virtues and sentiments of a good citizen."
5. See Michael Novak, *The Rise of the Unmeltable Ethnics* (New York:

Macmillan, 1972); Nathan Glazer and Daniel Patrick Moynihan, *Beyond the Melting Pot* (Cambridge, Mass.: M.I.T. Press, 1963); Lawrence H. Fuchs, ed., *American Ethnic Politics* (New York: Harper & Row, 1968); Edgar Litt, *Ethnic Politics in America* (Glenview, Ill.: Scott Foresman, 1970); Andrew M. Greeley, *Why Can't They Be Like Us?* (New York: American Jewish Committee, 1968); Andrew M. Greeley, *The American Catholic: A Social Portrait* (New York: Basic Books, 1977); Peter Schrag, *The Decline of the WASP* (New York: Simon & Schuster, 1971); and William M. Newmann, *American Pluralism: A Study of Minority Groups and Social Theory* (New York: Harper & Row, 1973).

6. Michael Novak, "The New Ethnicity," *The Center Magazine*, July/August, 1974, pp. 18–19.
7. Novak, p. 25.
8. Andrew M. Greeley, "The Ethnic Miracle," *The Public Interest*, Fall 1976, no. 45.
9. Greeley, *The American Catholic.*
10. Greeley, "The Ethnic Miracle," p. 29.
11. Robert Nisbet, *Twilight of Authority* (New York: Oxford, 1975), pp. 3–5.
12. Nisbet, p. 278.
13. Nisbet, p. 286.
14. See Bibliographical Notes (p. 401) for some of the major works. For a thoroughgoing criticism of the radical view, see Diane Ravitch, "The Revisionists Revised: Studies in the Historiography of American Education," *Proceedings of the National Academy of Education*, 1977, 4:1–84.
15. Michael B. Katz, *Class, Bureaucracy, and Schools* (New York: Praeger, 1971), Chap. 3; and Joel Spring, *A Primer of Libertarian Education* (New York: Free Life Editions, 1975).
16. Henry J. Perkinson, *Two Hundred Years of American Educational Thought* (New York: McKay, 1976), pp. 282–352.
17. Perkinson, p. 291.
18. Alan Graubard, "But Is It Interesting?" *The Review of Education*, May 1975, 1(2):168.
19. Perkinson, pp. 307–308. For an excellent brief bibliography of the major writings of the romantic critics, see pp. 310–312.
20. Seymour Itzkoff, *A New Public Education* (New York: McKay, 1976), pp. 333–334.
21. Itzkoff, p. 356.
22. Theodore Ryland Sizer, "Education and Assimilation: A Fresh Plea for Pluralism," *Phi Delta Kappan*, September 1976, p. 34.
23. Sizer, p. 34.
24. Vernon Smith, Robert Barr, and Daniel Burke, *Alternatives in Education* (Bloomington, Ind.: Phi Delta Kappa, 1976).
25. Smith et al., p. 23.
26. Panel on Youth of the President's Science Advisory Committee, *Youth: Transition to Adulthood* (Chicago: University of Chicago Press, 1974); National Commission on the Reform of Secondary Education, *The Re-*

form of Secondary Education (New York: McGraw-Hill, 1973); Task Force '74, *The Adolescent, Other Citizens and Their High Schools* (New York: McGraw-Hill, 1975); and National Panel on High Schools and Adolescent Education (Washington, D.C.: Government Printing Office, 1976); and National Association of Secondary School Principals, *Secondary Schools in a Changing Society: This We Believe* (Reston, Va.: NASSP, 1975).

27. *Ten Years of Teacher Corps, 1966–1976* (Los Angeles: University of Southern California); and special issue of *Journal of Teacher Education*, Summer 1975, 26(2).

28. Theodore Andersson and Mildred Boyer, *Bilingual Schooling in the United States*, 2 vols. (Washington, D.C.: Government Printing Office, 1970), Vol. II, p. 1; see also Francesco Cordasco, *Bilingual Schooling in the United States: A Sourcebook for Educational Personnel* (New York: McGraw-Hill, 1976).

29. Andersson and Boyer, p. 8.

30. *Lau v. Nichols*, 94 S. Ct. 786 (1974).

31. William A. Hunter, ed., *Multicultural Education Through Competency-Based Teacher Education* (Washington, D.C.: American Association of Colleges for Teacher Education, 1974), pp. 21–23.

32. Horace M. Kallen, *Culture and Democracy in the United States* (New York: Boni and Liveright, 1924), p. 124.

33. Horace M. Kallen, *Cultural Pluralism and the American Idea: An Essay in Social Philosophy* (Philadelphia: University of Pennsylvania Press, 1956), p. 87.

34. John Dewey, *The Public and Its Problems* (New York: Henry Holt, 1927). (Swallow Press, 1954, p. 149). Quotations by permission of the Center for Dewey Studies, Southern Illinois University at Carbondale.

35. Dewey, pp. 15–16.

36. Dewey, p. 63.

37. Dewey, pp. 76–77.

38. Dewey, p. 211.

39. George Z. F. Bereday, ed., *Charles E. Merriam's The Making of Citizens* (New York: Teachers College Press, 1966), Bessie L. Pierce, *Civic Attitudes in American School Textbooks* (Chicago: University of Chicago Press, 1930); Charles E. Merriam, *Civic Education in the United States* (New York. Scribners, 1934).

40. George S. Counts, *Dare the School Build a New Social Order?* (New York: John Day, 1932), pp. 31 and 37. (Reprint edition by Arno Press, 1969).

41. *The Social Frontier*, October 1934, pp. 4–5.

42. Educational Policies Commission, *The Purposes of Education in American Democracy* (Washington, D.C.: National Education Association and American Association of School Administrators, 1938), p. 108.

43. Report of a poll by the *New York Times* and CBS in the *Times*, November 16, 1976.

44. Daniel Yankelovich, *The New Morality: A Profile of American Youth in the Seventies* (New York: McGraw-Hill, 1974).

45. Study Commission on Undergraduate Education and the Education of

Teachers, Nebraska Curriculum Development Center (Lincoln: University of Nebraska, October 1974).

46. Education Commission of the States, *National Assessment Achievements; Findings, Interpretations and Uses*, Report #48, Denver, Col., June 1974, p. 1. See also NAEP *Newsletter*, December 1973 and January–February 1974. Details are contained in NAEP Report 03-55-01, *Political Knowledge and Attitudes*, December 1973.

47. Announcement by National Assessment of Educational Progress, reported in *The New York Times*, January 2, 1977.

48. "Political Education in the Public Schools: The Challenge for Political Science," *PS*, Newsletter of the American Political Science Association, Summer 1971, 4(3).

49. See National Task Force on Citizenship Education, *Education for Responsible Citizenship* (New York: McGraw-Hill, 1977).

50. Law, Education and Participation. *Education for Law and Justice: Whose Responsibility? A Call for National Action* (Los Angeles: Constitutional Rights Foundation, 1975), pp. 46–48; see also American Bar Association, Special Committee on Youth Education for Citizenship, *Law-Related Education in America: Guidelines for the Future* (St. Paul, Minn.: West Publishing Company, 1975).

51. See Edwin Fenton, ed., "Cognitive-Developmental Approach to Moral Education," *Social Education*, April 1976, 40(4).

52. Robert M. Hutchins, "The Schools Must Stay," *The Center Magazine*, January/February 1973, 6(1).

53. See, for example: R. Freeman Butts, "The Search for Purpose in American Education," *College Board Review*, no. 98, Winter 1975–76, pp. 3–19; "Once Again the Question for Liberal Public Educators: Whose Twilight?" *Phi Delta Kappa*, September 1976, pp. 4–14; "The Public School: Assaults on a Great Idea," *The Nation*, April 30, 1973, pp. 553–560; "Foundations of Education and the New Civism," *Educational Studies*, Fall/Winter, 1976; "Public Education and Political Community," *History of Education Quarterly*, Summer 1974, 14(2), pp. 165–183; "The Public Purpose of the Public School," *Teachers College Record*, December 1973, 75(2), pp. 207–221; "Public Education in a Pluralistic Society," *Educational Theory*, Winter 1977, 27(1).

54. *New York Times*, July 15, 1976.

55. John Rawls, *A Theory of Justice* (Cambridge, Mass.: Harvard University Press, 1971), p. 5. For criticisms of Rawls, see Robert Nozick, *Anarchy, State and Utopia* (New York: Basic Books, 1974); and William R. Torbert, "Doing Rawls Justice," *Harvard Educational Review*, November 1974, 44(4).

56. Rawls, p. 302.

57. Rawls, p. 61.

58. Rawls, p. 302.

59. Rawls, p. 61.

Bibliographical Notes On Recommended Reading

In the notes that follow I have not tried to compile a reference bibliography addressed to the research scholar in the history of American education. Neither do they summarize the books or articles cited in support of the arguments or quotations in the text. Instead, I have tried to provide suggestions that will encourage the interested reader to delve further into the substance or interpretation of the major themes dealt with in this book. I have therefore concentrated on listing books (and a few periodical articles) that are likely to be widely available in college, university, or general libraries. Extensive references to primary sources or to the monographic, periodical, unpublished, or textbook literature have not been included. Rather, I have concentrated on serious works of scholarship which themselves are based upon primary sources and which present readable and sometimes provocative interpretations of the history of public education in the United States.

The reader who wishes to probe more deeply into the issues raised in this book may do so in a number of ways in addition to pursuing the references cited at the end of each chapter. There are, for example, several recent volumes that seek to cover the entire period of American educational history; there are several excellent books of readings containing collections of documents and selections from primary sources; and there are the articles and books that focus on the historiographical debates of the past decade or so.

General Surveys

The most complete and scholarly history of American education by a single author is the three-volume study by Lawrence A. Cremin. Volume I, *American Education: The Colonial Experience, 1607–1783*, was published in 1970 by Harper & Row. Volume II will be *The National Experience, 1783–1876*; Volume III will be *The Metropolitan Experience, 1876–1976*.

Recent one-volume surveys of American education by single authors represent a wide range of outlooks and attitudes toward the past performance of public education. The most positive and enthusiastic is that of Fred M. and Grace Hechinger, *Growing Up in America* (New York: McGraw-Hill, 1975).

Among the more moderate but yet critical volumes are: David B. Tyack, *The One Best System: A History of American Urban Education* (Cambridge, Mass.: Harvard University Press, 1974); Alexander Rippa, *Education in a Free Society: An American History* (New York: McKay, 1967); and Robert L. Church, *Education in the United States: An Interpretive History* (New York. Free Press, 1976).

The least positive and most critical books are Clarence J. Karier, *Man, Society, and Education: A History of American Educational Ideas* (Glenview, Ill.: Scott, Foresman, 1967); and Henry J. Perkinson, *The Imperfect Panacea: American Faith in Education, 1865–1965* (New York: Random House, 1968).

Books of Readings

The most extensive recent collection of readings in the history of American education is contained in the five volumes by Sol Cohen, Ed., *Education in the United States: A Documentary History* (New York. Random House, 1974). More useful for the themes in this book are the three volumes (in five books) by Robert H. Bremner, Ed., *Children and Youth in America: A Documentary History, Volume I: 1600–1865; Volume II: 1866–1932;* and *Volume III: 1933–1973* (Cambridge, Mass.: Harvard University Press), vol. I, 1970; vol. II, 1971; vol. III, 1974).

The most rewarding of the recent single-volume books of readings for pursuing the themes of public education are: John Hardin Best and Robert T. Sidewell, Eds., *The American Legacy of Learning: Readings in the History of Education* (Philadelphia: Lippincott, 1967); David B. Tyack, Ed., *Turning Points in American Educational History* (Waltham, Mass.: Blaisdell, 1967); Daniel Calhoun, Ed., *The Educating of Americans: A Documentary History* (Boston: Houghton Mifflin, 1969); Rush Welter, Ed., *American Writings on Popular Education: The Nineteenth Century* (Indianapolis: Bobbs-Merrill, 1971); S. Alexander Rippa, Ed., *Educational Ideas in America: A Documentary History* (New York: McKay, 1969); Henry J. Perkinson, *Two Hundred Years of American Educational Thought* (New York: McKay, 1976); and Theodore Rawson Crane, Ed., *The Dimensions of American Education* (Reading, Mass.: Addison-Wesley, 1974).

Collections of readings designed to illustrate radical revisionism in the history of American education are: Michael B. Katz, Ed., *School Reform: Past and Present* (Boston: Little, Brown, 1971); Michael B. Katz, Ed., *Education in American History; Readings on the Social Issues* (New York: Praeger, 1973); and Clarence J. Karier, Ed., *Shaping the American Educational State: 1900 to the Present* (New York: Free Press, 1975).

Revisionism and Historiography

Though seldom recognized as such, one of the earliest revisionist attempts to relate the history of education to social, cultural, and intellectual history of the United States was R. Freeman Butts and Lawrence A. Cremin, *A History of Education in American Culture* (New York: Holt, Rinehart and Winston 1953). It is still a useful one-volume survey up to the early 1950s. The more commonly accepted view is that cultural revisionism began with Bernard Bailyn's *Education in the Forming of American Society* (Chapel Hill: University of North Carolina Press, 1960), followed by Lawrence A. Cremin's *The Wonderful World of Ellwood Patterson Cubberley: An Essay on the Historiography of American Education* (New York: Teachers College Press, 1965).

Those interested in the details of historical research and revisionism since the mid-1960s may do so in successive issues of *The Review of Educational Research:* articles by Paul Nash in February 1964, vol. 34; by Charles Burgess, February 1967, in vol. 37; and by Mark Beach, in December 1969, vol. 39. Other summaries of interest were made by David B. Tyack, "New Perspectives on the History of American Education," in Herbert J. Bass, Ed., *The State of American History* (Chicago: Quadrangle Books, 1970); John Talbott, "The History of Education," *Daedalus*, Winter 1971, 100(1); Sol Cohen, "New Perspectives in the

History of American Education, 1960–1970," *History of Education* (England), January 1973, 2(1); Douglas Sloan, "Historiography and the History of Education," in Fred M. Kerlinger, Ed., *Review of Research in Education*, I (Itasca, Ill.: Peacock, 1973); and Geraldine Joncich Clifford in *Review of Research in Education*, III (Itasca, Ill.: Peacock, 1975); Carl F. Kaestle, "Conflict and Consensus Revisited: Notes Toward a Reinterpretation of American Educational History," *Harvard Educational Review*, August 1976, 46(3); and Lawrence A. Cremin, *Traditions of American Education* (New York: Basic Books, 1977).

A recent guide to "doing history of education" contains several essays by different authors and interpretations by the editors: Robert R. Sherman and Joseph Kirschner, Eds., *Understanding History of Education* (Cambridge, Mass.: Schenkman, 1976). Extensive annotated and classified bibliographies are contained in Joe Park, *The Rise of American Education: An Annotated Bibliography* (Evanston, Ill.. Northwestern University Press, 1965); and Francis Cordasco and William W. Brickman, *A Bibliography of American Educational History* (New York: AMS Press, 1975). See especially Donald R. Warren, Ed., *History, Education and Public Policy* (Berkeley, Calif.: McCutchan, in press, 1978) for a collection of conflicting views.

Radical Revisionism

The most enlivening aspect of the past decade in the history of American education has swirled around the rise of radical revisionism and the critical attacks upon it. These debates can be followed in the pages of *The History of Education Quarterly*, the *Harvard Educational Review, The Review of Education, Educational Studies*, and *The Teachers College Record* since the late 1960s. It is generally acknowledged that the radical revisionist trend was initiated by Michael B. Katz, *The Irony of Early School Reform: Educational Innovation in Mid-Nineteenth Century Massachusetts* (Cambridge, Mass.: Harvard University Press, 1968). This was followed in rapid-fire order by Marvin Lazerson, *Origins of the Urban School: Public Education in Massachusetts, 1870–1915* (Cambridge, Mass.: Harvard University Press, 1971); Michael B. Katz, *Class, Bureaucracy, and the Schools: The Illusion of Educational Change in America* (New York: Praeger, 1971; expanded edition, 1975); Colin Greer, *The Great School Legend: A Revisionist Interpretation of American Public Education* (New York: Basic Books, 1972); Clarence J. Karier, Paul Violas, and Joel Spring, *Roots of Crisis: American Education in the Twentieth Century* (Chicago: Rand, McNally, 1973); Martin Carnoy, *Education as Cultural Imperialism* (New York: McKay, 1974); Walter Feinberg, *Reason and Rhetoric: The Intellectual Foundations of 20th-Century Liberal Educational Policy* (New York: Wiley, 1975); Joel Spring, *The Sorting Machine; National Educational Policy Since 1945* (New York: McKay, 1976); Samuel Bowles and Herbert Gintis, *Schooling in Capitalist America: Educational Reform and the Contradictions of Economic Life* (New York: Basic Books, 1976).

Critiques of the radical revisionist reviews grew in number and effect from 1974 onward. See, for example, R. Freeman Butts, "Public Education and Political Community," *History of Education Quarterly*, Summer 1974, 14(2); Wayne J. Urban, "Some Historiographical Problems in Revisionist Educational History," *American Educational Research Journal*, Summer 1975, 12(3); Rush Welter,

"Reason, Rhetoric, and Reality in American Educational History," *The Review of Education*, January/February 1976; book reviews by Charles Tesconi and Diane Ravitch in *Teachers College Record*, February 1977, 78(3); several articles in a special issue, "Education and History," *Harvard Educational Review*, August 1976, 46(3); R. Freeman Butts, "Once Again the Question for Liberal Public Education: Whose Twilight?" *The Phi Delta Kappan*, September 1976; Allan Horlick's review of Bowles and Gintis in *The Review of Education*, May/June 1977, 3(3); and Floyd Morgan Hammack, "Rethinking Revisionism," *History of Education Quarterly*, Spring 1976, 16(1). A full-scale critical analysis of ten revisionist books should be read by all who are interested in the debates: Diane Ravitch, "The Revisionists Revised: Studies in the Historiography of American Education," *Proceedings of the National Academy of Education*, 1977, (4).

Part I

The Promise of the American Revolution
(1776–1826)

chapter 1
The Formation of Political Community

One of the best ways to prepare for understanding the original meaning and purpose of public education in the United States is to gain insight into the meaning of the American Revolution and its aftermath. An excellent introduction is contained in Bernard Bailyn, David Brion, David Herbert, John L. Davis, Robert Wiebe, and Gordon Wood, *The Great Republic: A History of the American People* (Boston: Little, Brown, 1977), written by six of the foremost American historians, each a specialist in a particular period but each focusing on two persistent themes that unify the book: the constant testing of free political institutions in the United States and the tension between majority rule and minority rights. In part I, Bernard Bailyn deals with "Shaping the Republic" (to 1760); in part II, Gordon Wood deals with "Framing the Republic" (1760–1820).

For those who wish to go further into the formation of political community in the Revolutionary era, the following books have been seminal: Bernard Bailyn, *The Ideological Origins of the American Revolution* (Cambridge, Mass.: Harvard University Press, 1967); Gordon S. Wood, *The Creation of the American Republic, 1776–1787* (Chapel Hill: University of North Carolina Press, 1969); Stephen G. Kurtz and James H. Hutson, Eds., *Essays on the American Revolution* (Chapel Hill: University of North Carolina Press, 1973); Ralph Ketcham, *From Colony to Country: The Revolution in American Thought, 1750–1820* (New York: Macmillan, 1974); David Hackett Fischer, *The Revolution of American Conservatism: The Federalist Party in the Era of Jeffersonian Democracy* (New York: Harper &

Row, 1965); Clinton Rossiter, *The American Quest, 1790–1860: An Emerging Nation in Search of Identity, Unity, and Modernity* (New York: Harcourt Brace Jovanovich, 1971); and Richard C. Wade, *The Urban Frontier, 1790–1830* (Cambridge, Mass.: Harvard University Press, 1959).

The greatest failure of the Revolutionary promise of political community was the acceptance of the ideology and institution of black slavery. Several recent studies have probed deeply into this paradox: Winthrop D. Jordan, *White Over Black: American Attitudes Toward the Negro, 1550–1812* (Baltimore: Penguin, 1968); David Brion Davis, *The Problem of Slavery in the Age of Revolution, 1770–1823* (Ithaca, N.Y.: Cornell University Press, 1975); Eugene D. Genovese, *Roll, Jordan, Roll: The World the Slaves Made* (New York: Pantheon, 1972); Duncan J. McLeod, *Slavery, Race and the American Revolution* (New York: Cambridge University Press, 1974); Ira Berlin, *Slaves Without Masters; The Free Negro in the Antebellum South* (New York: Pantheon Books, 1974); Leon F. Litwack, *North of Slavery: The Negro in the Free States, 1790–1860* (Chicago: University of Chicago Press, 1961); and Thomas D. Morris, *Free Men All: The Personal Liberty Laws of the North, 1780–1861* (Baltimore: Johns Hopkins Press, 1974).

chapter 2
The Educational Dream: Unum

Excellent collections of early writings about education in the Revolutionary and post-Revolutionary era are contained in Frederick Rudolph, Ed., *Essays on Education in the Early Republic* (Cambridge, Mass.: Belknap Press, 1965); and Wilson Smith, Ed., *Theories of Education in Early America, 1655–1819* (Indianapolis, Ind.: Bobbs-Merrill, 1973). Jefferson's writings on education are quoted and interpreted in Gordon C. Lee, Ed., *Crusade Against Ignorance: Thomas Jefferson on Education* (New York: Teachers College, Columbia University, 1961); and Roy J. Honeywell, Ed., *The Educational Work of Thomas Jefferson* (Cambridge, Mass.: Harvard University Press, 1931).

A variety of interesting interpretive studies is represented in the following: David Tyack, "Forming the National Character; Paradox in the Educational Thought of the Revolutionary Generation," *Harvard Educational Review*, 1966, 36(1); Rush Welter, *Popular Education and Democratic Thought in America* (New York: Columbia University Press, 1962); Alice Tyler, *Freedom's Ferment: Phases of America's Social History from the Colonial Period to the Outcome of the Civil War* (New York: Harper Torchbook, 1962); Maxine Greene, *The Public School and the Private Vision: A Search for America in Education and Literature* (New York: Random House, 1965); Merle Curti, *The Social Ideas of American Educators*, c. 1935 (Totowa, N.J.: Littlefield, Adams, 1966); Jonathan Messerli, "The Columbian Complex: The Impulse to National Consolidation," *History of Education Quarterly*, Winter 1967, 7.

Two short Phi Delta Kappa "fastbacks" deal with this period: Abraham Blinderman, *Three Early Champions of Education: Benjamin Franklin, Benjamin Rush, and Noah Webster* (Bloomington, Ind.: Phi Delta Kappa, 1976) no. 74; and Jennings Waggoner, Jr., *Thomas Jefferson and the Education of a New Nation* (Bloomington, Ind.: Phi Delta Kappa, 1976), no. 73.

chapter 3
The Educational Reality: Pluribus

The role of religion in the transition from private education to political community and public education was one of the knottiest problems of the postrevolutionary era. Various facets are treated in R. Freeman Butts, *The American Tradition in Religion and Education* (Boston: Beacon, 1950); Timothy L. Smith, "Protestant Schooling and American Nationality, 1800–1850," *The Journal of American History*, March 1967, 53(4); Robert M. Healey, *Jefferson on Religion and Public Education* (New Haven, Conn.: Yale University Press, 1962); Herbert M. Kliebard, Ed., *Religion and Education in America: A Documentary History* (Scranton, Pa:. International Textbook, 1969); Vincent P. Lannie, *Public Money and Parochial Education* (Cleveland, Ohio: Case Western Reserve University Press, 1968); and Donald G. Mathews, "The Second Great Awakening as an Organizing Process, 1780–1830: An Hypothesis," *American Quarterly*, 1969, 21.

Three probing studies of the transition from private to public education in America's rapidly growing and major cities are Carl F. Kaestle, *The Evolution of an Urban School System, New York City, 1750–1850* (Cambridge, Mass.: Harvard University Press, 1973); Diane Ravitch, *The Great School Wars: New York City, 1805–1973: A History of the Public Schools as Battlefield of Social Change* (New York: Basic Books, 1974); and Stanley K. Schultz, *The Culture Factory; Boston Public Schools, 1789–1860* (New York: Oxford, 1973).

Various aspects of the practical conduct of schools are treated in such older and newer studies as Ruth Miller Elson, *Guardians of Tradition: American Schoolbooks of the Nineteenth Century* (Lincoln, Nebr.: University of Nebraska Press, 1964); *Noah Webster's American Spelling Book* (New York: Teachers College Press, 1962); Warren Burton in Clifton Johnson, Ed., *The District School As It Was* (New York: Crowell, 1928); Thomas Woody, *A History of Women's Education in the United States*, vol. I (New York: Farrar, Straus; Octagon Books, 1966); Howard K. Beale, *A History of Freedom of Teaching in American Schools* (New York: Farrar, Straus; Octagon Books, 1974); Willard S. Elsbree, *The American Teacher* (New York: American Book, 1939); Paul Monroe, *Founding of the American Public School System* (New York: Macmillan, 1940); David Madsen, *Early National Education, 1776–1830* (New York: Wiley, 1974); and John C. Crandall, "Patriotism and Humanitarian Reform in Children's Literature," *American Quarterly*, Spring 1969, 21.

Part II

Building Blocks of Public Education
(1826–1876)

Historical Setting

The tensions between the value claims of democratic political community and of segmental pluralisms are treated in *The Great Republic* (Boston: Little, Brown, 1977) by David Brion Davis in Part III, "Expanding the Republic," and by David Herbert Donald in Part IV, "Uniting the Republic." Germinal interpretations are made by Robert H. Wiebe, *The Segmented Society: An Introduction to the Meaning of America* (New York: Oxford, 1975); and Michael Kammen, *People of Paradox: An Inquiry Concerning the Origins of American Civilization* (New York: Vintage Books, 1973).

The worldwide meaning of modernization is treated by C. E. Black, *The Dynamics of Modernization: A Study in Comparative History* (New York: Harper & Row, 1966); and Gabriel Almond and G. Bingham Powell, Jr., *Comparative Politics: A Developmental Approach* (Boston: Little, Brown, 1966). The analysis of modernization is applied to the United States in C. Vann Woodward, Ed., *The Comparative Approach to American History* (New York: Basic Books, 1968); Seymour Martin Lipset, *The First New Nation; the United States in Historical and Comparative Perspective* (New York: Basic Books, 1963); Clinton Rossiter, *The American Quest, 1790–1860: An Emerging Nation in Search of Identity, Unity, and Modernity,* (New York: Harcourt Brace Jovanovich, 1971); Richard D. Brown, "Modernization and the Modern Personality in Early America, 1600–1865: A Sketch of a Synthesis," *The Journal of Interdisciplinary History*, Winter 1972; and Herbert G. Gutman, *Work, Culture, and Society in Industrializing America* (New York: Knopf, 1976).

Urbanization

For the specifically urbanizing aspect of modernization, useful documents are contained in Alexander B. Callow, Jr., Ed., *American Urban History: An Interpretive Reader with Commentaries* (New York: Oxford, 1969); Charles N. Glaab, Ed., *The American City: A Documentary History* (Homewood, Ill.: Dorsey, 1963); Kenneth T. Jackson and Stanley K. Schultz, Eds., *Cities in American History* (New York: Knopf, 1972). For a brief synthesis of urbanization, see Charles N. Glaab and A. Theodore Brown, *A History of Urban America* (New York: Macmillan, 1967).

The most useful recent studies of the role of education in the urbanization process are David B. Tyack, *The One Best System: A History of American Urban Education* (Cambridge, Mass.: Harvard University Press, 1974); Carl F. Kaestle, *The Evolution of an Urban School System; New York City, 1750–1850* (Cambridge, Mass.: Harvard University Press, 1973); Diane Ravitch, *The Great School Wars; New York City, 1805–1973: The History of the Public Schools as Battlefield of Social Change* (New York: Basic Books, 1974); Stanley K. Schultz, *The Culture Factory: Boston Public Schools, 1789–1860* (New York: Oxford, 1973); and Selwyn K. Troen, *The Public and the Schools: Shaping the St. Louis System 1838–1920* (Columbia, Mo.: University of Missouri Press, 1975). Ravitch and Troen are most favorably oriented to the public schools; Tyack and Kaestle moderately so; and Schultz least so.

chapter 4
The Common School: Palladium
of the Republic

The rise of the common school is treated sympathetically in two monographs, one older, one newer: Lawrence A. Cremin, *The American Common School: An Historic Conception* (New York: Teachers College Press, 1951); and Frederick

Binder, *The Age of the Common School, 1830–1865* (New York: Wiley, 1974). The two giants of the reform movement are considered in depth: Jonathan Messerli, *Horace Mann: A Biography* (New York: Knopf, 1972); Lawrence A. Cremin, Ed., *The Republic and the School: Horace Mann on the Education of Free Men* (New York: Teachers College, Columbia University, 1957); John S. Brubacher, Ed., *Henry Barnard on Education* (New York: McGraw-Hill, 1931); Vincent Lannie, Ed., *Henry Barnard: American Educator* (New York: Teachers College Press, 1974); and Richard Thursfield, *Henry Barnard's Journal of Education* (Baltimore: Johns Hopkins Press, 1946).

A generally "progressive" view of the common school revival is taken by Merle Curti, *The Social Ideas of American Educators* (Totowa, N.J.. Littlefield, Adams, 1966); Sidney E. Jackson, *America's Struggle for Free Schools* (Washington, D.C.: American Council on Public Affairs, 1941); Frank T. Carlton, *Economic Influences Upon Educational Progress in the United States, 1820–1850,* c. 1908 (New York: Teachers College Press, 1966); and Rush Welter, *Popular Education and Democratic Thought in America* (New York: Columbia University Press, 1962).

Generally, revisionist views are taken by Merle Borrowman and Charles Burgess, *What Doctrines to Embrace: Studies in the History of American Education* (Glenview, Ill.: Scott, Foresman, 1969); Michael B. Katz, *The Irony of Early School Reform: Educational Innovation in Mid-Nineteenth Century Massachusetts* (Cambridge, Mass.: Harvard University Press, 1968); Albert Fishlow, "The American Common School Revival: Fact or Fancy?" in Henry Rosovsky, Ed., *Industrialization in Two Systems* (New York: Wiley, 1966); Jay M. Pawa, "Workingmen and Free Schools in the Nineteenth Century: A Comment on the Labor-Education Thesis," *History of Education Quarterly,* Fall 1971; Robert H. Wiebe, "The Social Function of Public Education," *American Quarterly,* Summer 1969; and two articles in the *Harvard Educational Review,* November 1976: David K. Cohen, "Loss as a Theme in Social Policy," and Alexander James Field, "Educational Expansion in Mid-Nineteenth Century Massachusetts: Human-Capital Formation or Structural Reinforcement?"

Various angles of vision on pedagogy in the schools are given by Ruth Miller Elson, *Guardians of Tradition: American Schoolbooks in the Nineteenth Century* (Lincoln, Nebr.: University of Nebraska Press, 1964); Barbara Finkelstein, *Governing the Young: Teacher Behavior in American Primary Schools, 1820–1880* (Unpublished doctoral dissertation, Teachers College, Columbia University, 1970); Barbara Finkelstein, "Pedagogy as Intrusion: Teaching Values in Popular Primary Schools in Nineteenth-Century America," *History of Childhood Quarterly: the Journal of Psychohistory,* 1975, 2(3); Barbara Finkelstein, "The Moral Dimensions of Pedagogy," *American Studies,* Fall 1974; Bernard Wishy, *The Child and the Republic: The Dawn of Modern American Child Nurture* (Philadelphia: University of Pennsylvania Press, 1968); Howard K. Beale, *A History of Freedom of Teaching in American Schools,* c. 1941 (New York: Farrar, Straus; Octagon Books, 1974); Thomas Woody, *A History of Women's Education in the United States,* c. 1929 (New York: Farrar Straus; Octagon Books, 1966); and Barbara H. Cross, Ed., *The Educated Woman in America: Selected Writings of Catherine Beecher, Margaret Fuller, and M. Carey Thomas* (New York: Teachers College Press, 1965).

chapter 5
Segmental Pluralisms

Religious Controversies

Studies that concentrate on the Protestant role in public education include Timothy L. Smith, "Protestant Schooling and American Nationality, 1800–1850," *The Journal of American History*, March 1967, 53(4); David Tyack, "The Kingdom of God and the Common School," *Harvard Educational Review*, 1966, 36(4).

Studies that pinpoint the Catholic side of education include Robert D. Cross, "Origins of the Catholic Parochial Schools in America," *The American Benedictine Review*, 1965, 66(2); Vincent P. Lannie, *Public Money and Parochial Education: Bishop Hughes, Governor Seward, and the New York School Controversy* (Cleveland: Case Western Reserve University Press, 1968); and Charles E. Bidwell, "The Moral Significance of the Common School," *History of Education Quarterly*, Fall 1966.

The books (listed under "Urbanization" on p. 405) by Tyack, Kaestle, Ravitch, Schultz, and Troen also treat the religious controversies extensively.

Two older studies are still useful: R. Freeman Butts, *The American Tradition in Religion and Education* (Boston: Beacon, 1950); and Raymond B. Culver, *Horace Mann and Religion in the Massachusetts Public Schools* (New Haven: Yale University Press, 1929). See also Herbert M. Kliebard, Ed., *Religion and Education in America: A Documentary History* (Scranton, Pa.: International Textbook, 1969).

Ethnicity

Three extremely valuable studies of immigration, assimilation, and nativism are Milton M. Gordon, *Assimilation in American Life: The Role of Race, Religion, and National Origins* (New York: Oxford, 1964); Leonard Dinnerstein and David M. Reimers, *Ethnic Americans: A History of Immigration and Assimilation* (New York: Dodd, Mead, 1975); John Higham, *Strangers in the Land: Patterns of American Nativism, 1860–1925*, c. 1955 (New York: Atheneum, 1974). For several other references that deal in part with ethnicity and immigration in the pre-Civil War period, see the Bibliographical Notes for Chapter 9.

An especially illuminating view is given by Vincent P. Lannie, "Alienation in America: The Immigrant Catholic and Public Education in Pre-Civil War America," *The Review of Politics*, October 1970, 32(4). A fairly extreme revisionist view is set forth in Robert A. Carlson, *The Quest for Conformity: Americanization Through Education* (New York: Wiley, 1975).

Racial Segmentalism

An interesting collection of statements by blacks on education is contained in Earle H. West, *The Black American and Education* (Columbus, Ohio: Merrill, 1972). The general history of black education is treated by Horace Mann Bond, *The Education of the Negro in the American Social Order*, c. 1934 (New York: Farrar, Strauss; Octagon Press, 1966); Henry Allen Bullock, *A History of Negro Education in the South: From 1619 to the Present* (Cambridge, Mass.: Harvard University Press, 1967); and Carter G. Woodson, *The Education of the Negro*

Prior to 1861: A History of the Colored People of the United States from the Beginning of Slavery to the Civil War, c. 1919 (New York: Arno Press, 1968). A recent and excellent study of black education during Reconstruction is William Preston Vaughn, *Schools for All: The Blacks and Public Education in the South, 1865–1877* (Lexington, Ky.: University of Kentucky Press, 1974). See also the several references to blacks in both North and South (listed on page 403 under Chapter 1) by Jordan, Davis, Genovese, McLeod, Berlin, Litwack, and Morris; and Jane H. Pease and William H. Pease, *They Who Would Be Free; Blacks Search for Freedom, 1830–1861* (New York: Atheneum, 1974).

Easily available and readable general accounts of the early history of schooling among American Indians are rare. The story must still be pieced together from bibliographical and specialized studies. A very helpful guide is Brewton Perry, *The Education of American Indians: A Survey of the Literature* (Washington, D.C.: U.S. Government Printing Office, 1969) prepared for the Special Subcommittee on Indian Education of the Committee on Labor and Public Welfare, U.S. Senate. A good overall historical account that contains considerable information on education is William T. Hogan, *American Indians* (Chicago: University of Chicago Press, 1961). A more specialized but illuminating account of missionizing education is in Robert F. Berkhofer, Jr., *Salvation and the Savage: An Analysis of Protestant Missions and American Indian Response, 1787–1862* (Lexington, Ky.: University of Kentucky Press, 1965).

The Federal Effort

The best recent study of the federal government's role in public education to the end of Reconstruction is Donald R. Warren, *To Enforce Education: A History of the Founding Years of the United States Office of Education* (Detroit: Wayne State University Press, 1974). Still useful is Gordon C. Lee, *The Struggle for Federal Aid: First Phase* (New York: Teachers College, Columbia University, 1949). Also still useful for piecing together the growing role of the federal government between the 1820s and 1870s are Parts 2 and 3 of R. Freeman Butts and Lawrence A. Cremin, *A History of Education in American Culture* (New York: Holt, Rinehart and Winston, 1953).

Part III

The Burden of Modernization
(1876–1926)

Historical Setting

For a general interpretation of the continuation and heightening of the three-way tensions between the value claims of democratic political community, segmental pluralisms, and the modernization process during the last quarter of the nineteenth century and the first quarter of the twentieth century, see Parts IV and V of *The Great Republic* (Boston: Little, Brown, 1977): David Herbert Donald's "Uniting the Republic, 1860–1890" and John L. Thomas' "Nationalizing the Republic, 1890–1920." Robert Wiebe's two influential books are especially useful. *The Search for Order, 1877–1920* (New York: Hill and Wang, 1967); and *The Segmented Society: An Introduction to the Meaning of America* (New York: Oxford, 1975).

For detailed bibliographical analyses of recent important historical scholarship concerning the Gilded Age and the Progressive Era, see four chapters in William H. Cartwright and Richard L. Watson, Jr., Eds., *The Reinterpretation of American History and Culture* (Washington, D.C.: National Council for the Social Studies, 1973): Rudolph J. Vecoli, "European Americans: From Immigrants to Ethnics," pp. 81–112; Rodolfo Acuña, "Freedom in a Cage: The Subjugation of the Chicano in the United States," pp. 139–148; Walter T. K. Nugent, "Politics from Reconstruction to 1900," pp. 377–399; and Robert H. Wiebe, "The Progressive Years, 1900–1917," pp. 425–442.

Emphasis upon industrialization and urbanization as key elements in the modernization of the United States is given by Samuel P. Hays, *The Response to Industrialism, 1885–1914* (Chicago: University of Chicago Press, 1957); Herbert G. Gutman, *Work, Culture, and Society in Industrializing America* (New York: Knopf, 1976); Kenneth T. Jackson and Stanley K. Schultz, Eds., *Cities in American History* (New York: Knopf, 1972); Charles N. Glaab, Ed., *The American City: A Documentary History* (Homewood, Ill.: Dorsey, 1963); Alexander B. Callow, Jr., Ed., *American Urban History: An Interpretive Reader with Commentaries* (New York: Oxford, 1969); and Charles N. Glaab and A. Theodore Brown, *A History of Urban America* (New York: Macmillan, 1967).

chapter 7
The Push Toward Coherence

The general development of education in the cities during the middle decades of the nineteenth century is described in such recent studies as David B. Tyack, *The One Best System: A History of American Urban Education* (Cambridge, Mass.: Harvard University Press, 1974); Joseph M. Cronin, *Control of Urban Schools: Perspectives on the Power of Educational Reformers* (New York: The Free Press, 1973); William A. Bullough, *Cities and Schools in the Gilded Age: The Evolution of an Urban Institution* (Port Washington, N.Y., Kennikat Press, 1974).

Older but still useful studies are: Raymond E. Callahan, *Education and the Cult of Efficiency: A Study of the Social Forces That Have Shaped the Administration of Public Schools* (Chicago: University of Chicago Press, 1962); and Henry J. Perkinson, *The Imperfect Panacea: American Faith in Education, 1865–1965* (New York: Random House, 1968). A study that broadens the view to include rural as well as urban cases is that of Patricia Alberg Graham, *Community and Class in American Education, 1865–1918* (New York: Wiley, 1974).

Significant reasons why schooling spread so rapidly in rural areas of the North and West are given in John W. Meyer, David Tyack, Joane Nagel, and Audri Gordon, "Education as Nation-Building in America: Enrollment and Bureaucratization in the American States, 1870–1930," unpublished paper, Boys Town Center for the Study of Youth Development, Stanford University, 1977.

Studies that concentrate on specific cities or states are Diane Ravitch, *The Great School Wars, New York City, 1805–1973; A History of the Public Schools as Battlefield of Social Change* (New York: Basic Books, 1974); Sol Cohen, *Progressives and Urban School Reform: The Public Education Association of New York City, 1895–1954* (New York: Teachers College, Columbia University, 1964); Marvin Lazerson, *Origins of the Urban School: Public Education in Massachusetts, 1870–1915* (Cambridge, Mass.: Harvard University Press, 1971); and Selwyn K. Troen, *The Public and the Schools: Shaping the St. Louis System, 1838–1920* (Columbia, Mo.: University of Missouri Press, 1975).

On the rise of compulsory education the two most useful studies are Michael S. Katz, *A History of Compulsory Education Laws*, Fastback no. 75 (Bloomington, Ind.: Phi Delta Kappa, 1976); and David B. Tyack, "Ways of Seeing: An Essay on the History of Compulsory Schooling," *Harvard Educational Review*, August 1976, 46. Studies that take a more dim view of the history of the compulsory attendance idea are Charles Burgess, "The Goddess, the School Book, and Compulsion," *Harvard Educational Review*, May 1976, 46(2); and Robert A. Carlson, *The Quest for Conformity: Americanization Through Education* (New York: Wiley, 1975).

Compulsory attendance and the Americanizing role of the public schools should be seen in the light of the broader trends of immigration and assimilation as documented by Leonard Dinnerstein and David M. Reimers, *Ethnic Americans: A History of Immigration and Assimilation* (New York: Dodd, Mead, 1975); Milton M. Gordon, *Assimilation in American Life: The Role of Race, Religion, and National Origins* (New York: 1964); and John Higham, *Strangers in the Land: Patterns of American Nativism, 1860–1925*, c. 1955 (New York: Atheneum, 1974).

The cross currents of educational ideas and practices as applied to curriculum and pedagogy can be plumbed at greater depth in Edward Krug, *The Shaping of the American High School* [1880–1920] (New York: Harper & Row, 1964); Lawrence A. Cremin, *The Transformation of the School: Progressivism in American Education, 1876–1957* (New York: Knopf, 1961); and Theodore Sizer, *Secondary Schools at the Turn of the Century* (New Haven, Conn.: Yale University Press, 1964). An excellent succinct history of the social studies is given in Robert D. Barr, James L. Barth, and S. Samuel Shermis, *Defining the Social Studies* (Washington, D.C.: National Council for the Social Studies, 1977).

Debates over the role of the federal government in public education can be followed in Gordon C. Lee, *The Struggle for Federal Aid: First Phase* (New York: Teachers College, Columbia University, 1949); and Donald R. Warren, *To Enforce Education: A History of the Founding Years of the United States Office of Education* (Detroit: Wayne State University Press, 1974).

Two recent studies of organized teachers in the early twentieth century are illuminating: William Edward Eaton, *The American Federation of Teachers, 1916–1961: A History of the Movement* (Carbondale and Edwardsville, Ill.: Southern Illinois University Press, 1975); and Wayne Urban, "Organized Teachers and Educational Reform during the Progressive Era," *History of Education Quarterly*, Spring 1976, 16(1).

chapter 8
The Pull of Differentiation

The call for individual development in this period centered largely upon progressive education and its precursors. The ins-and-outs of progressive ideas and practices are dealt with in Jack K. Campbell, *Colonel Francis W. Parker: The Children's Crusader* (New York: Teachers College Press, 1967); Lawrence A. Cremin, *The Transformation of the School: Progressivism in American Education, 1876–1957* (New York: Knopf, 1961); Sol Cohen, *Progressives and Urban School Reform: The Public Education Association of New York City, 1895–1954* (New York: Teachers College Press, 1964); Patricia A. Graham, *Progressive Education: From Arcady to Academe; A History of the Progressive Education Association, 1919–1955* (New York: Teachers College Press, 1967); Timothy L. Smith, "Progressivism in American Education, 1800–1900," *Harvard Educational Review*, Spring 1961, 31(2); Claude A. Bowers, *The Progressive Educator and the Depression: The Radical Years* (New York: Random House, 1969); and Dom Cavallo, "From Perfection to Habit: Moral Training in the American Kindergarten, 1860–1920" *History of Education Quarterly*, Summer 1976, 16(2).

Widely variant contrasting views of Edward L. Thorndike are given by Geraldine Joncich Clifford, *The Sane Positivist: A Biography of E. L. Thorndike* (Middletown, Conn.: Wesleyan University Press, 1968); by Robert L. Church, "Educational Psychology and Social Reform in the Progressive Era," *History of Education Quarterly*, Winter 1971, 11(4); and by Clarence J. Karier, "Testing for Order and Control in the Corporate Liberal State," *Educational Theory*, Spring 1972, 22.

The call for vocationalism is heard differently by Arthur G. Wirth, *Education in the Technological Society: The Vocational-Liberal Studies Controversy in the Early Twentieth Century* (Scranton, Pa.: Intext Educational Publishers, 1971); Marvin Lazerson and Norton W. Grubb, Eds., *American Education and Vocationalism: A Documentary History, 1870–1970* (New York: Teachers College Press, 1974); Edward Krug, *The Shaping of the American High School* (New York: Harper & Row, 1964); Sol Cohen, "The Industrial Education Movement, 1906–1917," *American Quarterly*, 1968, 20(1); and Berenice Fischer, *Industrial Education: American Ideals and Institutions* (Madison, Wis.: University of Wisconsin Press, 1967).

chapter 9
Pathologies of Pluralism

The role of public education in assimilation and Americanization in the late nineteenth and early twentieth centuries has been heatedly debated in recent years as a result of much new historical scholarship on the subject of immigration. In addition to the references cited in earlier parts of this section of Recommended Readings (Vecoli, Acuña, p. 409; Dinnerstein and Reimers, Gordon, and Higham, p. 407), the reader could well examine such general studies as: Joshua Fishman, *Language Loyalty in America* (The·Hague: Mouton, 1966); and John Higham, "Another American Dilemma," *Center Magazine*, July/August 1974, 7(4); Stephan Thernstrom, *The Other Bostonians: Poverty and Progress in the American*

Metropolis, 1880–1970 (Cambridge, Mass.: Harvard University Press, 1973); Thomas Kessner, *The Golden Door: Italian and Jewish Immigrant Mobility in New York City, 1880–1915* (New York: Oxford, 1977); and Andrew Greeley, "The Ethnic Miracle," *The Public Interest*, Fall 1976, 45.

Studies that concentrate on the role that public education played as a result of immigration and nativism include several chapters in William W. Brickman and Stanley Lehrer, Eds., *Education and the Many Faces of the Disadvantaged: Cultural and Historical Perspectives* (New York: Wiley, 1972); Diane Ravitch, "On the History of Minority Group Education in the United States," *Teachers College Record*, December 1976; Timothy Smith, "New Approaches to the History of Immigration in Twentieth Century America," *American Historical Review*, July 1966, 71; Timothy Smith, "Immigrant Social Aspirations and American Education, 1880–1930," *American Quarterly*, Fall 1969, 21(3); David K. Cohen, "Immigrants and the Schools," *Review of Educational Research*, February 1970, 40(1); Michael R. Olneck and Marvin Lazerson, "The School Achievement of Immigrant Children, 1900–1930," *History of Education Quarterly*, Winter 1974, 14(4); Christopher Eisele, "John Dewey and the Immigrants," *History of Education Quarterly*, Spring 1975, 15(1); and Mark Krug, *The Melting of the Ethnics* (Bloomington, Ind.: Phi Delta Kappa, 1976).

The weight of the research represented by such studies as cited above seems to counteract the radical views of such authors as Colin Greer, *The Great School Legend: A Revisionist Interpretation of American Public Education* (New York: Basic Books, 1972); and Robert A. Carlson, *The Quest for Conformity: Americanization Through Education* (New York: Wiley, 1975).

The background for understanding the role of public education as viewed by, and as affecting, black Americans can be gained from such works as John Hope Franklin, *From Slavery to Freedom: A History of Negro Americans* (New York: Random House; Vintage Books, 1969); Herbert Gutman, *The Black Family in Slavery and Freedom, 1750–1925* (New York, Random House; Pantheon Books, 1976); and C. Vann Woodward, *The Strange Case of Jim Crow*, c. 1957 (New York: Oxford, 1966). For a general analysis of recent scholarship on the history of blacks in the United States, see John W. Blassingame, "The Afro-Americans: From Mythology to Reality," chap. 3 in William H. Cartwright and Richard L. Watson, Jr., Eds., *The Reinterpretation of American History and Culture* (Washington, D.C.: National Council for the Social Studies, 1973).

The most extensive histories of black education are Horace Mann Bond, *The Education of the Negro in the American Social Order* c. 1934 (New York: Farrar, Straus; Octagon Books, 1966); Henry Allen Bullock, *A History of Negro Education in the South from 1619 to the Present* (Cambridge, Mass.: Harvard University Press, 1967); and Louis R. Harlan, *Separate and Unequal: Public School Campaigns and Racism in the Southern Seaboard States, 1901–1915* (Chapel Hill: University of North Carolina Press, 1958); Louis R. Harlan, *Booker T. Washington: The Making of the Black Leader, 1856–1901* (New York: Oxford, 1972); Horace Mann Bond, *Black American Scholars: A Study of Their Beginnings* (Detroit: Balamp, 1972); and Kenneth J. King, *Pan-Africanism and Education: A Study of Race Philanthropy in the Southern States of America and East Africa* (New York: Oxford, Clarendon Press, 1971).

Significant periodical articles on specific aspects of black education include

David B. Tyack, "Growing Up Black: Perspectives on the History of Education in Northern Ghettoes," *History of Education Quarterly*, Fall 1969; James McPherson, "White Liberals and Black Power in Negro Education, 1860–1915," *American Historical Review*, June 1970; and Robert G. Newby and David B. Tyack, "Victims Without Crimes: Some Historical Perspectives on Black Education," *Journal of Negro Education*, Summer 1971, 46(3).

A recent and well-balanced study of native American Indians is in Wilcomb E. Washburn, *The Indian in America* (New York: Harper & Row, 1975). An older general study is in William T. Hogan, *American Indians* (Chicago: University of Chicago Press, 1961). More specialized studies can be tracked down in Robert F. Berkhofer, Jr., "Native Americans and United States History," chap. 2 in William H. Cartwright and Richard L. Watson, Jr. Eds., *The Reinterpretation of American History and Culture* (Washington, D.C.: National Council for the Social Studies, 1973). Similarly, specialized studies of Indian education are enumerated at length in Brewton Perry, *The Education of American Indians: A Survey of the Literature* (Washington, D.C.: U.S. Government Printing Office, 1969), prepared for the Special Subcommittee on Indian Education of the Committee on Labor and Public Welfare, U.S. Senate. An example of a recent but specialized study is in Irving G. Hendrick, "Federal Policy Affecting the Education of Indians in California, 1849–1934," *History of Education Quarterly*, Summer 1976, 16(2).

The historical plight of Mexican-Americans is portrayed by Rodolfo Acuña, *Occupied America: The Chicano's Struggle Toward Liberation* (San Francisco: Canfield Press, 1972). Many other studies are cited by Acuña in chap. 5 of Cartwright and Watson, *Reinterpretation of American History and Culture*. A wide variety of selections depicting life and culture is contained in Wayne Moquin, Ed., *A Documentary History of the Mexican Americans* (New York: Praeger, 1971).

Some historical generalizations about the education of Mexican Americans in the late nineteenth and early twentieth centuries are given in several books that concentrate on more recent periods: George I. Sanchez, *Concerning Segregation of Spanish Speaking Children in the Public Schools* (Austin: University of Texas Press, 1951); Herschel T. Manuel, *Spanish Speaking Children of the Southwest: Their Education and the Public Welfare* (Austin: University of Texas Press, 1965); and Thomas B. Carter, *Mexican-Americans in School: A History of Educational Neglect* (New York: College Entrance Examination Board, 1970).

Meyer Weinberg, *A Chance To Learn; The History of Race and Education in the United States* (New York: Cambridge University Press, 1977), brings together in one volume the history of education of blacks, Mexican-Americans, Indian-Americans, and Puerto Ricans; it contains extensive bibliographies.

In the past, most of the special studies of education for women have had to do with higher education. Bits of information about girls and women in elementary and secondary education can still be gleaned from the pioneer study by Thomas Woody, *A History of Women's Education in the United States*, c. 1929, vol. II (New York: Farrar, Straus; Octagon Books, 1966), but full-scale historical studies about women and public education are badly needed. Patricia A. Graham begins to fill the vacuum in her *Community and Class in American Education, 1865–1918* (New York: Wiley, 1974). Meanwhile, the interested reader needs to go to the periodical literature. Lois B. Merk, "Boston's Historic Public School Crisis," *The New England Quarterly*, June 1958, 31(2), describes the role of women in the school-board elections of the 1880s. Joan N. Burstyn and Ruth E. Corrigan report on "Images of Women in Textbooks, 1880–1920," *Teachers College Record*, February 1975. A reading of Ann Firor Scott, "Women in American Life," chap. 7 in Cartwright and Watson, *Reinterpretation of American History and Culture*, will reveal how little has been written about women and public education.

Part IV

The Trichotomy of Reform
(1926–1976)

For the general historical setting in the United States during its most recent half-century, see part IV of *The Great Republic* (Boston: Little, Brown, 1977) by Robert H. Wiebe, "Modernizing the Republic." This carries forward to the period 1920–1977 the analysis begun by Wiebe in *The Search for Order, 1877–1920* (New York: Hill and Wang, 1967) and in *The Segmented Society* (New York: Oxford, 1975).

In addition to the general readings on the history of American education (mentioned on pages 399–401 of these Bibliographical Notes) which include discussion of recent decades, several volumes pay special attention to the period since the 1920s. Those that concentrate on progressive education include Lawrence A. Cremin, *The Transformation of the School: Progressivism in American Education, 1876–1957* (New York: Knopf, 1961); Patricia A. Graham, *Progressive Education: From Arcady to Academe, a History of the Progressive Education Association, 1919–1955* (New York: Teachers College Press, 1967); Sol Cohen, *Progressives and Urban School Reform: The Public Education Association of New York City, 1895–1954* (New York: Teachers College Press, 1964); Claude A. Bowers, *The Progressive Educator and the Depression: The Radical Years* (New York: Random House, 1969); and Ronald K. Goodenow, "The Progressive Educator, Race and Ethnicity in the Depression Years: An Overview," *History of Education Quarterly*, Winter 1975, 15(4).

The usual conception of educational "reform" (in contrast to its meaning in this book) has concentrated largely on curriculum and pedagogy. Main trends in this kind of reform can be traced in Edward Krug, *The Shaping of the American High School, II, 1920–1941* (Madison, Wis.: University of Wisconsin Press, 1972); Harry Passow, "Once Again: Reforming Secondary Education," *Teachers College Record*, December 1975, 77(2); "Symposium on Educational Reform," *The Review of Education*, May 1975; and Daniel Selakovich, "The Failure of School Reform," *Educational Studies*, Spring/Summer 1975, 6(1/2). For short excerpts from scores of authors on a wide variety of reform efforts in the 1960s and 1970s, see Henry Ehlers, Ed., *Crucial Issues in Education* (New York: Holt, Rinehart, and Winston, 1977), 6th ed.

For radical views of reform in the recent period, see Edgar Gumpert and

Joel H. Spring, *The Superschool and the Superstate: American Education in the Twentieth Century, 1918–1970* (New York: Wiley, 1974); Joel H. Spring, *The Sorting Machine: National Educational Policy Since 1945* (New York: McKay, 1976); Martin Carnoy and Henry M. Levin, *The Limits of Educational Reform* (New York: McKay, 1976); and Ronald and Beatrice Gross, Eds., *Radical School Reform* (New York: Simon and Schuster, 1969).

For the changing role of the courts in educational policy making, see Betsy Levin, *The Courts as Educational Policymakers and Their Impact on Federal Programs* (Santa Monica, Calif.: Rand, 1977); and Clifford P. Hooker, Ed., *The Courts and Education*, Part I, 77th Yearbook, National Society for the Study of Education (Chicago: University of Chicago Press, 1978).

chapter 10
The Search for Freedom

Much of the most fundamental discussion of the meaning of freedom in education is contained in Supreme Court cases decided in the period from the 1920s to the 1970s. Handy access to many of the cases is made possible by a number of volumes in which pertinent cases are collected and analyzed: David Fellman, Ed., *The Supreme Court and Education* (New York: Teachers College Press, 1976); Clark Spurlock, Ed., *Education and the Supreme Court* (Urbana, Ill.: University of Illinois Press, 1955); Joseph Tussman, Ed., *The Supreme Court on Church and State* (New York: Oxford, 1962); and Sam Duker, Ed., *The Public Schools and Religion: The Legal Context* (New York: Harper & Row, 1966).

For a historical summary of the controversies over religion and public education up to the 1950s, see R. Freeman Butts, *The American Tradition in Religion and Education* (Boston: Beacon Press, 1950); and for discussion of more current issues, see Theodore R. Sizer, Ed., *Religion and Public Education* (Boston: Houghton Mifflin, 1967).

On various aspects of the freedom of parents to guide the education of their children and to receive public support through vouchers, see John E. Coons, William A. Clune III, and Stephen D. Sugarman, *Private Wealth and Public Education* (Cambridge, Mass.. Belknap Press of Harvard University Press, 1970); John E. Coons, "Law and the Sovereigns of Children," *Phi Delta Kappan*, September 1976, 58(1); S. D. Sugarman, "A Parent's Right to Decide," *Saturday Review/World*, November 6, 1973; Otto F. Krauschaar, *American Nonpublic Schools: Patterns of Diversity* (Baltimore: Johns Hopkins University Press, 1972); Mario Fantini, *Public Schools of Choice* (New York: Simon and Schuster, 1974); Vernon Smith et al., *Alternatives in Education* (Bloomington, Ind.: Phi Delta Kappa, 1976); and David Schimmel and Louis Fischer, *The Rights of Parents in the Education of Their Children* (Columbia, Md.: National Committee for Citizens in Education, 1977).

For discussion of the special rights and freedoms for children in education, see the entire issue, "The Rights of Children," *Harvard Educational Review*, November 1973, 43(4), and February 1974, 44(1), with an introduction by then Senator Walter F. Mondale; Alan Levine, *The Rights of Students: The Basic ACLU Guide to Students' Rights* (New York: Dutton, 1973); David Schimmel and Louis Fischer, *The Civil Rights of Students* (New York: Harper & Row,

1975); Vernon F. Haubrich and Michael W. Apple, Eds., *Schooling and the Rights of Children* (Berkeley, Calif.: McCutchan, 1975); Children's Defense Fund of the Washington Research Project, *Children Out of School in America* (Cambridge, Mass.: Children's Defense Fund, 1974); and Alan N. Sussman, *The Rights of Young People* (New York: Avon, 1977).

Radical proposals for extreme freedom for children in education are contained in Paul Goodman, *Compulsory Miseducation* (New York: American Heritage, Horizon Books, 1964); Ivan Illich, *Deschooling Society* (New York: Harper & Row, 1970); Everett Reimer, *School Is Dead: Alternatives in Education* (Garden City, N.Y.: Doubleday, 1970); Carl Bereiter, *Must We Educate?* (Englewood Cliffs, N.J.: Prentice-Hall, 1973); William F. Rickenbacker, *The Twelve-Year Sentence: Radical Views of Compulsory Schooling* (La Salle, Ill.: Open Court, 1974); John Holt, *Escape from Childhood: The Needs and Rights of Children* (New York: Dutton, 1974); and Joel H. Spring, *A Primer of Libertarian Education* (New York: Free Life Editions, 1975).

On the rights and freedoms of teachers, see Howard K. Beale, *A History of Freedom of Teaching in American Schools*, c. 1941 (New York: Farrar, Straus; Octagon Books, 1974); Louis Fischer and Daniel Schimmel, *The Civil Rights of Teachers* (New York: Harper & Row, 1973); Alexander Meiklejohn, *Political Freedom: The Constitutional Powers of the People* (New York: Harper & Row, 1960); Sidney Hook, *Heresy, Yes—Conspiracy, No!* (New York: John Day, 1953); Robert W. Iverson, *The Communists and the Schools* (New York: Harcourt Brace Jovanovich, 1959); National Education Association, Committee on Tenure and Academic Freedom, *The Freedom of the Public School Teacher* (Washington, D.C.: NEA, 1951); and Howard K. Beale, *Are American Teachers Free?* (New York: Scribner, 1936).

chapter 11
The Search for Equality

On dismantling the dual system of schools for blacks and whites the most complete and engrossing account is given in Richard Kluger *Simple Justice: The History of Brown v. Board of Education and Black America's Struggle for Equality* (New York: Knopf, 1976); see also Benjamin Muse, *Ten Years of Prelude; The Story of Integration Since the Supreme Court's 1954 Decision* (New York: Viking Press, 1964). Significant court cases are contained in David Fellman, Ed., *The Supreme Court and Education* (New York: Teachers College Press, 1976); and James Bolnar and Robert Stanley, *Busing: The Political and Judicial Process* (New York: Praeger, 1974). Statements by black spokesmen are collected in Earle H. West, Ed., *The Black American and Education* (Columbus, Ohio: Merrill, 1972).

The special controversy over the effects of busing as one means to achieve school desegregation is illustrated in James S. Coleman, Sarah D. Kelly, and John A. Moore, *Trends in School Segregation, 1968–1973* (Washington, D.C.: The Urban Institute, 1975); and in Thomas F. Pettigrew and Robert L. Green, "School Desegregation in Large Cities: A Critique of the Coleman 'White Flight' Thesis," *Harvard Educational Review,* February 1976, 46(1). Kenneth B. Clark, noted black educator and social scientist, is extremely critical of Coleman in "Social

Science, Constitutional Rights, and the Courts," *The Educational Forum*, March 1977, 41(3).

Evidence for gains made by blacks since the 1950s is contained in Sar A. Levitan, William B. Johnston, and Robert Taggart, *Still a Dream: The Changing Status of Blacks Since 1960* (Cambridge, Mass.: Harvard University Press, 1975); U.S. Commission on Civil Rights, *Fulfilling the Letter and Spirit of the Law: Desegregation in the Nation's Public Schools* (Washington, D.C.: The Commission, 1976); and Richard B. Freeman, *Black Elite, The New Market for Highly Educated Black Americans* (New York: McGraw-Hill, 1977).

At last there is a very useful historical summary of American Indian education for the recent period: Margaret Szasz, *Education and the American Indian: the Road to Self Determination, 1928–1973* (Albuquerque: University of New Mexico Press, 1974). This can usefully be supplemented by The National Study of American Indian Education, *The Education of Indian Children and Youth; Summary Report and Recommendations* (Minneapolis: University of Minnesota Center for Urban and Regional Affairs, 1970); by the views expressed by the Special Subcommittee on Indian Education of the U.S. Senate Committee on Labor and Public Welfare, *Indian Education: A National Tragedy—A National Challenge* (Washington, D.C.: U.S. Government Printing Office, 1969); and by Hazel W. Hertzberg, *The Search for an American Indian Identity: Modern Pan-Indian Movements* (Syracuse, N.Y.: Syracuse University Press, 1971).

A large-scale study of the status of Mexican-Americans in the United States was conducted in the 1960s by the Mexican-American Study Project of the University of California, Los Angeles: Leo Grebler, Joan W. Moore, Ralph C. Guzman et al., *The Mexican-American People: The Nation's Second Largest Minority* (New York: The Free Press, 1970); special attention was given to schooling in Thomas P. Carter, *Mexican-Americans in School: A History of Educational Neglect* (New York: College Entrance Examination Board, 1970). See also U.S. Commission on Civil Rights, *Mexican-American Education Survey*, Report No. 1: "Ethnic Isolation of Mexican Americans in the Public Schools of the Southwest" (Washington, D.C.: U.S. Government Printing Office, 1971); George I. Sanchez, *Concerning Segregation of Spanish Speaking Children in the Public Schools* (Austin, Texas: University of Texas Press, 1951); Herschel T. Manuel, *Spanish Speaking Children of the Southwest: Their Education and the Public Welfare* (Austin, Texas: University of Texas Press, 1965); and F. Chris Garcia, *Political Socialization of Chicano Children: A Comparative Study with Anglos in California Schools* (New York: Praeger, 1973).

Equalizing Financial Support

For recent studies of educational inequality in the states, see Joel S. Berke, *Answers to Inequity: An Analysis of the New School Finance* (Berkeley, Calif.: McCutchan, 1974); and Arthur E. Wise, *Rich Schools, Poor Schools: The Promise of Equal Educational Opportunity* (Chicago: University of Chicago Press, 1968). See also Nelson F. Ashline, Thomas R. Pezzulo, and Charles I. Norris, Eds., *Education, Inequality, and National Policy* (Lexington, Mass.: Heath, 1976); and Andrew Kopan and Herbert Walberg, Eds., *Rethinking Educational Equality* (Berkeley, Calif.: McCutchan, 1974).

Schooling and Economic Inequality

The original study was James S. Coleman et al., *Equality of Educational Opportunity* (Washington, D.C.: U.S. Government Printing Office, 1966). Coleman's more readable general interpretations are contained in James S. Coleman, "Equality of Opportunity and Equality of Results," *Harvard Educational Review,* February 1973, 43(1); and James S. Coleman, "The Concept of Equality of Educational Opportunity," *Harvard Educational Review,* Winter 1968, 38(1).

Very useful summaries of the principal issues and protagonists over inequality are contained in Donald Levine and Mary Jo Banes, Eds., *The Inequality Controversy: Schooling and Distributive Justice* (New York: Basic Books, 1975); Frederick Mosteller and Daniel P. Moynihan, Eds., *On Equality of Educational Opportunity* (New York: Random House, 1972); and special issues of the *Harvard Educational Review,* Winter 1968 and February 1973; and of *American Educational Research Journal,* Spring 1974.

Radical downgrading of the effects of schooling is illustrated in Christopher Jencks et al., *Inequality: A Reassessment of the Effect of Family and Schooling in America* (New York: Basic Books, 1972); Martin Carnoy and Henry M. Levin, *The Limits of Educational Reform* (New York: McKay, 1976); and Samuel Bowles and Herbert Gintis, *Schooling in Capitalist America: Educational Reform and the Contradictions of Economic Life* (New York: Basic Books, 1976).

Criticism of the Jencks thesis and reassertion of the values and potentials of schooling are contained in Benjamin S. Bloom, *Human Characteristics and School Learning* (New York: McGraw-Hill, 1976); Henry M. Levin, "Schooling and Inequality," *Saturday Review,* November 11, 1972; David Tyack, "Do Schools Make a Difference?" *Andover Review,* Autumn 1975; Herbert H. Hyman, Charles R. Wright, and John Shelton Reed, *The Enduring Effects of Education* (Chicago: University of Chicago Press, 1975); Kenneth B. Clark, "Social Policy, Power, and Social Science Research," *Harvard Educational Review,* February 1973, 43(1); and Ronald Edwards et al., "A Black Response to Christopher Jencks' *Inequality* and Certain Issues," *Harvard Educational Review,* February 1973, 43(1).

Compensatory Education

For the successes of compensatory education, see Ralph W. Tyler, "The Federal Role in Education," *The Public Interest,* Winter 1974; Samuel Halperin, "ESEA Ten Years Later," *Educational Researcher,* September 1975; National Assessment of Educational Progress, *Newsletter,* October 1976; and Peggy Gardner, "Good News in Reading," *American Education,* December 1976.

For the failures of compensatory education, see Sol Gordon, "The Bankruptcy of Compensatory Education," *Education and Urban Society,* August 1970; Richard H. Davis, "The Failures of Compensatory Education," *Education and Urban Society,* February 1972; and Daniel Selakovich, "The Failure of School Reform," *Educational Studies,* Spring/Summer 1975.

The National Institute of Education is conducting a large-scale study of compensatory education as required by law. See, for example, *Evaluating Compensatory Education* (Washington, D.C.: N.I.E., Dec. 30, 1976) and *Compensatory Education Services* (Washington, D.C.: N.I.E., July 31, 1977).

Affirmative Action

The neoconservative reaction against affirmative action is best illustrated by Nathan Glazer, *Affirmative Discrimination* (New York: Basic Books, 1975). A strong repudiation of Glazer's position is made by Kenneth B. Clark, "Social Science, Constitutional Rights, and the Courts," *Educational Forum*, March 1977, 41(3).

The case for equal rights for women in education is made by Patricia Sexton, *Women in Education* (Bloomington, Ind.: Phi Delta Kappa, 1976); Nancy Frazier and Myra Sadker, *Sexism in School and Society* (New York: Harper & Row, 1973); Judith Stacey, *And Jill Came Tumbling After: Sexism in American Education* (New York: Dell, 1974); Gordon Foster, *Equality of Educational Opportunity* (New York: General Learning, 1976); Iris M. Tiedt, *Sexism in Education* (Morristown, N.J.: General Learning, 1976); and Jill Conway, "Perspectives on the History of Women's Education in the United States," *History of Education Quarterly*, Spring 1974.

chapter 12
The Search for Community

Appeals to Pluralism

The germinal statement of the case for cultural pluralism was Horace M. Kallen, *Culture and Democracy in the United States* (New York: Boni and Liveright, 1924). It received further elaboration by Kallen and his admirers and critics in Horace M. Kallen, *Cultural Pluralism and the American Idea* (Philadelphia: University of Pennsylvania Press, 1956).

The case for applying cultural pluralism to education has grown rapidly in the 1970s: William Greenbaum, "America in Search of a New Ideal: An Essay on the Rise of Pluralism," *Harvard Educational Review*, 44(3); Charles A. Tesconi, Jr., *Schooling in America: A Social Philosophical Perspective* (Boston: Houghton Mifflin, 1975), part IV; Thomas F. Green, *Education and Pluralism: Ideal and Reality* (Syracuse, N.Y.: Syracuse University, 1966); Seymour Itzkoff, *A New Public Education* (New York: McKay, 1976); Edgar G. Epps, Ed., *Cultural Pluralism* (Berkeley, Calif.. McCutchan, 1974); Madelon D. Stent, William Hazard, and Harry N. Rivlin, Eds., *Cultural Pluralism in Education* (New York: Appleton-Century-Crofts, 1973); Theodore R. Sizer, "Education and Assimilation: A Fresh Plea for Pluralism," *Phi Delta Kappan*, September 1976; and Lawrence A. Cremin, *Public Education* (New York: Basic Books, 1976).

The New Ethnicity

Prominent authors who espouse the new ethnicity are Michael Novak, *The Rise of the Unmeltable Ethnics* (New York: Macmillan, 1972); Nathan Glazer and Daniel Patrick Moynihan, *Beyond the Melting Pot* (Cambridge, Mass.: M.I.T. Press, 1963); Nathan Glazer and Daniel Patrick Moynihan, Eds., *Ethnicity: Theory and Experience* (Cambridge, Mass.: Harvard University Press, 1975); Peter Schrag, *The Decline of the WASP* (New York: Simon and Schuster, 1971); Michael Novak, "The New Ethnicity," *The Center Magazine*, July/August 1974;

and Andrew M. Greeley, "The Ethnic Miracle," *The Public Interest*, Fall 1976, 45.

Cautions about possible excesses of ethnicity and pluralism are expressed in Harold Isaacs, "The New Pluralists," *Commentary*, March 1972; John Higham, "Another American Dilemma," *Center Magazine*, July/August 1974, 7(4); Milton H. Gordon, *Assimilation in American Life: The Role of Race, Religion and National Origins* (New York: Oxford, 1964); and Mark Krug, *The Melting of the Ethnics* (Bloomington, Ind.: Phi Delta Kappa, 1976).

Neoconservatism in political and moral philosophy is illustrated by Robert Nisbet, *Twilight of Authority* (New York: Oxford, 1975); Robert Nozick, *Anarchy, State, and Utopia* (New York: Basic Books, 1974); and the pages of *The Public Interest*, especially the issue entitled "The American Commonwealth," Fall 1975, 41.

Alternatives

See, for example, the special issue of *Harvard Educational Review*, August 1972; Vernon Smith, Robert Barr, and Daniel Burke, *Alternatives in Education* (Bloomington, Ind.: Phi Delta Kappa, 1976); Mario Fantini, *Public Schools of Choice* (New York: Simon and Schuster, 1973); Panel on Youth of the President's Science Advisory Committee, *Youth: Transition to Adulthood* (Chicago: University of Chicago Press, 1974); and National Commission on the Reform of Secondary Education, *The Reform of Secondary Education* (New York: McGraw-Hill, 1973); Mario Fantini, Ed., *Alternative Education: A Source Book for Parents, Teachers, Students, and Administrators* (Garden City, N.Y.: Doubleday; Anchor Books, 1976).

Bilingual and Multicultural Education

Theodore Andersson and Mildred Boyer, *Bilingual Schooling in the United States*, 2 vols. (Washington, D.C.: U.S. Government Printing Office, 1970); Francesco Cordasco, *Bilingual Schooling in the United States: A Sourcebook for Educational Personnel* (New York: McGraw-Hill, 1976); the several articles in *The Educational Forum*, May 1976; William A. Hunter, Ed., *Multicultural Education Through Competency-Based Teacher Education* (Washington, D.C.: American Association of Colleges for Teacher Education, 1974); Michael Kane, *Minorities in Textbooks: A Study of Their Treatment in Social Studies Texts* (Chicago: Quadrangle Books, 1970); a special issue of *Journal of Teacher Education*, Summer 1975, 26(2); and Herbert Teitlebaum and Richard J. Hiller, "Bilingual Education: The Legal Mandate," *Harvard Educational Review*, May 1977, 47(2). See also *Journal of Teacher Education*, May/June, 1977.

Appeal to Civic Community

Three fundamental statements of political philosophy that span the period from the 1920s to the 1970s are John Dewey, *The Public and Its Problems* (New York: Holt, Rinehart and Winston, 1927); Alexander Meiklejohn, *Political Freedom* (New York: Harper & Row, 1948); and John Rawls, *A Theory of Justice* (Cambridge, Mass.: Harvard University Press, 1971).

Key statements of social frontiersmen from the 1930s to the 1950s include George S. Counts, *Dare the School Build a New Social Order?* c. 1932 (New York: Random House; Arno Press, 1969); William H. Kilpatrick, Ed., *The Educational Frontier* (New York: Century, 1933); John Dewey, *Experience and Education* (New York: Macmillan, 1938); John L. Childs, *Education and Morals* (New York: Appleton-Century-Crofts, 1950); R. Bruce Raup et al., *The Improvement of Practical Intelligence* (New York: Harper & Row, 1950); Theodore Brameld, *Patterns of Educational Philosophy* (Yonkers, N.Y.: World Book, 1950); Harold Rugg, *Social Foundations of Education* (Englewood Cliffs, N.J.: Prentice-Hall, 1955); and William O. Stanley et al., *Social Foundations of Education* (New York: Holt, Rinehart and Winston, 1956). The appeal to democracy as the essence of civic community continues to the present in Francis T. Villemain, "The Significance of the Democratic Ethic for Cultural Alternatives and American Civilization," *Educational Theory*, Winter 1976, 26(1); see also note 53, Chapter 12.

Political socialization research snowballed in the final decade covered by this book: Robert D. Hess and Judith Torney, *The Development of Political Attitudes in Children* (Garden City, N.Y.: Doubleday, 1968); Byron G. Massialas, *Education and the Political System* (Reading, Mass.: Addison-Wesley, 1969); Robert C. Cleary, *Political Education in the American Democracy* (Scranton, Pa.: Intext Education Publishers, 1971); Jack Dennis, *Socialization to Politics: A Reader* (New York: Wiley, 1973); M. Kent Jennings and Richard D. Niemi, *The Political Character of Adolescence: The Influence of Family and Schools* (Princeton, N.J.: Princeton University Press, 1974); a special issue on political socialization, *Harvard Educational Review*, Summer 1968; and Richard E. Dawson, Kenneth Prewitt, and Karen S. Dawson, *Political Socialization,* 2nd ed. (Boston, Little, Brown, 1977).

The case for new approaches to civic education in the public schools is made by: National Task Force on Citizenship Education, *Education for Responsible Citizenship* (New York: McGraw-Hill, 1977); Law, Education and Participation, *Education for Law and Justice: Whose Responsibility? A Call for National Action* (Los Angeles: Constitutional Rights Foundation, 1975); American Bar Association, Special Committee on Youth Education for Citizenship, *Law-Related Education in America: Guidelines for the Future* (St. Paul, Minn.: West Publishing Co., 1975); Edwin Fenton, Ed., "Cognitive-Developmental Approach to Moral Education," *Social Education* (the Journal of the National Council for Social Studies, Washington, D.C.), April 1976, 40(4); Fred M. Newmann, *Education for Citizen Action: Challenge for Secondary Curriculum* (Berkeley, Calif.: McCutchan, 1975); Judy Gillespie and Stuart Lazarus, *American Government: Comparing Political Experiences* (Englewood Cliffs, N.J., Prentice-Hall, 1978). The American Political Science Association's Committee on Pre-Collegiate Education is preparing a volume of readings on political education under the editorship of Harmon Zeigler.

Name Index

Subject Index

429